THE WELSH PEOPLE

THE WELSH PEOPLE

CHAPTERS ON THEIR ORIGIN, HISTORY AND LAWS, LANGUAGE, LITERATURE AND CHARACTERISTICS

BY

JOHN RHYS, M.A.

Principal of Jesus College, and Professor
of Celtic in the University of Oxford

AND

DAVID BRYNMOR-JONES, LL.B.

Bencher of the Hon. Society of the Middle Temple, King's
Counsel, and Member of Parliament

WITH TWO MAPS

GREENWOOD PRESS, PUBLISHERS
NEW YORK

Originally published in 1923
by T. Fisher Unwin Ltd., London

First Greenwood Reprinting 1969

Library of Congress Catalogue Card Number 69-14053

SBN 8371-1960-X

PRINTED IN UNITED STATES OF AMERICA

WE DEDICATE THIS BOOK

TO

THE MEMORY OF

THE LATE

HENRY BARON ABERDARE

OF DUFFRYN

AND OF THE LATE

THOMAS EDWARD ELLIS

OF CYNLAS

IN RECOGNITION OF THE PUBLIC SERVICES
RENDERED BY THEM TO THEIR
NATIVE LAND.

PREFACE TO THE FOURTH EDITION.

WE have in this edition simply corrected some few errors that had escaped our notice.

JOHN RHYS,
D. BRYNMOR-JONES.

28th February, 1906.

PREFACE TO THE THIRD EDITION.

IN issuing a third edition of this book, we desire to say that we have tried to profit by the criticisms passed upon our work. We have not, however, deemed it expedient at present to enlarge its scope by dealing with topics to which it has been alleged, rightly or wrongly, we have not given sufficient space or attention. Errors which have been pointed out by reviewers or which we have ourselves discovered have been, we believe, duly corrected. We also wish to express our gratitude for the kindness with which these chapters have been received by all those who are interested in the past and present condition of the Welsh People.

JOHN RHYS,
D. BRYNMOR-JONES.

17th April, 1902.

PREFACE.

THE following chapters concerning the Welsh people consist partly of extracts from the Report of the Royal Commission on Land in Wales and Monmouthshire, and partly of matter which we have written since that body finished its work.

Chapters I., IV., X., XI., XII., and XIII. are based upon the Report, and were all (except some paragraphs in Chapter XII., for which the Commission was indebted to Mr. Lleufer Thomas, one of the secretaries) originally drafted by us, and were adopted with many changes by all the Commissioners. As now published they have, however, been greatly added to and altered, and though, as they appeared in the Report, they were signed by all our colleagues, we cannot hold them responsible for them in their present form.

Chapters II., III., V., VI., VII., and VIII. are new.

The greater part of Chapter IX. was written by Mr. Frederic Seebohm, LL.D., one of the Commissioners, the well-known author of "The English Village Community" and other works. This part of the Report appears to us so valuable a contribution to economic history that it ought to be made more accessible to students than it is at present. We accordingly republish it here with Mr. Seebohm's kind consent.

For permission to reprint such paragraphs of the Report

as we might deem necessary for this work, we are indebted to the Lords Commissioners of the Treasury, whose consent was courteously signified through the Right Honourable R. W. Hanbury, M.P.

In the Introduction which follows we give some necessary preliminary information, and explain briefly the scope and character of the work.

We have to acknowledge our obligation for help of various kinds to Professor Morris Jones, M.A.; Mr. Henry Owen, B.C.L.; Mr. Cadwaladr Davies; Mr. Edward Owen, F.S.A.; Lieut.-Col. Morgan, of Brynbriallu, Swansea; Principal Viriamu Jones, F.R.S.; Chancellor Trevor Parkins; Mr. Lleufer Thomas, M.A.; Mr. Cecil Owen, M.A.; Mr. T. E. Morris, LL.M.; and many other friends.

JOHN RHYS,
D. BRYNMOR-JONES.

St. David's Day, 1900.

NOTE TO THE READER.

IN this book where we refer to "the Commission," we mean, unless the context shows the contrary, the Royal Commission on Land in Wales and Monmouthshire, appointed on March 27, 1893. The Commissioners were :—Earl Carrington, G.C.M.G. (chairman); Lord Kenyon ; Sir John Talbot Dillwyn Llewelyn, Bart., M.P. ; Mr. Edwin Grove, chairman of the Monmouthshire County Council; Mr. John Morgan Griffiths, of Penally; Mr. Richard Jones, of Pertheirin ; Mr. Frederic Seebohm, M.A., LL.D. ; and ourselves. The secretaries were Mr. Lleufer Thomas and Mr. C. E. Owen.

The Minutes of the evidence taken by the Commission are contained in five Blue-books, the references to which are as follows :—Vol. I., (1894) C—7439; Vol. II., (1894) C—7439 ; Vol. III., (1895) C—7661 ; Vol. IV., (1895) C—7757 ; Vol. V., (1896) C—8222. In these volumes the questions put to the witnesses, with their answers, are numbered consecutively from the beginning to the end. So in referring to the evidence we do so by giving the number of the question and answer in these Minutes.

When we have occasion to refer to the Report of this Commission (which was signed and delivered on August 26, 1896, and is Parly. Paper (1896) C—8221), we use the word "Report" only ; and the words "Appendix to Report" mean the Appendix to that Report (Parly. Paper (1896) C—8242).

It has been found impossible to insure uniformity in the spelling of Welsh names in this work, as we have not thought it advisable to depart altogether from the spellings occurring in the documents consulted. This may occasion some inconvenience to the reader, but if he should happen to be a student of English history he will readily recognise in it an inconvenience with which he has had to struggle in his own field of study. As regards, however, the history of Wales and the Welsh, the case is somewhat aggravated by the fact that not only have we to deal with names belonging to widely different centuries, carrying with them phonetic modifications, but that in not a few instances a name may have besides several Welsh spellings, several English ones too. Take, for example, that of *Gruffud* or *Gruffyd*, of which the most usual English spelling is *Griffith*: the index shows a still greater variety. It will simplify matters for the English reader if he will bear in mind the following points of Welsh orthography and phonology :—

(1) *C* has always the sound of *k*, and formerly both *c* and *k* were used, though the present Welsh alphabet does not recognise *k*.

(2) *G* has never the English sound of *j* or *dzh* as in *John* or *James*.

(3) *F* is sounded *v*, and both letters were formerly used, but *v* is not included in the modern alphabet.

(4) *Dd* (printed Đ, đ in this work) has the sound of *th* in the English words *this* and *that*, while *th* is confined to the sound of the same digraph in *thick* and *thin*.

(5) *Ll* (here printed L, ŧ) represents the surd force of unilateral *l*, and its sound stands to that of *l* as that of *th* to *đ* or of *ph* to *v*. It is a single and simple consonant, though Englishmen sometimes seem to hear it as *thl*, which has now and then been their way of representing it, as, for instance, in "The Record of Carnarvon," in *Thlandrethloñ* for *Landriŧo*.

(6) *R* is trilled as in Italian, and in *rh* it is a surd strengthened by the aspirate.

(7) *S* is never sounded *z*.

(8) *W* may be either a vowel or a consonant, that is English *oo* (approximately) and *w*: a similar remark is in part applicable to the sound of *i*.

(9) *U* is sounded nearly like a thickish English *i*, as in the word *bit*, and so under certain circumstances is *y*. Thus *Gruffyd* or *Gruffud* is sounded very nearly as indicated by the English spelling *Griffith*, provided the final *th* have its soft sound. The inconsistency between *Gruffyd* and *Maredud* was observed too late to be corrected: the preferable spelling is *Maredyd* or *Meredyd*— the early forms were Gripp-iud and Marget-iud.

(10) The syllabic accent is ordinarily on the penultimate, except where the two last syllables of a word have been run into one in the more modern stages of the Welsh language: then the word is of course a perispomenon.

J. R.
D. B.-J.

TABLE OF CONTENTS.

MAPS.

TABLES.

INTRODUCTION.

THE Dominion or Principality of Wales may be described as a broad indented peninsula situated in the south-western part of Great Britain. Its greatest length from north to south is about 135 miles, and its breadth from east to west ranges from about 35 to 95 miles. On the north it is bounded by the Irish Sea and the estuary of the Dee, on the west by St. George's Channel, on the south by the Bristol Channel, and on the east by Cheshire, Shropshire, Herefordshire, and Monmouthshire. The eastern boundary was definitely fixed by the operation of the St. 27 Henry VIII. c. 26,[1] though some small variations have subsequently taken place.

The Principality is divided, as is the case with England, into counties, which, including Monmouthshire, are thirteen in number. The names of these counties with their Welsh equivalents are :—

Anglesey	Ynys Môn.
Carnarvonshire	Sîr Gaernarfon.
Denbighshire	Sîr Ðinbych.
Flintshire	Sîr Fflint.
Merionethshire	Sîr Feirionyð.
Montgomeryshire	Sîr Drefaldwyn.
Brecknockshire	Sîr Frycheiniog.
Cardiganshire	Sîr Aberteifi.

[1] See below, pp. 368–74.

Carmarthenshire .   . Sîr Gaerfyrdin.
Glamorganshire   .   . Sîr Forgannwg.
Pembrokeshire   .   .   Sîr Benfro.
Radnorshire   .   . Sîr Faesyfed.
Monmouthshire   .   .   Sîr Fynwy.

The first six form what is generally known as North Wales, and the remainder South Wales. Their boundaries preserve, to some extent, the ancient divisions of the Principality. There are also two large county boroughs—Cardiff and Swansea.

Monmouthshire is technically an English county, but it is often for administrative purposes, and sometimes by legislation, treated as part of Wales, or grouped with some of the Welsh counties.[1] This has been due partly to the

[1] Monmouthshire was constituted into a county or shire by 27 Henry VIII. c. 26, out of territory that was expressly stated to be part of the Dominion of Wales, but it was, however, by the same statute made subject to the courts at Westminster, while the rest of Wales was granted separate jurisdiction, which lasted until its abolition in 1830. See *infra*, p. 373.

The position of the county at present is in many respects anomalous. It forms part of the Oxford Circuit, and, therefore, is included in England in most matters concerned with the administration of law, but in the division of the, country into county court circuits, the whole of the county, along with Cardiff and Crickhowell (in Wales) and Ross (in Herefordshire), is grouped into what may be regarded as a Welsh circuit (No. 24). Its inclusion in Wales for executive purposes has been the general, though not universal, rule. It is so recognised by the Registrar-General for statistical purposes, by the Local Government Board for poor-law purposes, and by the Home Office for the purposes of the Mines Regulation Acts, the Factory and Workshop Acts, and the Quarries Act. In all matters educational, Wales and Monmouthshire have been treated as a unit distinct from England, *e.g.*, by the appointment of Commissioners to inquire into the state of Education in Wales in 1846, and of the Departmental Committee to inquire into Intermediate and Higher Education in Wales in 1880–81, as well as by the subsequent passing of the Intermediate Education Act of 1889. It was similarly dealt with by the Schools Inquiry Commission of 1864, which issued a separate report (vol. xx.) on the schools of "Monmouthshire and Wales"; by the Court of Chancery in Schemes for the re-organization of Charitable Trusts; by the Oxford University Commissioners in Statutes made under the Universities of Oxford and Cambridge Act, 1877; and by the Privy Council in the granting of charters to the University College of

similarity of its development to that of the adjoining county of Glamorgan, and partly to the fact that a large proportion of its inhabitants are Welsh as to their origin, language, and habits. In any historical inquiry as to the Cymric people it must be looked on as Welsh, and so in this work we generally use the term Wales as including Monmouthshire.

These thirteen counties are divided into hundreds, poor-law unions, highway districts, sanitary districts, and parishes for the purposes of local government; into petty sessional divisions, county court districts, and circuits for the administration of justice; and into borough and county constituencies for the appointment of parliamentary representatives. There are also ecclesiastical divisions similar to those that exist in England.[1] The most ancient political division of Wales about which we have any sure knowledge is that into cantrefs and cymwds. This must not be

South Wales and Monmouthshire, and to the University of Wales. Both the Education Department and the Charity Commissioners, in their superintendence and inspection of elementary and intermediate schools respectively, also include Monmouthshire in Wales, and reports specially dealing with Wales are reprinted, in separate book-form, from the annual general reports made by these two Departments. Monmouthshire was, however, treated as a part of England (and not of Wales) in the Welsh Sunday Closing Act of 1881, as it has also been in nearly all matters agricultural, *e.g.*, by the Royal Commission on Agriculture (1880); by the Royal Commission on Labour (in its inquiry as to the agricultural labourer in 1892–93), and also, we believe, by the Royal Commission on Agricultural Depression (1893–6), but not by the Commission on the Employment of Children, Young Persons, and Women in Agriculture (1867). The Board of Agriculture also treats Monmouthshire as a part of England in the preparation of their agricultural returns, as well as in all other matters.

[1] A list of the hundreds in each county, with the names of the parishes in each hundred, will be found in the Appendix to the Report, pp. 361 *et seq.* The student should compare this list with that of the Welsh parishes, according to cymwds printed in the "Myvyrian Archaiology," ii. 613–628. For a list of the poor-law unions, see the Appendix cited above, pp. 378–403, and of the highway districts, see the same Appendix, pp. 404–408. Much information as to Wales and its place names is given in Carlisle's "Topography of Wales," Lond. 1811.

confounded with the distribution of the Cymric land among the regal or princely families which resulted in small kingdoms or principalities. It was regarded as old in the time of Howel Ða (907-950), and the boundaries of the cantrefs and cymwds were then well enough ascertained for practical purposes. We think it useful to reproduce the map of Wales according to cantrefs and cymwds made by William Owen (known later as Dr. Owen Pughe) about the end of the eighteenth century. We ought to say that this map cannot be taken as representing boundaries with absolute accuracy, but it may be found of some service as showing the geographical relations of the various areas.

There is yet another division of Welsh land distinct in origin, and based on different conceptions from that into cantrefs and cymwds, which must be mentioned, though it has now little or no practical political significance—that into seigniories, lordships-marchers, lordships, manors, and fees. These feudal divisions were the result of the Norman Conquest of South Wales and the Marches, and of the final conquest of the Principality of Edward I. They are often conterminous with other areas.[1]

We think it well to add a few observations as to the population of Wales at different periods, for without bearing in mind the number of persons concerned it is not possible to appreciate historical events correctly, or to see the past conditions of things in true perspective.

Beginning with the known and proceeding to the conjectural statistics, we find that according to the census returns of 1891 the population of England and Wales was 29,002,525, and that of Wales (including Monmouthshire) was 1,776,405 ; so that the population of the latter area

---

[1] As to the lordships, etc., see the "Memorandum on the Lordships and Manors of Wales and Monmouthshire" in the Appendix to the Report, pp. 437 *et seq.* In the Principality, in the limited sense—the land acquired by Edward I.—the cymwds were treated as in effect lordships that passed by conquest into the hands of the Crown. See below, p. 281, n. 1, 305, 256, 403.

was about one-sixteenth of that of the former.[1] Coming
to the first complete and systematic enumeration of
England and Wales—the census of 1801—we find that the
figures for England and Wales are 8,892,536, and for
Wales and Monmouthshire 586,634. From them it appears
that the population of Wales and Monmouthshire was a
little over one-fifteenth of that of the whole of England
and Wales.[2]

Before 1801 no direct and trustworthy enumeration
of the inhabitants of this country had taken place, but
numerous estimates had been made from time to time.
Three such estimates of the population towards the close
of the seventeenth century have been made at different
times by three statisticians, acting without concert, and the
results differ but slightly. Perhaps the best known of
these computations is that made by Gregory King. The
basis of his calculation is the number of houses returned in
1690 by the officers who made the last collection of the
hearth money, and the conclusion at which he arrived was
that the population of England was nearly 5,500,000. We
find that the number of houses in Wales (excluding
Monmouthshire) according to the Hearth Book of 1690
was 77,921. Assuming that on a general average every
house so returned contained five persons, the population of
Wales amounted to 389,605. If we add this number to
the population of England, we get a total of 5,889,605, or
nearly six millions. So the population of Wales (excluding
Monmouthshire) was then a little more than one-fifteenth
of that of England and Wales, and if Monmouthshire be
added on this basis to Wales, the population of Wales
plus Monmouthshire would come out at nearly one-
fourteenth of that of England and Wales.[3]

---

[1] App. to Report, p. 272.   [2] *Ibid.*
[3] See King's "Natural and Political Observations" (1696). A second
calculation was made on the basis of returns made to William III. as to the

For periods earlier than the end of the seventeenth century, estimates of the population of this country are still more speculative. McCulloch puts the population of England and Wales at the time of the Domesday survey at 2,150,000.[1] Thorold Rogers came to the conclusion that from the fourteenth to nearly the end of the sixteenth century, it could not have exceeded two to two-and-a-half millions. He bases this opinion partly on the postulate that the number of persons in a country, chiefly subsisting on one kind of grain, will be almost exactly equal to the number of quarters of wheat which is annually produced, and on the estimate that during that time the maximum produce of wheat in any one year could not have been more than the higher figure just given ; and partly on the direct evidence of taxing rolls, and especially records of poll taxes.[2] We have seen that the ratio of the population of Wales and Monmouthshire to that of the whole of England and Wales, on Gregory King's estimate, was in 1690, 1:14. If we assume that ratio to have been constant (except for slight and temporary variations) from the beginning of the fourteenth century to the time of Elizabeth, and adopt the higher limit given

number of the adherents of the different religious denominations, and it puts the population of England and Wales at 5,200,000. (Macaulay, "Hist. of England," c. 3.) The third important estimate is that of Finlaison, who, after subjecting the ancient parochial registers to modern tests, calculates that towards the close of the seventeenth century the number was a little under 5,200,000. (See Population Returns, 1831; Macaulay, *ubi supra;* Lecky's "Hist. of England in the Eighteenth Century," i., p. 197; Macpherson's "Annals of Commerce," ii. 68, 634, 674, and iii. 134).

[1] McCulloch's "Statistical Account of the British Empire" (1847), vol. i. p. 396. Mr. York Powell estimates the population in the area covered by the survey at 2,000,000 : "Social England," vol. i. p. 240. Mr. A. L. Smith puts it at the same figure : *Ibid.,* p. 357.

[2] "Dictionary of English History" (Lond. 1885), art. Population. See too, Rogers' "History of Agriculture and Prices in England," vol. i. pp. 50 *et seq.;* and "England's Industrial and Commercial Supremacy," pp. 44–64.

by Thorold Rogers—2,500,000, the population of Wales and Monmouthshire could not during that period have been greater than about 178,000.

We are, however, not justified in assuming that the ratio 1:14 truly represents the proportion of the inhabitants of Wales and Monmouthshire to that of England and Wales at the time of the Edwardian conquest in 1282, or even in the sixteenth century. We could do so safely only if we found that the economic development of the two areas had proceeded at equal rates. The facts, however, indicate that this was not the case before the end of the great war. For instance, the total acreage of Wales and Monmouthshire is 5,121,013 ;[1] in 1795 the waste area was 1,696,827 acres[2]—that is, more than one-third of the whole was wild and uninclosed. The mountainous character and the climatic conditions place the country at a disadvantage in regard to the production of cereals as compared with the greater part of England, and the progress of agriculture was very slow until the beginning of this century. These and other considerations[3] lead us to believe that the population of Wales and Monmouthshire in comparison with that of England and Wales in 1282 was proportionally smaller than it is to-day, and that the rate of its increase has been slower than that of England and Wales as a whole. We think, therefore, that the population of Wales and Monmouthshire at the end of the thirteenth century was not greater than 150,000,[4] and if McCulloch's estimate as to the number at the time of the Domesday survey is fairly accurate, it was still less in the eleventh century.

[1] Report, p. 672.
[2] App. to Report, p. 214.
[3] *E.g.* The non-existence of any large towns. Cardiff (which had in 1891 a population of 128,915) had only 1,870 inhabitants according to the census of 1801.
[4] Thorold Rogers places it as low as 131,040. "England's Ind. and Comm Supremacy," p. 48.

No attempt to estimate the population of Wales or of the western part of the island at times earlier than the Norman Conquest can be made with success, for we have no materials at all on which to base any exact calculation. Giraldus, writing at the end of the twelfth century, says :— "For as the mountains of Eryri could supply pasturage for all the herds of cattle in Wales if collected together, so could the Isle of Môn provide a requisite quantity of corn for all the inhabitants ; on which account there is an old British proverb, 'Môn mam Gymru,' that is, 'Môn the mother of Wales.'"[1] If the saying was then really old and this explanation is correct, we may infer that in the far distant days of Cuneda and Cadwaladr the population was very scanty. In any case the notion which was formerly widely entertained, and still lingers in some quarters, that Wales was in early times very populous is quite unfounded.

It is, however, not only in regard to their numbers in the past that the view popularly taken of their own history by the Welsh is erroneous. It is not easy to state briefly, and at the same time quite accurately, the current theory ; but we think it may be fairly expressed thus : That they are the descendants of a great homogeneous nation called Cymry or Britons (now referred to as Ancient Britons); that in distant centuries they formed a mighty state or empire, the dominions of which comprised not only Britain but larger territories on the Continent as well ; that they were ruled over by a line of illustrious kings which stretched up to Brutus, son of Æneas, and from him to Noah, who ordered the world anew after the Deluge ; but that they, owing to unsuccessful wars, bad government, and all sorts of mischances, lost not only their continental possessions, but also the Crown of Britain ; and at last became confined in what is now Cymru, and reduced into subjection through the "fraud and rapacity" of the Saxon.

[1] Giraldus Cambrensis, "Descriptio," i. c. 6.

Now all this is not mere nonsense, and as to every proposition that goes to make up this bundle of historical ideas there is some sound basis of fact. It is true that the determining element in the composition of the Cymry of what is now Wales was Brythonic; that the Brythons belonged to a Celtic race which, before Cæsar's time, had spread over more than half this island and a considerable part of the Continent; that there were many British kings who were very important in their day, and who had long and well-known pedigrees; and that a confederation of Celtic tribes—Brythonic and Goidelic—did most stubbornly resist the Teutonic tribes which invaded the island and settled in it after the departure of the Roman legions, and that for a long time it maintained its domination in the western half of Britain. Yet the representation of the early history of the Welsh given by the theory we have summarised makes a picture in which things and persons are exaggerated and distorted, and by adopting it the chain of events is thrown out of gear—that is, if our conclusions are correct. For we feel bound to repeat, in regard to the Brythons and the Cymry, what a famous Greek historian said about the Hellenes, that judging from the evidence which we are able to trust, "after most careful inquiry," we should imagine that "past ages were not great either in wars or anything else."

So far as we can make out, the beginning of the history of the Cymry, considered as a separate and independent nation, must be associated with the migration into what is now North Wales of a Brythonic tribe, whose chief was Cuneda Wledig, and which came from the North. This invasion took place not long after the time when the Roman occupation ceased. Before this, however, there were both Goidels and Brythons in Wales. A glance at the map of Roman Britain below will show the relative positions of these two Celtic races. The former were settled over a part of North Wales and nearly the whole of the South, while the latter had spread over the central area to the coast; but we must add that there were in the same parts besides these Celts certain non-Aryan elements, which must be looked on as aboriginal, though more or less completely assimilated by the first Celtic conquerors. This was the position when Cuneda, who seems to have assumed the authority of the Roman military officer called the *Dux Britanniæ*, established his rule over Wales, and united the Celtic tribes of the west of Britain into a kind of confederation under his leadership, which was soon forced to defend the land against divers streams of Teutonic settlers, and which under his successors for a long time struggled to retain its supremacy.

It was during this contest that the term *Cymro* (which means compatriot), became a national name covering the members of all the Celtic tribes and kindreds who acknowledged the over-lordship of the line of Cuneda. Such, if the matter is looked at, not through the mists of Neo-Druidism or the bright yet delusive atmosphere of mediæval romance, but in the clearer light of the evidence afforded by inscriptions, language, laws, and reasonably trustworthy chroniclers, seems to us the true conclusion as to the origin of the Cymry. If we are right, the Welsh people of to-day have the satisfaction of knowing that they are not the decayed and disconsolate remnant of a once great nation, but that in the main they are the descendants of Celtic races which though absorbed into the English polity, after a prolonged struggle for independence, have steadily progressed by the side of their conquerors in regard to all that goes to make up civilisation, and by combining an obstinate vitality with a certain happy power of adapting themselves to new circumstances, have succeeded in retaining their language and some of the best characteristics of their ancestors.

We are well aware that there are grave imperfections in our treatment of many of the problems we discuss. We have, however, tried to give them true solutions, ever keeping before our minds the motto of the new-born University of Wales—*Goreu awen gwirioned (Optima musa veritas)*. That we have, as to every point, succeeded we do not of course assert ; and indeed we advance our conclusions on controverted questions in no dogmatic spirit, but in tentative fashion, though we cannot always be saying so in the text. Nor do we present this collection of chapters as a history of the Welsh people, but rather as a contribution to such a work, which may be useful to students at our national colleges and to others who are seriously interested in things Welsh. Yet there is a connecting thread of purpose running through the book, as will be seen by a brief description of the subject-matter of each chapter.

In the first, second, and third chapters we deal with the ethnology and origin of the Cymry, and in order to justify and explain our views, discuss minutely some of the questions connected with the so-called " Picts " and the distribution of tribes in this island during the Roman occupation. Having shown that the Cymry emerge as a separate nation under the rule of Cuneda and his descendants when that occupation ceased, we pass on to state very briefly in the fourth chapter their history down to the death of Cadwaladr, when their kingdom in its more extensive sense came to an end. In the next (the fifth) chapter we treat of the history of Wales from that time to the Norman Conquest of England. Then we stop to describe the legal organisation and social condition of the Cymry in the tenth and the immediately succeeding centuries. In the seventh chapter we describe the way in which the greater part of Wales was gradually conquered by the Normans, and sketch the history of the last and greatest Cymric principality to its transference by conquest to Edward I. From this event the history of the Welsh in regard to wars, foreign policy, and general affairs becomes so merged into that of Great Britain that it is hardly susceptible of separate treatment in a continuous narrative form. They have, however, a particular history as to many of the institutions, conditions, and activities, that create or maintain the life of a nation. It is with some of these things that our eighth, ninth, tenth, eleventh, and twelfth chapters are concerned. There we try to show how, for nearly all purposes of government, Wales has become organised in the same way as England; how the old Cymric tribal notions of land-holding and administration (which became by natural and easy stages very like to those of the feudal system) gradually disappeared under the influence of Norman-English officials, and by degrees developed into the land tenure of to-day ; how a religious movement commencing in the sixteenth century culminated in a great revival in the eighteenth, and brought about the predominance of Nonconformity in the Welsh counties, the preservation and growth of Cymraeg, and an intellectual renaissance ; and how this movement in its turn created a demand for schools and colleges, which has resulted in the formation of a system of Welsh public education as perfect as any to be found in the United Kingdom. After that we pass on to give some information as to the language and literature of the Welsh ; and finally in the thirteenth chapter we attempt to exhibit the characteristic features of the most typical classes of the population of the Principality in our own day.

THE WELSH PEOPLE.

CHAPTER I.

THE ETHNOLOGY OF ANCIENT WALES.

IN this chapter we propose to state briefly what comparative philology and ethnology have to say as to the
races of ancient Britain, especially those to be found in
what is now Wales, and what admixture has taken place
there in later times.

Archæologists who have studied the contents of the
ancient barrows or burial mounds of this country find that
the human remains which they detect in them belong to
more than one race. The barrows of the earliest date are
long, and yield long skulls, while the round barrows, which
are later, show the remains of a short-skulled people ; but
the round barrows sometimes contain long skulls as well
as short ones, a fact which suggests that the conquerors
began early to intermarry with the conquered population.
Looking at the same order of questions from the point of
view of language, one may say, that the first race as to whose
presence in this country in ancient times there can be no
manner of doubt is the Celtic ; and it is also a matter
admitting of no philological doubt, that the Celts of the
British Isles were Aryans, speaking related languages
which fall into two groups, the Goidelic and the Brythonic.
The Goidelic group embraces at the present day the Gaelic

of Ireland, of the Isle of Man, and of Scotland. The Brythonic group, on the other hand, is now represented by Welsh, and the Armoric dialects of Brittany or Llydaw. To this group also belonged old Cornish, which has been extinct as a spoken language for somewhat over a century.

These two groups of Goidelic and Brythonic languages may be regarded as variations of two ancient tongues, Goidelic and Brythonic respectively, which differed from one another somewhat in the same way as Latin and the Umbro-Samnite dialects of ancient Italy. Thus the Goidelic for *who* is in Manx Gaelic *quei, quoi*, but in Welsh *pwy :* compare Latin *qui, quis*, Oscan *pis*, accusative *pim*. Similarly the Goidelic for *five* is in Manx *queig*, but in Welsh *pump* (and *pimp*[1]) : compare Latin *quinque*, whence the derivatives *quintus*, "fifth," *Quintus* (for *quinctus, Quinctus*), and *Quinctius, Quintius*, which we have as an Oscan name in Πομπτιες, Latinised *Pomptius*, and *Pontius*, as in the well-known name of the Samnite *Pontius* Pilate. This distinction of *qu* and *p* is, it is needless to say, only one of the differences which must have existed between early Goidelic and early Brythonic ; but it has the advantage of forming a conspicuous and decisive mark wherever it happens to occur. Nobody, however, supposes that *qu* and *p* are equally original here : *qu* is the older, and where its equivalent occurs as *p*, this last is to be regarded as a simplification of the *qu*, but the simplification appears to date very early. Thus a Roman inscription[2] at Hexham was set up in honour of a god called therein Apollini *Mapono*, where *Mapono* may be regarded as cognate with

[1] *Pimp*, "five," and *pimphet*, "fifth," occur among the old Welsh glosses in the Bodleian manuscript, Auct. F. 4—32 ("Gram. Celtica," p. 1060, and "Transactions of the Philological Society," 1860-1, p. 237), and the regular spelling in modern Welsh would be *pymp* and *pymed*, which represent the actual pronunciation in the spoken language of most of South Wales.

[2] See the Berlin "Corpus Inscriptionum Latinarum," vol. vii., No. 1345.

a Brythonic or Gaulish nominative, *Mapono-s*,[1] a word which in old Welsh would have been *mapon*, now *mabon*, "a boy or youth," derived from the simple form *map*, now *mab*, "a boy or son." This is in Irish *macc* or *mac*, for an early Goidelic *maqua-s*, genitive *maqui*, which occurs frequently in the Ogam inscriptions of Britain and Ireland.[2] All this, however, only takes us back at most to the Roman occupation, but, as a matter of fact, we have no data from a time when Brythons and Gauls had not already made *qu* into *p*; and the question arises which of the two groups

[1] In Gaulish the nominatives corresponding to those in *us* and *um* (like *dominus*, *regnum* in Latin) ended in *os* and *on* respectively, as in Greek, and where the declension is fairly certain we shall write them so; but Latin authorities using *us* in two declensions leave us sometimes unable to decide between the *o* and *u* stems. In that case we shall follow the Latin in using *us*.

[2] Speaking more precisely, Ogam inscriptions occur (1) in Wales, mostly South Wales, but North Wales has two, one in Denbighshire and one at least in Carnarvonshire; (2) in Devon and Cornwall, and one remarkable instance occurs at Silchester, in Hampshire; (3) in Ireland, mostly in the south of that country; (4) in the Isle of Man; and (5) in Scotland, including Orkney and Shetland, but these are mostly late in comparison with the bulk of the others. The older Ogam characters consist of scores or notches on the edge of the stones used, and the following is the alphabet of the most ancient monuments, with the continuous line representing the edge of the stone inscribed :—

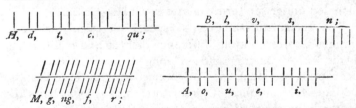

The classification of the vowels into broad and slender suggests that the inventor was a grammarian; and the group which stands second in the usual arrangement was probably the first to be fixed, as it is found that *h*, *d*, *t*, *c*, *qu*, represent the initials of the Goidelic words for 1, 2, 3, 4, 5, in the oldest forms which can be inferred for them, thus :—*a hóina-, a dŷou, a ttrĩ-, a ccetŷor, a qqŷenqŷe*. See Rhys's "Outlines of the Phonology of Manx Gaelic" (in vol. xxxiii. of the Publications of the Manx Society), p. 73, also pp. 41, 58, 59, 60, 88, 102, 178.

of Celts, Brythons or Goidels, came here first, and also whence they came. The answer to this latter question must be, that in all probability they first came from the nearest part of the Continent, from the land where the bulk of the Celts dwelt in the time of Cæsar, namely, Gaul, comprising ancient France, Belgium, Switzerland, and North Italy, also parts of Spain. To the question of the order of their coming the answer is sufficiently indicated by the relative positions of the peoples speaking Goidelic and Brythonic respectively at the present day. For it may be regarded as fairly certain that those who are found driven furthest to the west were the earlier comers, namely the Goidels.

Goidelic was a phase of the language of the Celtæ in Cæsar's restricted use of that word, and we may, in this context, call the language Goidelo-Celtic or Celtican ;[1] but we must suppose its place, at any rate as a dominant speech on the Continent, to have been taken by Gaulish some time anterior to Cæsar's Gallic wars. Gaulish belonged to the same group as Brythonic ; or, to be more exact, Brythonic may be treated as the Gaulish spoken in Britain, as we shall see presently. Both may be, however, included under the term Galatic or Galato-Celtic.

The ancient distinction of speech between the Celts implies a corresponding difference of race and institutions, a difference existing indeed long before Celts of any description are mentioned in connection with these islands. Perhaps few matters of prehistoric archæology have recently been more discussed than the distinction between Celticans or Celts of the older stock and the Galatic warriors by whom they were encroached upon. The two peoples are found to have differed in their manner of disposing of their dead, and each had weapons

[1] See the "Transactions of the (London) Philological Society " for 1891-3, pp. 104, 105

characteristic of its own civilisation. The interments with the most important remains of the older stock are found mostly in the neighbourhood of the Alps, including the upper portions of the basin of the Danube and the plains of North Italy.[1] This older Celtic world began, about the sixth century B.C., to be invaded by the Galatic Celts, whose home may be inferred to have consisted of Central and Northern Germany and of Belgium; and the remains of these Galatic Celts are to be studied in the great burial-places between the Seine, the Marne, and the Rhine—in the country, in short, from which they invaded Britain. It has been surmised that this movement was begun by the Brythons between the time of Pytheas, in the fourth century B.C., and the visits of Julius Cæsar. The latter mentions, ii. 4, a certain Diviciacos, king of the Suessiones, a Belgic people which has left its name to Soissons, as the most powerful prince in Gaul and as ruling also over Britain. This was, moreover, late enough to be within the memory of men living in Cæsar's time. We have also Cæsar's general statement as to the settlers from Gaul, that they belonged to the Belgæ or the tribes inhabiting Belgium, by which he meant, roughly speaking, the tract between the Seine and the Rhine and between the sea and the tributary waters of the Marne and the Moselle; also that their settlements here were known by the names which they already had on the Continent. This is borne out by those names themselves where they happen to be recorded. Thus the Atrebates, whose chief town was Calleva, supposed to be the site of Silchester, in Hampshire, probably came from the Atrebates of the Continent, where that name of theirs has been worn down to Arras, in the Pas de Calais. Then, as to the tribe called Belgæ,

---

[1] For the most recent and comprehensive account of this chapter in Celtic archæology, see Bertrand and Reinach's volumes " Nos Origines," especially vol. ii., entitled "Les Celtes dans les Vallées du Pô et du Danube" (Paris, 1894), pp. ii., 42, 180, 181. To this work, with its numerous illustrations, we are much indebted.

who appear to have once been important enough to impose their name on a whole group of peoples on the Continent, they seem to have come over here in a body, leaving to the Germans their old home in a country now indicated by such a place-name as that of *Billig*, in the government of Cologne, and that of Wasser-*Billig*, near where the Sauer joins the waters of the Moselle. In Britain the people called Belgæ took possession of a tract which included the sites of the towns now called Winchester and Bath. Similarly the Parisi of the south-east of what is now Yorkshire occupied a country which is remarkable for its interments, containing as they do remains of the iron war-chariots used by the conquerors. They were probably a division of the Parisii, who have left their name to the city of Paris, on the Seine. The first of the Belgic peoples to cross over to this country were probably those who dwelt nearest to it, namely, on the other side of the Straits of Dover. These appear to have been called Brittani or Brittones, whom Pliny[1] seems to have found so called in the valley of the Somme: the name of a town of theirs is duly perpetuated by that of the village of Bretagne, near the mouth of that river. In our country the history of their name was probably the following : from being exclusively that of the first settlers it came to be extended to the successive hordes, so that at the last it actually denoted all the settlers here of Belgic descent ; and we have probably to look for the Brittani proper under the geographical appellation of Cantii, or people of Cantion —"Kent." In its form of *Brittones* it yields in Welsh the name *Brython*, "a Briton or Welshman," and in its form of *Brittani* it yields the Irish plural *Bretain* (genitive *Bretan*), "Brythons or Britons, also their country." The prevalent

---

[1] See Detlefsen's Pliny, "Historia Naturalis," iv. 106: *A Scaldi incolunt extera Texuandri pluribus nominibus, dein Menapi, Morini ora Marsacis juncti pago qui Chersiacus vocatur, Britanni, Ambiani, Bellovaci, Bassi.*

spelling in Latin appears to have been *Britanni;* but the related forms, and among them the French *Bretagne,* show that it ought to have been written with *tt.*

Without enumerating the Belgic tribes which constituted the Brythonic group of Celts in this country, suffice it to say that the whole of the coast on the east and south was probably occupied by them from the Isle of Wight to the Firth of Forth. But how far inland they had overrun the country by the time of the Roman occupation, it is impossible to say with any precision. We have, however, in the Itinerary of Antoninus, evidence of their presence as far west as Staffordshire, to wit, in the name of the station of *Pennocrucion,* which is now represented letter for letter by *Penkridge.* The form in the Itinerary is the dative-ablative *Pennocrucio,* derived from the stem *penno,* represented in Welsh by *pen,* "end, extremity, head," early Goidelic *quenna,* whence Irish *ceann,* "end, head," and *crucio,* Welsh *crug,* "a heap or tumulus." So the whole compound, had it been Goidelic, would have been *Quennacrucio* m the Itinerary. But as that is not the case, we know that we have here to do with Brythons, not with Goidels. The spot was comprised probably in the territory of the Cornovii, who may accordingly be supposed to have been Brythons. Behind them towards the west wĕre the Ordovices, who were also probably Brythons, though we have no exactly similar evidence to prove it ; but we can account best for the facts which we have at our disposal, if we suppose the Ordovices to have divided what is now Wales into two parts, as it were with a wedge, and to have reached the shores of Cardigan Bay. Beyond the Ordovices, towards the south, the country was occupied by the Silures and the Demetæ, neither of whom can be supposed to have been Brythons, for their territory supplies inscriptions in Goidelic dating some time after the departure of the Romans. Similarly beyond the Ordovices in a northern and north-western direction in the country called Venedot, later Gwyned, there were likewise peoples who cannot have been Brythons, as is proved more or less explicitly by inscriptions found there showing traces of Goidelic.

We have some aid to the understanding of the early history of the tract of country which we may loosely call Mid-Wales in the dialects of Welsh actually spoken there. Welsh dialects are commonly treated as three : (1) the *Gwyndodeg*, or Venedotian Welsh ; (2) the *Powyseg*, or Welsh of Powys ; and (3) the Southwalian, consisting of the closely connected *Gwenhwyseg* (Gwentian or Silurian Welsh) and the Demetian or Welsh of Dyfed. But this is of little use as regards Mid-Wales, for the facts are briefly as follows :— The Demetian reaches northwards as far as the stream of the Wyrai at Llanrhystud, a little south of Aberystwyth, in Cardiganshire. North of the Wyrai and of Strata Florida the dialect is very distinct from the Demetian, and still more so from the contiguous dialect of the counties of Merioneth and Montgomery ; but, on the other hand, it resembles that of Penllyn as represented by Bala and other places in the neighbourhood of Bala Lake. We may add that the same dialect embraces, without any sudden variation, the Welsh of the Dee valley and some of the northern portion of Montgomeryshire. The inference to be drawn is probably this : at one time a uniform dialect prevailed in the region of Mid-Wales comprising North Cardiganshire, Radnorshire, Montgomeryshire, and the south-east of Denbighshire. Its northern boundary was probably the river Mawdach, the northern watershed of the Dee, and eventually the Clwyd and the Dee Estuary. The area indicated may be said to represent the conquests and settlements of the Ordovices. Later, however—not long probably after the departure of the Romans from Britain— another people came on the scene and established its own dialect in a great part of the Ordovic territory, but so as to leave the marginal districts of North Cardiganshire and Penllyn in the continued use of their old Ordovic speech. The intruding dialect, which severed them, is now no other than the Welsh of Powys, which prevails in Montgomeryshire and on the coast of Merionethshire from the river Dovey to Dolgelley and Harlech. It was introduced probably by Cuneda Wledig and his Sons, that is to say, by the people whose princes are collectively known to Welsh history and hagiology by that designation.

Now Cuneda was the ancestor to whom the kings of Gwyned traced their origin, and most of the best-known saints of Wales are represented as his descendants. The legend [1] of Cuneda represents him and his sons coming to Wales from the North, where he appears to have been at the head of a force of cavalry defending the Roman wall, and to have filled the post of the military leader, who, during the Roman occupation, used to be known as the *Dux Britanniæ* or *Dux Britanniarum*. The legend further represents Cuneda and his Sons as engaged in Wales in the expulsion of the Goidels ; so we may suppose that the Ordovices had been hard pressed by the Goidels on both sides of them, and that they had appealed for aid to Cuneda, who accordingly sent a force under the command of his sons to combat the Goidels. However that may be, Cuneda's men must have permanently settled in the country, and so did his sons, as we are told, except the eldest, who is said to have died some time before in Manau Guotodin, a district near the Firth of Forth. The share of the eldest son was given to his son Meirion, from whom it was called Cantref Meirion, "the Hundred of Meirion," which in its turn has given its name to *Meirionyd* and the county of *Merioneth*. This Hundred of Meirion, as the

---

[1] See San Marte's "Nennius," § 62, and the Harleian MS. 3859, published by Mr. Egerton Phillimore in "Y Cymmrodor," ix. 182, also Rhys's "Celtic Britain," pp. 118-21.

dominion of the eldest branch of the Cuneda family, is probably what was sometimes called simply *Y Cantref,*[1] "the Hundred." It was also that which an old tract on boundaries calls *Cantref Ordwyf,* which possibly meant the Hundred of the Ordovices, extending from the Dovey to the Mawdach, the southern boundary of Ardudwy, which belonged to Gwyned.[2] Now Meirion, grandson of Cuneda, as chief of the family, assigns to his uncles, the sons of Cuneda, their respective territories, and the list of them purports to represent the Brythonic conquests made by the family in various directions, including the carving out of Keredig's kingdom of Keredigion, which is, roughly speaking, the present county of Cardigan. Other members of the family have different parts of Gwyned, including Môn or Anglesey, assigned to them in this legend. One of the branches of the Cuneda family established in Gwyned became in the sixth century so powerful, to wit in the person of Maglocunos or Maelgwn Gwyned, that not only Wales, but also Cumbria, was, to a certain extent, forced to own his sway ; and it was perhaps in his time that the Hundred of Meirion first became a part of Gwyned.

We have suggested that the Brythons came over to Britain between the time of Pytheas and that of Julius Cæsar Their invasions probably spread over a considerable period of time, but we should perhaps not be far wrong in ascribing the mass of them to the second century before our era.[3] When, it may be asked, did the other Celts, the Goidels,

[1] See the "Iolo MSS." (Llandovery, 1848), pp. 85, 86, translated at pp. 475-7, but with serious errors; also pp. 120, 519 ; and Rhys's "Celtic Britain," pp. 308, 309.

[2] See the Mabinogi of Math, in which Math has the disposal of Ardudwy, probably as king of Gwyned, Oxford Mabinogion, p. 73.

[3] See M. d'Arbois de Jubainville's "Premiers Habitants de l'Europe." vol. ii., p. 295, where he expresses himself to the same effect, also in the "Revue Celtique," vol. xiii., p. 402 ; see also Holder's "Alt-Celtischer Sprachschatz," s.v., Brittani. Both, however, make the Brythons conquer this island from the Picts, not from Goidels.

whom they found here, arrive in this country? It is impossible to give any precise answer to such a question, but it may be supposed that the Goidels came over not later than the great movements which took place in the Celtic world of the Continent in the sixth and fifth centuries before our era.[1] We mean the movements which resulted in the Celts reaching the Mediterranean and penetrating into Spain, while others of the same family began to press towards the east of Europe, whence some of them eventually crossed to Asia Minor and made themselves a home in the country called after them Galatia. On the whole, we dare not suppose the Goidels to have come to Britain much later than the sixth century B.C.; rather should we say that they probably began to arrive in this country very much earlier. Before the Brythons came the Goidels had presumably occupied most of the island south of the firths of the Clyde and Forth. So when the Brythons arrived and began to press the Goidels in the west some of the latter may have crossed to Ireland : possibly they had begun still earlier to settle there. The portion of Ireland which they first occupied was probably the tract known as the kingdom of Meath, approximately represented now by the diocese of that name ; but settlements may have also been made by them at other points on the coast.

We have next to consider the question whether the first Celtic comers, the Goidels, were also the first inhabitants of this country. This may be briefly answered to the effect that there seems to be no reason to think so, or even to suppose that it may not have been uninterruptedly inhabited from a time before it ceased to form a continuous portion of the continent of Europe. By what race is a much harder question. Indeed, there is a previous question

---

[1] See the "Premiers Habitants de l'Europe," vol. i., p. 262, and Zimmer's "Mutterrecht der Pikten," in the "Zeitschrift für Rechtsgeschichte," vol. xv. (Röm. Abth.), pp. 233, 234. For later views see Read's British Museum Bronze Age Guide.

which might reasonably be asked, namely, Was it a single race or several ? This cannot be answered, but it would clearly be a waste of conjecture to suppose the pre-Goidelic inhabitants to have belonged to more than one race, until at any rate evidence is found to compel us to that conclusion. So we rest satisfied for the present to treat them as if belonging to a single race ; and we proceed to consider, very briefly, the nature of the relation in which that race is likely to have found itself placed as regards the new-comers. It is but natural to suppose that the Goidels, when they arrived, subjugated the natives, and made slaves of them and drudges. From the first the fusion of the two races may have begun to take place, but to what extent it proceeded it would be impossible to say. It is, however, fairly certain that the process of fusion between the Goidelic and native elements must have been quickened by the advent of a third and hostile element, the Brythonic. For it must have been to the advantage of the Goidels to have induced the natives to make common cause with them against the intruders ; and under the pressure exerted by the Brythons the fusion of the two other nations may have been so complete as to produce a new people of mixed Goidelic and native origin. To be more correct, perhaps, we ought to have restricted the term Goidelic to that mixed nationality, and applied some other designation, such as Celtican, to the early Celtic invaders of the island before they mixed with the Aborigines of these islands. Then as to the Brythons, coming later as they did, they had the Goidels between them and the Aborigines, and they were not likely to come in contact on any large scale with the latter before they had been to a considerable extent Celticised [1]

[1] Except perhaps in the North, where, for example, the Picto-Brythons of Fortrenn, with their headquarters eventually at Forteviot, on the banks of the Earn, seem to have spoken a kind of Brythonic. But that dialect is unknown with the exception of a few words like *Peanfahel*, given by Bede (" Hist. Eccles." i. 12) as the vernacular for Latin *pennae valli.*"

Accordingly, supposing the Aborigines not to have been Aryans, one might expect the language of the resultant Goidelic people to show more non-Aryan traits than the language of the Brythons : as a matter of fact, this proves to be the case.

The Goidels have already been represented as a mixed race, and when later this mixed-Goidelic population became one people with the Brythons, the result was still more composite; and one may say that the Welsh people of the present day is made up of all three elements: the Aboriginal, the Goidelic, and the Brythonic. And it would be unsafe to assume that the later elements predominate; for the Celtic invaders, both Goidels and Brythons, may have co ne in comparatively small numbers, not to mention the iact that the Aboriginal race, having been here possibly thousands of years before the first Aryan arrived, may have had such an advantage in the matter of acclimatisation, that it alone survives in force. This is now supposed to be the case with France, whose people, taken in the bulk, are neither Frankish nor Celtic so much as the representatives of the non-Aryan populations which the first Aryans found there. It thus becomes a matter of interest for us to know all we can about the earliest inhabitants of this country. Now the question of the origin of that race is, according to one view taken of it, inseparably connected with the Pictish question ; and the most tenable hypothesis may be said to be, that the Picts were non-Aryans, whom the first Celtic migrations found already settled here. The Picts appear to have retained their language and institutions latest on the east coast of Scotland in portions of the region between Clackmannan and Banff. But Irish literature alludes to Picts here and there in Ireland, and that in such a way as to favour the belief that they were survivals of a race holding possession at one time of the whole country. If the Picts were not Aryans, we could hardly suppose them to have been able to acquire possession of extensive tracts of these islands after the arrival of such a powerful and warlike race as the early Aryans. The natural conclusion is, that the Picts were here before the Aryans came, that they were, in fact, the Aborigines.

Now something is known of the manners and customs of the ancient Picts; for one of them at least was so remarkable as to attract the attention of the ancient authors who mention the peoples of this country. It was the absence among them of the institution of marriage as known to men of Aryan race. This is illustrated by the history of the Picts in later times, especially in the case of their kings, for it is well known that a Pictish king could not be succeeded by a son of his own, but usually by a sister's son. The succession was through the mother, and it points back to a state of society which, previous to the conversion of the Picts to Christianity, was probably based on matriarchy as distinguished from marriage and marital authority. Accordingly the Greeks and Romans who have touched on the manners and customs of the Picts show clearly that they could not understand the relations of the sexes among peoples of that race, except as mere licence and wanton promiscuity. Among others may be mentioned Dion Cassius, who in writing (lxxvi. 16) about the wars of the Emperor Severus introduces, for the evident benefit of Roman women, a Pictish lady, who replies to the strictures of Julia, the Emperor's wife, on Pictish morality, to the effect that she thought the Pictish custom the better, since, as she said, Pictish ladies openly consorted with the best warriors of the race, while Roman matrons privily committed adultery with the vilest of men. Further the Pictish succession cannot have always been confined to the Pictland of the North,[1] for the ancient literature of Ireland

[1] Since writing the above we have come across a passage showing that the same kind of succession once prevailed at Tara : see the Place-name Story of

abounds in allusions to heroes who are usually described with the aid of the mother's name. Take the case of Conchobar mac Nessa, " Conor son of Nessa " (his mother), Diarmait Ua Duibne, "Dermot descendant of Dubinn " (his ancestress), not to mention the gods called *Tuatha Dé Danann*, " the tribes of the goddess Danu or Donu," which *Donu* appears also in the old literature of Wales, to wit as *Don* in the names of such personages as "Gwydion son of Don," " Arianrhod daughter of Don," and others of the same family, all placed by the Mabinogion on the northern coast of Gwyneđ. This kind of nomenclature implies the Pictish succession as its origin, and probably all that such origin implied. If the Aryans ever had this kind of custom, a view which js not universally accepted, it was probably so very far back that we could not with any confidence invoke it to explain these designations and others like them ; so we are inclined to regard them as having originated in non-Aryan surroundings.

The same conclusion as to the probable non-Aryan origin of the Picts is warranted by facts of another order, namely, those of speech ; but the Pictish question is rendered philologically difficult by the scantiness of the remains of the Pictish language. It would seem to have been rapidly becoming overloaded with loan-words from Goidelic and Brythonic when we first hear anything about it. So, failing to recognise this borrowing of words by the Picts, some have been led to regard Pictish as a kind of

Druim Criaich, edited with a translation by Stokes in the "Revue Celtique," xvi. 148–50. The storyteller undertakes to explain the peculiarity of the succession : he first relates how the three sons of the Irish king, Eochaid Feidlech, rebelled against their father, and how they fell in the conflict. He then adds words to the following effect :—"Then before nightfall their three heads came to Druim Criaich, and there Eochaid uttered the word, that from that time forward no son should ever take the lordship of Tara after his father unless some one came between them."

Gaelic, and some as a dialect akin to Welsh. The point to have been decided, however, was not whether Gaelic or Welsh explains certain words said to have been in use among the Picts, but whether there does not remain a residue to which neither Gaelic nor Welsh, nor, indeed, any Aryan tongue whatsoever, can supply any sort of key. This has of late begun to be perceived,[1] and all the more clearly now that the ancient inscriptions found in the Pictland of the North have been more carefully studied.[2] The whole group of inscriptions, however, is a very small one, and it shows the manifold influence of Gaelic and Norse, especially in Shetland, for Pictish cannot have become extinct for some time after the earlier visits of the Norsemen to our coasts. Among those inscriptions and fragments of inscriptions, there are two or three which may be said to be fairly legible ; and one of them is punctuated word by word. Nevertheless the adherents to the view that Pictish is Celtic and Aryan have in vain been challenged to produce a convincing translation. Neither Gaelic nor Welsh seems to be of any material avail in the effort, and one may confidently surmise that any other Aryan language will be found of still less use, if possible. This being so, it is not too much to say that the theory of the non-Aryan origin of the Pictish language holds the field at present.

Precarious as the Pictish inscriptions must be admitted to be, they have supplied the key to the interpretation of certain other inscriptions, to wit, in Wales, Cornwall, and Ireland. Thus a short one in minuscules at St. Vigeans, near Arbroath, reads, *Drosten ipe uoret ett forcus*, which

---

[1] See the "Revue Celtique," vi. 398, 399, and Zimmer's article in the "Zeitschrift für Rechtsgeschichte," p. 217.

[2] Lists of them will be found in Lord Southesk's "Ogams at Brodie, Aquhollie, Golspie, and Newton" (Edinburgh, 1886), p. 38, and in the "Proceedings of the Society of Antiquaries of Scotland," vol. xxvi., pp. 267–304, to which may now be added vol. xxxii., pp. 324–98.

may be for the present rendered "Drost's offspring,[1] Uoret, for Fergus." Similarly a well-known monument at Newton, in Aberdeenshire, bears in Ogam what may be provisionally read *Vorrenn ipuai Osir*, which may, in the same way, be interpreted as "Vor's offspring Osir," that is to say, Osir son of Vor or Vaur, for the name is read *Vaur* in the script on the same stone. From these one learns how to construe the following, found at ILanfaglan near Carnarvon :[2]—

FILI LOVERNII

ANATEMORI.

That meant, no doubt, " (the monument) of Lovernias's son, Anatemoras," that is, of Anatemoras son of Lovernias. This inscription was written in Latin, and *Anatemori* was the Celtic genitive of a proper name which in Brythonic would have been Anatjomaros; Welsh *eneid-fawr*, "great-souled," μεγαλόψυχος. From this cannot be severed the following, which is to be seen at Helston, in Cornwall : *Cnegumi fili Genaius.*[3] Though meant to be Latin, it has to be construed according to the grammar of a different idiom, for *fili* is here treated as the crude stem of the word, so that *fili Genai-us* is to be regarded as doing duty for *filius* and *Genaius* in apposition, and with only one case termination. The whole means *Genaius filius Cnegumi*, but the syntax is not that of an Aryan language. It is familiar, however, in agglutinative languages like Basque, and it occurs in our inscriptions too frequently to be regarded as a slip. Thus we have it both in Latin and in Goidelic on a tombstone found at Clydai, in Pembroke-

---

[1] It will be seen later (p. 50) that a more probable rendering than "offspring" would be "kin" or "nephew," and so probably with the vocable *poi* of certain Irish Ogams.

[2] See Hübner's "Inscriptiones Britanniæ Christianæ," No. 147.

[3] Hübner, No. 5.

shire: the Latin reads ETTERNI FILI VICTOR,[1] where *fili Victor* is treated as one noun in the nominative, and enough of the Ogam remains to show that the construction in the Goidelic version was identical. The whole meant "Æternus's son Victor," that is, Victor son of Æternus. Another instance of the same agglutinative syntax occurs on a stone at Eglwys Cymun, in the southwest of Carmarthenshire: it reads in Latin,[2]

AVITORIA

FILIA CVNIGNI,

and in Goidelic *Inigena Cunigni Avittoriges*, " (the monument) of Avitoria, daughter of Cunignas." Here the nouns in apposition are *inigena*, "daughter," and *Avittoriga ;* so the genitive ending *es* is applied to the latter alone, while the genitive of the father's name is inserted between the two feminines. From Ireland may be mentioned an inscription at Dunloe, near Killarney, which runs thus: *Maqui Ttal maqui Vorgos maqui mucoi Toicac*, " (the monument) of MacTail, son of Fergus, son" &c. In correct Goidelic this should have been *Maqui Ttali maqui Vorgossos*[3] *maqui*, &c. ; but *Ttal* and *maqui*, *Vorgos* and *maqui*, being respectively in apposition, have only one mark of the genitive each. The same construction is shown in one of the northern Ogam inscriptions of Ireland : it stands at a spot some twelve miles north-east of Omagh, in Tyrone, and reads: *Dotoatt maqui Nan* . . .[4] " (the monument) of Dotoatt, son of Nainnidh." Here *Dotoatt-maqui* must be construed as an agglutination with

---

[1] Hübner, No. 110.

[2] See the "Archæologia Cambrensis" for 1893, p. 285.

[3] It is not necessarily *Vorgossos*, as *Vorgos* may have represented a genitive which in a later form occurs as *Forgo* or *Forco*.

[4] See the "Journal of the Royal Society of Antiquaries of Ireland" for 1895, p. 104.

only one genitive termination, to wit, the *i* at the end of
maqui, "son's, *filii.*"

The distribution of inscriptions with this non-Aryan
syntax suggests that the British Isles were once inhabited
by a people speaking a non-Aryan language, and that,
while that people learned the vocabulary of an Aryan
language, it continued the syntax of its previous speech.
This was so decidedly the case, that we trace it not only
in the Goidelic which that people definitely adopted, but
also in the Latin which its learned men now and then
wrote. There is nothing incredible in this, as habits of
pronunciation and the syntax peculiar to a language are
most persistent and difficult to eradicate, even when careful
teaching is directed to that end, as anybody will admit
who knows anything of the difficulties of teaching Welsh
boys idiomatic English. One sees accordingly how the
Goidelic of the west of Britain may have been profoundly
modified by the pronunciation and syntax of the non-
Aryan language of the Aborigines ; but to what extent
the Brythonic conquerors of Mid-Wales may have cleared
the latter area of its ancient inhabitants, whether mostly
Goidelic or native, it is impossible to say. Beyond those
conquests, however, the old inhabitants of the Venedotian
north on the one hand, and those of the Siluro-Demetian
south on the other, are not likely to have been displaced
on any considerable scale. We are accordingly at liberty
to regard the Ordovic territory of Mid-Wales as the most
thoroughly Brythonic. It might appear at first sight a
remarkable corroboration of this view, that Mid-Wales
shows no inscriptions in Ogam at all or any inscriptions
whatsoever in which Goidelic can be traced. But as to
the absence of Goidelic traces in Mid-Wales, it must be at
once explained, that this region has very few inscriptions
at all to show corresponding to the post-Roman ones to be
found more to the north and more to the south. That

very fact, however, is not without a significance of its own, for it seems to show that the burial customs of the ancient Brythons of Mid-Wales differed from those of the other peoples : add to this that Mid -Wales has few or no cromlechs to show. Possibly the inhabitants buried their dead in barrows, where there was less inducement to indulge in writing than in the case of peoples who put up stones as memorials of their departed.

It may be objected that these arguments as to Mid-Wales are mostly negative, but there is at least one argument of a more positive kind—an argument based on the actual pronunciation of Powysian Welsh. In that dialect the vowel *a*, whether short or long, has a narrow pronunciation resembling that of the narrow *a* in the standard English pronunciation of such words as *man* and *bad*. This vowel may be indicated as *ạ*, and we have it in such words as *cạm*, "crooked," *mạm*, "mother," *pạn*, "when," and *cạ̄r*, "a cousin." Further, *cạm* and *cạr* tend to become, and have, in fact, extensively become, *kiạm* and *kiạr*, combinations from which the analogy of other languages would lead us to expect eventually some such forms as *tshạm* and *tshạ̄r*, or even *shạm* and *shạ̄r*, that is, provided this dialect of Welsh continued long enough a spoken language not too much restrained by the yoke of the standard spelling. The change here indicated is just what has happened in France : the Gauls appear to have pronounced their *a* narrow, and when they adopted Latin they could probably not help continuing their old pronunciation with its *ạ*. The result has been that French has made Latin words like *nassus*, "nose," and *pratum*, "a meadow," into *nez* and *pré*, and *caput*, "head," into *chef*, pronounced with *tsh* as in its English form of *chief*, and later, with *ch* = English *sh* as in standard French at the present day. The same was the case with such a word as Latin *castra*, "a camp," which some of the Gauls and the Brythons of this country seem to have pronounced *kiạstra*, which the ancestors of the English borrowed and made into *ceaster*, whence the modern *Chester*, pronounced *Tshester*. The initiative in all these changes is the pronunciation of *a* as *ạ*, which is a sound with a tendency to become *e*; and the most natural explanation of the fact that *ạ* and *iạ* occur in Mid-Wales Welsh is, that some of the Brythons, like the other Celts of Northern Gaul, had *ạ* as the sound of *a* in their language when· they penetrated to the west of this island. To the extent here indicated by the pronunciation, the Welsh of Powys is more like that of ancient Gaulish, that is to say, it is more purely Brythonic, than any of the other dialects. The reason for this is, probably, that the language of the Ordovices had been modified by the gradual absorption of other nationalities into that tribe, as it extended its conquests towards the west, while the Sons of Cuneda came from a district called Manau in the land of the Guotodin, Ptolemy's Otadini, or better *Votadini*. It was in or near their territory that the Roman wall reached the North Sea, and to them also belonged the coast northwards to the Forth, including what is now known as the Lothians. It is possible that the Votadini were not the first Brythons to occupy that strip of country; and it is probable that the previous inhabitants were driven inland, either by them or by previous invaders of kindred nationality. In either case the Gaulish of the Votadini may have had the chance of remaining less influenced by the idioms of the country, than can have been the case with tribes whose assimilation of the peoples conquered by them in war proceeded on a larger scale and for a longer period of time.

South of the domain of Powysian Welsh we have Brecknockshire, giving a broad pronunciation to the vowel *a*, whether long or short. But in the Welsh of Monmouthshire and Glamorganshire as far as the Neath Valley and the western limit, approximately, of the Custom of Glamorgan

(p. 30), the short *a* alone is broad, long *a* being uniformly made narrow. This seems to indicate that at one time that part of the southern border of the Principality came under the influence of some Brythonic people pressing westwards, such, for anything known to the contrary, as the Dobunni near the mouth of the Severn may have been.

It is, however, not to be supposed that Brythonic was formed in Wales : we are compelled by the close similarity of Welsh with Old Cornish and Breton to suppose that the language in all its essential features was formed before the Ordovices reached the shores of Cardigan Bay ; and we have the means of gauging to some extent how far it has deviated from Gaulish. A certain number of sentences are extant in Gaulish, and they invariably observe the ordinary usage of Aryan syntax in not placing the verb before its subject : take for example the following—

Σεγομαρος Ουιλλονεος τοουτιους Ναμαυσατις ειωρου
Βηλησαμι σοσιν νεμητον

That is, "Segomaros son of Villonos, magistrate of Nîmes, made for (the goddess) Belesama this temple." Or this, *Ratin brivatiom Frontu Tarbeisonios ieuru ;* that is, "Propugnaculum pontilium Fronto, Tarbeisoni filius, fecit."[1] It is unfortunate that not one of the Gaulish sentences extant happens to come from the ancient Belgium; but there is no reason to suppose that the Gaulish of Belgic Gaul differed in its syntax from the Gaulish of other parts of the country. On the other hand, the normal syntax of the Neo-celtic languages requires the verb to precede its subject, and the question arises how this important difference began. It might be suggested as an explanation, that the earlier Celts mixed with a non-Aryan race, whose language had this syntactic peculiarity of Neo-celtic as regards the position of the verb, and that they thus evolved

---

[1] According to Stokes's "Celtic Declension" (Göttingen, 1886), pp. 60, 67.

the Goidelic language. The next stage might similarly be supposed to be a mixing of the Brythons with the Goidels of the description just suggested, when it became the turn of the latter to be conquered, the result being that Brythonic emerged, having indirectly acquired some of the linguistic peculiarities of the Aboriginal inhabitants of Gaul, of Britain, or of both. Whatever the real explanation may prove to be, it will, in all probability, have to take for granted a racial amalgamation on a considerable scale. But the linguistic conditions seem to us, it is needless to say, to postulate a pre-Celtic race whose language was characterized by the chief peculiarities distinguishing Neo-celtic from Gaulish.[1]

The foregoing remarks amount briefly to this : the Goidelic and the Aboriginal elements should be expected in their greatest strength in the south and in the north of Wales, while Mid-Wales is marked out by the Gaulish affinities of the Powys dialect, and by the absence of monuments betraying any traces of Goidelic influence, as the home of the Brythonic element in the west of the island. We are, however, unable to detect in the habits or physical characteristics of the people at the present day any salient features corresponding to these vanishing landmarks. Thus the Aboriginal non-Aryan ideas as to marriage might, conceivably, have survived long in the modified form of a tendency to take somewhat too lenient a view of immorality, but the statistics of illegitimacy in Wales do not represent its geographical distribution to be such as clearly to suggest any such permanence of influence. On the other hand, men of purely Aryan descent are supposed to have been, like the ancient Gauls and the ancient Germans, inclined to be of light complexion and tall stature, which would, perhaps, imply the requirement

---

[1] We are glad to be able to refer our readers to an elaborate treatment of this question in Appendix B.

of more food than in the case of men of smaller build. We have, however, no statistics to show whether the people of Mid-Wales are on the whole taller or blonder than other Welshmen, but the Land Commission heard some evidence to the effect that the former fare better in the matter of food, especially in the county of Montgomery.

When and how the comparative homogeneity of the Welsh people was produced, it is impossible to say with any approach to precision. First of all, however, the distinctive customs of the Aborigines must have given way gradually to those of their Goidelic masters, though hardly without affecting the latter themselves; and the native language yielded, no doubt, comparatively early to Goidelic. As to Goidelic itself, its turn to go came in due time. We have no evidence that it was spoken in any part of Wales in the eighth or ninth century ; but it was probably not dead till well into the seventh. Besides having a language of their own, however, the Goidels must have had also their own laws ; and these, it would seem, proved in some respects more tenacious than their language. Welsh literature speaks of one great and conspicuous legislator of this island in early times. He is called *Dyfnwal Moel-Mut*, but the name *Dyfnwal*, answering as it does exactly to the Irish *Domhnall*, Anglicised *Donald*, teaches us nothing precise as to his race. On the other hand, the epithet *Moel-mud*, in its oldest form *Moel Mut*, cannot be other than Goïdelic, and its historical form in Irish is *Moel Muaid*, which we have in *Ua Maol-muaidh*, in English spelling *O'Molloy*. It should mean "the tonsured man or slave of Muad," in the same way that *Mael-Patraic* or *Mulpatric* was made into *Calvus Patricii*.[1] In the vocable

---

[1] See Rhys's "Goidelic Words in Brythonic" in the "Archæologia Cambrensis" for 1895, pp. 299, 300; Nigra's "Reliquie Celtiche" (Turin, 1870), p. 19; Stokes's "Goidelica" (London, 1872), pp. 86, 91 ; and Rhys's "Celtic Britain," pp. 73-5.

Muaid, for an earlier *Mõti*, we have the genitive of the name, possibly of some forgotten divinity, and the formula is not Christian, but merely retained in use in Christian times. This personage, whose full name proves him to have been no thorough Brython, is the accredited legislator of the Cymry ; and, according to one of the manuscripts of the Venedotian version of the Laws of Howel, the former's laws continued in force to the time of Howel. But even Howel, descended as he was from Cuneda, and representing the Brythonic element as he did, thought it inexpedient to undo the whole of the work of the Goidel. He left undisturbed his reckoning of measurement from the barley-corn up to the acre and the mile, as he did also his divisions of the country into cantrevs and their subdivisions. The words are to the following effect :[1] " And he [Dyfnwal] was a man of authority and wisdom ; and he (first) made good laws in this country, which laws continued in force till the time of Howel the Good. Afterwards Howel enacted new laws and annulled those of Dyfnwal ; and (yet) Howel did not disturb the measurements of lands in this island, but [let them continue] as Dyfnwal left them ; for the latter was the best man at measuring." Without entering into the question how far the laws of the Goidels differed from those of the Brythons, and to what extent Howel really modified[2] the laws obtaining till then in any part of his kingdom, we cannot help suggesting that the statement we have quoted represents one of the last stages in the amalgamation of the two Celtic races in the west of the island.

[1] Compare Owen's "Ancient Laws and Institutes of Wales," i. 184, 185, where the different manuscripts have been diligently wrought into a patch-work most difficult to unravel. For this, however, the editor was probably not so much to blame as the perverse policy obtaining at the Public Record Office in his time.

[2] Possibly we have an instance in point in the law, said to have once obtained in Britain, that any animal transgressing should be forfeited to the person injured. See the article "Mug-Eime" in Cormac's Irish Glossary (Dublin, 1862, and [translated by Stokes at] Calcutta, 1868).

Something may be learned on the head of race amalgamation from the probable history of the national name of the Welsh, to wit, *Cymro*, "Welshman," plural, *Cymry*. This word *Cymro* stands for an earlier *Cumbrox* or *Combrox*, parallel to the Gaulish *Allobrox*, plural *Allobroges*, a name applied by Gauls to another people whose country they conquered ; and just as *Allo-brox* meant an alien or foreigner, Welsh *attfro*, "foreigner," so *Com-brox* must have meant "one belonging to one's own country, a compatriot." The choice of this term as the national name suggests that it was applied to men who did not all belong to one and the same race, or speak the same language. As the word is to be traced in *Cumbra-land*, *Cumber-land*, its use must have extended to the Brythons of Strathclyde, which renders it probable that it had acquired some popularity before the end of the struggle between the kings of Gwyneđ and the Anglian princes of Northumbria in the earlier half of the seventh century. On the other hand, as the name seems to have been unknown not only in Brittany but also in Cornwall, it may be conjectured that it cannot have acquired anything like national significance for any length of time before the battle of Deorham in the year 577, when the West Saxons permanently severed the Celts west of the Severn from their kinsmen in the country consisting now of the counties of Gloucester, Somerset, Devon, and Cornwall. Thus it is probable that the national significance of the term *Cymro* may date from the sixth century, and that it is to be regarded as the exponent of the amalgamation of the Goidelic and Brythonic populations under the high pressure of attacks from without by the Saxons and the Angles.

Thus far of the races which may be said to have constituted the Welsh people ; but some mention may now be made of others that have entered into the composition later.

Among the earliest may be supposed a certain admixture introduced by the legions of ancient Rome, chiefly at such places as Isca Silurum or Carleon on the Usk, and Segontium, the remains of which are partially visible at the Carnarvon of the present day. After the departure of the Romans there was probably nothing of any importance in the matter of foreign blood introduced till the visits of the Scandinavian rovers from the eighth to the twelfth century. They may have left small settlements here and there on the coast, as, for instance, at Angle, in Pembrokeshire, and in the neighbourhood of the Point of Ayre and other places in Flintshire. Their presence also at Fishguard and Solva (in Welsh *Solfach*) in Pembrokeshire, seems to be proved by those names, and perhaps the same remark might be made as to Harlech, in Merionethshire. But the Scandinavians must have lost their idioms and distinctiveness in the language and nationality of their Celtic neighbours. The next accession of foreign elements came in the course of the Norman conquests ; but it is not easy to say to what extent the conquerors contributed in flesh and blood to Welsh nationality, or even to ascertain to what extent they were Normans, and not Bretons similar in race to the Welsh among whom they arrived. But the descendants, whether of Normans proper or of Bretons, became eventually absorbed in the body of the Welsh people and adopted the Welsh language, even in the Vale of Glamorgan, where the conquest by the Normans was probably the most systematic and thorough in Wales.

Not quite so, however, with another race which the Normans are supposed to have established in the west : we allude to the Flemings, who deserve in this context to be mentioned at somewhat greater length. Even before the Norman conquest of England, Flemings seem to have been brought to this country, as, for instance, by Tostig in his contest with his brother Harold for the crown. William the Conqueror married Matilda, daughter of the Count of Flanders, and he appears to have had Flemings in his employ in England. His son, William Rufus, had Flemish mercenaries in his army in Normandy when he attacked his brother, and Stephen employed them in large numbers in England. In fact, there is reason to believe that in the time of the early Norman kings Flemings settled in considerable numbers in this country. They appear to have been unpopular with both Normans and Saxons, and it occurred to Henry I. to make use of them, first, as a check on the Scotch, and afterwards on the Welsh. He settled them first in waste lands on the Tweed, but later he is said to have transported them bag and baggage to the Hundred of Roose in Pembrokeshire.[1] It is observed that Roose is remarkable for its comparative absence of Welsh place-names, and it may be concluded that the Flemings cleared it of what Welsh inhabitants there may have been there. The settlers made themselves masters of the rest of South Pembrokeshire, but as more Welsh names survive there, it is not probable that the new-comers made a clean sweep of the previous inhabitants. The question how far this Flemish settlement was really Flemish and not English is one of considerable difficulty. In case it was purely or mainly Flemish, one is tempted to ask, why the language of the district is now a dialect of English any more than that of Flanders, where Flemish shows no innate tendency to become English. To this it has been replied, that the Fleming of Pembrokeshire now speaks English for the same general reason that the Dane of Lincolnshire speaks English; and it may be readily admitted that the influence

---

[1] The principal contemporary authorities for this are Florence of Worcester, Orderic, Alfred of Beverley, William of Malmesbury, and Brompton; the words of those authors and of others in point will be found brought together in a valuable paper contributed by Dr. Henry Owen, of Poyston, to the "Archæologia Cambrensis" for 1895; see, more particularly, pp. 98—100.

of the Church and of the castles[1] in the district, combined with an inveterate hatred of the neighbouring Welsh, must have amply made up for the isolation from the body of the English world. On the other hand, one[2] of the greatest authorities on English dialects has examined the linguistic evidence and declared that it breaks down. At most, he thought, there could only have been a subordinate Flemish element, which soon lost all traces of its original and but slightly different dialect, while the principal element must have been Saxon, as in Gower and in the Irish baronies of Bargy and Forth, forming the south-east corner of Ireland.

Settlements of a still more obscure history were made here and there on the rest of the coast from St. Govan's Head to the mouth of the Severn, but far the most important must have been the group which made most of the peninsula of *Gwyr* or Gower into a non-Welsh district, now known as English Gower, and in Welsh as *Browyr*, that is, *Bro- Wyr* "the march or country of Gower."[3] Gower and South Pembrokeshire, which are mutually visible and

[1] See Mr. Ivor James's "Welsh in the 16th and 17th Centuries" (Cardiff, 1887), p. 31.

[2] We allude to the late Mr. Alexander J. Ellis, in a paper to which we shall have occasion to refer again. It is "On the Delimitation of the English and Welsh Languages," and published in the "Cymmrodor" for 1882, see p. 178. See also Mr. Edward Laws's evidence received at Pembroke by the Welsh Land Commission, Questions 28,994–29,032. Mr. Laws is practically of the same opinion as Mr. Ellis; and Professor Rhys has recently submitted the linguistic evidence adduced in Mr. Henry Owen's paper, p. 106, to the greatest living authority on the history of English sounds, namely, Dr. Henry Sweet, and he finds no reason to qualify Mr. Ellis's account of the matter. On the other hand, Professor Joseph Wright, in the course of his editing his English Dialect Dictionary, considers that he has come across words which unmistakably point to the Belgic mother country of the Flemings : he instances the interjection *ackafi*, and *blease*, "a blister."

[3] For a summary of the evidence as to the Flemish origin, see the Rev. J. D. Davies's "West Gower," especially part i., chapter iv., entitled "The Colonization by the Flemings," pp. 95–115. See also an important article entitled "Anglia Transwalliana" in the "Saturday Review" for the 20th of May, 1876 ; it is, unless we are greatly mistaken, from the pen of the late Professor Freeman.

enjoy the same dialect of English, may be supposed to
have been at one time in close communication with one
another by sea. The establishment of Flemings and
Englishmen in Gower and the geographical position of
their country would naturally suggest a distinct lordship,
which we have as the Seigniory of Gower : it has been
referred to more than once in the evidence taken by the
Welsh Land Commission in Glamorganshire.[1] A great
part of the south of Glamorgan is called in Welsh *Bro
Morgannwg*, "the march, margin, or country of Glamorgan,"
a term incorrectly rendered into English as " the Vale of
Glamorgan." Here the district of Llantwit Major has been
thought to show traces of Flemish settlements ; but the
Vale is remarkable chiefly for being, as already suggested,
one of the earliest Norman conquests in Wales. This fact
is rendered conspicuous at the present day by two very
different features of the country, the Norman architecture
of its churches and the possession by its farmers of the
tenant-right known as the Custom of Glamorgan, which
excels any other customary tenure in Wales.

Lastly, Wales, situated as it is between England and
Ireland, has always received additions to its population
from both countries. As to England, the number of
Englishmen settling in Wales has perhaps at no time been
equal to the number of Welshmen migrating to the large
towns of England. Irishmen have probably at all times
been coming over to Wales, especially to the nearest
corner, namely, Pembrokeshire. Thus the Irish story of
the Déisi tells us how some of those people left the part
of Ireland represented by the Baronies of the Decies in the
county of Waterford, and gave to Dyfed, a line of kings
represented in the time of Gildas by Vortiporius, from whom
Elen, wife of Howel the Good in the 10th century, was

---

[1] Qu. 5,095, 6,189–6,404, 6,418–6,422, 23,359, 27,975, 27,980, 28,014,
28,029, 28,037.

descended. To come down to a later time, we read in the history of Pembrokeshire by George Owen, who lived in the reign of Elizabeth, that the Anglo-Flemish portion of his native county was so overrun by Irishmen, that in some parishes the clergyman was found to be the only inhabitant who was not Irish.[1] This, it is true, was an exceptional time, as it was at the end of the war known as Tyrone's Rebellion, but many of the exiles must have settled in Pembrokeshire. In fact, Mr. Henry Owen, the learned editor of George Owen's work, remarks[2] that the descendants of those Irishmen can still be traced.

Reverting for a moment to the chief races constituting the Welsh people, the Celtic or Aryan consisting of Goidels and Brythons, and the non-Aryan consisting of the Aboriginal population, we may say that their relative proportions to one another may be treated as little disturbed by immigrants from Ireland or even from England; for the average Englishman is at most not much more Aryan than the average Welshman. But the Scandinavian settlements, so far as they went, must have gone to strengthen the Aryan element, and in a qualified sense the same may be said of the Norman conquests in Wales. Then as to the Anglo-Flemish districts, the settler cannot be regarded as having to any large extent helped to modify the composition of the Welsh people, as he has partly resisted the temptation to merge his national individuality in the amalgam of races around him. As it is, he is there conveniently situated for the purposes of comparison, and in this connection he may be roughly described, at any rate so far as Pembrokeshire is concerned, as somewhat better fed than his Welsh neighbour, more plump and well-conditioned in point of personal appearance, more happy and contented with his

---

[1] See George Owen's " Pembrokeshire," p. 40.

[2] In the volume, to which reference has already been made, of " Archæologia Cambrensis," p. 103.

lot generally, and less troubled with social or political ideas as to the future.

Should it then be asked what the Welsh of the present day are, Aryan or not Aryan, the answer must be, we think, that, on the whole, they are not Aryan ; that, in fact, the Aryan element forms, as it were, a mere sprinkling among them. This is by no means surprising, as will be seen on comparing the case of France, to which we have already alluded. For the French of the present day, with the exception of the Teutonic element in the north-east of France, are, in the main, neither Gauls nor Aryans of any description so much as the lineal representatives of the inhabitants whom the Aryans found there. In fact, the Gauls were not very numerous, even when they ruled the whole country. It has been estimated, on the basis of the particulars given by Cæsar as to the numbers of the cavalry which the different Gaulish tribes were able to place in the field to meet the Roman legions, that the Gaulish aristocracy formed a surprisingly small proportion of a population whose numbers ranged somewhere between three and six millions.[1] There seems to be no reason to suppose that the dominant Celts in this country were relatively more numerous than in Gaul. They formed a ruling class, and led their dependents in war, which was their business above all other things.

Coming down to later times, we may say that their descendants retained the position of privilege and leading in the contests with the Normans, who either measured

---

[1] See Roget de Belloguet's "Ethnogénie Gauloise," ii. 308-314, and Bertrand and Reinach's "Celtes dans les Vallées du Pô et du Danube," ii. 41. See also M. d'Arbois de Jubainville's "Premiers Habitants de l'Europe," vol. ii., pp. 7-9, where the learned Frenchman estimated the aggregate of Gauls, inclusive of women and children, at 60,000, a figure which has always struck us as somehow too low. It has since been boldly challenged by Mr. W. H. (Bullock) Hall in his "Romans on the Riviera" (London, 1898), pp. 3-5.

swords with them on the field of battle, or entered into family alliances with them, as best suited their purposes for the time being. In any case, the Normans do not appear to have thought it beneath them to intermarry with the nobility of Wales, and that to an extent not to be, in the case of England, inferred from the history of their treatment of Saxon or Anglian families. As late as the Tudor period the able-bodied men of the Welsh families took part in raids on the Marches and in the interminable feuds which raged among them at home, in the course of which they waylaid one another or burnt each other's residences about their owners' ears. Witness, for instance, the state of Eifionyd, as represented by Sir John Wynne, in his History of the Gwydir Family. But from the moment that Wales was subjected to English law they began to find their occupation gone, and probably to dwindle in importance and power ; but it remained for the Civil War which broke out under Charles I. to complete their ruin, since they ranged themselves nearly all on the side of the King. Neither folly nor misfortune, however, could loosen the attachment felt for them by their dependents, an attachment which a perusal of the evidence taken by the Welsh Land Commission would show to be still strong among the tenants on the larger estates in Wales. There remained a difference of education, a difference of class, to mark off the squire and his family from the people on his land, but no conscious distinction of race.

Nevertheless, if a competent ethnologist were to be sent round Wales to identify the individual men and women who seemed to him to approach what he should consider the Aryan type, his report would probably go to show that he found comparatively few such people, and that those few belonged chiefly to the old families of the landowning class : the vast majority he could only label as probably not Celtic, not Aryan. To pronounce, from the point of view of race and history, on the social, political, or religious proclivities of that majority is rendered difficult by the fact that it is not easy to estimate correctly the influence on Wales of movements originated or developed in England. There is, however, one instructive instance : the Welsh people have largely deserted the Established Church, and they have done so in favour of more democratic forms of religion, just as their kinsmen have done in Cornwall and the Highlands of Scotland. Herein the Welsh can hardly be said to have been merely following the example of England, as England cannot be considered to have given a decisive lead in the matter. Religion, however, is not the only domain in which the tendency of the Welsh is democratic : it holds good of their attitude, on the whole, as regards social and political questions. And this cannot fail to be rendered more and more conspicuous by all movements calculated to weaken the attachment of the many for the class which supplied them with leaders in the past.

It may perhaps be convenient if we summarise here the views set forth in this chapter, somewhat as follows :—

The study of the skulls and other remains found in early interments in this country proves that it was inhabited by more than one race at the time when the Romans came here to conquer.

The study of language and institutions suggests the view, that the earliest inhabitants were of a non-Aryan race, namely, that represented probably by the Picts of history.

In the fifth or the sixth century before our era, or perhaps earlier, the first Celtic settlers came and overran most of the southern half of Britain. They were the Aryan ancestors of the Goidels, whose language is now represented by the Gaelic dialects of Ireland, Man, and Scotland.

In the second or the third century B.C. there arrived invaders belonging to the other branch of the Celtic family, namely, the Brythons, and they conquered from the Goidels most of the country which the latter had conquered previously from the Aborigines.

In what is now Wales the Brythonic conquests were represented by the territory of the Ordovices, covering the whole of Mid-Wales as far as Cardigan Bay.

The Goidels to the north and south of the Ordovices were never systematically displaced, and their Goidelic may have continued a living tongue down into the seventh century.

Soon after the Romans left Britain the Ordovices received an accession of Brythonic blood in the troops led by Cuneda and his Sons, to whom may be traced the political framework of Wales under the aspect which it presents to the historian of the Norman Conquest.

Conquests there must have been, but the study of the languages in point goes to prove more, namely, inter-mixture: the Brythons mixed with the Goidels, who were themselves an amalgam of the first Celtic settlers with the Aborigines ; but all conscious distinction of race had probably been obliterated before the eleventh century.

The admixture of other blood, Scandinavian, Norman, Flemish, and English, has not greatly modified the race, the predominant element in which has probably always been the substratum contributed by the earliest lords of the soil of these islands.[1]

---

[1] Since this chapter was written we have had occasion to read a remarkable book by the late Rev. W. D. Babington on "Fallacies of Race Theories as applied to National Characteristics" (London: Longmans, Green & Co., 1895). Among other things we may say that it confirms our view as to the mixture of races constituting each of the nations in the United Kingdom, and it disposes of the stock generalisations framed to flatter the German at the expense of the Celt.

CHAPTER II.

THE PICTISH QUESTION.

THE foregoing outlines will serve to suggest a picture of the ethnology of ancient Wales, and we have endeavoured not to crowd it with details. Some of these we now proceed to supply by elaborating a few of the points on which we have touched in passing. We begin by reverting to the Pictish succession and metronymic designations like that of *Gwydion son of Dôn ;* and when one comes to consider what the Pictish succession must have originally meant, one cannot overlook Cæsar's statement, that some of the inhabitants of Britain had their wives in common. Professor Zimmer, on analysing Cæsar's chapter in point, comes to the conclusion that the words were meant to apply to non-Aryan inhabitants in the interior—those, in fact, whom Cæsar represents as regarding themselves descended from the Aboriginal islanders in contrast to the later comers, who, according to the same authority, did not materially differ in their customs from the Gauls. Cæsar's words (v. 14) are to the following effect :—*Uxores habent deni duodenique inter se communes, et maxime fratres cum fratribus parentesque cum liberis ; sed qui sunt ex iis nati, eorum habentur liberi, quo primum virgo quæque deducta est.* The first sentence makes a clean sweep of the institution of marriage, and leaves no room for the idea of incest ;[1] but the

[1] As to the origin of that idea see M. S. Reinach's article "La prohibition de l'inceste et ses origines" in "L'Anthropologie," vol. x., pp. 59–70.

second sentence seems to us to have been dictated by the Roman's inability to realise a state of society exclusively based on birth. The idea of assigning the children each to its own father, if not entirely due to the working of Cæsar's own mind, reads in this context like an advance towards Aryan habits. At any rate, we shall as we proceed find traces of a stage of society betraying no perceptible tendency in that direction.[1]

The kind of social arrangement here in question suggests several curious points for consideration, and foremost among them this : who would be reckoned a man's nearest of kin ? Clearly one's own brothers and sisters by the same mother ; and looking backwards one's nearest relatives would be his mother and his mother's brothers and sisters similarly, while looking forwards it would be one's sisters' children. So one would naturally look for one's heir and successor in one's brother, and after him in a son of one's sister. This is the key to a good deal that is otherwise unintelligible in Celtic literature : let us take for instance the *Mabinogi of Math*, which has already been mentioned. There the leading family ruling over Gwyneđ consists of the following persons :—

Math the king, who is called son of Mathonwy, about whom nothing is known.

Dôn, Math's sister, about whom equally little is known, except that she had the following children :

Gwydion, Gofannon, (Amaethon), Gilfaethwy, and *Efeyd,* all called sons of Dôn ; and one daughter called

Aranrot, or Arianrhod, daughter of Dôn. Arianrhod had two sons, *Dylan* and *Lew Lawgyffes.*

Next to the king himself, Gwydion plays the most important *rôle* in Math's realm, and the king teaches him the

---

[1] Such a stage of society, together with well-known stories about virgin mothers, points back to a savage state in which the male element had never been supposed necessary to conception.

magic of which he was master : in fact, everything points to Gwydion as Math's successor, though that is not stated in the story. In due time ℓLew ℓLawgyffes is represented succeeding to the kingdom of Gwyneð. In other words, Math is succeeded by his sister's son, Gwydion, and Gwydion is succeeded by his sister's son, ℓLew. It is tacitly assumed that Gwydion was the father of ℓLew ; but the relationship between Gwydion and Arianrhod is never discussed, and the silence maintained on that point only becomes intelligible in the light of the social arrangement here supposed.

Similarly in the case of the *Mabinogi of Branwen* : there we have Bendigeitvran, or Brân the Blessed, as king of Britain, and he has a brother, Manawyðan, and a sister, Branwen : they are called sons of ℓLyr and daughter of ℓLyr respectively, while their mother is named Penarðim,[1] daughter of Beli, son of Mynogan.

Now Branwen is given to wife to Matholwch, who reigns in Ireland, and there she has a son by him called Gwern son of Matholwch ; but after some years have passed Brân hears of his sister being harshly treated, and he makes an expedition to Ireland. He leaves behind him Cradawc, or Caradog, his son, to take charge of this country, the kingship of which is, however, seized in the meantime by Caswaℓlawn, or Caswaℓlon, son of Beli. For this Caswaℓlon,

---

[1] She had two other sons, Nissien and Efnissien, whose father is called Euroswyð in the Mabinogi : he is said in one of the Triads (i. 50 = ii. 49) to have, some time or other, taken ℓLyr prisoner. The form *Penarðim* in the Mabinogi was an archaism ; and our narrator, had he understood it, would have put it into his own spelling as *Penardu*, which would be in modern Welsh *Penarðu* or *pen-arðu*, meaning " Her of the Black Head." Compare the variant *Dyf-lyn* for *Du-lyn* " Black pool," and Welsh *u* in verbal nouns like *credu* " act of believing " and *gohebu* " act of corresponding," as compared with Old Irish *cretem* " belief," *sechem* " act of following," and *sessom* " standing." The subject is too large to dispose of here in passing, but the reader should consult the learned articles of M. Ernault on " Les Formes de l'Infinitif Breton," in Meyer and Stern's " Zeit. für Celt. Philologie," vol. ij.

we are told, donned a coat of magic mail and slew Caradog's men without disclosing who it was that did it; but he
did not slay Caradog, as he was his relative. He is called
his nephew, son of his cousin; and we learn from an
ancient triad cited in the story that he died of grief and
vexation at the slaughter of his men. In Ireland the
coming of Brân and his host created a great commotion,
but, thanks to the intercession of Branwen, the two kings
Brân and Matholwch came to terms, and the concession
made by the Irish was to give Matholwch's kingdom to
Branwen's son Gwern. The concession consisted in the
fact implied that Gwern could not, according to the usage
of Matholwch's people, be Matholwch's successor, as he
would, according to the birth succession, be no recognised
relation of Matholwch's at all, whereas, according to the
same rule, he would be Brân's nearest of kin and his rightful
successor, as son of his sister. The editor or narrator of
the story as we have it does not show that he understood
this, and it is he probably that is to be held responsible
for an inconsistency which occurs in it. More than once
he makes Caswatton son of Beli cousin to Brân and
Manawyđan, though he treats them at the outset as sons of
Penardim, and her as daughter of Beli.[1] It all comes right,
however, if we treat Penardim, not as daughter of Beli, but
as his sister on the mother's side: then Brân's right to
succeed Beli, who is fabled to have been king of Britain,
becomes clear—he is the son of Beli's sister. But an editor

---

[1] We take it that the latest editor is responsible for this, but that he found
Caswatton made son of Beli in the version which he was using of the Mabinogi,
and that he forgot or hesitated to alter the relationship as indicated at pp. 41
and 44. The passage where Penardim is made daughter of Beli is the opening
of the Mabinogi of Branwen (p. 26), and the second line of it is remarkable for
the words *arderchabc o goron lundein,* which have been translated from some
such a phrase as *insignitus diademate,* common enough, for example, in
Geoffrey's Latinity, as in Lib. ij. 1, 20, iv. 11, vi. 4. In fact we suspect that
the Mabinogion had not assumed the form in which we have them till Geoffrey's
time.

not familiar with this kind of succession would naturally think that he improved Brân's position by making his mother daughter of Beli—that is to say, by making Brân a descendant of Beli.

The story originally implied the Pictish succession, and it is worthy of note that of the two men whom it represents succeeding their respective fathers contrary to it, the one, Caradog, dies of vexation,[1] while the other, Caswałton, is only enabled to secure by violence and magic a position which the tenor of the Mabinogi assumes to have rightfully belonged to Manawyđan after the death of his brother Brân.   In fact, the introduction of Caradog and Caswałton betrays the falsifying hand of a historian, for *Cradawc*, as we have assumed, is merely a form of *Caradawc*, the representative of *Caratācos*, in Latin *Caratacus*—sometimes distorted still into *Caractacus*—the name of the famous but unsuccessful leader of the Silures and Ordovices against the Romans.   As a matter of fact, he was no son of Brân, nor was he of his Goidelic race, as he was a Brython.   Yet this fiction has been widely accepted in Modern Welsh literature, according to which Caradog and Brân his father, together with their families, were taken captives to Rome, where Brân and others of his family were converted to Christianity, and on their return brought the Gospel to Britain.   Then as to Caswałton, by him we are doubtless to understand

---

[1] The exact meaning of the word used is merely inferred, as it occurs only in this triad.   The part relating to Caradog reads in the Red Book (Oxford Mabinogion, p. 41), *A h6nn6 uu y trydyd dyn a torres y gallon o niuyget*, where the two last words should probably be *o anniuyget.*   It seems to mean "And that was one of the three who broke their hearts of vexation or grief." Another of the three making up the original triad was Ffaraon, who is thus mentioned in "Ludd and Ļevelys," *ibid.*, p. 98: *Trydyd crynweissat uu h6nn6 a torres y gallon [o] anniuiged*, "That was the third chief guardian who broke his heart of grief."   It is there said that *Dinas Emreis* in Snowdon had been previously known from Ffaraon as Dinas Ffaraon Dande, and the name carries us back to an old world of legend now submerged.   The third limb of the triad, we are sorry to say, has never been discovered.

Cassivellaunos, the leader of the Brythonic tribes who had opposed Julius Cæsar in the south-east of Britain when that general paid his second visit to our shores: Geoffrey, at the end of his third book, chap. xx., introduces him as Cassibellaunus, son of Hely [*read* Bely]. The way in which Caradog's history is referred to an ancient triad, suggests that we have in the allusion to his death a touch of genuine tradition, based remotely on the real history of Caratacos, and preserved in the west of the island.

Lastly, as to Beli son of Mynogan,[1] his identity with *Bellinus* son of *Minocannus* in Nennius's Historia Brittonum, where he is made the native leader against Julius Cæsar, has been known for some time. Arid Professor Zimmer[2] has traced the Nennian *Bellinus, filius Minocanni*, back through Orosius's gibberish *Minocynobellinum Britannorum regis filium* to Suetonius's *Adminio, Cynobellini Brittannorum regis filio;* and from the latter historian we learn that Adminios was a fugitive from Britain, who gave himself up to the mad emperor Caligula. So much for the designation of Beli, or Beli Mawr, son of Mynogan ; but we cannot follow Professor Zimmer in thinking that his unravelling of this tangle of errors disposes of Beli. For we conjecture that the words translated "Son of Mynogan" were not to be found in the original of the Mabinogi, but that they were introduced by an editor who was acquainted with the Historia Brittonum of Nennius. What stood in the story previously was rather *Beli Maur map Aun, An*, or *Anau*, "Beli the Great, son of A.," which occurs as *Beli Ma6r m. Anna*, "Beli the Great, son of Anna," in one of the pedigrees in

---

[1] See Skene's "Four Anc. Books of Wales," ii. 204, 420 ; and San Marte's "Nennius und Gildas," pp. 40, 41, § 19.

[2] See Zimmer's "Nennius Vindicatus," pp. 271-3 : his references are to Suetonius's Caligula, cap. 44 *et seq.*, and Orosius's "Histor. advers. Paganos," vii. 5, 5 ; see also Evans's "Coins of the Ancient Britons," pp. 208, 284-348 ; and Rhys's "Celtic Britain" (2nd edition), p. 278.

Jesus College Manuscript 20, supposed to be of the thirteenth century. Further one reads two sentences respecting Anna, as follows : *yr anna honn oed verch y amhera6dyr rufein. yr anna honno a dywedei wyr yr eifft y bot yn gyfynnithder6 y veir vor6yn*,[1] which seem to represent two glosses from two different sources, as will be seen from the rendering of them, " This Anna was daughter to the emperor of Rome. That Anna used to be said by the men of Egypt to be cousin to the Virgin Mary." The latter statement is also made in the pedigree of Owen son of Howel the Good, who is traced back to *Aballac* son of *Amalech qui fuit Beli magni filius, et Anna mater ejus, quam dicunt esse consobrinam Mariæ Virginis, Matris Domini nostri Ihesu Christi*.[2]

The treatment of the ILyr pedigree in the matter of Penardim prepares us to understand the treatment of Anna in the pedigrees in question. The editor probably found Anna represented as Beli's wife or as his mother, but not feeling bound to say anything about her, he simply added to the name of Beli words meaning "Son of Mynogan," after the example of Nennius. With regard to the Christian Anna, the introduction of her name is due probably to àn early confusion of it with that of *Ána* or *Anu*, genitive *Ánann*, who figures in Irish mythology as *mater deorum hibernensium*.[3] This name would be treated in Old Welsh as *Aun* or *An* (possibly *Anau*), according to the quantity

---

[1] See "Y Cymmrodor," viij. 84; also p. 85.

[2] For the abbreviations used see Phillimore's edition of MS. A. of the " Annales Cambriæ," in " Y Cymmrodor," ix. 170 : the genealogies seem to have been compiled in the tenth century. Whether the scribe here meant one to regard Anna as the mother of Beli or of Amalech is not clear ; but a little later (p. 174) he undoubtedly takes the latter view—the wrong view, in fact ; for he there has "Amalech son of *Beli et Anna*."

[3] See Stokes's edition of O'Donovan's translation of "Cormac's Glossary" (Calcutta, 1868), s.v. *Ana*, p. 4 ; also p. 17, where an article is devoted to another female figure, *Buanann*, mother of Irish heroes, just as *Ána* was mother of Irish gods.

of the initial vowel in the Goidelic *Ána* or *Anu*, which is not certain.

To return to Beli, we read in the Red Book story called Maxen's Dream,[1] that he was in possession of Britain until Maxen and his legions came and drove him and his sons on sea ; and so closely does Beli appear associated with the sea that an ancient verse calls the brine of the ocean Beli's liquor.[2] This we cannot help regarding as a popular touch not to be explained by any amount of learned bungling on the part of Orosius or Nennius. We are led back to a legend in the west of Britain, which represented it enjoying a sort of a golden age which was only brought to an end by the advent of the Romans. We learn that the king's name was Beli, and we infer that he was a Goidel, who had ships on the Irish Sea. We know from the Chronicles that the name which was Beli in Welsh (borne by one of the kings of Gwyneđ and by others in historical times) was in Irish *Bile ;* further, there was an ancient Bile with whom we should identify our Beli the Great, and Irish legend represents him as the father of Míl, the leader of the last legendary conquest of Ireland and ancestor of all those of the Irish who called themselves *Milesians* after his name. The story as we have it makes Bile king of Spain, and by giving his son the name of *Míl*, genitive *Míled*, it brings us to the Latin *miles*, genitive *militis*, " a soldier": this seems to have been a synonym or translation of another name, *Galam* or *Golam*, by which Míl was known and described in Irish as a man of bravery and valour. The identity of the names Bile and Beli is, however, not all: the parallel is closer than it looks at first sight. Míl, son and successor of Bile, conquers Ireland, which is divided between his two

---

[1] See the Oxford Mab., p. 88.
[2] See the Book of Taliessin in Skene's " Four Ancient Books of Wales," ii. 150, where one reads *Gnaбt róyf yn heli Beli wiraбt*, "Familiar is the sight of oars in the brine of Beli's liquor." For a mistranslation of it see i. 300.

sons Eber and Airem, while the Mabinogi makes Beli's
heir and successor, Brân, obtain the practical disposal of
Ireland. The narratives otherwise differ, owing chiefly to
the Welsh one having gone off into a story which may be
regarded as forming a counterpart of that of the Nibelungen
Slaughter in the literature of Teutonic lands.

The tradition about Beli must be regarded as belonging
to the Goidels of Britain, and it was only by a *tour de force*
that Caswaḷḷon, the leader of Brythons—that is to say, of
the hereditary foes of the Goidel—could be made son of
Beli ; but it was natural enough that an editor of the
Mabinogion should wish to graft the later history of his
country on the legendary glories of the past, and it
was a step in that direction to place Caswaḷḷon among
the sons of Beli. Whether he set himself to do this, or
merely followed the example set by a previous writer,[1]
his readers, accepting the words which he has used,
could not help saying in effect : Yes, it was by craft and
violence that Caswaḷḷon secured supreme power ; but he
was after all son of the rightful king of Britain in her
golden age—that is, of Beli the Great. The same editor is
possibly also to be held responsible for the order of the
events, which is probably unhistorical, as we should rather
regard the aggressiveness of Caswaḷḷon's race as one at least
of the reasons for Brân's going to Ireland. But the dating
of Caswaḷḷon's conquests in Wales after Brân's departure
for Ireland is to be explained by the confounding of the
naming of Cadwaḷḷon Lawhir with Caswaḷḷon's ; for Welsh
tradition insists on that Cadwaḷḷon, who was grandson of
Cuneḋa and father of Maelgwn, as the final vanquisher of the

---

[1] Such as Geoffrey or the writer of the pedigree already mentioned (p. 42),
in which we have the descent of Owen son of Howel traced back not only to
Maelgwn and Cuneḋa, but to Beli. The former portion seems to reach back
to Tacit only : then comes a very Pictish looking portion beginning with *Cein*,
son of *Guorcein*, son of *Doli*, son of *Guordoli*, and terminating with Beli and
Anna. See also the "Proceedings of the Antiq. of Scotland," xxxij. 342.

Goidels in North Wales.[1] We may therefore still suppose
that the Brythonic tribe of the Ordovices pushing on to
the shores of Cardigan Bay may have been the cause of
an emigration of Goidels to the nearest coast of Ireland.
In fact, we have possibly a trace of this in the name
Eblanii, which Ptolemy gives to the inhabitants of the
coast north and south of the mouth of the Liffey, as
we seem to have closely related names in that of the
river *Elan* (a tributary of the Wye), and that of the
mountain region of Elenid, in which Giraldus[2] places
the sources of the Severn and the Wye, of the Towy, the
Teifi, and the Ystwyth. On the Irish side it is significant
that the story of Míl's two sons gives to Eber, the elder
brother and eponymous hero of the *Iverni*, the southern half
of Ireland, and to the younger brother, Airem (genitive
Aireman or *Eremon*), the northern half; and that it further
represents Airem slaying Eber and taking the whole of
Ireland to himself. The name *Airem* means *ploughman*,
and possibly conveys a reference to the triumphs of the
Aryan farmer over the ruder native. But even disregard-
ing all such connotation of the name, we still have the fact
that it has gathered round it legends reminding one of the
story of Arthur; and that the name Airem was borne by one
of the early kings of Tara, in Meath and the land of the
ancient Eblanii, the centre of Milesian rule over Ireland.

Let us now see in what way the custom of reckoning

---

[1] See Triad i. 49 = ii. 40 = iii. 27 and the "Iolo MSS.," pp. 78, 468.
Compare Nennius, § 62, and note the confusion of names in the "Iolo MSS."
See also the Oxford Bruts, where Kat6aïla6n ILa6ir at p. 200, stands possibly
for the same man as Kas6aïla6n at p. 232: in Geoffrey's Latin they are
respectively Caduallo ix. 12, and Cassibellanus xi. 2.

[2] See his "Descriptio Kambriæ" (Rolls Office edition), pp. 119, 138,
170-3, 175, where the spelling is *Elennyth* and *Elennith*; also the Oxford
Mabinogion, p. 62, where it is written *Elenit*: Lewis Glyn Cothi wrote
Elenid, III. iv. 43, 4 (p. 184). As to the phonology of the equation suggested
in the text, we have the similar reduction of *ebl* into *el* in the Welsh adverb
eleni (this year) from some form of the Welsh word *blyned*, "year."

descent by birth alone has left its impress on the language and monuments of those among whom it prevailed. Our attention is challenged in the first instance by inscriptions which suggest no father's name; and the earliest of that class is probably the bronze tablet found not very long ago at Colchester and read as follows :[1]—

DEO . MARTI . MEDOCIO . CAMP
ES[tr]IVM . ET VICTORIE ALEXAN
DRI . PII FELICIS AVGVSTI . NOS[tr]I
DONVM . LOSSIO . VEDA . DE . SVO
POSVIT . NEPOS . VEPOGENI . CALEDO.

"To the god Mars *Medocius* of the *Campes[tr]es* and to the victory of our Alexander Pius Felix Augustus (this) gift has been dedicated at his own expense by Lossio Veda, Vepogenos's nephew, a Caledonian."

The god Medocius who is here equated with the Roman Mars is otherwise unknown, as is also the precise meaning in this instance of the Latin *Campestres*, which usually has reference to the open field, and in particular to the Campus Martius in Rome : this has called forth the suggestion that perhaps Lossio Veda was a gladiator. However that may be, he has taken care to tell us that he was a Caledonian, which is for our purpose much the same as if he had called himself a Pict. We have indirect evidence to the same effect in the vocables *Veda* and *Vepogeni*, for both may be said to occur in the list of the Pictish kings. The former has there been read *Uecla*, a spelling due doubtless to the difficulty of distinguishing

---

[1] See the " Proceedings " of the Society of Antiquaries, 2nd S. xiv. 108, 183 ; also " The Archæologia," liv. 37. By reading *Campesium* one seemed to arrive at a native name *Campeses*, recalling *Campsie* in Stirlingshire, and the Linn of *Campsie* on the Tay. As we have, however, to treat NOSI as *nostri*, we seem to be bound to insert *tr* in CAMPESIVM likewise. For some further account of the bronze, together with a photograph of it, see the " Pro. of the Antiq. of Scotland," xxxij. 325-30.

in some kinds of handwriting between *d* and *cl;* and the
latter has in the same document yielded a nominative
Vipoig. The two entries occur also significantly near one
another, as follows :[1]—

> *Vipoig namet xxx. ann. regnauit.*
> *Canutulachama iiii. ann. regnauit.*
> *Wradech uecla i:. ann: regnauit.*

Lòssio Veda, though showing no inclination to be over brief
in describing himself, suggests no father's name ; and this is
the case with certain other inscriptions, such as the one
found on Winsford Hill, in Somerset, which reads[2] merely—

CARATACI
NEPVS.

But what did *nepos* (or *nepus*) mean ? For the Romans the
word is known to have meant a grandson, a descendant,
also a nephew, whether son of one's brother or of one's
sister ; but in a society with birth alone considered, only
one of those meanings is admissible—namely, a sister's son.
Thus *Carataci Nepus* would mean " Nephew (= sister's son)
of Caratacas." Where the language used is Goidelic, the
place of *nepos* is supplied by *avjas*, genitive *avi*, reduced in
Modern Irish to *úa* or *ó*, genitive *úi*, as for instance in the
following inscription from the Barony of Bere, co. Cork :
Maqui Decceddas avi Toranias " (The Stone) of Mac-Dechet
ó Torna." Or take the following, found at Dunbell, co.
Kilkenny : *Navvallo avvi Genittac[ci],*[3] " (The Stone) of *Núall*

---

[1] See Skene's "Chronicles of the Picts and Scots," p. 6 ; also the fac-simile of
the MS. Skene's account of the manuscript will be found in his preface,
pp. xviii.—xxiii., according to which it is a copy made in the fourteenth century
from one or more manuscripts of the tenth.

[2] See the "Archæologia Cambrensis" for 1891, p. 30 ; also the " Academy "
for Feb. 14, 1891, p. 168.

[3] "Journal of the Royal Society of Antiquaries of Ireland" for 1896,
p. 134.

ó Gentich." In one remarkable instance the word used is the etymological counterpart of the Latin *nepos*, genitive *nepotis*, in Irish Ogam *niotta*[*s*], later *nioth*, *niath* with a nominative *nie* or *nia*, Welsh *nei*, now *nai*, "a nephew."[1] The stone was found near Gortatlea, between Killarney and Tralee, and it reads thus, in two lines :[2]—

Dumeli maqui Glasiconas
Niotta Cobranor[*i*].

"(The Stone) of Dumel, son of Glasiuc, nephew of (the) Distributor." We take *Cobranor*... to stand for *com-rannori*, genitive of *comrannorias*, and to mean one who shares or divides, probably in the sense of carving and dividing meat at feasts and banquets. Among the Irish this was a position of distinction, claimed by the warrior who had performed most feats of valour. There is a well-known Irish tale entitled the Story of Mac Dáthó's Pig, which turns on a contest for the carving of that portentous beast by the braves of Ulster and Connaught. Mac Dáthó was king of the Leinstermen, but afraid of both Ulster and Connaught, on account of a remarkable hound of his which they coveted. Fearing trouble, he took his wife's advice and cunningly invited both the men of Connaught and the men of Ulster for the same day : then they would, he said, get the hound.

---

[1] The *p* which appears in the Latin *nepos* disappears, according to rule, in the Celtic equivalent ; hence Irish *nie*, genitive *nioth*. The Welsh setting out from ne(p)ot-s made it into *ne-o* or *ne-io*, whence *nei* and *nai :* compare *tleidr* "thief," from *latrio*, for the Latin *latro*. Other instances will be found in the "P-oceedings of the Society of Antiquaries of Scotland," xxvi., 309. Breton has *ní* and *níz* "nephew," and *nizez* "niece," where the *z* of *niz* probably stands for the earlier *s* = *ts* of the nominative *ne(p)ot-s*. Compare Breton *noz* = Welsh *nos* "night," from *not-s* = *noct-s*, reduced in Latin to *nox*.

[2] See the "Journal of the Royal Society of Antiquaries of Ireland" for 1895, pp. 1–4 ; but our reading is checked by a rubbing and a sketch kindly supplied by the Rev. P. Sweeny, A.M., Ballinacourty Rectory, Annascaul, and by a recent examination of the stone by Professor Rhys.

They came, and were filled with surprise at meeting one another so unexpectedly. Presently they prepared to sit down to feast on the host's great swine, and then arose the question who was to carve : it was agreed to give it to the bravest. So each warrior who had confidence in his record declared what that was, whereupon rose another and put him down by enumerating greater feats of his own. This went on for some time, when at length it looked as though the honour of carving would fall for certain to Cet mac Matach, a Connaught hero, and he had taken up the knife to begin the carving when a belated Ultonian, Conall Cernach, hurries into the room and asks, *Cia rannas dúib?* "Who is carving for you?" It was replied that Cet was going to do it, and a contest of words takes place between Cet and Conall, with the result that Cet reluctantly yields, with the remark that Conall would not carve had Cet's brother Anlúan been present. "But he is present," said Conall, who, after feeling in his girdle, brought forth the bleeding head of Anlúan and hurled it in his brother's face. Such was Conall's excuse for arriving late, and the passage is one of the most graphic and savage in the whole range of old Irish literature.

We have taken *Niotta Cobranari* to mean *Nepotis Partistæ*, as describing either *Dumeli* or *Glasiconas*, but it is possible that it should rather be taken as an independent proper name : at any rate, such names occur. Take, for example, such a later instance as *Nioth-Fruich*,[1] *Niath-Froich*, *Nat[h]-Fraich*, or *Nad-Fráich*, in which the first element owing to its proclitic position has suffered curtailment. It is to be noticed that *Fraech*, genitive *Fraich*, was a separate personal name of unknown signification, and that *Niath-Fraich* must have meant "Nephew of Fraech," or, more precisely speaking, "Son of Fraech's Sister." And this is not mere inference, for we have the positive statement of

[1] See Stokes's "Patrick," p. 331 ; also pp. 76, 194, 196, 214, 250, 468.

Cormac's Glossary that the meaning of the word *nie*, genitive *niath*, was *mac sethar*, " sister's son,"[1] and, as far as we know, that was its only meaning. In harmony with the foregoing interpretations, the St. Vigeans Stone (p. 17, above) should be rendered " Drost's nephew Voret for Fergus," rather than " Drost's kin, Voret and Fergus." Similarly in the case of the corresponding vocable[2] on the Newton Stone (p. 17, above), and of the *poi* of certain Ogam inscriptions in the south of Ireland.

The earliest existing manuscript of Adamnan's Life of St. Columba dates from the beginning of the eighth century, and it is found that he distinguishes as a rule between two kinds of clan designations. (1) He mostly uses *nepos* where the native usage of later times recognises *úa* or *ó*, with the plural *nepotes* rendered by *úi* or *húi* (Anglicised *hy* and *o*'), as for instance in *Nepos Lethani*, called in Irish *Ua Liathain*, Anglicised *Olethan*. So with the plural, as in *Nepotes Nellis = Ua Néill*, " the Hy-Neill or O'Neills"; but some of

---

[1] See Stokes's edition of O'Donovan's " Translation of Cormac's Glossary," p. 121 ; also Stokes's paper on the " Bodleian Fragment of Cormac's Glossary " (read before the Royal Irish Academy, November 30th, 1871), p. 8.

[2] Our last reading of it is *ipuai*, but we should treat *ipe* as a spelling of *ipai*, and equate it with *ipuai* ; that is, unless it should prove more correct to regard *ipuai* as a spelling of *ipue*. In either case we should treat both as accented on the final syllable (like *mucói*), and equate them with *poi* as a foreshortening of some such a vocable as *ipói* or *ápói*. In all instances *poi* appears *affixed* (contrary to the Celtic habit of *prefixing*) to the genitive of a personal name, as in *Broinienaspoi* (*Poi* of Broiniu), *Corbipoi* (*Poi* of Corb), and *Iacinipoi* (*Poi* of Iacin). These come respectively from the counties of Cork, Kilkenny, and Wicklow ; but the same formula must have been in use in the south-west of Britain. At any rate, it is thence we have to suppose it transported to Brittany, where we have it in the well-known name of the king *Érispoë* in the ninth century. It is made up of *poi* affixed to the genitive of a man's name which occurs now and then in the pedigrees in the Book of Leinster as *Aires*, genitive *Airiss* as on fol. 326d, 353d, 356a, 363c. See vol. xxxij. of the " Proceedings of the Antiq. of Scotland" for 1897-8, where, in a paper entitled a " Revised Account of the Inscriptions of the Northern Picts," Professor Rhys has dealt with several of the questions touched upon in this chapter : for this rendering see more particularly pp. 347, 370.

the race are found styled *Nieth-Néill*,[1] where *nieth* is the etymological counterpart of *nepotes*. So we learn not only the equivalence of meaning of *nieth* and *nepotes*, but of both practically with *ui*, treated in Modern Irish as meaning grand-children or descendants. (2) Adamnan leaves untranslated and undeclined in his Latin a certain word *mocu*, as in Mocu-Sogin, Mocu-Dalon, and Mocu-Alti. In Irish Ogam inscriptions this is a very important word, and its most usual forms in them are *moco*, genitive *mucoi;* but in Irish literature it appears as *maccu*, genitive *maccui*, which began comparatively early to be regarded as made up of *macc-ui* and meaning *filius nepotis*. As a matter of fact, however, it is nothing of the kind, but a distinct word meaning race or kin in the concrete. Thus a family or tribe called *Mocu Runtir* by Adamnan is called *Dál Runtir* in the Tripartite Life of Patrick,[2] and members of it are said in the Book of Armagh to be *de genere Runtir*. As to this last, it is to be noticed that the little word *de*, though necessary in the Latin, is not in the original *Mocu Runtir*, which literally rendered would be *genus Runtir*, as if each individual of the group personified the whole. The real explanation is that the Picts had not learnt to speak of any race apart from some individual member of it : to them "the kin of A. B." was "kin A. B." *Mocu* here followed by a genitive is Goidelic, while the Pictish inscription at Aboyne on the Deeside has the words in apposition.[3]

In order to get over the difficulty Adamnan sometimes interposes the word *gente*, as in the instance *Trenanum, gente Mocuruntir*, "Trenan, Mocu-Runtir by race or family." At other times he lets *mocu* do duty alone, as in his mention *de Erco fure Mocudruidi qui in Coloso*

[1] See Skene in his "Chronicles of the Picts and Scots," p. 352, where he copies the Annals of Ulster for A.D. 692.

[2] See Stokes's edition, p. 226 ; and as to the meaning of *mocu*, see Rhys's "Lectures on Welsh Philology," pp. 408, 409.

[3] See the "Proceedings of the Antiquaries of Scotland" 1898-9, pp. 351-3,

insula commanebat. The island was one of those now called Colonsay, and the clan to which Erc belonged took its name from a *druid*, somewhat like the Mactaggarts and MacPhersons of later times, so named after ancestors in holy orders. When the great person in the past of a family was a man and not a woman, the word offspring is inadmissible in the rendering, and the nearest approach to the original may be made perhaps by using "kin": thus *Miliuc mocu Buain*, the name of the king of Dáln-Araide (between Loch Neagh and Belfast Loch) who bought Patrick as a slave, might be rendered "Miliuc kin of Buan"; and so with the following inscriptions from the county of Waterford, *Catabor* [1] *moco Viricorb*[*i*], "Cathbar kin of Fer-Corb," and *Gosoctas mucoi Macorbi*, "the Monument of Guasacht kin of Macorb." A wider choice of words is permissible in a case like *ad Insolas Maccuchor* in the Book of Armagh, as we might render it "to the Islands of the family or tribe of Cor"—they are the isles at the Skerries, off the north-west corner of Antrim; and when a woman is the chief ancestral figure we are at liberty to use a word meaning progeny and lineal descendants. But what is one to make of the double genitive *maqui mucoi*, which frequently occurs in ancient Ogam inscriptions, and must mean *filii generis* or *filii gentis?* Take, for example, the following from Corkaguiny in Kerry: *Maqqui Erccias maqqui mucoi Dovinias*,[2] that is to say "(The Monument) of Mac Erce son of the kin of Dubinn," where the ancestress Dubinn (genitive *Duibne*) has given her name to *Corco Duibne*,

---

[1] We are not certain whether we should read *Catabor* or *Catabar ;* but compare Ptolemy's name— *Vellabori*—of a tribe in the south-west of Ireland, *Velvor filia Broho* of a somewhat late Cardiganshire inscription, and *Falbhar*, a champion's name mentioned in O'Curry's "Manners and Customs of the Ancient Irish," iii. 158.

[2] From a rubbing supplied by the Rev. Edmond Barry, and recently verified by Professor Rhys. The stone is at Lord Ventry's residence in the neighbourhood of Dingle.

Anglicised *Corkaguiny*, now the name of a barony in the west of Kerry. Or to come back to Wales, take the following Ogam at Brideŧŧ in the north of Pembrokeshire : *Nettasagru maqui mucoi Breci*, which may be rendered (*Monumentum*) *Nettasagrûs filii generis Breci.* These and the like inscriptions take us back without doubt to the words of Cæsar already cited : in fact they lead us back a little further, to wit, to a stage antecedent to the consideration of the paternity suggested by him. In Irish literature this state of society is found surviving in a form which looks like polyandry, as in the case of a king of Tara, supposed to have reigned about the beginning of the Christian era. He was known as Lugaid of the Red Stripes, and said to be the son of three brothers, the sons of Eochaid Feidlech.[1] Or take the Mac Lir family of Irish legend : one of its leading figures was the famous Manannán Mac Lir, and this is how he is introduced in the opening verses of a poem in the well-known story of Bricriu's Feast, in the Book of the Dun Cow, fo. 50a :

> *Fégaid mac læchraidi Lir,*
> *do maigib Éogain Inbir !*
> Behold the son of the heroes of Ler,
> From the plains of Eogan of Inver !

It is, perhaps, relevant also to mention here that a state of things in which the children were the children of the family, so to say, and owned no fathers in particular, rendered necessary some arrangement of the nature of fosterage, an institution known to have been of vast importance among the ancient Goidels, including among them the family of Pwyŧŧ, king of Dyfed, as mentioned in the Mabinogi already cited.

A man who styles himself *Nepos Vepogeni*, or Son of Vepogen's Sister, without naming her, leaves us no evidence

---

[1] See the " Book of Leinster," fol. 124b, 151a ; the " Revue Celtique," xvi. 148–50 ; O'Mahony's Keating, pp. 287–8, and the footnote on page 37 above.

that the community to which he belonged made much of its women. That community appears to have recognised no paternity, but to have reckoned descent by birth alone ; it is possible, however, that at a previous stage in its history the family was constituted on strictly matriarchal lines. At all events other cases occur, which seem favourable to the belief in the former existence of matriarchy. Certain Ogam inscriptions, for instance, have been found in the neighbourhood of Dingle, in Kerry, ending with the ancestress's name, nominative *Dovini[s]*, genitive *Dovinia[s]*, reduced in Mediæval Irish to *Dubinn* or *Dubind*, genitive *Duibne*, respectively, as already mentioned. In the next place, certain well-known characters in Irish literature are distinguished by the mother's name, such as *Conchobar son of Nessa*, and *Fergus son of Roig*, with which should be compared the Welsh *Gofannon son of Dôn*. Lastly, the legends of heroic Erin picture the ladies sitting with their husbands at their banquets, and treated by them as their equals ; and sometimes courtship is represented in Irish story as initiated by the woman, not to mention the doings of such personages as Queen Macha or Queen Maive. Supposing that proof were to be found that Irish society began with matriarchy, several things in Irish literature could be pointed out as admitting of easy explanation as survivals; but we dare not reverse the argument and say that they admit of no other explanation, and that we must therefore postulate matriarchy.

To say the least of it, however, there is nothing to suggest that individual women might not enjoy great consideration among the early Goidels : there is much to the contrary, and in this connection a question offers itself as to the nature of the theology evolved by a people of the kind. Clearly, if they reckoned descent by birth alone, and provided they were given to ancestor worship, they must have had female divinities. Unfortunately it happens that the whole range of Irish literature supplies extremely few references in express terms to divinities of any kind, and the few to be found are of the most meagre and precarious description. In other words, the Irish pantheon forms but a very dim background to Irish history; but in that vanishing picture it is very remarkable that the goddesses loom larger than the gods. Thus we have already referred to Ánu, said by Cormac to have been considered the mother of the gods, and we pointed out traces of her in Welsh pedigrees derived probably from Goidelic sources in Britain. Cormac mentions also an analogous figure whom we may call *Buanu*, genitive *Buanann ;*[1] and to this latter he gives the position of mother or nurse of Irish heroes, and of teacher who taught them feats of arms. We next come to the story of the Second Battle of Moytura,[2] which mentions a people who invaded Ireland at different points, and bore the name of *Fir Domnann*, or the Men of Domnu. They came from the west coast of Britain, where we shall presently find them to have borne the name *Dumnonii* or Dumnonians. But the interest of their name consists in the fact that the Irish form, *Fir Domnann*, is as it were *Viri Dumnonis*, taken from that of a goddess *Domnu* (genitive *Domnann*). She was presumably considered to

---

[1] The name is given as *Buanann*, making probably a genitive *Buanainne*, but this is a comparatively late declension, superseding the older *Buanu*, genitive *Buanann*. Cormac also gives *Anu* a genitive, *Anainne*, ·s.v. ána, and *Danann* is sometimes made into *Danainne*, while *Danann* or *Donann* occasionally functions as nominative : see the "Book of Leinster," fol. 11a.

[2] The story, which will be found published, with a translation by Stokes, in the "Revue Celtique," xii. 52—130, treats the Fir Domnann as belonging to the Fomori, a fabulous race of elves or demons whose name has been supposed by Stokes (pp. 128, 130) to be derived in part from the same source as the latter syllable of the English word *nightmare*, to which we may add that in Scotch Gaelic stories the singular occurs as *fomhair*, meaning a giant. On the other hand, popular etymology has associated the Fomori with the sea, *muir*, as if the meaning had been that of a people who were *fo muir*, "up and down the sea, all over the sea"; hence the term tended to mean invaders who came over the sea, and sea rovers or pirates generally.

be their ancestress, and their leader is styled *Indech ma Dé Domnann*, "Indech son of the goddess Domnu," where *mac*, "son," has probably to stand for a distant descendant. At any rate, Domnu does not figure as intervening in the story, and we may presume that many generations had passed away between her and Indech; not to mention that Fir Domnann is probably to be equated with Dumnonii, one of the most widely-spread designations of the Goidels of Britain.

Far more common, but just as little explicit, are the references to the goddess Danu, after whom were called the *Tuatha* or *Tuath Dé Danann*, "the goddess Danu's Tribes or Tribe"; also *Fir Dea*, "the Goddess's Men." No one of the leading figures in the many allusions to the Tuatha Dé Danann is styled Son or Daughter of Danu, and as the people called after her are usually spoken of in the plural as *tuatha*, "tribes," she was probably regarded as belonging to a distant past. Here we have the advantage of a Welsh identification: Danu is the Dôn of the Mabinogi of Mâth son of Mathonwy; but at the stage in which Dôn is there found she is no goddess: she is briefly referred to as sister to the king and mother of his successor, Gwydion son of Dôn, and of his brothers and sister, as already stated (p. 37). All this would have to be tumbled upside down by those who seem to think that the Mabinogion have been imported into Wales as Irish stories from Ireland.[1] The

---

[1] Such appears to be the view taken by Professor Kuno Meyer in an article on Gael and Brython in the "Transactions of the Cymmrodorion Society," 1895–6, especially where he speaks (pp. 71–3) to "the deposits of Irish legendary lore" which he finds, for example, in the *Mabinogion*. He instances the Irish story of *Mesce Ulad*, in which a party of Ultonians are induced to be entertained in an iron house, the iron of which is concealed by the timber covering it both inside and out. When they are found to have drunk freely, their attendants leave them one by one, and the door is shut. Then fuel is piled up round the iron house and set fire to. The story relates how the inmates at length realised their position, and how some of them forced their way out. Now an iron house story is referred to in the Mabinogi of Branwen; but, so far as the

view which recommends itself to us is that they are stories which were current among the Goidels of old in Britain, and, in such instances as that here indicated, they represent a far earlier state of things than can be said of any Irish story extant about the Tuatha Dé Danann.

In one case we see, perhaps, a little more closely the deification in process : this takes us back for a moment to the barony of Corkaguiny and the name of the ancestress Dubinn. A story,[1] which, as we have it, was committed to writing in surroundings where Aryan ideas had begun to prevail, makes Dubinn sister to Cairbre Musc, who appears to have been king in the west of Munster in the third century. They had a son called Corc Duibne, and the story relates how Cairbre's realm was visited with bad seasons in consequence of the incest, and how Corc Duibne had to be taken outside his father's realm by the Druid who undertook the boy's education. Now several of the Ogam inscriptions of Corkaguiny, which may be said to belong to the fifth or the sixth century, end with the name of the ancestress. Thus one at Ballintaggart, near Dingle, reads: *Maqqui Iaripi maqqui Mucoi Dovvinias*, "(The Stone) of Iarip son of the Kin of Dubinn." Another, preserved at Burnham House, Lord Ventry's residence in the same neighbourhood, has been read thus (p. 52): *Maqqui Erccias maqqui Mucoi Dovinias*, "(The Stone) of Mac Erce, son of the Kin of Dubinn." But the most remarkable one stands on a headland beyond Dunmore Head and looks out on the Atlantic Ocean as if prophetically appealing to the Gaels beyond :

---

brevity of the Welsh allows us to judge, it cannot have been the *Mesce Ulad* which the narrator had his story from : most likely the iron house had figured in more than one tale. Further, as the iron house incident is there avowedly Irish, one can hardly regard it as a very instructive sample of "the deposits of Irish legendary lore" in the Mabinogion: it is desirable to have more instances, and of a less self-confessed description.

[1] See the Book of the Dun Cow, fol. 54a ; and Rhys's "Celtic Heathendom," pp. 308, 9.

it may have been the monument of a son of the chief commemorated on the last-mentioned stone, as it reads on the one edge, *Erc maqqui Maqqui Ercias*, " The Stone of Erc, son of Mac Erce," and on the other, *Mu Dovinia*, " of My Dubinn." Here one would have expected a longer legend making " Erc son of Mac Erce, son of the Kin of My Dubinn," as that is probably how we are to construe. But what is most remarkable, if our reading should prove correct,[1] is the use of the prefix *mu* or *mo*, which is familiar to every student of Irish hagiology as a mark of respect and affection prefixed to the names of certain saints. Thus in Corkaguiny we have first simply *Dovinias*, "Dubinn's"; then *Mu Dovinia*[s], " My Dubinn's," with the reverential prefix ; and had not the deification been arrested by the advance of Christian ideas we should have probably had the name in a third stage : that is, Dubinn's son would have been known in Irish literature not as *Corc Duibne*, but as *Corc Dé Duibne*, or the progeny[2] of the goddess Dubinn.

The folklore of Ireland from Meath to Beare Haven and Corkaguiny abounds with allusions to an old woman of fabulous age called Bera, Béara, or Béirre, and she is probably to be identified with the Beara whom certain stories make the daughter of a king of Spain, and wife of Eogan Mór or Mog Nuadat, who, with Conn the Hundred-fighter, is fabled to have divided Erin into a northern and a southern half between them in the second century. But in those stories Bera's name is mostly given with the prefix

---

[1] It is only right to warn the reader that the reading of the Ogams on the same edge as *Dovinia* is contested by the Rev. Edmond Barry and by Mr. Macalister. Professor Rhys, having become aware that the former read it differently, took an opportunity of re-examining the stone in 1891, and the result only confirmed him in his former opinion. Mr. Macalister's remarks in point will be found in his " Studies in Irish Epigraphy," p. 56.

[2] It is not known precisely what the word Corc meant ; nor is it evident that *Corco* in Corco-Duibne (which also occurs as *Corca Duibne*) is the plural of Corc, as if *corc*, *corco*, meant *child*, *children*, or the like, respectively. See " Pro. Soc. Antiq. Scotland," xxxij. 355–7.

mo (or *mu*), as in the case of *Mu-Dovinia*, and then it is found written *Moméra*. The stories[1] have not been found so far as we know in any very ancient manuscript; but there appears to be no reason to suppose them to have begun late. They would seem, however, to have been developed relatively so late that Bera has only succeeded in attaining to the status of a witch or wise woman, of a nun or hag, of a revered person and a giantess, not quite to that of a goddess, unless it be in Argyll, where she rules the storm.

Here also attention may be relevantly directed to the great place which women occupy in the legendary account of the early colonisations of Ireland. Take, for example, Scota treated as chief ancestress of the Milesian Irish, and as giving her name to all the Scots. She is not, at any rate in this context, to be disposed of as a mere myth; for a cognate eponym of the other sex might have served equally well for mythic purposes. The most remarkable instance, perhaps, is the case of Cessair, said to have taken possession of Ireland before the Flood : her wanderings are made to begin with Noah refusing her and hers room in the ark which he was building. She is represented landing at *Dún na m-Barc*, "the Fortress of the Barks," somewhere between Bantry and Tralee. The Irish historian Keating apologises for mentioning Cessair, and suggests it as his reason for doing so, that he found her story in old books, such probably as the Book of Leinster, folios 4, 5, and those used by Duald mac Firbis, a well-known Irish antiquary of the earlier part of the seventeenth century, who compiled from old manuscripts his annals known as the *Chronicum Scotorum*. His first entry is under *Anno Mundi* 1599, and it runs thus: "In

---

[1] See O'Curry's volume containing "The Battle of Magh Leana" and "The Courtship of Moméra," pp. xx. 39, 166, and 31*n*, and compare O'Flaherty's "Ogygia," p. 274, where he has *Bera filia Ocha principis Britonum Manniæ*, whatever that may have exactly meant ; also Professor Kuno Meyer's "Vision of Mac Conglinne," pp. 131–4, 208–10, and Professor Rhys's "Celtic Folklore," p. 393.

this year the daughter of one of the Greeks came to Hibernia, whose name was Heriu, or Berba, or Cesar, and fifty maidens, and three men with her. Ladhra was their conductor, who was the first that was buried in Hibernia. This the antiquaries of the Scots do not relate."[1] This it will be seen equates or co-ordinates Cessair with *Eriu*, the eponym of *Ériu*, genitive *Erenn*, "Ireland," and with *Berba*, which there is no sufficient reason for altering into the better-known name Banba of another eponym of the island. Berba is elsewhere only known as the name of the river Barrow, in which we seem accordingly to have another ancestral name. The most reasonable view to take of the legend of Cessair is, that it was a local tradition of the Aborigines of the south-west of Ireland, who by making Cessair the first coloniser asserted their own priority of possession to all other peoples in the country. The synchronisers, not knowing what to make of this, accepted the alleged priority, and placed the whole story before the Flood. Thereby they rid themselves of difficulties from two possible sources, to wit, the context of the story with the other events occupying their attention, and the later fortunes of Cessair's descendants. The legend associates Cessair and her companions with various localities in the south and west of Ireland, together with others lying so far north as Slieve Beagh in Fermanagh ; not to mention that Ireland is occasionally found designated Cessair's Island.[2] We gather, therefore, that Cessair may have been the eponymous heroine of a race occupying the whole of the southern half of Ireland and more, together very possibly with the nearest portions of the west and south-west of

---

[1] See the opening of the Four Masters' Annals of the Kingdom of Ireland, and the editor O'Donovan's notes on the place-names involved ; Joyce's edition of Keating's "History of Ireland," part i., pp. 52–5 ; and Hennessy's (Rolls edition of the) "Chronicum Scotorum," pp. xxv.–xxxij. 2, 3.

[2] See *Tochmarc Monéra* [*read* Moméra] in O'Curry's "Battle of Magh Leana," page 154. Compare "Rhys's "Studies in Early Irish History," p. 23.

Britain as its earlier home.[1] However that may be, it proves to our satisfaction that to show a predilection for ancestresses over ancestors was Ivernian : that it was also Aryan we are inclined to doubt, but that, where it has been found among the peoples of these islands, it is to be traced rather to the Aboriginal element in a mixed population promiscuously termed Celtic.

The influence of Christianity must have by degrees put an end to the social system to which we have been referring, and this raises questions of great difficulty as to dates and localities, on which we cannot enter. So we return to our view, that if the reckoning of descent by birth alone was not Aryan, it must have been accepted by the Goidelic Celts from the Aborigines, which would go far to prove the numerical importance of the latter. It is known to have been Pictish, but was it also Celtic and Aryan ? We are disposed to think that it was not, though we readily admit that the negative cannot be proved. Moreover it is right to say that the following passage in chapter xxi. of the Germania[2] of Tacitus is redolent of the same ancient menage : *Sororum filiis idem apud avunculum qui ad patrem honor. Quidam sanctiorem artioremque hunc nexum sanguinis arbitrantur et in accipiendis obsidibus magis exigunt, tamquam etiam*

[1] The name *Cessair*, genitive *Cesra*, admits of being regarded as derived from a stem, *cestari*, and should M. Salomon Reinach's conjecture prove correct, that the Cassiterides originally meant the British Isles, and that κασσίτερος, "tin," was, like several other Greek names of metals, called simply after the country or the people of the country in which it was found, our Cessair would be found to supply a necessary link in the reasoning. For M. Reinach's view see "L'Anthropologie" for 1892, pp. 275–81 ; also Rhys's letter on *Cassiterides* in the "Academy," October 5, 1895, pp. 272–3, and see further pp. 298, 342, 366, 390, 414, 438, 524, 547.

[2] Compare chapter viii., which treats female hostages as more efficacious in the case of the Germans—*adeo ut efficacius obligentur animi civitatum, quibus inter obsides puellæ quoque nobiles imperantur ;* and also a passage in Suetonius's Augustus, 21, to the following effect : *A quibusdam vero* [the last people mentioned seems to have been Germans] *novum genus obsidum, feminas, exigere tentaverit, quod negligere marium pignora sentiebat.*

animum firmius et domum latius teneant. "There is the same regard shown for the sons of the sisters by the uncle as by their father. Some think this tie of blood more binding and closer, and insist on it more when they receive hostages, on the theory that it restrains their impulses more powerfully, and has a wider control over the family." The words are unfortunately so indefinite that we have no clue to the identity of the tribes the historian had in view; so it is impossible to say whether they were likely to have been mixed with any Aboriginal race practising the same customs and enjoying the same institutions as the Aborigines of the British Isles.[1]

We admit that the foregoing argument is not quite decisive, and we now turn to others of a more purely linguistic nature, and leading to a more decided conclusion. So we revert for a moment to the dedicator of the bronze tablet found at Colchester : we saw that he describes himself as *Lossio Veda, Nepos Vepogeni, Caledo,* and that *Veda* appears as part of the name of one of the kings in

---

[1] Say somewhere between the mouth of the Rhine and that of the Elbe, where there was an amber coast, and where Tacitus would seem to have heard of a people partly Celtic and partly Teutonic, whom he has mixed up with the Æstii of the amber coast of the Baltic. Witness the following passage in the Germania, 45 :—*Ergo jam dextro Suebici maris litore Æstiorum gentes adluuntur, quibus ritus habitusque Sueborum, lingua Britannicæ propior. matrem deum venerantur. insigne superstitionis formas aprorum gestant: id pro armis hominumque tutela securum deæ cultorem etiam inter hostis præstat : rarus ferri, frequens fustium usus. frumenta ceterosque fructus patientius quam pro solita Germanorum inertia laborant. sed et mare scrutantur, ac soli omnium sucinum, quod ipsi glesum vocant, inter vada atque in ipso litore legunt.* How well the allusion to the goddess would fit Goidelic surroundings need not be dwelt upon ; and, as to the language, *glesum* is as easily explained by means of Celtic as of Teutonic. Witness the Irish *glain, gloin,* "glass or crystal," Welsh *glein, glain* (*gemma, tessera*), for an older *gles-inu-s ;* while a language said to come nearer the *Britannica* would exactly describe the position of Goidelic as compared with Brythonic. The sort of people which the Germania suggests might be Aborigines who had first become Goidels in speech and later Teutons, while retaining habits and customs which they practised before they acquired any Aryan language at all.

the Pictish list, where also *Vepogeni* is to be found, curtailed, it is true, to *Vepog*, and written *Vipoig*. But while it is probable that *Veda* is not Celtic, it is certain that *Vepogeni*[1] is, and we compare it with Gaulish names like *Vepus* and *Vepo-talos*, of unknown meaning, and *Matu-genos*, "well-born," or *Camulo-genos*, "offspring of Camulos." Thus we seem to have in *Vepogeni* an early instance of the Pictish habit of borrowing names and other words from the Celts. The interest of the present instance centres in the way in which the name *Vepogenos* was treated. This would be the Brythonic and Gaulish form, while in Goidelic it would have been approximately *Vequagenas*. Now the study of the laws of mutation of initial consonants in the Neo-celtic languages goes to show that the ending of the nominative must have been dropped early, so that the foregoing forms would be shortened to *Vepogen* and *Vequagen*. Another process of curtailment would be to drop the thematic vowel of the first element in the compound, bringing the result approximately to *Veb-gen* and *Fech-gen*. But the reduction of *Vepogen* to *Vepog*, which is what underlies *Vipoig*, is impossible on Celtic ground, whether Brythonic or Goidelic, while Pictish offers a simple and natural explanation. In that language it can be shown that *enn* or *en* was a common ending of the genitive case, so that *Vepogen* must in the long run have sounded to the Picts as a genitive, whence was readily inferred a simpler form, *Vepog*, which we should call nominative in the case of Aryan speech.

This leads us to consider the Pictish genitive somewhat further, and to mention another instance in *Drosten*, which may be regarded as the genitive of the Pictish name Drost

---

[1] *Vepogenos* was, perhaps, the name represented by the abbreviation VEP on the native coins of the Brythons north of the Humber, reading VEP COR F, for, let us say, VEPOGENVS COROTICI FILIVS : see Rhys's "Celtic Britain," p. 41 ; and p. xv., coin 5.

on a stone already mentioned as being at St. Vigeans, near Arbroath. Take also the well-known Newton Stone in Aberdeenshire, which has in Ogam the genitive, *Vorrenn*,[1] of a name which occurs as *Vaur* in the other lettering on the same stone. This genitive occasionally appears in old Irish inscriptions, such as one on the island of Valencia which reads, *Logiri*[2] *maqui Erpenn*, "The Monument of Lugar son of Erp." Had *Erpenn* been Goidelic, it should, in order to be on a level with *Logiri* and *maqui*, have been *Erpennas*, or at least *Erpenna;* but the presence of the consonant *p* is very fair evidence that the name is other than Goidelic. The Picts appear to have had genitives also in *ann*, *on*[*n*], and *in*[*n*]. Instances of the first-mentioned occur in the mixed inscriptions found in the Shetlands, such as *Meqqddrroann*, which might be rendered probably *Filii Druidis;* and *dattrrann* on the same stone seems to be the Pictish genitive of the Norse word for *daughter*.[3] As to *onn*, the Book of Deer mentions a grant of land to the Church of Aberdour, in which among other names of men occur a nominative *Cultí*, and a genitive *Culéon :* they are probably cases of one and the same name.[4] We have it now and

[1] See the "Proceedings of the Society of Antiquaries of Scotland," vol. xxxij. pp. 360–4.

[2] This is a reading recently made out by Professor Rhys ; but it is not quite certain whether *Logiri* is to be equated with the *Lugir* of *Maccu Lugir*, or with *Loegairi*, the genitive of *Loegaire* mac Néill, the name of the king of Ireland in whose time Dubthach Maccu Lugir was chief poet (Stokes's "Goidelica," pp. 86, 126). Reeves in his Adamnan's *Vita Columbæ* (p. 350) cites, after Ussher, a passage the writer of which thought that *macu, mocu,* or *mucoi* had something to do with *muc*, "a swine," so that in his hands the chief poet, D. Maccu Lugir, becomes *subulcus regis Loigeri filii Nil ;* but compare Stokes's "Patrick," pp. 122, 324.

[3] "Pro. Soc. Antiq. Scotland," xxvi. 297–300, where the *dd* of *Meqqddrroann* should probably be pronounced *đ*, and *Nahhtvvddaθθs* taken to mean *Nahhtvuđđaθθs*, as a more likely antecedent of the curtailed form *Natdad's* or *Natdod's*, which became historical as the name of the man who discovered Iceland.

[4] From the same MS. one might quote Abber-deon (Aberdeen) but for the uncertainty that the Dee is the river implied and not the Don. The entries

then in the old inscriptions of Ireland, as, for instance, in an Ogam in the Kilkenny Museum, reading, in two lines :—

Mucoi Atr... ⎰ (The Monument) of the kin of A.,
Bivadon, ⎱ namely, Bivad.

Perhaps, however, the order intended was the reverse, "The Monument of Bivad, kin of A." Lastly, a remarkable instance of the genitive in *inn* occurs in the name of the district called the Mearns, approximately the county of Kincardine. *Mearns* is derived from a native name, *Mag Gerginn*, or *Gergind*,[1] which is also found as *Mag Cirgin*, the Plain of Gerg, Greg, Giric or Ciric ; for the name appears to have had several forms, between which it is not easy to decide, not to mention that it has been confounded with that of St. Ciricus. We have an unexpected instance of this genitive in an Ogam inscription from the townland of Ballinvoher in Corkaguiny, county Kerry. It reads, *Coimagni maqui Vitalin*, "The monument of Coemán

in Gaelic, including the names here in question, will be found printed and translated in Stokes's "Goidelica," pp. 106–111 ; and *à propos* of *Vepogen* and *abber* may be mentioned the old Welsh *Morgant* (mod. Welsh *Morgan*), which appears borrowed as *Morcunt, Morcunn, Morgainn* : all three occur in the genitive, and *Morgunn* in the nominative. Query, whether such Pictish names as *Talargan, Talorcen, Talorc*, and kindred forms are not all adaptations of a Brythonic *Talargent* or *Talargant*, "Silver-forehead"?

[1] "Book of Leinster," fol. 319c; Skene's "Chronicles of the Picts and Scots," p. 319 ; also Skene's "Celtic Scotland," i. 295, where he purports to give *Terra Circin* from the Irish annalist Tigernach. For *Gerg* see O'Curry, i. ccclxxv. ; III. 168, 307. The name Gerg occurs frequently in "The Tragic Story of the Courtship of Gerg's daughter Ferb" in the book of Leinster, fol. 253a–259b, where it is mostly nominative *Gerg*. genitive *Geirg* (also *Gerg*). His house was in Glen-Gerg in Ulster, but there was another Glenn-Gerg in Carlow : see the "Four Masters," A.D. 1015. We have the genitive also possibly in the patronymic of Munremur mac *Gerrcind*, an Ulster champion introduced to checkmate the Connaught magician Cúrói mac Dairi, in the *Táin Bó Cualnge*, in the "Book of the Dun Cow," fol. 71b. Various forms of this name occurred in Scotland, as will be seen under *Grig* in the index to Skene's Chronicles of the Picts and Scots ; and some of them were stereotyped in the name of the Mearns church, *Eccles-greig* or *Eglis-girg*, now called St. Cyrus, dedicated to St Ciricus : see Skene's "Celtic Scotland," i. 333, 4.

son of Fidlin," where correct Goidelic would seem to require *Coimagni maqui Vitalini*. The scores are all certain, and the third genitive never had a final *i* on the stone.[1]

All this has to do chiefly with the inflection of the names to which we have referred; and though it supplies convincing evidence to the presence of some element other than Celtic, whether Goidelic or Brythonic, Irish nomenclature provides us with a still more sweeping argument to the same effect. We allude to an important group of Irish names formed much in the same way as Hebrew names are represented chosen in the Old Testament. We begin with an instance from a comparatively late manuscript, namely, that which contains the story of the Battle of Magh Leamhna :—A certain Munster prince called Mogh Néid, " Slave of Ned," had a son called Eoghan Mór, or " Big Eoghan," who was fostered by one of his nobles called Nuadha. One day when Eoghan, in the company of the Druid, whose name was Deargdamhsa, were watching the building of a *ráth* for Mogh Néid, the workmen came upon a stone which they were unable to lift to its place, but the boy Eoghan Mór went and lifted it at once, to everybody's astonishment; whereupon the workmen exclaimed, " This is a noble slave that Nuadha has." The Druid then said, " That name shall be upon him for ever," that is, *Mogh Nuadhad*, "the Slave of Nuadha."[2] It is right to say that Néd and Nuadha were names of gods, the former a god of war of the ancient Goidels, and the latter a god the remains of one of whose temples have been found at Lydney, near the Severn,

---

[1] The stone is in the Irish National Museum in Dublin, where it has been examined repeatedly by Prof. Rhys. A paper on it by the Lord Bishop of Limerick will be found in the third series of the "Proceedings of the Royal Irish Academy," 1893, pp. 374-9, where he would identify *Fidlin* and Welsh *Gwythelin* with *Vitalin*.

[2] See Curry's " Battle of Magh Leana " (Dublin, 1855), pp. 1-3 : we have given the names in the late spelling in which Curry left them ; the older forms would be *Mug Net* or *Neit* and *Mug Nuadat*.

together with a representation of his person careering in a chariot over the waves of the sea; and from inscriptions in honour of him we know that his name had in Roman times the form Nodens or Nudens, genitive Nodentis, Nudentis, or Nodontis, the termination of which is doubtless Latin:[1] in Welsh the name has become *Nûd* and also *Lud*. It is needless to point out how such names as Mogh Néid and Mogh Nuadhad resemble such instances as Abdiel, " Servant of El," *Abdastartus,* " Servant of Astarte," and others from Semitic lands.

To go back to an older manuscript, namely, the " Book of the Dun Cow," which was written as we have it before the end of the year 1106, we have there one of the oldest and most weird of fairy tales, which relates how a fairy damsel came to entice Condla the Red, one of the two sons of Conn the Hundred-fighter, to go away with her to the Land of the Living, and how Conn sent for Corán, his Druid, to counteract her wiles. Corán tried to do so, and failed ; the youthful Condla leaps into the fairy's glass boat and away they sail till they are lost to the sight of Conn and his astonished friends. Before Conn had stirred from the spot his other son, called Art, came to them, when his father exclaimed, " Art is now solitary (*oenfer, oenur*), for he has no brother." " That is the word," said the Druid ; "that will be his name for ever, *Art Oenfer.*"[2] Here again the Druid does his part, though in this instance he seems only to add an epithet, but *Art*, though common enough as an Irish name, probably meant as an appellative " a

---

[1] See the Berlin Corpus, vol. vii. Nos. 137–141 ; also the numerous plates with which are illustrated a posthumous work on the " Roman Antiquities at Lydney Park," by W. H. Bathurst, edited by C. W. King (London, 1879) ; and a paper by Hübner on the Sanctuary of Nodens in the "Jahrbücher des Vereins von Alterthumsfreunden im Rheinlande," vol. lxvii. pp. 29–46.

[2] See the " Book of the Dun Cow," fol. 120 : the story will also be found printed in Windisch's " Kurzgefasste irische Grammatik mit Lesestücken (Leipsic, 1879), pp. 118–120.

bear," in Welsh *arth*; and its original use in this story may have been that of a nickname which was allowed to stand as part of the new name.

The next two instances come also from the " Book of the Dun Cow," but they belong to the Ultonian cycle of stories. The first to be mentioned relates to Derdriu, the heroine of the story of the Exile of the Sons of Usnech. Even before she was born there were forebodings of the troubles before her, and before her country on her account. For while yet unborn she screamed in a way that alarmed King Conchobar mac Nessa and his nobles as they sat banqueting in the house of her father and mother; and Conchobar's Druid, whose name was Cathbad, exclaimed on hearing the scream which the child had given (*derdrestar*) and said, " Verily it is a girl, and let *Derdriu* be her name." Here again it is the Druid of the party that fixes the name of the child, and the relation between the deponent verb *derdrestar*, "screamed," and *Derdriu*, purports to explain how he came to call her Derdriu. The rest of the story need not be reproduced here.[1] The other story is one related of Cúchulainn's infancy.[2] Conchobar and his nobles were gone one evening to feast at the house of Culann the Smith, who was a great man among them. Culann, when they were all supposed to have arrived, had his gates closed, and a famous war-dog of his was let loose, as was his wont, to guard his possessions. The boy Cúchulainn, however, had been forgotten, and when he arrived he was attacked by Culann's watch-hound ; but, to everybody's astonishment, the boy killed the formidable beast. Culann afterwards complained loudly of his loss, whereupon Cúchulainn said that until the smith had another hound of the same breed reared to guard his possessions he would guard them : he would be himself Culann's war-dog. Thereupon Cathbad

[1] For the text see Windisch's " Irische Texte " (Leipsic, 1880), pp. 67–69.
[2] See the " Book of the Dun Cow," fol. 60a–61a.

the Druid said, " Let Cú-Chulainn (Culann's Hound) be thy name "; for till then he had been known as Setanta Bec, or the Little Setantian, in reference probably to his race; for we know that he cannot have been altogether of Ultonian descent, as he and his father are represented as never liable to the *cess noinden* or couvade sickness[1] of the Ultonians, while on the other hand the opposite coast of Britain had, according to Ptolemy, a Port of the Setantii somewhere near the mouth of the Ribble. Before leaving the incident which fixed Cúchulainn's name, let us observe that the Druid Cathbad who gave it him was also the schoolmaster or tutor of the young nobles of the Ultonians : he had, we are told,[2] no less than one hundred at the same time learning *druidecht* or magic from him, and Cúchulainn is found afterwards boasting that, in consequence of the teaching of Cathbad, he was an adept in " the arts of the god of magic," or whatever the term *druidecht* may have precisely meant.

We now turn to the Mabinogion, which represent, though doubtless not very closely, the stories of the Goidels of ancient Wales; and there we have at least two instances in point. One of them relates how Ilew Ilawgyffes got that name given him by Gwydion from an exclamation made by Arianrhod, the boy's mother, when she saw him making a skilful hit at a wren. Thereby she unwittingly undid a destiny which she had put on her boy, that he should never have a name, whereby she had intended to protect her own reputation as a maiden. This is from the Mabinogi of Math,[3] but the other occurs in that of Pwyll, Prince of Dyfed. This latter Mabinogi relates how Rhiannon, his queen, had

---

[1] For the Irish account of this *cess* or suffering, see the "Berichte der k. sächs. Gesellschaft der Wissenschaften, philologisch-historische Classe," for 1884 (pp. 336–47), where Windisch discusses the question and gives some texts relating to it.

[2] See the "Book of the Dun Cow," fol. 61a and fol. 124b (printed in Windisch's Irische Texte, p. 325).

[3] See the Oxford Mabinogion, pp. 69–71; and Guest's Mabinogion, iii. 233–6.

her firstborn kidnapped by witches immediately after his birth, and how the child, a wondrously fine boy, was found by Teyrnon, a chieftain of Gwent, and brought up by his wife as her own child. When Teyrnon, however, who had been one of Pwyłł's men, heard of Rhiannon's trouble, it struck him that the boy was unmistakably like Pwyłł ; so he and his wife resolved to restore the boy to Pwyłł and Rhiannon at their court in Dyfed. When Teyrnon and the boy were being entertained at table by Pwyłł and Rhiannon, with the nobles of their court, Teyrnon related the wonderful story of his finding the boy, and appealed to all present to say whether they did not agree with him that the boy was Pwyłł's son. They responded with one accord in the affirmative, whereupon Rhiannon exclaimed, " I call heaven to witness that this, if true, would deliver me of my anxiety (*pryderi*)." Pendaran of Dyfed at once said, " Well hast thou named thy son *Pryderi*, and the name Pryderi son of Pwyłł Penn Annwn befits him best." He had been called by Teyrnon and his wife "Gwri of the Golden Hair," but Pwyłł insisted on his being now called Pryderi according to his mother's word when she got joyful news of him, and on his being fostered by Pendaran of Dyfed.[1]   Pendaran is not called a Druid—nobody is called a Druid in the Mabinogion—but both he and Gwydion remind one of the Druids of Irish tales ; and, furthermore, the latter portion of the name of Penn-Daran, " Chief Daran," is probably to be identified with that of the Irish Druid, *Dalan*, in the story called the " Wooing of Étáin," where also the name Étáin of the heroine happens to equate letter for letter with the latter part of the name *Rhiannon*, on the hypothesis of this last representing an earlier *Rig-Anton*,[2] meaning " King's Anton " or " Royal Anton."

[1] See the Oxford Mabinogion, pp. 18–24; and Guest's Mabinogion, iii. 60–70.

[2] The text of the " Wooing of Étáin " has been published in Windisch's

These stories transport us into an atmosphere more like Semitic than Aryan, and we notice—(1) first, that the permanent name is drawn from some incident in one's history, and that as a rule it supersedes any name or nickname of one's infancy; (2) secondly, that the name is fixed by the Druid or by the foster-father and tutor; (3) lastly, that in the Mabinogion the part played by the mother is regarded as essential; and it suggests that the giving of the name was originally her exclusive right, while the man who took it up only gave the transaction a certain stamp of ceremony and publicity. Now this plan of naming men and women could not help resulting in names differing widely from those given under the Aryan system of nomenclature; but before proceeding to consider the latter, let us for a moment take stock of the names we have been discussing. Their prevailing nature may be gathered from the following enumeration of the most common of them :—(1) First may be mentioned those formed with *mug* or *mogh*, " s¹ave," such as *Mogh Nuadhad*, " the Slave of Nuadha." (2) Those formed with *máil*, " cropped, tonsured," are analogous, such as *Máil-Patraic*, " the tonsured man (the slave) of Patrick," called in Latin *Calvus Patricii*. Names of this kind had a great vogue among Irish Christians, but the formula was doubtless pagan, and some of the names recorded appear to be so, such as *Mail-genn*, the name of the third century Druid who is related to have caused demons to kill king Cormac mac Airt, because he had become a Christian.[1] (3) The same view may be taken of names with *gille*, such as *Gilla-Muire*, " the gillie or servant of (the Virgin) Mary," Anglicised *Gilmore*. Names of this class also became very common among Goidelic Christians, but we appear to have a pagan instance in *Gilvaethwy* son of Dôn, in the Mabinogi

---

"Irische Texte," pp. 117–130, and a letter by Prof. Rhys on the equations here suggested will be found in the "Academy" for August 15th, 1896, p. 115.
[1] See the Four Masters, A.D. 266.

of Mâth. (4) Another vocable used for names of this kind
was *nia*, genitive *niath*, " a champion," as in *Nia Segamain*,
which appears in the genitive in Ogams as *Neta Segamonas*,[1]
"the Champion of *Segomo*," Segomo being in Gaulish
theology a divinity equated with the Latin Mars. (5) So
with *fer*, "a man, *vir*," as in *Fer Tlachtga*,[2] "the Man of
Tlachtga." (6) The same idea approximately was doubtless
expressed by *cú*, "hound," the meaning intended being that
of a watch-hound, champion, and protector, as in *Cú-chulainn*,
"Culann's Hound," *Cú-Chorb*, "Corb's Hound," *Cú-Chocriche*,
"the Hound of the Frontier, the Watch-dog of the Boundary." (7) *Mac*, " boy," was used in much the same way,
as for instance in *Mac Naue*, " Boy of the Boat or Ship,"
rendered by Adamnán *Filius Navis*,[3] and *Mac Táil*,[4] supposed to mean " Boy of the Hatchet" or "Son of the Adze."
(8) Feminine names with *der* are analogous, such as *Der-
Lugdach* and *Der-Fraich*, meaning probably the maid or
woman of *Lugaid* and *Fraech* respectively. (9) Names with
niott, such as *Niott-Vrecc*, and *Nióth-Fruich* or *Nad-Fraich*,
have already been sufficiently discussed.

The foregoing will suffice to show how this kind of
personal name forms a very striking feature of Goidelic
nomenclature, although the majority of Goidelic names are
of another description, remaining, as they do, true to the
Aryan system.   On the other hand, it is not to be supposed
that the above syntactic names are in any way the outcome
of a disintegration of Aryan names, or that as a group they
date later here than the Aryan ones.   The reverse would be

---

[1] See Rhys's "Celtic Heathendom," p. 33; and Stokes's "Celtic Declension,"
p. 87. It is to be noticed, that, though the later forms of the word for
" champion," *nia*, *niath*, become confused with the words for "nephew," *nia*,
nioth (p. 48 above), the Ogmic spellings were respectively *netta* or *neta*, and
niotta.

[2] See the " Book of Leinster," fol. 326ᵍ.

[3] Reeves's Adamnán's " Life of St. Columba," preface, p. 9.

[4] Stokes's " Martyrology of Gorman," June 11th and October 9th.

nearer the truth. Take, for instance, those names which consist of a noun followed by a genitive, such as Mug Néit or Mug Nuadat. How little we know about *Nét* or *Nuada* it is needless to suggest; and as for *Tlachtga* in *Fer Tlachtga* we know nothing, except that Irish story makes Tlachtga the daughter of a famous Druid called Mog Ruith, whom it brings in contact with the Simon Magus of Christian legend; and that it associates Tlachtga's name with an ancient *ráth* on the Hill of Ward (in Meath), where a fire used to be kindled at Allhallows, and distributed to the country round about.[1] Then who knows anything about Corb? And still we have not only *Cú Chorb*, "Corb's Hound," and *Fer Corb*, "Corb's Man," but also *Nia Corb*, "Corb's Champion," *Mac Corb*, "Corb's Boy or Son," *Mug Corb*, "Corb's Slave," *Art Corb*, "Corb's Bear." So we should probably not be far wrong in supposing that *Corb* was a divinity, fetish, totem, or ancestor of the Aborigines. In any case *Corb* must be regarded as antecedent to such personal names as *Cú Chorb*, *Fer Corb*, and the like. In other terms, these names are conglomerates involving elements derived from an ancient system, and the obscurity that surrounds them precludes, in most cases, one's regarding the class of personal names in which they are present as late.

The Aryan system of personal names differed from the foregoing very strikingly. They may be classed under two heads: first come the full names, consisting not of words in syntactic relation to one another, but of two elements forming real compounds, such as, Sanskrit *Candra-rája*, from *candra*, " shining, moon," and *rája*, " king," Greek Διογένης, " descendant of Zeus," Gaulish Πεννο-ουινδος, meaning " white-headed," from *penno-s*, " head," and *vindos*, " white," in Welsh *Pen-wyn*, and in Irish *Cenn-fhinn*, of the same meaning. The number of words employed for the purposes of this composition does not appear to have been at

---

[1] For references see Rhys's " Celtic Heathendom," p. 515, note 2.

any time very great, but the best use was made of them when the Greeks formed not only Ἵππαρχος but also Ἄρχιππος ; and similarly in Old High German, *Hariberht* (English Herbert) and *Berhthari*, Servian *Milodrag* and *Dragomil*, and so in some of our inscriptions, such as the one at Laugharne in Carmarthenshire reading BARRIVENDI FILIVS VENDVBARI.[1] The two names occur in later Irish as *Barrfhinn* and *Finnbharr* respectively, in Welsh *Berwyn* and *Gwynfar :* both seem to have meant white-topped or white-headed. These are instances of the Aryan full or compound name, but there was another class consisting of the full name reduced to one of the elements in the compound and supplied sometimes with hypocoristic or endearing terminations. Thus in Greek,[2] for instance, we find besides the compounds Νικόμαχος, Νικόστρατος, and the like, shorter forms such as Νικέας, Νικᾶς, Νίκων, Νικεύς, Νῖκυς, Νίκυλλος, and a good many more. Similarly, besides such names as *Cadwallaon, Cadfael, Cadfan* in Welsh, we have the shorter ones suggested by them, *Cadog* and *Catwg*. Many more might be added from all the Celtic languages, but the foregoing will serve to show what the Aryan system of names was, and how it would have taxed the ingenuity of the cleverest Druid to select many incident names which at the same time should sound Aryan of the approved type. Not only were the two systems different, they must have been incompatible, mutually destructive; and it is needless to say that the habit of giving children incident names cannot have been developed in Aryan surroundings. It is the less artificial of the two, and belongs to a ruder race ; and no evidence could well be more conclusive as to the former presence in these Islands of a population of natives of non-Aryan origin.

---

[1] See Rhys's " Lectures on Welsh Philology," pp. 279, 388.
[2] For a discussion of the whole subject of Greek proper names, see Fick's " Griechische Personennamen " (Göttingen, 1874).

CHAPTER III.

THE following chapter is intended mainly to do two things : to elucidate the map of Britain in the first century of our era which faces this page, and to lead up to the history of Wales proper. The facts, where they are not new or submitted to a fresh examination, are taken from Rhys's " Celtic Britain,"[1] checked by Mr. F. Haverfield's map of Roman Britain,[2] and the succinct account of the Province with which his map is accompanied.

From what has already been said it will be seen that Pytheas, when he visited this country in the 4th century before our era, is not likely to have found any Brythons here: the inhabitants of the south of the Island consisted then of the Aborigines, with Goidels as the race ruling over some or all of them. It is unfortunate that Pytheas's account of his visit is not extant; abstracts, however, from his diary have come down through such channels as the works of Diodorus, Strabo, and Pliny. But the evidence which principally concerns us is concentrated in a few proper names, such as *Albion, Belerium, Britanni, Cantium, Ictis, Morimarusam*, and *Pretanic* Islands. Of these *Cantium* and *Pretanic* must be regarded as Brythonic,

---

[1] Published by the Society for Promoting Christian Knowledge, 3rd ed., London, 1904.
[2] See Mr. Poole's " Historical Atlas of Modern Europe from the Decline of the Roman Empire" (Oxford, Clarendon Press, 1896), Plate XV.

Belgic, or Gaulish, and not Goidelic. The earliest existing work which alludes to the south-eastern portion of Britain as Cantium is Cæsar's account of the Gallic War, and then follows Diodorus with his Κάντιον.[1] The name has the same form in the pages of Strabo, who uses it in passages devoted to a criticism of the statements of Pytheas in such a way that it has been supposed that Pytheas had used it himself. On this, however, one can only surmise that Pytheas either employed a slightly different form of the word or else that it reached him from a Brythonic or Belgic source on the Continent. The same kind of remark would apply to *Pretanic*, if it could be shown that any such a term was known to Pytheas, for the Celtican or Goidelic form must be supposed to have been *Qv̆rtanic*. The form, for example, in which it occurs in Ptolemy's Geography is Πρετανικὴ Νῆσος or Πρετανικαὶ Νῆσαι, " Pretanic Island or Islands," the latter of which meant the British Isles generally, the largest of them being called *Albion*, " Albion, Britain," and the next in size and importance Ἰουερνία, or Ivernia, " Ireland." The collective name has its living cognates in the old Goidelic *Cruithni*, "Picts," *Cruithnech*, "Pictish," in Old Welsh *Priten*, later *Pryden*, *Prydyn* and *Prydein*, now *Prydain*,[2] " Scotland, Alɔa, or the Pictland of the North," and *Ynys Prydain*, " Great Britain," literally " Prydain's or Picts' Island." Thus the name of the Aborigines implied by these vocables would have been in Greek orthography Πρετανοί, with which eventually another and an unconnected name was confounded, namely that of the Brittani, and the confusion is to be detected in the ττ of Πρετταντκή, Πρετταντκαί, and in the ε of Βρεττανοί. The name of the *Brittani* was, as already suggested, more usually and less correctly made in Latin

---

[1] See Cæsar's Gallic War, v. 13, 14, 22; Diodorus, v. 21, 3; and Meineke's Strabo, i. 4, 3 (C. 63), iv. 3, 3 (C. 193).

[2] For *Priten* see "Y Cymmrodor," ix. 179 : the other forms occur in the plural, meaning Picts, in the Books of Aneurin and Taliessin: see Skene, ii. 92, 209.

orthography into *Britanni,* until at last it was ousted by the name as pronounced by those people themselves, namely, *Brĭttŏnes.* This last has regularly yielded the Welsh *Brython* and French *Bretons,* while French *Bretagne* similarly represents *Brittania,* not *Britania* or *Britannia;* and it cannot be regarded as an accident that the Latin *Brittani* corresponds exactly to the Mediæval Irish plural *Bretain,* genitive *Bretan.* In other words the form *Brittani* must have reached the Romans from the non-Brythonic Celts of these Islands or of the Continent.

Let us now take the other names, (1) beginning with Pliny's *Albion,* which is treated in Greek as Ἄλβιον, Ἀλβίων or Ἀλουίων, genitive Ἀλβίωνος or Ἀλουίωνος.[1] This name is unknown to the Brythonic dialects, except that Modern Welsh literature sometimes borrows *Alban* for Scotland; but it survives in the Goidelic dialects, namely, as *Alba, Alpa,* and *Elpa,* genitive *Alban* (also *Alba*[2]). Traces of its application to the whole of Great Britain[3] before it came to be confined to the northern portion of it occur' in Irish literature; and the fact of the Island being called *Insula Albionum* in the Ora Maritima of Avienus[4] makes it probable that the name is very ancient. Albion is supposed, and perhaps rightly, to mean the White Country, in reference to the appearance of the cliffs of the southern coast, and at first it was applied presumably only to the south. There is no evidence that the Brythons or Belgic Gauls used the word, but rather that they translated it into their own tongue as *Cantion;* for some believe that also to have meant the

---

[1] Pliny's "Historia Naturalis," iv. 30, 1.
[2] Rhys's "Manx Phonology," p. 85.
[3] See "Cormac's Glossary," *s.v.* "Mug-éime," and the instance in the Duan Albanach, quoted at the close of this chapter, p. 115; see also Stokes's "Urkeltischer Sprachschatz," p. 21, where he explains the name to mean White Land.
[4] See the lines in question quoted and explained in Müllenhoff's "Deutsche Altertumskunde," i. 91.

White Country.[1] Unlike the other name, however, *Cantion* remained confined to the south-east of the Island, so that it has yielded the Welsh *Caint* and the English *Kent*.

(2) *Belerium* is given twice by Diodorus as Βελέριον, which Ptolemy's manuscripts give as Βολέριον, and it is supposed to have meant some portion of the south-western peninsula, including probably the Land's End. In Old Irish we have a word which comes very near it, namely the neuter noun *bélre*, (Modern Irish *béurla*), which meant a language, and unqualified, perhaps, an alien or foreign tongue. This would explain how in Modern Irish it means "English"; and the inference suggested by the occurrence of the name Belerion is, that it became current among the Goidels at a time when the language of the Aborigines was still dominant over a certain area of the south-west of the Island. Perhaps, however, it was merely meant to describe the extreme south-west as a *tongue* of land.

(3) *Ictis* is the name recorded by Diodorus as given to one of the islands at high tide to which the inhabitants of the south-western peninsula of Britain brought their tin for sale to the merchants who traded with them. The same name was known to Pliny, for his *Insulam Mictim* is doubtless to be corrected into *Insulam Ictim*. But his account of Ictis differs from that of Diodorus, although both are supposed to have drawn their information from Timæus, a historian who was contemporary with Pytheas. There seems to be no sufficient reason for identifying *Ictis* with *Vectis*, "the Isle of Wight," or to sever it from the Irish name of the English Channel, namely, *Muir n-Icht*,[2]

[1] See Stokes's "Urk. Sprachschatz," p. 90, and Holder's "Alt-celt. Sprachschatz," *s.v. Cantion, canto :* compare the Welsh word *can*, "white." A certain school of English historians pretend that *Cantium* is in Welsh *y Caint*, "the Kent," and that it meant "the open country." This interpretation comes from Dr. W. Owen Pughe, but where the definite article has been found prefixed to this proper name we have not yet discovered. Both "*the* Caint" and "*the* Gwent" figure among the curiosities of Guest's "Origines Celticæ."

[2] "Cormac's Glossary," *s.v.* Mug-éime.

"the Sea of Icht, or Ictian Sea." *Ictis* and *Icht* represent possibly a Celtic pronunciation of the same Aboriginal word which the Romans made into *Pictus*,[1] plural *Picti ;* for if the Celts learned the word sufficiently early they would naturally treat it like any other word with the consonant *p*, that is to say, they would get rid of that consonant as in their own words. It is probably a mistake to suppose that in this name we have the Latin *pictus*, "painted," any more than in the name of the Pictones in Gaul. Had it been Latin it could hardly have been regarded as other than a kind of nickname, and no one would have expected the Aborigines of Caithness and Sutherland to give the Norsemen who first reached their shores a Latin nickname as their national designation. Rather must we suppose it an early name, which the Aborigines adopted, while the Celts sooner or later applied another name, *Qụrtani, Pretani, Cruithni* and *Prydyn*, to them in Goidelic and Brythonic respectively.[2]

[1] This may, perhaps, be regarded as confirmed by *Ictium*, given by Holder as an old name of a place now called L'Isle-Jourdain in the Dép. of the Vienne, covered by the eastern portion of the old province of Poitou. For *Poitou* represents an older *Pictavi*, another form of the name of the *Pictones*, and both claim close kinship with that of the Picts of this country. For the latter were not only called Picti, but also Pictones (see Stokes's "Annals of Tigernach" in the "Revue Celtique," xvii. 251, 253); and probably *Pictores*, which, under the influence of the genitive plural *Pictorum*, is not uncommon, is everywhere to be corrected into *Pictones*. The Paris document, published by Skene at the head of his collection of the Chronicles of the Picts and of the Scots, has, in that compilation, *Pictavia* and *Pictaviam* seven times. Skene's *v* is meant to represent the *u* of the manuscript; but on scrutinising the original (Latin, 4126) in the Bibliothèque Nationale, we find only one instance which looks like *Pictauia*. The others we should read *Pictania, Pictaniam*, with *ni* formed like *m*. The MS. appears to be a fourteenth century copy of an original of the tenth. Add to this that the Life of St. Cadroe calls the Aborigines of Ireland *gentem Pictaneorum :* see Skene's "Picts and Scots," p. 108 ; also p. 137, where the unusual form *Pictinia* is given.

[2] The words *Cruithni* and *Prydyn* have been regarded as derived, though the nasal has not been exactly accounted for, from the Irish and Welsh words for "form or shape," namely *cruth* and *pryd* respectively, and a reference in them has been assumed to the forms or outlines of the beasts which the Picts are

(4) *Morimarusam* is said by Pliny, after Philemon, to have been the name of the northern ocean from the Cimbri's country to a certain Cape Rubeas, and to have meant *Dead Sea*. The passage, somewhat carelessly given by Pliny, is repeated in a less ambiguous form by the later author Solinus, xix. 2 :—*Philemon a Cimbris ad promunturium Rubeas Morimarusam dicit vocari, hoc est Mortuum Mare : ultra Rubeas quicquid est Cronium nominat.*[1] Scholars are not inclined to regard *Morimarusam* as a specimen of the language of the Cimbri, whom they regard as a Teutonic people, while on the other hand it admits of being explained exactly as Celtic, *Mori Marusam*, which would make in Modern Irish *Muir Marbh*, Welsh *Mor Marw*, "Dead Sea." In the Latin of both Pliny and Solinus it looks like an accusative feminine, but as the word *mori*, Irish *muir*, was neuter like the Latin *mare*, it is probably to be treated as accusative neuter ; and the fact of *Marusam* ending in *am* shows that we have here to do with Goidelic, as Brythonic and Gaulish would have had *on* or *om*,[2] and the Latin would have been given accordingly as *Mori-Marusum*. Pliny's authority was a certain Philemon who

believed to have had tattooed on their persons. Should this prove tenable, one could scarcely avoid treating *Cruithni* and *Prydyn* as translations into Goidelic and Brythonic of the word *Pict* regarded as the Latin *pictus*, "painted." It is needless to say that this would not help us to the meaning of *Pict* as a word of the Pictish language to which it possibly belonged ; but the supposition here suggested as to *Pretanic* being merely a sort of translation of the Latin *pictus*, would compel us to regard the first use of *Pretanic* as dating no earlier than Cæsar's time and the spread of Latin in Northern Gaul. This would simplify the question if the chronology should make it possible, which looks hardly probable.

[1] Pliny's version runs thus, iv. 95 : *Morimarusam (eum) a Cimbris vocari, hoc est, Mortuum Mare, inde usque ad promunturium Rubeas, ultra deinde Cronium.* This we copy from Müllenhoff's "Deutsche Altertumskunde," i. 413, where the passage is discussed.

[2] The predilection of Goidelic for *a* instead of *o* as the thematic vowel is borne out by the most ancient Ogams of Britain and Ireland : thus the genitive ending corresponding to Greek *os* (Latin *is*) is always *as* or *a*.

appears to have lived in the last century before our Era and Philemon is supposed to have been using information obtained by Pytheas when he visited Britain.

With regard to these names *Albion, Belerium, Ictis,* and *Mori-Marusam,* it is probable that they were learnt in this country by Pytheas or some of the travellers who came here after his time. In other words, we may treat them for what they are worth as evidence of the occupation of the southern portions of Britain by a Celtican or Goidelic people at a time before the Brythons had obtained a footing on its shores. We have dwelt on these names at this point as another view is sometimes put forward, that everything Goidelic in Britain is to be traced to invasions from Ireland, and to a time subsequent to the second century of our era, especially the later years of the Roman occupation and those following the withdrawal of the Roman legions from the Island.[1] That men from Ireland invaded Britain at various points and at various times, and, further, that some of them settled here, is not to be disputed. Take, for instance, the case of the Dalriad Scots, who crossed from Ireland to Argyle in the fifth century, or that of the Déisi in the south-west of Wales at a still earlier date. This, however, proves in no wise that there was not previously a Goidelic population in the west of the Island; it rather favours the contrary supposition, for a native Goidelic population might well be credited with having appealed to men of their own race and language in Ireland for aid in their struggles with Brythonic tribes, and the response to such an appeal may have served as the beginning of a series of descents on the coasts of Wales and of the south of England. To such invasions we may possibly have to

---

[1] This view has been recently advocated by Professor Meyer in the " Transactions of the Hon. Society of Cymmrodorion " (64 Chancery Lane, London, 1897), 1895–6, pp. 55–86, where a number of facts illustrating the early intercourse between Wales and Ireland have been brought together in a very interesting fashion.

ascribe the destruction of such towns as Isca Silurum or Caerleon and Venta Silurum or Caer Went in Monmouthshire, and perhaps of Calleva or Silchester in Hampshire, where an Ogam inscription[1] testifying to the presence of a Goidel was discovered a short time ago. Nay, it is conceivable that Vortigern, whose name outside the Hengist story is found to have been more at home in Ireland and Brittany than in Wales, represented such an invasion, with its influence reaching as far as Kent.

The advocates of the view to which we have referred appear to be at one with us as to the existence of a considerable Goidelic population in the west of Britain from the second century onwards, and also as to the influence of that Goidelic element on the subsequent history of this Island, especially that portion of it which constitutes the Principality of Wales. The difference of view attaches to the previous question, whence came the Goidelic element admitted to have been present here? Our hypothesis regards it as for the most part resident and as partly drawn from Ireland, while the other derives it wholly from Ireland. The difficulty which we feel in estimating the respective merits of these hypotheses is enhanced by our lack of data to enable us to judge of the attitude of the advocates of the hypothesis of the exclusive Irish origin with regard to the question of the Aboriginal population. Nor can we hope to understand their position till they indicate how they suppose the Goidels of Ireland to have reached that country, also where and when they approximately think Goidelic nationality and Goidelic speech to have assumed their individuality. For our own part, we have already sufficiently sketched our conjectures as to the Aboriginal population ; and we have also indicated our conviction that

---

[1] See in the Archæologia, vol. liv., a paper by Mr. G. E. Fox and Mr. W. H. St. John Hope, entitled "Excavations on the Site of the Roman City at Silchester, Hants," in 1893, pp. 35-9.

Goidels and Brythons differed in speech before they left the Continent. We might probably add religion: for we understand Cæsar (vi. 13) to represent Druidism as being on the wane in Gaul, and as having originated in Britain, whither those who wished to study it thoroughly had to resort. But as there is no convincing evidence to identify it with any Brythonic tribe in this country, while there is evidence of its prevalence among the Goidels of Môn in the time of Agricola, and of its surviving in Ireland in that of Patrick, and in the Pictland of the north in that of Columba, we infer that it was a system evolved by the Continental Goidels, or rather accepted by them from the Aborigines. When, however, the Goidels of Gaul were conquered by the Galatic Celts, including the Belgic peoples, Druidism may well have found it impossible to hold its own for any great length of time, though it may have continued to flourish in remote corners of Britain, which we take to be the real meaning of the supposition that Britain was its native country.[1]

We now come to the question how the Goidels reached Ireland—that is to say, was it direct from the Continent or across Britain? In answer to this, we should say that the first Celts to land in Ireland embarked probably on the western shores of Britain ; in other words, they belonged to a race which had conquered southern Britain from sea to sea. In early ages the voyage from the nearest ports of the Continent to Ireland must have been a formidable undertaking ; but by the time, let us say, of Cæsar, it was probably well within the capacity of the mariners of the Veneti and of the other tribes belonging to the Armoric League. That in one instance at least this did take place

---

[1] Since this was written a most suggestive volume of " Nos Origines " has been published : it is the work of the veteran archæologist, M. Bertrand, and bears the title of " La Religion des Gaulois, les Druides et le Druidisme " (Paris, Leroux, 1897), pp. ix. 436, and numerous illustrations.

the following neglected indication is worthy of note : in the extreme north-west of Gaul—that is to say, on the westernmost peninsula of Brittany—there was in Pytheas's time a people called by him 'Ωστίαιοι, "Ostiæi." Another early form of their name appears to have been 'Ωστίωνες ; but later they were best known as 'Οσίσμιοι, the Osismi whom Cæsar mentions among the allies of the Veneti. Now a name which has all the appearance of being closely connected with that of the Ostiæi or Ostiones is given by Ptolemy to a people in the south of Ireland—namely, the Οὐσδίαι,[1] "Usdiæ," whose name in its turn is probably to be identified with that of Ossory. In Irish this latter is written *Osraighe*, and, roughly speaking, it means the county of Kilkenny ; but the Ossorians formerly claimed against Munster the whole of the country from the Suir to the Barrow, and from the mountains called Slieve Bloom in Queen's County to the Meeting of the Three Waters near Waterford.[2] Moreover, as Ptolemy represents the Usdiæ as reaching the coast, we should probably add to their territory the greater part of the County Waterford, on which the Déisi seized in the third century, together with the western portion of the Ossorians' country, north of the Suir, of which they got possession later.[3] The similarity of the names Usdiæ and Ostiæi naturally leads one to suppose that some of the Ostiæi or Osismi sailed from Brittany past the Land's End to the coast between Youghal and Waterford Harbour, and then gradually pushed inland,

---

[1] Οὐσδίαι is considered the best reading, and it has been adopted in the text of Ptolemy, by C. Müller, in the Firmin Didot edition of 1883 ; and as to the name Ωστίαιοι see Müllenhoff's " Deutsche Altertumskunde," i. 373–5. If the view suggested above should prove correct, one may propose that instead of correcting the οὖς τιμίους of the MSS. of Strabo into οὖς 'Ωστιμίους, as Müllenhoff does, it should rather be into οὖς Οὐστιμίους.

[2] See O'Donovan's "Book of Rights," pp. 17, 18.

[3] *Ibid.* pp. 49, 50 ; but for the whole story of the Déisi see the "Book of the Dun Cow," fo. 53, 54, and O'Curry's " Manners and Customs of the Ancient Irish," ii. 205–8.

taking possession of some of the best land in Ireland. Possibly this took place as late as Cæsar's Gallic War, and one's thoughts are naturally directed to the time when the Osismi found their powerful allies, the Veneti, being crushed by him on land and sea. The archæological discoveries of the future may perhaps supply evidence where we have at present only conjecture.

The south-east of Ireland seems also to have been occupied, at least in part, by settlers coming direct from the Continent. For next to the Usdiæ come, according to Ptolemy, a certain tribe of Brigantes, occupying the coast as far as Carnsore Point, and above them he places a people whom he calls the Coriondi or Coriondæ, who probably occupied a district to which the waters of Wexford Harbour and the River Slaney gave ready access. Then come the Manapii, with their town called Manapia, and situated somewhere near the mouth of a river called Modonnus, which may probably have been the Avonmore, at whose mouth stands the town of Arklow, called in Med. Irish Inber Mór, "the great River-mouth." Beyond the Manapii come the Cauci, occupying probably the north of the present County Wicklow, and extending, perhaps, towards the mouth of the Liffey. Of these four tribes, the Manapii point to the Menapii on the Lower Rhine as their mother state, and as to the Cauci their name reminds one of that of the Teutonic people of the Chauchi, Chauci, or Cauchi, but our Cauci are more likely to have been Celts—possibly Celts who had been under the Teutonic rule of the Chauci.[1] The

---

[1] In this connection it is worth while mentioning that there seems to have been a very ancient trade in amber between Britain and the coast, with its islands, between the mouth of the Rhine and that of the Elbe. Some of the amber found in the ancient burials south of the Thames seems to have been of that origin ; so one infers that there was active navigation between the country of the Chauci and the British Isles. On this amber question see Elton's " Origins of English History," pp. 65–6. Holder cites Kiepert as believing the Cauci connected with the Lower Rhine.

Brigantes of Ireland were very probably of the same origin as the Brigantes of Britain; but we have no evidence to help us to fix on their home on the Continent. We should, perhaps, not be greatly mistaken in looking for it not far from the territory of the Menapii; for instance, in the country at the mouth of the Rhine known as *Insula Batavorum.* The Batavi and Caninefates whom we find in possession of it in the first century are believed to have been Teutonic peoples; but that the country had been formerly inhabited by Celts is proved by *Lugudunum (Batavorum),* now *Leyden,* which is as Celtic a name as that of the other Lugudunums[1] in different parts of Gaul. Another Batavian town was known as *Batavodurum,* which, in point of name, was at least in part Celtic, and situated in the neighbourhood of Nymeguen, whilst a little higher up the Rhine seems to have been a place called *Burginatium,* which looks like a sort of Teutonic translation of some such a Celtic name as *Brigantio,* borne· by a place once perhaps inhabited by the Brigantes of whom we are in quest.

Now some, possibly, of the four tribes of this group were Brythonic or Belgic rather than Goidelic; but we have no means of tracing the influence of their language on the Goidelic which became the language of Ireland. They are also remarkable for the small scale of their territory: it cannot have extended much beyond the limits of the present counties of Wexford and Wicklow, and its area was probably far from covering them, as it presumably consisted of settlements surrounded by the Aboriginal population—that is, in case that part of the country had not already been Goidelicised. In any case the territory of these Leinster tribes and that of the Usdiæ had been carved probably in the first instance out of that of the Iverni, who may accordingly be represented as an Aboriginal

---

[1] For a list of these see Holder's " Alt-celtischer Sprachschatz," *s.v.* ; see also his *Batavoduron* and *Burginatio.*

population previously extending from the south-west of the Island to the mouth of the Liffey or the Boyne. This would help to explain why Munster used formerly to claim Ossory, which we have supposed to represent the Usdiæ, and why the Iverni gave their name to the whole Island— that is to say, Ivernia, Latinised Hibernia; and similarly in the case of the Ἰουερνικὸς Ὠκεανός, which still retains its name of the "Irish Sea." When these names came into vogue the Iverni must have been predominant in Ireland. It is probably from the northern half of the Island that we have the name *Scotti*, under which the first western invaders appear in the history of Roman Britain in the fourth century. Before leaving Ireland we wish to mention two or three[1] of the names identified in Ptolemy's Geography. Foremost comes that of the people whom he calls Οὐσλούντιοι or Οὐολούντιοι,[2] for the manuscripts differ. His figures admit of our locating them around Armagh, near which is the remarkable pre-historic fortress of Emain Macha, now known as the Navan Fort, and we detect their name in the Irish *Ulaid, Ultu*,[3] "the Ultonians, Ulster," which

[1] We take them from àn excellent paper on Ptolemy's Map of Ireland, by Mr. G. H. Orpen, in the "Journal of the Royal Society of Antiquaries of Ireland," 1894, pp. 115–128, with map.

[2] The editor of the Firmin Didot edition gives the preference to this reading, for the incredible reason, that the so-called Richard of Cirencester has *Voluntii* or *Volantii* in Britain. To make Οὐολούντιοι fit as well as Οὐσλούντιοι we should have perhaps to spell it Οὐλόντιοι; but Οὐσλούντιοι and the variant Οὐσλόντιοι, which also occurs, would do ; however, the declension of the word in Irish suggests -τοι rather than -τιοι.

[3] This was the accusative plural, and the dative was *Ultaib*, contracted, no doubt, from *Ulatu* and *Ulataib* respectively—no singular occurs : so the genitive should have been *Ulat* and the nominative *Ulait*, but from *Ultu* and *Ultaib* were, by false analogy probably, inferred *Ulad* and *Ulaid*. Compare such words as *ingnáth* or *ingnád*, "wonderful, a wonder," pl. *inganta, césad*, "a suffering or passion," ac. plural *cestu*, and *molad*, "praise," pl. *moita* and *moltha*. The Irish *Ulaid* occurs in Welsh as *Wleth* : see the Book of Taliessin, poem xiv. (Skene, i. 276, ii. 154), where Penren Wleth seems to mean some headland called after the Ultonians or their country. The reduction of *nt, nc* to *tt* (*t*), *cc* (*c*) is universal in Goidelic, and no certain instance from a previous stage has yet been discovered. *Brigantes*, for example, was Brythonic,

fits so well that there can be no serious doubt as to their identity. The name of Ptolemy's Ἐρδῖνοι survives in that of Lough *Erne* and of the ancient tribe of the *Ernai* associated by Irish legend with that water. His Βουουίνδα was undoubtedly the Boyne, and his Βίργος the Barrow, not to mention his Δαβρώνα, which is probably to be corrected into Σαβρώνα, and to be identified with *Sabrann*,[1] an old name of the river Lee, on the banks of which, somewhere about the position of Cork, stood Ivernis, which may be supposed to have been the capital of the Iverni in Ptolemy's time.

We now at length come back to Britain and the disposition of its populations under the Romans. Here we have to deal first with the question, whom the Romans had to contend with when they invaded the island. Cæsar's passage already mentioned (p. 5) as to the powerful Gaul Diviciacos who ruled over Britain supplies a clue to the answer. The statement of the Remi to Cæsar referred to a time which men then still alive remembered, and, since no hint as to a revolution is vouched, the probability is that the empire of Diviciacos in this country subsisted

---

and *Uoluntii* comes from a Pictish origin doubtless rather than a Celtic one. Compare Pictish *Uoret*, *-uorra:in* and *-uorrn* (Pro. of Antiq. Scot. xxxij. 347, 349, 372). On the other hand, not only Brythonic but also Pictish shows no aversion to *nt*: take, for instance, the names of the thirty Pictish kings mentioned in the Pictish Chronicle as ruling over Erin and Britain (Skene's "Picts and Scots," pp. 5–8); the list opens with Brute *Pant*, followed by Brute *Urpant*, and contains others called Brude *Gant* and Brude *Urgant*, Brude *Cint* and Brude *Urcint*, also such later names as *Entifidich* and *Custantin* (= *Constantinus*). Similarly Ptolemy places a tribe. called *Decantæ* in the northern reach of the Pictish country, while we have the *Decanti* of the *Arx Decantorum* of the Annales Cambria, later *Deganhwy* or *Deganwy*, near Llandudno, in North Wales : the Goidelic equivalent is found in the personal name which occurs in the genitive variously as *DECCETI*, *DECHETI*, and in Ogam *Decceddas*, *Decedda*, &c.

[1] This name is probably non-Celtic, and evidently identical with that of the Severn, in Welsh *Hafren*, from an earlier *Sabrīna*, which our classical scholars, so particular as to vowel quantity, are pleased to make into Sabrīna. Compare Irish *salann*, Welsh *halen*, "salt," and Irish *crann*, Welsh *pren*, "a tree, timber."

under his successors in Cæsar's time. But Diviciacos's people were the Suessiones and the Remi; so we should expect to find both of them represented in Britain, though their names have not been detected. Now we know from a couple of ancient inscriptions[1] that a favourite god of the Remi was Camulos, whose name is the etymological equivalent of the German word *himmel,* "heaven," and may be regarded as a synonym or translation doubtless of the god's common Aryan name, which is represented by Zεύς in Greek, *Jovis* in Latin, and *Dyaus* in Sanskrit. This was the supreme god of the ancient Aryans, and the Celts made him their god of war; so some of them when they settled in Britain called one of their fortresses *Camulodunon,* "the town of Camulos." This was near Colchester, in the country of the Trinovantes, in whom we are accordingly prepared to find the Remi we are seeking. The next neighbours of the Trinovantes were the Catuvellauni, in whom we probably have our insular Suessiones. At any rate, the name of the Catuvellauni was also that which, shortened into *Catelauni* or Catalauni, eventually became *Chaalons* and *Châlons,* the name of a well-known town on the Marne, in a district usually assigned to the Remi. But the fact is that the Remi and Suessiones formed a sort of twin state, the boundary between whose lands we have no data to enable us to draw. According to Cæsar's information, the Remi and the Suessiones regarded one another as kinsmen: they lived under the same laws and obeyed the same magistrates. But the Remi cultivated the friendship of Cæsar, while the Suessiones took part in various efforts made by the Gauls to throw off the Roman yoke; and when those efforts failed, the Remi came forward to intercede for the Suessiones and save them from ruin.[2]

---

[1] See the Berlin "Corpus Inscrip. Latinorum," vi. No. 46, and Hübner's "Exempla. Script. Epigraphicæ, No. 198."

[2] Cæsar, ii. 3, 12.

A somewhat similarly close relationship appears to have existed between their representatives in Britain—that is, if we are right in supposing these to have been the Trinovantes and the Catuvellauni respectively. Thus the Catuvellauni, under the lead of their chief Cassivellaunos, strenuously opposed Cæsar's second invasion, while the Trinovantes hastened to seek his protection, complaining that Cassivellaunos had slain their king, whose son fled to Cæsar on the Continent. The feud between these kindred peoples is perhaps to be detected also in the case of a certain prince named Dubnovellaunos, who in vain sought the aid of Augustus : at any rate, some of his coins seem to identify him with the country of the Trinovantes.[1]

In any case the Catuvellauni and the Trinovantes between them may be regarded as the upholders of the empire of Diviciacos, and for aught we know Cassivellaunos may have been lineally descended from Diviciacos. The power and influence of the Catuvellauni is sufficiently proved by the fact of their chief Cassivellaunos being entrusted with the conduct of the war against Cæsar; and Dion Cassius, speaking of the campaign of Aulus Plautius in 43, represents the Catuvellauni as ruling over a part or the whole of the people of the Dobunni on the Severn in Gloucestershire. On the other hand, the coins of Cunobelinos their king, who died before that year, show him occupying Camulodunon as his headquarters in the lifetime of his father Tasciovant,[2] who resided at Verlamion, now

---

[1] See Rhys's "Celtic Britain," pp. 27, 294.

[2] This name has a variety of forms on the coins : the nominative occurs as *Tasciovanus, Tasciovanius,* and *Tasciovans,* and the genitive as *Tasciovani, Tasciiovanii, Tasciovantis,* besides such abbreviations as *Tasciov, Tasciav, Tascio, Tascia, Taxcia,* and *Taxci;* but there must have been also some such a form as *Tacsivant-,* for we find it represented in Welsh pedigrees by a form which must have been Techuant, written *Tehvant,* which is the explanation of the form Teuhant in the Nennian genealogies : see "Y Cymmrodor," ix. 174, 176, also *Tecmant* for Techmant, with *m* for *v* (p. 174) : it is written *Tecwant* in Jesus College MS. 20, *Ibid.* viij. 84, and it is from *Tehvant,* by the easy

Old Verulam, near St. Albans. Thus at the time when the Claudian invasion took place the people of the Catuvellauni held sway from the North Sea to the mouth of the Severn. But to return to Tasciovant, the number of his coins seems to indicate that he had a long reign, terminating only in the earlier years of the Christian Era. Some of his coins suggest that his rule extended to Calleva of the Atrebates—that is to say, Silchester, in the north of Hampshire. He had two sons also whose coins are extant, namely, Cunobelinos already mentioned, and Epaticcos, whose coins induce one to believe that he held sway south of the Thames, in what is now Surrey.[1] But the tribes south of the Thames appear to have for some time retained a certain independence under three princes named Tincommios, Epillos, and Verica, each of whom styles himself on his coins "Son of Commios." Their father may have been Commios the Atrebat, who attempted to act as Cæsar's emissary in Britain, and who afterwards played the part of mediator when Cassivellaunos sued for peace. The subsequent career of this Commios in Gaul was a very chequered one. He joined with his countrymen in various attempts to free themselves from the yoke of Rome, and after narrowly escaping Roman treachery he withdrew to Britain. But whether Tincommios and his brothers were the sons of this Commios or not, there is evidence that Tincommios, who possibly ruled over the Regni, pursued a Romanising policy;

misreading of *h* into *n*, that Geoffrey's *Tenuantius* (iii. 20) arose. It is remarkable that we have in the pedigree of Rhun, son of Nwython (Cymmrodor, ix. 176) the correct succession *map. Caratauc. map. Cinbelin. map. Teuhant*, for *filii Carataci filii Cunobelini filii Taxivanti;* but this information which one obtains partly from the coins, above all the name of Tasciovant, is not to be got from any known author, whether Roman or Greek. So we have here probably traces of a Welsh pedigree representing a genuine tradition reaching back beyond the beginning of the Christian era.

[1] A coin with the letters CARA or CARAT is probably to be referred to Caratacos, the more famous brother : see Evans's "Coins of the Ancient Britons," Supplement (London, 1890), p. 553, and Plate XX. 8.

for Augustus having become emperor and styled himself on a coin *Augustus Divi Filius*, it was not long
before Tincommios had coins of his own inscribed in
Augustus's Latin formula : *Tinc[ommius] Com[mi] F[ilius]*.

A passage in Tacitus's Agricola, c. 14, is here in point.
He says that certain cities were given to a certain king
Cogidumnos, according to the received policy of Rome
when she wanted tools for the enslaving of other nations,
and he adds that Cogidumnos continued faithful to the
Romans even within the historian's own time.   An inscription, dating from the time of Claudius or Vespasian and
found at Chichester, helps to localise Cogidumnos there.[1]
Thus we seem to have glimpses of a Romanising policy
pursued among the kings of the Regni from the time of
Tincommios to that of Tacitus.   It originated probably
in fear and jealousy of the power of the Catuvellauni, and
in any case that is the key to the history of the Roman
conquest in 43, for the legions seem to have met with no
serious resistance till they neared the Thames.   The resistance then offered was organised by the Catuvellauni, while
the Eceni in their rear, that is to say, in the district between
the Trinovantes and the Wash, do not seem to have fought
at all, for Tacitus[2] represents them as having entered into
alliance with Rome of their own free will.   This makes it
appear all the more probable that we have the Eceni in
the Cenimagni of a previous age, who head Cæsar's short
list of tribes suing for peace.   The names of the others
were Segontiaci, Ancalites, Bibroci and Cassi, who were all
probably inhabitants of the southern side of the Thames,
and may have been forced or frightened into submission; but
it is hard to believe this of a warlike people like the Eceni,
located as they were beyond the Trinovantes and the

---

[1] See the Berlin "Corpus Inscr. Lat. " vii. No. 11 ; also Holder, *s.v.*
" Cogidubnus."

[2] See the Annals, xiv. 31.

Catuvellauni. One is left to conclude that they, in case we are to identify them with the Cenimagni, only followed the example of the Trinovantes out of fear or jealousy of the aggressive policy of the Catuvellauni. How far northwards the power of the Catuvellauni extended it is impossible to say, but it may have reached Uriconion, or Wroxeter, on the Severn, near Shrewsbury, and probably it took in the Coritavi or Coritani, whose country lay between the Trent and the North Sea, and contained the towns of *Lindon*, now Lincoln, and *Ratæ*, now Leicester. It is significant as to the power of the Catuvellauni that Suetonius (Caligula, 44) calls their king Cunobelinos, who died before the Claudian conquest, *Britannorum Rex*, "King of the Brythons."

Some further light is to be obtained on the disposition of these and neighbouring tribes from the history of the conquest of the south of Britain. According to Dion Cassius a prince named Bericos, having been driven into exile by troubles at home, sought for help from the Emperor Claudius, who then made up his mind to conquer Britain. Aulus Plautius was appointed leader of the expedition, and the war was prosecuted with vigour for the first ten years ; and Dion Cassius tells us that Aulus Plautius conquered two of Cunobelinos's sons, first Caratacos, and then his brother Togodumnos, who had probably succeeded his father as king. In the course of the war the Roman general's lieutenant, Vespasian, afterwards emperor, appears to have greatly distinguished himself, having, as it is said by Suetonius (Vespasian, 4), reduced two of the most powerful tribes in the island, together with more than twenty towns and the Isle of Wight. We can only surmise that his operations were conducted chiefly against the Belgæ and Dumnonii, the latter of whom were probably Goidels. The Romans, at any rate, appear to have lost little time in making their way to the Mendip Hills, where they had lead mines worked. In the year 50 the command was taken by Ostorius Scapula, and he proceeded to deal with the natives with a strong hand. He took measures to hold in check all the tribes living on his side of the Severn and the Trent;[1] and possibly it was then the Roman town of Uriconium came into existence, marking the limit reached by the province as well, perhaps, as that of the influence of the Catuvellauni. But the determined attitude of Ostorius would seem to have moved various widely severed tribes to take a sort of concerted action against him. The first to rebel were the Eceni; and after humbling the Eceni he marched to the coast of the other sea, namely, to the country of the Deceangli, whose name survives in that of the deanery of Tegeingl, in Flintshire. The attraction of that district was its mineral wealth, and it is the inscription on some pigs of lead from there, now in the Grosvenor Museum at Chester, that enables us approximately to fix the locality.[2] From the Deceangli, the general turned back to quell troubles caused by the Brigantes, who formed the dominant people in what is now the North of England. We next read of him establishing a strong colony of veterans at Camulodunon and undertaking to subdue the Silures, who occupied the eastern half of the region between Cardigan Bay and the Severn. The Silures were a warlike race, and they were at this time led by Caratacos, one of the sons of Cunobelinos. Caratacos had resisted the Romans from the beginning, which meant some nine years of experience in war against them. When his own people, the Catuvellauni, succumbed, he appears to have sought refuge among the Silures, to

---

[1] See Tacitus's Annals, xii. 31, where the passage in point has been emendated as follows by Dr. Henry Bradley; *Cunctosque cis Trisantonam et Sabrinam fluvios cohibere parat.* See the "Academy," April 28, 1883, p. 296. *Trisantona*, which was probably the early form of the name of the *Trent*, analyses itself into *Tris-antona*, and recalls *Rhi-annon* (for *Rig-anton-*), on which see the "Academy," Aug. 15, 1896, p. 115.

[2] See the "Academy," Oct. 31, 1891, p. 390 : see also pp. 412, 437.

whom he must have been well known for his opposition to the Romans, not to mention that the portion of his father's dominion entrusted to him may have been the western one bordering on the country of the Silures. However, he shifted the war into the country of the Ordovices, who were probably of the same Brythonic race as his own people, while the Silures are more likely to have been Goidels. The final battle was fought, as we gather, in the neighbourhood of the Breidin[1] Hills, between Welshpool and the English border. The legions prevailed, and Caratacos fled to the Brigantes, whose Queen Cartismandua gave him up to the Romans to adorn a triumph in the streets of Rome ; but the Silures continued unsubdued.

In the year 58, Nero sent here Suetonius Paulinus, who led his troops in 62 to Anglesey, and Tacitus's account of the battle which they fought there is remarkable for the Druids that figure in it. While Suetonius was reducing Mona and cutting down her sacred groves, Boudicca, queen of the Eceni, widow of the king whose name is given as Prasutagus, headed a determined revolt, which resulted in a terrible slaughter of the Roman colony at Camulodunon. In time, Suetonius supervened, and was able to avenge the Roman losses by inflicting others on a still larger scale. Nothing worthy of note seems to have occurred till Vespasian became emperor in 69 ; one of his generals effected the reduction of the Brigantes in the years 69 and 70. The Silures were also at last conquered, and Julius Agricola, who was sent here in 78, quickly crushed the Ordovices and led his troops as far as Anglesey. His subsequent achievements in war took place mostly in the north of the island, where he is supposed to have drawn a line

---

[1] This word put back into its early form would probably make *Bragidunon* or *Bragodunon*, meaning possibly the " Hill-fort." Dygen Freidin was the name of a stream in the same neighbourhood : see Skene's " Four Ancient Books of Wales," ii. 277, and the " Myvyrian Arch.," i. 193.

of fortifications from the Clyde to the Forth. One of his great victories was won at a place called Mons Granpius or Graupius, over tribes who fought from war chariots ; and on his way back he took hostages from a people called by the otherwise unknown name of Boresti, located somewhere between the Tay and the Forth. The fleet also co-operated with the land forces, and after passing a winter at a certain *Portus Trucculensis* or *Trutulensis*, it performed the circumnavigation of Britain. Agricola was recalled in 85 or 86, but had he been allowed to go on he would probably have conquered Ireland : he had calculated the cost, and he had an exiled chief ready to lead the way. He was not only a great general, but also an astute statesman, who conciliated the conquered and encouraged them to adopt Roman institutions and acquire the Latin language.

The Emperor Hadrian, who came here in 120, appears to have put down an insurrection, and he is represented building a wall from the Solway to the Tyne. In 139, his successor, Antoninus Pius, sent his general Lollius Urbicus here, and he reduced the Brigantes dwelling beyond Hadrian's Wall, and constructed in 143 a turf wall across the country from the Clyde to the Forth. The reason given for the war on the Brigantes was, that the latter had begun to invade the territory of certain Roman subjects described by Pausanias, the only writer who alludes to them, as ἡ Γενουνία Μοῖρα, " the Division or Cohort called Genunia," a thoroughly non-Brythonic designation, which recalls Adamnán's *Geona Cohors*, and such tribal names as *Dál-Riada* and *Dál-Cais*, the division of Riada and Cas respectively.[1] The Genunians probably occupied some part of Galloway,

----

[1] See Reeves's Adamnán's " Life of St. Columba," i. 33 (p. 62), p. 92, note. One is strongly tempted to identify the terms Γενουνία Μοῖρα and *Geona Cohors*: all that is necessary is to suppose the latter written *Geona*, that is *Genona* instead of *Geona*. But what would such an identification mean geographically and historically?

possibly that assigned by Ptolemy to a people whom he called Selgovæ, a name which meant hunters: they were probably a tribe of the Aboriginal Picts, more or less Goidelicised, and depending on the Romans for protection against the aggressiveness of the Brigantic Brythons. In 162 there were troubles again in the north, and under Commodus they became still more serious. The fortresses beyond Hadrian's Wall, and that Wall itself, fell into the hands of the northern enemy, who spread devastation in the province; it was repelled in 182. In the struggle for the purple of empire, following the death of Commodus, Albinus, who was in command of the forces in Britain, crossed to the Continent, where he met with his death. He had, in 197, succeeded in making terms with the tribes beyond Hadrian's Wall; but his successor found himself unable to keep them quiet, so he purchased peace from them at a great price.

It was not long, however, before they attacked the province with such determination, that the Emperor Severus resolved to make a great expedition in the north in 208. Severus penetrated, it has been supposed, as far as the Moray Firth, and he is credited with having built or rebuilt a wall from the Clyde to the Forth; in any case, as Britain figures little in history from the time of Severus's death in 211 to the reign of Carausius, his expedition must be pronounced very effective. It is to be noticed that in the time of Severus one finds the populations of the north grouped under the two names of Caledonii and Mæatæ. By the former, we are to understand the Caledonians, or native Picts of the Highlands, while the latter name appears to have comprised a mixed people of Picts and Celts occupying approximately the country assigned by Ptolemy to the northern portion of the Dumnonii, together with the tribes of the Lowlands nearest to them. Dion Cassius (lxxvi. 12) locates the Μαιάται close to the Wall which divided the island in two. If, as might be expected in his time, he meant Hadrian's Wall, the Mæatæ must be supposed to have included the Brigantes dwelling beyond that Wall and the tribes overshadowed by them, such as were probably the Votadini,[1] who occupied the coast from the southern Wall to the Firth of Forth. But we find it hard to accept this, and would prefer supposing that Dion was loosely following some previous author who meant the northern Wall. Otherwise one gets into difficulties as regards the subsequent history of the tribes involved, and runs counter to the later traces of the home of the Mæatæ; for their name is found to survive beyond the more northern Wall, to wit, in *Dun-Myat*, "the fortress of the *Mæatæ* or *Miati*," as the name is once given by Adamnán.[2] Dunmyat is now the name of one of the westernmost points of the Ochil Hills, over against Stirling, on the other side of the Forth. Other fixed points of the same kind are *May* Wäter, near Forteviot, and *Maya Insula*, well known as the Isle of *May*, off the north-east coast of Fife. So it may be supposed that the country of the Mæatæ comprised at least most of the tract covered by Stirlingshire and the whole of the Lowlands as far as the Tay, whatever may be said as to the region beyond that river.[3]

[1] The name of these people is given in most of the manuscripts of Ptolemy as 'Ωταδηνοί or 'Ωταδινοί, but the Welsh form, according to Nennius, was *Guotodin*, which should now be *Gododin ;* and it follows that the ancient form should have been more nearly Ούοταδηνοί or Ούοταδινοί, perhaps better still Ούοτοδινοί. Their country embraced the district around North Berwick, and the headland over against Fife is alluded to in Irish literature (Skene's "Picts and Scots," p. 57) as the promontory of Fothudán, which agrees, except in its termination, with the *Guotodin* of Nennius. We have a simpler form of the same origin in the Irish personal name *Fothad*, and in the leading element of the genitive *Voteporigis*, *Votecorigas*, on the bilingual stone of Castell Dwyran, Carmarthenshire. See the "Arch. Cambrensis," 1895, pp. 303-13; 1896, pp. 107-10, 138.

[2] See Reeves's Adamnán, i. 9 (p. 36) ; also i. 8 (p. 33), where the spelling is *Miathi*.

[3] See Skene's "Picts and Scots," pp. clxi. 423-4.

Carausius seized the reins of government in Britain in 287, and he is described as of the most plebeian descent, as a Menapian citizen, and as an alumnus of Batavia. His history was that of a man who had once worked for wages as a mariner, and by degrees made his way up to the very responsible position of commanding the Roman fleet charged to keep the sea opposite the Belgic and Armoric coasts clear of the Saxons and Franks who infested it ; among other distinctions he had earned a great reputation in the war against the Bagaudæ in Gaul. The headquarters of his fleet were at *Bononia* or Boulogne, and he did his work with great success, but at length he fell under the suspicion of conniving at the doings of the pirates and of receiving a share of the plunder. This resulted at last in an order that he should be put to death, whereupon Carausius declared himself Cæsar, and made Britain for a time independent of Rome, and not a little prosperous. He died in 294, assassinated by a certain Allectus, who is represented as one of his associates, and Allectus enjoyed power till he was slain in a battle fought in 296 with the army of Constantius Chlorus, who then re-united Britain to the Roman Empire.[1]

It will help one to understand the career of Carausius, if it be borne in mind that being a citizen of Menapia does not necessarily mean that he was a native of the Continental Menapia : he may have been born in the Manapian town which Ptolemy places somewhere between Wexford Haven and Avonmore, on the east coast of Ireland ; and when one comes to look into the name Carausius, this becomes probable. For it can hardly be an accident that *Carausius* admits of being equated with the

---

[1] For the history of Carausius see Aurelius Victor's Cæsars (edited by Pichlmayer) xxxix. 20, 39, Eutropius, ix. 21, and other authors cited by Holder, *s.v.* Carausius.

Irish name *Cú-rói*,[1] which, according to the analogy already discussed (pp. 68, 72), seems to have meant the Hound of the Plain or of the Field, probably of the Battlefield ; and it was borne by a personage well known in Irish literature. Cú-rói is represented in Irish literature as a consummate magician and a great warrior usually engaged in expeditions to Scythia and other distant lands; but he has unfortunately been inextricably confused with a great ancestral figure in the West of Ireland, whose name was Cú-rí, and his fortress has accordingly been identified with *Cathair Con-rí*, "Caher Conree, or the City of Cú-rí," in Kerry. The true position, however, of Cú-rói's stronghold is more correctly indicated by the circumstantial evidence of the locality of certain foes who made attacks on it at night: some come from Breg, the eastern portion of Meath, roughly speaking, and some from Sescenn Uairbeóil, "Marsh of Uarbél," somewhere on the east coast of Leinster. On the Welsh side, poem xlii. in the Book of Taliessin purports to be the elegy of Cú-rói, calls him Corroi, represents him holding a helm on the Sea of the South, and connects him seemingly with Dover.[2]

If this view should prove correct, it is easy to understand that, belonging to a colony which probably traded with

[1] The first part of *Cú-rói* consists of *cú*, " hound," the vowel of which is long; but in a compound like *Cú-rói* the stress accent being on the second element *rói*, the *u* of *cú* would lose a part of its length, yielding practically *Cǔ-rói* or *Cǒ-rói*. Then as to the spelling of *Ca-rausius* with *a*, compare *Kanovio* on a Roman milestone (now in the British Museum) for *Conovio*, now *Conwy*, Anglicised *Conway*, in North Wales. As to the other part of the name *Ca-rausius*, the intervocalic *s*, according to rule, disappears, yielding *rói*, concerning which see Stokes's "Urk. Sprachschatz," p. 235, where he traces *róe, rói*, "ebenes Feld," to the same origin as the Latin *rūs*, genitive *rūris*. *Corroi* in the Taliessin poem is derived from the Irish genitive *Con-rói*.

[2] See the story called Fled Bricrenn in Windisch's "Irische Texte," pp. 294–300. As to *Sescenn Uairbeoil*, this has been recently identified with the *Esgeir Oervel* of the Twrch Trwyth story (Oxford Mabinogion, pp. 135–6) by Prof. Meyer, in the "Transactions of the Cymmrodorion Society," 1895–6, p. 73. *Uarbél* seems to mean the " Cold-mouth," referring to some gap or gully where a cold wind usually blows : compare The Sloc, in the Isle of Man known in Manx as the Great Mouth of the Wind.

Britain and with the Belgic coast, including the Menapian mother-state, Carausius was used from his boyhood to the sea. If, moreover, the colony was, as we have supposed, Belgic or Brythonic, he could presumably pass as a Brython, but the fact of his name being Goidelic argues his being partly of Goidelic descent : in other words, he would seem to have been favourably situated to become popular with both Brythons and Goidels, and to make them consider him one of themselves, whether in Britain or on the Continent. During his time, at all events, we read of no difficulties with the tribes beyond the Roman Wall. The same remark applies to the three years of Allectus's rule ; but his name [1] points to the North of Britain, whence also his troops may have been largely drawn. No sooner, however, had Rome resumed possession of the province than the northern tribes began to be troublesome once more, and they are now, for the first time, spoken of as Caledones and "other Picts,"[2] against whom Constantius Chlorus undertook, in 296, an expedition beyond the Wall. The effect of the chastisement which he then inflicted on them appears to have lasted some time.

The next serious attack on the province took place in 360, when the Picts from the north were joined by a people from Ireland, figuring for the first time in history under the name of Scotti. They were probably mixed bands of Goidels, *Cruithni* or Picts of Ireland, and *Fír Ulaid* or True Ultonians. These last had been crowded into the north-east corner of that island in consequence of the conquest of Oriel or southern Ulster some years previously by Celts

---

[1] We have it in the name of the Perthshire town of *Alyth*, in an older form *Aleecht*, and probably also in the Welsh name *Elaeth*, borne, according to Williams's "Eminent Welshmen," by a sixth century saint and poet, who had, before he took to a saintly life, been a king in a district in the north of England. See also Skene's "Four Ancient Books," ii. 344.

[2] See Eumenius's "Panegyricus Constantino," c. 7 : *Non dico Caledonum aliorumque Pictorum silvas et paludes.*

from the direction of Meath. The Scotti presumably crossed at first into Galloway, where we have surmised the Genunians to have dwelt; and on this occasion the people of Galloway, the descendants of the Genunians of a former age, take part themselves in the attack on the province; these were probably the Atecotti represented as located between 'the southern and the northern Walls, and their name would seem to have meant the Old or Ancient Race. The Picts from the north are this time described as consisting of Dicaledonæ and Verturiones, in whom we seem for certain to have the Caledonii and Mæatæ of Dion Cassius respectively; for the term Dicaledonæ used by Ammianus Marcellinus (xxvii. 8) seems to have meant the inhabitants of the Highlands conceived of as forming two Caledonias, severed by the waters of Loch Linnhe, Loch Lochy, Loch Ness and Inverness Firth, or else as consisting of a Lowland and a Highland region. As to Verturiones, that is a name which gave rise ultimately to the designation *Fir Fortrenn*,[1] as it were *Viri Verturionis*, "the Men of *Fortrenn*," a district in which the Picto-Brythonic people of the Lowlands had their headquarters at Forteviot till the centre of gravity was shifted to the banks of the Tay by Kenneth mac Alpin and his dynasty. Thus the Verturiones seem to have been the Boresti of Tacitus and the Mæatæ of Dion. Whilst these tribes were attacking the province on one side, the Saxons were plundering it on another, especially the south-eastern coast. In 369 Theodosius arrived and put a stop to the devastation, which had extended to the heart of the province, and he renewed the stations on the Wall. Add to this that the Atecotti

---

[1] It is possible that we have a survival of the nominative in *Fothrev-e* or *Fothrif*, the name of a district embracing Kinross and a part of Fife : see Skene's "Picts and Scots," pp. lxxxiv., lxxxv., 136. This would imply that *Fothrif* stands for an earlier *Forthriu*, and that the old Brythonic forms were approximately *Vorthrio*, genitive *Vorthrionos*. See " Pro. Soc. Antiq-Scotland," xxxii. 396.

were subdued and their able-bodied men drafted into the Roman army in Gaul, where St. Jerome reports[1] having seen some of that race, which was in his time believed to be cannibals. The province continued to be attacked from without by land and sea, and to be cleared from time to time of the spoilers by the Roman soldiers, until at last the exigencies of the empire compelled Rome to withdraw her troops from the island altogether early in the fifth century.

A word now as to the administration. At the date to which the *Notitia Dignitatum* or the Table of Dignities belongs, the military command of Roman Britain was distributed as follows :—(1) There was the Count of Britain, *Comes rei militaris Britanniarum*, *Comes Britanniarum* or *Comes Britanniæ*, who with his troops was not fixed in any particular locality ; (2) the General or Duke of Britain, *Dux Britanniarum* or *Dux Britanniæ*, who had command of the troops on the Wall and in the country south of it to the Humber ; and (3) the Count of the Saxon Shore, *Comes litoris Saxonici per Britannias*, who had charge of the south-east of the island, where there were, from the fourth century, military posts placed at intervals from the Wash to the Isle of Wight, as a defence against invasions by the Saxons and other Teutonic tribes. Comparatively little is known concerning the civil administration of Britain under the Romans, but the organisation of it, at the head of which stood the Vicar of the Britannias, *Vicarius Britanniarum*, was practically subordinated to the military system, owing doubtless in a great measure to the continuous attacks to be expected from without. Roman Britain was treated as a single province till the year 210, when Severus divided it into two, called Lower and Upper Britain, *Britannia Inferior* and *Britannia Superior;* but we have no indication as to their respective positions beyond the fact that *Eburacum*, "York," was in Lower Britain ; while *Deva*,

---

[1] See "Hieronymus adversus Iovinianum," ii. 7 (p. 50).

"Chester," and *Isca Silurum*, "Caerleon," on the Usk, were in Upper Britain. This naturally suggests that Lower Britain was the area drained by rivers flowing to the North Sea and the English Channel, and that Upper Britain was so situated as to be reached by travelling up the valleys of the rivers of Lower Britain, in other words the region beyond the watershed and draining into the various parts of the Irish Sea. But Mr. Haverfield is of opinion that Upper Britain was the first portion of the island reached by the Romans, that it comprised the whole of the south as far as a line drawn from the Mersey to the Humber, and that Lower Britain lay north of that line : such a division would seem to have the advantage of fitting in better with the military arrangements already suggested. Possibly the explanation is, that Severus found the terms Lower and Upper Britain already in use in his time in the sense which we have suggested, and that he altered their application so far as to make Lower Britain comprehend all south of the Mersey and the Humber, and Upper Britain all the Roman territory beyond those waters ; for we are not convinced that the relative position of Lower and Upper Britain was the reverse.

In 297 Diocletian divided Roman Britain into four provinces called Prima, Secunda, Flavia Cæsariensis, and Maxima Cæsariensis ; but all that has been made out as to their positions is that Cirencester was in Britannia Prima. In 369 a fifth province was made, called Valentia, after the Emperor Valens, but the position of this also is uncertain ; it has been supposed to have been the district between the two Walls. In the second and third century the forces here consisted of three legions, one stationed at York, one at Chester, and a third at Caerleon. Besides these there were auxiliary cohorts, with their cavalry, mostly recruited in Germany, stationed on the Wall and at various points in the district between the Tyne and the Humber, which was largely given up to those troops. The Brigantes were not reduced to quietness till the end of the second century, and for another century native troops were seldom employed in garrisons in the island : they were drafted away to Germany.

When the Roman legions finally departed the provincials appear to have been on the whole equal to the task of repelling attacks from the north ; at any rate, there is no evidence that any Caledonians or other Picts were able to effect a single settlement south of the Clyde or the Forth. The question of invasions from Ireland is a more difficult one, as it cannot be severed from the other question, already touched upon : What Goidelic populations had their home in this country before the coming of the Romans, and remained here till after the departure of the legionaries ? But in spite of the threnody of Gildas over the ravages committed by Picts and Scots, the principal misfortunes of the Brythons came from a different quarter, namely, from the Continent ; we mean the permanent conquests effected here by the Teutonic peoples of the Saxons, the Angles, and the Jutes. In the continued effort to hold their own the Brythons may naturally be expected to have at first endeavoured to maintain the offices to which Roman administration had accustomed them. Thus they would probably have somebody filling the office of Count of Britain, or, perhaps more likely, of that and the office of Emperor all in one, now that the Emperor of Rome concerned himself no more with the affairs of the island. Welsh literature does not fail to supply us with a personage fitted for such a position, and that is Arthur, at any rate in so far as Arthur can be treated as a historical man and not a myth. He exerted himself, according to Nennius, as the *Dux Bellorum* of the kings of the *Brittones*, and his activity manifested itself in all parts of the country. In Welsh story he is called *Amherawdyr*, which is the Latin

word *Imperator* borrowed, and also *Penteyrned yr Ynys honn*,
"Chief of the Rulers of this Island,"[1] but not king till late.

With more confidence, however, one detects a post-
Roman officer filling the position of the *Dux Britanniæ*,
in command of the forces on the Wall and in the adjacent
district, namely, in Cuneda the Gwledig or Ruler, to whom
reference has already been made (p. 9). His pedigree
represents him as son of *Ætern* (*Æternus*), son of *Patern
Pesrut* (*Paternus* of the Red tunic, in reference probably to
the purple of office), son of *Tacit* (*Tacitus*); while one of
his own sons was called *Dunawd* (*Donatus*), and one of his
grandsons was *Meriaun* (*Marianus*), after whom is called
Meirionyd or *Merioneth*.[2] So the family of Cuneda
must have been Christian, and perhaps partly of Roman
descent. The most powerful branch of it supplied Venedos
or Gwyned with kings, and the most powerful of them
appears to have been Maglocunos or Maelgwn, who was
contemporary with Gildas, by whom he is called *Insularis
Draco*, meaning probably thereby the Dragon or Leader
of the Island of Britain. The explanation of the term is
presumably that the general or leader had as his ensign a
dragon, which had descended to him from the *Dux Britanniæ*
in Roman times. In the seventh century this dragon
figures, as heraldry teaches, as the Red Dragon of King
Cadwaladr, who was the last of the line of Cuneda and
Maelgwn to try to wield the power which Maelgwn enjoyed.
What that power precisely was, is only a matter of inference.
Maelgwn was King of Gwyned, but he seems also to have
exercised sway over the whole of the country from the
Severn Sea to the Firth of Forth. How he obtained this
wider power becomes intelligible on the supposition that
the office of *Dux Britanniæ* had been continued from

---

[1] See the Story of Kulhwch and Olwen, in the Oxford Mab., p. 105.
[2] See "Y Cymmrodor," ix. 170, 178, 182, and see the pedigree in the note
on p. 120 below.

Roman times, and that the Gwyneð branch of the Cuneda family had been able to keep it in their own hands. Thus however widely the east and south of the island had been wrested from the Brythons by Teutonic tribes, there still was what might be called Roman Britain, though it no longer owed allegiance to Rome, and its head would naturally be hailed by Gildas as the Dragon of the Island. It was more congenial to his style to describe him in that way than to call him simply *Dux Britanniæ.* Though Gildas had grave faults to find with Maelgwn, the latter was of his own race, and that must have counted for a great deal with one who hated Picts and Scots and Saxons with the bitter hatred of an irritable saint.

Maelgwn's son and successor, Rhûn, appears to have been less able than his father, but we read of him making war as far north as the river Forth,[1] probably in order to retain his father's power ; and it seems to have been successfully so retained, to be lost only to the Angles after a prolonged struggle. This may be said to have begun with the winning of the battle of Chester by Æthelfrith of Deira in the year 616, and to have been continued later in a war between Cadwaﬂon, king of Gwyneð, and Eadwine or Edwin, king of the Angles of Bernicia. Bede, in speaking of Cadwaﬂon, calls him oftenest *Rex Brettonum,* "King of the Brythons," but he is also found once using the term *Brettonum Dux,* "general or leader of the Brythons." Edwin triumphed for a time over Cadwaﬂon, and it appears from what Bede says that Edwin was the first of the kings of the English to have a banner carried before him when he rode forth and a tuft of feathers when he went on foot. This Roman fashion was probably also that of the *Dux Britanniæ* down to Cadwaﬂon, from whom Edwin would seem to have adopted it as a visible indication that he had taken the position of Cadwaﬂon. It was then also presumably that was first

[1] See Aneurin Owen's "Laws and Institutes of Wales," i. 104, 5.

heard the title of *Bretwalda*,[1] Ruler of "Britons," otherwise *Bryten-walda* or *Bryten-wealda*, *Breten-anwealda*, and
Bryten-weald, "Ruler of Britain;" for all these forms
of it are given in the manuscripts of the Saxon Chronicle,
when, in speaking of Ecgbryht, it enumerates those of his
predecessors supposed to have wielded more power than
the others. The diversity of form which the title shows in
English documents argues a certain amount of hesitation
between *Dux Brittonum*, which would in Welsh be *Gwledig
Brython*, and *Dux Britanniæ*, which Welsh poetry renders
Prydein Wledic.[2] Nay, one would not err perhaps in supposing that the term *gwledig* (earlier [*g*]*wledic, wletic*) had
something to do with the choice in Anglo-Saxon of the word
walda or *an-wealda*, "a ruler or sovereign," to translate the
title into that language. As it happens, the words are also
cognate, for *gwlad*, [*g*]*wlat*, meant the government or
power of the state, while Anglo-Saxon *wealdan* was "to rule,
or *wield* power."

The battle of Chester made no difference in the claims of
the kings of Gwyneð to be *gwledigs* or overlords ; and this
is the light in which should be read the epitaph of King
Cadfan, put up by his son Cadwaðon or by his grandson
Cadwaladr : *Catamanus rex sapientisimus opinatisimus
omnium regum*,[3] " King Cadfan the wisest, the most
renowned of all kings." It was inspired not so much by a
spirit of random flattery, perhaps, as by the ancient pretensions of the family. The final history of the struggle
between the kings of Gwyneð and the princes of the Angles
was this : Cadwaðon returned from exile in Ireland and
was for a time triumphant in the assertion of his ancient

[1] See the Oxford New English Dictionary, *s.v. Bretwalda*, where the
untenable nature of Kemble's interpretation of "wide ruler" is exposed, and
the equivalence of Æthelstán's *Brytenwalda ealles ðyses iglands* with *rector
totius huius Britanniæ insulæ* is advanced.

[2] See Skene's "Four Ancient Books of Wales," ii. 138.

[3] Rhys's "Lectures on Welsh Philology," p. 364.

right to the office of *gwledig* or overlord, Edwin having been slain by him in a great battle fought in 633 at Hethfield, somewhere near Doncaster. The Angles continued the struggle under Æthelfrith's son Oswald, and Cadwallon fell in a battle fought with him in 635 in the neighbourhood of Hexham. Cadwallon's son Cadwaladr tried for some time to recover the position of his ancestors, but his efforts failed and his personality passed into legend as that of Cadwaladr the Blessed. For some time afterwards the bards of the Brythons sang of the expected return of Cadwaladr to lead his people to victory, and to assert the ancient rights of his family, described in this context as *Kessarogyon* or Cæsarians.[1]

The *Dux Brittonum* had long been also *rex* and king, to wit, king of Gwyned, so the title of *Dux Brittonum* very naturally passed into that of *Rex Brittonum;* in the pages of Bede one finds this latter all but uniformly preferred. Henceforth also the domain of the *Rex Brittonum,* what was left of Roman Britain, dwindled down to the dimensions of Wales. There, however, the title continued in vogue : witness the oldest version of the *Annales Cambriæ,* compiled about the middle of the tenth century, which under the year 754 record the death of *Rotri rex Brittonium,* and in 950 that of *Higuel rex Brittonum.*[2] The Bruts continued for some time to use the same phraseology;[3] thus under 1056 is mentioned *Grufud vrenhin y brytanyeit,* "Griffith, king of the Britons." In 1091, with the death of Rhys, son of Tewdwr, the kingdom of the Britons (*teyrnas y brytanyeit*) is said to have fallen. Under the year 1113 allusion is made to the wish of certain Welshmen to renew the kingdom

[1] See Skene's "Four Ancient Books of Wales," i. 444–46, 487–90; ii. 25-8, 211–3.

[2] "Y Cymmrodor," ix. 161, 169.

[3] See Rhys and Evans's "Bruts" (Oxford, 1890), pp. 267, 270, 296, 309, 341, 355, 361, 365, 368, 369, 375, 379; and " Brut y Tywysogion " (Rolls, 1860), pp. 44, 54, 124, 158, 252, 288, 306, 316, 326, 356.

of the Britons (*brytanaöl teyrnas*). Under 1135 two of
the sons of Gruffuð ab Kynan are represented as jointly
holding together the whole kingdom of the Britons
(*hoꞇꞇ deyrnas y brytanyeit*). In the subsequent entries the
phraseology changes, *Kymry*, "Wales, Welshmen," being
introduced. In 1198 Gwenwynwyn, prince of Powys,
purposed an attempt to secure for the *Kymry* their ancient
rank, their ancient rights and boundaries. In 1216 Ꝇywelyn,
son of Iorwerth, summoned to him, at Aberdovey, all the
princes of Wales (*hoꞇꞇ tywyssogyon kymry*) to partition the
land of Wales ; and in 1220 he summoned most of the Welsh
princes to him in order to join in an attack on the Anglo-
Flemings of Roose and Pembroke. In 1228 the English
king, after making an expedition into Wales, makes peace
with Ꝇywelyn ab Iorwerth, and during the latter's lifetime
all the princes of Wales swore allegiance to his son David
in 1238, at Strata Florida ; lastly, when Ꝇywelyn died in
1240, he is called prince of Wales (*tywyssaöc kymry*). In
1258 we read of an assembly of the princes of the country
swearing allegiance to Ꝇywelyn, son of Gruffuð, and in 1267
we find the English king, Henry III., formally and solemnly
acknowledging the right of the prince of Wales to the
homage of the barons who held land in Wales. This
Ꝇywelyn ab Gruffuð proved to be the last of the line of
Cuneða and Maelgwn to occupy the position of prince of
Wales, for as is well known the military successes and
shrewd policy of Edward I. achieved the substitution of
the heir to the English crown for a native prince of the
race of Maelgwn and Cuneða. Even thus the Prince of
Wales of the present day is historically the actual representative of the *Dux Britanniæ* of Roman Britain ; but his
Roman Britain is Wales, and it differs in one important
particular from the Gaulish portions of the Roman Empire,
namely, in that it has not, like them, adopted the Latin
language. The number of Latin words, however, in the

vocabulary of the Celtic language of Wales shows that the latter began to give way to Latin; and this would have continued to go on had not the Latin firmly rooted in the east and south of Britain been submerged. Strange as it may appear, had it not been for the English language, by which the existence of Welsh is now threatened, the Welsh language would have long ago given way to a Latin idiom resembling French.

Lastly, another glance at the map of southern Britain and the position on it of some of the Brythonic tribes will enable us to infer the relative dates of their advent. Thus the Britanni from the opposite coast of the Straits of Dover probably took possession first of Cantion or Kent. Passing by the Regni of obscure origin and overshadowed by the woods of Anderida, we find next in order the Belgæ, who may have been preceded by the Dobunni; but these last may have made their way round Cornwall and sailed up the estuary of the Severn, or they may have drifted westwards from the Midlands. A similar uncertainty attaches to the Atrebates; they may have come up the Thames, but it is perhaps more likely that they came about the same time with the Belgæ and pushed inland from the neighbourhood of the Isle of Wight. We now come to a second group, some members of which must have made for the mouth of the Thames. The first of these were probably the Trinovantes, who posted themselves on the coast of Essex and the banks of the Thames as far, at any rate, as the site of London, which the fashionable Romans of a later day thought they had re-named Augusta for all time.[1] The

---

[1] See Tacitus, Ann. xiv. 33, and Ammianus, xxvii. 8; xxviii. 3. Luckily for the historian the ease with which a superior race thinks it consigns to oblivion a place-name current among its subjects often proves delusive, as in this instance of London; but it is a matter of regret that no Roman inscription discovered in London or elsewhere gives the full name of *Londinium*, or whatever the Latin spelling may have been: we have nothing more than the abbreviation LON.

Catuvellauni, coming about the same time, had to proceed higher up the river before landing to conquer the Midlands. Near the Trinovantes settled also the Eceni, who landed on the coast between the Trinovantes and the Wash ; we offer no guess as to their home on the Continent. The same remark applies to the Brythons beyond the Wash, namely the Coritavi, who arrived, presumably, by the way of the Humber, as did also, perhaps about the same time, the Parisi, the remains of whose iron chariots impart a special interest to the archæology of the opposite district between the Derwent and the North Sea.

If we look westwards, our attention is challenged by the Ordovices and the Cornavii, both of obscure origin. The former possibly acquired their individuality in the Midlands, and thence gradually pushed their way westwards to the sea, leaving in the possession of unnamed Goidels what is now the north-west corner of Wales, including Mona, or Anglesey, where Agricola found Druids. The latter, namely the Cornavii, seem to bear a geographical name describing them as the inhabitants of the *horn* or peninsula, as though they had landed between the estuaries of the Dee and the Mersey and thence penetrated inland. The same interpretation fits the Celtic *corn* (Latin *cornu*, English *horn*) in the name of *Cornwall* and in that of the *Cornavii*, in the extreme north. It need not be supposed to imply identity of race : thus the Cornavii on the Dee were Brythons, while the northern Cornavii were as probably a tribe of the Aborigines. The last groups of Brythons consisted of the Brigantes and the Votadini, that is unless we should include with them the Parisi from the banks of the Seine. This could hardly be correct if our conjecture (p. 86) fixing the home of the Brigantes in the country at the mouth of the Rhine should prove tenable. The position of the Brigantes in this country would seem to show, that they arrived comparatively late and landed probably from the Humber or the Tees, or from both. Last of all came the Votadini, who took up their abode on the coast from the Tyne to the Firth of Forth, together with the adjacent country as far, perhaps, as Bannockburn.

This, however, does not cover the whole Brythonic area towards the west and the north, since Brythonic speech is found to have acquired, previous to Kenneth mac Alpin's reign, a footing among the Picts of Forteviot, to which must be added the fact that Goidelic also appears, in later times, in the valley of the Tay possessed of such a hold there as to be difficult to account for. So we are forced to suppose that a considerable mixture of Pictish, Goidelic and Brythonic must have existed in the country extending from the Firth of Clyde to the banks of the Tay ; in other words, the Picts beyond the Forth were fairly well protected by the deep mud of the Forth[1] on one side and by the Ochil range on another, while their Celtic aggressors took one and the same path towards the Tay, namely, that passing between Stirling and Dunmyat, and now sufficiently indicated by the line of railway from Stirling to Perth : it became also the route of the Roman legions, as indicated by the camp at Ardoch.

But roughly speaking, the inland region from the Firth of Clyde to the basin of the Tay is that assigned by Ptolemy to the Dumnonii, and there were Dumnonii also in the south-west of the island:[2] neither appear to

[1] It is probably the muddiest river in the kingdom, and its name *Forth* may be supposed to refer to this peculiarity of its waters, if we may take the word to be Celtic and the etymological equivalent of its Welsh name *Gweryd*, which would seem to be the same word as Welsh *gweryd*, " soil, mould, or earth." Similarly, its ancient name of *Bodotria* seems to have its explanation in the Welsh *budr*, "dirty " : Ptolemy calls it Βοδερία, which does not harmonise with *budr* with its *u* for an older *ū* or *ō*. Skene's " Picts and Scots " gives *Forth* a dative *Forciu* (to be read probably *Forthiu*) and a genitive *Forthin*, pp. 10, 43.

[2] Holder, *s.v.* Dumnonii, mixes the two peoples up, and declares them to have been Brythons; but it is right to say that the article seems to have accidentally escaped revision.

have been Brythonic.   In fact, the position of the two peoples so designated suggests the hypothesis that their countries are to be regarded as extreme portions of the Goidelic area which had escaped conquest by the Brythons, and that the word *Dumnonii* was a collective name of the Goidels of Britain when the Brythons arrived. The adjective discloses the stem *Dumnon*, which, treated in a way not unusual with Irish names, would yield a nominative *Domnu*, genitive *Domnann;* and we are thus led back by easy steps to the *Fir Domnann*, that is, *Viri Dumnonis*, or Domnu's Men, already mentioned. We infer that one of the Fir Domnann's landing places in Ireland was the river-mouth known as Malahide River, between Howth and Balbriggan, in County Dublin ; for in Med. Irish it is called *Inber Domnann*, or the Domnu river-mouth, and from that point the *Dronga Domnand*,[1] or the Multitudes of Domnu, proceeded to the conquest of the fertile soil of Meath and adjacent districts. This we should have to regard as an attack on Ireland in front, but we are reminded that she was also assailed from behind, so to say : witness such a place-name as Irrus Domnann, "the *Iorrus* of Domnu," now the barony of *Erris* in the north-west of the county of Mayo, and witness also the Irish stories of early invasions of the north of Connaught from the sea. The explanation is probably that some of the Dumnonii, from their home near the Firth of Clyde, sailed round the north of Ireland, and landed in the nearest part of Connaught : hence the Fir Domnann of some of the Irish legends. Nor is this all, for they may have coasted further southwards ; and this may possibly be the key to the legend which represents Scota, the eponym of the Irish Scots of the Milesian group, as buried in Kerry, where her grave and that of one of her companions are pointed out in the barony of Troughanacmy, in that county.[2]

---

[1] See O'Curry's MS. Materials, p. 485, and Stokes's "Patrick," p. 34.
[2] See O'Donovan's notes to the Four Masters under the year A.M. 3500.

However that may be, the Fir Domnann on this side of the Irish Sea have left the name of the goddess Domnu to the county of Devon ; and in the North, likewise as Devon, it has become the name of a river rising within their natural boundary in the Ochil Hills. Even should these conjectures prove tenable, the tribes in the west of Roman Britain must be pronounced hard to classify, while on the eastern side, in spite of the usual scantiness of the data, there is little room for error in this respect. There the Brythonic settlements were continuous from Dover to the Forth, as it has been comprehensively put in the *Duan Albanach*, a historic poem concerning *Alba*, or Scotland, which is surmised to have been written in Ireland in the eleventh century and to represent the ideas of a still earlier time. The *Duan* begins with the Trojan story, and represents Albanus and Brutus, treated as eponymi of Alba and the territory of the Brittones respectively, taking possession of Britain. The third stanza runs thus[2] :—

Ro ionnarb a bráthair bras	To exile Brutus drove his big brother
Briotus tar muir n-Ioth n-amnas	Over the sea of the ungentle Ioth :
Rogab Briotus Albain áin	To himself Brutus noble Britain took
Go rinn fiadnach Fothudáin.	As far as Fothudán's . . . foreland.

This last doubtless meant, as already suggested, a promontory in the country of the Guotodin, somewhere

---

[1] In the transition from *Domnu* or *Domnann* to Devon it is to be remembered that Welsh has made *mn* into *vn* and Irish into *wn*. In the Anglo-Saxon Chronicle (with *f = v*) Devonshire is sometimes written *Def[e]nascîre* and sometimes *Def[e]nanscîre*. See Thorpe's Rolls ed., i., 120, 121, 146, 147, 166, 167, 246, 247.

[2] For the text see the Irish Nennius, pp. 272–3 ; and Skene's " Picts and Scots," p. 57—the original MS. appears to have been lost (*Ibid.*, pp. xxxvi–iii). We have substituted *Ioth* for *Icht*, which makes no sense here, as *Muir n-Icht* would be the English Channel. As to *Ioth* and *Iodeo*, see Rhys's Rhind Lectures in the " Scottish Review" for 1891, p. 101, where perhaps it might be more correct to say that *merin* was obtained by analysing into *tra merin* the Latin *transmarinus* ; as, for instance, in Gildas's *duabus primum gentibus transmarinis vehementer sævis, Scotorum a circione Pictorum ab aquilone* (Hist. § 14).

near North Berwick; and the whole of the island up to that point means all the country from the Straits of Dover to the Firth of Forth, which is here termed *Muir n-Ioth*, or Sea of Ioth. This is undoubtedly to be identified with the water called *Merin Iodeo* in the Book of Aneurin, and Iodeo further equates letter for letter with Nennius's name of a town of *Iudeu*, which Bede calls *Urbs Giudi*.[1] In Scotch history the Firth was well known as *Scottewatre* and *Scottis See*. Lastly, as will have been gathered from our previous remarks, the fact of giving the name Alba to Britain, when referring expressly to the southern half of the Island, from the English Channel to the Firth of Forth, argues a very respectable antiquity for the tradition set forth in the poem.

[1] As references here may be further mentioned—for *Merin Iodeo*, Skene's "Four Ancient Books," ii. 103; Thomas Stephens's "Gododin" (London, 1888), pp. 348-9. For *Iudeu*, see Rhys's "Celtic Britain," pp. 134, 152, 271, San-Martes "Nennius und Gildas," § 65 (p. 74); and for Bede's *Giudi* or *Iudi*, see Plummer's Bede's "Hist. Eccles." i. 12 (vol. i., p. 25). Here should be added *Muir n-Giudan*, quoted (from the book of Lecan) in Reeve's Culdees, p. 124, and to be explained probably as having *ni* modified into *ngi* (rather than influenced by Bede's *Giudi*). This sort of change is common enough, for example, in Manx Gaelic: see Rhys's "Manx Phonology," pp. 135-6. But more interesting philologically is the identity of the termination of *Iodeo* and *Iudeu* with the *evv* of such names as *Frobbáccennevv* in the Aboyne Ogam: see the "Proceedings of the Society of Antiquaries of Scotland," xxxii. 396; also the suggestion in the note, at p. 102 above, as to the name *Fothrif*.

CHAPTER IV.

EARLY HISTORY OF THE CYMRY.

In this and the following four chapters we propose to deal briefly with the history of the Cymric nation,[1] to give some account of the laws and customs of the people during the time of their independence, and to trace the steps by which Wales became politically assimilated to England. We do not affect to write a history of Wales and the Marches, for that is in our opinion a task that cannot be successfully performed with the aid only of the materials at present at our command.

Many of the sources of information as to the middle and later periods of the Welsh story which have survived to our day are to be found at the Record Office and elsewhere, but have not been published or even properly examined ; and even the well-known authorities have for the most part been only very indifferently edited and printed.[2] Under these circumstances any work dealing with the history of Wales must be looked on as merely tentative,

---

[1] It may be well to state here that *Cymru* means the land of the Cymry, *i.e.*, Wales ; and that *Cymry* means the Welsh people. Originally, of course, the latter term only included the men of the dominant tribes or clans, and not classes or persons subject to them. For the meaning and origin of the term see p. 26 above.

[2] Progress is being made. See the " Public Records relating to Wales," by R. Arthur Roberts, Barrister-at-Law, in "Y Cymmrodor," x., p. 157 ; and the " Ruthin Court Rolls" (in the Cymmrodorion Record Series), edited, with translation, notes, etc., by the same author (Chas. J. Clark, Lond., 1893), affords a good model for the treatment of the legal materials at the Record Office.

and we only present what follows as matter likely to be useful and suggestive to the student of things Welsh.

Most people have either forgotten or never observed that it was only in the century now ending that Wales was completely assimilated to England. Before the Norman Conquest we may truthfully say that Wales, though its rulers were in some sort of subjection to the kings of England, formed no part of the English realm, and it is only by gradual steps that it has been absorbed into the English body politic. Our principal aim is to point out the chief stages in the process by which the present constitutional position has been brought about.

The history of Wales, as distinct from other portions of the Island, commences after the departure of the Romans. The scanty and obscure character of the evidence relating to the fifth and sixth centuries does not enable us to speak with any confidence as to the commencement of the national life of the Cymry. What is now Wales appears to have been during the time of the Roman occupation part of the territory extending, roughly speaking, from the Bristol Channel to the Clyde and the Forth, under the charge of the military official called *Dux Britanniarum* The word Cymro means, according to the best philological authorities, "compatriot,"[1] as we have seen, and it was in the contests of Celtic tribes with Teutonic immigrants that it became a national name. It seems perfectly clear that for something over 200 years after the Roman occupation had ceased the western part of the Island, from the Bristol Channel to the Solway Firth and the Clyde, as well as the south-western peninsula, were in the possession of tribes who may, subject to what has been said above,[2] be described as " Celtic," and who succeeded in maintaining

[1] *Supra*, p. 26.
[2] *Supra*, pp. 34-5.

their predominance in that part of the Island till a few years after the middle of the seventh century. The evidence of the Welsh laws referred to below tends to show that the tribal system therein disclosed was similar in its main and fundamental particulars to a stage of society through which other Indo-European races have passed. It seems clear, too, that these tribes were bound together in some loose form of confederation, and that from the time they recognised the term Cymry they looked upon themselves collectively as one nation. They appear to have acknowledged the over-lordship or leadership of a king or ruler, who was called the "gwlędig," and whose office or dignity was sooner or later known as the "Crown of Britain." The authority of the gwledig appears to have been partly based on his claim to be the successor of the Roman officer called the *Dux Britanniarum*, and partly on earlier tribal notions of political and military organisation.[1]

In time the territory over which the confederation spread came to be called Cymru, and the predominant language Cymraeg. The earliest ruler of the Cymry and of Cymru of whom there is distinct evidence is Cuneda, whose name often occurs in Welsh literature. In an elegy in the "Book of Taliesin" he is said to be a man from Coelin, by which was apparently meant the district since called Kyle in Ayrshire. In Nennius' "Historia Britonum" there occurs the following passage :—"The great King Mailcun reigned among the Britons in the district of Guenedota because his great-great-grandfather Cuneda with his twelve sons had come before from the left-hand (or northern) part, *i.e.*, from the country which is called Manau Guotodin, 146 years before Mailcun reigned, and expelled the Scots with much slaughter from those countries, and they never again

---

[1] One of the ancestors of Cuneda is called Padarn Pesrud (literally, Paternus of the red tunic). See Rhys's "Celtic Britain," 2nd ed., p. 118. See the pedigree printed in note 2 on p. 138 below.

returned."[1] Guenedota here is obviously Gwyneḋ (speaking broadly, North Wales); Manau Guotodin is evidently the Manaw of the Gododin of Welsh poems, and appears to have been a district in Scotland situate somewhere south of the Forth, but we have no meʼans of determining its boundaries.[2] If the conjecture is true, Manaw was south of the northern Roman Wall, in the province of Valentia. The entry ɩn Nennius is confirmed by Welsh tradition and by many items of archæological, philological, and literary evidence So that we may take it that the Cymric kingdom was founded upon conquest, and that the aspect which society in what is now Wales presented in the centuries to which we are referring was that of an aggregate of Brythonic clans forming a tribal aristocracy superimposed upon Goideʼlic tribes, partly Celtic and Aryan in origin and partly Aboriginal, who had before occupied the land. The conclusion thus arrived at as to the early structure of Welsh society is borne out by the Welsh laws and customs of a later time.

It is unnecessary to trace in detail, even were it possible for us to do so with accuracy, the steps by which

----

[1] The date of Cuneda's occupation of North Wales cannot be exactly determined; but it probably took place early in the fifth century, and very near to the departure of the Romans. The passage cited does not give the date of Maelgwn's reigning. The "Annales Cambriæ" record his death as taking place in 547. He was a contemporary of Gildas' (see "Gild. Epist." s. 33). The most probable dates for the birth and death of the latter are 516 and 570 respectively (Smith's "Dict. Christ. Biog.," *s.n.* Gildas). The "Ann. Cam." assign his birth to 516, and the "Annales Tigernachi" his death to 570.

[2] In the genealogies annexed to the "Annales Cambriæ" (as to which see below, p. 132), the number of Cuneda's sons is put at nine. The entry (which deserves the notice of the student) is as follows : "[H]ec sunt nomina filiorum Cuneda quorum numeras erat. ix. Typipaun primogenitus qui mortuus in regione que vocatur manau guodotin. et non uenit huc cum fratribus suis. pre [dictis] meriaun. filius ejus. divisit possessiones inter fratres. suos. ii. Osmail iii. rumaun. iiii. dunaut. v. Ceretic. vi. abloyc. vii. enniaun. girt. viii. docmail. ix. etern." See "Y Cymmrodor," ix., p. 182, and below, p. 138.

invading Teutonic tribes advanced upon the western half of the Island, and by slow steps broke up the Cymric federation. Two well-ascertained events mark the process. By the loss of the battle of Deorham in 577, the Cymry of what is now Wales were severed from the Celtic tribes of the south-western peninsula, and afterwards, as a result of the battle of Chester in 616,[1] the Cymry of Wales were also cut off from their northern allies. The Cymry were thus enclosed by Teutonic kingdoms within that part of the west of the island which subsequently was called Cymru by the inhabitants themselves and Wales by the conquering Saxon.

Notwithstanding these disastrous battles, the Cymry proper maintained a vigorous struggle with very varying fortunes against the Saxon or English kingdoms. But the result of continuous warfare, though it did not bring about incorporation with the English kingdom till long after, was to create a state of complete disorganisation, from a military and a political point of view; and by the defeat of Cadwaladr, shortly after the middle of the seventh century, the Cymric kingdom in the older sense came to a melancholy end. This Cadwaladr is deemed by Welsh tradition to be the last king of the Cymry who wore the "Crown of Britain"; and that the result of the conflict of centuries was adverse to the Cymric nation is admitted by the brief but graphic entry in "Brut y Tywysogion," which says: "Cadwaladr died at Rome as Merdyn had previously prophesied to Vortigern of repulsive lips, and thenceforth the Britons lost the crown of the kingdom and the Saxons gained it."[2]

[1] The date is uncertain. The Annals of Tighernach (see O'Connor's "Scriptores rerum hibernicarum" and "Ann. Cam.") put the battle under 613. But the true date seems 616. See Plummer's "Bædæ Opera Historica," ii., pp. 76, 77. Tighernach antedates the battle of Dægsastan by three years, and probably does the same in regard to the battle of Chester.

[2] See Murray, "Eng. Dict.," s.v. "Bretwalda."

With this completion of a series of events the history of Wales in its limited and modern sense commences.

The subsequent history of Wales may be divided into the following periods :—

First.—From the death of Cadwaladr to the Norman Conquest of England.

Second.—From that Norman Conquest to the conquest and settlement of North Wales by Edward I.

Third.—From the settlement of Wales by Edward down to the incorporation of Wales into the English organisation, in the reign of Henry VIII.

Fourth.—From the time of Henry VIII. onward.

CHAPTER V.

HISTORY OF WALES FROM CADWALADR TO THE NORMAN
CONQUEST.

(A.D. 664—A.D. 1066.)

LITTLE is known of the history of Wales from the death
of Cadwaladr to the death of Gruffyd ab Llewelyn.
Literary tradition has preserved the names and a bald
account of the deeds (chiefly inconsiderable battles) of a
line of kings or princes, some of whom are represented
as kings of all Cymru or all the Britons ; but the persons
it hands down to us are for the most part as shadowy as
the ghosts of Banquo's issue. The account is colourless,
and the men it brings to our notice in this period have
hardly more living interest than the names in a genealogical
tree. No relation of the events that happened in Wales
during this time can be lively or dramatic unless one bases
it more on plausible efforts of imagination than on credible
evidence.[1] But though this is the case, in order to understand the subsequent history, it is necessary to see what
trustworthy authority has to say about this period, and
especially to discover as well as we can what were the
chief political divisions of Cymric territory, or, to put the
matter perhaps more accurately, how Cymric land was
apportioned among the leading royal or princely families.

[1] We have no assistance from bardic or poetic literature for the period from
the sixth century down to about 1080, when Meilir lamented Trahaearn (defeated
and slain by Gruffyd ab Kynan). Stephens's "Literature of the Kymry"
(2nd ed.), pp. 10, 11.

There is a considerable number of works dealing with the history of Wales, or with the history of Britain from a specially Welsh point of view. Passing over Geoffrey of Monmouth's[1] work, which cannot be treated as serious history, and for the moment Caradog of Ilancarvan's "Historie of Cambria," we may refer to the ambitious "Cambria Triumphans" of Enderbie as the principal example of an older type.[2] This writer carries back the Cymric story to Troy, and thence to the Tower of Babel. His fundamental conception is that all history may be reduced to a system of events radiating from Troy as a centre. For the early period dealing with this island he relies on Geoffrey of Monmouth, and for the events of the later period on Caradog of Ilancarvan. It is only in regard to the "modern estate" that the book is of any value to the student of history.

But besides works of this class there are other histories which discard older theories, though they are not adequately critical, of which Warrington's and Jane Williams'[3] are the best. Both are in the main founded on a sixteenth century compilation—"The Historie of Cambria, a part of the most famous ylande of Britaine, written in the British language

[1] For a recent account of Geoffrey and the character and value of his work, see Morley's "English Writers," vol. iii., pp. 44–57. See also Professor W. Lewis Jones' paper on Geoffrey in "The Transactions of the Hon. Soc. of Cymmrodorion," session 1898-9, p. 52.

[2] "Cambria Triumphans, or Britain in its perfect lustre, showing the origin and antiquity of the illustrious nation, the succession of their kings and princes, the description of the countrey, the history of the modern estate, etc., etc.," by P. Enderbie; folio (Lond., 1661); reprinted 1810. See also Lewis' "History of Great Britain, etc., to which is added the Breviary of Britayne by Humfrey Lwyd, and lately Englished by Thomas Twine," folio (Lond., 1729).

[3] "History of Wales in nine books, with an Appendix," by the Rev. William Warrington; 4to (Lond., 1786). "History of Wales," by Jane Williams, 8vo (Lond., 1869). Reference should also be made to the "History of Wales," by John Jones (barrister-at-law), Lond., 1824; and to "Hanes Cymru," by the Rev. Thomas Price, commonly called by his bardic name, *Carnhuanawc* (1842). See also his "Literary Remains" (Llandovery, 1854-5). See also O. M. Edwards' "Hanes Cymru," part i. (1895), an excellent text-book for Welsh students.

about two hundred years past : translated, into English by H. Lloyd,[1] gentleman, corrected, augmented, and continued out of records and best approved authors, by David Powel Doctor in Divinity."[2] Caradog of Lancarvan,[3] the friend and contemporary of Geoffrey of Monmouth, was one of the band of men of letters who gathered around Robert, Earl of Gloucester, the illegitimate son of Henry I. The date of his birth is unknown, but it is supposed he died in 1147. It was to him that Geoffrey left the history of the kings who succeeded the Ivor and Ini, who had "fiercely attacked the nation of the Angles" but to little purpose, just as he committed the kings of the Saxons to William of Malmesbury and Henry of Huntingdon.[4] That Caradog wrote a chronicle is clearly proved; but in its original form it is not extant. Professor Tout thinks (with the probability of the case on his side) that it was written in Latin.[5] According to the address to the reader given by Powel, Caradog collected the successions and acts of the British princes after Cadwaladr to 1156 ; several copies of the collection were kept in the abbeys of Conway and Strata Florida, which were "yearly augmented as things fell out," the two abbeys comparing the entries every third year. Powel says that the entries were continued to the year 1270, and

---

[1] Humfrey Lwyd (physician and antiquary) was born in 1527, and died in 1568. The MS. of his translation of Caradog's translation is preserved in the British Museum (Cotton MS. "Caligula," A. vi.),*v.* "Dict. Nat. Biog.," *s. nom.*

[2] Small quarto, London, 1584 ; 2nd ed. (Lond., 1811). See also Wynne's "improved edition" (Lond., 1697) ; 2nd ed. (Lond., 1774) ; 3rd ed. (Merthyr, 1812) ; 4th ed. (Shrewsbury, 1832). The edition of 1811 is the only exact reproduction of Powel's work. David Powel was born in 1552 (?), and died in 1598. He was vicar of Ruabon and rector of Lanfyllin. The living of the latter parish he exchanged afterwards for Meifod (*vide* Dict. Nat. Biog., *sub nom.*). He is honourably mentioned in "Strype's Annals," ii. 472-3 (ed. 1824).

[3] See Dict. Nat. Biog., *sub. nom.;* also Morley's "English Writers," vol. iii., pp. 95, 96, 97.

[4] See Geoffrey's "British History," book xii., ch. 19 and ch. 20.

[5] Dict. Nat. Biog., *sub nom.* "Caradog."

that transcripts of the work were made by divers, and that over a hundred copies were extant in Humfrey Lwyd's time. Lwyd translated the work into English, and a copy of the translation was bought by Sir Henry Sidney, President of the Court of the Marches, and he, desiring its publication, entrusted the work to Dr. Powel. The editor collated the copy with three versions of the Welsh work ; he added matter from other chronicles showing the additions by a change of type, prefixed a description of Wales by Sir John Prise, and added brief accounts of the Princes of Wales after the Edwardian Conquest. In this form the work was published in 1584, under the title set forth above.

In our judgment the statements made in a work thus compiled, and published so late as 1584, cannot be relied on unless confirmed by the Welsh chronicles, to which we refer below, or by the authorities accepted by competent students of English history as trustworthy—at any rate, so far as the pre-Norman period is concerned. At the same time we cannot deny to the work considerable value, and assuming that the main text is down to the middle of the twelfth century the work of Caradog, we may look upon that part of the history as representing the Welsh traditional view of the general course of Welsh affairs at a time when the memory of many of the events was comparatively recent.

But really for the period we are now dealing with, the principal Welsh authorities which are entitled to credence are "Brut y Tywysogion" and the "Annales Cambriæ."[1]

---

[1] "Brut y Tywysogion" (i.e., history of the princes) and "Annales Cambriæ" are the names given to two sets of chronicles which specially record affairs concerning Wales, and which in MS. seem to have been produced as a whole within the Cymric limits, though some of the entries in the "Annales Cambriæ" appear to have been written in Ireland, or at any rate to have been of Irish origin. The former set of MSS. is in Welsh, and the latter in Latin. The best critical account of the origin, the date, and the value of the MSS. is to be found in Mr. Egerton Phillimore's able paper entitled "The Publication

From these sources, supplemented by the authorities relied on for the early history of the island by competent English writers, the story of these pre-Norman Welsh kings and princes must (if it be possible to do so at all) be constructed.

It is clear from the entry in the Brut that we have quoted above and from other sources that the death of Cadwaladr was regarded by the Cymry as an event of great importance, but as to its exact date we have no certain evidence. The Brut puts it as taking place in 681, but the writer uses language which shows that for some reason he confounded Cadwaladr with Ceadwalla, king of Wessex, who did die in that year. If from the few data we have to rely on the matter is traced out there can be no doubt that the year 681 is too late, and that in all

of Welsh Historical Records" in "Y Cymmrodor," vol. xi., p. 133 (1892). The earliest known version of the "Annales Cambriæ" is printed in "Y Cymmrodor," vol. ix., pp. 152—169, under Mr. E. Phillimore's editorship. The portion of the "Annales" dealing with the events up to the Norman Conquest is also printed in "Monumenta Historica Britannica," vol. i. (1848), under the editorship of Petrie (really under that of Aneurin Owen, the editor of "The Ancient Laws and Institutes of Wales"). The "Annales Cambriæ" were also published in the Rolls series in 1860 (edited by Ab Ithel). The "Brut y Tywysogion" up to 1066 is also printed in "Monumenta Historica Britannica," and the whole of it was published (ed. Ab Ithel) in the Rolls series in 1860. The versions of the "Annales" and the "Brut" in the Rolls series are subjected to severe but just criticism by Mr. Phillimore. In 1890, however, the text of the "Brut," as transcribed in the "Red Book of Hergest," was published in the series of Welsh texts produced at Oxford under the editorship of Professor J. Rhys and Mr. Gwenogvryn Evans (Clarendon Press). For further information as to the MSS. see Mr. Evans' preface to the "Red Book of Hergest," vol. ii., and Aneurin Owen's posthumously printed introduction to the "Gwentian Chronicle" in "Arch. Cambr." (1864). The so-called "Gwentian" or "Aberpergwm Brut" is printed in "Myv. Arch." (vol. ii., pp. 468—582), and a copy made by Aneurin Owen from the "Myv. Arch." is printed in "Arch. Camb" for 1864. The date of its compilation was not earlier than 1550, and it has not the authority of the genuine and older "Brut" (see Egerton Phillimore's paper cited above, "Y Cymmrodor," xi. 163–168). As to the genealogies appended to "Annales Cambriæ" in Harl. MS. 3,859, and printed in "Y Cymmrodor," xi., p. 169 *et seq.*, see pp. 132, 138, below.

probability it was in or very near to 664 that Cadwaladr died.

If we assume that this date is correct, the period now under consideration comprises 402 years, and the scantiness of the direct evidence as to what took place may be estimated from the fact that there are in the Brut only about 200 entries up to the Norman Conquest, and only 43[1] for the 180 years that elapsed from the time the Britons lost the crown of Britain to the accession of Rhodri Mawr in 844, and that these entries are always brief and often obscure. We have, however, some incidental help for the construction of this direct evidence from other sources, amongst which the Laws of Howel Ða and other legal treatises must be given the first place,[2] for from them we can discover with reasonable certainty the structure of Welsh society in these times from a legal and economic point of view ; and the " Liber Landavensis "[3] properly and

---

[1] Forty-one in "Annales Cambriæ" (Phillimore, *ubi supra*).

[2] For an account of the legal treatises see below, p. 176 *et seq.*

[3] "Liber Landavensis" is the name given to a work supposed to have been compiled by Galfrid (Jeffrey or Geoffrey), the brother of Urban, the last Bishop of Llandaff mentioned in it.   This Galfrid is identified by Mr. Gwenogvryn Evans with Geoffrey of Monmouth (see preface to the Oxford text mentioned below).   It is a chartulary or collection of documents concerning the Bishops of Llandaff, the endowments of the Church, and events connected with the history of the diocese.   There are several MSS. of the work.   The oldest and, as it seems, the original one is the Gwysaney MS. (belonging to Mr. P. B. Davies-Cooke, of Gwysaney, Flintshire, and Owston, Yorkshire).   For information as to the MSS. see the prefaces to the printed texts by W. J. Rees and Mr. Gwenogvryn Evans.   The book was first printed in 1840, under the auspices of the Welsh MSS. Society.   The Gwysaney text has been recently published in the Oxford series.   See "The Liber Landavensis Lyfr Teilo, or the Ancient Register of the Cathedral Church of Llandaff, from MSS. in the Libraries of Hengwrt and of Jesus College, Oxford, with an English translation and explanatory notes by the Rev. W. J. Rees, M.A., F.S.A., &c." (Landovery, 1840).   This has been, however, superseded by the Oxford work, in which the Gwysaney text is diplomatically reproduced under the editorship of Mr. Gwenogvryn Evans, "The Text of the Book of Llan Dâv, reproduced from the Gwysaney Manuscript by John Gwenogvryn Evans, Hon. M.A. Oxon., with the co-operation of John Rhys, M.A.,

critically used is not to be ignored. From Welsh literature (other than the Brut and the Laws) no help is to be obtained for this period.

The task of the historian of Wales has, however, been lightened by the excellent work of those who during this century have devoted themselves to clearing up the early history of England, and it is only by labouring in the light of what they have made known, and according to the methods they have adopted, that he can succeed in getting at the truth about the story of the Cymry.

As pointed out above, the break-up of the older Cymric kingdom left Wales in a state of complete political dis-organisation. Memories of the old kingship and of the old bonds undoubtedly survived in theory and sometimes reappeared in fact; but, speaking broadly, the aspect that Wales presents during the succeeding centuries is that of a disunited, or very loosely connected, aggregate of clans, or petty kingdoms, or lordships engaged in perpetual war-fare both among themselves and with English kingdoms and English rulers. It would be untrue to state that there was absolutely no conception of a collective nation or of a united kingdom, but, so far as we can ascertain, on no occasion was the whole country effectively under the rule of one sovereign. The material is so scanty that it would be dangerous to make any general assertion in other than a tentative fashion.

In an endeavour to clear up the history of a country thus disorganised one of the first questions that must occur to

Professor of Celtic in the University of Oxford " (Oxford, 1893). The " Liber Landavensis " is also called " Lyfr Teilo " (the Book of Teilo). Teilo is one of the principal traditional saints of Wales. He is represented as a cousin of St. David's and as Bishop of Llandaff, but he seems to have advanced archiepiscopal claims. For an account of him see Smith's " Dicty. Christ. Biog.," *sub nom.* The chief authority for his life is a portion of the twelfth century MS. with which this note deals. See " Lib. Land." (Oxf. ed.), pp. 97 *et seq.* There is no life of, but there are several references to, Teilo in Rees' " Lives of the Cambro-British Saints " (Landovery, 1853).

one's mind is, what were its divisions for the purposes of such government as existed, especially when as in the case of Cymru one finds the names attached to various areas ancient. We have in the introduction pointed out that Wales was in the times of its practical independence of the English monarchy undoubtedly divided into cantrefs and cymwds. In the laws of Howel Ða, which are legal treatises once in practical use, the land divisions and measurements are ascribed to Dyfnwal Moelmud, who was king "before the crown of London and the supremacy of this island were seized by the Saxons, and who first established good laws in this island . . . and after that Howel enacted new laws, and abrogated those of Dyfnwal; yet Howel did not, however, alter the measurement of the lands in this island, but continued them as they were left by Dyfnwal; because he was the best measurer."[1] Now "the cause of his measuring of the island was that he might know the tribute of this island, the number of the miles, and its journeys in days."[1] What is expressly ascribed in the laws to Dyfnwal is the determination of the units of measurement and the division of the area called the cymwd into smaller parts, having some, though to us not quite clear, significance in a tribal system. It is not said that Dyfnwal marked out the Cymric land into cantrefs and cymwds, but as the cymwd is represented as an aggregate of smaller divisions, themselves having reference to the prescribed units of measurement, it seems to be implied that he did in fact constitute the division into those larger areas.

The matter is not, however, free from difficulty, for if we are to read the text literally as a division of the whole of Cymru, the area of each cymwd ought to have been of equal superficial extent. In fact, the

---

[1] "Ancient Laws and Institutes of Wales," vol. i., pp. 182–185 (1841, Rolls series, ed. A. Owen).

cantrefs and cymwds varied very greatly in size. We cannot profess that we have discovered any final solution of the difficulty thus created. It would seem that the primary purpose of the division was to facilitate the equitable assessment of the food-rents due to the chieftains as well as in the first instance to secure a fair apportionment of a conquered territory among the new settlers. It may be that in the time of Dyfnwal the different families of Cymric origin took possession by arrangement among themselves; that they, as was natural, made their first establishments on the more developed and fertile areas; that each cenedl on whom the liability for customary dues fell became associated with a particular area; that in some cases the area came to be called by the name of the head of the cenedl at the time of its settlement,[1] and in others that the name of some pre-existing division survived ; and that what Dyfnwal the legislator really did was to create a system of measurement and division applicable roughly to an established order of possession with a view to making the incidence and rendering of the customary food-rents fair and easy. However this may be, it is certain, that in the tenth century Cymru was divided into cantrefs and cymwds, with boundaries ascertained well enough for practical purposes, and that the division was then deemed to be ancient.

Dyfnwal Moelmud is generally supposed to have reigned about 400 years before Christ. This seems due to the place given to him by Geoffrey of Monmouth in his line of British kings. According to Geoffrey he gained the sceptre of Britain after a civil war that followed the slaying of Porrex, and on his death his sons Belinus and Brennius became kings of Britain.[2] If we were to assume this to be true, the date of Dyfnwal's flourishing and legislation

---

[1] *E.g.*, Meirionyd. Meirion was a son of Cunedda.
[2] " British History," book ii., cc. 16 and 17 ; book iii., c. 1.

might be about B.C. 400.[1] But there is nothing to support
Geoffrey's narrative, while there is credible evidence that
about the time of Cuneda (who, as leader of the Cymry,
conquered Wales) there was a Dyfnwal Moelmud who,
whether or not he was ever head-king of the Cymry, or
simply a member of a ruling family, was so closely connected with the line of Cuneda, that his name may have well
become associated with legislation over Cymric territory.
It fortunately happens that there are several pedigrees
appended to the earliest MS. of the " Annales Cambriæ," and
as they are undoubtedly old, and came into being at a time
when every one's genealogy was most religiously preserved
and remembered as a kind of title-deed to his status in the
then existing legal and social system, we may with a high
degree of confidence look upon them as in substance
accurate.[2]   The name of Dyfnwal Moelmud occurs in
Pedigree X.   He was son of Garbaniaún, and grandson of
Coel Hen, whose daughter was Cuneda's wife, and his
pedigree was traced "to Beli et Anna."[3] He may therefore
have been a contemporary of Cuneda's, and may have
survived during the lives of one or two generations of his
descendants.   Save so far as we may infer it from the
statement in the Welsh laws, that he was king before the
loss of the crown of Britain, there is nothing to show that
he was king of all the Cymry ; and in fact the text does not

---

[1] Geoffrey's Brennius took the city of Rome, and seems to be meant for
Brennus, who, according to current computation, in B.C. 390, did capture the
city and besiege the citadel. Mommsen, "History of Rome," i., p. 366
(English translation).

[2] " The annales and genealogies in their present form show marks of having
been composed in the last half of the tenth century" (E. Phillimore, " Y
Cymmrodor," xi., p. 144).   " But the date of the MS. is upwards of a century
later than that of the composition of the Annales and Welsh Genealogies"
(*ibid.*, p. 145).   See also "The Welsh Pedigrees," a paper by Henry F. J.
Vaughan, B.A., S.C.L., printed in "Y Cymmrodor," x. 72 (1890).

[3] "Y Cymmrodor," ix., p. 174. As the pedigree is not very accessible to
the student we reproduce it :—

necessarily give him the position of a head-king or gwledig ; and there is nothing inconsistent between what is stated in the laws, and the inference that he was a king of some territory subject to Cuneda, and that he was authorised by the gwledig, upon the conquest of Wales, to settle the affairs of the newly-won lands. This conjecture accords well with the ascertained facts. There were in all probability earlier divisions of Wales, and we need not assume that they were entirely superseded by Dyfnwal's work. His main object was evidently, as we have said, to make an arrangement for the fair imposition of the food-rents of the occupiers of Cymric land. Under his system, confirmed by Howel, the families in each cymwd were liable for the same food-rent, that is, the same amount was levied on each cymwd, irrespectively of the number of the families or its size ; and as the occupied land varied very greatly in fertility and productiveness, the operation of practical

[X]

	[M]orcant.	map.	Vrb.
map.	Coledauc.		an.
map.	Morcant.	map.	Grat.
	bulc.	map.	Iume-
map.	Cincar.		tel.
	braut.	map.	Riti-
map.	Branhen.		girn.
map.	Dumngual.	map.	Oude-
	moilmut.		cant.
map.	Garbani	map.	Ou-
	aún.		tigir.
map.	Coÿl hen.	map.	Ebiud.
map.	Guotepauc.	map.	Eudof.
map.	Tec ma-	map.	Eudelen.
	nt.	map.	Aballac.
map.	Teu-	map.	Beli *et* anna.
	hant.		
map.	Telpu-		
	il.		

The map before Guotepauc should, says Mr. Phillimore, be cancelled. Guotepauc (now Godebog) was Coÿl's epithet. The pedigree is Northern. The patronymic of Dumngual Moilmut seems Goidelic ; see above, p. 24.

causes may well have led to great difference in the relative extents of the rent-paying units.

In the "Chronicles" and the "Liber Landavensis" we find individuals represented as kings or princes of areas larger than cantrefs, to which names other than those of the cantrefs are given. These may have been, probably were, aggregates of the smaller divisions. They represented lands over the inhabitants of which certain regal or princely families descended from, or assumed to be descended from, Cuneda, or it may be the descendants of other founders of ancient and pure-blooded tribes of the Cymric race exercised a tribal sway, and possessed customary privileges. In the "Brut" we find mention of the following areas for the most part in terms implying that they were kingdoms :— Gwyneð, Powys, Ceredigion, Dyfed, Morgannwg, Gwent, Brecheiniog, Buallt, Ystrad Towi,[1] Rhuvoniog, Cidweli, Gwyr, Môn.

We need not assume the list to be exhaustive. There were very likely other kingdoms or principalities which do not happen to be mentioned. The names of other districts are certainly to be found (e.g., Gwentlwg, Lleyn, Meironyð), but not in terms necessarily suggesting they were under separate sovereign families.

It is worthy of notice that before Rhodri's time there is no mention of a king of Deheubarth (ordinarily used as equivalent to South Wales), though the word Deheubarthwyr (men of Deheubarth) occurs once.

To the rulers of these larger areas the names "brenin" (king) and "tywysog"[2] (prince) are applied. In the earlier times the former title is liberally accorded. The king is usually described as king of a particular district, e.g.,

---

[1] Ab Ithel in the Rolls edition of the "Brut" translates this as the "Vale of Towi," but it practically means *district* of the Towi. Ystrad literally means strand, "strath."

[2] See *s.a.* 856: "Y bu uar6 Ionathal tywyssawc Abergeleu."

Gwgaun, son of Meurug, king of Ceredigion ;[1] but some of the chieftains are described as "king of the Britons."[2] Now later writers proceed on the theory that Cymru was divided into three principal parts, Gwyneð, Deheubarth, and Powys, with three royal residences—Aberffraw in the first Dinefwr in the second, and Mathrafal in the third, and an over-lordship is ascribed to the king of Gwyneð. There is nothing in the "Chronicles" absolutely inconsistent with this, but on the other hand there is nothing directly to support it ; but some of the later legal treatises accord a pre-eminence to the king of Gwyneð, and many isolated facts tend to support this view, so far as the kingdoms of Deheubarth and Powys are concerned ;[3] but there seems no evidence proving with certainty that the regal families of South-eastern Wales, which was divided into the kingdoms of Morgannwg, Gwent, Brecheiniog, and Buallt, generally acknowledged the over-lordship of Gwyneð. There is, however, no improbability in the view that the chieftains of Cymru at one time regarded themselves as forming a kind of hierarchy of kings ;[4] and certainly the organisation of each kingdom, as described in the codes, seems to involve a gradation of lordships very nearly resembling a feudal system. But though the supremacy of Gwyneð and the subordination of one ruler to another, in some settled manner grouping all Wales into a collective nation, may have been a legal first principle, the actual facts, as gathered or inferred from the "Chronicles," hardly seem to square with the theory,

[1] "Brut," *s.a.* 871. "Ann. Cam.," *s.a.* 871.

[2] *E.g.*, "Brut," *s.a.* 998 : "Mareduð, son of Owain, the most celebrated King of the Britons."

[3] Mr. Seebohm adopts the theory. "Tribal System in Wales," pp. 134—139.

[4] Cf. the case of Ireland, where there seem to have been recognised an Ard-rí Érend and three classes of subordinate kings. O'Sullivan's Introduction to O'Curry's "Lectures on the Manners and Customs of the Ancient Irish," pp. ccxxix–xxxi. See also Ginnell's "The Brehon Laws" (London, 1894), pp. 63 *et seq.*

and what we do find is an aggregate of small states under separate kings or ruling families continually quarrelling among themselves.

The period now under consideration—that from the death of Cadwaladr, in 664, to the Norman Conquest—may itself be conveniently divided at the accession of Rhodri Mawr. For the one hundred and eighty years that elapsed from the loss of the crown of Britain to 844, when Rhodri became chief king of the Britons, we know little of what took place in Wales, and all we can gather from trustworthy sources is the names of certain kings and battles, and the general conclusion that the limits of the Welsh area were further contracted.

According to Caradog of Llancarvan, Ivor, son of Alan, king of Armorica (who becomes strangely confounded with Ine, king of Wessex), succeeded Cadwaladr on his death in 681, and reigned till 720. Then Rhodri Molwynog, son of Edwal Ywrch, became " King of the Brytains," and survived till 750, and was followed by his son, Conan Tindaethwy, who continued chief king till 817, when he died (after chasing his brother Howel out of Môn in that year), leaving a daughter, Esyllht, married to Merfyn Frych ab Gwriad. Merfyn and his wife took possession of the kingship, and Merfyn reigned till 841. In that year ("as some do write") he was killed in a battle at Cetteff between the Welsh and the Mercians under Burchred, and then his son Rhodri succeeded. This account is usually followed by Welsh historians, but it is barely credible. For a period of one hundred and fifty-three years (*i.e.,* 664 to 817), only four chief kings (one following the other immediately) are assigned, and Conan is made to reign nearly seventy years.

Caradog appears to have been trying, very likely honestly enough, to represent a continuity in the devolution of the Cymric over-lordship that had had no existence except in the imagination of later rulers and those who were connected with them as bards and genealogists. The "Brut," while not absolutely inconsistent with the view of Caradog, can hardly be described as entirely supporting it. It says that after Cadwaladr, Ivor, son of Alan, king of ILydaw, which is called little Britain, reigned not as king, but as a chief or prince,[1] and after him Rhodri Molwynog reigned. The entries down to 844, when it records the death of Merfyn Frych, are very brief. Rhodri Molwynog died in 754. The earliest reference to a Kynan is in 812, when it is recorded that a battle took place between Howel and Kynan, and that the latter was beaten, and three years later (815) Howel expelled Kynan from Môn.[2] Then, in 817, Howel was "a second time" driven from Môn, and Cynon (who, we may fairly assume, was identical with Kynan) died, and the Saxons ravaged the mountains of Eryri, and took the kingdom of Rhuveniog.[3] No mention is made of Esyllht, but it is stated that Merfyn Frych died in 844. We may therefore look upon the existence of Ivor, Rhodri Molwynog, Kynan, and Merfyn Frych as proved, and we may believe that they were very important chieftains of the Cymry in the time after the death of Cadwaladr and before Rhodri Mawr's accession. But there are other kings mentioned, such as Caradog, king of Gwyned, Maredud and Rein, kings of Dyfed, Arthen, king of Ceredigion, and Cadell, king of Powys.[4] To Rhodri Molwynog, indeed, the title of "brenin y Brytanyëit" is accorded, but the deaths of Conan and Merfyn are mentioned as if they were simply kings of districts; and we cannot avoid noticing that if Gwyned

---

[1] The words in the text of the "Brut" (Oxford edition, p. 257) are "ac nyt megys brenhin namyn megys pennaeth neu tywyssauc." They are important as showing clear recognition of the change in the position of the Cymry in the island, which had been brought about by the events that led up to the death of Cadwaladr and the loss of "the crown of Britain."

[2] "Brut," *s.a.* 815.

[3] "Brut," *s.a.* 817.

[4] See under the years 798, 796, 807, and 808, "Ann. Cam.," 798, 807, 808.

had at that time a practical pre-eminence, it is strange that Caradog (a king of that part of Wales) should find no place in the succession of kings of all Wales as traced by Caradog of Llancarvan.

The sources of information by means of which we may check or correct the traditional or usually adopted account of this period are not limited, however to the Chronicles. The first of the pedigrees appended to the MS. of the "Annales Cambriæ," edited by Mr. E. Phillimore, is that of Owain, the son of Howel Đa, and great-grandson of Rhodri Mawr, and it carries back his genealogy a very long way. It is a genuinely old compilation, and however much we may doubt, or rather be in a state of indifference as to the more remote stages, yet if we bear in mind the legal structure and general complexion of the community in which it was produced, it would be an excessive display of the sceptical spirit to deny its accuracy for many generations, especially as there is evidence from many sources that most of the nearer ancestors of Owain whom it discloses really lived and played their parts among the Cymry in a sequence of events that is not inconsistent with the order of the names in the pedigree in question.[1]

According to this pedigree, the names of the successors of Cadwaladr were :—Iutgual, Rotri, Cinnan, Etthil, Mermin, Rotri (Mawr).[2] Iutgual is probably the Idwal Ywrch of Caradog ; the first Rotri is evidently Rhodri Molwynog, king of the Britons, who, according to the "Brut," died in 754 ; Cinnan seems to be the Kynan or Cynon of the "Brut," who fought with Howel in 812 and 815, and died in 817, and Caradog's Conan Tindaethwy ; Etthil, daughter of

---

[1] In Mr. Phillimore's opinion, "up to the date when all Welsh records necessarily became more or less fabulous, these genealogies have every claim to rank beside the 'Annales' and the 'Saxon Genealogies' as a valuable historical authority." "Y Cymmrodor," ix., p. 149 (1888).

[2] This important pedigree deserves the most careful study. It is printed in the preface to Aneurin Owen's "Welsh Laws," etc. (vol. i., Preface, p. xiv,

Cinnan, is the Esyllht who, in his account, was married to Merfyn Frych; Mermin, son of Etthil, is probably identical with the Merfyn Frych whose death is assigned by the Brut to the year 844, and the Mermin whose death is mentioned in the Annales as taking place in the same year. The second Rotri is Rhodri Mawr.

We may, then, take it that the existence of Idwal Ywrch, Rhodri Molwynog, Conan Tindaethwy, Etthil, Merfyn or Mermin Frych is confirmed by the pedigree, and that they were descendants of Cadwaladr; but the interval between 754, when Rhodri Molwynog died, and 817 or 816, when Conan died, is very long. A Caradog, king of Gwyneđ, is stated to have been killed by the Saxons in 798.[1] He may have been a son of Rhodri Molwynog, and have

note). We reproduce it as edited by Mr. E. Phillimore in "Y Cymmrodor" (vol. ix., pp. 169, 170).

[O]wen map. iguel.
 map. catell.
 map. Rotri.
 map. mermin.
 map. etthil merch.
  cinnan.
 map. rotri.
 map. Iutgual.
 map. Catgualart.
 map. Catgollaun.
 map. Cat man.
 map. Jacob.
 map. Beli.
 map. Run.
 map. Mailcun.
 map. Catgolaun.
  Iauhir.
 map. Eniaun girt.
 map. Cuneda.
 map. Ætern.
 map. Patern pefrut.
 map. Tacit.

map. Cein.
map. Guorcein.
map. doli.
map. Guordoli.
map. Dumn.
map. Gurdumn.
map. Amguoloyt.
map. Anguerit.
map. Oumun.
map. Dubun.
map. Brithguein.
map. Eugein.
map. Aballac.
map. Amalech qui fuit.
 beli magni filius.
 et anna mater ejus.
 quam dicunt esse
   [conso.
 brina MARIÆ.
 uirginis matris.
 d'ni n'ri ih'u xp'i.

[1] "Brut," *s.a.* 798. "Caratauc rex guenedote apud Saxones iugulatur," "Ann.," *s.a.* 798.

been omitted by the compiler of the genealogy, but there can be no certainty about the question. Nor can we speak positively as to the district over which this line held sway, though the mention in the Brut and Annales of kings of various districts,[1] who do not appear to have been descendants of Cadwaladr, leads us to the opinion that Iutgual and his immediate successors were rulers of Gwyneð.

In addition to the scanty information we have as to the names of these kings, we know, from the Welsh and other sources, that there was almost continual warfare between the Cymry and their English neighbours, and very frequently among themselves, and that, as a result, the Cymric area was again diminished.

It is with the name of Offa of Mercia that the further and definite lessening of the Cymric land is chiefly associated. He began his reign in 757.[2] Of his deeds during its earlier years little is recorded, but later on he engaged in seemingly fierce contests with the Welsh. In 776 the destruction of the South Wales men took place,[3] and some years after he pushed over the Severn, "and spoiled the Britons in summer time."[4] The king of Powys was driven from Pengwern (Shrewsbury), till then the capital of his realm, and the boundaries of Mercia were practically carried to the Wye. It was probably about this time that the Mercian king caused the earthwork known as Clawð Offa, or Offa's dyke, to be constructed. Speaking roughly, this work extended from the estuary of the Dee to the mouth of the Wye. Whether it was intended for military purposes or simply as a visible mere

---

[1] *E.g.*, "Arthgen rex cereticiaun," "Regin rex demetorum; et catel, pouis moriuntur," " Ann.," *s.a.* 807, 808.

[2] " Dictionary of National Biography," *sub nom.* Offa.

[3] " Brut," *s.a.* 776. "Vastatio Brittonum dexteralium apud Offa," "Ann.," *s.a.* 778.

[4] " Brut," *s.a.* 779. *Cf.* "Vastatio Brittonum cum Offa in estate," " Ann.," *s.a.* 784.

between England and Wales, it became recognised as the boundary line of Cymru. The dyke is not mentioned in 'he Oxford text of the "Brut," though in one of the MSS. on which the Rolls edition is based, it is stated that Offa caused the dyke to be made to enable him more easily to withstand the attacks of his enemies. Probably this is a iate addition to the Brut, but the making of the dyke is mentioned by Asser,[1] and its existence is an indisputable fact. Portions of it were a few years ago noticeable. In Radnorshire at the beginning of this century its remains were "almost as fresh as if cut yesterday, excepting the edges, which are clothed with a fine verdure."[2]

The consolidation of the Teutonic kingdoms in England under Ecgbryht (the first Saxon king who called himself Rex Anglorum) in the early years of the ninth century had an immediate effect upon the fortunes of the remnant of the Britons. In his reign the Cornish people were subdued, and henceforth, though they maintained some kind of separate organisation, they never successfully threw off the yoke of Wessex. After the reduction of Mercia and Northumbria, it seems clear that he extorted the submission of the Cymric princes[3]—the English certainly made temporarily successful invasions into the heart of the Cymric land.[4]

[1] Asser, M. H. B. 471.

[2] Williams's "History of Radnorshire," 58. See also Pryse's "Descriptio" prefixed to "Caradoc of Llancarvan," ed. 1584; also Guest's "Origines Celticæ," vol. ii., p. 273; and Longueville Jones's article in *Arch. Cambr.* (3rd series, vol. ii., pp. 1-3, and pp. 151-4); also Earle's paper, *Arch. Cambr.*, 3rd series, vol. iii., pp. 196-209. Most of what is known about the dyke is well stated by Mr. A. N. Palmer in his paper, "Offa's and Wat's Dykes," in "Y Cymmrodor," vol. xii., p. 65 (1897). [3] Freeman, N. C. i., p. 42.

[4] In 817, "The Saxons ravaged the mountains of Eryri and took the kingdom of Rhuvoniog," "Brut," *s.a.*

In 818, "A fight took place in Mona, called the action of Llanvaes."

In 819, "Kenulf ravaged the kingdoms of Dyfed."

In 823, "the Castle of Deganwy was destroyed by the Saxons, and then the Saxons took the kingdom of Powys into their possession." "Brut," *s. a.* 823.

The reign of Ecgbryht marks a distinct step in the development of the English monarchy ; but just as the English state was attaining to considerable power, its own existence, as well as that of all the kingdoms of the island, was threatened by the formidable invasions of the Northmen or Danes, who were still outside the pale of Christianity. Sporadic incursions had taken place before the accession of Ecgbryht. The Welsh Chronicle says that 790 was the year of Christ when the Pagans first came to Ireland.[1] At the beginning of the ninth century their raids became more frequent and more effective ; but shortly before his death Ecgbryht defeated the invaders and the Cornish Britons (who had joined them) in a great battle at Hengestendun in Cornwall.[2]

Freeman makes the Danish invasions of England to fall into three periods—one of mere plunder, one of settlement, and one of political conquest. The first extended from the first appearance of the Scandinavians in the later years of the eighth century to 855 ; the second, from that year to 897 ; and the third from 980 to 1016, when Cnut commenced to reign as king of the English.[3] In the first period the Welsh seem to have suffered much as the English did, though to a less extent. As to the second period, there was no large settlement of Northmen in Cymru.[4] As to the third, the Danish Conquest did not materially alter the relations of the Welsh princes to the government of England. However much the people settled on the coast of Wales may have suffered from the Danish raids, it seems clear enough that for the Cymry, as a whole, the arrest of the growth of the English monarchy and the incoming of fresh settlers was an advantage. The

---

[1] *Cf.* " Ann.," *s.a.* 796.
[2] In 836, Freeman, " Norman Conquest," i. 43.
[3] Freeman, *ubi supra*.
[4] See above, pp. 27, 35.

incursions of the Northmen assisted the preservation of practical independence by the Welsh nation for a long time, and by distracting the English gave an opportunity for the operation of forces which were slowly tending to the consolidation of the little British kingdoms beyond the dyke. Probably it was due to the absorption of the English in the conflicts of the ninth century that Rhodri Mawr found it possible to extend his dominion over a very large part of Wales, and make his house the really predominant power there.

While Merfyn Frych was still reigning, some cessation of Danish attack enabled Burchred, king of Mercia, to turn his attention to the Welsh. In 844 he engaged and defeated them at a place called Cetyll in the Brut; Merfyn was slain, and was succeeded by his son Rhodri, who came to be known as "the Great" (Mawr). With his accession we reach ground somewhat surer.

By the death of Merfyn he had become head of the line of Gwyned. Afterwards, by his marriage with a daughter of Meurig ab Dyfnwallon, he became lord of Ceredigion and Ystrad Towi on the death of her brother Gwgan;[1] and he is said to have become possessed of Powys through his grandmother, Nest, sister and heiress of Congen ab Cadell, king of Powys.[2] Whether Rhodri ever directly ruled over Powys is not clear,[3] but it is certain that his dominions included the rest of Wales except Dyfed, Morgannwg, Gwent, and the principalities roughly corresponding to the modern Brecknockshire and Radnor. It is, of course, possible that he may have exercised some kind of over-lordship even over these territories. We know so little of Rhodri that it is not very plain why he came to be

---

[1] See Jesus Coll. MS. 20: "Cymmrodor," viii. 87; Harleian MS. 3859; "Cymmrodor," ix., p. 180: Pedigree xxvi.

[2] The death of a Cadell, king of Powys, is recorded in the "Brut," *s.a.* 808. See Pedigree xxvii. in "Y Cymmrodor," ix., p. 181.

[3] In 823 the Saxons took possession of Powys. "Brut," *s.a.* The "Brut" is silent as to Powys from this time to the Norman Conquest.

called the Great,[1] unless it be from the fact that he ruled
over an area much larger than any then recent predecessor,
and that this, coupled with military successes of which we
have no sure evidence, made him an exceptionally powerful
king among his contemporaries. He had continual conflicts with the Mercians and the Danes. According to Irish
authorities, he slew a Danish chief called Horm in 855.
The end of his reign was clouded in misfortune ; for in 876
he sustained a great defeat at the hands of the English, and
was obliged to flee to Ireland. Returning in the following
year, he and his brother Gwriad were slain by the Saxons.[2]

Great importance is attached by the later writers on
Welsh history to Rhodri's reign, for with it, or its conclusion, is associated the division of Wales into the three
kingdoms we have mentioned — Gwyneð, Powys, and
Deheubarth. Some say that Rhodri made the division
during his lifetime, but the earlier authorities attribute the
division to his sons after his death. The text of Caradog
of Ilancarvan says that Rhodri had divers sons, as Anarawd,
to whom he gave Aberffraw with North Wales ; Cadell, the
second son, to whom he gave Dinevwr with South Wales, also
took Powys land by force from his brethren after the death of
Merfyn, the third son, to whom his father had given the same.

Powel, in his note, amplifies this statement in substance
thus :[3] Rhodri was the undoubted owner and possessor of
all Wales ;[4] Gwyneð he had through Esyllt,[5] his mother ;

---

[1] This is a convenient place for our calling attention to the excellent
biographies of Welsh princes in the "Dictionary of National Biography."
They deserve the attention of all students of Welsh history. Most of them
are written by Professor Tout, Professor J. E. Lloyd, or Mr. Lleufer
Thomas.

[2] "Brut," *s.a.* 877. "Ann. Camb." 877. According to the latter, Gwriad
was Rhodri's son.

[3] "Car. of Ilan.," p. 35.

[4] This is certainly not true if the term Wales is used to cover the present
thirteen counties.

[5] Seemingly the Etthil of the pedigree cited above is meant.

Demetia, or South Wales, came to him by his wife, daughter of Meurig ab Dyfnwal, king of Ceredigion ; Powys he had by Nest, his grandmother. These three dominions he appointed under their meares and bounds, with a princelie house in every of them, which he named "y tair talaeth," and left the same unto three of his sons, Anarawd, Cadeŧ, and Merfyn, which were called "y tri thywysog taleithiog " (the three diademed princes).[1] The historians of Wales generally accept this account, often speak as if the division amounted to a splitting up of all Cymru, and deplore it as an impolitic act.

There is, however, something wrong in the aspect it gives to the division of Rhodri's dominions, whether it took place during his life or after his death. Gwyneđ and Powys (as we have seen) were separate kingdoms before Rhodri's time. So also were Dyfed and Ceredigion, as we know from the Welsh chronicles, which are, however, silent as to any division by Rhodri.[2] The principalities or kingdoms of the south-eastern part of Wales—Morgannwg, Gwent, Brecheiniog, Buaŧt, and smaller areas—clearly preserved separate organisations. The evidence of Asser confirms this.[3] In the "Life of Ælfred" he says that King Hemeid,with all the inhabitants of Demetia, compelled by the violence of Rhodri's six sons,⁴ submitted to Ælfred. Howel also, son of Rhys king of

---

[1] Giraldus, writing more than 300 years after Rhodri's death, gives the tripartite division as ancient, and says that Rhodri was the cause of the division. "Descriptio," i. c. 2.

[2] S.a. 796, we hear of Mareduđ, king of Dyfed ; s.a. 798, of Caradog, king of Gwyneđ ; s.a. 808, of Rein, king of Dyfed, and Cadeŧ, king of Powys ; s.a. 819, of kingdoms of Dyfed ; s.a. 817, of the kingdom of Rhuvoniog ; s.a. 823, of the kingdom of Powys ; s.a. 848, of Ithel, king of Gwent ; s.a. 856, of Ionathal, prince of Abergeleu ; s.a. 871, of Gwgawn ab Meurug, king of Ceredigion and the Vale of Towi.

[3] We are aware that the worth and genuineness of Asser's "Life" have been seriously attacked, and give the extract with this caution.

[4] We can only find four mentioned in the "Brut." See the genealogical table at the end of this chapter.

Gleguising, and Brocmail and Fernmail, sons of Meurig, kings of Gwent, compelled by the violence and tyranny of Earl Ethered of the Mercians, sought his protection ; while Elised, son of Teudyr, king of Brecknock, compelled by the force of the same sons of Rhodri, sought the government of Ælfred. Now, of course, it is quite possible that Rhodri, after adding Ceredigion and Ystrad Towi to the parcels of his immediate dominions, had obtained some kind of submission from the kings or princes of the smaller areas here mentioned, and that he was recognised as king of all the Britons or all Cymru. But it is certain that he was not possessed of all the Cymric land. He was king of Gwyneð, with seemingly Aberffraw as his home demesne, and of Deheubarth, with Dinevwr as its chief seat ; but for the notion that Deheubarth was equivalent to what we now call South Wales there is no warrant at all, and no *kingdom* of Deheubarth is referred to in the chronicles, though the word Deheubarthwyr is used. Dinevwr seems to have been the palace of the king of Ceredigion and Ystrad Towi, which roughly corresponded to the present Cardiganshire and the greater part of the modern Carmarthenshire. Neither Cidweli nor Gwyr (answering to Gower in Glamorganshire) which are both mentioned in the Brut, are shown with any certainty to have been part of Rhodri's dominions as matter of right ; while we find that Dyfed, Morgannwg, Gwent, and Brecheiniog, and probably other smaller areas, were under other rulers. Some time afterwards the line of Dyfed came to an end, and the district was incorporated in some fashion, at any rate temporarily, into the kingdom of Dinevwr or Deheubarth ; but its subsequent history—its rapid development into a county palatine, without any apparent violent breach of the continuity of its story— seems to show the survival of a separate organisation. Morgannwg, Brecheiniog, and Gwent remained as " separate entities," if we may use a modern phrase, and by a gradual process became counties under the English or Norman system.

Though there is no early authority on the question, and though the complexion given to the transaction by Caradog is probably wrong, yet there is ground for thinking that something unusual did take place in regard to the devolution of the regal rights upon the death of Rhodri. The Cymric kingship was originally, and probably down to a late time, not a personal monarchy; but a tribal or family chieftaincy.[1] The so-called king was the chief of the royal family (penkenedl) in whom the tribal sovereignty was vested. If we may assume that the laws of Howel Ða apply to earlier times, then we should expect that on Rhodri's death Anarawd, the eldest son, would become chief (if he had the necessary legal qualifications of a penkenedl) without any division of the family dominions of a permanent character, though CadeII (*e.g.*) might be made arglwyð (lord) of a particular district of the family lands for reasons of convenience. Then on the death of Anarawd one would expect his eldest son or some other member of the cenedl (kindred) to become chief and rule over the whole dominion. In fact, however, the devolution of Rhodri's possessions was different. Anarawd became king of Gwyneð, and handed it on to his son Idwal; and CadeII became king of Deheubarth, and was succeeded by his son Howel. Merfyn does not seem to have transmitted any claims to Powys. The two former undoubtedly founded the princely lines of Gwyneð and Deheubarth. The facts, therefore, seem to show that the succession to Rhodri's dominions did not proceed in the ordinary way; and, perhaps, what took place may have marked a stage in the change from a tribal chieftaincy to a territorial sovereignty.

Upon the death of Rhodri his eldest son Anarawd, as we have said, succeeded to Gwyneð; CadeII to Deheubarth,

---

[1] See below, pp. 202–3.

and perhaps Merfyn to Powys. Of the south-eastern principalities we learn practically nothing on trustworthy authority. No grave internal troubles seem to have occurred during Anarawd's long reign of thirty-eight years. In 880, three years after his accession, there was an English invasion, and Anarawd defeated the Saxon enemy. "for God to avenge Rhodri."[1] The battle was fought near Conway, and came to be referred to as "Dial Rhodri" (Rhodri's revenge).

During the later years of the ninth century the house of Rhodri was undoubtedly the predominant power in Wales. We have seen how the kings outside the pale of Rhodri's possessions were compelled by the oppression of his "six sons" to seek the protection of Ælfred the Great; but now Anarawd himself, with a brother (seemingly Cadell of Deheubarth), abandoned close relations with the Northumbrians and came into the great king's presence and sought his friendship. He was received by the king with honour as his son by the Bishop's confirmation, and was presented with many gifts.[2] Probably Anarawd at first pursued a policy of friendship and alliance with the people of Northern Britain as against the Mercians and West-Saxons, as he did with the Danes for a time. His submission to Ælfred, and that of his brother, no doubt paved the way to that usually friendly relation which existed between the chief rulers of Wales and the kings of the house of Ælfred during the greater part of the tenth century. We know not when Anarawd and Ælfred met; not even whether it was before or after a temporary quarrel with Cadell which led, in 893, to an inroad into Ceredigion and the Vale of Towi by the North-Welsh prince. Probably, however, the meeting took place

---

[1] "Brut," *s.a.* 877; "Ann. Cam.," 877.
[2] Asser, M. H. B., p. 488.

after the defeat of the Danes under Hasting by Ælfred in 897.[1]

The remaining years of Anarawd's reign were quite barren of any events of importance. He died in 915, and was succeeded by his son Idwal Voel. Cadell had predeceased his brother, and Howel afterwards called Đa (the good) became king of Deheubarth, and later on of Gwyneđ as well. Under the rule of Idwal and Howel the Cymry enjoyed unwonted peace.[2] They were contemporaries of Eadward the Elder and Æthelstan, and thus lived when the power of the house of Ælfred was at its greatest height. Howel throughout his whole career remained[3] on peaceful terms with the English court, and so far as we know (except in regard to a dispute with Morgan Hen of Morgannwg) with the other Welsh princes. Both Idwal and Howel did homage to the English kings, and seem to have behaved as faithful vassals.

To appreciate the significance of the isolated facts which we can gather concerning Idwal and Howel it is necessary to bear in mind the change that had been wrought in England by the settlement of the Danes. By the peace of Wedmore England north of the Thames had been divided by a line roughly drawn from north to south from the Ribble to the upper valley of the Thames. This involved the division of the ancient and important kingdom of Mercia into an English and Danish Mercia. The former

---

[1] Green, " Conquest of England," pp. 172-3, 183 ; " Eng. Chron.," *s.a.* 897. The fact, however, that Gwyneđ and Deheubarth escaped the ravages of the Northmen in 894 suggests that the house of Rhodri was then in alliance with them.

[2] In the " Brut " only four battles are mentioned between 914 and 948 :—

914. The people of Dublin (*i.e.*, Norsemen) made a descent on Môn.

919. A battle took place at Dinas Newyđ. (Ann. Cam., 921.)

935. The battle of. Brun took place. (Ann. Cam., 938.)

944. Ystrat Clut (Strath Clyde) was devastated by the Saxons. (Ann. Cam., 946.)

[3] At any rate, after the first five years of his reign.

was a stretch of country from the Ribble to the Thames and the Avon, and it seems clear that it was one of Ælfred's objects to separate the Danes from the Welsh by this English Mercia. At the beginning of the tenth century this remnant of the older Mercia was ruled by the Ealdorman Æthelred and his wife Æthelflaed, and after the death of the former, by the latter, the celebrated " Lady of Mercia."

No marked change took place in regard to the Welsh principalities during the latter part of the ninth or earlier part of the tenth century. There is nothing to show that either Idwal Voel or Howel extended his dominions over Morgannwg, Brecheiniog, Buallt, or Gwent. Of Powys we hear nothing, but it may be presumed with probability that the lordships into which, as we gather from later sources, it was divided were in some sort of subjection to Mercia. As to Deheubarth, it is likely that Howel became possessed of Dyfed, for he married Elen, daughter of Loumarc ab Hymeid, king of Dyfed. This Hymeid was seemingly the king of Dyfed who sought the protection of Ælfred.[1] We hear no more of kings of Dyfed, though it seems to have kept a separate character. On the east Howel extended his rule peaceably over Kidweli and Gwyr, and thus became the immediate neighbour of Morgan Hen (king of Morgannwg), for we find that the undoubted possessions of Maredud ab Owain—the grandson of Howel Da—included those two districts in addition to Ceredigion and Ystrad Towi.[2] Gwyned certainly included Môn, the present shire of Carnarvon, and part of Merionethshire, and

[1] See above, p. 145. In pedigree ii. appended to the " Ann." ("Y Cymmrodor," ix. p. 171), Elen is daughter of Ioumarc (a mistake for Loumarc), son of Himeÿt. Loumarc is the Welsh Llywarch.

[2] The "Brut," *s.a.* 991, with a videlicet, describes the kingdoms of Maredud as—Dyfed and Keredigion, and Gower and Kydweli. Ystrad Towi is not specifically mentioned, but probably it was covered by the term " kingdom of Keredigion."

probably North Wales up to the Dee, but at this time it did not comprise Chester.[1]

Pursuing the policy adopted by Ælfred, of completely interposing an English kingdom between the Welsh and the Danes, the rulers of Mercia early in the tenth century proceeded to re-fortify that city. Since its surrender to Æthelfrith in 616 the city had lain waste and desolate. Situate on the Dee, being the point of junction of ancient ways, and commanding the old coast route from England to Anglesey, it was a place of military importance, and its effectual occupation cut off the shortest communication between the Welsh of Gwyneđ and the Danish Mercians. Its Roman walls still existed in a damaged condition, and little exertion must have been necessary to make it a comparatively strongly-defended centre of operations. In 907 the Ealdorman of Mercia "renewed" Chester, though we are not informed as to the extent of the new fortifications he erected. A small settlement was made, and a secular house of St. Werburgh was founded in the city. The event was of consequence in Welsh history, and henceforth Chester played a considerable part in the military and the economic fortunes of the men of Gwyneđ and Powys.

Bearing these general considerations in mind, we now return to the personal history of Idwal and Howel.

Few facts are known concerning Idwal's reign over Gwyneđ. In 922, when Eadward the Elder had subdued all Mercia (Danish as well as English), Idwal, together with Howel Đa and a Welsh king called Clydaiwc,[2] received him as their lord,[3] and the two former did homage to Æthelstan in 926[4] at Hereford and, it is said, rendered tribute to him.

---

[1] We can find no evidence of a re-peopling of Chester by the Welsh.

[2] We know not where he reigned. The death of a Clydog is recorded in the "Brut," *s.a.* 917, and in "Ann. Cam.," *s.a.* 919.

[3] "Eng. Chron.," *s.a.* 922.

[4] "Eng. Chron.," *s.a.* 926.

A word or two ought here to be said as to the submission
of the Welsh kings to these kings of the English. There can
be no reasonable doubt that the entries in the English
chronicles, confirmèd as they are by authentic charters
and by the documents relating to the litigation between
Howel Đa and Morgan Hen referred to below, recount real
historical events. But there is danger of misunderstanding
what took place. The kings of the English did not by
reason of the commendation of the Welsh kings obtain the
right of directly interfering in the affairs of the Welsh
kingdoms. Though Idwal and Howel became his men, their
subjects—under-kings or lords or uchelwyr—stood in no
legal relation to the English king. The effect of the commendation was that the over-lord took upon himself the
duty of protecting his vassals from their enemies, while on
their side they incurred the obligation of fighting against
their lord's enemies. The tie was necessarily, in those times,
a loose one, and was often broken.[1] The reality of the
relationship in the first half of the tenth century is shown
by the attendance of the Welsh princes at the meetings of
the Witenagemot. If we can trust a charter (which is, however, of doubtful authenticity), Idwal was taking part in the
proceedings of the English assembly at Exeter in 928.[2]
That Howel Đa attended these meetings on several
occasions is certain. The silence of the Brut about Idwal
till 943 affords some indication that nothing of any importance took place in Gwyneđ between 926 and that time ;
but as in that year Idwal and his brother Elised were killed
by the English,[3] we may presume that Idwal had revolted,
or perhaps had refused to pay tribute, but there is no
certainty about the matter.

We have somewhat fuller information about Howel Đa,

[1] See as to the effect of "commendation" Freeman, N. C. i., pp. 131-2.
[2] See charter, "Cod. Dipl.," 1101.
[3] "Brut," s.a. 941 ; "Ann. Cam.," s.a. 943.

though of the earlier years—that is, the years before the submission to Eadward the Elder—we know nothing. Whether or not he took part in the actions of Dinas Newyđ or of Brun we cannot determine. After doing homage to Æthelstan he is said to have made a pilgrimage to Rome.[1]

There seems no reason to doubt this, but if he did so we may infer that there was an unusually stable position of things in Wales, and no internal events seem to have made such a journey necessary. Upon his return he resumed peaceable exercise of his regal rights. From that time to the year before his death he was a frequent attendant at the meetings of the Witenagemot of his English over-lords. We know from his subscription of charters that he did so in 931, 932, 933, 934, 937, 946, and 949.[2] In the earlier charters he attests as " sub-regulus " ; in the later ones he subscribes as " regulus " and " rex." Perhaps the difference is due to his having on Idwal's death succeeded to Gwyneđ and becoming recognised as king of the Britons or of the Cymry.

The nature of Howel's relations with the English kings is made clearer by the account, preserved in the Book of Llandaff, of a dispute between him and Morgan Hen,

---

[1] " Brut," *s.a.* 926 ; " Ann. Cam.," *s.a.* 928. The date is uncertain ; see below, p. 182–3.

[2] The following are the dates of the charters, and the references to them in Kemble's " Cod. Diplom." :—

21 July, 931 (" Cod. Dipl." v. 199).
12 Nov., 931 (*ib.*, ii. 173).
30 Aug., 932 (*ib.*, v. 208).
15 Dec., 933 (*ib.*, ii. 194).
28 May, 934 (*ib.*, ii. 196).
16 Dec., 934 (*ib.*, v. 217).
937 (*ib.*, ii. 203).
946 and 949 (*ib.*, ii. 269, 292, 296).

There are also subscriptions of Howel's to doubtful charters of the 17th June, 930, and the 1st Jan. and 21st Dec., 935 (" Cod. Dipl." ii. 170 ; v. 222 ; ii. 203).

king of Morgannwg. The entry in the Book is not, however, free from ambiguity. It says Eadgar and Howel Ða and Morgan Hen were kings of all Britain, and those two were subject to King Eadgar, and Morgan enjoyed the whole of Glamorgan in peace and quietness, but Howel would take from him Ystradyew and Ewyas if he could. Then Eadgar summoned his under-kings and Morgan's son, Owain, before him, and having examined the matter in dispute, gave judgment in favour of Morgan, and with the common assent and testimony of all the archbishops, bishops, abbots, earls, and barons of all England and Wales granted to Owain, the son of Morgan Hen, "the said two districts of Ystradyew and Ewyas, declared by name to be in the diocese of Llandaff, as his own proper inheritance." [1] There are several points of difficulty connected with this document—points which we do not affect to solve. Eadgar, though he had ruled in Mercia before, was not king of England till 958, some eight years after Howel's death. Morgan Hen survived Howel, for he was a witness to a charter of Eadwig's in 956, together with Eadgar, sub-regulus of Mercia. There is a Welsh version of the same Latin document to be found in the Myvyrian Archaiology, among the collection called "Y cwta cyfarwyđ o Forganwg." It is clearly impossible that Howel could have appeared before Eadgar, king of England. It is, of course, possible that the dispute may have arisen during the time of Howel, and, lingering on for years, may have been decided by Eadgar. But, on the other hand, it is quite possible that the dispute may have been decided, not by Eadgar, but by Eadward the Elder, and that the mistake may have occurred in the transcription of the account of the dispute and of the grant, especially as we find it expressly stated that it was inserted in the Book

---

[1] "Book of Llan Dâv" (Oxford, 1893), p. 248; "Liber Landavensis" (Llandovery, 1870), p. 237; Palgrave, "English Commonwealth," v. 2, p. ccxliv.

of Llandaff because the paper on which it had been written had nearly perished from its great age.[1]

It is, however, on his legislation that the fame of Howel Da chiefly depends, for to him is attributed the setting down in writing of the laws and customs of the Cymry. The preamble prefixed to each of the codes that have been handed down to us in substance (though in varying language) records that Howel summoned four men from each cantref in his dominions to the Ty Gwyn, which is identified by far-reaching tradition with Whitland in Carmarthenshire. We deal with these laws in the following chapter. Though there is no mention in the Brut of the summoning of this meeting at Ty Gwyn, there is no reason to doubt that the preambles of the Code preserve a historical transaction.[2] It is probable that the compilation of the work took place after Howel had become king of Gwyned upon Idwal's death, and therefore some time between 943 and 950. These facts are all that we can glean upon trustworthy evidence concerning a king who was, to use the words of a later writer, "for his godlie behaviour, discreet and just rule, beloved of men." They are too few to enable us to draw a vivid picture of his character or personality, but they corroborate the view of him popularly entertained among the Welsh people, and justify us in inferring that he was an able and politic prince, under whom Wales enjoyed a period of unusual repose and prosperity.

The peace that Howel had kept disappeared at his death. There was war at once between his sons (Owain, Dyfnwal, Rhodri, and Edwyn) and the sons of Idwal Voel (Ieuaf and Iago), and the eighty-nine years that elapsed from the

---

[1] Palgrave, *ubi supra*, says that according to usual custom the Welsh scribe omitted the final *d* and substituted a *g* for a *w*, relying, he observes, on the authority of a genealogical MS. ("Bibl. Harl.," 4181).

[2] See the next chapter.

commencement of this conflict to the accession of Gruffyd
ab ILewelyn in 1039 form a time of almost inextricable
confusion.   In a battle fought at Carno in the very year
that Howel died his sons sustained a defeat at the hands
of Ieuaf and Iago, who, setting aside their elder brother,
obtained joint possession of Gwyned.[1] In 952 they
ravaged Dyfed twice, and slew Dyfnwallon, who was
probably the prince of that region.[2] The sons of Howel
in 954 invaded North Wales, but were again apparently
unsuccessful, being beaten in an engagement at ILanrwst,[3]
by the sons of Idwal, who thereupon devastated Ceredigion—
whence, however, it is said they were driven back with
great slaughter.[4] After this there was an interval of peace
between Gwyned and Deheubarth, but raids of the Danes
gave some trouble.

There was a quarrel with the English in 965, and Alvryd
invaded and ravaged Gwyned; while in 970 Godfrey son
of Harold subdued and for a time held Môn.[5] Before
this latter event, however, the brothers of Gwyned had
quarrelled. Iago seized Ieuaf and caused him to be blinded
and then hanged. The relations between the Welsh
princes and Eadgar (958—975) were fairly peaceable,
though there seems to have been an invasion of Gwyned
in 968,[6] but the English hold on Wales was gradually
relaxing. No fewer than four Welsh princes attended a
Witenagemot held by Eadred. During Eadgar's time,
so far as we can tell, the Welsh no longer attended the
English Court, and their dependence on the English Crown,

[1] " Brut," *s.a.* 948, 950, 951, 952.
[2] He may have been Dyfnwal ab Howel Đa; but the " Brut " places the
death of this Dyfnwal in the following year.
[3] " Brut," *s.a.* 952.
[4] Gwentian " Brut " (Myv. Arch. ii., 468 *et seq.*).
[5] " Brut," *s.a.* 965 and *s.a.* 970.
[6] " Ann. Cam.," *s.a.* 968. It is possible this is the same invasion as that
by Alvryd noted in the " Brut," *s.a.* 965.

which had been real enough, as we have seen, earlier in the century, was now becoming nominal as the power of the house of Ælfred was waning.[1]

In later chronicles it is said that Eadgar went to Chester and summoned eight under-kings—including five Welsh princes—to his presence, that they did homage and swore fealty, and that as a mark of their subordination he caused his vassals to row him in his barge on the Dee from the palace to the monastery of John the Baptist, and after divine service there back to the palace.[2] Possibly the invasion of Gwyneđ mentioned above may have led to a renewal of oaths of fealty and payment of tribute; but this twelfth-century story cannot be accepted as certain history, and a similar observation must be made as to the imposition by Eadgar of a tribute of three hundred wolves.[3]

Returning to the affairs of Gwyneđ, the murdered Ieuaf had left a son called Howel, who was not long in avenging his father's death, for in 972 he succeeded in expelling Iago and taking possession of Gwyneđ in his stead. Iago was captured by Danes in 978, and we hear of him no more.[4]

Howel's rule was soon challenged, for the cause of the defeated chieftain was espoused by his son Kystenin, and in the year after the capture of his father he, with the help of Godfrey son of Harold (of whom we have already heard), made a raid on Ileyn (in the modern South

---

[1] Green, "Conqu. of Eng.," p. 323. There is one charter to which Iago's name (as Iacob) appears dated at Bath, Whitsuntide, 966, but the document is suspect. Kemble, "Cod. Dipl.," 519.

[2] "Will. Malm. Gest. Reg." (Hardy) i., p. 251 ; "Flor. Worc." (Thorpe) i. 142.

[3] "Will. Malm. Gest. Reg." (Hardy) i. 251. Palgrave prints a charter (the date of which must have been before 971, since one of the subscribers, Oscytel, died in that year) which Iukill and Jacobus attest. "Eng. Com." ii., p. ccliii. They may have been Ieuaf and Iago ; but Iukill does not look like Ieuaf at all.

[4] The dates are quite uncertain. See "Brut," *s.a.* 972 and 978.

Carnarvonshire) and Môn, but he was met by Howel ab Ieuaf at Hirbarth, and fell in the battle.[1] Howel, who acquired (in curious antithesis to the case of Howel Ða) the epithet of Ðrwg, or the Bad, does not seem to have been attacked by other Welsh claimants to Gwyneð; but the Godfrey son of Harold (who had taken the side of Cystenin, as we have seen) still vexed the Welsh kingdom. In 981 he ravaged Dyfed, and in the next year Brecheiniog, and the territories of Einion ab Owain ab Howel Ða were overrun by the Saxons under Alvryd. In 984 Howel was killed by the "Saxons through treachery."[2] He left two sons —at least—Maig, who was killed in the following year, and Cadwaïon, who took possession of Gwyneð, but who was almost immediately defeated and slain[3] by Mareduð ab Owain, king of Deheubarth (a grandson of Howel Ða), who played a considerable part for the next few years.

We must now turn for a moment to the affairs of Deheubarth. Upon Howel Ða's death Owain and his three brothers succeeded to ʾthat kingdom, but failed to make good whatever claim they may have had to Gwyneð as against the sons of Idwal. Dyfnwal, Rhodri, and Edwyn died very soon,[4] and Owain reigned alone till he died in 987 or 989,[5] and was succeeded by the Mareduð just mentioned.

From an incidental statement in the Brut[6] we know that Mareduð's possessions included Dyfed, Ceredigion, Gwyr, and Kydweli, and no doubt Ystrad Towi, which had long

[1] "Brut," s.a. 979.
[2] "Brut," s.a. 984. Probably, however, a year or two later.
[3] "Brut," s.a. 984.
[4] In 951 and 952, according to the "Brut." Probably in either case later.
[5] "Brut," s.a. 987. In "Ann. Cam." Owain's death is placed in the next entry after 987.
[6] "Brut," s.a. 991. It is curious that this is pretty nearly the kingdom of Pryderi ab Pwyïł, as described at the end of the story of Pwyïł, prince of Dyfed, in the "Mabinogion." See Oxford edition of the Red Book, i. 25.

been connected with Ceredigion. Gwyr may have passed from Howel's sons on his death, for we have it recorded that Einion ab Owain, his grandson, devastated that district twice—the first time, according to the Brut, in 968, and the second time in 976. Probably Einion was extending the family territory to the east, and under his father Owain was able to annex some of the smaller lordships or areas to Deheubarth. We hear that Brecheiniog and all the territory of Einion were devastated by the Saxons in 982[1]—an entry which seems to show that Einion's territory extended to south-eastern Wales. The year after this raid Einion was killed through "the treachery of the nobles of Gwent."[2]

Apart from such exploits as may have been performed by Einion and Maredud, the only events of Owain's long reign were the usual raids of Danish leaders, and some conflicts with the English. Of his relation to Powys we know nothing certain. We may conjecture with some probability that he shared some of the qualities of his father, for upon his death he handed on to Maredud the kingdom of Deheubarth with its area undiminished, and before that event, as we have recounted, his son Maredud, taking advantage of the fall of Howel Drwg, had founded a claim to Gwyned by attacking and killing that king's brother, Cadwatton ab Ieuaf.

Maredud does not seem to have been able to obtain real possession of Gwyned, though Caradog places him in the line of kings or princes of all Wales.[3] He was

chiefly occupied in repelling the Danes (to whom he paid
tribute on at least one occasion),[1] and in attacks upon
Gwyneđ and Morgannwg.[2]   It is said he ruled Powys in
right of his mother, but there is no sufficient authority for
this.[3]   However this may be, he fairly maintained the
prestige of the house of Howel Đa in a very disturbed
period, and died a natural death in 998 or 999,[4] leaving
only one child—a daughter, married to Ịlewelyn ab Seisyịłt,
who, apparently in right of his wife, assumed the government
of Deheubarth.

Ever since the retreat of Mareduđ from Gwyneđ, after
his victory over Cadwałłon, that kingdom had been in a
condition of extreme confusion ; and there was probably
from the death of Cadwałłon ab Ieuaf to Iago ab Idwal's[5]
accession a kind of interregnum.[6]   Meurig ab Idwal Voel
(apparently he who was ousted by his brothers Ịeuaf and
Iago) "fell sick" and died,[7] but he left issue.   Among his
sons was an Idwal, who fled to Ịlancarvan in Morganwg,
in the lifetime of Mareduđ, who made an attempt to seize
him.   Idwal's claims on Gwyneđ seem to have been just,
according to the legal rules of succession, and Mareduđ's
attempt on his person having failed, he secured some
adherents, and in 992 returned to Gwyneđ.[8]   In the
following year, 993, a battle took place between him and

---

[1] "Brut," *s.a.* 988.

[2] In 990 he devastated also Maes Hyfeid (roughly equivalent to the present
Radnorshire).   See "Brut," *s.a.* 990.

[3] Warrington, p. 20, cites "Brit. Antiq. Revived," by G. Vaughan of
Hengwrt, pp. 5, 14.

[4] "Brut," *s.a.* 998.

[5] *I.e.*, 984 to 1021.

[6] Caradog, however, fills the time up with Idwal ab Meurig, Conan ab Howel,
and Aedan ab Blegored.

[7] "Brut," *s.a.* 972 ; but *cf.* "Ann. Cam.," "Meuric filius Idwal cæcatus est"
(974).

[8] "Brut," *s.a.* 992 : "the sons of Meurig made an inroad into
Gwyneđ."

his brothers[1] and the sons of Mareduḍ, in which the former triumphed, with the result that Idwal ab Meurig became king of Gwyneḍ;[2] but he did not enjoy his success long, for two years after he was killed, probably by the Danes.[3]

He left a son of tender years, Iago, who, though passed over for the moment, many years after obtained Gwyneḍ. Upon Idwal's death Cynan ab Howel, Aeḍan ab Blegored, and others, with little or no show of right, "did aspire to the government," and sought the rule of the land.[4] There was again a contested succession, but Kynan was killed (presumably in a battle with Aeḍan) in 1003,[5] and Aeḍan seems to have usurped the throne. We know nothing more of him except that he and his four sons were killed in 1016 in a fight with ILewelyn ab Seisyłt, who once more joined Gwyneḍ to Deheubarth.[6] The troubles of England under Æthelred the Unready, culminating in the fall of the house of Ælfred and the accession of Cnut, seem to have afforded some relief to Wales from attacks from the English border as well as by Danish forces, and with the reign of ILewelyn begins a fresh growth of Cymric power that attained its greatest development in the reign of his son, Gruffyḍ ab ILewelyn. It is assumed that ILewelyn ruled over Powys,[7] but for this there is no certain warrant. Though Deheubarth seems to have been fairly quiet under his rule, he had one rising at least to contend with. The uchelwyr of South Wales "loved not ILewelyn,"[8] and, led by one

---

[1] In the "Brut" Idwal's party is described as the sons of Meurig. The only one of the sons of Meurig besides Idwal whose name we know seems to be the Jonaval who was killed by Cadwałon ab Ieuaf in 984. Brut," *s.a.* 984. *Cf.* "Ann. Cam.," p. 24.

[2] "Brut," *s.a.* 993.

[3] "Brut," *s.a.* 995. Three years after, according to "Ann. Cam.," p. 21.

[4] Caradog, p. 74.

[5] "Brut," *s.a.* 1003.

[6] "Brut," *s.a.* 1016.

[7] Warrington, p. 205.

[8] Caradog, p. 83.

Meurig ab Arthvael, revolted in 1019, but they were at once subdued.[1]

In the following year there was a more formidable rebellion, when a pretender called Rein Yscot, affecting to be a son of Maredud ab Owain, got together the strength of Deheubarth at Abergwili, and waited the coming of the king. Llewelyn, "daring and fearless," with the host of Gwyned engaged in battle and conquered Rein, who, though brave and confident in assault, "retreated shamefully in a fox-like manner, and never thenceforward, made his appearance."[2] The men of Gwyned wrathfully pursued the enemy, and devastated the country to the Mercian border. In 1023 Llewelyn at the height of his power died.[3] It is said by Caradog he was slain by two descendants of Howel Da, but the " Brut " simply records that he died. His son Gruffyd, who was destined to play a great part in the years just before the Norman Conquest, must have been at this time very young, and did not succeed to either kingdom. Gwyned fell to Iago, the son of that Idwal who had possessed it in defiance of Maredud ab Owain ; but possibly he did not make good his claims till some time after Llewelyn's death.[4] But it was only to Gwyned that he succeeded, for Deheubarth was seized by Rhyderch ab Iestyn.[5] Though possessing neither of the two principal divisions of his dominions by a legal title, Llewelyn's rule left a marked impression upon the Welsh people. According to the " Brut," " In his time it was usual for the elders of his kingdom to say that his dominion was from one sea to the other complete in abundance of wealth and inhabitants ;

---

[1] Meurig was killed. " Brut," *s.a.* 1019. "Book of Lan Dâv " (Oxf.), p. 200.

[2] " Brut," *s.a.* 1020.

[3] " Brut," *s.a.* 1021. " Ann. Cam.," *s.a.* 1023. Caradog, p. 86.

[4] " Brut," *s.a.* 1031, says : "And then Iago ab Idwal held the government of Gwyned after Llewelyn."

[5] We infer this from later events recorded in the " Brut."

so that it was supposed there was neither poor nor destitute in all his territories ; nor empty trev nor any deficiency."[1]

Though we cannot fix the exact year in which Iago ab Idwal obtained a real possession of Gwyned, it seems clear that his reign was uneventful. Nor did anything of special consequence happen in the south. Great events, however, had been taking place in England, for the Danish king Cnut had become in 1016 ruler of all England,[2] which he divided into the great ealdormanries of Wessex, Mercia, East Anglia, and Northumbria. Cnut's accession brought peace to the whole country. The Danish pirate fleets (speaking broadly) ceased to ravage the coast of the island, while indirectly the vigorous government of Cnut benefited Wales as well as the territories under his more direct rule. English manufactures and trade began to make some progress. Worcester was growing to be a place of importance, and Gloucester was rapidly rising to a position which enabled it in the years after the Norman Conquest to exercise a marked influence on the development of South Wales. In the north, Chester, restored as we have seen some one hundred years before by Æthelflaeda, was now a centre of commerce and the common meeting ground of Irish, Welsh, Cumbrians, English, and Danes. The quiet of Iago's reign is probably largely explained by these and other more general circumstances. Deheubarth and the small principalities to the south-east enjoyed an unwonted immunity from external attack, but there was as usual internal trouble. Rhyderch of Deheubarth was slain, it is said by Irish-Scots, in 1031 or 1033.[3] Howel and Maredud, sons of Edwin,[4] took his place, but a year

---

[1] S.a. 1020.
[2] Green, " Conqu. of Eng.," pp. 411 et seq.
[3] " Brut," s.a. 1031. " Ann. Cam.," s.a. 1033.
[4] Apparently this Edwin was son of Einion, one of the grandsons of Howel D.1 : see the genealogical table at end of this chapter.

afterwards the sons of Rhyderch revolted, and a battle was fought at Hiraethwy, in which the latter were probably defeated. Maredud ab Edwin was soon after killed in an obscure conflict,[1] and Howel, his brother, was left in sole possession of Deheubarth, though Gruffyd ab Rhyderch survived to create further disturbances in after years.

The peace of Gwyned was some six years after these events broken by the assertion of his claims by Gruffyd ab Llewelyn ab Seisytt, who had, though still young, by that time reached manhood. Of his early years nothing is known. The immediate occasion of his attack upon Gwyned appears to have been that one Iestyn ab Gwrgant, having ravished Gruffyd's cousin Arden, the daughter of Robert ab Seisytt, fled to Iago, who gave him his protection. Gruffyd thereupon raised a force, engaged the army of Iago, slew the king, and seized his kingdom.[2]

It was during the reign of Gruffyd ab Llewelyn—extending from 1039 to 1063—that the Cymry reached the point of greatest strength since the death of Cadwaladr, and that for the first time for many years their leader was able to exercise an appreciable influence on affairs beyond the border. In 1035 Cnut had died. At the meeting of the Witan at Oxford held after his death, notwithstanding the resistance of the powerful Godwine, Earl of Wessex, who endeavoured o enforce the will of Cnut in favour of Harthacnut, Harold Harefoot was chosen king, with the aid of Leofric, Earl of Mercia. Godwine's influence was, however, strong enough to secure part of the late king's dominions for the younger son of Cnut, who was recognised as king of Wessex. It was after England had been once more divided, and the house of Godwine had received a temporary check in its path of aggrandisement, that Gruffyd became king of Gwyned. Nearly ninety years had passed since

<hr>

1 "Brut," *s.a.* 1033.   "Ann. Cam.," *s.a.* 1035.
2 "Brut," *s.a.* 1037.   "Ann. Cam.," *s.a.* 1039.

the death of Howel Đa. They had been for the most part, as the bald narrative we have been able to give shows, years of almost continued internal confusion, of border troubles, and of vexatious invasions from beyond the sea. But the career of Gruffyđ ab ILewelyn seems to show that the conflicts that had been waged and the events that had taken place had not sensibly affected the power of the Cymric clans as a whole. It is difficult to avoid the inference that the wars during this disturbed period, of which the recollection is preserved in the " Brut," were on a merely petty scale—an inference strengthened, of course, by our knowledge that the population was very small.[1]

However this may be, there can be no doubt that under the leadership of Gruffyđ the Cymry suddenly developed an amount of military capacity and activity which had not been displayed for centuries, and which resulted in their becoming a factor of some considerable importance in the affairs of the whole island. The divisions of race in England, the rivalries of the great Earls, and other circumstances, combined to assist Gruffyđ in uniting the forces of Wales, consolidating his own position, and making himself not only the predominant chieftain in Wales, but a dangerous and powerful foe to the English king, or at any rate to the house of Godwine. One reason no doubt was that after the first year of his reign his policy—one consistently pursued—was to remain on friendly terms with the Earl and people of Mercia, or rather the English part of the old kingdom of Mercia, then forming the ealdormanry of Leofric. Of the personal characteristics of this the greatest military chief of the Cymry (except, perhaps, ILewelyn ab Iorwerth, who was to exhibit similar qualities two hundred years later), we know nothing except what may be inferred from his deeds. The burst of literary activity which commenced among the Cymry shortly after the

[1] See the Introduction, above.

Norman Conquest has preserved for us much information about later and far less important princes and warriors; but though Gruffyd, like them, had bards in his train and at his court, not even fragments of their poems have come down to enlighten us concerning the lord whom they doubtless delighted to honour. For Gruffyd's life, as in regard to those of his predecessors, we must rely simply on the short entries in the chronicles.

Gruffyd's character showed itself at once. In the very year of his accession he led a raid over the border into Mercia, and beat the English forces in a battle at Rhyd-y-Groes,[1] on the Severn, in which Eadwine, brother of Earl Leofric, was slain. This event does not seem to have embroiled him with the Mercian Earl, for henceforth we find him in alliance with the house of Leofric, and many years elapsed before he again invaded England. He immediately turned his attention to Deheubarth. Howel ab Edwin, who was now possessed of South Wales as a result of the defeat of the sons of Rhyderch, was, without any considerable pause, attacked by Gruffyd, and defeated in an encounter at Llanbadarn. Howel was forced to fly to the Irish Norsemen for assistance. Two years afterwards, with their support, he returned to Wales, and penetrated into Keredigion, but was again beaten by Gruffyd in an engagement at Pencader, which was of a decisive character, and in which the victor captured Howel's wife, whom he took as his mistress. Howel's resources were not, however, exhausted, and, by one of the sudden changes of fortune characteristic of the period, in the following year (1042) Gruffyd was himself beaten, with the aid of the "black Pagans," and taken prisoner, at Pwll Dyvach. Somehow— probably by payment of a ransom—Gruffyd regained his

[1] Literally "the ford of the Cross." The chief authorities for the life of Gruffyd are the "Brut." and "Ann. Cam.," with the English Chronicle. See his life in "Dict. Nat. Biog."

liberty, and returned to his kingdom. Two years after
Howel, who seems to have once more gone to Ireland, came
back with a fleet, and, sailing round Dyfeđ, proceeded to
the Towy, but was defeated and lost his life in a battle with
the army of Gruffyđ at Abertowy.[1]

This victory secured Deheubarth for the king of
Gwyneđ, though his troubles in that part of Cymru
were not over. Howel, as we have seen, had himself
violently usurped the crown of Deheubarth, after expelling Rhyđerch. Two sons of the latter, Gruffyđ and
Rhys, saw in Howel's overthrow an opportunity of
asserting the claims of their house. How far they were
able to obtain actual possession of the whole or any part of
South Wales is not clear; but probably it was Gruffyđ ab
Ilewelyn who was the actual ruler, while the sons of Rhyđerch from time to time attacked him or his subordinate
lords. About ten years, however, elapsed from the defeat
of Howel before Gruffyđ was able finally to suppress the
house of Rhyđerch. That he was strengthening himself
with prudence is shown by his peaceful attitude towards
Edward the Confessor's government, and his close relation
to the Mercian Earl; and when Swein son of Godwine, in or
about 1045, was Earl of the south-western part of the old
kingdom of Mercia, he joined Gruffyđ ab Ilewelyn in
an expedition against the sons of Rhyđerch. His friendship with the house of Mercia was cemented by his marriage
with Ealdgyth, daughter of Ælfgar, the son of Leofric, who
afterwards became the wife of Harold II. Gruffyđ also

---

[1] This place is not to be confounded with Aberteivi in Keredigion, nor with
Abertawe. Abertowy occurs in the Twrch Trwyth hunt. At "Aber Tywi"
it was that Twrch Trwyth turned to bay and killed Kynlas son of Kynan, and
Gwilenhin, king of France. See Rhys's paper in "Transactions of Cymmro-
dorion Society," 1894–5, p. 16. Abertowy was on the peninsula between the
Towy and the Gwendraeth. About three years ago a storm, carrying away
parts of the sandbanks there, exposed the foundations of a row of houses.
(Account furnished to Professor Rhys by Mr. Drummond, agent for Lord
Cawdor.)

succeeded in obtaining a grant from the English king of all the lands west of the Dee that had theretofore been taken possession of by the English.

In 1047 he had to deal with a more than usually serious revolt in Deheubarth. The uchelwyr of Ystrad Towi suddenly rose and slew one hundred and forty of his men. Gruffyđ thereupon laid waste that district, as well as Dyfed. This rising had probably some connection with the claims of Gruffyđ ab Rhyđerch and his brother. Two years later there was further trouble in the south. The Irish allies of Gruffyđ ab Rhyđerch are said to have ravaged Deheubarth. We hear nothing further of this Gruffyđ, except that he was slain by Gruffyđ ab Llewelyn in 1055, and his brother Rhys, too, disappears from the story.

Even before the death of Gruffyđ ab Rhyđerch the power of the North-Welsh king had become very considerable. He felt himself strong enough once more to invade England. Of the circumstances that led to this course of action we have no information. Whatever the reason for the raid, Gruffyđ in 1052 penetrated into the land of Hereford, very nigh to Leominster, and fought the " landsmen as well as the Frenchmen of the Castle " on the same day on which, thirteen years before, Eadwine had been slain.[1] Ælfgar was outlawed in 1055, without, as the English chronicler says, any guilt.[2] He fled to Ireland and collected a fleet of eighteen ships, and with that force proceeded to Wales to Gruffyđ, who received him into his protection. Gruffyđ and his father-in-law, having gathered together a great force, invaded England, and defeated the English under Ralph the Earl near Hereford. " Before there was any spear thrown the English people fled because they were on horses, and there great slaughter

---

[1] "Eng. Chron.," *s.a.* 1052. "And there were slain of the English very many good men, and also of the Frenchmen."

[2] "Eng. Chron.," *s.a.* 1055.

was made about four hundred or five, and they made none on the other side."[1] The Welsh then took Hereford, burnt the town and the minster that the venerable Bishop Æthelstan had built, and even slew the priests that were within it and many others, and retired carrying away much booty.[2]

The incapable Ralph was replaced by Harold son of Godwine, and the importance of the Welsh victory is shown by the fact that a great force was gathered "from well nigh all England."[3] The English army met at Gloucester, and started against the Welsh. Gruffyđ appears to have retreated, or at any rate avoided an engagement, and Harold either did not desire or was not able to bring about a battle. Some obscure negotiations took place between Ælfgar and Gruffyđ on the one side, and Harold on the other. The result was that peace was restored ; Ælfgar was in-lawed, but Gruffyđ lost the lands beyond the Dée that had been granted to him by the king. One of the copies of the English Chronicle says that when the Welsh " had done the utmost evil this counsel was counselled : that Elgar (Ælfgar) the Earl should be in-lawed and be given his earldom and all that had been taken from him." The fact that peace in accordance with this counsel was made is the strongest evidence of the formidable influence of the Welsh king. Harold forthwith rebuilt Hereford, and Bishop Æthelstan having died, he appointed Leofgar, his mass-priest, to be Bishop on February 7, 1056.

The peace between Gruffyđ and Harold was not long kept. In the summer of 1056 Gruffyđ (who was probably dissatisfied with the arrangements of the year before) again

---

[1] "Eng. Chron.," s.a. 1055.

[2] "Eng. Chron.," s.a. 1055. Cf. "Brut.," s.a. 1054. This entry describes the engagement as a "severely hard battle," and says the Saxons took to flight unable to bear the assault of the Britons, and fell with a very great slaughter.

[3] "Eng. Chron.," s.a. 1055.

invaded south-west Mercia.   He was met by the new
Bishop—who had worn "his knapsack during his priesthood till he was a bishop," and then "forsook his chrism
and his rood, his ghostly weapons, and took to his
spear and sword after his bishophood"—and Ælfnoth,
the Sheriff, at the head of the Mercian forces, eight days
before Midsummer.[1]   Gruffyd was again victorious; both
the Bishop and the Sheriff were slain, and with them
"many good men."   Gruffyd seems to have followed up
his success, for the English chronicler found it "difficult
to tell the distress, and all the marching and all the
camping, and the travail and destruction of men and
also of horses which all the English army sustained."
But Leofric, Harold, and Bishop Ealdred of Worcester
came to Gruffyd and succeeded, though we know not on
what terms, in quieting him.   A reconciliation was effected,
and Gruffyd swore oaths that he would be to King
Edward "a faithful and unbetraying under-king."[2]

Two years after this event, however, it is recorded in the
"Brut" that Magnus, son of Harold, described as "king of
Germany," came to England and ravaged the dominions of
the Saxons, and that Gruffyd was his "conductor and
auxiliary."[3]   The English Chronicle says that a fleet came
from Norway in 1058, but does not connect this event with
Gruffyd; but that there were hostilities between him and
the English in that year is clear, for Ælfgar the Earl, who
succeeded his father on his death in 1057, was banished, but
soon returned, with the aid of his son-in-law.[4]   The Welsh
king was now at the height of his power.   So long as Ælfgar
lived, however, he seems to have kept the peace.   Harold himself had taken possession of the earldom of the Magesaetas

---

1 "Eng. Chron.," *s.a.* 1056.
2 "Eng. Chron.," *s.a.* 1056.
3 "Brut," *s.a.* 1056.   In "Ann. Cam.," seemingly 1058.
4 "Eng. Chron.," *s.a.* 1058.

and the course of the Severn (*i.e.*, south-west Mercia), no doubt with the intention of holding Ælfgar and Gruffyd in check. The exact date of the former's death is not known, but it is probable that he died in 1062. Very likely border raids into England were made by the Welsh, or some other provocation was given by Gruffyd, for in 1063 Harold determined to make a strong attempt to crush his dangerous and now too formidable neighbour. The chief palace of Gruffyd was at Rhudlan, which was a site of military value, since it dominated the Vale of Clwyd, and was then a seaport. It was against Rhudlan that Harold directed his first blow. With a small band (probably his own house-carls) he hastened there at the end of 1062, and surprised Gruffyd, who, however, escaped by sea. Unable to follow, and not strong enough to winter in North Wales, Harold contented himself with burning the house and the remaining ships, and set out back for Gloucester on the same day.[1] It may be conjectured from the subsequent course of affairs that this event did much to damage Gruffyd's prestige among the loosely united Welsh clans, and especially among the uchelwyr of South Wales. Such a career as his, in the circumstances of his time, must have created jealousies and involved the enmity of many families among the Cymry. Only six years had elapsed since the final overthrow of the house of Rhyderch. Many men must have been waiting for the time when a reverse gave a favourable opportunity for revolt.[2]

It was immediately after his sudden raid on Rhudlan that Harold, now the most powerful subject of England—indeed, its real ruler—planned a systematic invasion of Wales. He collected a fleet at Bristol with a view to coasting round the country, while he arranged that his brother Tostig[3] should

[1] Fl. Wigorn, 1063.
[2] Note Giraldus' reference to Gruffyd as one "who by his tyranny for a long time had oppressed Wales": "Itin. Cam.," book i., ch. 2.
[3] Tostig had become Earl of Northumbria.

cross the border from Northumbria with a land force. At
Rogation-tide (in 1063) Harold left Bristol with his fleet and
sailed along the coast, presumably landing at points where
damage could be inflicted on the Welsh.[1]   Tostig, acting
in conjunction with his brother, crossed the border.   For
several weeks the English carried on a vigorous and far-
reaching harrying of Gruffyd's dominions.   There is no
record of any pitched battles, and the warfare was clearly
of the guerilla kind.   Taught by experience, the English
leaders changed their method of fighting.   They made
their men discard armour and give up the close array.[2]
Lightly armed, they fought on the same terms as their
active enemies.   The Cymry defended themselves with
stubbornness, but the English won many skirmishes and
gave no quarter.   The former suffered more severely than
at any time since the death of Cadwaladr.[3]   The campaign
seems to have been carried on over a large part of Wales.
The result was that "the people" (so says the English
Chronicle) made a truce with Harold and delivered
hostages.[4]   Of Gruffyd himself during these weeks in the
summer of 1063 we hear nothing.   Later authority says
the Welsh sentenced him to deposition.   What is certain
is that he was slain in August by Welshmen—slain,
according to the English chronicler, because "of the war
he waged with Harold the Earl"—slain, according to the
Brut, by the treachery of his own men.   "The shield and
defender of the Britons . . . the man who had been hitherto
invincible, was now left in the glens of desolation, after
taking immense spoils and after innumerable victories and
countless treasures of gold and silver, and jewels and purple

---

[1] "Eng. Chron.," *s.a.* 1063.

[2] See Freeman, "N.C.," ii. 480.

[3] Giraldus (writing about 140 years later) says that Harold left scarcely a
man alive in Wales.

[4] "Eng. Chron.," *s.a.* 1063.

vestures."[1] The effects of Harold's merciless ravaging were long felt. His victory plunged Wales once more into confusion, and no doubt contributed to the comparatively swift conquest of a great part of the South by the Normans a few years afterwards.

However ruthless Harold had shown himself in the campaign, so soon as Gruffyd had been got rid of he proceeded to arrange a new settlement of Welsh affairs. The kingdom of the dead chieftain was divided between Bledyn ab Cynfyn and his brother Rhiwatton,[2] but further considerable portions of Cymric land were added to the shires or earldoms on the border. The Vale of Clwyd, or the greater part of it, was added to the shire of Chester, and seemingly passed under the rule of Eadwine, son of Ælfgar, Earl of Mercia. The whole or a large part of what is now Radnorshire became an English possession. Part of Gwent, though we cannot define what part (probably the land between the Wye and the Usk), was united to the earldom of Harold.[3] How far, or in what sense, these lands

---

[1] "Brut.," *s.a.* 1061. "Ann. Cam.," *s.a.* 1063.

[2] The "Brut" and "Ann. Cam." are silent as to this, but the subsequent entries confirm the transaction. The "Worcester Chronicle" (1063) records it—making Bledyn and Rhiwatton *brothers* of Gruffyd; and in the "Brut," *s.a.* 1068, they are referred to as still reigning, and are mentioned as sons of *Cynfyn.* They were really half-brothers of Gruffyd. Their mother was Angharad (daughter of Maredud), who married Lewelyn ab Seisytt, and also Cynfyn. Probably the latter was her second husband. The "Brut," *s.a.* 1112, explains the relationship. See Freeman, "Norman Conquest," ii., p. 483, n. 1. In the "Brut," *s.a.* 1073, Bledyn ab Cynfyn is referred to as "the man who after Gruffyd his brother nobly supported the whole kingdom of the Britons." The Gruffyd referred to is Gruffyd ab Llewelyn.

[3] See Freeman, "N. C.," v. ii., p. 483-6; and note (*uu*) in App., p. 707 (third edition, London, 1877). Harold, it seems, began to build a hunting seat at Porth Iscoed. Caradog, son of that Gruffyd who claimed Deheubarth and who was slain by Gruffyd ab Lewelyn, made a raid upon the workmen engaged in the building, slew nearly all of them, and carried away the provisions and other things that Harold had collected. "Chronn. Ab. et Wig.," 1065; "Domesday," 162: "Sub iisdem præpositis sunt iiii. villæ wastatæ per regem Caradnech."

(except the Vale of Clwyd) had been part of Gruffyd's possessions we have no means of determining ; but it is clear that one of the results of the Earl's successful war was that the English made a further advance on Welsh territory.

There can be no doubt that this comparatively great Welsh campaign largely increased the prestige of Harold and his house, and was one of the circumstances which led to his being elected king on the death of Eadward the Confessor early in 1066. He did not enjoy his high office long, for on the 14th of October in the same year he fell in the battle of Hastings or Senlac, resisting the Norman invasion, and shortly afterwards William, Duke of Normandy, became king of England. We need say nothing for our purpose as to the general circumstances and effect of this Norman conquest, but he who looks at it from a Cymric standpoint will note with curious interest the satisfaction of the Welsh chronicler who records that Harold, who had been previously "vauntingly victorious," was despoiled of his life and kingdom by William the Bastard "Tywysog" of Normandy, and that "that William" defended the kingdom of Loegr in a great battle "with an invincible hand and his most noble army."[1]

As appendices to this chapter we insert in face of this page :—

(A) A Chronological Table of the Kings of England and the Kings or Princes of Gwyned and Deheubarth. The dates of the accession of the latter are taken

---

[1] "Brut," *s.a.* 1066. The last sentence is, "Ar G6ilim h6nn6 dr6y dirua6r ur6ɔ lyr a ymdiffynna6d teyrnas Loegr o an orchyfegedic la6 a uonhedickaf lu" (see "Red Book of Hergest," vol. ii., p. 268 : Oxford edition). Though at the time Loegr denoted much the same area of the island as England at present, yet it did not connote, when the chronicler wrote, all that the word England does now to us. The notion that William was defending Loegr should be observed. The student should also notice that the application of the term *tywysog* to William in regard to Normandy shows it was then used in a very general sense.

mainly from the " Brut y Tywysogion," but in some instances from the dates placed in brackets in Mr. E. Phillimore's edition of the "Annales Cambriæ."

(B) A Genealogical Table of the House of Rhodri Mawr. This is compiled from the "Brut" and the "Annales," and is, in regard to some of the persons, conjectural, owing to the paucity of the names in use among the Cymry. Where the letter " d." is prefixed in this table to a date it signifies " died." Where a date alone is given it refers to the year of entry in the " Brut."

CHAPTER VI.

THE ANCIENT LAWS AND CUSTOMS OF WALES.

WE have in the preceding chapters set down the scanty facts concerning the history of the Welsh princes before the Norman Conquest that can be gleaned from the authorities to which credit may be reasonably given. Standing alone these facts tell us little; they form only a barren record of men who played their parts in a remote district of Western Europe. Even if we knew them far better, their real interest would lie in the circumstance that they were the chieftains of clans and families which had survived from a distant past, and had established themselves in Wales before the English nation was formed; and to a greater extent still in the further circumstance that, though their descendants have become an integral part of the United Kingdom, they have not lost their national characteristics or the consciousness of their national individuality. Fortunately, manuscripts containing the laws of the people living in some of the small Welsh kingdoms have been handed down to us, and from them we can obtain a fairly clear picture of society in Wales before the conquest of Gwyneđ by Edward I.; and, besides what we can gather from their formal documents, we have in the works of Giraldus Cambrensis much information as to the habits and character of the Cymry in the twelfth century.

Caradog of Ћancarvan states that "Howel Đa constituted and gave lawes to be kept through his dominions which were used in Wales till such time as the inhabitants received the lawes of England in the time of Edward the first, and in some places long after. These lawes are to be seen at this daie both in Latine and in Welsh." To this Powel, the editor, adds a statement of the circumstances attending Howel's legislation.[1]

Though there is not a word of all this in the Brut or Annales, there seems no doubt that the tradition handed down by Caradog of Llancarvan records a real historical transaction. The supersession of Celtic by Latin Christianity led to the spread of the Roman organisation into Wales, and to the more extensive knowledge and use of collections of canons and penitential books among the Cymry.[2] It must thus have had the effect of familiarising the minds of tribal rulers with the advantage of having a written law. Furthermore, some conflict between the Roman code of morals and the tribal or customary system naturally arose, and the clergy found the reduction

---

[1] This seems taken from the preface to one of the codes.

[2] It should be observed, too, that there were canons and penitentials of Welsh or British origin earlier than the submission of the Welsh clergy to Rome. The *Prefatio Gildae de penitentia* is a fragment that is assigned to a date before 570 (Haddan and Stubbs's "Councils, &c." i., p. 113). *Excerpta quaedam de libro Davidis* consists of sixteen canons supposed to be extracted from the *Liber* of St. David, and to be of a date between 550 and 600 (*ibid.*, i., p. 118). *Sinodus Aquilonis Britanniæ* and *Altera sinodus luci Victoriæ* contain canons apparently affecting to have been adopted at two synods held in 569, during the lifetime of St. David, at Landewi Brefi, in Cardiganshire, and not far from the Roman station called Loventium in the Itineraries (*ibid.*, i., p. 117 ; Lewis's Topographical Dict. of Wales). The date 569 comes from the " Ann. Cambr.," as printed in Mon. Hist. Brit., but in the MS. of the same chronicle, edited and published in " Y Cymmrodor," v. ix., by Mr. E. Phillimore, there is no entry as to these synods. *Canones Wallici* form a collection of laws of a civil rather than ecclesiastical character. They probably belong to the first half of the seventh century, and in Haddan and Stubbs's opinion are of Welsh origin ("Councils, &c.," i., p. 127). Several of these canons are identical, or nearly identical, with texts to be found in one of the Latin MSS. of the Welsh Laws, printed in A. Owen's edition of the " Ancient Laws, &c., of Wales." See " Anc. Laws," ii., pp. 875-6 ; and *cf.* " Councils, &c.," i., pp. 127 *et seq.*

of traditional rules to writing one means of increasing their power. Even if a powerful and progressive chieftain had no example to follow, one would not be surprised to find that under the circumstances in which Howel was placed, the idea should occur that it would be expedient to set down the principal rules governing his own household, and regulating the concerns of the district over which he exercised tribal rights. In fact, however, any chieftain who had the opportunity of coming in contact with kings and lords of countries or districts in which the laws had been, to a greater or less extent, written down, and had obtained the sanction which in those days was attached to manuscripts, might naturally feel a desire to act upon the precedents set by those neighbours for whom he had either admiration or respect. Howel had, as we have seen, opportunities of meeting the English kings, and perhaps he had made a pilgrimage to Rome.

We find, too, that there was throughout the whole of Western Europe in the ninth and tenth centuries a strong tendency to the making of so-called codes. Probably this tendency had its immediate origin in the foundation of the Karlovingian Empire, in the legislation of Karl the Great, and in the notion that smaller rulers and chieftains could not do better than imitate one whose deeds and fame were so great, and whose prowess and wisdom were fast becoming legendary and heroic. Certainly we find in the most unexpected places in the two centuries that follow the coronation of Karl the Great, attempts to reduce customary law to written law. There is, therefore, a fair probability in favour of the genuineness of the tradition that couples the name of Howel Ða with the reduction of Welsh tribal customs into a rigid and formal written system.

The preamble prefixed to each of the codes that has been handed down to us in substance (though in varying language) records that Howel summoned four men from each cantref in his dominions to the Ty Gwyn, which is identified by modern antiquaries and far-reaching tradition with Whitland in Carmarthenshire. It is unnecessary to inquire whether the details given in the different recensions of the code are absolutely accurate. The notion that there is any similarity between such a gathering and later mediæval Parliaments is obviously unfounded. Not only does our general knowledge prohibit the placing of any such interpretation upon the transaction, but the specific information afforded to us from later sources that the making of laws was a prerogative of the princes clearly shows it to be untenable. Moreover, the similarity of these preambles with those prefixed to other compilations, collectively called, in opposition to the civil and canon law, *leges barbarorum*, is inconsistent with this idea, and leads to the inference that some churchman, probably the Blegywryd (archdeacon of Llandaff), mentioned in the manuscripts of some of the codes, acquainted with similar books, had a large share in the actual transcription of that compilation which by the Welsh is called "hen lyfr y Tygwyn." This ancient manuscript has not come down to us, and what we have is a number of manuscripts of considerably later dates, presenting a general similarity in substance combined with considerable differences in detail.

These manuscripts appear to be transcripts of older books, which had probably received additions from time to time either authoritative, as coming from a ruler, or as being the notes of judges or lawyers who had become the possessors of documents which were naturally, from the difficulty of reproduction and the paucity of their number, extremely valuable.

The earliest edition in print of these laws is the work published in 1730 by Wotton with the assistance of Moses

Williams and Clarke.[1] In this volume no attempt is made
to separate or classify those manuscripts which apply to
different parts of the Principality. It was reserved for
Aneurin Owen, who was commissioned to edit and publish
the Welsh laws for the Record Commissioners, to make
the discovery that in fact the MSS. fell into three classes
—namely, those embodying the customs of Gwyned, of
Demetia, and of Gwent respectively.[2]

The work of Aneurin Owen, entitled "The Ancient Laws
and Institutes of Wales," was published in 1841, and is at
present the best and authoritative edition of these laws.[3]

We cannot describe at any length the contents of these
volumes. The first contains (a) the Venedotian Code ; (b) the

[1] Wotton (William), D.D. "Cyfreithyeu Hywel Dda ac eraill seu leges
Wallicæ Ecclesiasticæ et Civiles Hoeli Boni et Aliorum Walliæ Principum
quas ex variis Codicibus Manuscriptis erint, Interpretatione Latina, Notis et
Glossario illustravit Gulielmus Wottonus, S.T.P., adjuvante Mose Gulielmo,
A.M., R.S. Soc. Qui et Appendicem adjecit." Londini : Typis Gulielmi
Bowen, mdccxxx. fo.

[2] See as to this point App. D.

[3] Owen (Aneurin) : "Ancient Laws and Institutes of Wales ; comprising
Laws supposed to be enacted by Howel the Good, modified by subsequent
regulations under the native Princes prior to the conquest by Edward the First ;
and anomalous laws consisting principally of Institutions which by the Statute of
Ruddlan were admitted to continue in force : with an English translation of the
Welsh Text. To which are added a few Latin transcripts containing Digests of
the Welsh Laws, principally of the Demetian Code. With indexes and glossary."
Lond. : Record Commissioners, 1841, fo. Another edition, 2 vols., 8vo,
1841. Something had been done towards making these laws known between
the publication of Wotton's and Owen's work. A portion of the laws was
published in the "Cambrian Register," vols. i. and ii. (Lond., 1795 and
1796), and in the 3rd vol. of the "Myvyrian Archaiology" (Lond. 1807), a
MS. of the Laws, which is termed E in Owen's Preface, was printed, and also
certain pieces headed "Trioedd Cyfraith" and "Trioedd Dyfnwal Moelmud."
See also 2nd ed. of "Myv. Arch." (Denbigh, 1870) ; also Probert (William),
"Ancient Laws of Cambria," &c. (Lond. 1823, 8vo), and Hoüard, "Traités
sur les coutumes Anglo-Normandes publiés en Angleterre depuis le onzième
jusqu'au quatorzième siècle," and "Tableau de mœurs au dixieme siècle, ou la
Cour et des lois de Hoel le Bon, Roi d'Aberfraw de 907–948," &c., by
E. G. Peignot (Paris, 1832). See note above, p. 25, n. 1, as to Owen's
unsatisfactory method of dealing with the MSS.

Demetian Code, and (c) the Gwentian Code. The first is given in the main according to a version in the Black Book of Chirk, a MS. now in the Peniarth collection, which appears to belong to the later part of the twelfth century.[1] The other MSS. of the Venedotian Code belong to the two succeeding centuries. The Demetian Code is printed from a MS. of about the end of the thirteenth century, now in the British Museum. The Gwentian Code comes chiefly from a MS. of the ·fourteenth century. In his second volume, Owen prints two fairly full versions and one incomplete version of these laws from Latin MSS. These Latin texts are of exceptional importance, because the technical terms, which are rendered into Latin, connect the Cymric system in an intelligible way with the systems of other parts of Western Europe. They indeed suggest the question whether, as a result of the celebrated convention of Howel Ða, the laws were not first of all set down in Latin. Blegywryd, archdeacon of Llandaff, mentioned above, was the scribe selected to write the law, as being the most learned in all Cymru (*yr ysgolheic huotlaf o Gymry oll*), after twelve of the wisest of the Assembly had been set apart to make the law (*y deudec doythaf o hyny arneilltu y 6neuthyr y gyfreith*).

Assuming, as we must, that Blegywryd was conversant with the Welsh language, it may be that he recorded the result of the formation of the law by these twelve wise men in Latin, and that the laws so settled were afterwards translated into Welsh. If it be true, as stated in the Preface to the Demetian Code, that Howel and others went to Rome to read the law before the Pope that he might see if there was anything contrary to the law of God in it,[2]

---

[1] So says A. Owen, but we understand that Mr. Gwenogvryn Evans thinks it is later. See, however, App. D. below.

[2] See Owen, i., p. 343. *Cf.* in the Ven. Code the Preface to Book iii., Owen, i., p. 217. The Venedotian Code (Book ii., c. xvi. 2) says, "The ecclesiastical law says again that no son is to have the patrimony but the *eldest*

and obtained the Pope's confirmation, there must have been a Latin version in existence at that time. But according to the Demetian Preface, the king ordered three law-books to be prepared; one for the use of the daily Court, to remain continually with himself; another for the Court of Dinevwr; the third for the Court of Aberffraw,[1] and in one of the MSS. of the Demetian Code, towards the end of the Preface, the names of the twelve laymen who were set apart to make the law—a kind of committee—are given.[2] The statements of this Preface (seemingly compiled at different times, and not affecting to be the Preface of the original book) are to some extent confirmed by the Preface to the third book of the Venedotian Code.[3]

There Iorwerth. ab Madog is represented as having collected the Book (*i.e.*, the third or Proof Book) from the Book of Cyvnerth ab Morgeneu, and from the Book of Gwair ab Rhuvon, and from the Book of Goronwy ab Moreidig,[4] and the old Book of the White House ("a hen lyfr y Ty Gwyn"); and, in addition to those, from the best books he found likewise in Gwyned, Powys, and Deheubarth. There is no improbability in all this; for the books of the lay Welsh judges or lawyers cannot have

born to the father by the *married* wife; the law of Howel, however, adjudges it to the youngest son as well as the eldest, and decides that sin of the father or his illegal act is not to be brought against the son as to his patrimony." This important difference between the law of the Church and the law of Howel, of course, is evidence against the story that the latter had received Papal confirmation.

[1] Owen, i., p. 340.

[2] It may be worth while to note them :—" Morgeneu, the judge; Cyvnerth his son; Gwair, son of Rhuvon; Goronwy, son of Moreidig; Cewyd, the judge; Idig, the judge; Gwiberi the aged; Gwrnerth the grey, his son; Medwon, son of Cerisc; Gwgon of Dyfed; Bledrws, son of Bleidyd; Gwyn, the maer, the man who was the owner of Glantavwyn, to whom the house belonged in which the law was made."

[3] Owen, i., pp. 216—218.

[4] It will be noticed that Cyvnerth, Gwair, and Goronwy are three of the twelve laymen referred to in the Demetian Preface. See note 2 above.

been in Latin, and so we may take it that men who had actually taken part in the convention at the White House had in their possession MSS. of the law in the Welsh language. This is not, of course, inconsistent with there having been a contemporary Latin version.[1]

There is, however, great reason for doubting whether Howel's visit to Rome had any connection with his legislation. The story as given in the Preface to the Demetian Code is as follows :—"After the law had been made and written, Howel, accompanied by princes of Cymru, and Lambert bishop of Menevia, and Mordav bishop of Bangor, and Cebur bishop of St. Asaph, and Blegywryd archdeacon of Llandaff, went to Rome to Pope Anastatius to read the law and to see if there were anything contrary to the law of God in it ; and as there was nothing militating against it,[2] it was confirmed, and was called the law of Howel Da from that time forward." The only Anastatius who was Pope during Howel's time was Anastatius III., who held the Papacy from 909 to 911. Both the Brut and Annales record that Howel went to Rome ; the former puts the date as 926 and the latter two years later. The Venedotian and Demetian Prefaces describe Howel as king of all Cymru,[3] but it seems clear he was not in possession of Gwyned till Idwal died in 941.[4] Even,

---

[1] For some further observations on the question whether the laws were first written down in Latin, see App. D.

[2] This was not, however, the case. See below, p. 210.

[3] The Gwentian Preface simply calls him king of Cymru.

[4] The Demetian Preface adds to the account of the journey to Rome : " The year of the Lord Jesus Christ at that time 914. And here are the verses composed by Blegywryd thereupon in testimony of that event :—

> Explicit editus legibus liber bene finitus
> Quem regi scripcit Blangoridus et quoque fuit
> Hweli turbe doctor tunc legis in urbe
> Cornando cano tunc judice cotidiano
> Rex dabit ad partem dexteram nam sumerat artem."

These verses, in a very slightly different form, are to be found in a Latin MS. in the Bodleian (A. Owen's Preface, p. xxxiii.). The text adds " Gornerth

therefore, if the story of the visit to Rome to get the Pope's confirmation be true, we cannot accept the date assigned or the name of the Pope as accurate. We see no reason to doubt that Howel paid a visit to Rome, as mentioned in the Chronicles; but, seeing that Idwal was then reigning in Gwyneđ, we think it unlikely that the Ty Gwyn convention could have been held before that event, for men from the cymwds of the North were summoned by Howel to attend it—a course which could hardly have been taken by the South Welsh prince without difficulties with his North Welsh cousin had the latter been then alive. The most probable date of the transaction we are considering is therefore 942 or 943, and the notion that Howel's visit to Rome had anything to do with his law-making looks like a later invention.[1]

The contents of Owen's second volume (apart from the Latin versions of the laws of Howel Đa and the statute of Rhuđlan) are not of the same interest or importance as the codes. They consist of comparatively late legal maxims, commentaries, and illustrations, which supplement and explain, without essentially modifying, the codes. He also prints specimens of pleadings and other matter of interest. From a literary point of view Book xiii., entitled "Trioeđ Dyvnwal Moelmud a elwir Trioeđ y cludau a Thrioeđ y cargludau" (*i.e.*, "the triads of Dyfnwal Moelmud, which are called the triads of motes and triads of car-motes"),[2]

ħ6ýd mab G6yberi bach (cornandus canus filius gwiberi parvi) erat judex curiæ de Dinevwr in tempore Hywali Da." As to the status of the Judge of the Court. see below, p. 198.

[1] It should be noticed that in the Venedotian Preface there is not a word said about the visit to Rome or the Papal confirmation.

[2] See Owen, vol. ii., p. 474. For further remarks on these triads and Owen's translation of the title, see Appendix D, below, p. 648. On p. 482 the second set of triads are called "the triads of the social and federate state; and which are the ancient triads of the privileges and customs of the Cymry before they lost their privilege and their crown, through the rapacity, fraud, and treachery of the Saxons."

naturally attracts attention. The tract is printed from a MS. which concludes thus: " And I, Evan son of Evan oi Trev Bryn in Morganwg, transcribed this from the old books of Sir Edward Mansell of Margam, when the year of Christ our Lord was 1685." We may believe that Evan ab Evan was not the author; but the style and the internal evidence show that the work is not one to which any great age can be ascribed. The whole production is unlike in style to the genuine law-books that have survived, and seems more a literary exercise than a practical treatise. The author, however, was acquainted with the old Welsh legal system and its technical terms, and many of the triadic texts embody really ancient maxims. No great weight can, however, be attached to the treatise. So far as it agrees with the codes it has no special value; when its texts differ from the codes, or extend the doctrines they state expressly or impliedly, they cannot be deemed to have any more authority than may be given to a late commentary not prepared for practical use; especially as there is a good deal that suggests that the real object of the writer was to magnify the importance and status of the bards in the old Welsh polity.

To sum up, we may say :—

The oldest MS. of the laws of Howel being of the twelfth century, we may be sure that we have no authentic copy of the old Book of the White House. The earliest MSS. bear marks of having had themselves a history. The Black Book of Chirk refers to amendments made by Bleđyn ab Cynfyn, who reigned from 1063 to 1073, and the thirteenth century MS. of the Demetian Code makes mention of alterations and additions by Lord Rhys ab Gruffyđ, who flourished from 1137 to 1197. But there is no reason for not carrying back the first setting down in writing of the Welsh customs to the time of Howel Đa.

Nor is there any real doubt that these bodies of law consist of custumals which were once in actual operation.

In support of this the high authority of Sir Henry Maine[1] may be cited, and apart from authority the fact that the documents disclose a fairly complete system of legal terminology in the Cymric language, while the general contents describe a tribal system such as what is known of other races leads us to think may have been in force among the Cymric people, is practically conclusive of the genuineness of these laws.[2]

Much controversy has arisen upon the question whether the English law is, as a whole, derived from Welsh law, or whether these Welsh laws are simply conscious imitations of the Anglo-Saxon laws. We do not affect to enter upon this question, but we may observe that we think it extremely likely that there were survivals of British customs among the people who afterwards became consolidated into the English-Norman kingdom. On the other hand, we think it quite probable, and in some instances certain, that Howel or those who assisted him intentionally adopted some rules or descriptions either from English or foreign bodies of written law. It cannot escape notice that in precisely that part of the codes where we might expect imitation and legislation in the modern sense of the term, that is, the making of new rules for changed

---

[1] "Early History of Institutions," pp. 5, 6.

[2] As to the interpretation of these Welsh Laws the following works should be consulted :—Seebohm's "Tribal System in Wales," and "The English Village Community" ; Palmer's "History of Ancient Tenures in the Marches of North Wales" ; Hubert Lewis's "Ancient Laws of Wales," edited by Professor Lloyd, M.A. ; Ashton's "Hywei Ða a'i Gyfreithiau" ; Walter's "Das Alte Wales" ; De Valroger's "Les Celtes : La Gaule Celtique" ; Skene's "Celtic Scotland" ; Fowler's "Some Account of the Ancient Laws and Institutes of Wales" ; Brynmor-Jones's "The Study of the Welsh Laws" (articles in Cymru Fyð, 1889), and "The Criminal Law of Mediæval Wales" (South Wales University College Magazine, 1890). See also Glasson's "Histoire du Droit et des Institutions de l'Angleterre," iii., pp. 609 *et seq. ;* Warrington's "History of Wales," pp 164-190 ; and Meyrick's "History of Cardiganshire," Int., pp. lxvii.-lxxi. For particulars of some of these works see Appendix to Report, pp. 81-2.

circumstances, there is a remarkable similarity with the corresponding part of the Karlovingian system. If it be true, as indicated above, that Howel had obtained the rule, or rather over-lordship of the whole of Wales, we might easily understand that one of the first things which would occupy his attention would be the organisation of his own Court or household ; and it is, in at least one of the codes, the completeness with which the rights and duties of the king himself, of members of his family, of his servants and attendants, are set forth that first strikes the reader. Now, here in this organisation we find a noticeable resemblance to the organisation created by Karl the Great. Probably this emperor and his advisers had themselves before their eyes the model of the Byzantine Court, but, however this may be, one cannot help coming to the conclusion that, directly or indirectly, the Welsh organisation was very largely influenced by intentional imitation of the Karlovingian precedent. We have no means, of course, of determining whether the model which Howel and his assistants set before them was the Frankish system or the Court of Æthelstan, but we are inclined to think that what is found in these Welsh books is not wholly derived from observation of the l tter.

But in regard to other portions of the customary system disclosed in what we may, without inaccuracy, call Howel's legislation, the traces of conscious imitation from other sources are few, if any. One is rather struck, when comparing them with the so-called Anglo-Saxon laws, say the laws of Edward the Confessor, with dissimilarities rather than with similarities. No doubt many notions and conceptions are very like in or common to both sets of laws, but the same is true as between the Welsh laws and the Irish laws. It would be in our judgment entirely wrong to infer an English derivation from mere identity or similarity of usage and idea. The truth seems rather to be that

all the races forming part of the Indo-European group
started with common ideas of duty and of tribal organisation
In some cases the process of disintegration of the tribal
system proceeded more rapidly than in others ; in one
case the line of development went in one, and in another
in another direction.   Or, possibly, while the process of
evolution was the same in every case, while every race went
through the same typical changes or stages of growth, circumstances interfered to alter the rate of the process.
Howsoever this may be, forming the best judgment we
can, we think that these ancient Welsh laws are truthful
evidence of the condition of society during the centuries
in which they were in operation in Wales and Monmouthshire, and that, apart from the organisation of the Court,
they represent a natural and spontaneous growth of
civilisation among the Cymric tribes.

Treating, then, these compilations as authentic evidence
of the condition of the Cymry in the tenth century, we are
enabled to draw a picture of society in its broad outlines in
the days of Welsh independence.   Looking at the system
as a whole it must be described as still tribal. Political
and property rights, as well as the status of individuals,
depended upon a theory of blood relationship.   The whole
community is looked upon as an aggregate of tribes or
clans and families, forming a ruling aristocracy, under whom
other classes of lower status are grouped.   The form of
government, so far as the term " government " can be used
at all, was monarchical.   In theory the king of Gwyneð or
Aberffraw was head of the organisation.[1]   He himself

---

[1] This seems to have been a principle of the Welsh law.   It is Mr. Seebohm's
view ("Tribal System in Wales," pp. 135—6) ; but the codes give no certain
evidence on the point.   The most explicit text seems that in Book x. of the
"Anomalous Laws" (Owen, vol. ii., p. 585).   There Aberffraw is said to receive
Mechdeyrn dues from Dinevwr (South Wales) and from Gwynva (Powys), and
the king of Loegr is to receive three-score and three pounds from the king of
Aberffraw.

recognised the over-lordship of the king of England. Regularly, all other chieftains, princes, or kings in Cymru were subject to the lord of Aberffraw. The result is that there was a more or less well-understood hierarchy of kings or princes, which presents remarkable analogies to a feudal kingdom. In the chronicles sometimes one individual is represented as king over the whole of Wales. We have seen that Howel Ða is an instance in point, but there were always other kings or princes who are represented as exercising power in different districts of the territory, and enjoying various regal privileges and prerogatives. There does not appear to have been any alteration in theory caused by the division and re-division of the existing Cymric districts among the kingly families. What is really meant by saying that Howel Ða was lord of all Wales is that certain districts usually held by kings or princes of other royal or princely kinsmen were possessed directly by Howel, who received the dues and enjoyed the privileges ordinarily received and enjoyed by the latter. That is, it really amounted to Howel's taking possession of all the rights and privileges of the king of Powys and the king of Gwyneð as well as those of the king of South Wales. The kingship of Powys and the kingship of Gwyneð were assumed to continue to exist, though the kingship was in the hands of one man. Similar later instances of an analogous kind readily present themselves, *e.g.*, after the conquest of Wales the mere attainder of a lord of Glamorgan, and the consequent forfeiture of his possessions to the Crown, followed by the king's taking possession, did not amount to an extinction of the lordship; it simply came to the king's administering Glamorgan until he re-granted it to one of his subjects. Whatever the theory, the state of Cymru was as a rule very unsettled and sometimes anarchical. The position and rights of its kings and its political organisation, cannot be understood without reference to the territorial divisions of and the different classes of persons in the country.

Cymru was divided into the districts called *cantrefs* and *cymwds*, the origin and character of which we have discussed above. The exact significance of the cantref it is very difficult to determine, for in the laws we are dealing with it is the cymwd which is the unit of organisation. In the time of Howel the boundaries of the cantrefs and cymwds were evidently known and settled for practical purposes. To understand the method of government from day to day the cymwd is the area on which one must fix one's eye. The cantref, as it then existed, was in all probability a district over which a lord (*arglwyd*), appointed by the king of the country (*gwlad*) of which it formed part, ruled with a set of officers whose rights and duties corresponded with those of the king's household. The lord of a cantref or cymwd must not be confounded with another kind of chieftain, the head of a kindred (*cenedl*) with whom the laws make us acquainted. The lord might, of course, be a *penkenedl* in reference to his own kindred, but his position as *arglwyd* was due, as it would seem, to his appointment by the king of, or the royal kindred ruling over, the country in which the cantref or cymwd was situate. Sometimes several cantrefs were combined under one lord who called himself *tywysog* (prince) or *brenin* (king), but in any case, if we may judge from the laws, each cymwd and cantref maintained its separate organisation. The lord delegated to certain officers the discharge of some of his functions. In every cymwd there was a *maer* (in the Latin text, *præpositus*) and a *canghettor* (in the Latin text, *cancellarius*), discharging prescribed governmental duties, and in each cymwd a court was held by them with the aid of other officers.

We cannot here attempt to give a complete analysis or full exposition of the legal system developed in these treatises; nor do we think it necessary, until they have been further examined and studied, to suggest the points of comparison between them and the Irish and early English laws. We do not in the least wish to disparage the value of "the comparative method" in its application to the history of institutions; but before we can compare systems with a view to generalisation we ought to know a good deal about the systems themselves—a thing surely obvious enough but often forgotten. So what we wish to do now is to show the leading features of the Cymric law as we find them in these old books.

As might have been expected, the codes disclose communities containing different classes of persons, or perhaps we ought to say, different castes. Speaking broadly, *braint* (status) depended on birth. The primary distinction is between tribesmen and non-tribesmen, between men of Cymric and those of non-Cymric blood. The Cymry themselves were divided into: (1) a royal class consisting of men belonging to families or kindreds (*cenedloed*) of kingly or princely *braint* (status) who had over divers areas of Cymru special rights; (2) a noble class called in the codes sometimes *uchelwyr* (literally, "high-men"), sometimes *brëyriaid*, sometimes *gwyrda*, and in the Latin versions *nobiliores* and *optimates;* and (3) innate tribesmen styled *bonedigion* (gentlemen).

Below the tribesmen in the scale were unfree persons denominated *taeogion* or *eilltion* (in Latin, *nativi* or *villani*), corresponding roughly to the villeins of English law. Lowest of all was a class of menial or domestic slaves (*caethion*).[1]

---

[1] *Taeog* is of the same origin as *ty* (house), and was probably suggested by *villanus*. *Alltud* means one of another people or country—a foreigner, and is equivalent to Anglo-Saxon *el-theod*. It has nothing to do with *aillt*, which in the early laws is usually *mab eyllt* (*eigyll*), or *mab eill* or *mab eillt*=a shaven fellow—*i.e.*, a slave, plural *meybyon eillion*. The later spellings *mab aillt* and *aillt* without the *mab*, plural *eillion*, make their appearance in the Triads. The word has its congeners in *eillio* (the act of shaving), and *ellyn* (a razor), Irish *altan*.

But quite apart from these—the primary classes contemplated—forming the legal organisation, the laws deal with strangers residing temporarily in or settling within the limits of a Cymric area. Such strangers were called *alltudion*, and though there was some similarity in the position of the two classes, they must not be confounded with the *eilttion*.

The degree of the *alltud* in his own country made no necessary difference to his position in the Cymric system. If a Mercian, whether noble or non-noble, settled in Gwyned, he was in either case an *alltud*. For the individual the line that separated him and the Cymro could not originally be passed.[1] But there is evidence to show that, in regard to South Wales, the residence in Cymru of an *alltud* and his descendants continued till the ninth generation conferred Cymric status upon the family ; and also that intermarriage with innate Cymraeses generation after generation made the descendants of an *alltud* innate Cymry in the fourth generation. Late texts give also examples of artificial methods of securing Cymric kinship, *e.g.*, by joining a kindred in the work of avenging the death of a kinsman.

The Cymry of full blood deemed themselves descended from a common ancestor ; but they were divided into numerous kindreds, each of which formed a kind of privileged oligarchy, but subordinate to the kindreds of royal status.

The kindred (*cenedl*) was an organised and self-governing unit, having at its head a *penkenedl* (chief of the kindred). The Welsh *cenedl* comprised the descendants of a common ancestor to the ninth degree of descent. The penkenedl, say the Laws, must not be either a maer or canghellor of the king, but an uchelwr of the country; and his status must not be acquired by maternity. He has to pay a

---

[1] It would seem, however, that if the king conferred office on him, he assumed the *braint* (status, privilege) attaching to it.

tribute yearly to the arglwyđ or higher chieftain. He must
be an efficient man, being the eldest of the efficient men of
the kindred, and being the chief of a household (*penteulu*),
or a man with a wife and children by legitimate marriage.
He was assisted by three other officers, the representative
(*teisbanteulu*) whose duty was to mediate in Court and
assembly, and in combat within the tribe, and to act for
the kindred in every foreign affair ; the avenger (*dialwr*) who
led the kindred to battle, and pursued evil-doers, brought
them before the Court, and punished them according to its
sentence ; the avoucher (*arđelwr*), who seemingly entered
into bonds and made warranty on behalf of the kindred.

Under the penkenedl were grouped the chiefs of household belonging to the kindred, and every one of the kindred
was a man and a kin to him (*yn wr ac yn gar iđo*).

We are now, in the light of these legal rules, able to form
a fairly clear notion of the original Cymric *cenedl*. Considered at any one moment in the abstract, it consisted of
a group of blood relations descended from a common
ancestor. Observed in more concrete fashion, it was an
aggregate of families residing in separate homesteads, at
the head of each of which was a *penteulu* (chief of the
household). It was a self-governing unit under the chieftainship of the penkenedl, assisted by the officers and for
some purposes by a council of elders.

There seems to have been some kind of court for
redressing wrongs done by members of one household to
members of another household within the *cenedl ;* but the
discipline of each household was maintained by its *penteulu*
(chief of the household). The household in its structure
resembled the "patriarchal family" under a *patria potestas*
more nearly than the "joint family" of some systems, with
its joint ownership under a chief who is only *primus inter
pares.*[1] The sanctity of each hearth was respected, and

[1] Seebohm, "Tribal System," p. 95.

each *penteulu* had a right of *nawd* (protection) within
defined limits, which varied according to his status.

It should be noticed that according to the fundamental
ideas of this system the *cenedl* was not a rigid or final
corporation or entity formed once for all ; it was an
ever-changing organism ; every *penteulu* was a possible
founder of a complete *cenedl.* As Mr. Seebohm says, the
tribal system was "always forging new links in an endless
chain, and the links of kindred always overlapped one
another."[1] Furthermore, it should be remarked that the
kindreds, the chiefs of which were uchelwyr, were subordinate in the complete structure of Cymric society to kindreds
built up in analogous fashion of the privileged or royal
status, the members of which in theory could trace their
descent from Cuneda the gwledig.

Such being, so far as we may infer it with some confidence from these laws, the original structure of the Cymric
cenedl, we observe that the system (except, perhaps, so far
as the theory of *tir gwelyawg*[2] is an essential part of it) has
no necessary connection with any particular area. It seems
indeed as well adapted for a nomadic as for a settled race,
and is a personal rather than a territorial organisation. But
it is evident the final settlement of the kindreds in a given
territory, even if that territory were previously unoccupied,
would lead to gradual modifications of custom, and the alterations would come more speedily when the tribe or tribes to
which the kindreds belonged conquered and settled upon
land already in the possession of men of other races who
were not extirpated, but placed in an inferior position by the
victorious immigrants. This probability is confirmed by the
laws of Howel. As we have seen, when the laws were set
down in writing, the Cymry had been settled in Wales for
several centuries, and the codes show that great changes

[1] "Tribal System," p. 85.
[2] *I.e.*, family-land. See below, p. 220.

must have taken place in the legal system. Many of the privileges and functions formerly appertaining to the *penkenedl* had come to belong to the *arglwyd* (lord) of the cymwd. There had arisen a court of the cymwd regulated by a *maer* and *canghellor* (officers appointed by an *arglwyd* or the king or prince above him); the canghellor had the right to appoint a *rhingyll* (the summoner of the court—seemingly a registrar or clerk). The two chief officers superintended the eilltion or taeogion, and they had to see that the king's rights in his waste land in the cymwd were respected. The son of an uchelwr[1] or innate bonedig at fourteen became the man of the *arglwyd* of the cymwd, and at twenty-one received land from him in consideration of military service.[2] In South Wales the uchelwyr of the cymwd were judges in its court.[3] The chiefs of household had become practically landowners as against all the world, except members of the household. The rights of the chief of household to his *tydyn*, and the lands in the occupation of himself and other members of his household were termed his *gwely* (literally, "bed or couch"), and on his death the family land was divided between his descendants in the manner described below.[4] So that it seems safe to say that the

---

[1] See the chapter on the Duties of the Maers and Canghellors, "Anc. Laws," i. p. 188.

[2] "Anc. Laws," i., p. 90; ii., p. 211.

[3] "Anc. Laws," ii., p. 567. In Gwyned and Powys, it is said, in the Demetian Code, the king placed five officers in each court—a *maer*, *canghellor*, *rhingyll* (summoner), a priest to write pleadings, and one judge by virtue of office; and four like the preceding in each court in South Wales, and many judges, that is, every owner of land, as they were before the time of Howel the Good, by privilege of land without office. "Anc. Laws," i. 405.

[4] There might be several *tydynau* (homesteads) on the land occupied by a penteulu and his family. They seem to have had grazing rights over sometimes several and distant districts. The descendants of the penteulu were, during his life, in a subordinate position as to land. They had rights of maintenance, and were capable of owning *da* (cattle or movable property), and they had rights of grazing cattle in the common herd and of co-aration with the other members

cymwd approximated to the manor or lordship of English law, though its structure in the tenth century appears to have been a natural development, and not an imitation of other systems ; and that the relations of the king to the *arglwydi*, and of the latter to the men óf the cymwd, were tending to become of a feudal character.

But though the *cenedl* was by the time of Howel to some extent disintegrated, and the general organisation of Cymric society had assumed a territorial aspect, it still played an important part in the legal system and was recognised for certain purposes. Now we may here mention that within the *cenedl* (*i.e.*, kindred to the ninth degree from the common ancestor), smaller groups of kinsmen were looked upon as what we may call, for want of a better term, legal entities. These were groups of the kindred to the fourth and the seventh degrees of descent from a common ancestor. The first group included a given person, his sons, his grandsons, and his great-grandchildren. This group formed the unit within which succession to land of the *gwely* of the given person could take place according to certain rules. It was also the group of kinsmen upon which joint responsibility for personal injuries short of homicide rested ; or in other words if a man did a wrong

of the gwely (Seebohm, "Tribal System," p. 91). *Tydyn* seems to mean a "house-hill," *i.e.*, a place suited for a house. *Ty* (a house), in Old Welsh, *tig*, is for *tegios*, corresponding to the Greek, τέγος (a house). From the word *tig* is partly derived the word *tydyn*, pl. *tydynau*. *Tydyn* occurs in the Laws (ii. 780) as *tygdyn*, and its *dyn* is perhaps the Welsh equivalent of the Irish *dinn* (a place, *i.e.*, *edificia patris sui*). The Gwentian version has *eissydyn* (Laws, i. 750, 760) : see also Laws, ii. 686, 688, where we have *essydyn*, which is in the present day reduced to *sydyn*. This involves an *s* form corresponding to Greek στέγος as contrasted with τέγος with, perhaps, a prefix *ad* or *ecs ;* but *eissydyn*, *sydyn* seems to have the same meaning as *tydyn*, the difference being one of dialect. In modern Welsh place-names *tydyn* is reduced to *tyn*, as in *Tyn yr Onnen* for *Tydyn yr Onnen*, and *Tyn Siarlas* for *Tydyn Siarlas* (Charles' tenement). See as to the meaning and use of *din*, Professor Lloyd's paper on "Welsh Place-names" in "Y Cymmrodor," xi. 22 ; and Mr. E. Phillimore's note, *ibid.*, p. 60.

to another which came within the definition of *saraad* (literally, "insult"), his kinsmen, as far as second cousins, were jointly liable with him for the payment of the prescribed compensation in cattle or money.[1] It also seems that this group was responsible for the marriage of daughters.[2] Lastly, as will be made clear below, there was no re-division of the ancestor's *gwely* after the second cousins had divided it, but the members of the group were still liable to jointly warrant their common title to their respective shares.[3]

The functions of the group of kindred extending to the seventh degree of descent can only be properly understood after the law relating to homicide between kindreds has been explained.

Bearing these general principles in mind, let us see what these laws have to say about the royal or princely kindreds. Each of the codes deals first of all with the *Cyvreithiau y Lys* (Laws of the Court), that is, with the organisation of the household of the king, but it is in the Venedotian Code that the matter is best and most fully dealt with. According to that treatise Howel appointed twenty-four servants of the Court, of which the following is a list :—

    (i) PENTEULU (*Chief of the Household*).
    (ii) EFFEIRYAT TEULU (*Priest of the Household*).
    (iii) DYSTEYN (*Steward*).
    (iv) PENHEBOGYT (*Chief Falconer*).
    (v) BRAHUDUR LYS (*Judge of the Court*).
    (vi) PENGUASTRAHUT (*Chief Groom*).
    (vii) GUASTAVEL (*Page of the Chamber*).

---

[1] " Anc. Laws," i., pp. 231 and 703.

[2] It seems to have formed for this purpose a kind of family council. If they gave a daughter of one within the circle to an attud, and her sons committed a wrong for which *saraad* was payable, the group became liable (" Anc. Laws," i., pp. 208—212). Mr. Seebohm aptly refers to the tale of " Kulhwch and Olwen " in the " Mabinogion." When Yspadaden Penkawr is asked to give his daughter in marriage, he answered, " Her four great-grandmothers and her four great-grandfathers are yet alive ; it is needful that I take counsel of them."

[3] " Anc. Laws," ii. 657 ; and see i., pp. 208-10.

(viii) Bart teulu (*Bard of the Household*).
(ix) Gostechur (*Silentiary*).
(x) Penkynyt (*Chief Huntsman*).
(xi) Medyt (*Mead Brewer*).
(xii) Medyc (*Mediciner*).
(xiii) Trulyat (*Butler*).
(xiv) Drysaur (*Doorward*).
(xv) Coc (*Cook*).
(xvi) Kanuylyt (*Candle-bearer*).

And eight officers of the queen :—

(i) Dysteyn (*Steward*).
(ii) Effeiryat (*Priest*).
(iii) Penguastrahut (*Chief Groom*).
(iv) Guastavel (*Page of the Chamber*).
(v) Lavoruyn (*Handmaid*).
(vi) Drysaur (*Doorward*).
(vii) Coc (*Cook*).
(viii) Kanuylyt (*Candle-bearer*).[1]

The rights, privileges, and duty of each of these officers are gone into with great detail. The names of the offices give sufficient indication of the sphere of work assigned to their holders, except in the case of the chief of the household. The penteulu was required to be of the blood royal, and appears to have had, subject to the king, and especially in the king's absence, the superintendence of the Court. The judge of the Court must not be confounded with the judges of cymwds or cantrefs. He was judge of the king's Court ; "he is to administer justice to the Court, the household, and to whoever pertains to them without fee," but he also on occasion examined other judges, and heard appeals from them, or dispensed justice in conjunction with them.[2]

Besides the twenty-four officers we have enumerated

---

[1] We have given the translation of the Welsh names, following A. Owen. But, of course, the nature of the chief offices becomes more intelligible when we use more courtly terms. Thus, the *Penteulu* is the "Mayor of the Palace," the *Brahudur Lys* "the Chief Justice" or "Justiciary," and the *Penguastrahut* the "Master of the Horse," of corresponding Western European Courts. *Dysteyn*, in Mod. Welsh *distain*, is the Anglo-Saxon *disc-thegn* or *disc-thēn*, literally dish-servant, but meaning at Court "seneschal."

[2] Ven. Code, i., c. xi. ; "Ancient Laws," i., p. 29.

there were eleven servants who are described as officers in the Court by custom and usage: (i.) groom of the rein; (ii.) foot-holder; (iii.) land maer; (iv.) apparitor; (v.) porter; (vi.) watchman; (vii.) woodman; (viii.) baking-woman; (ix.) smith of the Court; (x.) chief of song; (xi.) laundress. The distinction drawn between the first set of officers—those "appointed" by Howel, and the latter class, the customary officers—and the descriptions of the two sets of ministers, indicate that Howel's innovations were intended to increase the pomp of the Court, and also that the authority of the kingly office was being enlarged.

One of the most interesting texts of this Book of the Law is that on *Priodolion Leoed* (appropriate places). It is what in modern times we should call a "table of precedence," and though nominally it only applies to the arrangement of the household at the meals in the king's hall, it really determined and indicated the order of the different officers. The arrangement cannot be understood without stating the character of the house of a Welsh chieftain. Fortunately Giraldus Cambrensis has given us a fairly minute description of the typical Welsh house of his time, and further material for its reconstruction is also furnished by the laws we are considering, so that we can ascertain what it was like in the later period of the tribal system.

The evidence of these two authorities has been summarised by Mr. Seebohm, and we cannot do better than quote his description:[1] "The tribal house was built of trees newly cut from the forest. A long straight pole is selected for the roof-tree. Six well-grown trees with suitable branches, apparently reaching over to meet one another, and of about the same size as the roof-tree, are stuck upright in the ground at even distances in two parallel rows, three in each row. Their extremities bending

[1] See "English Village Community," pp. 239-40; "Report," p. 691.

over make a Gothic arch, and crossing one another at the top each pair makes a fork, upon which the roof-tree is fixed. These trees supporting the roof-tree are called *gavaels*, forks, or columns, and they form the nave of the tribal house. Then, at some distance back from these rows of columns or forks, low walls of stakes and wattle shut in the aisles of the house, and over all is the roof of branches and rough thatch, while at the aisles behind the pillars are placed beds of rushes, called *gwelyau* (*lecti*), on which the inmates sleep. The footboards of the beds between the columns form their seats in the daytime. The fire is lighted on an open hearth in the centre of the nave between the two middle columns."[1] This tribal house was the living and the sleeping place of the household. The kitchen and buildings for cattle and horses were separate and detached, and it seems that, if not the whole set of buildings, yet the set of buildings with more or less completeness was duplicat d for summer purposes on the higher grazing grounds. The house of persons of smaller importance was not, of course, so extensive. Giraldus describes the ordinary house as circular, with the fireplace in the centre and beds of rushes all round it, on which the inmates slept with their feet towards the fire.[2]

In the king's house screens extending from each middle pillar to the side walls divided the hall into an upper and a lower part; the former part appears to have been raised so as to form a daïs, upon which the king and nine of his officers were seated, while in the other part four officers and the rest of the household were placed.[3] The text is curious and deserves attention :—

---

[1] See also "Arch. Cambr." 3rd ser., vol. iv. (1858), p. 195 ; and 4th ser., vol. x. (1893), p. 172. There is some confusion in the words "*gavaels*, forks, or columns" in this passage. *Gavael* means a grasp or hold ; the Welsh for fork is *gavl*.

[2] "Report," p. 692 ; "Gir. Desc. Camb.," i., c. 10 and c. 17.

[3] See "Ancient Laws," vol. i., p. 11, note.

"There are fourteen persons who sit on chairs in the palace; four of them in the lower portion and ten in the upper portion. The first is the king; he is to sit next the screen; next to him the canghellor; then the osb; then the edling; then the chief falconer; the foot-holder on the side opposite the king's dish; and the mediciner at the base of the pillar opposite to him on the other side of the fire. Next to the other screen, the priest of the household, to bless the food and chaunt the *Pater;* the silentiary is to strike the pillar above his head; next to him the judge of the Court; next to him the chaired bard; the smith of the Court on the end of the bench below the priest. The chief of the household is to sit at the lower end of the hall with his left hand to the front door, and those he may choose of the household with him; and the rest on the other side of the door. The bard of the household is to sit on one hand of the chief of the household; the chief groom next to the king, separated by the screen; and the chief huntsman next to the priest of the household, separated by the screen."[1]

These were the rules for Gwyned; in the Demetian Code, as we have it, there is no such elaborate statement, though there is a chapter on appropriate places applying to the ceremony at the three principal festivals, Christmas, Easter, and Whitsuntide.[2]

In regard to this order of precedence we notice first of all the absence of all reference to the queen or other ladies, and we feel inclined to infer from this fact that it has reference, not to the ordinary life of the chieftain and his establishment, but to the formal occasion of some ceremonial Court, probably the solemn meetings of the household on the three principal festivals, of which we have mention, or other similar assemblies. It will

[1] Ven. Code, i., c. 6; "Ancient Laws," i., p. 11.
[2] Dem. Code, i., c. 6; "Ancient Laws," i., p. 351.

in the second place not escape observation that, besides
the officers named in the list we have given above,
there are places assigned to the "canghellor," the "osb,"
and the "edling." The canghellor was not a minister
of the Court (in the sense of the household), but a
territorial officer of the cymwd, though we may assume
that he attended the king's Court when in the due course
of the royal progress it was held in his particular district.
The word "osb" or "hosb" is derived from the Latin *hospes*,
guest, and though used in the singular is to be looked on
as a generic word to cover all guests of high degree present
on any formal occasion on which the full ceremonial was
observed. The "edling," to use the word employed in
Aneurin Owen's translation, is in the Welsh text, "*Gwrthdrych*" (the words "*id est edligg*" are added), and signifies
the heir-apparent—"he who is to reign after the king," and
who "ought to be son or nephew to the king."

In the status of the edling, as described in the Venedotian
Code, we seem to perceive a new order of ideas. Originally
the kingship or chieftainship appears to have been the
"prerogative of a family rather than of a person, and the tie
of blood relationship bound together the head chieftains
and the sub-chieftains and the chiefs of kindred and heads
of households, and whilst the continuity of kindred so
secured throughout the whole hierarchy of chieftains bound
the whole body of tribesmen together by the tie of blood,
the gulf remained as great as ever between the tribesmen
and the strangers in blood." [1] The regal rights were vested
in a *cenedl* (kindred) of royal privilege. [2] This family, as
exhibited in the Codes, consists of the king and his near
relations, and the near relations are defined as his sons,
nephews, and first cousins. The Code says:—

---

[1] Seebohm, "Tribal System," p. 148.
[2] The Welsh word is *braint*. Perhaps *status* is the most correct juridical
term to express what is meant.

"When the edling dies he is to leave his horses and his dogs to the king, for that is the only *ebediw*[1] he is to render; and the reason why he ought to render no other is because he is a near relation of the king. The king's near relations are his sons, his nephews, and his first cousins. Some say that every one of these is an edling; others say that no one is an edling except that person to whom the king shall give hope of succession and designation. . . . The edling and those whom we have above mentioned shall possess that privilege until they obtain land; after that their privilege shall be identified with the privilege of the land they obtain, except they obtain land in villeinage; in that case the privilege of the land shall augment until it become free."[3]

The near relations of the king thus formed an exclusive royal class, and on the death of a king it was from this class that the new king legally came. Seemingly, the king had the right to nominate his successor. The similarity of the position of the Welsh "*Gwrthdrych*" with that of the Irish "*Tanaiste*"[3] should not escape attention.

[1] A render in the nature of a heriot or relief.

[2] "Ancient Laws," i., pp. 9, 11.

[3] With the Cymric family of royal privilege, compare the *ríg domna* (*i.e.*, "the makings" or "materials of a king") or royal class among the Irish. See O'Sullivan's Introduction to "O'Curry's Lectures," pp. ccxxx—ccxxxi. Our information as to the proper devolution of the kingship or chieftaincy is scanty. It seems, however, clear that the royal privileges did not descend according to the rule of primogeniture, and that the lands appurtenant to the kingship were not divided on death like *tir gwelyawg*. The new chieftain was either the *gwrthdrych* nominated by the deceased king from among his "near relations," or else was elected by the members of the royal *cenedl*. Theoretically, the bundle of rights forming the kingship belonged to the *cenedl* collectively. The members of the *cenedl* were entitled to maintenance at court; but the king could grant to any of them the rule over one or more cymwds, or settle them on *tir gwelyawg*, to the possession of which he might be entitled. Such were the rules as we infer them from the Codes, and from what we know as to the actual course of succession in the more peaceable times; but we cannot advance these propositions with certainty. Some light is perhaps thrown on the matter by the Irish system as described in "Le cas de gavelkind," where it is said :—"Before the establishment of the

Any one of the "near relations," until he settled upon land in some cymwd, was maintained at Court. When he settled on land from which a free tribesman's dues issued, he lost his royal status and became a *breyr* or *uchelwr*. But there are indications in the laws that he might be placed at the head of a court (*tỹs*) of a cantref or cymwd, and exercise (subject to the king) regal rights.[1] If, instead of settling on that kind of land which was called *tir gwelyawg* (*i.e.*, family land), he was established on bond land, he lost his status, but in that case his land became free, and he was only liable to pay the *gwestva* and other dues of an *uchelwr*.

The Cymric king, like other monarchs of mediæval times, made progresses through his dominions, which imposed obligations on his subjects. There seems to have been a distinction between the progress for hunting or hawking, or military purposes and the great progress of the household after Christmas. The king's *gosgordᵗ* (retinue) consisted of thirty-six horsemen—the twenty-four chief officers and twelve *guestey* (*i.e.*, probably the persons who brought the entertainment dues, *gwestva*, from each free *maenol* in the cymwd)—together with the rest of the household, the king's *gwyrda* (literally, "good men"), his inferior servants, his ministers, and his almsmen.[2]

Passing on from the men of royal or princely degree we come to the rest of the Cymry proper, the *uchelwyr* and *boneđigion*. They, of course, formed the majority of the race. Their status cannot be fully understood till the rules relating to the possession of land and the way in which it

(English) common law all the possessions within the Irish territories ran either in course of Tanistry or in course of gavelkind. Every Signory or Chiefry, with the portion of land which passed with it, went without partition to the Tanist, who always came in by election or with the strong hand, and not by descent; but all inferior tenantes were partible between males in gavelkind" ("Davis's Reports," Hil. 3 Jac. 1).

[1] See Seebohm, "Tribal System," p. 147.
[2] "Ancient Laws," i., p. 9.

was distributed in each cymwd have been explained. The *uchelwyr* and *boredigion* were all free tribesmen; they were true Cymry; they were, like their royal superiors, grouped into cenedloeđ. They occupied *tyđynau* (homesteads) on the *tir gwelyawg* (free or family land) of the cymwd; and by the time of Howel Đa some of the *uchelwyr* had on their land *eiłłtion* or *taeogion* cultivating the soil on terms analogous to those on which the bond tenants of the bond or register land of the cymwd stood towards the *arglwyđ*. They were liable to military service for six weeks in the year outside the country, and at any time within it. They were competent to take an oath for legal purposes and to be members of the *rhaith gwlad* (literally, "right of the country "),[1] which meant that they were fully entitled to the privileges of the common law of the Cymry. In dealing with the law of property (if we may use the term), we shall make the position of the free tribesman more clear.

The acquisition by the son of a Cymro of full privileges in the cenedl was marked by two stages. First, the infant son was solemnly received into the kindred by his father, or if the father was not alive by the penkenedl with six kinsmen, or if there were no penkenedl, by twenty-one of the best men of the cenedl.[2] From the time of his reception into the kindred the son was maintained by his father, who was "responsible for him in everything," until the child attained the age of fourteen years. Then his father took him originally (as it seems) to the penkenedl, but in the Codes, as we have them, to the arglwyđ, and commended

---

[1] *Rhaith* is a term that is used in more than one sense. Originally it seems to have been used to signify the notion conveyed by the juridical terms, *jus, droit, recht.* It is cognate with German *recht* and English *right*, and is represented in Irish by the neuter *recht*, which is as if we had in Latin, besides *rectus,-a,-um,* a neuter *rectu,* genitive *rectūs.*

[2] The ceremony is described in the Venedotian Code, "Ancient Laws," i., p. 207.

the youth to him, and the youth became the man of, and
' was placed on the privilege" of the penkenedl or arglwyd;
and thenceforth the young Cymro was to be supported by
the chief or lord, and became himself liable to answer claims
made upon him, and capable of possessing *da* (cattle and
movable property). The status so acquired was that of an
innate bonedig ; and even if his father was an uchelwr he
did not obtain that degree till the father died.[1]   The right
of maintenance by the chief or lord to whom the young
Cymro was commended seems to have involved the giving
of cattle to the latter, and a share of the free land of the
kindred ;[2] but on the other hand he became liable to
military service.[3]

The transfer of the son to the care of the lord of the
cymwd did not, however, confer on the former the right to
receive his *cyvarwys* at once, but the lord undertook the
obligation of providing for him till his settlement and of
doing what we should now call completing his education.
This he performed by quartering the lad on one of his
eitltion.

The *gweision bychain* (little youths) or *gwestion bychain*
(little guests), as they were called, were no doubt troublesome visitors in a farmer's house, and as they approached

---

[1] See Ven. Code, "Ancient Laws," i., pp. 203–5; also *ibid.*, i., p. 91.
The text adds "and no one is a *marchog* (horseman or knight) till he shall
ascend," *i.e.*, to the status of his father.

[2] The rights of the kinsman against the chief, as representing the kindred,
were collectively called *cyvarwys*. A late triad says, "Three *cyvarwysau* of an
innate Cymro ; five free erws ; co-tillage of the waste ; and hunting." See
"Anc. Laws," ii., p. 516. *Cyfarwys* or *cyfarws* is used in the Mabinogion
to signify a boon or the right to ask for a gift of one's own choice. Whether
that is the original meaning may be doubted. Its employment in the laws
suggests that its primary signification was a right to quarters or lodging. If
that is so it may be analysed into *cyf-ar-wys*, from the root *ues* ("to abide,"
also "to be," in Eng. *was, were*), from which we have *ar-os* (to "remain" or
"wait"). From it, too, comes *gwas* ("a residence") in Welsh mediæval
poetry.

[3] And, of course, entitled to bear arms.

manhood formed those companies of youths whom Giraldus mentions as moving about the country. According to the same author, the princes entrusted the education of their children to the care of the principal men of their country each of whom, after the death of the father, endeavoured by every possible means to exalt his own charge above his neighbours, and he points out that on that account friendships were found to be more sincere between foster-brothers than between those who were connected by the natural ties of brotherhood.[1] It looks as if the rules as to youths and the usages we have referred to had some connection with the widely-diffused custom of fosterage,[2] of the existence of which in Wales definite proofs are to be found in the Welsh laws. In the Venedotian Code it is laid down that if an *uchelwr* place his son to be reared with an *aillt* of a lord by the permission or sufferance of the lord for a year and a day, that son is to receive a son's share of the *aillt's* land, and ultimately of his property.[3]

Here we must notice that, besides the rights possessed by the innate *bonedig* to his *cyvarwys* (rights acquired by him as one of the kin, and claimed by kin and descent), he had a right of succession to a share of the *tir gwelyawg* (family land) possessed by his father, grandfather, or great-grandfather, and the possibility of attaining a position of privilege as a landed person and chief of his family within the *cenedl*

---

[1] "Desc. Cambr." ii., cc. 4, 9.

[2] See Maine, "Early History of Institutions," p. 241 ; and the tract on the Law of Fosterage in the "Senchus Mor."

[3] "Anc. Laws," i., p. 195. *Cf.* Dem. and Gwent. Codes, pp. 543 and 767. In this connection, see the text as to the rearing of a *bonedig* when he was nursed by his mother and brought up at home ("Anc. Laws," i. 519). There can be little doubt that the character of the marriage contract and the division of the children on separation of husband and wife afford some explanation of the custom of fosterage. But, as Mr. Seebohm points out, it was "one of the several means used under the tribal system for the purpose of tying strangers as closely as possible to the tribe, quite consistently with the tribal policy of keeping the class of strangers in blood as loosely organised as possible *inter se.*" "Tribal System," p. 128.

(*i.e.*, becoming an *uchelwr* or *breyr*). His possible accession to that position depended on the rules relating to *tir gwelyawg*, with which we deal below, and his right was claimed by a process called *dadenhud* (*i.e.*, the uncovering of the family hearth).[1] The hearth was the symbol of family ownership, and "the covering and uncovering of the fire had a picturesque significance. Whether the fire were of wood or turf, the hearth was swept out every night. The next thing was to single out one particular glowing emblem —*the seed of fire*—which was carefully restored to the hearth and covered up with the remaining ashes for the night. This was the nightly covering of the fire. The morning process was to uncover the seed of fire, to sweep out the ashes under which it was hid, and then deftly to place back the live ember on the hearth, piling over it the fuel for the new day's fire. This was the uncovering of the fire, which thus, from year end to year end, might never go out."[2]

So much as to the sons of the free tribesmen. In regard to a daughter, the law was that she was to be maintained by her father till she attained twelve years of age, and thenceforward she was not to remain "at her father's platter" unless he should will it. There is some ambiguity as to her position if her father refused to maintain her ; but the text says that from her twelfth year she is to possess her own *da* (chattels, movable property), which may simply mean that she is capable of owning movable property, or (as is more probable) implies that she had a right to a share in the *da* of the household or of the larger group of kindred, to the fourth degree, of which she was a member.[3]

It is said that a daughter is to have of her father's *da*

---

[1] A man could not claim by dadenhud except by the hearth he himself, or his father before him, uncovers. "Anc. Laws," ii., p. 141.

[2] Seebohm, "Tribal System," p. 82.

[3] See the Ven. Code, book ii., c. 30, on the "Law of a daughter and her rights." "Anc. Laws," i., p. 205.

only half the share her brother is to have.[1] Whether this was on the father's death or on attaining the age of twelve years is not clear. One of the noticeable things about the status of woman in these laws is the freedom accorded to her both before and after marriage. "Every woman is to go the way she willeth freely, for she is not to be home-returning."[2] Upon the marriage of a Cymraes, or upon her having connection with a man, a fine, called *amobr*, was payable to the lord of the cymwd.[3] The amount of the fine varied according to the status of her father. If her father or other relative gave her away in marriage, he was liable to pay the *amobr;* if the woman disposed of herself, she was bound to pay the fine.[4] The head of the household in which a woman slept was also liable to the lord, presumably in case of default on the part of the person primarily responsible.[5]

The young daughter, in the first instance, does not seem to have been entirely at the disposal of her father, nor to have been, in theory, entirely free. The laws refer to the giving of a daughter in marriage by her kindred as well as by her father.[6] She seems also to have been entitled to a marriage portion or settlement (*gwaddol*) from her father or kindred, which consisted, perhaps, of the half of a brother's share of *da*, or, perhaps, of chattels agreed between her father or kindred and the bridegroom.

The *gwaddol* usually included not only things of utility for a new household, but also *argyvreu* (special ornaments, paraphernalia). It is not perfectly clear whether a sister's share of *da* was necessarily handed over on marriage, or

---

[1] "Anc. Laws," i., p. 99.

[2] "Anc. Laws," i., p. 97.

[3] *Amobr* became due in three modes : one, by gift and delivery before the woman be slept with; secondly, by openly cohabitating, though there might be no gift or delivery; thirdly, by her pregnancy. Ven. Code, ii., c. i., "Anc. Laws," p. 95.

[4] "Anc. Laws," i., p. 88.

[5] "Anc. Laws," *ibid.*

[6] See above, as to the functions of the group of kindred to the fourth degree.

receivable on the death of the father, but on the whole the texts seem to indicate that it was usual for the family of the bride to give some kind of portion.

Daughters did not take any share in the land of the *gwely*. But if a woman were given in marriage to an alltud, her sons could claim in due course to share by privilege of maternity.[1]

The position of women in the system can, however, only be made intelligible by reference to the law as to the marriage contract and its consequences, which shows a serious conflict between the law of the Church and the law of Howel.

Thus we read in the Venedotian code that: "The ecclesiastical law says again that no son is to have the patrimony but the eldest born to the father by the married wife; the law of Howel, however, adjudges it to the youngest son as well as the eldest ; and decides that sin of the father or his illegal act is not to be brought against the son as to his patrimony."[2] By the "married wife" in this passage we are probably to understand a woman married according to the rites of the Church, and therefore not within the prohibited degrees of consanguinity; and by the "illegal act" is meant a marriage invalid according to the doctrines of the Church. The general tenure of the Welsh laws and the provisions of the Statute of Rhudlan[3] show that to a late period the old Cymric customs prevailed. The laws did not permit polygamy ; a man at one time could have only one "espoused" wife.[4] But the contract was not necessarily of life-long duration, and each party had a right of repudiation or separation exercisable without any liability, except a loss of *da* (goods and chattels),

---

[1] "Anc. Laws," i., pp. 97 and 175.
[2] "Anc. Laws," i. 179.
[3] See below, p. 353.
[4] "No man is to have two wives" ("Anc. Laws," i., p. 97).

varying with the time and circumstances of the parting. The marriage ceremony is not expressly described, but, as we infer it from texts scattered throughout the codes, it was a verbal contract between the kindred or father of the bride and the bride herself of the one part, and the bridegroom of the other, entered into in the presence of witnesses.[1] We are not told whether it took place in the house of the bridegroom's or that of the bride's kindred, but in its essence it was a formal delivery of the woman, together with her *gwadol* and *agwedi*, by her kindred or father to the bridegroom. At the time of the delivery mutual warranties or suretyships were exchanged. On behalf of the bride her kindred or parent gave sureties that she would do nothing culpable against her wedded husband, and the bridegroom gave sureties for his wife's *gwadol* and *agwedi*.[2] There is some obscurity as to the term "*agwedi*." Aneurin Owen translates it "dower," but it is clear that the Welsh wife was not entitled to dower in the English sense till the Statutes of Rhudlan came into force; and *agwedi*, strictly, was a payment made by the kindred or parent of the bride to the bridegroom,[3] but the word sometimes seems to be used to include the marriage portion of the bride as well.

One other incident of the marriage must be mentioned,

---

[1] See an incidental reference to the contract, " Anc. Laws," i., p. 519.

[2] " Anc. Laws," i., p. 529. The Ven. code gives a chapter to suretyship (*mechniaeth*), but it is very obscure. It seems to have been a contract entered into verbally, in formal terms, before witnesses or arbitrators (*ammodwyr*), whom the parties empowered to enforce the contract in the form they had agreed. Ven. Code, book ii., cc. 6, 7; " Anc. Laws," i., p. 112.

[3] "There are three legal *agwedi*: the *agwedi* of a King's daughter, 24 pounds ; . . . the *agwedi* of a gwrda's daughter, 3 pounds ; . . . the *agwedi* of an aillt's daughter, 1 pound " (Ven. Code, ii., c. i. 32; " Anc. Laws," i. 91). In modern dictionaries both *gwadol* and *agwedi* are translated into "dower." *Gwadol* = *gwo-dawl* (Irish *fo-dail*; Latin *divisio*) is a portion or dowry as a division of something. *Agwedi* seems to mean all that the *dy-wedi* (the betrothed woman) brings with her to the husband ; but in the laws it is limited, as in the text just quoted, to a pecuniary sum given to the bridegroom by the bride's parent or kindred.

the *cowyll* of the bride ; this was a gift payable the morning after the consummation of the marriage by the husband to the wife, the amount of which depended on the status of the wife's father.[1]

Each of the three codes contains a chapter dealing with the law relating to women. They are very similar in substance, though they vary in detail. That in the Venedotian code is the fullest and, on the whole, the more archaic. It describes some usages of a barbaric character which one is somewhat surprised to find surviving to so late a period in a country in which the Church had been established for many centuries and was a powerful force. The laws deal very minutely with the relations of husband and wife *inter se*, and it is impossible for us to follow them into particulars.

We can only attempt to seize the salient points, but we are by no means sure that we have construed the texts aright. It is however clear that the marriage tie was loose, and that the wife had far greater freedom than was afforded to her by the law of the Church or the English common law. Practically either husband or wife might separate whenever one or both chose. There seems to have been no legal method of bringing the parties again together; but the time and circumstances of the separation entailed

---

[1] The *cowyll* of a king's daughter was 8 pounds ; of a gwrda's daughter 1 pound ; and of an aillt's daughter six-score pence ("Anc. Laws," i., p. 91). Probably at an early period the *cowyll* was not thus accurately measured, for one of the texts says, "If a maid be given in marriage to a man and her *cowyll* be not specified before she rise from her bed in the morning, he is not answerable to her for it thenceforward. If a maid declare not her *cowyll* before she rise from her bed in the morning, the *cowyll* is to be thenceforward in common between them" ("Anc. Laws," i. 91). There seems some inconsistency between these two sentences, and it is not easy to see what they mean if the *cowyll* was already fixed by law. *Cowyll* is probably of the same origin as the Welsh word *cawell*, "a basket or creel," and to be compared with the French term, *corbeille de mariage*, which Littré explains as meaning "parure et bijoux que le futur envoie à sa fiancée dans une corbeille d'ornement."—Littré, Dict., *s.v. corbeille*.

different consequences in regard to the division of the household goods. Separation of husband and wife might take place by agreement or by the act of one party without lawful cause. In regard to separation by agreement, the period of seven years less three days was crucial. If the separation was voluntary on both sides, and took place before the wife had attained " three nights of the seventh year," the wife was only entitled to take away from the house her *agwedi* (seemingly including her *gwadol*, her *argyvreu* (paraphernalia), and her *cowytt*). If they cohabited till after there were three nights wanting of the seventh current year, and afterwards separated by agreement,[1] everything belonging to them was divided into two portions. The laws set out minutely the things that were to go to the wife and to the husband respectively, and as to the things which the law did not specifically allot, the wife had the right to divide them, and the husband chose which portion he would take.[2] Of the children two shares went to the father and one to the mother—the eldest and the youngest to the former, and the middlemost to the mother. The debts were payable in equal shares; and the household goods that were to go to the wife and husband respectively are enumerated with particularity. If a wife left her husband before the seventh year without good cause, she lost all her property except her *cowytt* and her right to any fine due from the husband for having committed adultery.[3] The good causes for which she might repudiate her husband without any loss of property were—his being affected with leprosy, his having fetid breath, or his impotence.[4]

1 It is not clear whether this division was made when the separation after seven years of cohabitation took place by the will of one party without misconduct on the part of either the husband or wife. We are inclined to think not, yet the other view is arguable, at least so far as the Ven. code is concerned.

2 " Anc. Laws," i., p. 81.

3 " Anc. Laws," i., p. 85.

4 Aneurin Owen's modesty induced him to translate some of the usages described in the laws relating to women into the comparative obscurity of the

On the other hand, if a wife were "guilty of an odious deed along with another man, whether by kiss, *aut coitu aut palpando*," the husband could repudiate her, and she forfeited all her property rights.[1]   Many other rules as to the relations of the sexes are given which we cannot stop to explain.   The separation of husband and wife under these rules does not seem at once to have operated as a complete divorce, and it seems that it was only on the subsequent marriage to another person of one of the parties that the relationship was finally determined.[2]

We pass on now from the rules as to the status of the Cymry proper to those dealing with men of the subordinate classes (called *eilltion, taeogion,* and *alltudion*), who though not endowed with tribal privileges were allowed certain rights and a recognised place on Cymric land. They could not possess *tir gwelyawg* (family land), but were settled (at least originally) only on *tir cyfrif* (register land—the bond or servile *maenolyd* of the cymwd), of which we say more below.   Their evidence was of no worth against a Cymro,[3] and to them were denied the right to bear arms, and the privileges of horsemanship and hunting.[4] An ailt could not without his lord's consent become a clerk, a smith, or a bard, but if the lord did not object

Latin tongue.   We follow his example.   The method of deciding whether the husband was or was not impotent is thus given :—" Si femina ob desiderium se sejungendi diceret quod vir non potest copulare, lex requirit id probari hoc modo : linteamen album recens lotum sub illis expandi, et virum in illud ire pro re venerea et urgente libidine eam super linteamen projicere ; et si fiat vel conspiciatur in linteamen satis est ei et illa postea non potest ob istam causam se sejungere ab eo ; et si non possit potest se sejungere ab eo, et abire cum omnibus rebus suis."

[1] "Anc. Laws," i., p. 527.

[2] So we infer : " If the husband take another wife after he shall have parted from the first, the first is free.   If a man part from his wife and she be minded to take another husband, and the first husband should repent having parted from his wife, and overtake her with one foot in the bed and the other outside the bed, the prior husband is to have the woman " ("Anc. Laws," i., p. 87).

[3] " Anc. Laws," ii., pp. 515, 557.

[4] " Anc. Laws," ii. 515.

before he was tonsured as a clergyman, or set up a smithy of his own, or graduated in song as a bard, the lord could not enslave him again.[1]

There is in the laws (though the rules we have just set forth apply to both classes) some confusion between the eilltion or taeogion on the one and the alltudion on the other hand. The explanation of the difficulties caused by the indiscriminate use of the words "aillt" and "alltud" in the manuscripts that have come down to us is easy if the views as to conquest of Wales by Cuneda and his Sons, and its settlement or division by Dyfnwal Moelmud, stated in the preceding chapter, are accepted. If that account be true in substance (as we think), the conquerors made arrangements that continued to exist for centuries; and the laws we are considering seem to prove that they had forcibly grouped the vanquished peoples of the land in the areas that became the bond-maenols of the cymwds as marked out by Dyfnwal, and put them into the category of the eilltion or taeogion. But so soon as the Cymry had established themselves, their rulers and the officers of the cymwds must have had to consider the legal position of strangers coming to reside on the then sparsely populated Cymric territory from England or Ireland, or of men of different grades, for one reason or another, leaving districts in which they were born and seeking a new place of settlement—especially those of Cymric blood who, because of their misdeeds, had become the "kin-wrecked" men with whom the Welsh texts make us acquainted. No alltud came within the purview of Cymric law till he placed himself in some way under the protection of a Cymro; before he had any rights recognised by that law he must have entered into relationship with a man of Cymric blood. The tie did not necessarily imply serfdom. An Englishman might commend himself to a Welsh king and become

[1] "Anc. Laws," i. 436.

his man; the matter.might go no further; he simply entered into the king's *nawd* (peace or protection). But if such an alltud desired to settle permanently in Cymru, he could not obtain *tir gwelyawg;* he could only be allowed to occupy land in the *maer-dref* of the king's demesne or be placed in a *taeog-tref*, in some cymwd belonging to his protector.

If he did so and lived on his land he did not lose his freedom to go away when he might will, but if his descendants remained there till the fourth generation, then those of that generation became eilltion and *adscripti glebæ.* Till the fourth generation his descendants might leave their land and its lord on penalty of forfeiting half their personal property (*da*).[1] But in some cases, at any rate, or in some parts of Wales, this settlement was not without compensation, for the recognition of kindredship then began, though it was not till the ninth generation that an *aillt genedl* was legally formed. The effect of this was not (except perhaps in South Wales) to make the members of such a kindred Cymry, but it altered their status and enabled them to claim galanas for the slaying of a kinsman.[2]

Another general distinction between the status of individuals was founded upon religious profession. The community was divided by these laws into lay and spiritual or ecclesiastical persons. The clergy formed a kind of separate estate. It is clear that in Howel's time the Church possessed a large amount of landed property with various immunities, which seem to have depended principally on the terms of the original donation. All possessors of Church land were to come to every new king who succeeded,

---

[1] " Anc. Laws," i. 183.

[2] As to the position of strangers in the system—a very obscure and doubtful topic—see Seebohm's " Tribal System," pp. 115—126. Till the period at which aillt kindredship was allowed, the worth of a slain man of the family went to the lord, as in the case of an hereditary taeog (" Anc. Laws," ii. 403).

to declare to him their privilege and their obligation; and after they had declared to him their privilege, if the king saw their privilege to be right, he allowed them to continue their *nawḋ* (right of sanctuary or protection) and their privileges or immunities.[1] The land of the Church seems to have been divided into abbey land, bishop land, hospital land, and land of a church.

As a general rule the king seems to have had jurisdiction in regard to some offences committed by and the right to certain dues and services from laymen settled on such land.[2] It is said, however, that Howel permitted every ecclesiastical lord, such as the archbishop of Menevia (St. David's), or other bishops or abbots, royal privilege for holding pleas among their laics according to the common law (*cyfraith gyffredin*) of Cymru.[3] The clergy were, it appears, exempt from the jurisdiction of civil courts, though they might sue laymen in them. On the other hand, in general, the spiritual court could not deal with suits against laymen; but in regard to tithe, *daered* (income or fees), etc., and to *saraad* (*injuria*) and open violence done to a clerk, the Church had jurisdiction over laymen.[4] There was no worth established by Howel for the limb or the blood or the *saraad* of a clerk, and every "unworthy" injury done to the clergy was to be repaired to them in the synod according to ecclesiastical law.[5] Abbots, bishops, and masters of hospitals were permitted to make capitular regulations according to their own law for their establishments, provided the rules did not contravene the law of the king.[6]

Other distinctions between persons were based upon

[1] "Anc. Laws," i. 139.
[2] "Anc. Laws," i., p. 171.
[3] "Anc. Laws," ii., p. 365. But this seems a late theory; see below, p. 240.
[4] So we interpret the texts in a chapter entitled "Suits of Court and Church" ("Anc. Laws," ii., p. 367), but the MS. is somewhat late.
[5] "Anc. Laws," i. 477.
[6] "Anc. Laws," i. 171.

official position or the status (*braint*) of office.   The rights
and duties of the ministers of the king's and queen's
establishments, to whom we have referred above, and of the
maer and canghellor of the cymwd, are set forth with great
minuteness.

We now turn to consider briefly the law relating to
property in or possession of land.   Here again in the
codes we find the cymwd treated as a legal unit, and
its divisions give us a key to the explanation of the
system.   The divisions are ascribed to the laws of Dyfnwal
Moelmud ; and though at first sight they look, as explained
in the codes, to be rigid territorial areas, yet on further
consideration it seems they were created in order to adjust
the rights of the king or chieftain, the uchelwyr, the tribesmen, and the eilltion, of separating the inferior classes from
the Cymric tribesmen, and especially for the purpose of
aggregating the homesteads of the free Cymric tribesmen
into groups for the assessment of the *gwestva* (food-rent) due
to the chieftain.   There was some difference in the arrangements in Gwyned and Deheubarth.   According to the
Venedotian code the cymwd was thus divided :—Four
erwau [1] in every *tydyn* (homestead), four *tydynau* in every
rhandir (shareland), four *rhandiroed* in every *gafael* (holding), four *gafaelion* in every *tref* (vill or township), four
trefyd in every *maenol*, [2] and twelve *maenolyd* and two

---

[1] *Erw* (literally, "what has been tilled") was a measurement applicable
to arable land.   It contained about 4,320 yards.   A. Owen's " Glossary."

[2] Sometimes spelt *maenor*.   *Maenol*, according to Dr. Pughe's guess, a
"dale" or "manor," is best explained as "heredium" or "praedium."
Maenol (adj.) means "stony."   *Maenawr* (for that is the old spelling) becomes
maenol in Gwyned and *maenor* in Powys and South Wales, and being
feminine it becomes with the article *y Faenol* and *y Faenor*, "the maenawr" ;
whence in place-names it is written *Vaenol* or *Vaynol* in the North, and
Vaenor or *Vaynor* elsewhere.   Without the article it is written *Manor*,
as in Manordeifi (= *Maenor Deifi*), and Manorbeer (= *Maenor Byr*)—both
in Pembrokeshire.   The latter was so called after a certain Porius or Pŷr
after whom Caldey was named Ynys Bŷr (Pŷr's island).   The word *maenawr*
has nothing to do with English *manor*, to which it is often assimilated, but

trefyd in every *cymwd*. So, there being fifty trefyd in each cymwd, and two cymwds being normally equal to a cantref, there were one hundred trefyd in the cantref; and there were twelve maenolyd and two trefyd in a cymwd, which were thus apportioned :—the two "supernumerary" trefyd were possessed by the king—one as *maer - dref* land (*i.e.*, demesne land), and the other as his waste and summer pasture ; four of the maenolyd were assigned to eilltion to support dogs and horses and for progress and *dovraeth* (quarters); of the remaining eight maenolyd, two were assigned to the canghellorship and maership of the cymwd, and the rest to the free uchelwyr. Such is the arrangement ascribed by the code of Gwyned to Dyfnwal, and though there seems no reason to doubt that it represents a system that once had real significance, there are some obvious difficulties arising from the language of the code. The *erw* is defined as a definite and constant area, and if the text is to be taken literally, all the cymwds would be of equal size, but this was certainly not the case ; and so, whatever may have been the intention of the ancient legislators, we must look on the larger areas mentioned as not being uniform in size, but as representing groups of households connected together for the purpose of adjusting the rights of the king as against the men of different classes residing in the cymwd. Whatever the original object of these divisions, the aspect presented by the cymwd in Howel's time, if we may judge by the codes, was this—it was divided into recognised maenolyd; a portion of the cymwd was possessed by the king, or an arglwyd appointed by him, as demesne land, and another part was recognised as the king's waste ; the maer and the canghellor occupied

---

appears to come from *maen* (a stone). Originally it probably meant a particular spot in its district, which was distinguished by stone buildings or some sort of stone walls ; this seems to us more likely than the conjecture of A. Owen that it meant a district bounded by stone land-marks. See Professor Lloyd's remarks in " Y Cymmrodor," xi., 32–3, and Mr. E. Phillimore's note x., p. 57.

other areas within it; the residue of the land was divided into *tir gwelyawg* (occupied by uchelwyr and bonedigion) and *tir cyfrif* (occupied by eilltion); and an acute distinction is drawn between the free land of the true Cymry and the bond land of the unfree persons, and it should be noticed that the legal attributes free and bond are given not only to persons, but also to specific areas of land.

The king's demesne (*maer-dref*) was cultivated by his eilltion under the superintendence of his land-maer, but it also seems that parts of it were occupied by subordinate officers of the court holding their land free by privilege of office in return for their services.[1]

We have already had occasion to advert to the relation of the *gwely* to the *cenedl* in dealing with the constitution of the latter as it existed in Howel's days; we have now to consider its relation to the king as lord of the cymwd.

So far as we have observed, the codes nowhere speak of the uchelwyr as holding their land of the king, but their position was in Howel's time, or when the codes were in operation, hardly distinguishable from that of tenants. The first obligation of the possessors of *tir gwelyawg* was to pay a *gwestva* (food-rent) to the king. Originally this was paid in kind for the entertainment of the king and his court on his progress.[2] He did not quarter himself on the Cymric tribesmen, but, as we shall see, the eilltion had to provide him with certain necessary buildings, while the former had to furnish the food and drink. According to the codes,

---

[1] See a survival of this in the case of the manor of Aberffraw. Seebohm's "Tribal System," p. 12.

[2] From the phrase "naw nos gwesty" (*i.e.*, nine nights of the guest-house) it would appear that the original obligation of the cymwd was to entertain its chieftain for nine nights. *Naw-nos* means eight days bounded by nine nights, just as *wythnos* (eight nights = a week) is our ordinary Jewish week of seven days. *Cf. huitaine*, and *pythewnos* (fortnight, *quinzaine*). *Naw-nos* is the old Celtic nine-night week of eight days. See Rhys' "Celtic Heathendom," pp. 360, 365. See "Anc. Laws," ii., p. 345; and Seebohm's "Tribal System," p. 158.

this service was no longer rendered in kind, but had been commuted into a money payment—the tunc pound. The Venedotian code says: "And from eight (*i.e.*, the two maenolyd of the maer and canghellor and the six of the Cymric tribesmen) the king is to have a gwestva every year; that is, a pound yearly from each of them : threescore pence are charged on each trev of the four that are in a maenol, and so subdivided into quarters in succession, until each erw of the tydyn be assessed : and that is called the tunc pound; and the silentiary is to collect it annually."[1] The maenol therefore appears as the tuncpaying unit, and the gwestva or tunc pound was a rent issuing from the whole *tir gwelyawg* of the cymwd, and not a personal due from the uchelwyr or heads of households; and the required amount was assessed among the uchelwyr and heads of household according to the number of the subdivisions of the maenol in their possession.

The uchelwyr and other Cymric tribesmen were also, as we have said, liable to military service.[2] Though they were not subject (except so far as the tunc pound in lieu of the gwestva was concerned) to liability in regard to the king's progresses, they had also to submit to the great progress of the household once a year.[3] Lastly, the free tribesmen, like other classes in the community, were obliged to pay on death an *ebediw* (a relief) to the king or lord.

The mode of succession on the death of an *uchelwr* or chief of a household was as follows :—The land of the deceased was first of all divided between all his sons. If there were no buildings on the land, the youngest son was to divide all the patrimony, and the eldest was to choose which portion he would take, and each in seniority chose unto the youngest. If there were buildings on the land, the

---

[1] "Anc. Laws," i., p. 189.
[2] "Anc. Laws," i., p. 79. See above, p. 205.
[3] See above, p. 204.

youngest brother but one was to divide the *tyddynau* (homesteads), and the youngest was to have his choice among them ; and after that he was to divide all the patrimony, and by seniority they were to choose unto the youngest. That division was not final, but only continued during the lives of the brothers. After the brothers were dead their sons (first cousins) divided the patrimony again *per capita*, and not *per stirpes;* the heir (*etifed*) of the youngest brother divided, and the heir of the eldest brother chose, and so by seniority unto the youngest. This division again was not final, but only continued till all the first cousins were dead ; when that time arrived there was a final division *per capita* among the second cousins—*i.e.*, the great-grandchildren of the original head of the *gwely*.[1]

Thus every one of the male descendants to the fourth degree of a possessor of *tir gwelyawg* had an interest in the family land, which became an interest in possession to a share in his father's land when his father died, and which was liable to be enlarged or lessened when the next division of the whole land of the *gwely* took place.

It was a logical result of this position of things that a chief of a household could not alienate or dispose of any part of his *tir gwelyawg* except for his own life ; if he did so, it was recoverable by his sons. Where, however, there was an agreement between father, brothers, cousins, and second cousins (seemingly the whole *gwely*) and the lord to yield land as bloodland (*i.e.*, in lieu of the composition for homicide), the head of the household might assign his land or part of it, and his son could not recover, and the reason given is that peace was bought for the son as well as for the father—*i.e.*, there was valuable consideration to the son.[2] This case is mentioned as the only one in which

---

[1] " Anc. Laws," i., p. 168.   This is from the Ven. code, but the Demetian code is in practical agreement.

[2] " Anc. Laws," i., p. 177.

a father could defeat his sons' rights. It seems, however, that a man who had no sons could, with the consent of his brothers, first cousins, second cousins, and the lord of the cymwd, alienate his land.[1]

We have now explained the principal rules relating to *tir gwelyawg* as they appear in the codes. They seem to us, in the form there presented, to indicate that the *tir gwelyawg* in each cymwd consisted of definite geographical parcels, though the uchelwyr and bonedigion occupying them had rights over waste and woodland, and our opinion is confirmed by the existence of rules concerning boundary disputes.[2]

We now pass on to consider the law as to the servile or villein maenolyd. According to the original scheme, four maenolyd were set aside for occupation by eilltion or taeogion. As a result of the application of the old regulations, we find that in Howel's time certain parts of each cymwd were in the possession of occupiers or tenants not looked upon as Cymric tribesmen, but as unfree persons (*adscripti glebæ*), whose services to the king or lord and whose rights were different from those of the owners or holders of *tir gwelyawg.*

---

[1] This is an inference. The Ven. code speaks of the grades just mentioned as the "persons without whose consent land cannot be assigned" ("Anc. Laws," i., p. 177), and another text says that "no man can sell land or engage it without the permission of the lord" (i., p. 181). He might let it annually without such permission.

[2] "Anc. Laws," i., p. 537 : "If a dispute as to boundaries be commenced between the land of co-inheritors, privilege is to meer ; if between occupied land and a waste, pre-occupation (*cynwarchad*) is to meer." The text goes on to say that "building and tillage denote occupation." The meaning is obscure ; but it seems to amount to this—that in the first case that one of the contending parties whose *braint* (status or privilege) was higher had the right to define the boundary ; that in the second case the prior occupant had that right. Another text says : "If there be contention between two persons of equal braint as to meers, and the truth between them be not known, let each swear to his meer, and afterwards the debateable land is to be divided between them" ("Anc. Laws," i. 537).

The bond maenolyd (the parcels of land to which a non-tribal character was given) were liable to furnish a dawn-bwyd food-gift) twice a year to the king—one in the winter and one in the summer.[1] Apart from the food-gifts, the eilltion were not bound to support the king or his household ; but they had to submit to the progresses of the maer and canghellor. These, with their servants, were to make two progresses a year, in parties of four. The villeins were also obliged to erect the hall and eight subsidiary buildings for the king on his progresses, though whether this was done afresh every year, or when built only repaired from time to time, is not clear.[2] The king was also entitled to have for his military expeditions from every villein-tref a man, a horse, and an axe, to form encampments at his own cost.[3] They had also to furnish pack-horses for the king for such expeditions.[4] Once a year they were to present the queen with meat and drink ; and upon them fell the duty of supporting the dogs, the huntsmen, the falconers, and the youths, all of them once a year. The king might also quarter strangers on his eilltion according to their abilities.[5]

The regulation of matters in the bond maenolyd or as to *tir cyfrif* was entrusted to the maer and canghellor of the

---

[1] "Anc. Laws," i., p. 199. According to the Venedotian code they were the following :—

(i) In the winter—a three-year-old swine ; a vessel of butter 3 handbreadths in depth and 3 in breadth ; a vat full of bragot 9 handbreadths in depth diagonally ; a thrave of oats of one band for provender ; 26 loaves of the best bread grown on the land ; a man to kindle the fire in the hall that night or one penny.

(ii) In summer—a three-year-old wether ; a dish of butter ; 26 loaves ; a cheese of one milking of all the cows in the tref.

The gifts in the other cases are similar in general character, though not identical.

[2] "Anc. Laws," i. 79, 487.
[3] "Anc. Laws," i., p. 79.
[4] "Anc. Laws," i. 193.
[5] *Ibid.*

cymwd.[1] Upon the death of an aillt possessing a *tyáyn*
the land which had been in his occupation was not divided
between his sons as in the case of *tir gwelyawg;* but the
tref in which the *tyáyn* of the deceased was situate was
re-divided between all the eilltion settled in the *tref*.[2] The
land-maer of the king's *maer-dref* is directed to proceed in
the same way as to the king's eilltion settled thereon. The
incident of *ebediw* (relief) applied to the eilltion as to the
Cymric tribesmen, but the amount was less.[3]

We can only give very brief attention to the law of
contracts. The laws recognise the sale, loan, deposit, and
pledging of *da* (movable property). But besides obligations resulting from such transactions as these, duties might
be created by entering into a suretyship (*mechnïaeth*), a
briduw, and a legal contract (*ammod deáfol*). Suretyships
and legal contracts were verbal agreements entered into
in solemn form before witnesses or contract-men (*ammodwyr*). The mutual undertakings were spoken by the con-
tracting parties, and in sign of the conclusion of the contract
there was "a mutual pledging of hands," which we gather
was a joining of hands.[4] A promise given without witnesses
present was of no avail if denied on oath by the alleged
contractor.[5] The *briduw* seems to have been a contract

---

[1] The general name of the land on which taeogion or eilltion were settled, is
in the codes *tir cyfrif* (reckon-land, *i.e.*, land accounted for). The *taeog-tref* or
maer-dref of the codes is equivalent to the *trefgeuery* (subdivided *tref*) of the
Record of Carnarvon. H. Lewis's "Ancient Laws," p. 41 ; Seebohm's
"Tribal System," p. 116.

[2] "Anc. Laws," i. 169. Seemingly for reasons of convenience no one was
to remove from his legal *tyáyn* if an equivalent could be obtained for it of
other land.

[3] It was for a king's aillt 6 score pence ; for an uchelwr's aillt 4 score and
10 pence ("Anc. Laws," i., p. 493). That of a breyr (= uchelwr) was
6 score pence.

[4] See "Anc. Laws," i., pp. 137–8 : also the chapter on Suretyship, *ibid.*,
p. 113. "There is no surety nor gorvodawg unless the three hands meet,"
ibid., p. 135 ; and also p. 133. See the texts as to "delusive suretyships."

[5] *Ibid.*

entered into with the sanction of the Church, a promise on oath taking God to witness that a man would do or abstain from doing some act. It could only be entered into by baptised persons.[1]

The same fundamental notions as to the punishment of wrongs that prevailed among the Irish and Saxon nations in early times are disclosed in the Welsh laws. The rules as to offences of different kinds are most completely developed in the third book of the Venedotian Code, which is called the Proof book (*Lyfr prawf*). The preamble shows that it was compiled after Howel's time;[2] and as the text refers to alterations made by Bleynd̄ ab Cynfyn, it must have been originally written not earlier than the middle of the eleventh century, and in fact probably a good deal later. It treats of the "three columns of law" (*teyr kolovȳn kyvreȳth*)—the law of murder or homicide (*galanas*), of theft (*ƚƚadrad*), and of fire (*tan*); and then with very great minuteness goes on to settle the worth of wild and tame animals, of the different limbs and members of the human body, of domestic utensils, agricultural implements, and many articles coming under the head of movable property.

The treatise shows clearly that as in regard to property arrangements, so also in regard to wrongs, the effect of settlement in a particular district for centuries had been to alter very materially the older tribal system, and to vest in the lord and court of the cymwd a territorial jurisdiction in regard to what we should call crimes. The distinction between civil injuries (offences against an individual or individuals) and crimes (offences against the state or community at large) is not developed, though for many wrongful

---

[1] "Anc. Laws," i., pp. 133-5. It was probably entered into in church or in the presence of a priest.

[2] "And this book Iorwerth son of Madog collected from the book of Cyfnerth son of Morgeneu, and from the book of Gwair son of Ruvon, and from the book of Goronwy son of Moreid̄ig, and the old book of the White House, &c." ("Anc. Laws," i., p. 219).

acts the lord has the right to exact fines called *dirwy* and *camlwrw*, and for some the wrong-doer might be sold, or exiled, or put to death. Apart from homicide, what we find is an elaborate system whereby the injured person might sue for money compensation fixed by law beforehand in respect of each kind of offence, though in some cases the offender was also directly punished. The texts of the codes are very obscure, and we do not affect to be able to interpret them with certainty or summarise them with absolute correctness.

The rules relating to *galanas* (homicide) are set forth with tolerable clearness, and are of great importance to students of the history of legal institutions, for they are evidently derived from notions common to all or nearly all races at certain stages of their development, and the working of the system is explained at unusual length. In very early communities the moral ideas of their members were limited to men of their own tribe or clan or family. The words stranger and enemy were practically synonymous. The slaying of a man outside one's community might or might not be counted for righteousness, but it was not thought of as wrong. But the killing of a man within the pale—belonging to one's own tribe—was quite another thing, and the nearer relations of the murdered man were prompted to vengeance, not only by natural emotions of anger and pride, but by powerful impulses connected with primitive religion. It was the right and duty of the kindred of the murdered man to prosecute a blood-feud against the murderer and his kindred. At some time amongst progressive races, to put a stop to strife within the tribe, a system of ending the feud between kindreds or families within the larger aggregate of kinsmen was devised. In all probability expediency suggested the settlement of the quarrel without further bloodshed between the kindreds by a payment of cattle. The termination of the vendetta was very likely originally brought about by a voluntary treaty between the kindreds at feud; but in the codes we find a rigid system, carried out according to a settled procedure, under which one group of kinsmen made to another group of kinsmen a payment in cattle or money, which varied with the status of the murdered man, and which was carried out under the auspices of the lord of the cymwd. "There was thus, so to speak, a kind of international law and authority superseding the lynch-law or blood-feud between the kindreds."[1]   The Irish laws describe an analogous system as "a middle course between forgiveness and retaliation," and the essential character of the whole proceeding is emphasised by the text of the Venedotian Code, which says that "on that day"—the day on which the worth of the murdered man is completely paid—"everlasting concord is to be established and perpetual amnesty between them (*i.e.*, the kindreds at feud)."[2]

Let us now try as briefly as possible to explain the system as it appears in the Venedotian Code. To do so we must first of all define two technical terms, *galanas* and *saraad*. The former word is now used for homicide or murder; in the codes it is employed not only in that sense, but also for the worth measured in cattle or money of the murdered man. *Saraad* (literally "disgrace") was in like manner a term used to signify a wrongful act involving insult to the person whose right was infringed, as well as the compensation payable for the wrong. It was a very general term, and included both direct trespasses to the person and indire t attacks upon a man's honour, privileges, or rights.[3]   *Saraad*, therefore, was much broader than *galanas*, and no one could commit *galanas* without doing

[1] Seebohm, "Tribal System," p. 105.
[2] "Anc. Laws," i., p. 229.
[3] *E.g.*, *saraad* was done to a queen by snatching anything out of her hand, or violating her protection or peace (*nawd*). So *saraad* was done to a king by seducing his wife or violating his protection ("Anc. Laws," i., p. 7).

saraad to the deceased.[1] Accordingly the law quite logically imposed on the murderer and his kinsmen compensation for *saraad* as well as *galanas*.

The amount of the *galanas* was generally thrice that of the *saraad* of the deceased,[2] and the amount was fixed by law for each kind of man, so that we have incidentally valuable information as to the grades of aristocracy and status.

The *galanas* of the king of Aberffraw was his *saraad* threefold. His *saraad* was—"a hundred cows from each cantref in his dominion, and a white bull with red ears to each hundred cows, and a rod of gold equal in length to himself and as thick as his little finger, and a plate of gold as broad as his face and as thick as the nail of a ploughman who has been a ploughman for seven years."[3] Gold was only paid to the king of Aberffraw. As to other men the following were the amounts of *galanas* :—

The penkenedl	189 cows.
An uchelwr	126 ,,
Man with a family without office (penteulu) .	84 ,,
Innate bonedig	63 ,,
Alltud of a brenin	63 ,,
Alltud of an uchelwr	31½ ,,
Caeth " slave " of the island : 1 lb. of silver .	4 ,,
Caeth from beyond the sea : 1½ lb. . . .	6 ,,

The *galanas* of a woman was half that of a man.[4]

The murderer or wrong-doer was not alone liable for the payment of *galanas* and *saraad*, but jointly with him a group of his kinsmen. The group liable for *saraad* was limited to the fourth degree from the common ancestor— *i.e.*, the group of descendants among which *tir gwelyawg*

---

[1] " No one is killed without being first subjected to *saraad* " (" Anc. Laws," i. 231).

[2] " Anc. Laws," i. 223.

[3] " Anc. Laws," i., p. 7. But as to the latter statement, see the Demetian Code (" Anc. Laws," i. 347).

[4] " Anc. Laws," i., p. 85.

was divisible and re-divisible. The responsibility for *galanas* lay upon a much larger group : the kinsmen to the seventh degree of descent from the common ancestor —*i.e.*, all the kinsmen of the murderer to that degree of relationship which, for want of a better term, we must call sixth cousinship.[1]

The *galanas* was assessed on such kinsmen not only on his father's side, but also on his mother's side. The mode of assessment was as follows :—One-third of the whole amount fell upon the murderer and his father and mother, if living, in the proportion of two parts on himself and one part on his father and mother. If he had children, and they were of age liable to pay, the murderer himself paid two-thirds of his own share, and the children the remaining third of that share. The residue (two-thirds) of the whole *galanas* fell upon the groups of kinsmen on the father and mother's side just described in the proportion of two-thirds for the father's kin and one-third for the mother's kin.

But the liability of his kin was not wholly exhausted within this grade, for if by assessment in the manner described the full *galanas* was not collected, the murderer could call upon the remaining men of his kindred (*cenedl*)— *i.e.*, his kinsmen to the ninth degree—to assist him by a payment called the spear-penny (*ceiniog baladyr*). Beyond the ninth degree liability ceased, and the Welsh lawyer asks, " Is there a single penny for which a person's life is

---

[1] The following was the group thus formed :—

1. Brothers	. . . . . .	*braut*
2. First cousins	. . . . .	*keuenderu*
3. Second cousins	. . . . .	*keuerderu*
4. Third cousins	. . . . .	*keÿuÿn*
5. Fourth cousins	. . . . .	*gorcheÿuen*
6. Fifth cousins	. . . . .	*gorchau*
7. Sons of a fifth cousin	. . .	*mab gorchau*

There is, however, some obscurity, if not confusion, in the mode of counting degrees of relationship in the codes. See " Anc. Laws," i. 225.

forfeited ? " and sternly answers, " There is ; a penny wanting for *galanas*."[1] Neither women nor clerks were liable for the spear-penny, for "they were not avengers."[2]

The manner in which the spear-penny was collected is curious. The murderer, accompanied by a servant of the arglwyd of the cymwd, carrying with him a relic, went forth, and wherever he met a man not known to be related to him within the seventh degree, was entitled to require such person to take an oath on the relic that he was not descended from any of the four kindreds from which the murderer was descended. If he took the oath, he was exempt ; if he did not, he was assessed.[3]

Turning now from the consideration of the individuals or groups liable to pay *saraad* and *galanas*, we find that the *galanas* obtained from the murderer and his kin was thus divided : the first third was taken by the lord for exacting it ; the second third was distributed between the father and mother of the murdered man, their children, and his children, if any ;[4] the third went to the groups of kinsmen of the murdered man on the father's and mother's side who would, in case he had been the murderer, have been liable to pay the corresponding shares of *galanas*—the third being divided between these groups in the proportion

---

[1] "Anc. Laws," i., p. 600. The method of communicating the law by question and answer is not infrequent in these Welsh treatises. It is interesting to notice that the ninth degree is still looked on as a limit among the Welsh. If a witness in Court is asked (*e.g.*), "Are you a relative of the defendant's ? " it is not unusual for him to reply, "*Dim perthynas o fewn y nawfed ach*," which means "not related within the ninth degree." Mr. S. T. Evans, M.P., heard the phrase quite recently in Carmarthenshire. Another phrase in use is, "I am not related '*hyd y nawfed ach*,'" *i.e.*, as far as the ninth degree.

[2] "Anc. Laws," i., p. 227.

[3] "Anc. Laws," i., p. 225.

[4] The division of the second third within this group took place thus : "two shares to the father and one to the mother . . . and of what remains for the children, if there be children of the murdered man, two shares to them." Two versions of the division of *galanas* are given in MSS. of the Ven. Code. We follow the older MS., which was taken by A. Owen as the principal text.

of two parts for the father's kin and one for the mother's kin.[1] As to the division of the *saraad* of a murdered man there is some conflict of authority, but the usual way seems to have been to give one-third to his widow if he was married, and to divide the remainder among the group of kinsmen liable in the converse case to pay *saraad ;*[2] but if his father were alive the father received in the distribution a share equal to twice that of a brother ; and similarly if the mother were alive she received a share equal to twice that of a sister.[3] If the *galanas* was not duly paid, the injured kindred were at liberty to exercise the right of vengeance seemingly without becoming in turn liable for *galanas.*[4]

It is evident that these arrangements applied to the case of the murderer and his victim being members of different kindreds. If a man murdered his near kinsman—a man of the same cenedl—no *galanas* was due, but the murderer appears to have forfeited his rights as a member of it ; he became a kin-wrecked (*carttawedrog*) man, and though not put to death, he was an object of hatred,[5] and obliged to flee and find shelter and protection among strangers.

It should be noticed that there is in the codes no definition of murder (*galanas*). It seems that the term was not imited to cases of intentional homicide. The gist of the wrong seems to have been the causing the death of a man, but the matter is not clear. One text says that there was no liability if the alleged murderer could prove that he acted in self-defence.

The procedure for determining liability is not fully

---

[1] "Anc. Laws," i., p. 227.
[2] "Anc. Laws," i., p. 231.
[3] *Ibid.*
[4] But in the time when the codes as we have them were in operation it seems that the right of revenge was limited to the slaying of the murderer. "No one," says one version of the Ven. Code, " is to be killed on account of another but the murderer " ("Anc. Laws," i., p. 229).
[5] "Since the living kin is not killed for the sake of the dead kin, everybody will hate to see him " ("Anc. Laws," i. 791).

explained, and raises questions of a character too detailed for us to enter upon here. It was evidently, however, a trial by compurgation. The oaths of three hundred men of a kindred were required to deny " murder, blood, and wound, and the killing of a person."[1] When the liability for *galanas* was admitted, or the kindred charged failed to absolve themselves, the amount was collected by the lord thus :—
" The period for *galanas* is a fortnight after being summoned for each lordship in which they (*i.e.*, the kinsmen liable) live to apportion the payment, and twice that time for exacting the payment and assembling them to pay it. At three periods and in three thirds the *galanas* is to be paid : two periods for the kindred of the father, and one period for the kindred of the mother ; . . . at the first period for the kindred of the father to pay one of their thirds, they are to have the oaths of one hundred of the best men of the other kindred that their relation is forgiven ; and at the second period, on their paying their second third, they are to have the oaths of another hundred men of the other kindred that their relation is forgiven, and those of the best men of the tribo ; and at the third period the kindred of the mother are to pay their third ; and then they are to have the oaths of a hundred men of the other kindred that their relation is forgiven ; and everlasting concord is to be established on that day and perpetual amnesty between them."[2]

The codes do not make the rules relating to trespass to the person not causing death, but dismemberment or other bodily injury, a " column of law " ; but assaults and batteries came under the head *saraad;* and the offender and his kindred of the circumscribed degree had not only, when

---

[1] A distinction was drawn between an ordinary murder and a murder "with savage violence." No explanation is given of the latter term, but to deny the charge the oaths of six hundred men of the kindred were necessary ("Anc. Laws," i., p. 231).

[2] "Anc. Laws," i., p. 229.

the wrong was admitted or proved, to pay the amount prescribed as the *saraad* of the complainant, but also. in case of maiming or definite injury to a part of the body the worth as fixed by law of the limb or part destroyed or affected.

The second "column of law" (*Hadrad*, literally theft) is treated of in a chapter in the Venedotian Code. Its contents are not simply rules for the punishment of theft in our sense, but rather a collection of rules relating to property in movable things and interference with a man's right of possession. The texts indicate difference of opinion on some points, and give an account of the law not easily intelligible. *Da* (chattels) were divided into things animate and inanimate. The claim or title (*ardelw*) to an animal was of three kinds—birth and rearing, possession before loss, and the. warranty (*arwaesav*) of another person ; to inanimate things, of two kinds—possession before loss, and warranty. Several kinds of wrongful taking of another man's *da* are given. The consequences of taking a thing in a man's presence were different from a taking in his absence—*i.e.*, secretly or without his knowledge.

Theft (*Hadrad*) is defined as the taking of a thing in the owner's absence, coupled with denial of the act. Surreption (*anghyfarch*) was the taking of the thing secretly, but without any subsequent denial of the act. Violence (*trais*) was the taking of a thing in a man's presence and against his will. Savage violence (*fyrnygruyd dywuynau*) was committed when a man rendered useless the property of another. Mistake or inadvertence (*annodeu*) was the taking of "one thing for another"—that is, the taking of a thing that one had no right to possess under the belief that one was acting legally. These distinctions were apparently of importance in regard to the procedure for recovering *da* which one man claimed from another.

If a man was in possession of property and another

claimed it, the procedure before the court was this:—The possessor asked, "Who owns this?" then the claimant said he did, and that "It is wrong for thee to own what is mine"; then the defendant said, "It is altogether denied; for nothing of thine have I : and since I have not, by what means did thy loss happen, and at what time didst thou lose it?" Then if the claimant alleged a loss by theft, by negligence, or by surreption,[1] he was entitled to swear to the thing being his property in the prescribed manner— which varied according as the chattel was animate or inanimate—and was obliged to state with particularity the time of its loss. Upon his taking the proper oath on the relic, what we should call the burden of proof was shifted to the then possessor, who was not, however, put to a *rhaith* (compurgation) in this proceeding,[2] but only on proof in a prescribed form of his title (*ardelw*). The title or claim he might take his stand on was either warranty (*arwaesav*)[3] or possession before the time sworn to by the claimant as the time of loss, and also, in the case of animals, birth and rearing. In case the defendant relied on a warranty he had to call for a warrantor, and if no one was produced he lost his cause; if the warrantor came forward the claimant

---

[1] There were six ways in which a man might lose his possession : theft, surreption, or negligence, deposit and loan, hire, or by favour (= gift). In the three former cases he could swear in legal form to the property ; in the latter he could not, and seemingly his suit failed. The reason given is that in the three latter cases he had voluntarily given up the thing, and, as we understand the law, it was for the bailee to sue, not the original possessor or owner. *Sed qu. ?* ("Anc. Laws," i. 249.) As we understand the matter, the action dealt with under the second column of law was one against a defendant alleged to be illegally possessing the plaintiff's *da*. It was not founded on contract, but on a wrong. An action as between a bailor and bailee was regarded as based on the real contract.

[2] "It is not right that there should be a rhaith after detention and swearing only, arwaesav, or custody before loss, or birth and rearing " ("Anc. Laws," i., p. 249).

[3] In this connection it ought to be observed that there was a special kind of warranty, which might be given on sale, called *dilysrwyd* (literally, affirmation), and which was a warranty of title.

recommenced the proceedings. If the defendant relied on prior possession he took an oath, in the way the claimant had done, that the thing was his, and then having said that the thing had been in his possession "either a week or a month or two or a season" before the time of loss deposed to by the claimant, he produced "guardians" (*geitweyt*[1] —seemingly witnesses) to lawfully prove his possession as alleged, and on doing so obtained judgment. If he alleged that he had bred and reared the animal in dispute he was to produce "guardians" who would depose to the mother of the animal having been his property, and that the latter was born in his possession and had not been parted with till that day. The production of two "guardians" sufficed if one was of status higher, and one of status lower, than that of the defendant.[2]

This proceeding for recovering possession is not to be confounded with what is described as a legal prosecution (*gyrr kyueythyaul*) for theft; the claimant in the former action, though he might allege he had a right to take the oath and put the defendant to his *ardelw*, did not swear the latter was a thief. A legal prosecution for theft could only be commenced by the claimant's taking an oath that a person accused by him had "really stolen the goods."[3] Upon this the accused was put to his *rhaith* (compurgation). At the time when the Venedotian Code as we have it was in operation it was customary to require for theft the oaths of twelve men, and "the half of them nodmen (*gwyr nod*)."[4] If the accused failed to secure the required rhaith he was convicted.

---

[1] The word is not now used. It is translated "guardians" by A. Owen ("Anc. Laws," i., p. 251).

[2] "One above his hand and another below his hand" ("Anc. Laws," i., p. 251).

[3] "Anc. Laws," i. 243.

[4] "Anc. Laws," i. 243. The term *gwr nod* (literally, man of mark) is very ambiguous. Sometimes it looks as if it meant a *taeog* or *aillt*. But here

There was a distinction drawn between theft of a thing worth fourpence or less, and a thing worth more than that amount. In the former case the convicted thief became a "saleable thief" (*lleidr gwerth*) ; in the latter the thief forfeited his life, but not his property.[1] The worth of a saleable thief was fixed at seven pounds, and it would seem that if the seven pounds were paid by the thief or on his behalf he was let off. If he or his friends did not redeem him he was exiled, and if he remained in the country beyond the time assigned (a day being allowed for him for passing through every cantref in the lord's dominions) was liable to lose his life unless some one bought him—that is, he became an outlaw.[2]

The third column of law was *tan* (fire), and the rules concerning it are curious. We can only glance at them. The important position given to this topic was due to the fact that the houses were timber-built, and probably also to the difficulty of kindling fire. *Tan* is dealt with as if it were an object of property rights. If a man gave fire to another to burn therewith, and he admitted the gift, the donor was to pay one third of any damage caused by its user.[3] To take fire from a house without leave was an offence against the owner for which payment was to be made to him, and

gwyrnod would seem rather to mean men of distinction, of higher status. *Cf.* "Nod y genedl" (= mark of the kindred), used for a sign on a boundary stone, and *di-nod* (obscure), "Anc. Laws," i. 242. See A. Owen's glossary ("Anc. Laws," ii., p. 1118).

[1] "Anc. Laws," i. 253. The property stolen was, however, restored to the owner. There is some diversity of view as to these rules.

[2] "Anc. Laws," i., p. 245. It is said that a bondman (*taeog*) is not to be put to death if his lord will redeem him (*ibid.*, i. 255). We ought to say that the codes show considerable difference of practice as to the law of theft. The Church in some cases seems to have claimed to play a part ; see Dem. Code, "Anc. Laws," i. 419. In trying to get at the first principles we have mainly followed the Ven. Code.

[3] "Anc. Laws," i., p. 259. But another text says, "Whoever shall ask to *borrow* fire : let it come to him without claim against the lender." The distinction seems fine.

was also punishable by a fine (*camlwrw*) to the lord.   If a man set fire to a house he was liable to pay its worth, and that of any other houses burnt in consequence.[1]   If in consequence of the carelessness of the owner of a house in a tref it caught fire, he was liable at any rate for damage done to the two nearest houses, but if the fire spread further it was deemed an uncontrollable fire for which no one had redress.[2]   There were three fires for which no indemnity could be claimed, even if they did harm : burning the heath in March ; the fire of a smithy in a hamlet which was seven fathoms from the nearest houses, and which was covered with shingles or tiles or sods ; and the fire of a bath in a hamlet seven fathoms from the other houses.

The elaborate distinctions made among those who were accessory to the offences dealt with in the three columns of the law deserve the attention of the student of legal history, but we cannot do more than call attention to them.

There is no reason to doubt that the essential principles of the criminal system of which we have been treating had their origin in a state of society much earlier than that of the Cymry in the time of Howel ; but as the whole 'aw is presented to us, it is clear that long strides had been made towards the development of a true criminal law, and the recognition of a distinction between injuries to individuals, and grave offences against the community or the king or lord as its visible representative.   This is most clearly shown by the liability to pay for various offences fines (called *dirwy* and *camlwrw*) directly to the lord of the cymwd, by the distinction between offences which amounted to a breach of the king's *nawd* (protection or peace) and that of other men, and to some extent by the punishment of treason

---

[1] "Anc. Laws," i. 259.   This explains the necessity for the rules as to the worth of buildings and their different parts.   See *ibid.*, p. 293.   Different values are set on the houses of a king, of an uchelwr, and of an aillt.

[2] "Anc. Laws," i. 259.

(*brad*) to a king (not merely as a wrong against a *pen-kenedl*), and the forfeiture by a traitor of patrimonial rights, which was roughly equivalent to the attainder of English law.[1]

We do not propose to deal at length with the administration of justice among the Welsh under these laws. The usual distinction between lay and spiritual courts is certainly to be found, but if we may safely judge from the codes we should say that the jurisdiction of ecclesiastical courts was not developed to so great an extent as in England at the same time. The highest lay court was the court of the king or prince. The king or the judge of the court (*ynad llys*) presided, but there were apparently other assistant judges. This court decided all disputes between officers of the household.[2] Certain other matters were reserved to it; for instance, if an ecclesiastic held land by title under service to be performed to the king, he was to appear in case of dispute in this high court. The same tribunal had a kind of appellate jurisdiction. If a suitor who had lost a cause in a court of local jurisdiction complained that the judgment was wrong, he entered into a "mutual pledge" with the judge against the decision. If he wished to appeal, he was obliged to demand the pledge before the judge left his seat or passed on to the next cause. The appeal came on in due course in the king's court. It seems the judgment could only be questioned on the ground that the judge had applied a wrong law, that the proceedings had not been conducted with the right formalities, that the judge was partial or interested in the result, or that he had exacted fees

---

[1] It should, however, be mentioned that though the fines (*dirwy* and *camlwrw*) were inflicted in Gwyneđ, the evidence as to *treason* comes from the Dem. Code. But *dirwy* for offences committed within the king's palace was doubled even according to the Ven. Code ("Anc. Laws," i. 13. See also *ibid.* 436, 550).

[2] See "Anc. Laws," i., pp. 27–28, pp. 369–371, p. 469.

illegally.[1] If the decision went against the judge, he lost his office, his status as one of the order of judges, and his tongue or its worth as settled by law.[2] If the appellant failed, he had to pay the judge's *saraad*, and to redeem his tongue by paying its value.

Besides the king's court (which moved about with the household) there were local courts—those of the cantref and those of the cymwd. The distinction between the two sets of fixed territorial courts is quite obscure. Perhaps the cantref court adjudicated in cases where the disputants resided in different cymwds. The officers of the court of a cymwd were the canghellor, the maer, a judge or judges, a priest who acted as registrar, a clerk, and a bailiff or usher. The composition of the court, so far as the judges were concerned, varied in different parts of the country. In Gwyneð and Powys, it is said, there was one judge appointed for each court of a cymwd or cantref; but in the south every landed person (owner of *tir gwelyawg*) was a judge, and the right or duty of sitting in the court was an incident attached to the land.[3]

In a treatise entitled "additional law" of a date subsequent to the subjugation of the principality by Edward I., it is said that Howel "permitted every ecclesiastical lord such as the archbishop of Menevia or other bishops and abbots, royal privileges for holding pleas among the laics by the common law of Cymru. And likewise, he permitted every chief (*pennaeth*),[4] to whom there might belong a cymwd or cantref or more, to hold a daily court of privileged officers, in number as he should think proper, in a similar

---

[1] " Anc. Laws," i. pp. 475, 479.
[2] "Anc. Laws," i. 116. The tongue's worth was that of all the other members of the human body. It was assessed at four score and eight pounds (*ibid.*, pp. 311, 505, 699). Lawyers and judges seem to have had some kind of organisation, and to have formed, like the bards, an order with various privileges.
[3] " Anc. Laws," i., p. 469.
[4] Seemingly the *arglwyð* of whom we hear in other contexts.

manner to himself; and privilege to hold a royal court of pleas (*dadleuoeɗ breninawl*) in his country among his uchelwyr."[1] Jurisdiction conferred by the king in this way finds no countenance in the codes. The courts of the cymwd appear in them as part of a regular system of no recent origin; but as the authority of the court of the cymwd covered in practice all the ordinary suits in its area, as by legal theory every cymwd had over it some brenin, tywysog, or arglwyɗ, and as the process was to a late period oral, it can have mattered little whether the presiding officer affected to proceed in the name and by the privilege of the king himself or of some lord appointed by him.

Though the granting of practically complete immunity to the Church from the authority of lay chieftains was very likely common enough in the earlier years of Cymric history,[2] the conferring on laymen of privileges analogous to those of the lords-marchers of a later time is not probable, and is inconsistent with some of the regulations in the codes; so we think that the statement which we have just quoted is simply a reproduction of a theory later than the time of Howel (perhaps of the fourteenth century), which attempted to account for a state of things then existing by referring it to the positive enactment of Howel.

On the subject of judicial procedure we must content ourselves with mentioning just a few salient points. As might be expected, the codes are very full of the subject,[3]

---

[1] This is in c. 13 of book x. of the "Anomalous Laws," entitled, the "Charter of Howel Ɖa." The chief text is printed from the MS. which is denominated Q by A. Owen (Preface, "Anc. Laws," i., p. 30), and in his opinion was written about 1401.

[2] See Seebohm's "Tribal System," c. 8; and "Book of Llan Dâv" (Oxf. ed.), pp. 118 *et seq.*, 364-5.

[3] See, *e.g.*, the lengthy chapter on the laws concerning landed property and how one pleads (*datlewýr*) in respect thereto, in the Ven. Code, "Anc. Laws," i. 141 *et seq.* We take *datlewýr* from the Code. It should be spelt *dadleuir* in Mod. Welsh.

W.P.

and any attempt to briefly summarise difficult and confusing texts would lead to error. Notwithstanding some striking analogies with the early judicial procedure of the English, we see no reason to doubt that in the main the rules disclosed in these codes were not imitations, but were naturally developed among the Cymry themselves. The court sat in the open air, the pleadings were oral (though there are references to a record—*cof ttys*), and the progress of civil actions (at any rate) was evidently slow and tedious. The year was divided for legal purposes, so far as actions about land were concerned, into four periods ; in two the law was "open. for landed property," and in two it was " closed." This resulted in there being two terms in which claims to land might be made, prosecuted, and tried. The first was from the ninth of the calends of winter to the ninth of February ; the second was from the ninth of May to the ninth of August.[1] There was a class of professional lawyers. The parties had the assistance of a *cynghaws* (literally, "pleader ") and a *canttaw* (a "guider," literally, a "hand-rail").[2]

It is in regard to real actions and to suits for *galanas* that we have the most detailed information, though even in regard to them it is hardly possible to give a clear and sure account of the whole procedure, and we cannot here attempt to do so. But the particulars the laws give as to the arrangement of the court for the decision of a claim to land on the day of trial are interesting. At the time appointed all concerned came " upon the land "

---

[1] " The reason why the law shall be closed in autumn and spring is because the land is cultivated during those two periods ; lest ploughing in the spring and reaping in the autumn be impeded " (" Anc. Laws," i., p. 143).

[2] The distinction was analogous to that between barristers and attorneys in the English courts. There is no reason for thinking it was taken from English practice, for it is found in the Irish laws. The *cynghaws* was there called " *aighne* " (arguer), and the *canttaw* appears as " *fir ebe.*" See O'Sullivan's Introduction to " O'Curry's Lectures," p. cclxxiii.

(*i.e.*, the land in dispute), and then proceeded to " sit legally." The litigants and their assistants, with their witnesses, compurgators, and sureties, divided themselves into two parties, and stillness being proclaimed on the field, the members and officers of the court arranged themselves and the parties in the manner represented in the following table [1] :—

Gurda—Gurda—Heniuid—BRENIN—Heniuid—Gurda—Gurda.

Effeyrat—Egnat Kymwd.	Egnat Lys—Effiriatt.
Kanłłau—Amdiffenur—Keghaus.	Keghaus—Haulur—Kanłłau.
Rigyłł.	Righiłł.

After the court was thus constituted very formal oral pleadings took place, and the judges (who seem to have been the spokesmen and controllers of the court, even if the king were present), after giving the parties an opportunity of amending their pleadings, re-stated the contentions, and then retired to deliberate with a priest or priests and an usher. When they had taken their seats "in a judgment place" a priest prayed, and the judges chanted their *Pater ;* they then recited the pleadings a second time, and having done so, decided whether by law there was any necessity for the giving of evidence ; if they decided not, judgment was given simply on the pleadings, *i.e.*, to the effect that

---

[1] We print the table as it appears in " Anc. Laws," i., p. 146. We must, however, translate the Welsh terms : *Brenin* = king ; *heniuid* (*hynefy*) = elder ; *gurda* (*gwrda*) = good-man, uchelwr, breyr ; *effeyrat* and *effiriatt* = priest ; *egnat kymwd* = judge of the cymwd ; *egnat łłys* = judge of the king's court, the chief justice ; *kanłłau* (*canłław*), literally, hand-rail = guider ; *keghaus* (*cynghaws*) = pleader ; *amdiffenur* (*amdiffynnwr*) = defendant ; *rigiłł* (*rhingyłł*) = bailiff, apparitor, usher. It is clear this table is only a skeleton form. There might, for instance, be more than two gwyrda on each side. So, also, more than two elders. The gwyrda were the uchelwyr of the cymwd who had to attend the king on his progress through their district. Probably the elders were men of the king's cenedl, his near relations, accompanying him in his progress. The table represents the arrangement of the king's court ; but, no doubt, when an arglwy presided it afforded a precedent ; and, perhaps, also one for the ordinary court of the cymwd. The king sat with his back to the sun or the weather, lest the weather should incommode his face.

one or the other contention as set forth was correct in law, and that there was no need to interrogate, *i.e.*, to call witnesses. If, however, they held they could not decide simply on the pleadings they returned to the field and announced the fact, seemingly saying on whom lay the burden of proof, and two judges were appointed to question the parties and demand the production of their witnesses respectively. At this stage there might or might not be an adjournment, but ultimately the whole matter was decided by a trial by witnesses sworn on relics.[1]

We may here remark that there were three actions in regard to land : (i.) a suit to recover possession of land from which the plaintiff himself had been ousted ; (ii.) the suit called *dadenhudd*, by which the plaintiff sought to recover a share of *tir gwelyawg* belonging to him in right of his father or ancestors within the smaller group we have described above ;[2] and (iii.) the plaint by kin and reckoning (*o ach ac edryu*[3]), by which one sought to establish his right to such land as he might be entitled to as a member of a cenedl (in the large sense as a group of descendants to the ninth degree from a common ancestor).[4]

The rules we have been considering were those applying to disputes about land, but it would seem that methods fundamentally similar were applied to other controversies. There were actions for the recovery of movable property or its value (to which we have adverted above), for enforcing suretyships, pledges, and obligations incurred by contract, as well as the more serious processes in regard to *galanas, saraad*, personal injuries, theft, and damage by fire. In regard to all these the normal mode of settlement was a

---

[1] It is hardly necessary to say that it was not everyone who could be a witness in regard to a suit concerning Cymric land, *e.g.*, an attud could not ; nor a woman as against a man, etc. ("Anc. Laws," i., p. 153.)

[2] See specially "Anc. Laws," i. 171–2 ; and above, p. 196.

[3] This would be "ach ac edrif" in modern Welsh.

[4] See "Anc. Laws," i., pp. 173–5 ; p. 467.

trial by witnesses or by *rhaith* (compurgation). The rules as to the number and value of the members of the *rhaith* are complicated and obscure. The oath entered very largely into the administration of justice. It was taken in divers ways, sometimes on the gospels, sometimes on relics. The place of swearing varied; it might be in a church or before the court. Trial by combat or other ordeal is not mentioned in the codes, but in a late treatise it is said Dyfnwal Moelmud established for cases of theft, *galanas*, or treason, three ordeals, those of boiling water, hot iron, and combat, and that Howel did not deem them just and substituted for them proof by men and *rhaith;* [1] but all this is doubtful, though one may believe that trial by ordeal (*i.e.*, an appeal to a divine authority) sometime existed among the Cymry, since it was a very ancient and widespread way of settling disputes.

We have now given an outline of the legal organisation of the Cymry in the days of their independence as it may be gathered from their law-books, and to some extent we can fill it in by means of the information handed down to us in the works of a celebrated Welshman of the twelfth century. Gerald de Barri (usually called Giraldus Cambrensis) was born in 1147 in the castle of Manorbeer, the ruins of which still stand on the rocks of the South Pembrokeshire coast. He came of a Welsh family which had a Norman strain, and his grandmother was the Nest— the " Helen of Wales "—who had been the mistress of Henry I., and afterwards wife of Gerald de Windsor, lord of Pembroke. His father, William de Barri, and other members of his family had joined in warfare in Ireland. We must not linger over the details of his life or of his persistent struggle to secure archiepiscopal status for St. David's, or in other words the independence of the Welsh Church. In that effort he failed, but he has left for us valuable books, of

[1] " Anc. Laws," ii., p. 623.

which the most relevant for our present purpose are the "Itinerarium Cambriæ" and the "Descriptio Cambriæ."[1]

In 1188 Baldwin, archbishop of Canterbury, journeyed through Wales to preach a crusade. He was accompanied by Giraldus, who recorded their experiences in the Itinerary. The second work is, as its name applies, a description of the country and the people. Notwithstanding some attempt at fine writing which may have led to undue emphasis on particular points, we have, no doubt, in these books a true record of the characteristics of the mediæval Cymry from the pen of an able and honest observer.

These and the laws being our principal authorities, we find that the condition of society in Wales was removed by very many degrees from a barbaric or nomadic stage, but it was backward as compared with the south-eastern Britain of that time. It may be that the economic progress of the scanty population of Wales had been checked by the war with Harold, the collapse of Gruffyd̄ ab Llewelyn's power, and the subsequent course of events. Gerald deals with a people who had sustained many reverses, and who had been driven from the most fertile portions of their country by bands of Norman adventurers ; and it is obviously likely that these things told for a time against any great social advance, though it may be noted as a curious fact that it was in the eleventh century that modern Welsh poetry has its beginning, and that in that region of culture contact, whether friendly or inimical, with the Norman lords had a stimulating effect. Neither Howel

---

[1] The works of Giraldus are to be found in the Rolls series, vols. i., ii., iii., iv. (ed. by Professor Brewer), vols. v., vi., vii. (ed. by the Rev. J. F. Dymock). "The Topography and History of the Conquest of Ireland " (translated by Thomas Forester), and the "Itinerary through Wales," and the "Description of Wales" (translated by Sir R. Colt Hoare, Bart.) are published in vol. vii. Bohn's Antiquarian Library (ed. by Thomas Wright, F.S.A.). For his life, see "Dict. Nat. Biog.," *sub nom.* ; the introduction to vol. i. in the Rolls series ; and "Gerald the Welshman," by Henry Owen, B.C.L., F.S.A. (Lond., 1889).

Ða nor Gruffyð ab Ilewelyn, the only two chieftains of the
Cymry who, after Rhodri Mawr, had played any really
considerable part in the affairs of the island, were celebrated
by contemporary bards whose works have come down to
our time; but from the end of the eleventh century we
find many poems devoted to the praise (often in extravagant language) of princes some of whom were hardly of
a position higher than that of a petty lord-marcher.

In the centuries with which we are dealing Wales
presented a physical aspect very different from that which
it does to-day. The greater part was waste land on which
the foot of man rarely trod, mere boulder-strewn moorland, or
boggy tract; and large portions of the estates now divided
into farm holdings and highly cultivated were covered with
trees that have disappeared. The roads (if we exclude the
few which seem to derive their origin from the time of
Roman occupation) were mere mountain tracks. There
were practically no enclosures apart from the mounds or
wooden fences which were made around the houses of the
more important families.[1]

When Giraldus wrote, towns were beginning to arise
under the shelter of some of the Norman castles, but there
were no truly Cymric towns. Caerleon on Usk was in
ruins, and Chester was in Norman hands.[2] The social and

---

[1] Rice Merrick, in his "Booke of Glamorganshire Antiquities" (1578),
(new ed. by James Andrew Corbett, fol., Lond., 1887), referring to the Vale
of Glamorgan, says it was "a champyon and open country without great store
of inclosures," and that the old men reported that "their ffore-fathers told
them that great part of th' enclosures was made in their daies" ("Cambrian
Register" (1796), pp. 96–8; "Report," p. 663).

[2] Giraldus says, "This city (Caerleon) was of undoubted antiquity and
handsomely built of masonry, with courses of bricks, by the Romans. Many
vestiges of its former splendour may still be seen; immense palaces formerly
ornamented with gilded roofs in imitation of Roman magnificence, inasmuch
as they were first raised by Roman princes, and embellished with splendid
buildings; a tower of prodigious size, remarkable hot baths, relics of temples,
and theatres all inclosed within fine walls, part of which remain standing, etc."
("Desc.," i., c. 5.) The castle of Cardiff was surrounded by high walls, and

domestic life of the Welsh centred round the timber-built
houses of the kings, princes, lords or uchelwyr which were
scattered in the valleys and on the lower slopes of the hills.
Except, perhaps, in some of the villein-trefs, there were no
villages or clusters of dwelling-houses close adjoining one
another, though the principal hall of men of higher position
had the usual out-buildings. The dwellings of some families
were duplicated ; in the summer they lived in a house on
the higher part of their property called the *havod-dy*
(literally, "summer-house"), and in winter returned to the
principal residence (*hen-dref*, literally, the "old-stead") set
up in a more sheltered place below.

The broad conclusion we draw from the sources we have
mentioned is that in the twelfth century the Cymry were a

Giraldus refers to the *city* as containing many soldiers. The "Brut," in one
of its versions, says, under the year 1080, "the building of Cardiff began."
This is not in the "Brut" reproduced in the Oxford series. It occurs in the
MS. called D, by Ab Ithel (see preface to Rolls ed., p. xlvi). The MS. is in
the B. M. Cottonian collection, marked "Cleopatra, B. v.," and is of the
fifteenth century. Whether this entry means that the building of Cardiff castle,
or that of the town, began, the date seems too early (see below, as to the
conquest of Glamorgan). The date of the foundation of Swansea castle is
uncertain, but it was later than that of Cardiff. Colonel Morgan, of Bryniaɬlu,
has been good enough to send us an interesting communication as to Swansea
(in Welsh Abertawe), which is, however, too long to reproduce here. He
argues that (i) Swansea, Sweyneshe, Sweineshe (the two latter are the earliest
forms) is to be identified with the Sein Henyd of the "Brut" (*s.aa.* 1215,
1221) ; and (ii) that the name Sweyneshe, etc., is derived from Sein Henyd.
We are of opinion that the first of these propositions is true, but we do not
think that the place-name Sweyneshe, etc., and Sein Henyd have anything
to do with one another. The "w" in the accepted English name is one of
the most considerable difficulties in the way of adopting Colonel Morgan's
second suggestion. There are place-names of Danish or Scandinavian, or at
any rate non-Welsh, origin to be found on or near the sea-coast of South
Wales. Consider Sully, Haverford, Stackpole, Hulberston, Angle, Herbrand-
ston, Gateholm, Stockholm, Skimer, Musselwick, Haroldston, Ramsey, and
Strumble. See Clark's "Mediæval Military Architecture in England," p. 15
(Lond., 1884). Giraldus calls Carmarthen an "ancient city," and notices
that it was strongly enclosed with walls of bricks, part of which were still
standing ("Desc.," i., c. 10). Dinevwr, higher up the Towy, was the seat of
the South Welsh princes.

warlike pastoral people, who had been settled on their lands
for centuries, but who had made only slight progress in
agriculture and the other practical arts, and who had
advanced more quickly in regard to intellectual exercises,
poetry, and music than in regard to material prosperity
and higher morality.

We have only space to mention a few details concerning
them from which we think this generalisation will appear
to be true. The principal crops referred to in the laws
and Giraldus's works are wheat, barley, and oats. The
plough, the scythe, and other farming implements (which
were, however, of primitive construction) are mentioned.
The ridges were generally ploughed straight upward, and
the Commissioners found their form still visible in some
places.[1] They also saw indications that slopes and even
summits of hills, which are not now and have not been for
a very long period arable land, had at some former time
been ploughed.

In the laws yokes of four different lengths are mentioned :—The *ber-iau*, or short yoke of three feet, for two
oxen ; the *mei-iau*, or field yoke of six feet, for four oxen ;
the *ceseil-iau*, or auxiliary yoke of nine feet, for six oxen ;
and the *hir-iau*, or long yoke of twelve feet, for eight oxen.[2]
The Welsh farmer seldom, however, yoked less than four
oxen to the plough. The driver walked backward, and
instead of a small sickle in mowing he made use of a
moderate-sized piece of iron formed like a knife with two
pieces of wood fixed loosely and flexibly to the head.[3] In
the month of March only the soil was once ploughed for
oats, and again in the summer a third time, and in the
winter for wheat.

[1] "Report, p. 657.

[2] See "Report," p. 657 : The measurements are in the English standard.
Pughe, in his "Welsh Dictionary," says the Welsh used four sorts of yoke until
about 1600.

[3] Giraldus Cambrensis, "Desc. Camb.," book i., c. 17.

Giraldus's remarks seem, for the most part, to apply to the Cymry proper, though there is a good deal to show that by his time there was considerable admixture of classes or races.

Hospitality and liberality were among the first of their virtues. The house of the Cymro was common to all. The traveller was not offered, nor did he beg entertainment. He simply delivered up his arms : he was then under the *nawd* (peace) of the *penteulu* (head of the household). Water was brought to him, and if he suffered his feet to be washed, he became a guest of the house ; if he refused water, he was understood to be simply asking for morning refreshment and not lodging for the night. Strangers arriving early were entertained by the conversation of the young women of the household and the music of harps. The principal meal was served in the evening. It varied according to the number and dignity of the persons assembled and the degrees of the wealth of different households. In any case it was a simple repast ; there were no tables, no cloths, no napkins ; the guests were seated in messes of three ; all the dishes were at once set before them in large platters on rushes or grass spread on the floor. The food consisted of milk, cheese, butter, meat plainly cooked. " The kitchen did not supply many dishes nor high-seasoned incitements to eating." The bread was served as a thin and broad cake, fresh baked every day,[1] and broth with chopped-up meat in it was sometimes added. The family waited on the guests, and the host and hostess stood up until their needs were satisfied. The evening was enlivened by songs and recitations by the bard of the household or by minstrels who in their wandering had joined the company, and seemingly also by choral singing.

---

[1] Giraldus says it was "lagana" in the old writings. It was evidently like the "bake-stone" bread—*bara planc* or *bara ttech*—of modern days.

A bed made of rushes and covered with a coarse kind
of cloth made in the country called *brychan*, was then
placed along the side of the hall, and the family and guests
lay down to sleep in common.[1] The fire on the hearth in
the centre continued to burn all night.

From Giraldus we get little information as to the clothes
of the Welsh ; he says that at all seasons they defended
themselves from the cold only by a thin cloak and tunic ;
but the laws give the worth of other articles of wearing
apparel, *e.g.*, a mantle of rich dark colour; a town-made
mantle ; a town-made cap ; a town-made coat *(pais);* a
home-made covering ; shirt and trousers ; a head-cloth ;[2]
robes of the king and queen, and of an uchelwr and his
wife, etc.[3]

As to their personal habits the Cymry seem to have been
cleanly.[4] In the laws we have allusions to the bath ; the
custom of offering water to guests has just been referred
to. Both sexes cut their hair short—close round to their
ears and eyes. The men shaved all their beard except the
moustache. All paid great attention to their teeth, which

[1] Giraldus does not mention pillows, but in the Ven. Code, iii., c. 22, a legal
price (*gwerth*) is placed on the pillow (*gobennyd*) of the king and on that of an
uchelwr, thus showing they were in use. A price is also put on a sheet (*Hen*,
or in the laws *Henllyeyn*). As late as the fifteenth century the English
"gentry, who slept on down beds, or beds stuffed with rabbits' fur and other
materials which passed for down, still went naked to their slumbers ; the poor,
who slept on bundles of fern or on trusses of straw spread on the ground, slept
in the dress they had worn during the day, and the cloak or cassock of the
ploughman was his only counterpane " (Denton, "England in the Fifteenth
Century," p. 206). Down to the early years of this century it was not unusual
in Wales for people to go to bed naked.

[2] Giraldus says the women covered their heads with a large white veil folded
together in the form of a crown.

[3] See Ven. Code, iii., c. 22 ; but book iii. was collected from books later
than Howel's time as well as from the old book of the "White House." See
the prefaces to it.

[4] The account given by Giraldus of the Cymry in this regard is very favourable as compared with his remarks on the barbarism of the Irish ("Top.
Irel.," iii., c. 10).

they rendered like ivory by constantly rubbing them with green hazel and wiping them with a woollen cloth.

For the Cymry proper—the leading families—the chief business of life was warfare. "They were entirely bred up to the use of arms;" but the language of Giraldus is general, and according to him "all the people are trained to war." When "the trumpet sounds the alarm, the husbandman rushes as eagerly from his plough as the courtier from his Court." We have seen that in the laws of Howel it was only the tribesmen who formed the host; to the eilltion only the subordinate duties of a campaign were entrusted ; but the words we have quoted seem to indicate that the settlement of the Normans in the land had brought about a change in the military arrangements, and this is confirmed by indications from other sources.

The higher classes (*nobiliores, i.e.,* uchelwyr) went forth to battle on horseback, though they did not hesitate to dismount if necessary, either for marching or combat. The great majority of the men of the host fought on foot. The armour of all was so light as not to impede the quick movements on which they depended for success. The uchelwyr, and seemingly most of the foot soldiers (of tribal privilege) as well, wore small coats of mail, helmets, and sometimes greaves plated with iron. In marching they often walked barefoot, but in battle array they appear ordinarily to have worn high shoes roughly made with untanned leather.[1]

---

[1] It is clear that even men of the upper class did not wear boots on many occasions, even of some importance. On the morning after leaving the house of Strata Florida, the archbishop and Giraldus met one Cyneuric ab Rhys (evidently of noble descent), accompanied by a body of light-armed youths. Giraldus describes him thus : "This young man was of a fair complexion, with curled hair, tall and handsome, clothed only according to the custom of his country, with a thin cloak and inner garment, his legs and feet, regardless of thorns and thistles, were left bare ; a man not adorned by art but by nature ; bearing in his presence an innate, not an acquired, dignity of manners" ("Itin.," book ii., c. 4). In the laws a price is set on wadded boots (*botessau kenhenlauc*), shoes with thongs (*eskydyeu careyauc*), and on buskins (*guyntesseu*).

Their chief weapons were the sword, the lance or spear, the battle-axe, and the bow and arrow; and in the time of Giraldus the men of Gwent were deemed more expert in archery than those of the other parts of Cymru.[1]

The fighting in which the Cymry excelled was of the guerilla kind. They did not shine much in open engagements or regular conflicts, but were skilful in harassing the enemy by ambuscades and nightly sallies. As a rule they made no determined struggle for the field of battle.[2] In their onset they were bold and rapid; they filled the air with horrid shouts[3] and the deep-toned clangour of very long trumpets; if repulsed, they were easily thrown into confusion, and trusted to flight for safety. But though defeated one day they were ever ready to resume the combat on the next; they were active and hardy; able to sustain hunger and cold; not easily fatigued by warlike exercise, and above all not despondent in adversity. Giraldus sums up the matter by saying that they were "as easy to overcome in a single battle as difficult to subdue in a protracted war."[4] We ought to add that it is probable

---

[1] The Ven. Code sets a price on "a bow and twelve arrows" (*bua a deudec saet*), a spear (*guaeu*), a battle-axe (*aref buyaⱨ*), and on a sword (*cledyf*) rough-ground, a sword dark-bladed, and a sword white-bladed ("Anc. Laws," i., p. 305). In one passage Giraldus refers to the lances as long ("Desc.," i., c. 8); in another he mentions frequent throwing of darts ("Desc.," ii., c. 3). The Welsh, therefore, probably had two ki..ds of spear. "A sword, and spear, and bow with twelve arrows in the quiver," was the traditional equipment of the head of a Cymric household ("Anc. Laws," ii., p. 557).

[2] Gruffyd̄ ab Lewelyn in his Hereford campaigns against Ralph acted exceptionally. But notice how he avoided a pitched battle with Harold when the latter changed the conditions by lightly equipping his men. See above, p. 172.

[3] So says Giraldus ("Desc.," ii., c. 3). *Cf.* the poem in praise of Lewelyn ab Madoc, ascribed to one Lywarch Lew Cad. The bard calls Lewelyn "commander of the men of terrible shout" (*Lawr gawr goruchel y wir*). Stephens's "Lit. of the Kymry" (2nd ed.), p. 53.

[4] See "Desc.," book ii., c. 3. It should be noticed, further, as an illustration of the character of the warfare, that the Cymry gave no quarter ("Desc.," book ii., c. 8).

that during the period of about one hundred and forty years that elapsed between the death of Gruffyd ab Lewelyn and the time at which Giraldus wrote, intercourse and fighting with the Normans had done much to improve the equipment and military methods of the Cymry.[1]

Giraldus bears warm testimony to the proficiency of the Cymry in the art of music. They used three instruments —the harp, the pipes, and the crwth.[2] In their concerts they did not sing in unison, but in different parts. He remarks that the people in the northern district of Britain beyond the Humber and on the borders of Yorkshire made use of the same kind of "symphonious harmony," but with less variety, singing only in two parts, one murmuring in the bass, the other warbling in the acute or treble.

Much attention was paid by them to poetry. Bards were important members of the community, as we know also from the laws. They were organised in some fashion into a kind of separate order, though we have no certain evidence as to the rules of their craft or guild in those early days.[3] Every considerable household had its domestic bard (*bard teulu*). Besides the duty of entertaining by song he had care of any documents that concerned the family of his patron; he was the preserver of the genealogy of the kindred; and often the teacher and companion of his chieftain's children. Whether by positive enactment or by usage, the practice of making tours of the country arose.

---

[1] See "Desc.," book ii., c. 7.

[2] Gir. "Top. Ireland" Dist., iii., c. 11; "Desc. Camb.," i., c. 12. The crwth or crowd was a kind of early violin. The pipes seem to have been bagpipes, and were objects of ridicule to the bards. For a summary of what is known as to early Welsh music, see Stephens' "Literature of the Kymry" (2nd ed.), pp. 55–69.

[3] It is traditionally believed Gruffyd ab Kynan, king of Gwyned, made rules for the government of the bardic order, but the proof is not satisfactory. See as to the Eisteddfod, p. 516, below. The Brut (*s.a.* 1176) records that Lord Rhys held a grand festival, at which there were musical competitions, in the castle of Aberteivi.

The bards went from house to house, quartering themselves on the households : the higher grade of bards only went to the palaces of princes and the greater nobles ; the lower grades had the range of the establishments of meaner men.

Extravagant pretensions as to the antiquity of this Cymric bardic order have been advanced ; it has been claimed for the bards of the twelfth century that their organisation was a direct survival of that of thê Druidic hierarchy ; and that they were the depositories of a mysterious system of religion and philosophy orally handed down to them from the priests of the oak, and thence transmitted without break to our own day. There is, however, no proof of any formal connection between the Druidic priesthood and the bardic system as it appears in Wales in' the twelfth century. There is no certain evidence that Druidism had spread to that part of the island whence Cuneda and the ancestors of the Cymry came. Centuries before their settlement in Wales Druidism had been suppressed by the Roman government, and there is nothing to show that the sacerdotal class, practically destroyed by Paulinus, ever regained its authority or maintained its organisation.[1]

From the Roman conquest of Môn to the time of Gruffyd ab Kynan over one thousand years had elapsed. Christianity had for a long period been the only legally recognised religion, and was probably professed by Cuneda and his followers. It had, first in its Celtic, and afterwards in its Roman form, obtained a secure and undisputed position in the land. If to these considerations we add the facts that none of the bardic MSS. are older than the twelfth century, and that competent criticism of the bardic remains leads to the conclusion that this so-called

---

[1] Môn, "the last asylum of the Celtic priesthood," was conquered by G. Seutonius Paulinus in A.D. 61, and finally subdued by Julius Agricola in A.D. 78. Mommsen's "Provinces of the Roman Empire" (Eng. Tr.), v. 1, pp. 179, 182.

Druidism was confined to the bards themselves, and that as an institution it was then of recent origin,[1] we must dismiss the claims we have been discussing as mere inventions or efforts of the imagination which have been ignorantly and uncritically adopted and developed in after times. On the other hand, it must be conceded that the office of domestic bard is one which is found in the earliest historic times among Indo-European nations; that there are many items of evidence which show an intimate connection between singers, story-tellers, and the like, and the priesthoods of early forms of religion; and that the memory may be so cultivated that rites, formulæ, poems, and tales may be orally handed down from generation to generation for an indefinite time. It must also be admitted that many pagan notions and customs survived among the people long after Christianity had obtained its formal hold on the community. The bardic poems of later date may be the genuine echoes of the conceptions of the religion of a distant past, and contain the dim recollections of true historical events;[2] but there is nothing in all this that need alter the opinion we have expressed, that there is no proof of any direct connection between the bardic order in mediæval Wales and the Druidic system described by Cæsar. However this may be, the genuine laws and the words of Giraldus give to the bards of Wales a very respectable position in the society of the time, and accord their profession a reasonable and satisfactory antiquity.

Among the characteristics of the Welsh, Giraldus notices their wit and pleasantry. They were fluent and bold in conversation; in their rhymed songs and set speeches they were so subtle and ingenious that they produced

---

[1] See the chapter on "Bards and Bardism," in Stephens's "Lit. of the Kymry," p. 84.

[2] See Matthew Arnold's "Essay on the Study of Celtic Literature" (Lond., 1867); Skene's "Four Ancient Books of Wales" (Edin., 1868, 2 vols.).

"ornaments of wonderful and exquisite invention, both in the words and sentences."

They greatly esteemed noble birth and generous descent. All retained their genealogy and could readily repeat the names of their ancestors to the sixth or seventh generation or beyond, and when we think of the laws we can readily understand this to have been the case.[1] They were, at any

---

[1] As late as the time of Norden's survey of Abenbury, a township adjoining Wrexham (1620), a gentleman of estate gave his name as Humfridus ap Robert ap Will'm ap Rob't ap David ap Griffith ap Robert. (Seebohm, "Tribal System," p. 85, note.) This is stated on the authority of Mr. A. N. Palmer. Though it was not every one who could give his style with this fulness, the method of identifying a person by coupling his christian name with those of his immediate ancestors lingered long in Wales. It is not easy to fix the time when the use of surnames became general among all classes. The noticeable thing now is the paucity of surnames in this populous area. Those that usually occur are mostly baptismal names taken from the Bible spelt in divers ways. This is especially so in the Welsh-speaking districts. The number of Joneses, Davieses, Williamses, Thomases, etc., on public bodies and juries is often the subject of jest, and sometimes the cause of inconvenience. The usual explanation of the fewness of surnames in the Welsh area is that the officials of the Welsh courts, the coroners, and lawyers found the Welsh custom of stringing together a series of baptismal names troublesome, and that in the jury process, etc., they abridged the style of the person with whom they were dealing. Thus they summoned a juror, not by the style he would have given himself, but as, *e.g.*, William ap John, or Gulielmus ap Johannes, which often repeated became William Jones, and was acquiesced in by a too patient people. In rural districts, to avoid ambiguity, farmers often referred to one another by the names of their holdings (*e.g.*, John Maeseglwys, where the latter word is the name of John's holding), and we have known this recently done by witnesses in the courts. In later times the inconvenience has been to some extent met among the professional and middle classes by the conferring of a second and distinctive christian name (*e.g.*, W. *Tudor* Howell, T. *Eynon* Davies, John *Morlais* Jones—where the intermediate names are the only distinguishing marks). The use of bardic names is not uncommon. Thus, the late Dr. William Rees, of Chester, is always spoken of as "Hiraethog," and Mr. William Abraham, M.P., is called by most Welshmen "Mabon," in public and private. People are reluctant to change their surnames, because they do not wish to lose touch with their relations, and fear that in property matters there may be difficulty later on in proof of identity, birth, etc. It would be a great advantage if some method of formal registration of change of name could be established in each county. For information as to Welsh surnames see a series of papers by Mr. T. E. Morris, LL.M., B.A., in "Byegones" for Oct., 1893, Feb., 1894, April, 1897, and Jan. and Feb., 1900.

rate outwardly, very religious ; when one of them met a priest or monk he asked his blessing "with extended arms and bowing head"; they showed greater respect than other nations to churches and the clergy, to relics, bells, holy books, and the cross.

So far our account gives a pleasant view of the Welsh people in these mediæval times, but there is a darker side to Giraldus's picture. In language which recalls in some degree the rhetoric of Gildas, he points out very grave blemishes in the character and mode of life of the Cymry He describes them as wanting in respect to oaths, faith and truth ; as so indifferent to the covenant of faith that they went through the ceremony of holding forth the right hand on trifling occasions and to emphasise mere ordinary assertions ; and worse still as not scrupling to take false oaths in legal causes. He says they habitually committed acts of plunder, theft and robbery, not only against foreigners but against their own countrymen. They were addicted to trespassing and the removal of landmarks, and there were continual disputes between brothers. They were immoderate in their love of food and intoxicating drinks.

Though the language of Giraldus is strong, and his strictures are severe, there can be no doubt that there is substantial truth in what he says, but by way of qualification it must be pointed out that he was a stern and imperious ecclesiastic, that he was looking at the condition of things from the point of view of the Norman-English government, so far as civil matters were concerned, and that he completely ignores the injustice that had been done by the conquest of the greater part of the south by Norman adventurers. What he meant by false swearing was almost a necessary result of a legal system, which made an oath an incident of ordinary transactions, and which in judicial proceedings multiplied the number of compurgators to an unusual degree. Especial allowance must be made for this kind of perjury in the case of men who regarded the tie of blood as the strongest social bond, and in a time when a trial was not an inquiry into issues of fact to be decided by witnesses in our modern sense, but one depending on a complicated method of swearing and counter-swearing by rheithwyr, who came to regard themselves not as being charged with the duty of saying what they had actually seen or heard, but of standing by a kinsman in trouble. So too much may be urged in extenuation of their trespassing and plundering. For in the early years of the conquest, at any rate, the men of the Norman lord were quite as ready to seize any cattle they could lay hands on as any Cymric youths, and many violent acts of the Welsherie were justifiable, because the cattle they carried off in their raids were looked on as being taken in lieu of those of which they had been despoiled. Their trespasses on and " ambitious seizures " of land in the occupation of invaders need from an impartial standpoint no justification ; but the continued litigation about land among themselves and the habits of forcible entry (as we should say) by one relative as against another, though easily to be explained as the consequence of the rules concerning succession to *tir gwelyawg*, must be condemned as a proof of those serious defects in the typical Cymric character, of which such striking illustration is afforded by the failure of the nation to effect any stable and lasting political combination.

But when every allowance is made, the Cymry proper, whom Giraldus describes, were a wild and turbulent race, dangerous neighbours, and impatient of settled control from any quarter,[1] a set of men very unlike the singularly

---

[1] Read the adventures of Owain ab Cadwgan, in the " Brut," *s.a.* 1106, and in following entries and pp. 293 *et seq.* below. See also Wynne's "History of the Gwydyr Family," which shows how disorderly were the habits of a later day.

law-abiding Welsh people of to-day.[1]   They were a quick, impulsive race, wanting in moderation, indulging in extremes of conduct, and we readily follow Giraldus when in ending his first book he says that "this nation is earnest in all its pursuits, and neither worse men than the bad nor better than the good can be met with."

[1] The comparative absence of crime in the distinctively Welsh counties has been noticeable for many years, and is often a topic of comment by judges of assize and chairmen of quarter sessions.

CHAPTER VII.

IT was the Norman conquest of England that led to the absorption first of large areas, and later on of the whole, of Wales into the English system. This absorption did not fully take place for about 500 years; and some 220 years elapsed before the whole of the country was placed in a position of actual and practical dependence on the English Government. It is a circumstance worth noting that while the English counties were conquered by the Normans in a comparatively few years, and almost by a single stroke, the Norman-English kings and their followers were only able to effect the subjugation of Cymru in a very gradual and tedious manner.

An eminent historian says in reference to the commencement of the Norman invasion of Cymru, "The conquest which now began, that which we may call either the English or the Norman conquest of Wales, differed widely both from the English conquest of Britain and from the Norman conquest of England. It wrought far less change than the landing at Ebbsfleet; it wrought far more change than the landing at Pevensey. The Briton of those lands, which in the Red King's day were still British, was gradually conquered; he was gradually brought under English rule and English law, but he was neither exterminated, nor enslaved, nor wholly assimilated. He still abides in his ancient land, still speaking his ancient tongue.

The English or Norman conquest of Wales was not a national migration, like the English conquest of Britain, nor was it a conquest wrought under the guise of an elaborate legal fiction, like the Norman conquest of England."[1]

The process by which the conquest of Wales was effected is one that cannot be described as simply military, but rather as being both military and economic. If we may judge from the records of the twelfth and thirteenth centuries, the Welsh chieftains were in the battles fought from time to time nearly as successful, and often more so, than the Norman invaders; but the greater resources and wealth of the latter gradually led to their military predominance, while such evidence as we possess in the work of Giraldus Cambrensis leads to the conclusion that when he wrote not only a relative, but an absolute, diminution of the Cymric or Welsh-speaking population had taken place. However this may be, it was by the building of castles on the Norman plan and by actual settlement that the process became successful. What appears to have been done was this:[2] at points conveniently situated near the more fertile lands, and most suitable for military defence or operations, a castle was built and garrisoned. Gradually the Cymry were ousted from the cultivated area, or else became, on some terms or other, the tenants of the Norman lord. From the coign of vantage afforded by the castle, the Norman lord waged continual warfare against the natives, and as he gradually forced them further and further into the less desirable areas of the country he

---

[1] Freeman, "William Rufus," vol. ii., p. 72. Though the generalisations in this paragraph are (we agree) substantially true, we cannot help pointing out that the phrase " English conquest of Britain " is not strictly accurate. Unless a very unreasonable extension is given to the terms "English" and "conquest," the English had conquered only a part of Britain before 1066.

[2] See the account of the Lords Marchers in Clive's "Ludlow" (London, 1841) from a manuscript in the Lansdowne collection (now in British Museum), p. 101.

extended his power, seizing cymwd after cymwd and cantref after cantref. In time towns began to spring up under the shelter of the castle walls, settlement from England was encouraged, charters conferring municipal privileges were from time to time conferred upon the settlers, and most of the early charters of the Welsh boroughs, drawing, as they do, an acute distinction between Englishmen and Welchmen, mark the nature of the struggle which went on during these years.[1]

The ultimate outcome of the process was that by the middle of the thirteenth century nearly the whole of what is now Wales, except the counties of Anglesey, Carnarvon, part of Denbighshire, and Merionethshire, the area roughly corresponding to the ancient kingdom of Gwyned, had passed into the hands of the Norman-English king or Norman lords, who came to be described by lawyers as "lords marchers," who were feudal vassals of the king of England, though they exercised in their respective lordships practically supreme power. As Freeman observes, "Wales is, as every one knows, pre-eminently the land of castles. Through those districts with which we are specially concerned, castles great or small, or the ruins or traces of such castles, meet us at every step. . . . The castles are in truth the leading architectural features of the country. The churches, mostly small and plain, might, themselves, with their fortified towers, almost count as castles. The towns, almost all of English foundations,

---

[1] Before the Norman Conquest, the Cymry did not for their defence build stone castles or fortresses. Their defensive works consisted "of a mound with a moat, and a timber building protected by palisades on the mound." (See Clark's "Mediæval Military Architecture in England," Lond. 1884, pp. 23, 24.) Clark says there is not a shadow of evidence that they (the Welsh) constructed any new defensive works in masonry upon the Roman models, or even repaired those that were left to them in the same material. (*Ibid* p. 12.) See, however, the Rev. S. Baring-Gould's paper on "Early Fortifications in Wales" in "Trans. of the Hon. Soc. of Cymmrodorion," Sess. 1898-99, p. 1.

were mostly small ; they were military colonies rather than seats of commerce. As Wales had no immemorial cities, like Exeter and Lincoln, so she had no towns which sprang up into greatness in later times, like Bristol, Norwich, and Coventry. Every memorial of former days which we see in the British land reminds us how long warfare remained the daily business alike of the men in that land and of the strangers who had made their way into it at the sword's point." [1]

The significance of the castle is that it is the mark of a lordship which formerly existed, and which may even at the present day remain for legal purposes, as forming the root of title to the possession of land or the exercise of some seigniorial right.

The detailed history of this gradual conquest has never been written with an adequate comprehension of the facts as a whole, though the county histories and many books written concerning Welsh families or particular lordships preserve the story with substantial accuracy. One general comment we have to make : that we are immensely struck with the continuity of the whole history. The evidence that the Commission obtained with regard to different estates and much of the information that they collected indicate that the settlement of the Norman in a particular cantref did not operate so as to cause an absolute break in local organisation and local life. The lordship or the sub-lordship oftentimes appears to have become coterminous with a cantref or a cymwd, and probably in its actual visible working the individual conquest from a legal point of view only led to the Norman conqueror's exercising a right and jurisdiction very analogous to that of the Welsh *arglwyd* in lieu of the dispossessed Cymro, and the holding of the court in the new castle instead of the older timber-built house of the Welsh chieftain, under the officers of the former instead of those of the latter.

[1] Freeman, "William Rufus," vol. ii., p. 777.

Another general observation which our experience
enables us to make is that Wales as a whole for a long
time presented a striking want of constitutional uniformity,
and the traces of that condition of things still remain.
The historian whom we have more than once quoted says:
—"Wales for a long time after the time with which we
are now dealing was as far from uniformity as any land
east of the Adriatic. Here was the castle of the Norman
lord, with his following, Norman, English, Flemish, anything but British. Here was the newly founded town, with
its free burghers, again Norman, English, Flemish, anything
but British. Here again was a whole district from which
the British Briton had passed away as thoroughly as he had
passed away from Kent or Norfolk, but which the Norman
had not taken into his own hands. He had found that it
suited his purpose to leave it in the hands of the hardy and
industrious Fleming, the last wave of Low Dutch occupation in the isle of Britain. And alongside of all there was
the still independent Briton, still keeping his moors and
mountains, still ready to pour down from them upon the
richer lands which had been his father's, but which had
passed into the stranger's grasp. Those days have long
passed away; for three centuries and more Briton and
Englishman have been willing members of a common state,
willing subjects of a common sovereign. But the memory
of those days has not passed away; it abides in the most
living of all witnesses. England has for ages spoken a
single tongue, her own ancient speech, modified by the
coming of the conquerors of 800 years ago; but in Wales
the speech of her conquerors, the speech of England, is
still only making its way slowly and fitfully against the
abiding resistance of that stubborn British tongue which
has survived three conquests."[1]

[1] Freeman, "William Rufus," vol. ii., p. 74. As to the settlement of
Flemings in Wales, see above, pp. 27–9.

The next remark that we have to make is that if we want to form a true picture of the actual facts taking place from year to year during the times with which we are dealing, we must notice the different interpretations placed upon events by those who approached their consideration from the Norman or English and from the Welsh point of view. We have seen above that before the Norman had placed his foot as conqueror upon English soil Wales, or, to speak more accurately, the cantrefs and cymwds, the areas and the names of which had been handed down from generation to generation, was parcelled out among lords, princes, or kings, exercising customary rights over their own portions. We have seen that the whole of this region was governed or regulated by a tribal system as strong as any statutory laws. The mere fact of a particular cymwd or cantref being violently taken possession of by a Norman or English stranger in no way, from the Welsh point of view, affected status and rights. The pretensions of the heads of the Welsh families remained precisely the same and were recognised to the same extent by their relations and dependants after the building of a new castle by an intruder or the loss of a series of battles, as before. The Welsh *arglwyd* retreated to the higher ground, fortified as well as he could his house, and sometimes imitated with skill the fortress of the stranger. The contest, when once the castle was built and adequately garrisoned, was however a hopeless one for the Welshman. The point to be noticed is that, though practically defeated and ousted from his cymwd, his cantref, or his gwlad, the Welshman still maintained his legal theory, and did not recognise the stranger's rights. In fact superseded, the Welshman at first still called himself and deemed himself justly the lord of the conquered territory, and to such an extent as the occupiers of the soil, whether free tribesmen or taeogion, recognised him, he was so in fact. Probably, however, the actual cultivators within the area of the castle's power were evicted one after another if they did not become the tenants of the Norman lord or were not slain in the ceaseless petty warfare that resulted from the efforts of the Norman lord to feed his garrison. It is not difficult, therefore, to understand the position of the Welsh chieftain. Sometimes he retook the castle and the adjacent lands, and for a brief period again enjoyed his accustomed rights. But whatever were the vicissitudes of the particular case, the Welsh chieftains long maintained their old tribal and customary rights, and did not, except as the result of generations of conflict, in the course of which many of them forfeited their lives, acquiesce in the counter-theory of the Norman lords.

Turning now to the side of the invader, we find a distinct order of ideas. We need not stop to inquire whether the theory which is a first principle of English land tenure is founded upon a solid fact when it is represented as springing from the recognition of the right of William the Conqueror to be the paramount lord of all land in the island at the assembly in which the chief English vassals and tenants swore fealty to the new monarch. Tradition hands down the story that after the great survey had been made the Conqueror summoned all the witan and landowners of England to meet him at Salisbury, and that the men assembled at this great meeting numbered 60,000, and that they one and all, "whose men soever they were, all bowed down to him and were his men, and swore to him faithful oaths that they would be faithful to him against all other men."[1] Whether this is true or not, it has been the undoubted principle of English law ever since, that all land is held either of the king or of some one who holds land immediately or mediately from the sovereign.[2]

---

[1] Freeman, " Norman Conquest," vol. iv., p. 693.

[2] " Every acre of English soil and every property right therein have been

Now when the Norman adventurer, acting with more or less cognisance on the part of his Norman sovereign, endeavoured to carry the conquest beyond the bounds of the English kingdom, he did so actuated very largely with the object of personal gain, but he did so under the influence of ideas which found a practical expression in the celebrated meeting at Salisbury. It is commonly assumed that in times in which human life was little regarded, and which appear to be times of mere violence, men knew no law except the law of the strongest. No greater blunder can be made than that which is involved in such an assumption. One of the remarkable things about the history of Europe at the close of the Dark Ages, and at the commencement of the mediæval period, is the immense influence of law and custom, and the most rapacious Norman adventurer, whatever his private vices and the turbulence of his disposition, never seems to have acted without endeavouring at least to do so under the colour of a legal right and a legal title. The theory which the conquerors of Wales adopted, the theory according to which the man who, following the Welsh view, was an *alltud* acted was this—that he was carrying out the commands of his sovereign, and that his title to any land that he won with his sword was his either by the express or the implied grant of the Norman king of England.

One other observation before leaving this part of the subject ought to be made. As the settlement of the Norman lords gradually became more fixed and permanent, the hostility between them and such of the Welsh princes or lords as retained any cantrefs or cymwds became modified in a sensible and continually increasing degree; and it was not unusual to find Norman lord and Welsh lord combining

brought within the compass of a single formula which may be expressed thus :—
Z tenet terram illam de . . . domino rege." Pollock and Maitland, "Hist. of English Law," i. 210.

for military purposes against some other chieftain of either race, while intermarriage between members of the Norman families and those of the more important and powerful Welsh cenedloeđ became, in the course of time, not infrequent. Probably, though this approximation between the rulers of the country became very marked by the middle of the thirteenth century, it must not be assumed that, speaking broadly, there was any such *rapprochement* among the lower orders. The small Welsh tenants, the servile occupiers of the land, the Welsh bards, and the Welsh-speaking clergy, continued to entertain racial prejudices and to advance national claims quite regardless of the interests and intrigues of the princely families.

Such appears to us to have been the general course of events that led to the final subjugation of Wales by Edward the First. The Welsh naturally regarded the overthrow of their enemy Harold as a·matter of congratulation ; but they soon found that their position was not improved by the Norman Conquest. Bleđyn and Rhiwałton, who had received the possessions of Gruffyđ ab Lewelyn, combined with Eadric the Wild, who was in possession of lands in Herefordshire and Shropshire, and had refused to submit to the new king. The allies laid waste the former county, though they did not take the town and fortress of Hereford, which were in Norman hands.[1] Almost immediately, however, there was internal war in Wales. Mareduđ and Ithel (or Idwal), sons of Gruffyđ ab Lewelyn, assailed the chieftains whom Harold had invested. The forces of the rival families met at Mechain. Ithel was killed in the battle ; Mareduđ fled and died of cold ; Rhiwałton, too, fell. Bleđyn held his own, and reigned alone over Powys, and probably over the greater part of Gwyneđ ; but we find that one Mareduđ ab Owain ab Edwyn now held Deheubarth—a fact which indicates that there had been

[1] Freeman, N. C., iv. 110, 111.　"Flor. Wig." and "Chron. Wig." 1067.

some partition of the great possessions of Gruffyđ ab
Lewelyn.[1] It is clear that the friendly feelings between
the Welsh and the Mercians shown by the durable alliance
between them in the great days of Gruffyđ still existed,
and Bleđyn joined in the abortive revolt of Eadwyne and
Morkere.[2]

After the submission of these earls to William we hear
of no further efforts of Bleđyn against the king, but
during the next few years Normans, on one pretext or
another, are found raiding in the south. In 1070 the
Mareduđ ab Owain who had assumed, as we have seen,
the chieftaincy of Deheubarth, was attacked by Caradog
ab Gruffyđ ab Rhyđerch.[3]   The latter, with the aid of the
French (so the Normans are called in the " Brut "), defeated
and slew the former in a fight on the banks of the Rymney,
and probably obtained a hold on some part of the south-
eastern district. In the next year we find the Normans
ravaging Dyfed and Keredigion, and in 1072 they devastated
the latter principality a second time. Probably these raids
were made in conjunction with the Caradog ab Owain who
had claims to Deheubarth, and who fought a battle in 1073
with Rhys ab Owain, who, as we gather, was his brother.
The state of things in that kingdom (if we may still use
the word), as well as in Dyfed and Morganwg, is very
obscure, but there can be no doubt that the continual
feuds in which the princely families of the south continued to indulge were among the main causes of the
rapid conquest of that part of Cymru a few years later.
In the significant fact that this Caradog ab Owain (following
a generally fatal precedent) sought the help of strangers—

[1] "Brut," *s.a.* 1068.   "Ann. Camb." 1068.

[2] Ord. Vit. 511B.

[3] " Brut," *s.a.* 1070. This Caradog was apparently the son of the Gruffyđ
ab Rhyđerch slain by Gruffyđ ab Lewelyn (above, p. 168). If so, he was
the man who destroyed Harold's hunting-seat at Porth Iscoed (Yscewin,
Portskewet).

" Freinc," in the " Brut "—in an internal dispute,[1] we may
see a further explanation of the ease with which the new-
comers established themselves at many important points
in South Wales before the end of the eleventh century.

Rhys ab Owain, with one Rhyderch ab Caradog, notwithstanding the efforts of Caradog ab Owain, maintained
themselves in Deheubarth. From the time of the submission of Eadwyn and Morkere, Bledyn had remained in
effective possession of Powys, and probably of a considerable
part of Gwyned, and he is regarded by the chronicler as
the man who after Gruffyd his brother " nobly supported
the whole kingdom of the Britons," " the gentlest and
most merciful of kings," " a defence to every one."[2] But
his reign was not long, for in 1073 he was killed, under
circumstances of which no information is given in detail,
by Rhys ab Owain, " through the deceit of evil-minded
chieftains and of the noblemen of Ystrad Tywi."[3] He
was succeeded in Gwyned by a cousin, Trahaiarn ab
Caradog.[4] We may presume, from what we know of the
subsequent history of Powys, that the cenedl of Bledyn
remained in possession there.

The death of Bledyn strengthened the position of
Rhys ab Owain in Deheubarth. Acting jointly with
Rhyderch ab Caradog, he put down in the same year
a rising led by Goronwy and Lewelyn ab Cadwgan,[5] and
was able, after the murder of Rhyderch in 1074, to defeat
them again in 1075. But in the next year Trahaiarn

---

[1] " Brut," *s.a.* 1070.

[2] " Brut," *s.a.* 1073 and 1076.

[3] " Brut," *s.a.* 1076. We have heard of similar conduct on the part of the
" uchelwyr of Ystrad Tywi " before (above, pp. 161, 168).

[4] Bledyn left sons, among whom Cadwgan, Iorwerth, and Maredud came to
the front. There is no explanation of the succession of Trahaiarn, except that
he was chosen from among "near relations," unless it was simply a case of
coming in " by the strong hand " ; see p. 203, n. 3, above. Nothing is said in the
" Brut " as to Trahaiarn's relation to Powys.

[5] The battle took place at " Kamdwr." " Brut," *s.a.* 1073.

(who was then for the moment firmly in possession of the north) attacked Rhys ab Owain; and by decisively defeating him at the battle of Pwłł Gwdyc avenged the blood of Bleđyn. There all the family of Rhys fell; he himself fled "like a timid stag before the hounds through the thickets and rocks," only, however, to die before the end of the year by the hand of Gruffyđ ab Caradog. Upon the overthrow of this Rhys, his kinsman Rhys ab Tewdwr, a lineal descendant of Rhodri Mawr, succeeded to Deheubarth without any opposition of which evidence is handed down, and for about fourteen years was the leading chieftain in the south, though as events turned out he was the last man who can really be regarded as king or prince of the ancient kingdom of Deheubarth.

Gwyneđ, though Trahaiarn's sway was at this time seemingly acquiesced in, had not been wholly free from internal trouble. Cynan, the son of Iago and grandson of Idwal, who came of the direct line of Rhodri, years before had taken refuge in Ireland. He married Raguell (daughter of Auleod, an Irish king), who became the mother of Gruffyđ, born about 1055. On the death of Bleđyn, with the aid of his Irish kinsmen, Gruffyđ ab Cynan made a descent on Môn, and effected some kind of settlement in the island. This, according to the "Brut," wasˢ in the year 1073, and he immediately crossed over to the mainland, attacking Trahaiarn at Bron yr Erw, in the cantref of Dunodig. Gruffyđ retreated to Môn, where he and his followers for a time remained. At this time, as we have seen, Rhys ab Tewdwr was ruling in Deheubarth. He allied himself to the cause of Gruffyđ (who had in the meantime₀ received reinforcements from Ireland); the allies attacked Trahaiarn, and ultimately a battle was fought at Mynyđ Carn between the two princes and the king of Gwyneđ, in which the latter was defeated and slain.[1]

---

[1] "Brut," *s.a.* 1079. For the life of Gruffyđ ab Cynan see "Dict. Nat.

Thus once more we find two princes lineally descended from Rhodri Mawr ruling respectively over Gwyneḍ and Deheubarth. Gruffyḍ was more fortunate than Rhys, and though the earlier years of his reign were far from being prosperous, by prudent conduct he succeeded in maintaining his rule and died peacefully, as we shall see, in what was for those troublous times extreme old age.

William the Conqueror in 1080 or 1081 made an expedition into Wales, by which, according to some, he subdued the country.[1] He and his army penetrated as far as Saint Davids, but since we find Rhys ab Tewdwr still reigning afterwards, the campaign can have had no great practical result, though it marks a stage in the conquest of South Wales, especially as with it seems to have been closely associated the foundation of a castle at Cardiff.[2] The Welsh chronicles represent that William, king of the French, Saxons, and Britons, came for prayer on a pilgrimage to Menevia; but it is clear from other sources and from subsequent events that his journey through the south was made with political intent and had political consequences.[3]

During the next few years no events of importance happened in Wales itself, but in 1087 William the Conqueror died, and we may stop for a moment to see how far his rule of twenty-one years had in fact altered the relations of England and Cymru. We will state what we can gather from trustworthy sources quite simply. William founded two palatine earldoms that directly

Biog." *s.n.* As to the situation of Mynyḍ Carn, see "Y Cymmrodor," xi., p. 167. It must not be confounded with Carno in Montgomeryshire or the Carno near Crickhowell. The best opinion locates it in South Cardiganshire.

[1] Chron. Petr., 1081. R. Wendover, ii. 20. Freeman, N. C., iv. 675-7, and his valuable notes.

[2] "Brut," *s.a.* 1080.

[3] "Brut," *s.a.* 1079 (this date is wrong) says : "Y deuth Gwilim vastard vrenhin y Saeson ar Freinc ar Brytanyeit wrth wediaw drwy bereniṛdawt y Vynyw." "Ann. Camb." (1079) simply record : "William Rex Angliæ causa orationis Sanctum David adiit."

concerned Wales—those of Chester and Shrewsbury[1]—and quickly made Worcester, Hereford, and Gloucester important military stations for operations in the west. William entered Chester (restored as we have seen by Saxon rulers) in 1070, and founded a new castle, the custody of which he entrusted to his stepson Gerbod.[2]

Shrewsbury (the Welsh Amwythig) had long been in English possession, but we do not know when first it was seized by the Normans. It must, however have been in their power before 1069, for in that year it was besieged and burnt by Eadric with the assistance of men from many quarters, noticeably from the regions of Chester, Gwyneð, and Powys.[3]

The date of the conquest of Worcester is not known, but Urse of Abetot held the city and shire for the king as early as 1068 or 1069.[4]

A Norman colony had been planted in the region of Hereford in the time of Eadward the Confessor. It is not clear when the castle was built, but Osbern the sheriff defended the city and the adjoining lands against the attacks of Eadric the Wild immediately after the Conquest, and in 1070 William Fitz-Osbern was appointed Earl of Herefordshire.[5]

The year of the conquest of Gloucestershire is uncertain, but it was probably occupied by the Normans and the building of a castle commenced in 1068 or the following year. It did not become an earldom at once, but later on Henry I. conferred the county on his son Robert.[6]

At the time then of William's death the Welsh were

---

[1] Counties palatine differed from other counties in that the earls thereof had certain royal privileges and prerogatives.

[2] Freeman, N. C., iv. 309–316.

[3] *Ibid.* iv. 272–278.

[4] *Ibid.* iv. 173–4.

[5] *Ibid.* iv. 64.

[6] *Ibid.* iv. 173.   Wm. R., ii. p. 89.

hemmed in and checked by the forces of the counties palatine of Chester and Shrewsbury, by the Earls of Worcester and Hereford, and by the Normans forming the garrison of Gloucester. The English frontier had, before the Conquest, been considerably advanced. At Rhuðlan, which, it will be recollected, had been one of the seats of Gruffyð ab Lewelyn and burnt by Harold, a castle had been built from which Robert of Rhuðlan (under the Earl of Chester) waged continuous warfare with the Welsh.[1] Similarly a fortress had been erected on a height which came to be called Montgomery among the English, after the name of Earl Roger of that place, and Tre Faldwin among the Welsh.[2] Some part of what is now Radnor-shire had passed into Harold's possession, and was still English or Norman land. The king held the castle of Monmouth. Cardiff Castle was either completed or in course of erection, and the better opinion is that the lands between the Wye and the Usk had for some time been in English hands.[3]

It is evident that during the greater part of William's reign Wales was in a state of extreme disorder. There was continual internal and border warfare. The fights (they can hardly be called wars) between the princely kindreds were incessant, and were repeated on a still smaller scale between the uchelwyr occupying adjacent lands. Quarrels were continually taking place on the border between the Welsh and the Norman earls, and the latter were of course quite ready to make temporary alliances with those of the Cymric chieftains who sought their assistance.

[1] Freeman, N. C., iv. 489–90. "Ord. Vit.," 670. "Domesday," 269.

[2] *Ibid.* iv. 501. "Ann. Camb." 1072 : "De Muntgumeri Hugo vastavit Keredigium." The land around the site of the castle seems to have been held by Englishmen as a hunting-ground in Eadward the Confessor's time. "Domesday," 254.

[3] Freeman, N. C., ii. 708, *et seq.*

Such was the position of things when William Rufus succeeded his father. The following year (1088) was marked by a rebellion in which the Norman conquerors took different sides, and the Cymric chieftains to some extent profited by the opportunity thus afforded.[1] Earl Hugh of Chester and Robert of Rhudlan were in opposite camps, and while Robert was assisting at the siege of Rochester, Gruffyd ab Cynan seized the occasion to invade his territory. The Welsh king, with Irish allies, advanced as far as Rhudlan itself, and slew many men and carried off many captives. Robert soon returned, however, and we hear of his being at Deganwy, an old British stronghold at the mouth of the river Conway, traditionally supposed to have been the seat of Maelgwn. It now seems to have been an advance post of the Earl of Chester, and a castle of some kind had been already erected by Robert. While the Norman chief was at this fortress Gruffyd with three ships entered the Conway, and, daring even in the very presence of Robert to raid the adjacent territory, carried off prisoners and cattle to his vessels. Robert in anger, and taken by surprise, bade his men, who were evidently few in number, to follow him; he himself, attended by only one knight, rushed to the shore of the river. He was immediately surrounded by the enemy and borne down by darts and arrows. His head was smitten off and placed as a trophy on the mast of one of the ships; but Gruffyd ordered it to be taken down and thrown into the sea, and then escaped with his booty.[2]

About the time when this considerable success was being obtained by Gruffyd trouble was taking place in the south. Three sons of Bledyn (Madog, Cadwgan, and Rhirid), who, as we gather, were among the joint rulers of

[1] For an account of this rebellion see Freeman, Wm. R., i. 22, *et seq.*
[2] The story comes from "Ord. Vit.," and is fully told by Freeman. See Wm. R., i. 124-7.

Powys, expelled Rhys ab Tewdwr from Deheubarth. Rhys escaped to Ireland, and immediately collecting "a fleet of the Gwyðyl," returned and landed. He gave battle to the sons of Bleðyn at a place called Lych Crei. Madog and Rhirid were killed, but Cadwgan survived to take an important part in Welsh affairs for many years. Rhys was evidently a wealthy chieftain, for the gifts he gave to his Irish mercenaries were so large as to attract special attention. His victory, as far as the cenedl of Bleðyn was concerned, was decisive, but he was assailed by others, and his failure to keep peace in the south, though he maintained a predominant position for some time, was one of the causes which made the conquest of South Wales easy and rapid.[1]

Soon after the overthow of the sons of Bleðyn a forward movement on a large scale was made by the Normans in central and south Wales which speedily resulted in the occupation of very large areas by Norman adventurers, and in the disappearance as real entities of Deheubarth and the kingdoms or principalities of south-eastern Wales. For the sake of clearness we must separate the conquests of Morgannwg, Brecheiniog, and Dyfed, though they seem to have been very nearly simultaneous, and it is likely that the movements which resulted in these events were more or less concerted. Whether this is so or not, Rhys ab Tewdwr was killed by the Normans in 1093 in an engagement at a place not particularly stated in the Chronicles somewhere near the borders of the present Brecknockshire.[2]

[1] For these events, see " Brut," *s.a.* 1087 (really 1088). As to Rhys' gifts the entry is : " Ac y rodes Rhys ab Tewdwr diruawr swllt yr Hygheswyr yscotteit ar Gwyðyl a deuthant yn borth idaw." According to the "Brut" (*s.a.* 1089), Lewelyn ab Cedivor, who, as we think, was of the line of Dyfed, with the Gruffyð ab Mareduð of whom we have already heard, fought with Rhys ab Tewdwr near Landydoch. Lewelyn was slain ; "Brut," *s.a.* 1089. The true date of Rhys' victory is probably 1091. Freeman suggests that Cedivor was a vassal prince of Dyfed under Rhys. Wm. R., ii. 78.

[2] " Brut," *s.a.* 1091, " Ann. Cam." 1093.

Morgannwg in earlier times seems to have been the name of a very large district, but the Morgannwg of the tenth and eleventh centuries was much smaller. It roughly corresponded to the present county without Gower on the west, but with the present shire of Monmouth up to the Usk included. The northern boundary cannot be determined. We have seen that a king called Morgan Hen had ruled in this part of the country in the tenth century, and had had a dispute with Howel Ða which was decided by an English king in favour of the former. Perhaps it was from his time that the place - name Gwlad Morgan (land of Morgan), which survives in Glamorgan, came into vogue. There was, however, a clear distinction between Morgannwg and Glamorgan, and long after it was reflected in the style assumed by the chief lords of the south-east of Wales—of lords of " Morgania et Glamorgania." No authentic record preserves for us the line of Morgan Hen, but at the time at which we have now arrived one Iestyn ab Gwrgan emerges as a ruler of Morgannwg, and perhaps of Gwent—no doubt the smaller Morgannwg and a sadly-curtailed Gwent. It was while he was reigning, if we may use the term, that the greater part of the tract of territory between the Usk and the Neath passed into Norman hands. As to the way in which this came about we have no information from really trustworthy sources ; but there is no doubt that by the end of 1093 it had happened, and that Robert Fitz-Hamon, a trusted companion of the Conqueror, was the man who brought it about. Neither in the "Brut" nor in the "Annales Cambriæ" is there any reference to the conquest of Glamorgan ; but in the so-called Gwentian "Brut" and in Caradog's History the story of the conquest is given with some pomp and circumstance.

We must tell Caradog's story in an abridged form. According to him, Lewelyn and Eineon, sons of Cedivor of Dyfed, were defeated by Rhys ab Tewdwr at Landydoch. Eineon fled to Iestyn, lord of Morgannwg, who also was at feud with Rhys. Iestyn promised his daughter in marriage to Eineon, who had served in England before, and undertook to bring an army of Normans to assist Iestyn in his quarrel with Rhys. Eineon thereupon prevailed upon Robert Fitz-Hamon and twelve knights to come into Morgannwg. A great army of Normans was gathered together, and shortly afterwards landed in Glamorgan. Joining forces with Iestyn, Robert burnt and spoilt the land of Rhys and his people. Rhys gathered his power and met the allies not far from Brecon. There was a terrible battle ; Rhys was slain, and with him "decaied the kingdom of South Wales." The Normans, after receiving "their promised salarie and great rewards" from Iestyn, returned to their ships. Eineon then demanded Iestyn's daughter, but was "laughed to scorne," and told that the daughter would be bestowed otherwise. Full of anger, Eineon followed the Normans and found them all a-shipboard. Going to the chiefest of them, he showed his grievance, and how easy it would be for them to conquer the land. Easily persuaded, they returned, despoiled Iestyn of his country, took "the fertile and valley" land to themselves, and awarded to Eineon the " barren and rough mountain." The knights that accompanied Robert were : Londres or London ("as the Brytish booke nameth him"), Stradlyng, St. John, Turberville, Grenuile, Humffreuile, S. Quintine, Soore, Sully, Berkeroll, Syward, and Fleming. Caradog adds "that these men and their heires have enjoyed that countrie to this daie, who were the first strangers that ever inhabited Wales since the time of Camber."[1]

Another version of the story is interpolated by Dr. Powel in the 1584 edition of Caradog's History. It is headed "Of the winning of the Lordship of Glamorgan or

[1] "Caradog" (1584 ed.), 119–122.

Morgannwc." Powell gives the tract from a manuscript delivered to him by Mistress Blanch Parry (" one of the gentlewomen of the Quaenes Majesties Privie Chamber, a singular well-wisher and furtherer of the weale public of that countrie "), and which had been " set in writing by some skilful and studious gentleman of that countrie." [1] The account in this tract does not materially differ from that in the main text, though a more definitely chivalrous complexion is given to the transaction.

It is evident that this story cannot be accepted with all its detail, but there is no reason for rejecting it altogether.[2] Robert Fitz-Hamon undoubtedly conquered Glamorgan.[3] Iestyn ab Gwrgan was lord of the whole or part of Morgannwg.[4] Some of the knights mentioned did settle in the county. We may take it as certain that Morgannwg was occupied about 1091 to 1093, though the exact date (no chronicle gives us information on the point) cannot be fixed. It is likely enough that the event was connected with the overthrow of Rhys ab Tewdwr in 1093, but the " Brut " ascribes his death to the " French who inhabited Brecheiniog." [5] This looks as if when Rhys' last battle was fought the conquest of Brecheiniog had taken place or was proceeding, and as if he were trying to oust the Normans, and not engaging in civil war with Iestyn, but there can be no certainty on the matter. It is not, however, probable

---

[1] "Caradog," 124, et seq.

[2] This is Freeman's view. Wm. R., ii. 81.

[3] He was on the side of William Rufus in the rebellion. He had great possessions in Gloucestershire and Somersetshire. His daughter Mabel became wife of Robert, Earl of Gloucester, son of Henry I. " Dict. Nat. Biog.," sub nom., and Freeman, Wm. R., ii., 83.

[4] See Giraldus, " Itin. Camb.," i. 7 : " Quatuor Caradoci filii Iestini filius, et Resi principis ex sorore nepotibus, his in finibus herili portione, sicut Gualensibus mos est, pro patre dominantibus, Morgano videlicet, et Mereducio, Oeneo, Cadwallano." The children of Iestyn held Aberafan (Aberavon) after the Conquest. Freeman, Wm. R., ii. 87.

[5] " Brut," s.a. 1091, probably in truth 1093.

that the conquest of Morgannwg was so sudden an affair as
the story represents. The building of Cardiff Castle, if we
may trust the "Brut," had begun some ten years before,
and the conquest by the Normans was gradual, though no
doubt in the Vale their settlement went on rapidly. It is
to be noticed that the number of castles, and therefore of
lordships, manors, or sub-manors, in Glamorganshire is
proportionally very large, and as the evidence the Land
Commission received shows the district was strictly
organised on feudal principles, and suggests some former
intentional and definite apportionment, it indirectly tends
to support the substantial accuracy of the story of the
conquest of Glamorgan.[1]

Brecheiniog also speedily passed into Norman hands. It
was probably in the early years of Rufus' reign that Bernard
de Neufmarché or Newmarch seized a central position in
that region and built a castle at Aberhonďu. He married
(we know not the date) Nest, who was the daughter of
Gruffyď ab Lewelyn by Ealdgyth, and therefore the step-
daughter of King Harold. It was probably in fighting
against him that Rhys ab Tewdwr was slain.[2] The defeat
of the Welsh king took place early in the year. Cadwgan
ab Bleďyn, the same who had survived the defeat at Lych

---

[1] *E.g.*, the Duke of Beaufort is lord of the seigniory of Gower. In this
area (182 square miles) there are a number of mesne manors, and besides these
fees or sub-manors, the lords of which hold of the lords of the mesne manors.
The Duke holds of himself, as lord of Gower, the mesne manors of Swansea,
Oystermouth, Loughor, Kilvey, Gower Wallicana, Gower Anglicana ; while
he holds the fee of Trewyďfa of the lord of the mesne manor of Pennard held
of the Duke himself. See Mr. Glynn Price's evidence, qq. 6425, *et seq.* ;
6626—6630. The contrast between this state of things and that which exists
in Gwyneď, where there are comparatively few manors (except, of course, the
Crown lordships formed by treating the cymwds on the conquest as equivalent
to lordships), is very marked.

[2] Bernard first married a daughter of Osbern of Hereford, settled there, and
established a stronghold at Aberhonďu (Brecon). The dates of his birth
and death are not known. "Dict. Nat. Biog.," *sub nom.*; and Giraldus,
"Itin. Camb." i. 2.

Crei, and who now begins to play a considerable part in the affairs of Wales, immediately despoiled Dyfed, and two months afterwards we find the Normans invaded both Dyfed and Keredigion, which, says the chronicler, "they have still retained." [1] They fortified the castles, and seized " all the lands of the Britons." This conquest was effected by Arnulf of Montgomery, and he immediately caused some kind of castle to be erected at Pembro (later Pembroke), and confided the defence of it to Gerald of Windsor. [2] It is to be noted, however, that at this time (1093-4) Gower, Kidweli, and most of the territory between the Neath and the Towi had not yet been occupied by the invaders.

The events in the north during the time the conquests we have described were taking place cannot be surely or clearly stated. The death of Robert of Rhudlan had only a momentary effect, and Rhudlan and Deganwy continued to be firmly held by Hugh of Chester or his subordinate officers, and he probably controlled the whole of the coast-line to the Menai Straits. Earl Roger of Shrewsbury had not been idle, and was strengthening his hold on Powys, and by the king's command a castle had been raised at Rhyd y Gors. [3]

---

[1] Rhys' son Gruffyd possessed only "one cymwd, namely, the fourth part of the cantref of Caeoc, in the cantref Mawr, which in title and dignity was esteemed by the Welsh equal to the southern part of Wales called Deheubarth, that is, the right-hand side of Wales." Giraldus, "Itin. Camb." i. 2. Caeoc is a mistake for Caeo, which was a cymwd in cantref Bychan, not cantref Mawr. Giraldus remarks that though Gruffyd's "inheritance was diminished, his ambition and dignity remained." It is in this connection he tells the well-known story of the Welsh prince's proclamation by the birds of the lake of Brecheiniog.

[2] The words of the "Brut" seem to indicate that some castles already existed—they are : "Ac y gadarnhayssant y kestyll." In modern Welsh *cadharnhau* means "to strengthen," and *castell* is used as equivalent to "castle." "Ann. Camb." say "circiter kalendas Julii Franci primitus Demetiam et Keredigion tenuerunt, et abinde totam terram Britonum occupaverunt." Pembroke is mentioned in the "Brut," *s.a.* 1092, as holding out against Cadwgan ab Bledyn.

[3] "Brut," *s.a.* 1092 (probably in truth later).

In Gwyneđ we may presume that Gruffyđ ab Cynan was still the recognised ruler, but we have no mention of him in the " Brut " after 1073 till the year 1096, and in the stirring events of the next two years it is Cadwgan ab Bledyn who comes to the front as the chief leader of the Cymric nation.[1]

The year 1094 is celebrated in Welsh annals for a general attempt to shake off the Norman yoke. Cadwgan, it may be fairly conjectured, effected some temporary combination among the Welsh chieftains.[2] There certainly was a widespread rising. The Welsh, unable to bear the cruelty of the Normans, began the movement under the leadership of Cadwgan by an attack on the newly-made castles in Gwyneđ and Môn, which resulted in their destruction or capture.[3] The " French " made a fresh expedition into Gwyneđ, but were defeated, according to the " Brut," in the wood of Yspwys. Cadwgan and his allies, taking the offensive, ravaged Chester, Shropshire, and even Herefordshire ; they burnt towns, slew many men, and carried off much booty.[4] Having as they deemed freed Gwyned, the Welsh chieftains marched south into Keredigion and Dyfed. They demolished all the fortresses except two. Pembroke held out under Gerald of Windsor, and William son of Baldwin succeeded in retaining Rhyd y Gors.[5] Cadwgan, it is said in the " Brut," " the people and all the

---

[1] He is mentioned in the epitaph of Robert of Rhuđlan that is given in " Ord. Vit. Hist. Eccles. ": " cepit Grithfridum regem." Gruffyd was at large in 1087, for he led in that year a raid against Robert (see above, p. 276), in which the latter was killed. Gruffyđ's captivity must therefore have ended before that event.

[2] See " Eng. Chron.," *s.a.* 1097 : " They (the Welsh) chose them many elders of themselves ; one was Cadwgan hight that of them worthiest was : he was brother's son of Grufyđ the king." (" Chron. Petrib.")

[3] " Brut," *s.a.* 1092. See " Flor. Wig.," 1094 : " fregerunt et castellum in Meoania insula."

[4] " Flor. Wig.," 1094.

[5] " Brut," *s.a.* 1092.

cattle of Dyfed brought away, leaving Dyfed and Keredigion a desert."[1] This statement must be taken with some qualification, but we may believe that there was a considerable migration of the scanty population of those districts to the safer and more mountainous regions of the northern and central parts of the country ; but in after times North Pembrokeshire and Cardiganshire are found to be, and still remain, Welsh-speaking areas. For the moment the work of the Norman adventurers seemed to be undone ; but in the very next year (1095), while the Cymry of the north were still in possession of the lands they had reconquered, the Normans of Morgannwg made a fresh advance to the west and overran Gower, Kidweli, and Ystrad Towi, into which they had not, except perhaps sporadically, up to that time penetrated. William of London settled at Kidweli, and commenced building a strong castle.[2] Within the next few years castles also arose at Abertawe (Swansea), Aberllwchwr (Loughor), Oystermouth, Penrice, and Lanrhidian in Gower.

In the same year (1095) the Cymry of Powys, with probably the men of Gwyneď, were fighting in the valley of the Severn, and suddenly achieved a success which, however, led to their undoing. They took the important castle of Tre Faldwin, and killed its garrison.[3] Matters now became sufficiently serious to demand the personal attention of William Rufus himself. Much disturbed, he called out the fyrd of his English kingdom, and made an expedition into Wales.[4] Crossing the border soon after Michaelmas, and dividing his force into parties, he is said to have marched through Wales. The Cymry, following their usual tactics,

---

[1] " Brut," *s.a.* 1092 ; "Ann. Cambr.," *s.a.* 1095 : "Demetia et Caretica et Stratewi deserta manent."

[2] So says the Gwentian " Brut," *s.a.* 1094.

[3] By this time Hugh son of Roger had succeeded his father in the earldom of Shrewsbury.

[4] " Chron. Petrib.," 1095.

avoided a pitched battle ; they took to the " moors and dales " and " the fastnesses in the woods and glens." [1]   Ultimately the Norman parties reunited somewhere near Snowdon, and, finding winter approaching, William ordered a retreat, and he and his army returned home " empty without having gained anything." [2]   In the next year, 1096, probably encouraged by the ill-success of . William's expedition, the Cymry of Brecheiniog, Gwent, and Gwenllwg " resisted the domination " and " threw off the yoke of the French." [3] The tide of Welsh success rose yet higher.   Some time in the same year William son of Baldwin, the founder of the castle of Rhyd y Gors, died.   Till now, under his personal direction or that of his officers, this castle had held out against all the efforts of the Welsh ; but no sooner had he died than its garrison deserted, leaving the fortress empty and open to the enemy.   Following up this fresh success, Uchtrud ab Edwin and Howel ab Goronwy, with many chieftains of the cenedl of Cadwgan, marched again against Pembroke. They failed to take the castle, but they despoiled its territory of its cattle, ravaged the whole country, and with immense booty returned home. [4]

At the same time there was fighting in the lands between the Usk and the Wye, and between the Usk and the Rymney, though how far there was any concert between the chieftains of the south-east and of the north we cannot say.   The result was evidently for the moment favourable to the Welsh, and made the positions of the Normans in those parts dangerous.   For we read that the French (operating we know not from where) sent an army into Gwent, but, like the forces of William, empty and without

[1] " Brut," *s.a.* 1093.   "Ann. Cambr.," 1095.
[2] " Brut," *s.a.* 1093.   " Ann. Camb.," *s.a.* 1095 : "**vacuus ad sua rediit**."
[3] " Brut," *s.a.* 1094.   " Ann. Camb.," *s.a.* 1096.
[4] *Ibid.*   Giraldus ("Itin. Cambr.," i. 12) gives some stories about this siege. His dates are wrong.   See Freeman, Wm. R., ii. 109, note.

having gained anything they were obliged to retreat. Less fortunate than the forces of the king, on the return march they were cut off and defeated at Kelli Carnant. Soon after a larger force, raised with a view of crushing the whole of the country, sustained a like fate, being defeated at Aberllech by the sons of Idnerth ab Cadwgan.[1] So far the success of the Cymry in the rebellion had been singularly great ; but early in 1097 Gerald of Windsor took the offensive, and ravaged the land of Dyfed up to the boundaries of the church of St. David. Once more William Rufus determined to go to the aid of his vassals in the west. Gathering an army, soon after Easter he entered Wales ; led by native guides, he penetrated far into the country, but with no practical result, though some of the Cymric lords made formal submission. He returned to England for the Whitsuntide festival, but before Midsummer he again set forth with an army of cavalry and foot soldiers, and for the third time entered and proceeded far into Wales. He remained there for several weeks. To the Welsh chiefs this new host seemed invincible ; following their usual practice, they avoided any engagement. Great though was the number of the Norman host, they were not able, or else did not dare, to seek out their enemies in the mountains and forests to which they prudently retreated, and, to use the words of the Welsh chronicler, they only "skulked about the level plains." According to the "Brut," the Welshmen, evidently conscious of their weakness in numbers, not confiding in themselves, " placed their hope in God, the Creator of all things, by fasting and praying and giving alms and undergoing severe bodily penance." Though we know that the Cymry were religious enough upon occasion, yet, reading between the lines of the English and Welsh sources of information, it is not unreasonable to infer from all this that the clergy were in league with Cadwgan and

[1] " Brut," *s.a.* 1094.   "Ann. Camb.," *s.a.* 1096.

were properly rewarded, and probably also that the "native guides" led the invincible host along the ways which the Cymric leaders desired them to go. Anyhow, William's third campaign ended like the others : he lost much in men and horses, and "eke in other things," and returned some time in August. William's three campaigns were failures ; he and his commanders had not learned what experience had taught Harold.[1] Cavalry—especially knights in armour —could do nothing against lightly-armed and agile infantry led by men who knew every inch of the land they were defending. But now the Norman warriors gradually took to heart the lessons of recent campaigns, and saw that it was in castle-building on every coign of vantage that this Welsh land was to be really subdued. They persevered, and in the long run attained their object.

Up to this time the revolt of the Cymry against the rule of the invaders had been attended with unexpectedly great success. They had recovered for the moment the control of the greater part of the land that had been Cymru before the conquest of England. But in 1098 the whole scene changes. Till then Cadwgan seems to have been able to keep the Cymric chieftains in active alliance for a longer period than usual, but suddenly he (the "Brut" joins Gruffyd ab Cynan with him) appears to have been obliged to take a defensive attitude. The great border earls, Hugh the Fat of Chester and Hugh the Proud of Shrewsbury, of whom we have heard nothing for some time, determined to make an expedition to Môn. Cadwgan and his allies according to the "Brut" retreated to the strongest places, but according to the "Annales" to the island itself. They enlisted into their service a fleet of pirates or vikings (gentiles de Ybernia). Whether this was before or after this new Norman expedition had reached Môn is not clear, but

[1] "Brut," *s.a.* 1095. "Ann. Camb.," *s.a.* 1097. "Eng. Chron.," *s.a.* 1097.

it is said that the Cymric leaders agreed in council to save
the island. The two earls reached Aberlleiniog, and entrenching themselves began the rebuilding or repair of the
castle. Whatever were the efforts made by the Welsh
leaders, they were made in vain. There were influences
of the usual character at work undermining the power of
the military leaders of the Cymry, and, "for fear of the
treachery of their own men," Cadwgan and Gruffyd fled to
Ireland.[1] Môn was at the mercy of the earls. They and
their followers behaved with a cruelty excessive even in
this period ; they did not simply slay, but blinded and
ferociously mutilated those of the native enemy on whom
they could lay their hands.

The sequence of events in this year is quite obscure,
but the result is plain enough. The combination which
the authority and ability of Cadwgan had brought about
fell to pieces (perhaps only from the inconstancy of the
people, but perhaps also from reverses of which we are
not informed), and the work of the last four years was
quickly undone. The Cymry, however, had some revenge,
for the Norman earls, while mercilessly punishing the
natives of Môn, were called upon to reckon with Magnus
son of Olaf of Norway, who was roving about the west
coast of Britain.[2] He one day appeared off Aberlleiniog
with some of his ships, and an engagement was brought
on between the Normans and the crews of his vessels.
Magnus by an arrow sped from his own bow killed Hugh
of Shrewsbury, who was leading his men on the sea-shore.
The viking, however, did not stay to succour the Welsh,
but sailed off, and so, according to the words of the Brut,
"the French reduced all, as well great as small, to the level

---

[1] "Brut," s.a. 1096.   "Ann. Camb.," s.a. 1098.   "Flor. Wig.," s.a.
1098.

[2] As to the expedition of Magnus, see Freeman, Wm. R. ii., 126.

of Saxons."[1]   Of what went on in the south we know little, though the later events show that the Norman lords recovered and strengthened the position they had already occupied, and continued to extend their dominions. The slaying of Lewelyn, one of the sons of Cadwgan, in the next year (1099), in a conflict with the men of Brecheiniog (probably the men of Bernard of Newmarch), seems to mark the end of the revolt in south-east Wales.[2]

Some time in the course of 1099 Cadwgan and Gruffyd returned from Ireland. The former made peace with the Normans, and received Keredigion and part of Powys.[3] Gruffyd obtained possession of Môn, whether by force or not is uncertain, but it seems clear that he did not obtain a grant from the king, at any rate at this time. Matters remained in this position in Wales during 1100—the year in which William Rufus was killed and Henry I. became king. In 1101, however, the revolt of Robert de Bellême had important effects on the affairs of the west. Robert and Arnulf his brother, on breaking with the king, asked for the assistance of Cadwgan and his brothers Iorwerth and Maredud, whom they regarded, and seemingly legally, as their vassals. The Welsh princes complied with the request or command of the rebel earls, and repaired to them at Shrewsbury, where they were received " magnificently

[1] Freeman thought these words had a strange sound. So they have, if the Rolls translation is taken literally. There Ab Ithel translates the Welsh text thus : " The French reduced all . . . *to be* Saxons." But the Welsh words are : " A dœyn aoruc y Freinc oll a maœr a bychan hyt ar y Saeson." What the Welsh writer meant was that the Normans reduced the Cymry to the level of the conquered Saxons. " Hyt ar y Saeson " is equivalent to " usque ad Saxones." The word " Saeson " was long a term of contempt among the Cymry.

[2] " Brut," *s.a.* 1097. " Ann. Camb.," *s.a.* 1099.

[3] " Brut," *s.a.* 1097 (really 1099). " Ann. Camb.," *s.a.* 1099. Cadwgan seems to have received the lands as feudal tenant from Robert de Bellême, who was now Earl of Shrewsbury. See " Brut," *s.a.* 1100 : " Robert .nd Arnulf invited the Britons who were subject to them in respect of their possessions and titles, etc."

and honourably." The earls made great promises, and "gladdened the country with liberty." Cadwgan called together the host of the territories of the house of Bleḋyn, and together with the earls obtained temporary successes. Henry, however, speedily laid siege to Bridgenorth, the principal castle of Robert, and at the same time astutely resorted to arts of diplomacy. William Pantulf was on the side of the king, and opened negotiations with Iorwerth with a view to detaching the Welsh from the Norman rebels. The result of the dealings between William and Iorwerth was that Henry promised Iorwerth, if he would come over to his side, with the Welsh forces, that he would grant him for his own (Henry's) life Powys, Ceredigion, half of Dyfed,[1] Ystrad Towi, Cidweli, and Gower, without homage and without tribute. Iorwerth was taken in, and, without informing his brothers, accepted the king's terms. Iorwerth went to the castle of the king, and sent orders to the Welsh forces to turn against Robert. They obeyed, and thoroughly despoiled the territory of the earls, collecting immense booty. Their work was probably made easier by the fact that Robert was taken by surprise, and the spoil was greater because the earl had placed such confidence in his Welsh allies that he had sent his "dairies, cattle, and riches" amongst them for safety.

Before the end of the year Robert submitted, and was allowed to cross over to Normandy. We have no explanation of the way in which Iorwerth induced the Welsh to follow him without any apparent sanction on the part of Cadwgan or Mareduḋ, but there was an immediate quarrel among the brothers. Iorwerth seized Mareduḋ and caused him to be confined in one of the king's prisons, but conferred on Cadwgan a portion of that great area which he assumed the king would grant him. Henry,

[1] "As the other half had been given to the son of Baldwin." "Brut," *s.a.* 1100.

however, had been simply using Iorwerth as a tool, and refused to perform his bargain. Pembroke was given to one Saer, from whom it passed in 1104 to Gerald of Windsor, who had been for some years holding it as steward. Ystrad Towi, Cidweli, and Gower were granted to Howel ab Goronwy. Unless there is some explanation, Henry was guilty not only of a mean duplicity, but of brutal cruelty as well. He caused Iorwerth, now apparently no longer in command of any force, to be brought before the Council at Shrewsbury on a charge of treason. The Welsh prince was convicted, fined, and cast into prison, not as the Welsh chronicler justly says, according to right, but according to might. He was kept in confinement till 1109, when the king "remembered the imprisonment of Iorwerth," and released him on hard conditions.[1]

The settlement of Welsh affairs made by Henry in 1102 was then this:—The Norman lords retook or retained the fortresses that they had built; the land of Deheubarth and Powys not actually in Norman hands was divided between Howel ab Goronwy and the descendants of Bleḋyn. The former received Ystrad Towi, Cidweli, and Gower as fiefs from the king, and Cadwgan and other former members of the cenedl of Bleḋyn were expressly or tacitly confirmed in the possession of Ceredigion and parts of Powys on terms of vassalage. In the north Gruffyḋ still held Môn, and probably some parts of Gwyneḋ on the mainland. Except the North Welsh prince, the members of the Welsh princely families were now practically in the position of tenants *in capite* of Henry. Cadwgan's temporarily successful attempt to shake off the Norman yoke had failed, and the new settlers had a still firmer grip on Welsh territory.

---

[1] The main authorities for these events, so far as the Welsh were concerned in them, are the "Brut," and "Ann. Camb."

Howel ab Goronwy did not long enjoy the possessions he had received from the king. He was a grandson of Rhys ab Tewdwr, but had been false to the cause of Cymric independence. He was at feud with the house of Bleḍyn, and was soon in trouble with Richard son of Baldwin as to Rhyd y Gors Castle. As we gather, Howel claimed it as part of his dominion, but it is not likely that this claim was acquiesced in, though when we last heard of it it had been deserted by its Norman garrison. It was now, however, again in "French" hands. Through this quarrel Howel was expelled from his dominions, but he quickly retaliated, raided the Norman territory and killed many of the "French who were returning home," and regained possession of his land. But in the following year (1105) he fell a victim to a conspiracy formed among his own surroundings, which, without an undue stretch of imagination, we may believe to have been instigated by Cadwgan or some of his kinsmen. Howel, following the custom of the times, had given one of his sons in fosterage to Gwgawn, "whom of all men he most trusted." From some motive (but as if to give point to the observations of Giraldus as to foster-fathers) Gwgawn either began or joined in a plot against Howel. According to the story handed down to us, he invited Howel to his house, having in the meantime arranged with the "French" that a band should be in a place near the house, where they were to wait till the appointed time. They agreed ; Howel, without suspicion, accepted the invitation and went to Gwgawn's residence. The "French," as arranged, about daybreak surrounded the house where the prince was sleeping ; at the given signal they gave a loud shout ; Howel awaking sought for his sword and spear, but found they had been taken away ; he called for his men-at-arms, but they had deserted. He escaped from the house, but was pursued and captured by Gwgawn and his men. They brought him, already nearly dead from strangling, to the Norman band, by whom h⸗ was unmercifully beheaded.[1]

The considerable area given by Henry to this Howel was not, it would seem, again granted to one man, but we subsequently find diverse portions of it in the possession of Welshmen. They indulged, as usual, in raiding adjoining territories and in killing and sometimes mutilating one another. But now the process of fusion between them and the Norman lords was going on, and the whole of the south was rapidly assuming a frankly feudal aspect. While the princes and the more important uchelwyr were ruining themselves by their incessant quarrels, the men of smaller possessions or pretensions and the inferior orders over a good deal of the country generally stuck to their lands, notwithstanding the changes among their overlords. When the lord over them was a Cymro, the Welsh customs continued in force; when he was Norman, the Norman-English laws prevailed as a rule, though in some instances Welsh law, more or less modified, was recognised over the whole or part of the lordship.

In 1108 Cadwgan was still in undisturbed possession of Ceredigion and the parts of Powys which he had received from Henry. He had in his earlier years displayed capacity above the average, but from causes which can only be conjectured he had now become a somewhat weak and incompetent ruler. His few remaining years were clouded in misfortune, and especially disturbed by the turbulent conduct of his son Owain. This man (whose career is fully enough told in the Chronicles, and is the most romantic handed down to us) was typical of the race from which he sprang. He possessed the best and the worst characteristics of the Cymric princely families. His first recorded feat is the slaying of the sons of Trahaiarn ab Caradog. His next adventure was an attack on Pembroke

[1] "Brut," *s.a.* 1103 (really 1105).

Castle and the abduction of Nest,[1] then the wife of Gerald of Windsor—one that influenced the whole of his after life. The story goes that in 1107 Gerald of Windsor was still holding Pembroke. He had deposited there " all his riches, with his wife, his heirs and all dear to him, and he fortified it with a ditch and a wall and a gateway with a lock to it." The next year at Christmastime Cadwgan made a feast in honour of God, at which Owain was present. The conversation turned upon the charms of Nest. Owain, fired by the accounts of her beauty, paid a visit to Pembroke, and being received as her kinsman (as in fact he was) made the acquaintance of the lady. Soon afterwards with a small band he made a raid at night on the castle, set fire to the houses near it, and perhaps to the fortress, itself. Forcing an entrance, though Gerald escaped by the connivance of his wife, Owain carried away Nest as well as the children, and returned with them and the more usual booty to his own land.

Cadwgan was greatly disturbed at such an outrage against a man high in the king's favour. He tried to induce his son to return to the great steward, his wife and the spoils, but in vain. The children were, however, sent back, but Nest herself was for the time retained.

Richard, steward for the king at Shrewsbury, hearing of this misdeed, sent for Ithel and Madog, sons of Rhirid ab Bledyn, and persuaded them by large promises to try to seize Owain, or, if not, to expel both him and Cadwgan from their country. Richard promised to procure for them the assistance of Lywarch ab Trahaiarn (who was at feud with Owain by reason of the slaying of his brothers), and also that of Uchtryd ab Edwin. Ithel and Madog collected their men and entered Cadwgan's country. Uchtryd met them, but seems to have played a double part. The

---

[1] Nest had been a mistress of Henry I. She has been called the "Helen of Wales."

inhabitants fled in various directions. Cadwgan and Owain took refuge in a ship at Aberdovey. The expedition did not achieve much beyond creating the usual confusion, and nothing except a few murders, the burning of houses, and the desecration of the church at Landewy Brefi was accomplished. Owain with some companions thought it prudent to retire to Ireland, while Ithel and Madog seized the part of Powys that the king had granted to Cadwgan. The latter secretly went to some lands in Powys which he possessed in right of his wife. He soon, however, made peace with the king, and on the payment of one hundred pounds was allowed to return- to Ceredigion on condition that there should be neither communication nor friendship between him and his son.

Owain thereupon returned from Ireland and hied him to Powys. He attempted to send a message to the king, but no man was bold enough to carry it. In the meantime Madog ab Rhirid had quarrelled with the Normans on account, as he alleged, of robberies committed by the Saxons, and refused any further to obey the commands of the steward of Shrewsbury. In these circumstances he sought the friendship of his former enemy Owain, who, nothing loth, came to an understanding with him. They mutually vowed upon sacred relics that neither would be reconciled to the king without the other, and that neither would betray the other. They then cast aside all pretence of ruling by any law or obeying any lord ; with armed forces they wandered about the country wherever their destiny might lead them. Making their headquarters among the mountains and forests of Powys, they set their hands against every man. They burned the hamlets of the gwyrda around, stole horses and cattle, and did not disdain to carry off clothes or whatever they could find.

This line of conduct was continued into the following year (1109). They were in the habit of carrying off their booty into the lands which had formerly been the share of the then captive Iorwerth. In that year, however, the king, as we have mentioned, released Iorwerth upon his making promises the performance of which he was not wholly able to compass, but he, however, was allowed to return to his lands. He made kindly representations to the two lawless chieftains, pointing out the danger in which Cadwgan and he himself were placed by their wild lives ; he asked them as a relative and commanded them as their lord not to enter his or his brother's territories. But Owain and Madog were now desperate men ; they treated Iorwerth's messages with scorn, and frequented the forbidden lands all the more. Iorwerth, sincerely anxious to carry out the king's wishes and restore some degree of order, took stronger measures and attempted to capture them.

Hunted from place to place, they, with their followers, went over the border of Meirionyð, then possessed by Uchtryd. Before they had left Cyfeiliog they were met by the sons of that chieftain, who were, however, not strong enough to repel them. Uchtryd found it necessary to assemble the host of Meirionyð, and came forward to defend his territory in well-ordered array. Some part of the forces of the invaders seem to have fled—probably the men of Madog ; but Owain advanced bravely, and the men of Meirionyð, apparently awed either by the number of his followers or his fame as a warrior, suddenly took to flight.

Owain and Madog then ravaged as usual, burning houses, but this time killing the cattle because they had no place to which to take them. They however now separated ; the latter went into Powys and the former into Ceredigion. There Owain with his band remained, "dwelling where he thought proper," in defiance of Cadwgan's orders. He made a raid into Dyfed, and terrorised the whole country. Finally, his misdeeds

culminated in the murder of a Fleming, one William of
Brabant, on the highroad.   Cadwgan and Iorwerth, seriously
alarmed, and unable to curb Owain's lawlessness, 'repaired
to the king and obtained an interview.   Even while they
were conversing news of the murder of William of Brabant
was brought by his brother to the king.   Henry sternly
questioned Cadwgan, and, though satisfied that he was not
aiding Owain, deprived him of his lands, and, on condition
that he should not set his foot on his native soil, pensioned
him.   The king bestowed Ceredigion on Gilbert son of
Richard, the founder of the house of Clare, who, having
collected a force, took possession of that region, and for a
time strengthened the Norman hold by building two castles :
one at Lanbadarn, and another near Aberteivi at a place
called Dingeraint.

When Owain heard that his father was dispossessed he
once more retreated to Ireland.   His associate Madog had
gone there before him, and it is not without a smile that
we can read in the Chronicle " that not being able to endure
the savage manners of the Gwyðyl" he soon returned,
leaving Owain to bear the ills of life in Ireland as he might.
Iorwerth had not, like Cadwgan, been detained by the king,
and when Madog returned was occupying his land in Powys.
Madog sought there an abiding-place, but he was not
welcomed by Iorwerth, and not daring to seek his presence
he " skulked here and there."   Iorwerth's anger was such
that he ordered that no man should even venture to mention
the name of Madog.

Underlying these events we can see two currents of
opinion among the Cymric chieftains.   The older men,
like Cadwgan and Iorwerth, saw that their only course was
to retain possession of as much of the Cymric land as
possible as vassals of Henry.   The younger men were
imbued with notions of an impossible independence.   The
deeds of Owain and Madog could hardly have been

performed if there had not been a latent and perhaps, on occasion, overt sympathy with them on the part of a section of the Cymric inhabitants. We are now coming to the close of the story. Madog, smarting under his ill reception by his uncle Iorwerth, planned a terrible revenge. He had maintained friendship with Lewelyn ab Trahaiarn, of whom we have already heard. They jointly determined to kill Iorwerth, and, finding at last a favourable time, Madog, with the assistance of Lewelyn's men, attacked him at Caereinion, where he was staying for the night. Iorwerth bravely defended himself, but the timber building in which he was reposing was fired by Madog. Iorwerth's attendants fled, and seeing the house falling in he, already sorely burnt, tried to escape, but rushing out of the house he was slain by the spears of his enemies. Madog retreated into the mountain lands and lurked in woods and recesses, for he had yet another uncle to kill.

When tidings of the murder of Iorwerth were brought to Henry he released Cadwgan and granted Powys to him, at the same time requesting him to send messages of forgiveness to Owain, who was still a fugitive in Ireland. The messages arrived too late to save his father from the wrath of Madog. Cadwgan proceeded to Powys and stayed at Trallwng Lewelyn, " never supposing that any man could intend him mischief." Madog had, however, determined that he should die, and one day he and his band set upon Cadwgan. The aged prince's men deserted or were overcome, and Cadwgan, who conducted himself " weakly," was put to death. Madog now boldly demanded from Richard of Shrewsbury a grant of Cadwgan's land, for which, so the Chronicle says, the crimes had been committed. Richard temporised, but ultimately gave him the share of the country which he and his brother Ithel had formerly possessed. The fact is that neither Henry nor his officers on the borders took much interest in the feuds between the Welsh princes, and were evidently quite ready to condone the destruction of such inconstant vassals.

The remaining son of Bleđyn, Mareduđ, on hearing of the death of Cadwgan, obtained from Henry the custody of Iorwerth's lands till Owain should return from Ireland. These events had taken place in 1110, and later on in the same year Owain returned from Ireland. Both he and Madog had interviews with Henry, and were invested with lands on giving pledges and promising "much money."[1] But their friendship had now ceased, owing to the murder of Cadwgan, and "each of them avoided the other" for a time. Peace was maintained in Powys during 1111, but in the year after we find Mareduđ making an incursion into the lordship of Lywarch ab Trahaiarn. The expedition passed through Madog's territory. Mareduđ's men by torturing a man of the country discovered the whereabouts of Madog; they decided to attack him, and by a sudden effort made him a prisoner, slaying many of his companions. He was brought to his uncle Mareduđ. Owain, hearing of the affair, came in haste to the prince, who delivered Madog into his hands. Owain spared his prisoner's life, but ruthlessly caused him to be blinded, thereby destroying his capacity for further mischief. We hear nothing more of him, and Mareduđ and Owain divided between them his share of Powys.[2]

During these events Gruffyđ ab Cynan was ruling in Gwyneđ, and consolidating the power of his family. In 1114, however, Hugh, Earl of Chester, accused him of

---

[1] Madog's portion was Caereinion, and a third of Deuđwr and Aberrhiw. Caereinion and Deuđwr were cymwds in Powys. Y Rhiw was a cantref in that ancient kingdom, but does not seem to have been identical with Aberrhiw.

[2] The "Brut" and "Ann. Camb." are the authorities for the events we have been narrating. See the excellent lives of Cadwgan, Iorwerth, and Owain in "Dict. Nat. Biog."

various misdeeds, and about the same time Gilbert Fitz-
Richard (who, as we have seen, had become lord ·of
Keredigion) complained of robberies made by Owain ab
Cadwgan.[1]   The king, believing the charges against
Owain at any rate to be true, made an expedition into
Wales.   Owain took refuge in the mountains of Snow-
don region; Maredud submitted at once.   There is no
record of any fighting, and Owain not only made terms
with the king, but was received into favour and accom-
panied him in an honourable capacity to Normandy.
Gruffyd made peace on payment of a large tribute.   The
kingdom or principality of Powys was now practically at an
end, and the surviving members of the Welsh princely
cenedloed of that region had become vassals of the king.
The whole of Cymru except Gwyned was divided between
Norman and Welsh lords, who came to be called Lords-
Marchers.   The subsequent history of the south and central
Wales resolves itself into the records of quarrels between
these lords and the rise and fall of baronial families.

The end of Owain ab Cadwgan's stormy career may be
told in a few words.   Gruffyd, a son of that Rhys ab
Tewdwr who had fallen in 1093, had been taken for safety
with some of his kin to Irèland.   About 1112 he returned
to what the "Brut" calls his patrimony, but for two years
he led a somewhat wandering life.   The spirit of independence was not yet wholly quelled in the south, and the
hopes of the Cymry were now set upon this young prince.
How far Gruffyd actually encouraged these aspirations at
this time we do not know, but the fact that he was or
might be dangerous to the Norman interests was brought
to the notice of Henry.   Hearing of this circumstance, he
took refuge with his namesake in the north, who received
him with favour.   Henry now summoned Gruffyd ab

---

[1] The "Brut" places this in 1111, but the "Eng. Chron." in 1114 ("Chron.
Petrib." *s.a.*), which is the right date.

Cynan to his presence. With his usual prudence he obeyed
the call, met the king, and at his instance promised to
secure Gruffyđ ab Rhys and send him a prisoner to
England, or else to compass his death. The young Gruffyđ,
however, had received tidings of this treachery, and he
escaped, first to the church of Aberdaron, and thence to
Ystrad Towi, where he collected a force. In 1116 he was
raiding in various directions in South Wales. Owain ab
Cadwgan was still with Henry, who commissioned him and
Lywarch ab Trahaiarn to expel "that thief" Gruffyđ ab
Rhys. They promptly collected an army and proceeded to
Ystrad Towi. Owain harried the country, and some of
the people fled to Carmarthen. At this time a force of
Flemings led by Gerald of Windsor, apparently acting
independently of Owain and Lywarch, was marching from
Rhos in Dyfed towards Carmarthen, as we understand
with the intention of putting down Gruffyđ ab Rhys.
The inhabitants, who had fled at the approach of Owain,
complained to Gerald of their having been attacked and
robbed. The story reads as if the fugitives did not understand that it was not Owain the bandit, but Owain in a
new character, who was coming into the country, nor is it
clear whether Gerald knew of the king's commission, but
it may be that there was treachery on his part or perhaps
that the king had led Owain into a trap. However this
may be, Gerald, who had of course never forgotten the
insult that in earlier days had been put upon him, incited
his Flemings against Owain. The forces met. The
Flemings were the attacking party; Owain bore the assault
bravely, but in the first discharge of arrows he himself fell
wounded; dismayed by the fall of their leader, his men
fled, and he was promptly despatched.

"Thus," says Warrington, "died this bold and profligate
chieftain agreeably to the tenour of his life." We cannot
deny the boldness and the profligacy; but perhaps a broad

consideration of the circumstances under which he ran his
short and violent course may lead to a lenient judgment
on the character and conduct of a man of great energy and
bravery. For the Norman conquest of England there was
some show of justification. The claims of Harold to the
crown were not legally stronger than those of the Conqueror.
But for the overrunning of Cymru by the more needy
or ambitious of the followers of William and his successors
there was no moral justification. The Cymric leaders
had welcomed the overthrow of Harold, and neither mere
border foray nor intestine quarrel could excuse the wholesale seizure of the lands of the Welsh princely and noble
families which had been in the possession of their cenedloed
for centuries, or justify the breaking-up of a social and
legal organisation which contained in itself the elements
of national progress, and which would in all probability
have resulted in a stable polity, had it been allowed to
develop without interference, under men like Gruffyd ab
Lewelyn, Bledyn, and Cadwgan. Owain and Madog were
men who were suffering under the sense of grievous wrong,
and though we, writing calmly, may condemn them as
impolitic and imprudent, or, judging by modern standards,
censure many of their acts as criminal, a truer criticism will
accord some tribute of admiration to their intrepidity in
fighting fearful odds—odds against them at home and odds
against them beyond the borders of their native land.

For some years longer Maredud ab Bledyn and the
remaining sons of Cadwgan upheld the claims of their
cenedl to the sovereignty of so much of Powys as was
not in the hands of Norman-English lords. Encouraged,
perhaps, by the drowning of Richard, Earl of Chester, in
the White Ship, they, in the course of 1121, rose and gave
cause of offence. Henry, deeming the matter serious enough
to make another expedition necessary, entered Wales with
an "immense and cruel army." Maredud and his friends

appealed to Gruffyd ab Cynan for help, but he, with a prudence unusual among the Welsh chieftains, refused to join them, and even threatened active opposition if they came over the border of his dominion.[1] The lords of Powys took counsel together, and decided to adopt the defensive attitude. The king marched into Powys, and there was at any rate one engagement, during which an arrow struck the king, but, owing to the strength of his breast-plate, glanced off. It is doubtful whether the arrow was sped by a Welsh archer or by one of Henry's force, though the "Brut" is probably right when it claims that it was directed by one of "the young men" sent forward by Maredud to harass the enemy in their advance. Henry behaved with cowardice, and, greatly disconcerted, entered into negotiations, which led to the renewed submission of the Welsh leaders. Maredud and his allies "came under the king's peace."[2] He did not again imbroil himself with the king, but he was involved in many domestic quarrels, and behaved with great cruelty to his relatives. He died in 1129 or 1130 in the odour of sanctity. The "Brut" describes him, with more generosity than justice, as the "ornament, and safety, and defence of all Powys."[3]

The ruin of the house of Bledyn, so far as any claim to sovereignty was concerned, was now complete. The kingdoms of Deheubarth and Powys, like the smaller regions of Dyfed, Morganwg, Gwent, Brecheiniog, and the rest, were destroyed as existing entities, save so far as occasional pretensions, the imagination of bards, or the friendly flattery of the adherents of the Cymric lords can be said to have kept them alive. In the south and in Powys the possession of the descendants of the princely houses dwindled down to cymwds or cantrefs, largely those of the more

1 "Brut," *s.a.* 118.
2 *Ibid.* "Ann. Camb.," *s.a.* 1120. Freeman, "Norm. Conq.," v. 212.
3 "Brut," *s.a.* 1129.

mountainous parts of the country, held more or less voluntarily as vassals of the Norman king ; but in these sadly-
diminished areas the *cyfraith gyffredin* (common law) of
Cymru was still the rule of right. The chieftains, though
reduced in power, kept up according to their means the
household state found in Howel's laws, haughtily cherished
the memories of a departed greatness, and alternately
sullenly acquiesced in the new state of things and eagerly
seized an opportunity for revenge against Norman, Saxon,
and Cymric neighbour alike. Notwithstanding that during
the twelfth century the line of Rhys ab Tewdwr, in the
persons of the two of its members who most clearly emerge
to our view—Gruffyd ab Rhys and Rhys ab Gruffyd—
carried on, with occasional very considerable successes,
warfare with the intruding Norman lords, and even the
king of England, the hold of the central government was
never permanently relaxed, except during the seventeen
years of Stephen's unhappy reign, and the policy of conquest
by settlement went on relentlessly.

We must here pause for a moment to make a few
observations on the legal aspect of the events that we have
been narrating. As will be seen by-and-by, the whole of
the Cymric lands, except that portion of the north which
remained in the possession of Gruffyd ab Cynan and his
descendants, became known as the Marches of Wales. By
the time that we have reached it seems to us that the whole
of the country except Gwyned had, as we have said, now
been feudalised, for there is a great deal of evidence that
the Welsh chieftains in the territories which became the
Marches had familiarised themselves with the notion that
they held their lands of the king of England on terms
analogous to those of the Lords-Marchers. Certainly this
was the case over the greater part of Powys. It will be
remembered that by Welsh law the uchelwyr and free
tribesmen did not, according to theory, hold their land of

any king or prince, though the system was approximating to the Norman-English notions of tenure. The introduction of the first principle of feudal law was encouraged and made easy by the organisation of the cymwd as it had developed from the time of the Cymric settlement many centuries before.[1]

The transition from the ideas of land ownership found in the Welsh codes to the Norman-English system was not difficult. The kingship, as we have pointed out, under Cymric law was originally vested in a family ; it was not an office handed down from person to person in a defined order. Primogeniture was not a recognised principle. The chieftaincy of the kingly families was in early times probably transmitted according to the rules which governed the election to the headship of any cenedl; but in the Venedotian Code the heir was to be sought in the last king's near relations, and was to be one marked out by him. Each gwlad was composed of an aggregate of cantrefs or cymwds. As the territorial idea became stronger and stronger, the chieftain of the ruling family of the gwlad found it expedient for the administration of his territory to place his sons or other kinsmen over this or that cantref or cymwd. Gradually these lords and their descendants so planted about the country got to look upon themselves as permanently

---

[1] Mr. A. N. Palmer says: "The cymwd or commote became almost invariably the civic hundred, and it often became the feudal lordship. Very often, however, the feudal lordship was formed by a group of commotes, each of which long retained a separate organisation and many old Welsh forms of procedure, but was gradually assimilated to the English manor. It was quite unusual for the bounds of the commote to be changed." He gives as examples of lordships formed by grouping cymwds those of Chirk, Denbigh, and Duffryn Clwyd. See his learned note in App. to Report, 447. See also the "Memorandum on Lordships and Manors," compiled by Mr. Lenfar Thomas (App. to Report, 437); and especially notes contributed by Mr. Cobb, F.S.A. (438), Mr. Trevor Prkns (449), Mr. Williams (451), Mr. John Lloyd (452), Mr. J. Hobson Matthews (459), and the late Mr. J. Stuart Corbet (465).

settled in the cantref or cymwd assigned to them, though recognising their allegiance to the head of their princely cenedl. The grants made from time to time to the Church, with the immunities of which we have spoken above, were also factors in familiarising the minds of men with defined territorial government. When the Cymric families came into contact with the Normans, with their fully-developed ideas of tenure, the transition from the old Cymric tribal idea of the right to possession of land to that of the invaders was very rapid, and not long after the beginning of the twelfth century there is ample evidence of the recognition by the Welsh princes over the greater part of Wales of this great change.

In Gwyneđ the position was, and remained for a long time, somewhat different, though it is not very easy to state precisely the legal relation of its prince to the Norman king. As far back as the time of Ælfred, Welsh princes had commended themselves and afterwards repeatedly did homage to English kings; but this commendation in the eighth, ninth, or tenth centuries was a very different thing from the receiving of a definite area of land from a Norman-English king in the twelfth century, as for instance did Cadwgan and his brothers. Bleđyn and Rhiwaħon had undoubtedly been invested by Harold, and so far as central and south Wales were concerned this fact was never lost sight of by the rulers of England. But Gruffyđ ab Cynan was not of the house of Cynfyn, but a lineal descendant of Rhodri Mawr. He conquered Môn, and seems gradually to have obtained possession of various parts of the old kingdom of Gwyneđ on the mainland, and we can find no evidence that he ever received his possessions by any grant from a Norman king, though he did homage to Henry I. His position, therefore, was different from that of the lords of the south. This view is confirmed by subsequent events, and by the preamble of the Statute of Rhudlan. The prince of Gwyneḋ continued to regard himself as a sovereign owing allegiance to the king of England in a personal capacity, but not admitting any jurisdiction of the royal court. As the power of the house of North Wales increased, some of the Welsh lords in areas outside Gwyneḋ acknowledged its prince as their immediate lord, and even after the final conquest by Edward I., and as late as 1354, an Act of Parliament was deemed necessary to declare that all Lordships-Marchers were held of the king and not of the Prince of Wales. Whether these observations are well-founded or not, there is no doubt that Gwyneḋ did occupy a special position, and that it was for nearly two hundred years after the downfall of the house of Bleḋyn practically independent. Henceforth the interest of Cymric affairs, notwithstanding the fitful struggles of the descendants of Rhys ab Tewdwr in the south, centres round the line of Gwyneḋ.

Gruffyḋ ab Cynan's long reign came to an end in 1137,[1] when he died (having survived Henry I. by two years) at the age of eighty-two, after assuming the monastic habit. Though his attitude of isolation, his conduct in not joining the lords of the centre and the south in resisting the Norman invasion, and his open desertion of the cause of Gruffyḋ ab Rhys have been censured, yet subsequent events justify his prudent policy, and prove him to have been a wise and competent ruler in a very difficult time. But for his steady resolve to avoid wasting the strength of Gwyneḋ in a fruitless attempt to hold all the Cymric land and to concentrate all the energies of the people on preserving the independence of the north-western districts, it is probable that Gwyneḋ might even thus early have sustained the fate of Deheubarth and of Powys. Gruffyḋ made Gwyneḋ for the time the centre of national life, and the eagerly-sought refuge of Welshmen dispossessed by

[1] "Brut," *s.a.* 1136. "Ann. Cambr." 1137. The latter is the true date.

Norman intruders. The result of his policy was a great revival of Cymric power under a line of princes whose capacity gives interest, and even lustre, to the annals of Wales from this time to the final conquest of the principality by Edward I. The space at our command does not enable us to deal at length with the fortunes of the house of Gwyneđ during this period, and we must content ourselves with a mere outline of the course of events.[1]

Gruffyđ ab Cynan left several sons. Owain (usually called Owain Gwyneđ) succeeded to the principality, and his brothers (we may assume) received shares of their father's provisions in the customary manner. He and Cadwaladr had, before the aged prince's death, distinguished themselves by raiding in the territories of the lords-marchers, and had even retained, for the time, some of the fortresses which had been built by the invaders. In the very year of his accession Owain and his brother Cadwaladr again marched to the south, and destroyed several castles.[2] During the seventeen years of Stephen's troubled reign the Welsh were left much to themselves, and the Norman lords who had settled in Wales had generally to depend on their own resources. Owain was later on troubled by a dispute with Cadwaladr, who was forced to flee into England, and there were, of course, constant feuds between the Welsh lords. It would be tedious to recount the vicissitudes of petty local quarrels which had no important consequences,

---

[1] For an excellent account of Gruffyđ see " Dict. Nat. Biog." Consult (in adoption to the usual sources) " Historia hen Gruffud vab Kenan vab Yago, Myv. Arch. ii., 583–605 ; Arch. Cambr., 3rd series, 1866. A Latin translation of this life of Gruffyđ by Robinson, Bishop of Bangor (1566–85), is preserved in the library at Peniarth, and is printed in " Arch. Cambr.," *ubi supra.* To Gruffyđ is popularly ascribed the making of regulations regarding minstrelsy and minstrels. See the " Historia hen " ; J. D. Rhys' "Cambro-Brytannicæ Cymræcæve Linguæ Institutiones" (1592), translated in " Y Cymmrodor," i. 283–293 ; Stephens' " Lit. of the Kymry," 2nd edition, p. 56. The bard Meilir composed an elegy on Gruffyđ. (Stephens, *ubi supra,* p. 12.)

[2] " Brut," *s.a.* 1136—really 1137.

and we will content ourselves with stating that when, after the peace of Wallingford and the death of Stephen, Henry II. became king the prince of Gwyneð had materi ally added to the resources of his country and re-occupied several places or districts from which the Welsh had been expelled earlier in the century; while in the south Rhys ab Gruffyð, who came of the princely line of Deheubarth, had obtained several comparatively important successes.[1]

Some three years elapsed before hostilities broke out between the new king and Owain, but in 1157 Henry invaded North Wales. It is not clear what provocation had been given by the Welsh, but it is probable the king was induced to take this step at the instigation of Cadwaladr and of Madog ab Mareduð (one of the lords of Powys), who had both quarrelled with the prince of Gwyneð.[2] Henry advanced through "the champaign land of Chester." Owain, entrenching himself at Basingwerk, awaited him. The king divided his forces; the main body was directed to proceed along the coast and attack the Welsh in front, while the king himself, intending to take the enemy in flank and to cut off his retreat to the mountains, turning to his own left, went into the forest of Kennadlawg; but his tactics were anticipated. He was surprised in "the trackless wood" by Davyð and Cynan, two of Owain's sons, and defeated. It was only with difficulty and loss that he escaped into the open country.[3] Owain did not, however, risk a pitched battle, but retreated to Kil Owain, near St. Asaph. The king gathered his army together and proceeded to Rhuðlan. Owain then moved to Lwyn Pina, and from there, with the help of Madog ab Mareduð (one of the chief barons of

---

[1] His father, Gruffyð (who is described by the " Brut " as " the light and strength and gentleness of the men of South Wales "), died in 1137.

[2] The formal pretext for the invasion was very likely that Owain had not done homage.

[3] It was probably in this engagement that the Earl of Essex, overcome by terror, abandoned the royal standard.

Powys), harassed the king by day and night. Henry's army was supported by a fleet which sailed along the coast ; a force of seamen and " youths fit for battle " effected a landing in Môn, but, after some pillaging of churches, was defeated with heavy slaughter by the men of the island.

Henry's attempt was a failure, but still was not without effect. Peace was quickly made on the terms of Owain's doing homage and restoring Cadwaladr to his share of the possessions of the late prince. In the same or the following year all the Welsh princes or barons except Rhys ab Gruffyd submitted to the king.

Rhys had been waging a sporadic warfare against the neighbouring lords-marchers from the recesses of Ystrad Towi. Henry sent him a message ordering his attendance at Court to do homage. Rhys, acting on the advice of his uchelwyr, went to the king, and made his peace on condition of receiving Cantref Mawr, and such other cantref as the king should be pleased to give him, " whole and not scattered." Henry agreed, but did not literally perform the condition. For some years there was comparative quiet in Wales, and in 1164 both Owain and Rhys appeared at the council at Woodstock and renewed their homage.

Rhys, however, soon began to raid the lands of the Norman lords, because, as the " Brut " says, the king did not fulfil his promises. Having regard to the general character of the Norman-English kings, we see no reason to doubt this view, or to believe that Rhys, who, on the whole, was one of the best of the later South Welsh princes, and afterwards became Justiciar of South Wales under Henry, was in the wrong in this quarrel. Rhys took, dismantled, and burnt the castle at Aber Rheidol, and overran Keredigion a second time.

Probably encouraged by this success, and influenced by circumstances of which we have no knowledge, the Welsh barons, with Owain at their head, combined and joined in the revolt begun by Rhys. Davyd ab Owain ravaged Tegeingl, and Henry, apprehending a further attack in force on the castles of that cantref, hastened to Rhudlan, but, finding matters more serious than he expected, after staying there only three nights, returned to England. Having collected a mixed but large force, he marched to Oswestry. The combined Welsh hosts (under Owain and Cadwaladr, as well as Owain Cyfeiliog and other lords of Powys) encamped at Corwen. There was, however, no considerable engagement. The Welsh adopted a defensive attitude; the king hesitated to attack. He ultimately moved into the wood of Ceiriog, causing ways to be cut in advance through the forest, and penetrated to the country near the Berwyn range; but the weather having become tempestuous and his supplies having failed, he was compelled to lead his men to "the open plains of England," and thence to Chester. Angry and disappointed, he cruelly blinded some of the Welsh hostages who were in his custody, and abandoned for the time being further attempts to crush the Welsh.

Later in the year Henry left England, and was absent for about six years, during which, though there were the usual disputes and occasional raidings among the Welsh lords, there was no warfare of consequence. The most serious quarrel was one in 1167 between Owain and Rhys on the one side, and Owain Cyfeiliog on the other, in which, after some fighting, the latter, with Norman aid, came off the better; but in the course of the year Owain and Rhys took and destroyed the castles at Rhudlan and Prestatyn. Nothing which tended to retard the growing power of Gwyned occurred until the death of Owain in 1169 led to a contest between his sons. His later years had been clouded by a quarrel with the Church, caused partly by a disputed election to the see of Bangor and partly by his marriage with Crisiant, his cousin, who was within the prohibited degrees of consanguinity. In the end he was excommunicated by Archbishop Thomas à Becket, but, notwithstanding this, he received the last sacraments and Christian burial. The Welsh chronicler praises him as a man of " the most extraordinary sagacity, nobleness, fortitude, and bravery." [1]

Upon Owain's death the succession to the principality was disputed among his sons. Cadwaladr did not advance any claims, though he survived his brother for three or four years.[2] Howel ab Owain, the late prince's eldest son, and Davyđ, his son by Crisiant, were both deemed illegitimate by the clergy. Iorwerth, the eldest legitimate son, was for some reason passed over altogether, though, as we shall see, his son Lewelyn later on obtained Gwyneđ, and raised the principality to its highest point of power and renown. Howel had, as early as 1144, taken part in military affairs, but he is better known as the author of some graceful poems than as a warrior. Immediately after Owain's death he seized or was elected to the inheritance. But his hold on the country was very slight (perhaps on account of the Irish origin of Pyvog, his mother), and Davyđ, who claimed the throne, overcame and slew him in 1170.[3] The victor, however, only made good his claim to part of the territories of Owain. His brother Maelgwn seized Môn, and othei members of the family refused to submit. In 1173 Davyđ expelled Maelgwn from that island, and by 1174 had

---

[1] The poet Gwalchmai celebrates his prowess in an ode upon which Gray founded his fragment "The Triumph of Owen." Stephens' "Lit. of the Kymry," 2nd edition, p. 18.

[2] According to the " Brut " he died in 1172.

[3] Howel ab Owain is celebrated among the bards of the twelfth century. Stephens says he is "the most sprightly and charming poet" he has to mention. (Stephens, *ubi supra*, p. 41.) An ode to him by Kynđelw, and a lament on his death by Periv ab Kedivor, are extant. Kedivor was Howel's foster-father.

captured or driven into exile all his brothers or near relations who refused to recognise his paramount position.

When the barons revolted against Henry II., Davyd, instead of pursuing the usual policy of the Welsh and siding with the rebellious and discontented men of the realm, remained faithful to the king; and it was due to this fact that he was permitted to marry, in 1175, the king's bastard sister Emma, the daughter of Geoffrey Plantagenet by a lady of Maine. He thought, no doubt, that this alliance would not only make his position in Gwyned more secure, but that it would in other ways be of advantage. But while such a connection did enhance the position of his family among the great houses of the whole country it did him no good at home, and almost immediately there were signs of coldness and disaffection towards him on the part of the barons of North Wales. Before the end of the year his brother Rhodri (whom he had treated badly) escaped, and, finding followers, possessed himself of Môn and part of the mainland, while his nephews, the sons of Cynan ab Owain, occupied Meirionyd. Davyd was unable to protect himself, and was driven over the Conway. He then turned for assistance to the English Court, and attended the Council at Oxford in 1177 with some of the Welsh barons who were still well affected to him, where they swore fealty to Henry. Apparently by way of compensation for the losses he had sustained, he received a grant of Ellesmere. But his power over Gwyned now became nominal; the leaders of the Welsh were completely alienated, and his real sway was limited to Rhudlan and the Vale of Clwyd with his newly-acquired estate. Nothing is known about him for some years, but we find that in 1188 he entertained Archbishop Baldwin and Giraldus Cambrensis very handsomely at Rhudlan, on their journey through Wales.[1]

[1] Giraldus describes Rhudlan as a very noble castle. "Itin. Cambr.." ii. c. 10.

Giraldus notes, however, that even then Davyđ was beginning to be harassed by Lewelyn ab Iorwerth or his adherents. Henry II. died in 1189, and was succeeded by Richard Cœur de Lion, whose prolonged absence for many years prevented much interference with Welsh affairs. Lewelyn's friends became more and more numerous; he allied himself with Rhodri, his uncle, and expelled Davyđ even from the Vale of Clwyd. Taking refuge in England (probably residing in Ellesmere), Davyđ lived on in obscurity, and died unnoticed in 1203.[1]

During the years after the death of Owain Gwyneđ, in which Davyđ attempted and failed to secure the actual rule of the principality, Rhys ab Gruffyđ (the representative of the old princely line of Deheubarth), to whom we have had occasion to refer more than once as the ally of Owain, pursued a more successful career in the south, though the success was purchased by a complete submission to the English crown. After reluctantly doing homage to Henry, as we have stated above, Rhys, finding the king's promises not to be trusted, and that "he could not preserve anything of what the king had given him except by force of arms,"[2] made his headquarters in Cantref Mawr, and for many years engaged in almost continual warfare with the lords-marchers within his reach, and sometimes with his Welsh neighbours. In 1171, after a campaign against Owain Cyfeiliog, at the end of which the latter submitted, there occurred a sudden change in the policy of Rhys. Henry, returning after a prolonged absence to England, forthwith planned and proceeded to carry out an invasion of Ireland. Rhys, apparently on his own initiative, sought the friendship of the king, and made offers of assistance. His overtures

---

[1] In 1200 John undertook to protect the lands of Ellesmere and Hales, which belonged to Davyđ or his wife (Rotuli Chart. 44 a). He left a son, Owain, who exchanged Ellesmere for lands in Lincolnshire.

[2] "Brut," *s.a.* 1157.

were accepted, and on his appearing before the king at Pembroke, where the English forces were awaiting a favourable opportunity of crossing the channel, he "obtained grace," and was received into high favour. Henry granted to him Keredigion and other lands, and handed back his son Howel, who had been given as hostage some time before. Though the Irish expedition was a failure, Rhys remained then and thenceforward true to his allegiance, and the king on his return made him Justiciar of South Wales. The holding of this office, far from alienating the Welsh, added to his authority ; he was called emphatically "the lord" Rhys, the style by which he is still known among the Welsh-speaking people. He rebuilt the castle of Aberteifi (Cardigan) " with stone and mortar," whence for many years he ruled over a large part of South Wales in comparative peace, and died at an advanced age in 1197.[1]

For some years before the death of Davyd, his nephew Lewelyn had obtained possession of the greater part of Gwyned. The son of that Iorwerth ab Owain who had been ousted by his brother Howel in 1169, Lewelyn, who was born about 1176, commenced his military career at an early age,[2] and soon secured the devoted support of the Welsh, who viewed with dislike and suspicion the close relations of Davyd with the English court.[3] He does not appear to have come in contact with Richard I., but when John came to the throne Lewelyn quickly made peace with the new king on terms that gave him a good title, according to Norman-English law, to the principality, but which made him a feudal vassal. This submission was an act of policy on

[1] See for further details his life in the " Dict. Nat. Biog."
[2] Giraldus says that Lewelyn was at the time of his journey twelve years old. " Itin. Cambr.," ii. 8. His partisans were even then asserting his rights.
[3] The chief authorities for Lewelyn's life are of course the " Brut " and " Ann. Cambr.," but English sources give us many additional facts. Lewelyn's life is dealt with exhaustively by Professor Tout in " Dict. Nat. Biog."

his part. His relations with the king continued friendly for several years, and in 1206 he married Joan (the daughter of John), who received as her marriage portion Ellésmere, which Owain ab Davyd had exchanged for lands elsewhere. Soon after (1207), John and Lewelyn fought against Gwenwynwyn (one of the sons of Owain Cyfeiliog), a considerable lord in Powys. Lewelyn seized the lands of Gwenwynwyn, who was captured by the king, and in the same campaign conquered all Keredigion north of the Aeron, which was then in the possession of Maelgwn ab Rhys. Most of the Welsh barons now acknowledged Lewelyn as their immediate superior. The old theory of the supremacy of Gwyned was of material help to him in his claim to the homage of the Welsh ; but his growing power soon excited the jealousy of the most powerful of the descendants of the other princely families, and the attack on Gwenwynwyn and Maelgwn was probably caused by their hostile attitude towards the claims of the prince of Gwyned. In the next year there was a quarrel between John and Lewelyn. The immediate cause was probably the release by the former of Gwenwynwyn, who in 1209 recovered his lands with the aid of the king. John and his son-in-law were never again really friendly. The latter appears to have been well-informed as to the course of events in England, and to have begun to form relations with the barons, whose discontent with the government was day by day increasing. But his position was for a time full of difficulty, and even critical. He ravaged the land of Chester in 1209, and made very successful attacks on the English within his reach. Ranulph, Earl of Chester, retaliated, and John himself, with the intention of deposing the prince, took the field in 1210, with a large army. He was joined by Gwenwynwyn, Maelgwn, Rhys Grug, and other Welsh lords. After some delay, owing seemingly to imperfect preparations, John marched right into Gwyned.

The combination was too much for ILewelyn. He retreated into the mountains, and was obliged to allow John to capture Bangor, and to build or restore many castles. Ultimately he sued for peace, which, owing to Joan's intercession, was granted on not unreasonable terms. ILewelyn retained the greater portion of Gwyneđ, but ceded Perfeđwlad, made large gifts of cattle, and delivered hostages.

Notwithstanding the fact that by allying himself for some years with John, and by his marriage, he had seemed to be following the same course as Davyđ I., the majority of the Welsh barons did not lose confidence in him, and even the terms on which peace was concluded did not alienate his supporters.

The position of John himself was now fast becoming desperate, and the discontent of the English barons was soon to become expressed in open rebellion. ILewelyn, with true insight, took the popular side, formed friendly relations with the disaffected magnates of the English realm, and, dropping former feuds, induced Gwenwynwyn, Maelgwn, and others to join forces with him. Then, not being able " to brook the many insults done to him by the men of the king who had been left in the new castle at Aberconway," he renewed the war, and with his allies took, in 1211, all the castles the king had made in Gwyneđ, and also achieved some successes in Powys.

Hostilities of the same sort being continued in 1212, John became so irritated that he caused twenty-eight of the Welsh hostages to be hanged at Nottingham, and made hasty preparations for another expedition into Wales. Before, however, he could carry out his plans of conquest in the west, he discovered the existence of the wide-spread conspiracy against him, and was forced to give up the design of another Welsh invasion. Owain ab Davyđ, however, tried to obtain possession of the ceded district of

Perfedwlad (which the king had granted him), but ignominiously failed, and the four cantrefs were soon regained by Lewelyn.

John's affairs went from bad to worse, and he was reduced to asking the aid of his son-in-law, but Lewelyn was too astute to desert the winning side. By steadily acting with the barons he increased his power, and, on the triumph of their party, he was able to secure the insertion of clauses in the great charter intended to remedy the grievances of the Welsh.

The death of John, the war with Louis, and the general confusion in England gave the Welsh prince opportunity of pursuing his successes. The Welsh lords of the south revolted ; Lewelyn came to their aid, and in 1215 took Carmarthen, demolished the castle of Lanstephan, and many others ; marched through Keredigion and obtained possession of the castles of Aberystwyth and Cilgerran. He was equally successful in the two next years, and as a result of his operations became the recognised feudal chief of all Wales not in the actual occupation of the lords-marchers. Gwenwynwyn alone questioned his position, but the prince swiftly expelled him from Powys, and though he escaped, he never himself obtained his lands again.

John died in October, 1216, and was succeeded by his infant son, Henry III. William Marshal, Earl of Pembroke, was made "governor of king and kingdom," and after the expulsion of Lewis, Lewelyn pursuing his usual policy did homage to the boy-king at Winchester in 1218. William Marshal died, however, in 1219, and his great possessions descended to his son William, the second Earl of Pembroke, while the management of English affairs passed into the hands of Pandulf, the papal legate, Stephen Langton, the Archbishop of Canterbury, and Hubert de Burgh.

For reasons that do not clearly appear, a quarrel took place between the new earl and Lewelyn which resulted in a private war of some six years' duration. In the earlier campaigns the latter was very successful in attacks on Dyfed. In 1221, Rhys Gryg, who had submitted to Lewelyn, rose and joined the earl, but was defeated by the prince, who confiscated his lands and compelled him again to do homage. Henry III. made in the same year an expedition in the interest of the earl, but with little result. William Marshal himself, however, in an encounter with the Welsh defeated them with great slaughter. The Archbishop of Canterbury excommunicated Lewelyn, and placed his lands under an interdict, but his power remained unshaken. The king led another army into Wales, but without the happening of any decisive operations peace was made. In 1223, Lewelyn and the earl attended the Council at Ludlow, but their feud was not composed, and it was only in 1226, after the prince had met the king at Shrewsbury, that some kind of reconciliation was effected between them.

For some years there was peace, but in 1228, for reasons which are not clear, war between the prince and the English again broke out. Lewelyn kept up his connection with many of the disaffected barons of England, and probably much of his conduct may be explained by their secretly inciting him to embarrass the king and his government. Henry III. and the Justiciar marched to Montgomery, which the Welsh were attacking. There was at least one engagement, but the campaign was not fruitful of any important result. The prince quickly made terms. He agreed to pay 3,000 marks as compensation, and, with other Welsh lords, renewed his homage.

William de Braose (the heir to the estates of the powerful marcher house of de Braose) was, however, captured by the Welsh. The prisoner was released in

1229 on his paying 3,000 marks, giving his consent to the marriage of his daughter Isabella to Davyđ, Lewelyn's son by Joan, and undertaking not to fight against the prince again. It so happened that while in captivity he had an intrigue with Joan, which seems to have been carried on after he obtained his freedom, and which was discovered by the prince. Lewelyn seized William (catching him, it is said, in his own chamber), and caused him to be publicly hanged.[1] It is strange to find that this affair did not prevent Davyđ's marriage to Isabella, which was soon afterwards celebrated. The prince's eldest son, Gruffyđ, had already shown considerable military capacity, but his unruly conduct not only cost him the loss of his father's affection, but led to his disgrace and imprisonment in 1228, and it was made plain to all that Davyđ was the son whom Lewelyn proposed to designate as his heir.

In 1231 Lewelyn again invaded the marches, burnt the castle of Montgomery, marched to Brecon and Gwent, destroying castles and cruelly devastating the districts. Avoiding Morganwg, he advanced to Neath and Kidweli, and then with the help of some south Welsh lords took Cardigan. This brilliant campaign alarmed the English government. The spiritual weapons of excommunication and interdict were again employed against the prince, and Henry once more marched into central Wales, but effected nothing decisive. A truce for three years was soon arranged on the terms of the suspension of the excommunication and interdict. Before, however, the three years had elapsed Richard Marshal (who had succeeded William, the prince's former enemy, in the Earldom of Pembroke) revolted against Henry. Lewelyn did not scruple to join him, and after raiding in Gwent and Morganwg besieged Carmarthen,

---

[1] The "Brut," *s.a.* 1230, says that "William Brewys was hanged by Llewelyn ab Iorwerth, having been caught in the chamber of the prince with the Princess Jannett."

but after a prolonged attempt to reduce the castle this time failed. In the next year the truce was renewed on terms favourable to the Welsh. The prince's active career now virtually ended, for though he was not old his health was bad, and the direction of affairs soon passed to Davyd. Lewelyn was henceforth chiefly concerned with securing the succession to his principality for Davyd. He liberated Gruffyd from prison after six years' confinement, and again acknowledged the king as his feudal over-lord. In 1238 he convened his Welsh vassals to a meeting at Strata Florida, at which they swore fealty to Davyd. Gruffyd received lands in Leyn. The prince, having arranged his affairs, soon afterwards assumed the monastic habit and retired from the world. He died on April 11th, 1240, in the Cistercian monastery at Aberconway.

The Welsh accorded to Lewelyn with justice the title of Mawr (the Great), and the epithet was recognised as appropriate among his Norman-English contemporaries. The melancholy fate of his grandson—another Lewelyn—has attracted to the personality of the last Cymric prince of Wales popular interest and sentiment to a degree that has been somewhat detrimental to the fame of the grandfather. There can, however, be no doubt that the latter was the most brilliant and capable ruler the Cymry produced after the time of Gruffyd ab Lewelyn or Howel Da—perhaps, indeed, the ablest of all the line of Cuneda. He saw that the true policy for a Welsh prince of his period was to frankly admit the suzerainty of the English king ; to devote his energies, not to regaining a shadowy crown of Britain, but to protecting the remaining Cymric land from encroachment, and preserving the independence of his people in internal matters. From the time when he obtained a firm hold on Gwyned he steadily pursued this course of action, and took his place among the great vassals of the realm. While it may have cost him something to assume openly a position of formal dependence, he was more than repaid by the increase of his real power. Unfortunately for the Welsh, his successors followed him with steps unequal, and the principality which he consolidated and handed on to his son Davyđ was destined not long afterwards to pass from the line of Cadwaladr to the greatest of the Plantagenet kings.

For some time before the death of his father, Davyđ II. had been the real ruler of the principality. The homage of the Welsh barons already done in 1238 went a long way to ensuring his succession; but he had taken "time by the forelock" in another way, for in the course of 1239 he had treacherously seized and imprisoned his half-brother Gruffyđ with whom he had been long at feud. Immediately after Lewelyn's death he was recognised as prince, again received the submission of the Welsh vassal lords, and himself attended at Gloucester, where he did homage to Henry, and was knighted. Lewelyn's territories were granted to him, and it was agreed between the king and him that any matters in dispute should be referred to the arbitration of the Papal legate, Otto, who however shortly afterwards left the kingdom. The imprisoned Gruffyđ had, however, some partisans in Gwyneđ. Foremost among them was Richard, Bishop of Bangor, who excommunicated Davyđ, and then, either from fear for himself or zeal for Gruffyđ, hurried to the king, and induced him to take an interest in Gruffyđ's grievances. In pursuance of the agreement come to at Gloucester, Davyđ was summoned to Worcester to arrange for the appointment of arbitrators in place of Otto. He took no notice of the summons, but fresh arbitrators were chosen, or rather appointed (for it does not appear that the prince ever consented to the new names), and being summoned to Shrewsbury for the decision of the question between him and his brother, he again neglected the call. Senena, the wife of Gruffyđ, was, however, at Shrewsbury pressing her husband's claims, and made an arrangement with the king. Quite apart, however, from his conduct towards Gruffyđ, Davyđ, not content with strengthening his hold over the lands granted to him, had been imprudent enough to receive the homage of rebellious royal tenants and to give aid to the enemies of Roger Mortimer. Under these circumstances Henry decided to make a punitive expedition. "Having assembled an army," he advanced towards Gwyneđ as far as Diserth Castle in the Vale of Clwyd. Davyđ was either taken unprepared or did not think it prudent to engage in war and submitted without striking a blow on August 29th, 1241, at Alnet, near St. Asaph, and came at once to terms with his over-lord. Under the arrangement made, the unfortunate Gruffyđ was transferred to the king; the Welsh prince agreed to submit the quarrel between him and his brother to the king's court, to give up Mold to the seneschal of Chester, to yield up to Gruffyđ ab Gwenwynwyn his lands in Powys, and to concede to other Welsh lords their claims to parts of Meirionyđ. He was ordered to attend the court in London, and went there in October. During his visit a further agreement was forced on him by the king's government by which it was stipulated that the principality should be surrendered to the English crown if he died without heirs of his body.

Davyđ returned to North Wales, and the next two years were years of peace. Gruffyđ was kept a prisoner in London. The English court had readily enough used his claims and grievances as weapons to justify interference with Davyđ; but when they had attained their object it was seen that his release would only mean more trouble in the west. He was therefore detained, and no steps were taken to bring on his cause before the king's court. He had been taken to London and confined in the Tower, where he was well treated. In 1244, having no doubt come to the conclusion that he could not count on redress from the king, he tried to escape by means of a rope, but fell in the attempt and broke his neck. Probably relieved by his brother's death from fear of internal disaffection, and influenced by the desire to repair a reputation damaged among subjects ever eager for war by his hasty conclusion of peace with the king, Davyđ, instead of waiting till the discontent of England with the despotic but weak personal government of Henry had burst into flame, took overt steps which showed that he.did not intend to regard the obligations into which he had entered.[1] He summoned in 1244 all the Welsh lords to join him—apparently to do homage with a view to a general rising. All obeyed except three, who were promptly assailed and compelled to submit. Davyđ not being able to secure allies among the English, and conscious of his inability single-handed to shake off the control of the English government, intrigued with the Papal court, and appears to have offered to submit the questions between him and the king to the judgment of commissioners appointed by the then Pope. But though the Pope did nominate two abbots as arbitrators Henry would have nothing to do with them ; and Innocent IV. on further representations cancelled the commission.

Border warfare continued into 1245. The Welsh sustained a considerable defeat at Montgomery, but Davyđ retook Mold.

Henry then made preparations for another invasion of Wales. With a sufficient army he advanced to Deganwy, while Món was ravaged by a force from Ireland. The Welsh prince avoided a decisive engagement, and was compelled to retire in the usual way to the mountains of Snowdon. There he awaited the development of events.

---

[1] "Brut," *s.a.* 1244, after recounting Gruffyđ's death, abruptly says Davyđ "became enraged and summoned, &c.," but his anger was surely not caused by the removal of one who was at once an enemy and a rival.

Henry was not able to follow the enemy into the mountains. When winter came his army fell short of supplies, and he had to retire without having obtained the submission of Davyd; but he strengthened Deganwy, and in the campaign inflicted much loss on the Welsh. The prince's plans were cut short by his death in March, 1246.

Davyd II. died without issue; but Gruffyd had left three sons, Owain Goch (who had shared his captivity for a time, but had been released and received into favour by the king), Lewelyn (who it is said had already been occupying parts of Perfedwlad in defiance alike of his uncle Davyd and the English authorities),[1] and Davyd (destined to be the last reigning prince of his line). Ignoring the agreement of 1241, by which the principality was to pass to the English crown in case Davyd II. should die without issue, Owain and Lewelyn, with the consent of the Welsh barons, assumed the sovereignty, and divided the possessions of their house (making provision for their younger brother Davyd). They were at once treated as rebels. Nicholas de Myles, seneschal of Carmarthen, seized the lordships in the south that were appurtenant to Gwyned, and promptly marched to the north as far as Deganwy. Owain and Lewelyn retreated to the mountains. The king, not wishing at the moment to push things to extremities, did not insist on the exact terms of the bargain with the late prince. An understanding was arrived at between him and the princes, in pursuance of which they did homage to him at Woodstock in 1247. A treaty was thereupon signed by which Henry pardoned their rebellion, retained all Welsh land east of the Conway, as well as the southern districts which had been occupied by De Myles (except a part allotted to Maelgwn Vychan), but conferred on them the residue of the principality.

[1] Warrington's "History," p. 428, citing Wynne's "History of the Gwydir Family," p. 28.

For several years the settlement of 1247 was loyally adhered to, and there was a period of unwonted peace, during which Lewelyn steadily increased his influence, and attracted to himself the devoted attachment and the still retained hopes of the Welsh. It was probably owing to the jealousy roused by his growing popularity that in 1254 his brothers Owain and Davyd quarrelled with and took up arms against him. Lewelyn and his men confidently awaited the " cruel coming "[1] of the rebels at Bryn Derwin, where after a brief engagement the latter were decisively beaten. Owain was captured, thrown into prison, and kept in confinement for many years, but Davyd escaped to England to work much mischief against his brother and the cause of the Welsh. Lewelyn took possession of their lands, and on the death of Maredud ab Lewelyn, one of his vassal barons, seized Meirionyd. This last act estranged Gruffyd ab Gwenwynwyn, lord of the neighbouring cymwd of Cyfeiliog, and induced him to ally himself to the English.

While matters were in this position in Wales an event which had a direct effect on the fortunes of Gwyned took place. Edward, the eldest son of Henry III., was married to Eleanor, daughter of Ferdinand the Saint, in October, 1254, and the king, as part of the provision made for his son, conferred on him the earldom of Chester and all his lands in Wales.

We have pointed out above the exceptional position of the county of Chester. From the time of William I. it had been a practically independent state. It was now the strongest and most valuable of all the lordships in the marches of Wales. By becoming Earl of Chester the heir to the English crown came directly into contact with Welsh affairs. The vague grant of the king's lands in Wales included the four cantrefs of Perfedwlad, and

[1] " Brut," *s.a.* 1254.

three lordships in the south that, though not without intermission, had been in the possession of the English crown for many years.[1] Edward and his wife came to England in 1255. Boy though he was—being only sixteen—Edward took some part in the administration of his possessions in the west, though the real government was no doubt left to ministers, who were arbitrary and often unjust in their treatment of the Welsh tenants in the earl's lands. Their conduct after Edward's assumption of his earldom gave rise to great irritation in the four cantrefs and the other parts of Wales in his jurisdiction. In the course of 1255 a survey was made by his officers or those of the king on his behalf of his castles and lands in Gwynedd ; steps were taken to annex the four cantrefs to the county of Chester ; while the earl's deputy, Geoffrey Langton, consti-tuted three parts of Keredigion and the lands attached to or held with the castle of Carmarthen into shire-ground, with an organisation similar to that of the English shires. The Welsh tenants, seeing clearly enough that the effect of these measures would be the introduction of Norman-English law and the suppression of customs to which they were attached, not only because of their substantial consonance with their ideas of justice, but also because their use was a symbol of practical independence. The smaller Welsh barons, as well as their tenants, looked on the action of Edward's officers in a very different way from that in which they regarded a change of prince or lord. It mattered little to them whether their superior lord or prince did homage to the king of England or any one else, so long as the incidents of tenure remained the same. The changes now made, as they instantly saw, might, and probably would, be detrimental to them from a pecuniary point of view, and

---

[1] Thus practically all the areas that are now Flintshire and Denbighshire, and large parts of the present Carmarthenshire and Cardiganshire passed to Edward.

tend to their having to endure new burdens. But apart from mere fears of the consequences of the changes attempted, the Welsh of the districts in question had also reason to complain of much actual injustice to individuals, of illegal imprisonment, violent evictions, and oppression in every possible form at the hands of the English local authorities.

In their distress, the Welsh now turned to Lewelyn, and besought him to come to their assistance. Moved, it is said, by their tears,[1] he determined to make an effort to regain the territories he had lost in consequence of his former rebellion. He took the field in 1256, and for about eleven years there was almost continuous warfare between him and the English—warfare that was ended by the peace of 1267.

Once determined on a fresh war, Lewelyn acted with vigour and promptitude. In the autumn of 1256 he suddenly invaded Perfeďwlad. His forces, no doubt received with gladness by the inhabitants, subdued it within a week; but the castles of Diserth and Deganwy remained in the hands of Edward's officers. Lewelyn then turned south, overran the parts of Keredigion that had been lately made shire-ground, and also took the cantref of Bualŧt in Powys, which belonged to the Mortimers. He did not, however, keep these conquests in his own possession; but, desirous of attaching the Cymric lords of the south, and through them the Welsh-speaking tenants of the Norman-English lords-marchers to himself, granted them to Mareduď ab Owain, who was a descendant of Rhys ab Teudwr, and therefore represented the ancient princely line of Deheubarth, and restored to Mareduď ab Rhys Gryg lands from which the latter had been ousted by his nephew, Rhys Vychan ab Rhys Mechyŧ. The new Earl of Chester had no force at his disposal adequate for an attack

1 "Brut," *s.a.* 1255.

upon the victorious Lewelyn. He appealed to his father, but, for the moment, in vain, and the Welsh prince, in his next campaign (1257), expelled Roger Mortimer from the cymwd of Gwrthryn in Powys, and Gruffyd ab Gwenwynwyn (who still remained aloof from the Welsh cause) from Cyfeiliog. Lewelyn, actively helped by his allies, ravaged a large part of South Wales, taking and burning many castles that were in English hands. Henry, in the summer of the same year, came to his son's assistance, and, with a considerable force, reached Deganwy, but did not cross the Conway. The king remained there for several weeks, but no engagement of importance took place, and the English army retired, after having effected nothing that altered the situation in a material degree in favour of Edward ; and in 1258 a truce for a year was concluded between Lewelyn and Henry on the terms that the latter should have free communication with Deganwy, and the former remain in possession of the four cantrefs. The fame of Lewelyn was now spreading far, for he was able to effect an alliance with the Scotch nobles against the king, and to enter into friendly relations with the English barons, whose discontent with the tyrannical and yet weak government of Henry was now coming to a head.

Lewelyn's military career and domestic rule had been so successful that now nearly all the Welsh barons openly took their stand on his side, and at a formal assembly a large number of the nobles of Wales took oaths of fealty to him.[1]

It was a fortunate circumstance for Lewelyn that the long-smouldering resentment of the English people against Henry and his practically foreign ministry burst

---

[1] Maredud ab Rhys, though he was indebted to Lewelyn for his restoration to his estates, and though he had taken the oath, intrigued with the Seneschal of Carmarthen—De Sayes ; but he was quickly attacked and captured, and his castle of Dinevwr seized.

into open revolt, and resulted in the Provisions of Oxford, the rule of Simon de Montfort, and civil war. In the troubled condition of things in England the war against Wales was not prosecuted with any vigour. Notwithstanding the truce, Lewelyn, in 1259 and 1260, made some border raids, justifying himself on the ground that its conditions were not observed by the English ; but peace was substantially preserved till 1262, when he took the offensive in earnest. This time he began by attacking Roger Mortimer, one of the principal lords-marchers in the cantref of Maelienyd, and then seized several castles in that region. The Welsh inhabitants of the cantref did homage to him, and he pressed on to Brecheiniog, and, having received the submission of the people there, returned to Gwyned. This bold incursion, which was probably made in concert with the disaffected English barons, caused general alarm in the west and a speedy renewal of operations in the marches Edward, with such a force as he could command, early in 1263 advanced into Wales, but his campaign was fruitless ; and the breaking out of actual civil war between the barons, headed by Simon de Montfort, and the king, made it impossible for him to give attention to Welsh affairs. Lewelyn, just as his grandfather had done many years before, threw himself on the side of the barons, and formed a close alliance with Simon de Montfort, who promised him his daughter Eleanor in marriage.

The disputes between the king and the barons were referred for settlement to St. Louis, king of France, who decided in favour of Henry III., and annulled the Provisions of Oxford. The Earl of Leicester repudiated the award of the French king, and took up arms again. The events of 1264 and 1265 are too well known to need retelling here. The battle and Mise of Lewes made Simon de Montfort the real ruler of the realm for the time. Edward was taken prisoner. A new constitution was drawn up. The celebrated Parliament of 1265 was convened and met. The earldom of Chester was assigned to Simon, who early in the year 1265 proceeded to the marches, which were now well under the control of Lewelyn and his allies. In 1263, seizing the occasion afforded by the commencement of the barons' wars in England, Lewelyn had again overrun Perfedwlad, and this time had succeeded in taking the castles of Diserth and Deganwy, which had so long resisted his attempts. His position was now very strong in Wales, and even his former enemy, Gruffyd ab Gwenwynwyn, came over to his side and did homage ; but just as the principal Welsh lord in Powys submitted, Lewelyn had to deal with a fresh revolt by his brother Davyd. The rebellion was at once suppressed, and Davyd himself was forced to take refuge again in England. The incident in no way weakened the prince, who continued to act with, and give powerful support to, the Earl of Leicester and his party. Simon rewarded Lewelyn for his services by forcing the king to sign a convention, which conferred on the Welsh prince large territories (including even Maud's Castle, Hawarden, Ellesmere, and Montgomery), and formally granted him the principality with the right of receiving the homage of the Welsh barons.[1]

Fortune, however, soon deserted the great earl. On August 4th, 1265, he was defeated and slain by Edward at the battle of Evesham. The loss was very great to Lewelyn, but he continued the war, and in September made an inroad into Chester, which had been restored to Edward ; but, notwithstanding the Welsh efforts and the prolonged resistance of the remainder of the baronial party in England, its cause was now lost, and shortly after the surrender of Kenilworth there was a general submission by the barons to the king and Edward.

[1] Rymer's "Fœdera," i. 457.

Lewelyn had formed an alliance with Gilbert de Clare, Earl of Gloucester, but the 'latter made peace with the king, and by the intervention of the papal legate, Ottobon, terms were also arranged between Lewelyn and Edward, which were so favourable to the former as to amount to a real triumph for the Welsh nation. By a treaty concluded at Montgomery, the king granted the principality to Lewelyn and his heirs, to be held on the terms of doing homage ; Lewelyn was authorised to receive the homage of all the Welsh barons (except that of Maredud ab Rhys, the representative of the old line of South Welsh princes, which the king reserved to himself and his heirs) ; the limits of the principality were defined in a way liberal towards the Welsh prince ; the four cantrefs of Perfedwlad were granted to him ; and Davyd was restored to the lands he had possessed, but Lewelyn was to pay 24,000 marks by way of indemnity. The treaty was ratified by papal authority. Practically it left to Edward no part of his Welsh estates except Carmarthen and its appurtenant lands.

It is useless to speculate on what might have happened if Lewelyn had thenceforth adhered faithfully to the terms of this treaty, and reinstated the far-seeing yet practical policy of his grandfather, which was concentrated on the maintenance of Gwyned as a separate entity among the great lordships or feudal states of the realm, and frankly based a position of vassalage under the English crown ; but one can hardly help thinking, when one looks back on the uncertain and devious devolution of the English kingship, that if Lewelyn ab Gruffyd had abided by the terms of the treaty, thrown over the De Montforts and their friends, and steadily allied himself to Edward, the crown of Britain might have been regained by a descendant of his house before the time at which a Welsh prince, in the person of Henry VII., became king of England. Things, however, turned out quite otherwise. Lewelyn not only continued on friendly relations with the sons of Simon, but intrigued with them against Henry. He did not understand the trend of events in England, and seems to have looked upon the treaty of Montgomery, not as marking the limit for a time of a prudent ambition, but as the immediate stepping-stone to the realisation of dreams of conquest, which were encouraged by the recollection of prophecies supposed to be ancient and continually fostered by the flattery of those around him, especially of the bards, to whom the somewhat backward conditions of life in North Wales still allowed an influence which was highly pernicious in practical concerns.

Till the death of Henry III. in 1272, Lewelyn did nothing overt to give offence. Peace was fairly well kept on the borders, there was internal repose, and no dispute with the English central authority. Edward (who had taken the cross in 1268, and had gone to the East to join in a crusade) was, when his father died in 1272, still abroad, but he was proclaimed king at Westminster without opposition, and the government carried on by the Archbishop of York, Edmund of Cornwall, and others, on his behalf. Lewelyn did not attend the assembly of the magnates of the kingdom at Westminster, and the regents having appointed a commission to receive his homage, summoned him on the 29th November, 1272, to render his service ; but the Welsh prince took no notice of the message.

It is clear he was continuing negotiations with the sons of Simon de Montfort, and he was probably encouraged by some of the English barons to resist Edward. In 1273 he was betrothed to Eleanor de Montfort, the late earl's only daughter, in accordance with the promise made some years before. He also entered into communication with the Roman court, and obtained from Gregory X. a decree

absolving him from obedience to citations to places
outside Wales.

Lewelyn was now called upon to meet an internal
revolt. Davyd entered into a conspiracy with Gruffyd
ab Gwenwynwyn and others against his brother. The
prince, however, was able at once to seize the lands of the
rebels. Davyd and Gruffyd fled to England, but Owain
was captured. The fugitives seem to have been well
received by the king, and Lewelyn found in that circumstance another reason for neglecting to perform his duty
as vassal, ignored all messages, and finally openly defied
his over-lord. Edward I. was crowned on August the 18th,
1274, but though Alexander III. of Scotland attended the
ceremony and did homage, Lewelyn was conspicuous by
his absence, and still delayed to make his submission.
Edward determined to compel him to submit, and proceeding to Chester, summoned his recalcitrant vassal to
come to him there. Lewelyn convened his own vassals,
and took counsel with them. In accordance with the
general assent of the Welsh barons, he refused to comply
with Edward's command on the ground that the latter had
committed a breach of the mutual feudal obligations by
harbouring his enemies, Davyd ab Gruffyd and Gruffyd ab
Gwenwynwyn. Edward returned to England in anger.
The De Montforts still kept up a connection with some
of the English barons as well as with the prince, and it
looks as if the action of the latter was taken in contem-
plation of some combined action. Edward, however,
checked any movement in England by proclaiming a full
pardon to the survivors of the barons who had sided with
Simon in the recent war. It was about this time that
Eleanor de Montfort, under the escort of her brother
Amaury, sailed for Gwyned to marry Lewelyn; but the
vessels of her party were captured by some Bristol sailors.
Amaury was thrown into prison, and Edward, meanly and

unchivalrously, caused Eleanor to be detained in captivity as one of the queen's household. Lewelyn sent many messages to the king with the view of obtaining the release of his bride and forming a durable peace ; but they were fruitless, for Edward was greatly incensed at what he deemed the prince's faithless and shifty conduct. The latter found the only terms on which Edward would set Eleanor at liberty too hard to be entertained. Border hostilities took place in 1276, and in November of that year Edward formally declared war against Lewelyn, and summoned his army to Worcester. He divided his whole forces into three armies. The first, led by himself (with whom served Davyd), entered Wales from Chester, while the fleet co-operated by sailing along the coast with the ultimate object of cutting off supplies for the Welsh from Môn. The second, under the command of Hugh de Lacy and Roger Mortimer, advanced from Shrewsbury to Montgomery, while the Earl of Hereford retook possession of Brecheiniog. The third, under Edmund of Lancaster, invaded the district of the south occupied by the vassals or allies of Lewelyn. Most of the South-Welsh barons speedily deserted and made submission to the king.

Lewelyn was obliged to abandon the south and confine his efforts to the defence of Gwyned by the usual tactics. But Edward had made his plans carefully ; he advanced cautiously, causing ways to be cut through the forests, and gradually forced Lewelyn, who did not venture on a pitched battle, to the mountainous districts of Snowdon. Blockaded there, surrounded on all sides by the enemy, deprived of provisions from Môn, Lewelyn, though he struggled long, was, when winter came, starved into submission and compelled to make peace on terms which were dictated by Edward, and embodied in the Treaty of Conway.

This treaty, in effect, completely undid the work of 1267, and reduced Lewelyn to the position of a petty baron. He agreed to pay 50,000 marks as a fine or indemnity, and to surrender all prisoners ; the four cantrefs and his former South-Welsh estates were to go to the king ; Môn, of which Edward was in possession, was granted to him at a yearly rent of 1,000 marks, but was to revert to the Crown on his death without heirs ; the homage of the Welsh barons (except the five barons of Snowdon) was transferred from him to the king. Provision was made for Davyd by a grant of land in Perfedwlad. Owain Goch, who had so far as we can find been in captivity since 1256, was released and given territory in Leyn. The adherents of the king in Wales were restored to the lands they had possessed before the war. Lewelyn was to come to London on a day to be appointed to do homage, and to attend in England every Christmas to renew that act of submission. On the other hand, it was stipulated that outside the four cantrefs justice should be administered according to the laws and customs of the districts in which the lands might lie ; that all tenants holding lands in the four cantrefs and other Welsh places in the king's possession should possess them as freely and enjoy the same customs and liberties as they did before the wars ; and that disputes between the prince himself and other persons were to be decided according to the law of the marches. The complete failure of the war and the conclusion of peace on these terms amounted to the ruin of the house of Gwyned, though an attempt, and as it proved a last attempt, was made by Lewelyn to recover the ground he had lost.

Edward, having shown his power, did not exact full performance of the treaty. He remitted the fine, and returned the hostages delivered by the prince. Lewelyn did homage at Rhudlan, and went to London at Christmas when the ceremony was repeated. His promised wife was still at court, and his conduct at this time was, no doubt, very largely determined by the natural desire that her

marriage to him should take place, and by the belief that
close connection with the family of the great earl would
strengthen him in an effort to recover the authority and
territories he had lost. Whatever his motives, he behaved
with such conciliatory prudence that in 1278, on the
occasion of his going to Worcester to renew his submission,
the king allowed the wedding to take place. Lewelyn and
Eleanor were married "at the door of the great church"
there in the presence of Edward and his court, and next
day "joyfully returned"[1] to Wales. The union thus formed
did not, however, last long. Eleanor died in childbirth in
1280, leaving a daughter, Gwenllian, surviving. The loss of
his wife tended to estrange Lewelyn from the English
court, and made him more ready to listen to the complaints
of the Welsh against the tyranny of the king's officers, but
it was not until the spring of 1282 that there was again a
formal rupture of the peace.

After taking possession of the districts ceded by the
treaty of 1277, Edward vigorously proceeded with the conversion of Perfedwlad into shire-ground, and renewed the
county organisations of Cardigan and Carmarthen, which
had been first created many years before. Many of the
castles which had been built in the early days of the
Norman invasion were strengthened or erected anew on a
larger and more formidable scale. These proceedings
caused general alarm and indignation among the Welsh of
the four cantrefs and the southern counties. They soon
saw that the new system in effect involved the substitution
of Norman-English laws for the Welsh customs, which by
the treaty were to be retained in regard to the lands of
the Welsh inhabitants. In any case the immediate change
from one system to another, however gently brought about,
would have caused some loss or injury to individuals; but
the conduct of the king's subordinates was such as to

" Brut," *s.a.* 1278.

aggravate very greatly the ills sustained by the Welsh.
The royal officers were not only violent and arbitrary in
their dealings with Welsh holders of land, but also grossly
extortionate and corrupt, while the provisions inserted in
the treaty for the protection of the latter were ignored.
Whatever allowance may be made for Edward on the score
of his being badly served, or of the acts of his officers being
unauthorised, he was guilty of bad faith, for when complaints were made to him, he declared that he would maintain the Welsh laws only so far as they were good.   In
fact, he had determined to impose English laws in the
ceded lands without regard to the treaty.   Lewelyn, too,
had grievances of his own.   Thus he laid claim to some
land in Arwystli, and brought the case before the king's
court at Rhudlan.   According to the treaty (so the prince
contended) the matter should have been tried and decided
according to the Welsh law, but it was, in fact, dealt with
according to the Norman-English procedure.   Davyd also
had complaints to make against the authorities in
Perfedwlad.   The anger and resentment kindled first
among the Welsh outside the remnant of the principality
left in the possession of Lewelyn quickly spread among his
own subjects and the whole Welsh-speaking people.   It
was felt by all that another effort to secure independence
ought to be made ; but the independence now sought for
was not the severing of all ties with the English king, but
freedom to carry on their affairs in accordance with their
own conceptions of right.   Just as the English clamoured
for the laws of Edward the Confessor, the Welsh national
demands focussed themselves into a claim that the laws of
Howel Ða should be maintained, and into resistance to the
innovations of the English government.   The movement in
favour of revolt rapidly spread in 1281.   A reconciliation
was effected between Lewelyn and his brother Davyd, and
the latter agreed with him never again to serve under the

English king. An understanding was also arrived at between the prince and the aggrieved barons of the south, and from what subsequently took place we may infer that a general insurrection was planned.

The rising was commenced by Davyd, who, on the eve of Palm Sunday, 1282, suddenly attacked and took Hawarden Castle and captured Roger Clifford the Justiciar. Lewelyn at once crossed the Conway, ravaged the country up to Chester itself, and besieged Rhudlan and Flint. Almost simultaneously, the chiefs among the southern barons, Gruffyd ab Maredud and Rhys ab Maelgwn, rose and took Aberystwyth, burnt the castle, and destroyed the rampart that had been made round the town. Edward, profoundly angered by the news from Wales, made very extensive preparations for the final subjugation of the principality. The events that had just happened left Edward no option but to invade it again, and we cannot blame him for taking that course. Yet the outbreak of a fresh rebellion at a time and under circumstances which (as the better informed of the Welsh leaders must have known) made its success impossible shows not only that the Welsh grievances were real and hard to be borne, but that Edward had neglected to make adequate inquiry about them, and to exercise efficient control over his local ministers. He made no attempt to negotiate, unless indeed it was by his desire that the Archbishop of Canterbury (Peckham) tried to effect a peaceful settlement. Either acting under the direction of the king or simply in his own episcopal capacity he visited North Wales, and having addressed a letter to the prince, met and conferred with him and his council. Lewelyn laid before him a written answer to his letter on behalf of himself and his people, adding particulars of "the greefes" of Davyd and other barons, and of the men of Rhos and other districts. The written complaints of the Welsh were

taken by Peckham to the king, who, though he did not
categorically refuse to hear the Welsh complainants, made
unconditional submission a preliminary step to investigating
the matters in dispute, for he would promise to those who
might come to him liberty to return to Wales only if "by
justice they deserved to depart." The archbishop again
went to Wales and saw Lewelyn, who resolutely refused
to place himself at the king's mercy. Returning to England he reported what had taken place, and Edward sternly
said he wanted no other treaty of peace than that the
prince and his people should simply submit themselves.
Such a submission was demanded in a message to Lewelyn
and his council, which was, however, accompanied by secret
offers to the prince of an estate worth £1,000 a year in
England, and to Davyd of adequate provision according
to his degree. The Welsh princes declined both the open
and the private terms of accommodation suggested to them,
and in a dignified and touching epistle to the archbishop
explained that they dare not trust to the king, as he had
kept "neither oath nor covenant nor grant by charter,"
and in effect expressed their determination to defend their
rights at all hazards.

Finding that his friendly negotiations had failed, the
archbishop excommunicated Lewelyn. Edward, fully
prepared, marched into Gwyned, repeated the tactics of
1277 with a similar result, and having occupied Môn, compelled the Welsh to retreat into the mountainous district
of Snowdon, though not without sustaining considerable
losses. In the south, the Earl of Gloucester and Sir
Edmund Mortimer advanced against the Welsh force,
under the command of Gruffyd ab Maredud and his friends,
and met and defeated it at Landeilo Fawr. Lewelyn,
remembering his fate in the last war, left Davyd to defend
himself in the north, and himself, with a small body of
men, escaped, in the hope of securing fresh adherents,

encouraging the Welsh in the marches, and of effecting
some kind of diversion.   He passed through and ravaged
Cardigan and the estate of Rhys ab Maredud, who was
serving with the king.   He then proceeded into the valley
of the Wye, apparently with the intention of inducing
the Welsh of southern Powys to join him when the winter
was further advanced in an attempt to cut off Edward's
communications with Chester ; but he was met not far from
Bualtt Castle by Mortimer, who was lord of the cantref,
and an engagement took place on December 10th, in which
the small Welsh force was beaten.   Lewelyn was killed by
Adam de Francton on the same day, but whether in the
actual battle or while waiting unattended for the coming
of some of the Welsh barons of the country with whom he
had made a secret appointment is not certain.   His head
was sent to Edward, and was afterwards exhibited in
London, encircled with a crown of ivy in mocking allusion
to a prophecy current among the Welsh that he should
be crowned there.   He is usually regarded as the last
Cymric Prince of Wales, and this popular view is substantially true, for he was the last lineal descendant of
Rhodri Mawr, who ruled over the whole, or nearly the
whole, of the ancient kingdom of Gwyned ; but technically
Davyd III. must be accorded the melancholy honour.
Left, as we have seen, in command in Snowdon on his
brother's death, he was acknowledged by the Welsh barons
as their prince.   For a time he held out, but he was soon
obliged to conceal himself in the recesses of the mountains,
and after some months was betrayed into the king's hands.
He was imprisoned at Rhudlan Castle ; the other Welsh
barons surrendered, and the whole of Wales and the marches
was soon reduced to subjection.   The king determined to
make an example of Davyd, who was tried as a baron
of England by a Parliament held at Shrewsbury, and,
having been convicted, was, on October 3rd, 1283, hanged,

drawn, and quartered.[1] Edward's brutal treatment of the
remains of Lewelyn (who, though a rebel according to the
law of the king's realm, was slain in honourable war), and
his utter want of magnanimity in dealing with Davyd,
were long remembered among the Cymry, and helped
to keep alive the hatred with which the Welsh-speaking
people for several centuries more regarded the English.

We deal in the next chapter with Edward's settlement
of Welsh affairs and his organisation of the principality
The possessions of the Cymric house of Gwyned were not
simply added to England. The principality was still
maintained, but annexed to the English Crown. During
the time Edward resided in Wales two sons were born
unto him. The younger one, Edward of Carnarvon (who
became his successor as Edward II.), was in 1301 created
Prince of Wales, and it became the custom for the king
of England to grant the principality to the heir to the
Crown with a special limitation which made it appurtenant
to the rightful succession to the throne.

But though the principality survived in a new form, and
under new rules, all was now over with the last of the
princely Cymric lines. Lewelyn and his brothers were
the representatives of one of the very oldest reigning
families of western Europe—one that could trace its origin
to the time when Britain still formed part of the Roman
Empire, and which had with some brief intervals ruled
in Gwyned for nearly nine hundred years. Lewelyn's
daughter, Gwenllian, lived on, was brought up in a convent,
and ultimately took the veil, it is said, against her will.
She was his only child legitimate according to English law,

---

[1] For full details as to their careers see the excellent lives of Lewelyn and
Davyd in "Dict. Nat. Biog.," by Professor Tout. Lygad Gwr wrote a long
ode to Lewelyn not long after the prince's success of 1267 (Stephens' "Lit. of
the Kymry," 2nd edition, p. 346) ; and Bledyn Vard and Gruffyd ab yr Ynad
Coch wrote elegies upon him. (*Ibid.*, pp. 365, 368.) Consult too "The
Welsh Wars of Edward I.," by J. E. Morris (Clar. Press, 1901).

but there is little doubt the Madog who led a vigorous
insurrection in 1294, which was put down in the following
year, was his son.[1] Davyd left sons surviving him, and Owain
Goch perhaps did so, but so far as we know none of the
descendants of the three brothers, except Madog, played a
noticeable part in political or military affairs, unless a distinguished soldier called Owain Lawgoch, with whom Welsh
literature and the pages of Froissart make us acquainted,
may be counted, as seems to us not unlikely, among them ;[2]
for neither Owain Glyndwr nor Henry VII. could substan-
tiate a claim to anything more than a remote and indirect
connection with the cenedl of Lewelyn ab Iorwerth.   In the
Record of Carnarvon we find that, at a court held at
Conway in the 44th year of Edward III., a certain Griffid
Says was adjudged to forfeit all his lands which he held in
Anglesey of the Prince of Wales (that is, Edward the Black
Prince) for the reason that he had been an adherent of
Owain Lawgoch.[3] This shows that Owain Lawgoch was
a real man, and it so happens that one Yewaines, Ievains
or Yvain de Galles (*i.e.*, Owain of Wales) was fighting on
the French side against the English in Edward's continental wars.   Froissart has a good deal to say about him,
for he distinguished himself very greatly on several critical
occasions.   From the French chronicler's account [4] we learn
that the king of England (Edward III.) had slain Owain's
father, and given his lordship and principality to his own
son, the Prince of Wales.   The name of the father is given
as Aymon, which is regarded as equivalent to Edmond, but
may be Einion.   Owain escaped to the court of Philip VI.,
who received him with favour, and had him educated with
his own nephews.   He was engaged at Poictiers in 1356,

[1] See under "Madog," Dict. Nat. Biog.
[2] See below, p. 593.   Owain Lawgoch means Owain " of the red hand."
[3] The words are : — " Adherens fuisset Owino Lawgoch inimico et preditor
praedicti Domini Principis et de consilio."   Record of Carnarvon, p. 133.
[4] See " Chroniques de J. Froissart," i., cc. 306-7, 311 ; ii., cc. 6, 17.

and when peace was made he went to serve in Lombardy, but returned on the breaking out of war again between France and England. He sometimes fought on sea and sometimes on land, but he was always entrusted by the French king (by this time Charles V.) with important commands. Thus, in 1372, he was placed at the head of a flotilla, with 3,000 men under him, and ordered to operate by sea against the English ; he made a descent on Guernsey, and while besieging the castle of Cornet there he was charged by the king to go to Spain to invite the king of Castile again to send his fleet to help in the attack on La Rochelle. Whilst staying at Santander, the Earl of Pembroke was brought thither to him, having been taken prisoner in the course of the destruction of the English fleet in 1272. Owain, seeing the earl, asked him if he had come to do him homage for his land which he had taken possession of in Wales, and threatened to avenge himself on him as soon as he could, and also on the Earl of Hereford and Edward Spenser, for it was by the fathers of these three men that, as he said, his own father had been betrayed to death. Owain survived the Black Prince and Edward III., and was actively engaged in besieging Mortagne-sur-Mer, in Poitou, when he was assassinated by one Lamb, who had insinuated himself into his service and confidence by pretending to bring news from his native land, and telling him that all Wales was longing to have him back to be lord of the country ("et lui fist à croire que toute la terre de Gales le desiroient mout à ravoir à seigneur "). So Owain fell in 1378, and was buried in the church at St. Leger, and Lamb returned to the English to receive his reward.

With the conquest of the principality by Edward I. it ceased to exist as an independent or semi-independent state, though its political institutions were not made the same as those of England in all respects until 1830,

Henceforth the history of Wales is merged in that of Great Britain, and save for the brief period during which Owain Glyndwr over a hundred years later revived the claims of the old princes of the country, and defied the authority of Henry IV., cannot with any advantage be treated in general as distinct from that of the whole island.   But yet the Welsh-speaking people have a particular history of their own.   Edward, by the building of great castles, of which that of Carnarvon is the best known example, and by the foundation of towns in which English traders and artisans were encouraged to settle, not only made the hold of the central government too strong to be relaxed for any length of time, but made the centres of the more progressive industrial and social life hostile to all things Cymric.   The conquest and the consequential changes did not, however, oust the Welsh cultivators of the soil ; but the loss of their independence, the change from the rule of native princes to that of unsympathetic foreigners, and their isolation in a mountainous part of the island, remote from the centre of affairs, retarded for a time their intellectual development.   Notwithstanding this, and the lapse of more than six centuries, Cymraeg is spoken habitually by nearly a million of persons in the thirteen counties, and is thus the only one of the ancient tongues of the island that has survived as a living language by the side of English among any considerable number of our fellow-subjects in the United Kingdom ; while the descendants of the Cymry still retain many of their national characteristics, and preserve the consciousness of their national identity.   To explain, so far as we can, how this has come about, and to describe briefly the condition and habits of the Welsh of to-day, are the principal aims of the remaining chapters of this work.

CHAPTER VIII.

LEGAL AND CONSTITUTIONAL HISTORY OF WALES.

HAVING traced the process and briefly narrated the events by which the Cymric princes lost all political power and Cymru its practical independence, we next propose to give an outline of the subsequent legal and constitutional history of Wales.

We may here describe shortly its legal position about the middle of the thirteenth century. The area that was called Wales—*i.e.*, which formed part of no English shire—had not been very largely curtailed since the time of William the Conqueror. The western limits of Gloucestershire, Herefordshire, and Shropshire, the three adjacent shires, were in the time of Henry I. only very vaguely defined. The result of the gradual formation of the lordships-marchers was, of course, to make the boundary line more and more precise, since their lords took care that the authorities of the shires should not trespass on the lands they had won by the sword. That line was not in the thirteenth century the same as the present one, which dates only from the time of Henry VIII. The former line included considerable portions of land that are now English, while the county palatine of Chester included the modern Flintshire and a great part of Denbighshire.[1] The

---

[1] We ought to point out that the district called Perfedwlad (the middle country), and sometimes the "four cantrefs," included the greater part of the modern Flintshire and Denbighshire, and frequently changed hands.

boundary did not then, any more than in the earlier days of the Norman conquest, correspond with the territorial distribution of the two languages or races.[1]

From the point of view of legal organisation the Welsh territory was at that time divided into :—

(i.) The Principality, roughly corresponding to the modern counties of Anglesey, Carnarvon, and Merioneth, in the possession of the house of Gwyneď.

(ii.) Portions of land in the king's hands (which passed to Edward I. under the grants made to him by his father), of which the chief were the towns and castles of Carmarthen and Cardigan, with the lands usually held with them. In these places Edward in 1256 tried to establish an organisation similar to that of the English shires ; but they hardly became effective till the Statute of Rhuďlan came into force, though we may assume he created a county court and appointed the usual officers.[2]

(iii.) The county palatine of Pembroke and the lordship of Glamorgan. Pembroke had been a county palatine since the grant to Gilbert de Clare in 1138, and is thus the oldest Welsh county.[3] The county palatine was not,

---

[1] See Professor Tout's paper on "The Welsh Shires : A Study in Constitutional History," "Y Cymmrodor," vol. ix., p. 201 ; and the same author's "Edward the First" (Lond. 1893), p. 16. Enderbie, writing in the seventeenth century, says :—"Welsh is commonly used and spoken Englishward beyond these old meares a great way, as in Herefordshire, Gloucestershire, and a great part of Shropshire" ("Cambria Triumphans," ed. 1661, p. 209).

[2] See Tout's paper (cited above), p. 211. Professor Tout has several bits of evidence in support of this statement : *e.g.*, in 1270 Pain de Chaworth was ordered to do homage to Edward's brother "for the lands which he holds of the castles and *counties* of Cardigan and Carmarthen" (35th Rep. of the Deputy, Keeper of Public Records, p. 11). In 1280 the "counties" of Carmarthen and Cardigan were granted to a certain Bogo of Knovill, the King's Justice of West Wales (Carmarthen Charters, collected by Daniel Tyssen and Alcwyn Evans, published by Spurrell, Carmarthen, 1878).

[3] See c. 24 of Owen's "Description of Pembrokeshire," headed "That Pembrokeshire was in ancient tyme a Countye Palatyne, and noe part of the Principalitie of Wales, &c.," in "Owen's Pembrokeshire" (edited with

however, so extensive as the county as delimited by the Tudor legislation. Haverfordwest, Walwyn's Castle, Slebech, and Narberth were not within its area, nor were Lamphey, Kemmes, or Dewisland at this time among its parcels.[1]

The lordship of Glamorgan, though not strictly a county palatine, was one in substance. An organisation similar to that of Pembroke or Chester was created perhaps by Robert Fitzhamon, but certainly not long after his time. As Professor Tout suggests, the fact that it did not become an earldom is very likely due to its close connection with the earldom of Gloucester, with which it was usually held. The Glamorgan of the thirteenth century was not so large as the present county. Gower was outside its western limits, and some districts in the Vale were excepted from its jurisdiction, while the uplands were for the most part in the hands of Welsh chieftains.[2]

(iv.) The rest of Wales was divided into lordships-marchers held of the king by Norman lords or Welsh chieftains, who held their lands on terms of vassalage. These lordships, with the characteristics of which we deal below, ultimately numbered about 140.[3]

---

notes by Henry Owen, B.C.L.), part i. (Lond. 1892), pp. 190 *et seq.* The "Description" is also printed in the Cambrian Register, vol. iii. (Lond. 1799), pp. 53–231. See also Tout's paper, p. 206.

[1] Tout's paper cited above, and Owen's "Description." Before the Act of Henry VIII., however, the limits of the county had seemingly been extended. See the table made by Geo. Owen, printed in "Owen's Pembrokeshire," part ii. (Lond. 1897), p. 374, headed "How the Counties of Pembroke and Carmarthen were made up." There "Narberth Baronia," "Haverfordwest Baronia," "Walwinscastle Baronia," "Kemes Baronia," are placed in "Oulde Pembrokeshire"; but "Dewisland" and "Slebech" are described as added by the statute.

[2] See Tout's paper cited above, and G. T. Clark's "The Land of Morgan" (reprinted from the "Archæological Journal"), Lond. 1888.

[3] The principal sources of information already published as to the courts, legal procedure and practice, and the government of Wales and the Marches from the Edwardian Conquest to the beginning of the seventeenth century, are the chapter on "The Government of Wales" in Clive's "Ludlow" (Lond. 1841); an essay printed in Hargraves' "Law Tracts" (Lond. 1787), from

Bearing these things in mind let us now see how Edward proceeded to organise his newly won lands. Even before he had finally subdued Lewelyn he had taken some preliminary measures for the settlement of Welsh affairs. In 1280 he had issued a commission[1] to Thomas, Bishop of St. David's, Reginald de Grey, and Walter de Hopton,

an anonymous MS. entitled, "A Discourse against the Jurisdiction of the King's Bench in Wales by Process of Latitat"; "An Historical Account of the Ancient and Modern State of the Principality of Wales, Duchy of Cornwall, and Earldom of Cornwall, &c.," by Sir John Dodridge, Knight (2nd ed., Lond. 1714; 1st ed., Lond. 1630); Owen's "Pembrokeshire," cited above; G. T. Clark's "Cartae et alia Munimenta quae ad Dominium de Glamorgan pertinent," 4 vols., vol. i. (1885), 1102–1135; vol. ii. (1890), 1348–1730; vol. iii. (1891), 441–1300; vol. iv. (1892), 1215–1689; G. G. Francis's "Charters granted to Swansea, the Chief Town in the Seigniory of Gower" (privately printed, 1867), and other collections of borough charters, such as the "Carmarthen Charters" already cited; Rice Merrick's "A Booke of Glamorganshire Antiquities" (1st ed. 1578; new ed. by James Stuart Corbet, Lond. 1867); "The Ruthin Court Rolls," cited above, p. 117; "A Descriptive Catalogue of the Penrice and Margam Manuscripts in the Possession of Miss Talbot of Margam," with an introduction and notes by Walter de Gray Birch (1st series, Lond. 1893; 2nd series, 1894, and 3rd series, 1895, all three privately printed), for the loan of which we are indebted to Mr. Charles Cheston, of Wyndham Place; Coke's "Fourth Institute," and other legal treatises. See also "The Record of Carnarvon" (Record Commissioners, 1838), and the extents appended to Seebohm's "Tribal System." The county histories also contain useful information, notably Theophilus Jones's "History of the County of Brecknock" (Brecknock, vol. i. 1805; vol. ii. 1809). But the fullest description of the political and legal institutions of Wales (in the broad sense) in Tudor times, and of their history, is to be found in a work printed but not yet published—"The Dialogue of the Government of Wales" (written about the end of the sixteenth century by George Owen, the author of the "Description"), edited by Henry Owen, B.C.L., who has kindly lent us the proof-sheets. It is a dialogue between Barthol, a doctor of the Civil Law, and Demetus, a Pembrokeshire man, in the course of which the Doctor interrogates the country gentleman as to the state and history of his country, and is courteously and fully answered by the latter.

[1] The commission is dated at Westm., 9 Edw. I., 4th Dec. For a fuller account of the commission and its proceedings see Lewis's paper on "The Court of the Council of Wales and the Marches" (cited above), pp. 4, 5, and Mr. E. Phillimore's note on p. 5. See also the "Historical Account of the Statute of Rhuddlan" in the "Literary Remains of the Rev. Thomas Price" (*Carnhuanawc*), i. 352–371, for a translation of part of the document. The evidence is printed in the Appendix to Wotton's "Leges Wallicae."

directing them to examine upon oath persons Welsh and
English in order to obtain information respecting the laws
and usages by which the kings, his predecessors, had been
accustomed to govern and order the Prince of Wales and
the Welsh barons of Wales and their peers and others their
inferiors, and all particulars connected with such laws and
usages. The heads of inquiry comprised fourteen inter-
rogatories to be put to each witness. The commissioners
sat and examined witnesses at Chester, Rhuḍlan, the White
Monastery (probably Oswestry),[1] Montgomery, and Lanbadarn Fawr, and in due course reported the answers. If
the evidence is true, there can be no doubt that in the area
of inquiry Norman-English procedure and law had already
almost entirely ousted the Welsh customs; but there is
reasonable ground for suspecting it. The frequent profession of absolute ignorance and some rather evasive replies
suggest that the witnesses were either carefully selected, or
else under the influence of fear or motives of self-interest
gave replies which they thought would be satisfactory to
the English authorities. The survival of Welsh customs, as
to which there is ample testimony even as late as Tudor
times, tends to confirm one's suspicions, but on the other
hand the commission's questions dealt chiefly with procedure
and the rights of barons and landed proprietors; and it
may be urged that the supersession of Welsh law in regard
to that part of the *corpus juris* was not inconsistent with
the retention of Welsh usages in regard to other parts, or as
to holdings of land by inferior tenants in particular lordships.

Edward remained in Wales for about two years after the
downfall of Llewelyn, reducing the Principality to order,
and ultimately, partly as a result of the commission, promulgated in 1284 the Ordinance of Rhuḍlan, consisting of a
series of regulations which a recent writer has felicitously
compared to the laws made by the British Government for

[1] See Mr. E. Phillimore's note (b) at the end of Lewis's paper, *ubi supra*.

the settlement of the affairs of the North-West Provinces of India. It is not strictly speaking a statute, but it is always treated as one, and is included in the Statutes of the Realm.[1]

It recites that :[2]—

"Edward by the grace of God, King of England, Lord of Ireland, and Duke of Aquitaine, to all his subjects of his land of Snowdon and of other his lands in Wales, greeting in the Lord. The Divine Providence, which is unerring in its own government, among other gifts of its dispensation wherewith it hath vouchsafed to distinguish us and our realm of England, hath now of its favour wholly and entirely transferred under our proper dominion the land of Wales, with its inhabitants heretofore subject unto us in feudal right, all obstacles whatsoever ceasing, and hath annexed and united the same unto the Crown of the aforesaid realm as a member of the same body. We therefore, under the Divine will, being desirous that our aforesaid land of Snowdon and our other lands in those parts like as all those which are subject unto our power, should be governed with due order to the honour and praise of God and of Holy Church and the advancement of justice, and that the

---

[1] It is in Latin, and has been printed several times in collections of the statutes. The authoritative version is that in the Statutes of the Realm (published by the Record Commissioners, 1810, vol. i., p. 55), with a translation. In this version the abbreviations of the MSS. are not expanded. In Pickering's Collection of the Statutes the Latin text is printed in expanded form. The text of the 1810 version is from a roll, then in the Tower of London, now at the Record Office, and the various readings are from two rolls, written in the time of Edw. I., preserved among the Records in the Treasury of the Court of the Receipt of Exchequer in the Chapter House at Westminster (which also are now at the Record Office). The statute is also printed in A. Owen's "Ancient Laws," vol. ii., p. 908.

[2] We feel it incumbent on us to explain that we make several lengthy citations from statutes and other authorities in this chapter because we hope that this work may be found useful to students in Wales, and we know that even at the National Colleges the statutes and some of the other books cited are either not at all or not easily accessible.

people or inhabitants of those lands who have submitted themselves wholly unto our will, and whom we have thereunto so accepted, should be protected in security within our peace under fixed laws and customs, have caused to be rehearsed before us and the nobles of our realm the laws and customs of those parts hitherto in use, which, being diligently heard and fully understood, we have, by the advice of the aforesaid nobles, abolished certain of them ; some thereof we have allowed and some we have corrected, and we have likewise commanded certain others to be ordained and added thereto, and these we will shall be from henceforth steadfastly kept and observed in our lands in those parts according to the form underwritten."

After generally providing that the justice of Snowdon is to have the custody and government of the king's peace in Snowdon and the lands of Wales adjoining, and that he is to administer justice according to original writs of the king and the laws and custom underwritten, the statute constitutes the counties of Anglesea, Carnarvon, Merioneth, Flint, Carmarthen, and Cardigan. It ordains for each county a sheriff as well as coroners, and also bailiffs for each commote.[1] It then describes the duties of the office of sheriff and the manner of holding courts (both the county court and the sheriff's tourn in each commote), and goes on to deal with the mode of electing the coroner for each commote, his duties, and the way in which he is to discharge them. It then sets forth the form of some of the principal writs : novel disseisin for a freehold and also for a common of pasture ; for nuisance ; writ of mortdancestor ; writ of general disseisin ; writ of dower ; writ of debt ; covenant. Rules for the trials of pleas or causes are then given ; some are to be determined by the assize and some by inquest or jury. Pleas of lands in those parts, it is said, are not to be determined by battle

---

[1] *Sic.* "Commote" is generally used for *cymwd* in English books.

nor by the grand assize. The county court is given jurisdiction in all trespasses wherein the damages do not
exceed forty shillings: other trespasses before the justice
of Wales.

The statute also provides that—

" Whereas heretofore women have not been endowed in
Wales, the king granteth that they shall be endowed. The
dower of a woman is two fold, one is an assignment of the
third part of the whole land that belonged to her husband
which were his during coverture, whereof there lieth the
writ of reasonable dower, elsewhere described in its place
with the other writs for Wales. . . . The other dower is
when a son endoweth his wife by the assent of his father."

As to succession the statute proceeds thus :—

" Whereas the custom is otherwise in Wales than in
England concerning succession to an inheritance inasmuch
as the inheritance is partible among the heirs male, and
from time whereof the memory of man is not to the
contrary, hath been partible. Our lord the king will not
have that custom abrogated, but willeth that inheritance
shall remain partible among like heirs as it was wont to
be, and partition of the same inheritance shall be made
as it was wont to be made, with this exception, that
bastards from henceforth shall not inherit, and also shall
not have portions with the lawful heirs nor without the
lawful heirs. And if it happen that any inheritance should
hereafter, upon the failure of heir male descend unto
females the lawful heirs of their ancestor last seised
thereof, we will of our special grace that the same women
shall have their portions thereof to be assigned them in
our court, although this be contrary to the custom of
Wales."

The statute concludes thus :—

" And whereas the people of Wales have besought us
that we would grant unto them, that concerning their

possessions immovable, as lands and tenements, the truth
may be tried by good and lawful men of the neighbourhood chosen by consent of the parties ; and concerning
things movable as of contracts, debts, sureties, covenants,
trespasses, chattels, and all other movables of the same
sorts, they may use the Welsh law whereto they have
been accustomed which was this, that if a man complains
of another upon contracts or things done in such a place
that the plaintiff's case may be proved by those who saw
and heard it, when the plaintiff shall establish his case by
those witnesses whose testimony cannot be disproved,
then he ought to recover the thing in demand, and the
adverse party be condemned, and in other cases which
cannot be proved by persons who saw and heard, the
defendant should be put to his compurgation sometimes
with a greater number, sometimes with less, according to
the quality and quantity of the matter in deed. And that
in theft if one be taken with the mainours he shall not be
permitted to pay it in but be holden for convict. We, for
the common peace and quiet of our aforesaid people of our
land of Wales, do grant the premises unto them. Yet so that
it hold not place in thefts, larcenies, burnings, they murders,
manslaughters, and manifest and notorious robberies, nor
do by any means extend unto these ; wherein we will they
shall use the laws of England as is before decreed.

" And therefore, we command you that from henceforth
you do steadfastly observe the premises in all things. So
notwithstanding that whensoever and wheresoever, and as
often as it shall be our pleasure, we may declare, interpret,
enlarge, or diminish the aforesaid statutes and the several
parts of them according to our mere will and as to us shall
seem expedient for the security of us and our land aforesaid.

" In witness whereof our seal hath been affixed to these
presents. Given at Rothelan on Sunday in Mid-lent in
the twelfth year of our reign."

In regard to this statute it is to be noticed—

That it applied only to the area of the Principality enjoyed by the last Lewelyn, prince of Wales ; it did not extend to the marches, *i.e.*, the districts in the possession of lords marchers. The term "marches" subsequently in common parlance was limited to the districts or counties on the borders of Wales in the large sense, but strictly, and for legal purposes, it included all the lordships marchers, even those in the very heart of what is now Wales, or situate in the most remote counties, *e.g.*, the lordship of Kemes in Pembrokeshire was a lordship marcher.[1]

The Principality extended only to those cymwds or lordships of which Prince Lewelyn was seised. His possessions, or to use the legal term *parcella principalitatis Walliae* were the cymwds grouped by the statute into the counties of Anglesea, Carnarvon, Merioneth, Cardigan, with part of Flintshire, and part of Carmarthenshire (West Towy).[2]

The effect of the statute was to create formally an important distinction between the Principality land and the marchers. In the former, save so far as the statute makes express exceptions, English law was introduced ; in the latter no express enactment made English law the rule to be applied by the courts. In the Principality justice was administered by the justices appointed under the statute ; in the marches it was dispensed in each lordship by officers appointed by the lord according to the law of the lordship.[3]

In regard to the tenure of, and succession to land, Welsh customs were preserved. Upon death land was allowed to continue partible according to the Welsh custom which was called by the Norman-English " gavelkind." We deal

---

[1] See Clive's "Ludlow" (cited *supra*), p. 135, and Owen's " Pembrokeshire," pt. ii., pp. 425 *et seq.*

[2] See Clive's " Ludlow " (cited *supra*), p. 117, and Dodridge's " Principality of Wales," p. 6.

[3] See Clive's " Ludlow " (cited *supra*), p. 103.

in the next chapter with the difficulty which the lawyers had in applying English law modified by this custom to property in land in the Principality.

The Act only became fully and really operative very gradually, and even in the time of the Tudors (as appears from the Acts of Parliament referred to below) many notions and practices found in the Welsh laws survived. In regard to the formal political organisation, it appears to have been put in force at once. It is clear from the statute that the organisation of the cymwd had survived, and probable that it had become almost indistinguishable from that of an English manor. The Norman-English lawyers seem to have treated the cymwd as a seigniory, and applied the English rules in its administration; and the definition of a cymwd to be found in the books is that it is " a great seigniory." [1]

The general constitutional effect was that the Principality was considered a distinct parcel of the kingdom of England, ruled however by English laws save so far as these were not modified by the provisions of the statute. The courts at Westminster did not affect to exercise any jurisdiction over it ; *breve regis non currit in Walliam.*

Let us turn now to the marches which were left untouched by Edward's legislation. From the time of the conquest a lordship-marcher was recognised by the king's courts and the English lawyers as a special kind of seigniory or honour. The distinctive marks of a lordship-marcher, as compared with the ordinary manor, were these :—

First, the lord-marcher had *jura regalia* or royal rights, his own chancery and his own courts, and appropriate officers.

See the case of *The Queen* v. *Reveley* and others, in which the right of the Crown to treat Penllyn as a lordship was in dispute and was affirmed. Report, p. 180. The case was privately reported and published for the Commissioners of Woods and Forests, Lond. 1870.

Secondly, all writs within the seigniory ran in the name of the lord and were *contra pacem* of the lord and not of the king of England.

Thirdly, the lord-marcher had judgment of life and limb in all kinds of criminal cases, and also the power of pardoning all offences.

Fourthly, he had a right to hold plea of all actions, real, personal, and mixed within his seigniory.

Fifthly, the king's writ did not run into the marches, for they were not parcel of the realm of England, nor could the king intromit into any of the lordships for the execution of justice. The only sorts of causes in which the king's court could hold plea, though the cause of action arose within the marches were :—

(*a*) Those to which the lord-marcher was a party, either in respect of the title to the lordship itself or its boundaries.

(*b*) Those causes in which it was necessary to write to the bishop, *e.g.*, *quare impedit* and issues of marriage and bastardy. In these cases an appeal was open to the king and his privy council.

Sixthly, the lord-marcher had the power of constituting boroughs.

Seventhly, for the purpose of exercising his powers the lord-marcher had the power of appointing officers, usually the following : Justiciary, chancellor, seneschal, mareschal, chamberlain, and constable, all of whom usually held their office *durante bene placito.* The courts were generally held at the castle and the possession of a castle was deemed to be necessary to a lordship-marcher, whence the maxim "No lordship-marcher without a castle," and it was a condition of his tenure that a lord-marcher should supply his castle with sufficient men and munition for the keeping of the king's enemies in subjection.

The picture, therefore, that Wales presented in the time

of Edward I. was very similar to that which one gathers to have been the condition of the larger part of France and Germany at the same time.   It is not difficult to see the evils naturally incident to the conflicting rights of so many petty sovereigns, and in fact their castles became the homes of disaffected and factious subjects of English kings and Welsh princes, as well as of mercenary adventurers.

With regard to the law administered in the courts of the lordships, there appears to have been considerable diversity of practice, but in the main the best authorities lead to the conclusion that for the most part it was the Norman-English law that was adopted, though many particular customs, especially in regard to the tenure of land, were recognised by the local courts.[1]

Lord Herbert of Cherbury in his history of Henry VIII. gives the following account of the lordships marchers :—
"As the kings of England heretofore had many times brought armies to conquer that country (Wales), defended both by mountains and stout people, without yet reducing them to a final and entire obedience, so they resolved at last to give all that could be gained there to those who would attempt it, whereupon many valiant and able noblemen and gentlemen won much land from the Welsh, which as gotten by force was by permission of the kings then reigning held for divers ages in that absolute manner as *jura regalia* were exercised in them by the conquerors. Yet in those parts which were gotten at the king's only charge (being not a few) a more regular law was observed. Howsoever, the general government was not only severe, but various in many parts ; insomuch, that in about some 141 lordships marchers, which were now gotten, many strange and discrepant customs were practised."[2]   Lord

[1] See Clark's "Cartae et alia Munimenta," *passim*.   Consult also Owen's "Description."

[2] "History of Henry VIII.," printed in Kennet's "Complete History, Lond. 1719.

Herbert's statement is no doubt true as to parts of South Wales, especially the counties of Pembroke and Glamorgan, but considerable parts of the marches must have been in the hands of Welshmen who had never been finally conquered at all by the invader, but had submitted to hold of the king or of a lord marcher. Lord Herbert's account agrees with that given in the MS. printed in Clive's " Ludlow " :—

" The said lord marchers being English lords, executed the English lawes for the most parte within their lordships, and brought the most parte of the landes of the said lordships to be English tenure, and passed the same according to the lawes of England, viz., by fine, recovery feoffment and seisin as in England, and such part as they left to the auntient inhabitants of the country to possesse, being for the most part the barrenest soiles was permitted by some lordes to be holden by the old Welsh custome, as to passe the same by surrender in court."[1]

In Jones's History of Breconshire substantially the same view is presented. He says :—

" In some lordships there were two courts, one for the English inhabitants called Englishcheria, or the rights of an Englishman, and Wellescheria, or the rights of a Welshman The former was abolished in the 14th of Edward III."

" There were also in some lordships a mixture or jumble of the laws of both countries ; thus Leland tells us that : ' Blain Levein (Blaenllyfni in Welscherie) though it be in Welsh Talgarth yet keep the Englishe tenure.' So also in Welsh and English Penkelley, English and Welsh Hay and many others, lands are frequently said to be holden of English tenure and Welsh Dole ; Cyfraith saesneg a rhan Cymraeg ; and here the lord had the wardship of all the children both sons and daughters; in many of the lordships none of the Welsh customs were permitted to be

[1] Clive's " Ludlow," p. 103.

retained, and the English laws entirely prevailed; the whole jurisprudence in fact depended on the will of the first conquerors."[1]

Some account of the jurisdiction of the lords marchers is to be found under *Quo warranto* in Coke's entries (549-551, No. 9 *Quo warranto*). He there gives the pleadings in a proceeding on a *Quo warranto* in 42 Elizabeth (1600) against Thomas Cornewall of Burford in Shropshire. The information alleges that Burford without warrant uses in the manor of Stapleton and Lugharneys in the county of Hereford, the franchise of taking the goods and chattels of felons. To this the defendant pleaded that before and up to the statute of 27 Henry VIII., and from the time of legal memory, Wales was governed by Welsh laws and Welsh officers in all matters, whether relating to lands and tenements, or to life and limb, and all matters and things whatever. Also at the passing of the statute of 27 Henry VIII., divers persons were seised of divers "several lordships," called in "English lordships marchers in Wales, and held in them royal laws and jurisdiction as well of life and limb as of lands and tenements and all other things, and they could pardon and had full and free power . . . of pardoning all treasons, felonies, and other offences whatever, and also to do and execute all things whatever within their separate lordships aforesaid, as freely and in as ample a manner and form as the king may in his aforesaid dominions; and that moreover the king ought not and could not interfere in any of the said lordships belonging to any other person for the execution of justice." The plea further states that the lords marchers were entitled to all forfeitures, goods of felons, deodands, etc., according to the laws and customs of Wales without any grant. It was further pleaded up to the date of the statute

---

[1] Jones, vol. i., p. 247, citing Camden, vol. ii., p. 401 ; and see vol. i., p. 246, for conveyances, etc.

the king's writ did not run in the lordships marchers. The plea then goes on to aver that the manors in question were lordships marchers, to which Cornewall and his ancestors had been entitled at the passing of the statute of 27 Henry VIII. c. 26, and that neither that statute, nor the statute of Philip and Mary, c. 15, deprived him of the particular franchise in question, but confirmed it to him. To this plea the attorney-general demurred, thereby admitting the truth of its averments. "Shortly, the pleadings come to this, that so much of Wales as had not been brought under the *Statutum Walliae* by Edward I. continued till the 27 Henry VIII. (1535) to be governed by a number of petty chiefs called lords marchers—chiefs who might be compared to the small rajahs to whom much of the territory of the Punjab and the North-West Provinces still belong."[1]

To conciliate the Welsh, Edward I., as we have seen, conferred the Principality upon his son Edward, who was born in Carnarvon Castle, and it became usual to confer this dignity upon the heir to the Crown. It has been sometimes imagined that the revenues of the Principality necessarily belonged to the Prince of Wales, but this view is erroneous. The revenues of Wales form part of the hereditary revenue of the Crown and whenever a Prince of Wales has enjoyed them it has been by virtue of a special charter or grant. The earliest grant given by Dodridge in his account of the Principality is that by which the Crown lands and lordships in Wales were conferred by Edward III. on the Black Prince. The last grant of that nature was made in the first of George I. to George (afterwards George II.) by virtue of a special Act of Parliament.[2]

---

[1] Stephen, "History of the Criminal Law," vol. i., p. 142. There is a tract entitled "Cornwall's Case" in the Harleian MS., 141, in Brit. Mus.

[2] See the 12th Report of the Commissioners appointed under 26 George III. c. 27.

It was probably during the period from the Edwardian Conquest to the time of Henry VIII. that the condition of the Welsh people as a whole was most unhappy, at any rate since the troubled period that followed the reign of Howel Ða. It was marked by several abortive insurrections, and by the temporarily successful revolution, in the latter part of the fourteenth century, of Owen Glyndwr. The black death appears to have ravaged the marches and the Welsh counties with much the same severity as England.

Neither life nor property was safe in the marches. Probably the condition of things in the Principality was slightly better than in the greater part of the marcher land. Private wars between the lords marchers continued to be very frequent. Their castles had become the haunts of men of disreputable character, ready to place their swords at the disposal of any one willing to employ them. They sometimes conspired together to despoil the Welsh, sometimes they quarrelled among themselves, involving in the dispute their tenants and their vassals, and sometimes they rebelled against the king of England; and while in the course of the two centuries which succeeded the conquest of Wales, their power and influence from various causes gradually declined, their administration of justice became a mere mockery, and the number of the courts and the clashing of jurisdiction involved the holders of land in vexatious litigation as expensive as it was corrupt.[1]

The venality and rapacity of the courts of the lordships marchers, the general disorder that prevailed, and the difficulty of punishing crime in consequence of the conflicts of jurisdiction and the flight of accused persons from one lordship to another, led to the establishment of a new court, that of " The President and Council of Wales and the

[1] See Wynne's "History of the Gwydir Family" (1st ed. 1770; 2nd ed. 1780; 3rd ed. 1827; 4th ed. 1878).

Marches." Its origin is not quite clear, but it seems to
have been created in Edward IV.'s time—in 1478, and
was probably intended to be of a merely temporary
character ; but Henry VII. made it permanent, and
extended its jurisdiction over the counties of Chester,
Salop, Worcester, Hereford, Gloucester, and the city of
Bristol, while its seat was fixed at Ludlow.[1] This was
done, not by statute, but by an exercise of the royal prerogative which gave rise to question in later years. Of the
composition of the court in the time of Edward IV., we
only know that it consisted of John, Bishop of Worcester,
and Anthony, Earl Rivers, the uncle and governor of the
young Prince of Wales, Edward of Westminster, and others
of his council,[2] who are said to have sat at the " town hall of
Salop," and to have made certain ordinances. This language
suggests that the new court really grew out of the council
of the Prince of Wales—a body the ordinary authority of
which could of course only extend to the Principality.
Whatever its earlier composition, when it became a fixed
institution, or at any rate after Henry VIII.'s legislation,
its members were the Lord President (who was "the
chiefe and supreme governor of all the Principalitie and
Marches of Wales"[3]), the Chief Justice of Chester, three

---

[1] For much information concerning the earlier history ot this court see a
paper by the late Judge David Lewis (edited and annotated by Mr. Egerton
Phillimore), entitled, "The Court of the President and Council of Wales and
the Marches " ("Y Cymmrodor," xii., p. 1), and "Further Notes on the
Court of the Marches," by Mr. Lleufer Thomas in "Y Cymmrodor," vol. xiii.,
p. 97. See also Powel's "Historie" (ed. 1584), pp. 389 and 391-2 ; the
Preface to Bacon's "The Argument on the Jurisdiction of the Council of the
Marches " in Spedding, Ellis and Heath's edition of Bacon's Works, vol. vii.
(1859), p. 569 ; and Wright's "History of Ludlow and its Neighbourhood"
(Ludlow, 1852), pp. 378 *et seq.* ; Clive's "Ludlow" and Owen's "Dialogue,"
cited above ; also Coke's "Fourth Institute," c. 48.

[2] Powel's Hist., ed. 1584, p. 389, and Lewis's paper, p. 22, *ubi supra*, citing
a MS. copy of the original Shrewsbury record referred to by Powel—Vitellius,
c. i., fo. 2.

[3] The words are George Owen's : "Dialogue," p. 21.

others of the justices of Wales ; together with such extraordinary members " both lords and knights and such others
as were learned in the lawes, and were called to councell
when the Lord President should think requisite." [1]   The
powers and methods of procedure of the court were defined
in Instructions which were renewed and amended from time
to time.   Briefly put, it had a criminal jurisdiction much
like that of the Star Chamber, but more extensive than
that court originally possessed ; an equitable jurisdiction to
mitigate the rigours of the law, especially for the benefit of
poor suitors ; and a common law jurisdiction both as to real
and personal actions.[2]   Its procedure was analogous to that
of the Star Chamber and the Court of Chancery.   In regard
to crimes its methods were inquisitorial, and it had power
to subject persons suspected of felony on proper grounds
to torture.[3]

Whatever doubts may have existed as to the legality of
this court were set at rest, so far as Wales and the marches
were concerned, by the stat. 34 & 35 Henry VIII. c. 26,
s. 4, which enacted that there should be and remain a
president and council in the dominion and principality
of Wales and the marches thereof, in manner and form as
hath been heretofore used and accustomed, which president
and council should have power and authority to determine
by their wisdoms and discretions such causes and matters
as were or should be assigned to them by the king as
theretofore had been accustomed and used.   There is no
reference here, it will be noticed, to the English shires

---

[1] Dodridge (*ubi supra*), p. 54.   *Cf.* Owen's " Dialogue," p. 21.

[2] See Owen's " Dialogue," pp. 21-23 ; Lewis's paper (*ubi supra*), p. 18,
citing Gerard's Discourse to Walsingham.

[3] See the Instructions of 1574 cited by Wright (*ubi supra*), p. 376.   So late
as James I.'s time this power was retained in two sets of instructions
revised by Coke.   The Instructions of 1607 and 1617 contain no express
power to torture, but there are general words which are capable of being
construed to cover the practice.   See Preface to Bacon's " Argument " (*ubi
supra*), p. 569.

included by Henry VII. in the area of the council's authority—a very material point in the controversy which took place in the reign of James I.

Except as altered by the formation of this new court the organisation of Wales and the marches remained much in the same condition down to the time of Henry VIII. As a consequence of the insurrection of Owen Glyndwr, a very oppressive series of statutes, upon which we need not dwell, was passed in the reigns of the Lancastrian princes ; but as bearing upon the history of tenure, we may mention that by the 28 Edward III. c. 2, lords of the marches of Wales were made attendant to the crown of England and not to the principality of Wales.

The accession of Henry VII. was the commencement of a brighter epoch for Wales and the marches. The power of the lords marchers had greatly declined ; in consequence of the Wars of the Roses many of the lordships were in the king's hands, but it was not till the latter part of Henry VIII.'s reign that legislative steps were taken to improve the political and judicial organisation of that part of the country. The performances of Henry VII. did not by any means fulfil the expectations which the Welsh people formed from the accession to the throne of a prince of Cymric descent. Though some relief was given to the tenants in parts of the country, no determined effort was made to remedy the grievances the people suffered at the hands of the surviving lords marchers, or to reduce the country into a more settled condition. No doubt Henry intended the continuance or renewed establishment of the Council of Wales and the Marches to be a step in that direction, but under William, Bishop of Lincoln (the first president mentioned in the records of the court), and Geoffrey Blyth, Bishop of Lichfield and Coventry, and John Voysey, Bishop of Exeter, who succeeded him, the court seems to have been by no means efficient in putting down the abuses of the lord-marcher system, or able to make punishment swift and certain.[1] For instance, Rowland Lee, who followed Voysey in the presidency in 1535, writing[2] to Cromwell about the condition of the lordship of Magor in 1534-5, says he found that there were living unpunished, under the protection of Sir Walter Herbert, five men who had committed wilful murder, eighteen who had committed murder, and twenty thieves and outlaws who had committed every variety of crime from the robbing of a man and his mother and putting them "on a hotte trevet[3] for to make them schow," to a robbery of the cathedral of Llandaff, perpetrated by Myles Mathew (a friend of Sir Walter's), and other persons unknown.

It was under Rowland Lee that the court became a terror to the evil-doers in the marches and a powerful weapon for keeping the peace and dispensing justice throughout the West. Lee was a very severe, even a cruel judge, but he was wise in counsel and active in the discharge of his duties.[4] His tenure of office (which lasted until 1543) prepared the way for the practical application of the great statutes by which Henry VIII. united Wales and the marches to England.[5]

[1] See Lewis's paper, *ubi supra*, pp. 21-24 ; p. 28.

[2] See Wright's "Ludlow," p. 383.

[3] This is obviously for "trivet." Mr. Phillimore suggests it is equivalent to the Welsh *trybedd* (a support ; a three-legged utensil put over an open fire). Lewis, *ubi supra*, p. 33.

[4] He did not content himself with sitting at Ludlow for the hearing of causes, etc. ; but made circuits in, or rather visited, such districts and places within his jurisdiction as specially required attention. See Lewis's paper, *ubi supra*.

[5] It is said by Ellis Griffith ("a soldier of Calais"—so he describes himself) in his "History of England and Wales from William the Conqueror to the Reign of Edward VI.," preserved in MS. in the Mostyn Collection (see Gwenogvryn Evan's "Report on MSS. in the Welsh Language," vol. i. (1898), pp. x. and 214, Parly. Paper, 1898, C.—8,829), that Lee caused over 5,000 men to be hanged during six years. We cannot accept so high

In the year of Lee's appointment no fewer than five Acts relating to Wales were passed. The first was one for the punishment of jurors in the lordships marchers, obviously designed to check the giving of verdicts friendly to the accused flagrantly against the evidence. There is reason to believe that the practice of bribing or otherwise corrupting juries in the lord-marcher courts prevailed very largely. The second was an Act prohibiting the ferrying of persons and goods over the Severn at night. This, of course, was designed to put a stop to the flight of criminals accused or convicted from the area of jurisdiction in which the crime was triable or punishable to another in which it was not, and also, of course, to prevent the carriage and disposal of stolen goods. The third was an Act for the amendment of the administration of justice, the details of which we cannot stop to give. One of its most important provisions, however, was the allowance of appeals from the courts of the lords marchers to the king's commissioners or the President and Council of the Marches. Certain old Welsh customs were abolished, *e.g.*, *Commorthas*, or collections. It also prohibited "congregations" by Welshmen in any place in Wales, unless for evident and necessary cause, and by the licence of the chief officers and ministers of the seigniory, and in their presence—a provision remarkably like recent

a figure as accurate ; it is evidently simply a reflex of popular belief some years afterwards. But even if we assume the true figure to be only one-fifth (1,000), that would be, having regard to the paucity of population and the comparative smallness of the area concerned, a terrible record, and must have involved great injustice. We must remember that no jury intervened, that perhaps torture was resorted to, and that Lee held office during what Green calls "the English Terror" under Thomas Cromwell. Notice, too, "the apparent relish" (the words are Lewis's) with which Lee and his brother judge write to Cromwell as to certain batches of convicts. We think Judge Lewis's view of Lee too favourable. His cruel and arbitrary administration may perhaps be justified by political considerations ; but neither its necessity nor its success prove him to have been a good or upright judge. There can be no doubt that the reduction of the marches to order and the suppression of the power of the lords marchers was part of Cromwell's policy.

legislation concerning public meetings in Ireland. The
fourth was an Act for punishing Welshmen for making
assaults or affrays on the inhabitants of Shropshire, Herefordshire, and Gloucestershire ; and the fifth one entitled
" An Act for the Purgation of Convicts in Wales," which dealt
chiefly with the plea of benefit of clergy.[1]   In the following
year an Act was passed instituting the office of justice of
the peace and providing for the appointment of justices in
Chester and the eight then existing Welsh counties.[2]

The legislation of 1534 shows that the affairs of Wales
were occupying much of the time of the central government ;
but its energy was not exhausted, and the Acts of that year
were only first steps towards the suppression of the political
and judicial authority of the lords marchers, and the complete merging of Wales and the marches into the English
polity.[3]

Under the rule of Thomas Cromwell, by the 27
Henry VIII. c. 26 and the 34 & 35 Henry VIII. c. 26,
the arrangements for the legislative and executive government of Wales were practically assimilated to those of
the English counties, and an improved judicial system
introduced.

The first Act was one entitled " An Act for Laws and
Justice to be ministered in Wales in like form as it is in
this Realm."   The preamble recites :—

" Albeit the dominion, principality, and country of Wales
justly and righteously is, and ever hath been incorporated,
annexed, united, and subject to and under the Imperial
Crown of this realm, as a very member and joint of the

---

[1] These Acts are the stats. 26 Henry VIII. c. 4, c. 5, c. 6, c. 11, and c. 12.

[2] Stat. 27 Henry VIII. c. 5.   But as to Welsh justices, consult the later
Act, 34 & 35 Henry VIII. c. 26.   See p. 377 below.

[3] How far these measures were desired by the body of Welsh-speaking
people we cannot tell.   Lord Herbert of Cherbury inserts in his "History of
Henry VIII." a speech by a Welsh gentleman advocating the union (" History."
ubi supra, p. 171).

same, whereof the King's most Royal Majesty of meer droit, and very right, is very head, king, lord, and ruler; yet notwithstanding, because in the same country, principality, and dominion divers rights, usages, laws, and customs be far discrepant from the laws and customs of this realm, and also because that the people of the same dominion have and do daily use a speech nothing like ne consonant to the natural mother tongue used within this realm, some rude and ignorant people have made distinction and diversity between the king's subjects of this realm and his subjects of the said dominion and principality of Wales, whereby great discord, variance, debate, division, murmur, and sedition hath grown between his said subjects; his highness therefore, of a singular zeal, love, and favour, that he beareth towards his subjects of his said dominion of Wales, minding and intending to reduce them to the perfect order, notice, and knowledge of his laws, of this his realm, and utterly to extirp all and singular the sinister usages and customs differing from the same, and to bring the said subjects of this his realm, and of his said dominion of Wales, to an amicable concord and unity, hath by the deliberate advice, consent, and agreement of the Lords Spiritual and Temporal, and the Commons in this present Parliament assembled, and by the authority of the same, ordained, enacted, and established, that this said country or dominion of Wales shall be, stand, and continue for ever from henceforth incorporated, united, and annexed to and with this his realm of England; and that all and singular person and persons born, and to be born in the said principality, country, or dominion of Wales, shall have, enjoy, and inherit all and singular freedoms, liberties, rights, privileges, and laws within this his realm and other the King's dominions, as other the King's subjects naturally born within the same have, enjoy, and inherit."

The statute then enacts *inter alia :—*

"And that all and singular person and persons inherit-able to any manors, lands, tenements, rents, reversions, services, or other hereditaments, which shall descend after the feast of All Saints next coming, within the said principality, country, or dominion of Wales, or within any particular lordship, part, or parcel of the said country or dominion of Wales, shall for ever, from and after the said feast of All Saints, inherit and be inheritable to the same manors, lands, rents, tenements, reversions, and heredita-ments, after the English tenure, without division or parti-tion, and after the form of the laws of this realm of England, and not after any Welsh tenure, ne after the form of any Welsh laws or customs ; and that the laws, ordinances, and statutes of this realm of England, for ever, and none other laws, ordinances, or statutes, from and after the Feast of All Saints next coming, shall be used, practised, and executed in the said country or dominion of Wales, and every part thereof, in like manner, form, and order, as they be and shall be had, used, practised, and executed in this realm, and in such like manner and form as hereafter by this Act shall be further established and ordained; any Act, statute, usage, custom, precedent, liberty, privilege, or other thing had, made, used, granted, or suffered to the contrary in anywise notwithstanding.

"III. And forasmuch as there be many and divers lordships marchers within the said country or dominion of Wales, lying between the shires of England and the shires of the said country or dominion of Wales, and being no parcel of any other shires where the laws and due correction is used and had, and by reason whereof hath ensued, and hath been practised, perpetrated, committed, and done, within and among the said lordships and countries to them adjoining, manifold and divers detest-able murthers, brenning of houses, robberies, thefts, trespasses, routs, riots, unlawful assemblies, embraceries, maintenances, receiving of felons, oppressions, ruptures of the peace, and manifold other malefacts, contrary to all laws and justice; and the said offenders thereupon making their refuge from lordship to lordship, were and continued without punishment or correction; for due reformation whereof, and forasmuch as divers and many of the said lordships marchers be now in the hands and possession of our sovereign lord the king, and the smallest number of them in the possession of other lords. It is therefore enacted by the authority aforesaid, that divers of the said lordships marchers shall be united, annexed, and joined to divers of the shires of England, and divers of the said lordships marchers shall be united, annexed, and joined to divers of the shires of the said country or dominion of Wales, in manner and form hereafter following. . . ."

"XX. Also be it enacted by the authority aforesaid, that all justices, commissioners, sheriffs, coroners, escheators, stewards and their lieutenants, and all other officers and ministers of the law shall proclaim and keep the sessions, courts, hundreds, leets, sheriff's courts, and all other courts in the *English* tongue; and all oaths of officers, juries, and inquests, and all other affidavits, verdicts, and wagers of law, to be given and done in the *English* tongue; and also that from henceforth no person or persons that use the Welsh speech or language shall have or enjoy any manner, office, or fees within this realm of *England, Wales*, or other the King's dominion, upon pain of forfeiting the same offices or fees, unless he or they use and exercise the English speech or language."

"XXXI. Provided always, that this present Act nor anything therein contained shall not take away or derogate from any laws, usages, or laudable customs now used within the three shires of North Wales, nor shall not deprive nor take away the whole liberties of the Duchy of

Lancaster, but the said liberties shall continue and be used in every lordship, parcel of the said duchy, within the dominion and country of Wales as the liberties of the said duchy be used in shire-ground, and not county palatine, within this realm of England."

"XXXV. Provided always, that lands, tenements, and hereditaments lying in the said country and dominion of Wales, which have been used time out of mind by the laudable customs of the said country, to be departed and departible among issues and heirs males, shall still so continue and be used in like form, fashion, and condition as if this Act had never been had nor made, anything in this Act to the contrary thereof notwithstanding."

By section 36 the king was empowered to suspend or revoke any part of this statute "at any time within three years after the end of the Parliament, so as such suspension, &c., be made in writing under the Great Seal, and be annexed to the Parliament roll of this statute, and proclaimed in every shire in Wales;" and by section 37 it was enacted that "for five years the king may erect in Wales so many courts and justices, &c., as he will."

The effect of this statute was to convert the whole of the marches into shire-ground, and to introduce into all the parts of the "dominion and principality" of Wales that were outside the limits of the old eight counties the county organisation of England. It struck a fatal blow at the power of the lords marchers; though then it did not expressly abolish all their peculiar powers, yet the result of the whole Act seems to amount to a supersession by the ordinary courts of the distinctive courts of these lordships, and the withdrawal of most of the *jura regalia*. The thirteenth section, indeed, preserved certain liberties to the temporal lords marchers, namely :—(i.) the accustomed mises and profits at the first entry into their lands ; (ii.) the right to hold courts baron, courts leet, and law-days in

their lordships ; and (iii.) certain ancient privileges, such
as "waife, straife, infanthef, outfanthef, treasure trove
deodands, goods and chattels of felons," &c. Such lords
marchers were also by section 25 allowed half the forfeitures
of their tenants.[1]

It will be seen from the third section, which is printed
above, that by its operation five new counties are created—
Monmouth, Brecon, Radnor, Montgomery, and Denbigh—
by grouping together divers lordships marchers. The lordships marchers not included in these new units were added
to existing English and Welsh shires. Sections 3 to 19
inclusive deal with the details of the operation, which may
be summarised in a table thus :—

No. of lordships marchers dealt with in regard to each county.	How dealt with.
24	United to form Monmouthshire.
16	United to form Brecknockshire.
16	United to form Radnorshire.
11	United to form Montgomeryshire.
9	United to form Denbighshire.
7	Added to Shropshire.
10	Added to Herefordshire.
3, and all honours, &c., lying between Chepstow Bridge and Gloucestershire	Added to Gloucestershire.
17	Added to Glamorganshire.
8	Added to Carmarthenshire.
13	Added to Pembrokeshire.
1	Added to Cardiganshire.
1	Added to Merionethshire.[2]

Monmouthshire was placed in a category apart, and
annexed to England ; while for the easier administration
of justice, having regard to the distance of the Welsh
counties from London, by section 9 Chancery and Exchequer
offices were established at Brecknock and at Denbigh ;

---

[1] These provisions (ss. 25, 30) were confirmed and extended to spiritual
lords marchers by 1 & 2 Ph. & Mary, c. 15.

[2] For a list of the lordships marchers thus dealt with, see Appendix C.

and by section 10 it was provided that justice should be
ministered and exercised in the new counties, by judges to
be appointed by the king, according to the law of England
and such Welsh customs as might be allowed by the king
and his council.

The manner of descent of manors, lands, and other hereditaments is described in section 2, and the Welsh method of
partition is done away with in the broadest way; but it should
be noticed that section 35 provides expressly that "lands,
tenements, and hereditaments" in Wales, "which have been
used time out of mind by the laudable customs of the said
country to be departed and departible among issues and
heirs male," shall still be so used.   There seems at first sight
a discrepancy here; but the intention seems to have been
to make the English rules apply in general, and to throw
on any one relying on the Welsh custom the burden of
proving its existence in regard to the land in question
before the time of legal memory.   But all doubt as to the
construction of these sections was finally set at rest by the
abolition, by the 34 & 35 Henry VIII. c. 26, of the Welsh
rules of descent.

The statute 27 Henry VIII. c. 26, also conferred Parliamentary representation on the Welsh counties and boroughs.
So far back as the reign of Edward II. members had been
returned for the counties of Anglesey, Carnarvon, and
Merioneth, and the boroughs of Beaumaris, Carnarvon, and
Conway, to the Parliament summoned to meet at Westminster on the 14th December, 1326, and by prorogation
on the 7th January, 1327.[1]   No members were afterwards

---

[1] See Introduction to W. R. Williams's " Parliamentary History of Wales "
(Brecknock, 1895).   Hughes's " Parliamentary Rep. of Cardiganshire " (1849)
contains a writ, dated 18th April, 15 Edw. II., to Edmund, Earl of Arundel,
Justiciar of Wales, directing him to choose twenty-four persons from South
and a like number from North Wales to attend the Parliament summoned to
York for May 2, 1322.   The writ summoning members for the Parliament of
1326 is dated at Kenilworth, the 8th January, 1326-7 (Williams, *ubi supra.*)

summoned until the passing of the Act of 1535, by the 29th section of which it was enacted that one knight should be elected for each of the twelve Welsh counties created or newly delimited by it, and one burgess from every borough therein being a shire-town (except the shire-town of Merioneth) ; while to the county of Monmouth two knights were allotted, and one burgess to the borough of Monmouth (section 26). Whether Welsh members attended the Parliaments of 1536 and 1539 is doubtful, as the returns have been lost, but members were certainly returned from Wales and served in the Parliament of 1541.

Important as this Act was, it did not complete the new organisation of Wales, and further legislation was contemplated. By section 26 it was enacted that a commission under the Great Seal should be appointed to inquire and view all the shires except the three North Welsh ones created by the Statute of Rhudlan, and upon such view to divide the former into hundreds, and certify with the commission such hundreds into the Court of Chancery ; and by section 27 it was directed that a like commission should be appointed to inquire into and report upon the Welsh laws and customs, that the report should be certified to the king and his council, and that the king and council, upon deliberate advice, might allow such laws, usages, and customs as they might deem expedient, requisite, and necessary to remain in full strength and vigour. These commissions and their reports are lost.[1] It is certain that the first was appointed and reported, for section 3 of the 34 & 35 Henry VIII. confirms the limitations into hundreds made by it for each of the nine

See also Stubbs's " Constitutional History," vol. ii., pp. 382, 392. Dr. Stubbs evidently assumes the summonses for the 1322 Parliament were complied with.

[1] See Oldnall's " Practice of the Great Sessions on the Carmarthen Circuit " (Lond. 1814), Introduction, p. xxvi. He is mistaken in thinking that Rowlands in his *Mona Antiqua* (p. 114) is referring to these commissions ; it is to certain extents that Rowlands refers.

counties to which its power extended. It is doubtful whether the provision of section 27 was put into force.

After a pause of some years another Act, which reorganised the Welsh judicial system, made important provisions that were rendered necessary by the new arrangements of the statute of 1535, and enacted supplemental sections as to the law of property, was passed in the 34th and 35th years of Henry VIII.

It is entitled "An Act for certain ordinances in the King's Majesty's Dominion and Principality of Wales." We extract the more relevant parts.

It recites that—

" Our Sovereign Lord the King's Majesty, of his tender zeal and affection that he beareth towards his loving and obedient subjects of his dominion, principality, and country of Wales, for good rule and order to be from henceforth kept and maintained within the same, whereby his said subjects may grow and arise to more wealth and prosperity, had devised and made divers sundry good and necessary ordinances, which his Majesty of his most abundant goodness, at the humble suit and petition of his said subjects of Wales, is pleased and contented to be enacted by the assent of the Lords Spiritual and Temporal and the Commons in this present Parliament assembled, and by the authority of the same, in manner and form as hereafter ensueth " ; and enacts—

" II. First, that his Grace's said dominion, principality, and country of Wales be from henceforth divided into twelve shires ; of the which eight have been shires of long and ancient time, that is to say, the shires of Glamorgan, Caermarthen, Pembroke, Cardigan, Flint, Caernarvon, Anglesea, and Merioneth ; and four of the said twelve shires be newly made and ordained to be shires by an Act made at the Parliament holden at Westminster in the twenty-seventh year of our said sovereign lord's most noble reign, that is to say, the shires of Radnor, Brecknock, Montgomery, and Denbigh, over and beside the shire of Monmouth and divers other dominion, lordships, and manors in the marches of Wales, united and annexed to the shires of Salop, Hereford, and Gloucester as by the said late Act more plainly appeareth.

"III. *Item,* That the limitations of the hundreds, of late made within the said shires by virtue of his Grace's commissions directed out of his Highness's Court of Chancery, and again returned into the same, shall stand in full strength, force, and effect, according to the said limitation; except such of the same as sith that time hath been altered or changed by virtue of any Act or Acts of Parliament already made, or that shall be altered or changed by any Act or Acts in this present session to be made."

After thus confirming the formation of the shires, and adopting the divisions of the shires into hundreds as certified by the commissioners, the Act by section 4 placed the Court of the President and Council of Wales and the Marches on a sure and legal foundation. The statute then constitutes courts, to be called the "King's Great Sessions in Wales," which were to sit twice a year in every one of the twelve counties, and for this purpose were grouped into four circuits. The Justice of Chester was to keep the sessions of Denbigh, Flint, and Montgomery; the Justice of North Wales those of Carnarvon, Merioneth, and Anglesey; one person learned in the laws (to be appointed by the king) those of Radnor, Brecknock, and Glamorgan; and one person learned in the laws (to be similarly appointed) those of Carmarthen, Pembroke, and Cardigan.[1] Within the local limits of their several commissions, the jurisdiction of these Justices was made as "large and ample" as that of the Courts of King's Bench and Common

[1] 34 & 35 Henry VIII. ss. 5 to 11.

Pleas in England.[1] Provision was made for the devising
and custody of an original seal for each circuit.   The seals
of the three shires of North Wales and of Carmarthen, Pembroke, and Cardigan were to be kept by the chamberlains of
North and South Wales respectively ; those of Brecknock,
Radnor, and Glamorgan, and of Denbigh and Montgomery,
by the stewards and chamberlains of Brecknock and
Denbigh respectively ; and the seal of Chester was to be
and stand for the seal of Flint and to be kept by the
chamberlain.[2]   These directions practically fixed the principal offices of the courts at the offices of the chamberlains.   Besides these seals, there were to be four judicial
seals devised by the king, one for each circuit, to be kept
by each Justice for the sealing of judicial process.[3]

For the discharge of the official business it was enacted
that there were to be four prenotaries, one for each circuit,
to be appointed by the king by letters patent, whose duty
it should be to make out all judicial process, to enter all
pleas and matters of record, and to attend upon the Justices
on circuit.[4]   There were also to be marshals and criers for
each circuit, who were to be appointed by the Justices.[5]
These are the chief sections regulating the Great Sessions,
but there are of course many others of a consequential
character, dealing with fees and other matters necessarily
requiring attention in creating new or reforming old courts.
Besides the President and Council, and the Justices of the

---

[1] *Ibid.*, ss. 12, 13.   These sections made the Great Sessions " Superior
Courts." Local equity jurisdiction had long existed in the old three North
Welsh counties and the three south-western shires ; while section 9 of the
27 Henry VIII. c. 26, provided for the creation of a Chancery and Exchequer
at Brecknock for the three south-eastern counties, and at Denbigh for Denbighshire and Montgomeryshire.   Flintshire was subject to Chester in regard to
Chancery matters. o
[2] *Ibid.*, ss. 16–20.
[3] *Ibid.*, ss. 29–31.
[4] *Ibid.*, s. 44.
[5] *Ibid.*, s. 45.

Great Sessions, there were to be justices of the peace and *quorum*, as well as one *custos rotulorum* for each shire. These officers were to be appointed by the Lord Chancellor of England by commission under the Great Seal, by the advice of the President, Council, and Justices, or three of them (the President being one); but the number of justices of the peace was not to exceed eight (excluding the President, the Council, the Justices, and the King's Attorney and Solicitor-General. of each circuit, who were to be *ex officio* on the commission).[1]

These justices of the peace, or any two of them (one of whom was to be of the *quorum*), were directed to keep and hold their sessions four times a year (*i.e.*, Quarter Sessions), and at other times for urgent causes, as was done in England; and like "power and authority in all things" as was possessed by English justices of the peace was conferred upon them.[2]

The Act also dealt with the offices of sheriff and coroner of the county, and constable of the hundred. In regard to the office of sheriff, it enacted that it should be only tenable for one year ; that the President, Council, and Justices of Wales, or three of them (whereof the President was to be one), should yearly nominate three substantial persons in each county for the office, and certify their names to the King's Council, so that the king may appoint one of the three so nominated ; and that the sheriff so appointed shall have the like patents and commissions as the sheriffs of English shires, but shall take the oaths and knowledges of recognizances before the President and Justices, or one of them. The authorities and duties of the Welsh sheriffs were made similar to those of their English colleagues. They were to keep their county courts monthly, and their hundred courts for pleas under forty shillings, and to

---

[1] *Ibid.*, ss. 53–55.
[2] *Ibid.*, ss. 53–59.

hold their tourn twice a year (after Easter and Michael-mas), as in England. It is also provided too, that in the county and hundred courts, as well as in courts baron, the trial of issues should be by wager of law or verdict of six men at the pleasure of the party pleading the plea.[1]

Further, there were to be two coroners in every county, appointed as in England by writ *de coronatore eligendo*, issuable, however, in the case of Welsh counties out of the Exchequer at Chester; and two constables specially charged with the maintenance of the king's peace were to be appointed for each hundred by the justices of the peace, or two of them (one of whom was to be of the *quorum*), of each county.[2]

To complete this brief account of the new or modified arrangements for the government of Wales, we ought to add that stewards of any lordships or manors were empowered to continue to hold the accustomed courts—leets, law-days, or courts baron—and to hold pleas by plaint up to forty shillings in every court baron, and exercise the same authority as the like stewards in England, and also that the mayors, bailiffs, and officers of corporations in Wales might hold courts according to their lawful grants or the custom of the towns, so long as they followed the law of England and not Welsh customs, and that issues joined in personal actions might be tried in such towns by a jury of six men.[3]

Besides these matters of formal organisation, this Act declared or altered certain rules of law. The sections relating to the real property are worthy of attention. They made the laws of descent the same as that of England, and

[1] *Ibid.*, ss. 61–64; ss. 73–75.
[2] *Ibid.*, ss. 68–70.
[3] *Ibid.*, ss. 23 and 26. The manorial courts were not to try felonies (section 24). The king, by section 27, took power to dissolve boroughs and create others.

finally abolished the Welsh system of partition. They are as follows :—

"XXV. And that from henceforth no leet nor law-day be kept by the steward or other officer of any lordship or manor in the said dominion of Wales, but in such lordships and places where it was accustomed to be kept before the making of the Act of Parliament concerning Wales, made in the twenty-sixth year of our said Sovereign Lord's reign ; so always the place where such court shall be kept, be meet and convenient for that purpose."

"XCI. *Item*, That all manors, lands, tenements, messuages and other hereditaments, and all rights and titles to the same, in any of the said shires of Wales, descended to any manner, person, or persons sith the feast of the Nativity of St. John Baptist in the thirty-third year of our said Sovereign Lord's reign, or that hereafter shall descend, be taken, enjoyed, used, and holden as English tenure, to all intents according to the common laws of this realm of England, and not to be partable among heirs males after the custom of gavelkind, as heretofore in divers parts of Wales hath been used and accustomed. And that the same law, from and after the said feast of St. John Baptist, in the said thirty-third year, be used, taken and exercised in the said county of Monmouth, and in all such lordships and other places, as by virtue of the said Act made in the twenty-seventh year, or by any other Act or Acts made or to be made, were and shall be annexed, united, or knit to any of the shires of Salop, Hereford, Gloucester, or other shire ; any laws, usages, or customs heretofore had or used to the contrary thereof notwithstanding.

"XCII. *Item*, That no mortgages of lands, tenements, or hereditaments made or had after the said feast of St. John Baptist, which was in the said thirty-third year of the reign of our said Sovereign Lord, or that hereafter shall be had or made within any of the said shires or places, shall be hereafter allowed or admitted, otherwise than after the course of the common laws or statutes of the realm of England ; any usage or custom heretofore had to the contrary thereof notwithstanding.

"XCIII. *Item*, It shall be lawful to all persons to aliene, sell, or otherwise put away their lands, tenements, and hereditaments within the said country or dominion of Wales, the county of Monmouth, and other places annexed to any of the shires of England, from them and their heirs, to any person or persons in fee-simple of fee-tail, for term of life, or for term of years, after the manner and according as is used by the laws of the realm of England ; any Welsh law or custom heretofore used in the said country or dominion of Wales to the contrary thereof notwithstanding. This article to take effect from and after the said feast of the Nativity of St. John Baptist, which was in the said thirty-third year of our said Sovereign Lord's reign."

" CI. *Item*, where divers lordships marchers, ' as well in Wales, as in the borders of the same, now being by Act of Parliament annexed to divers shires of England, be lately come to the king's hands by suppression of houses, by purchase or attainders, and now be under the survey of the court of augmentations, or of the king's general surveyors, the liberties, franchises, and customs of all which lordships be lately revived by Act of Parliament, made in the thirty-second year of his most gracious reign ; ' nevertheless his Majesty willeth and commandeth, that no other liberties, franchises, or customs shall from henceforth be used, claimed, or exercised within the said lordships, nor any other lordships within Wales, or the county of Monmouth, whosoever be lord or owner of the same, but only such liberties, franchises, and customs as be given and commanded to the lords of the same lordships, by force and virtue of the said Act of Parliament made for Wales in the said twenty-seventh year of his Grace's reign, and not altered nor taken away by this ordinance; the said Act made in the said thirty-second year, or any other Act, grant, law, or custom to the contrary thereof notwithstanding."

"CXXVII. Provided always, that all lands, tenements, and hereditaments, within the said dominion of Wales, shall descend to the heirs, according to the course of the common laws of England of the realm of England, according to the tenor and effect of this Act, and not to be used as gavelkind; anything contained in these provisions or any of them to the contrary thereof notwithstanding."

This measure (the clear drafting of which has won the commendation of eminent lawyers) completed the incorporation of Wales and the marches into the realm of England. It assimilated the Welsh to the English counties for political and executive purposes, but left the former with a separate judicature. The new judicial system seems to have begun its work very quickly, and after a few years' trial, owing to the amount of the work and the difficulty of the questions that arose, it was found expedient to appoint an additional judge on each circuit. Power to do so (which was duly acted on) was given to the Crown by the stat. 18 Eliz. c. 5 (1576), and the number of the judges was thus raised to eight. The Great Sessions absorbed the bulk of the more considerable business done in the old marcher courts, and no doubt also many matters that would have gone to the Court of the President and Council. They continued in active operation until 1830, and developed a special practice of their own, which varied but little on the different circuits, and which was based on the same fundamental principles as that of the English Superior Courts.[1]

[1] The earliest printed book on the practice of the Great Sessions is R. Rice Vaughan's "Practica Walliæ" (Lond. 1672). See also Foley's "Practice of the Courts of Great Sessions for the several counties of Carmarthen, Pembroke, and Cardigan" (Lond. 1792); Abbot's "Jurisdiction and Practice of the Court of Great Sessions of Wales upon the Chester Circuit" (Lond

It is clear, notwithstanding the creation of the Great Sessions, that the Court of the President and Council, though not nearly so active as in the days of Lee, continued during the closing years of the sixteenth and the earlier part of the seventeenth century to deal with a great many causes; but it must be borne in mind that these causes came not only from Wales, but also from the four English counties over which its jurisdiction had been extended since the time of Henry VII.[1] These four shires and Bristol were not mentioned in the fourth section of the 34 & 35 Henry VIII. c. 26. The jurisdiction of the Court over the English counties therefore rested on an act of the prerogative, unless those counties were included within the term "marches" in that section. An agitation against the Court, so far as it exercised authority over any part of England, of which the principal leader was Sir Herbert Croft, a Herefordshire landowner and justice, arose in the early years of James I.'s reign. In 1605-6 a Bill to exempt the four counties passed through the House of Commons, but was dropped in deference to a conciliatory speech from the king. A like fate awaited a similar Bill in the next session.

In 1607 Lord Eure was appointed Lord President, and fresh instructions were issued. These to some extent met the alleged grievances of the opponents of the English jurisdiction of the Court. The extraordinary powers of the President and Council were confined to Wales, but a civil

1795), and Oldnall's "The Practice of the Court of Great Sessions on the Carmarthen Circuit" (Lond. 1814). The last book is the most valuable. Oldnall, afterwards Sir W. Oldnall Russell, became Chief Justice of Bengal. Much information as to the history and the methods of these courts will be found in the Reports and Minutes of Evidence of the Select Committee of the House of Commons appointed in 1817, 1820, and 1821; and in the first Report of the Common Law Commissioners, issued in 1829.

[1] See the remarks of Demetus hereon in Owen's "Dialogue"; and the extracts from Gerard's Discourses to Walsingham, printed in Lewis's paper, *ubi supra.*

jurisdiction in cases of debt and trespass where the damages were laid under 10*l.* was retained in the four shires. Croft and his friends were not, however, satisfied, and ultimately the validity of the English jurisdiction was submitted to the Privy Council, and by them referred to the judges. The king propounded the question ".whether the article of the instructions touching hearing causes within the four shires under 10*l.* be agreeable to the law?" The case was argued in 1608 for six days. The opinion of the judges was given in writing on February 3rd, 1609, but was never published, and was therefore probably adverse to the Crown.[1]

The instructions were not, however, withdrawn, and the agitation was continued. A fresh attempt at legislation proved abortive; but the movement was carried on in the country. The process of the Court was set at nought; a petition signed by five thousand persons alleged it to be a nuisance; it was presented as such by a grand jury; numerous actions were threatened, and some brought, against its officers. But the king was firm in resisting what he looked at as an attack on his prerogative, and the resistance gradually died away, notwithstanding some revival of the agitation in 1614. In 1617 Lord Compton succeeded Lord Eure as President of the Court, and fresh instructions were issued. By these new articles the concessions made in 1607 were withdrawn; no distinction was made between Wales and the four shires; in both areas civil jurisdiction (limited to 50*l.* in personal actions) concurrent with that of the Superior Courts at Westminster was granted, and an unlimited jurisdiction where the plaintiff's poverty was duly certified; a full equitable and Star Chamber jurisdiction was also conferred, with the saving that no injunction was to be issued to the Superior

---

[1] Coke led for those who attacked the legality of the jurisdiction, while Bacon did so for the President and Council.

Courts.[1] It has been said on good authority that the abolition
of the Court of Star Chambers by stat. 17 Charles I. c. 10, in
effect took away those powers of the President and Council
which were analogous to those exercised by the former
court, and that it thenceforth only determined civil causes.[2]

Whether this view is right or not, the Court during the
Commonwealth and the two succeeding reigns declined in
importance, and immediately after the Revolution of 1688
was abolished by the stat. 1 William & Mary, sess. i. c. 2,
which recited that " the powers of the Lord President had
been much abused, and that the institution had become a
great grievance to the subject."

Between 1688 and 1830 a considerable number of statutes
affecting the Welsh courts were passed, but as they dealt
chiefly with procedure and have now no importance it is
unnecessary for us to mention them specifically.[3] No
change of any moment was made by these Acts as to
the constitution and jurisdiction of the Great Sessions.[4]
Though the Welsh courts were Superior Courts, the King's
Bench had long affected to exercise a power of regulation and review over them, and by the end of the eighteenth
century, by a series of judicial decisions, it had become
settled law that plaintiffs might bring in the courts at
Westminster actions concerning lands in Wales, and also
personal actions (which might have been commenced in the
Welsh courts) where the damages claimed exceeded 50*l*.[5]
Notwithstanding, however, the encroachments on their area
of authority, the Welsh courts continued to do an increasing

---

[1] See Heath's preface to Bacon's " Argument," *ubi supra*, for all these facts.
[2] So says Heath, *ubi supra, sed quære?*
[3] See Oldnall's " Practice," *ubi supra*, Introduction.
[4] One of the Acts, however, it may be well to mention—that of 20 Geo. II.
c. 42, which enacted that in all Acts of Parliament in which "in England" is
mentioned, Wales shall be deemed to be included.
[5] See the argument referred to above in Hargrave's " Law Tracts," as to the
encroachments of the King's Bench, &c.

amount of business, seemingly without any greater complaints against their procedure than was indulged in against
that of the courts at Westminster. It is not clear when the
movement for the abolition of the Welsh courts began, but it
probably first arose (except merely by way of suggestion)
as part of the larger agitation for reforms in all branches of
the law, and in the procedure of all the courts, which distinguished the first quarter of this century. It is, however,
interesting to note that Burke, speaking in the House of
Commons on the 18th December, 1780, and referring to the
Welsh judicial system, said it had been proposed to add a
judge to each of the courts at Westminster, and thought
that arrangement would be sufficient for Wales ; but that
his original thought was to suppress five out of the eight
Welsh justices, and to throw the counties into districts.[1]
Burke was, however, not attacking the Welsh courts on
general grounds, but on account of their alleged unnecessary
expense to the Crown.

It was not till 1817 that some definite step was taken
in regard to the matter. In that year a select committee
was appointed by the House of Commons to inquire
into the condition of the judicial system of Wales and
Chester, and in 1820 and 1821 like committees sat. The
evidence taken by and the reports of these bodies contain
full information about the Welsh courts, their merits and
their defects. Nothing was done, however, until after the
first report of the Common Law Commissioners, who
were appointed in consequence of the attack led by
Brougham on the abuses and defects of the courts and
the whole judicial system in his celebrated speech of
February, 1828. The first report of the Commissioners
dealt chiefly with the Welsh judicature. It recommended

---

[1] Speech of Edmund Burke on a "Plan for the better security of the
independence of Parliament, and the economical reformation of the civil and
other establishments."

the extension of the jurisdiction of the Superior Courts
of England to Chester and Wales, the appointment of
three additional judges (one to each of the common law
courts), the abolition of the Courts of Great Sessions, as
well as certain subsidiary steps.

The Government adopted the principal recommendations
of the Commissioners ; and on the 9th March the Attorney-
General (Sir J. Scarlett), after a somewhat perfunctory
speech that showed little grasp of the real issues, moved
for leave to bring in "a Bill for the more effectual Administration of Justice in England and Wales," embodying
in substance the plan of the Commissioners. O'Connell
opposed the Bill as useless to the public. Sir J. Owen[1]
protested against it ; but C. W. Wynn[2] on the other hand
supported the Government. The best speech was made by
John Jones,[3] who pertinaciously opposed the Bill, on the
main ground that while the need for a reform of the Welsh
system was admitted, that did not involve the need for
its abolition ; he defended the Welsh judges ; he objected
to the interests of Wales being made the ladder by which
ambitious barristers might climb to such preferment as
three additional judgeships necessarily included ; the Welsh
people, he said, were attached to their institutions, and
did not desire the abolition of these courts ; the Bill
was being forced upon them. After a brief debate the
motion was agreed to without a division, and the Bill read
a first time.[4]

---

[1] Then M.P. for Pembrokeshire (born 1776 ; died 1861, having sat fifty-one
years in the House). Williams' "Parl. Hist.," p. 159.

[2] M.P. for Montgomery (Privy Councillor 1822 ; member of Lord
Liverpool's Administration ; Secretary at War and in Cabinet 1830–1 ; died
1850). Williams' "Parl. Hist.," p. 145.

[3] M.P. for Carmarthen (b. 1792 ; d. 1857 ; barrister-at-law, and Chairman
of Quarter Sessions for Cardigan ; afterwards member for Carmarthenshire).
Williams' "Parl. Hist.," pp. 49, 55.

[4] Hansard (2nd series), vol. 23, col. 54.

The second reading was taken on April 27th. Frankland Lewis[1] and Colonel Wood[2] made criticisms on the Bill. The latter, while not denying that the time had come for the assimilation of the Welsh to the English system, pointed out the characteristic of the Welsh people, and how largely the Welsh language was used by the lower classes; he thought the juries ought to be Welsh, and asked how many gentlemen in the House would like to give evidence in French in a case in which the life of a fellow-countryman was at stake? John Jones subsequently spoke, attacking the Commissioners, with very considerable reason on his side, as being completely ignorant of Wales and its inhabitants, and complained of their unfair treatment of him and other Welshmen who had assisted them, and again insisted that there was no demand for the Bill in Wales. C. W. Wynn argued in its favour. Rice Trevor[3] urged that the Bill would entail great additional expense on Welsh suitors. The Attorney-General briefly replied, and the Bill was read a second time without a division, passed through Committee, but was re-committed on June 18th, and read a third time on July 17th;[4] and subsequently passed through the Lords without difficulty—notwithstanding the adverse opinion of Lord Eldon, then no longer the autocrat of that House—and duly became law.

By this Act (the 11 George IV. and 1 William IV. c. 70) an additional judge was appointed to each of the three

[1] M.P. for Radnorshire (b. 1780; d. 1855; Privy Councillor 1828; held various offices, and was Chairman of the Poor Law Commission, 1834–9; a member of the Commission of Inquiry into the Rebecca Riots, 1843; created a baronet 1846). Williams' "Parl. Hist.," p. 176.

[2] M.P. for Breconshire (b. 1778; d. 1860). Williams' "Parl. Hist.," p. 20.

[3] M.P. for Carmarthenshire (b. 1795; d. 1869; only son of George Lord Dynevor, and succeeded his father as second Lord Dynevor in 1852). Williams' "Parl. Hist.," p. 49.

[4] Hansard (2nd series), vol. 24, col. 104.

Superior Courts—the King's Bench, the Common Pleas, and the Exchequer of Pleas. The jurisdiction of these and other English Superior Courts was extended over Chester and Wales, while that of the Great Sessions was to cease from the commencement of the Act. It was enacted that assizes should thenceforth be held by the judges of the superior Courts, as in England. It was arranged that there should be two circuits—a North Wales and Chester, and a South Wales and Chester circuit. A single judge was to do the work in the six counties of North Wales, and another to go alone through the counties of South Wales (except Glamorganshire), and that both judges should unite for the assizes of Cheshire and Glamorganshire. Proper provisions were inserted for the pensioning of the officials of the Welsh courts and effecting the change without delay or inconvenience, and certain useful amendments in regard to the procedure of the common law courts were also made.

It can hardly be said that the Welsh members made the most of their case. The majority sat on the Government side, and most of them were country gentlemen who rarely took part in debate ; but a meed of praise is due to the stand made by John Jones of Carmarthen against the Bill at a time when the very courts which the Government proposed to substitute for the Welsh ones were themselves unreformed and carried on their work under a system of practice universally condemned. The broad questions, whether it is or is not expedient to centralise the administration of justice (in regard to all except the more trivial disputes) so completely as was, and in a less degree still is, the case in this country ; whether the English circuit system is better than a system of provincial courts of first instance controlled by a Court of Appeal ; whether it was fair to deprive of its separate judicial organisation, a part of the country where a different language was, in most of the counties, habitually spoken by the large majority of the inhabitants, and to allow Scotland, where English was even then almost exclusively spoken, to retain its own courts, were not raised with any clearness. No doubt there were many abuses, grievances, and defects connected with the Welsh system. The judges were permitted to sit in Parliament, and to practise at the Bar off their own circuits; the appointments to the Bench were often made for political reasons; no pensions being attached to their office, the judges often clung to their posts when they were really too infirm to do their duties properly; they did not change their circuits, and some became too familiar with the barristers who came before them, and the country gentlemen in the neighbourhood, thus giving rise on occasion to grave suspicion of partiality; the term of the sessions (six days) was often not long enough for the cautious and patient trial of the causes; the procedure was antiquated and complicated; the territorial limits of jurisdiction gave rise to difficulties. All those things are true, and show that a reform of the system was quite necessary; but every one of those ills could have been removed by legislation, and not one of them (except perhaps the possibility of too great familiarity with a particular neighbourhood) affords an argument against a properly-constituted system of provincial courts.

For some years the Act inflicted considerable hardship on Welsh suitors. There being no county courts on the modern basis till the Act of 1846 had passed, and the local courts having only jurisdiction up to forty shillings, it was necessary to bring an action in London even to recover trivial debts, and as the local equitable jurisdiction had been determined, the administration of the smallest estate had to be effected through the medium of the Court of Chancery. The proceedings, too, in an action commenced in a Superior Court and tried at a Welsh assize, were much more dilatory and expensive than those in a suit of the same kind in the Great Sessions. Again, though the Welsh judges were not the equals of the English judges in status at the Bar, or, as a rule, in legal attainments, they came in a very little time after their appointments into close touch with the people and generally secured their confidence. For many years the want of sympathy of the English judges going the Welsh circuits, their ill-concealed assumption that Welshmen were beings inferior to Englishmen, their apparent total inability to understand that a man who could speak a few words of a foreign language in the market-place or society might decline to give evidence in it in a court of justice and yet be an honest man, produced very often great popular (though in those days not overt) indignation, and sometimes grave miscarriage of justice. The establishment of the modern county courts, and the gentler and more tactful treatment of Welsh witnesses by the judges of the High Court during recent years, have done much to remove any grievances special to the people of Wales in regard to the administration of justice.[1]

We have now only to add a few words about the legal profession in Wales as affected by the Act of 1830. The statute enabled the attorneys and solicitors of the Welsh courts to obtain like positions in the common law courts at Westminster and in the Court of Chancery. A considerable but not numerous Bar had been in the habit of attending the four old circuits.[2] What took place on the coming

---

[1] The more vigilant action of the Welsh members in the House of Commons since 1868 has no doubt contributed to this more satisfactory state of things.

[2] We are indebted to Mr. W. Trevor Parkins, of the North Wales Circuit, Chancellor of the diocese of St. Asaph, for he following information. Before 1830 there was a Bar mess for each Welsh Circuit. A book in MS. containing the " Records " of the Chester Circuit from 1788 to 1830 (now in the possession of Sir Horatio Lloyd) seems to be the only minute-book of the old circuit messes extant. From 1790 the minutes of the Chester Circuit were regularly kept. The Attorney-General of the Circuit, or in his absence his deputy, presided at the High Court. The " Records " contain the names of the

into operation of the new Act is not quite clear;[1] but it seems that two Bar messes[2] were formed, on much the same plan as, and with rules very similar to, those of the English circuits[3]—one for the North Wales and the other for the South Wales Circuit, which united to form one mess at Chester and in Glamorganshire respectively. The number of barristers practising on the Welsh circuits was at first and for many years very small;[4] but of late years, principally

members present at each High Court, an account of the expenses of the wine, of the fines imposed, and of the jokes that were made and deemed worth setting down. Among the more eminent members whose names occur are :— Richard Richards, afterwards Lord Chief Baron of the Exchequer ; Charles Abbot, Speaker of the House of Commons ; Charles Wetherell, who became Attorney-General of England ; C. W. Williams Wynn (see note 2, p. 388, above) ; John Jervis, afterwards Chief Justice of the Common Pleas. The members of the mess frequently held mess dinners in London. The last of such meetings took place at the Thatched House Tavern, on May 19th, 1830. The Bar of the Chester Circuit was composed of men who belonged to other Circuits (usually the Northern or Oxford), and a few equity barristers. Many of them did not follow the Circuit into Wales. In addition to the judges mentioned above, Mr. Justice John Williams, Mr. Justice Littledale, Baron Parke (Lord Wensleydale), Mr. Justice Wightman, and Mr. Justice Crompton practised at Chester Great Sessions. After 1830 Chester became the common ground for all the members of the old Welsh Circuits. Thus Vaughan Williams (afterwards Justice of the Common Pleas), who belonged to the Carmarthen Circuit, exercised his right to come to Chester.

[1] When I became junior of the South Wales Circuit in 1877 the books of the mess handed to me only contained the minutes of business from about the middle of the fifties.—D. B. J. Mr. Trevor Parkins informs us that the existing minute-book of the North Wales Circuit (in the narrower sense) only goes back to 1872, and that of the Chester mess only to 1880. There are no records of either mess for the period from 1830 to 1872.

[2] This is substantially true, but we are informed that technically the members of the North Wales Division regard the Bar mess in the Welsh counties as a distinct mess from that of Chester.

[3] *E.g.*, members of the mess were not allowed to travel on circuit in any public conveyance ; nor to reside during the Assizes at any hotel or inn, but had to take private lodgings ; members were not permitted to dine with solicitors during the Assizes, &c. The two former rules were modified before 1877. Members were then allowed to go to hotels, provided they engaged private sitting-rooms, and to travel by rail, but only in a first-class carriage after joining circuit.

[4] They can, however, boast of three members who joined after 1830 and have

owing to the great increase of the work in Glamorganshire, has been greatly augmented.[1]   The business in the other counties since the large extension of the county court jurisdiction has very greatly diminished, and there is a tendency to putting down the more substantial cases for trial at Swansea or Cardiff; and the great amount of work done in the industrial and commercial centres of South Wales has led to the "localising" of several members of the Bar.[2]

Having touched upon the principal points in the constitutional and legal development of the Welsh counties from the time of Edward I., we must now turn to the history of land tenure in Wales, looked at from an economic rather than from a legal standpoint.

reached high judicial office—Lord Halsbury, the present Lord Chancellor; the late Sir William Milbourne James, Lord Justice of Appeal; and the late Sir William Grove, Judge of the High Court of Justice.

[1] In 1843 we find from a letter of Carlyle's (Froude's "Life of Thomas Carlyle in London," vol. i., p. 312) that about twenty barristers were attending the summer Assizes at Carmarthen.   Carlyle was staying at Abergwili with the Bishop, and, the Assizes being on, the Bishop, following a not unusual custom, had invited the Judge and Bar to dinner.   C. calls the entertainment "an explosion of dulness, champagne, and *ennui*," and makes the ill-natured and conceited remark that "the advocates generally filled me with a kind of shudder !   To think that had I once had 200*l*. I should have been that !"

[2] The technical name of the former North and South Wales Circuits is now "The Welsh Circuit," but the North Wales and South Wales "Divisions" are recognised.

CHAPTER IX.

HISTORY OF LAND TENURE IN WALES.

§ 1.—*The Welsh Tribal System.*

IT is not proposed to enter at great length upon the history of ancient land tenures in Wales. But it seems a necessary part of our duty to offer the best explanation we are able of the main facts in Welsh economic history which, commencing with the general prevalence throughout the greater part of Wales of the tribal system above described, have resulted in the present conditions of ownership and tenure.

It may be well to mention at the outset that the evidence of the main facts of the Welsh tribal system prevalent under the chieftains or princes before the conquest is not by any means confined to vague tradition, or even to the codes and treatises of various authority in which from the time of Howel the Good the customs and customary law prevalent in different districts of Wales were from time to time collected. The evidence for the main facts relevant to the object of this inquiry rests upon the solid ground of the actual surveys or extents made by Norman surveyors in great detail and with the especial object of recording the condition of things as to tenure which was found to exist in North Wales after the conquest by Edward I. and which was the result of the customary tribal law prevalent before the conquest.

The extent of greatest value and detail is that of the

Lordship of Denbigh made in 8 Edward III., but other extents embrace Anglesey, Carnarvonshire, and Merionethshire and the scattered possessions of the see of St. Davids in four counties of South Wales.

The main facts relevant to this inquiry are those which relate to the customary law as to land under the tribal system itself, and the results it left behind it as regards land tenure in Wales after the English conquest.

So far as the part of Wales conquered by Cuneda and his sons is concerned, the Cymry appear not to have been the original inhabitants, but a conquering tribe ; and it appears most probable that their coming into Wales in the fifth and sixth centuries partook of the nature of a tribal migration from Cumbria.[1]

The result naturally followed that a permanent division of classes was established according to tribal custom, between the conquering tribesmen and the conquered people, so that the inhabitants of Wales from that time onward were divided into two classes—the free tribesmen and the non-tribesmen, or strangers in blood.

First, as to the free tribesmen. They were bound together from the chieftain down to the humblest tribesman by the tie of blood relationship. They carefully guarded their pedigree and purity of blood, and the several kindreds or groups of kinsmen within certain degrees of relationship were mutually liable to one another for injuries and crimes.

It is not needful to enter into details as to the structure of tribal society, except so far as to explain the result of the tribal organisation upon the occupation of land ; and the main point about this is the fact that the tribal unit of occupation of land was the kindred or family group and not the individual. The rights, moreover, of the family group

[1] See above, pp. 118—120, as to the conquest of Gwyned by Cuneda and his sons.

were vested in its patriarchal head, and during the lifetime
of this head of the group all the surbordinate members of
it, down to great-grandchildren or second cousins, instead
of being joint tenants of the family rights as regards land
had apparently only tribal rights of maintenance. They
were regarded not as, in the modern sense, joint owners
with equal shares in the land, but rather as the sons and
grandsons of a patriarchal family under the patriarchal
rule of its head.

Thus tribal society was in no true sense a republic or
democracy in the modern sense of the term, but rather an
aristocratic group of families organised on a patriarchal
basis.

When the English surveyors, therefore, in the fourteenth
century made their extents after the conquest, they found
and described this or that district as occupied, not by
individuals, but by this or that family group, or, using the
Welsh term, this or that *wele* or *gwely* (*i.e.*, bed or family
stock), consisting of the *progenies* or descendants down to
great-grandchildren of the original head of the family
group. Each of these family groups held together till a
final division took place amongst the great-grandchildren
of its original head, and it was called by the surveyors the
" wele of so-and-so," although he and his sons may have
been long dead. And the reason why the " wele " of the
original head of the family thus held together long after
his death and the death of his sons is given in the codes.
It was the tribal rule that on the death of the original head
the original wele was divided into the equal weles of his
sons, who were brothers, that after the death of all the sons
the tribal rights of the family were subject to a re-division
among the grandsons or cousins *per capita* and not *per
stirpes*, and that, lastly, on the death of all the sons and
grandsons, a final re-division could be claimed by the great-
grandsons or second cousins *per capita* and not *per stirpes*.

Hence the original wele of the great-grandfather **was** retained as the unit of the family rights until all the grandsons were dead, on which event the final division of family rights among great-grandsons took place and fresh family groups were formed. Thus it came to pass that the *gwely* or family so constituted under tribal custom continued after the conquest, and was described in the extents by the English surveyors as the ordinary tribal unit of land occupation.

The result was that the surveyors describe this district, and that as in the occupation, not of individuals, but of the *wele* or *gwely* of so-and-so, or, as mostly happened, of several such family groups, having undivided shares in the tribal occupation of the district.

The surveys or extents enable us further to realise that this occupation in most districts was that of a pastoral, rather than agricultural, people. The tribal rights of land occupation held by the family groups were thus mainly rights of grazing over considerable districts in common with other family groups. Each *wele* or family group, no doubt, held in severalty its own roughly constructed homesteads or *tyđynàu*, with cattle-yards and crofts for winter protection and feeding, whilst the mass of the land, mountain and moor and waste, was held by them in common. And, further, these families of tribesmen, with their cattle, often had both winter and summer homesteads and grazings, and were easily shifted from one district to another when changes of population or otner necessities of tribal life might require it.

Another peculiarity of this tribal system of land occupation may be noticed as increasing the difficulty of description by English surveyors, who approached it full of English and manorial notions. All the landed rights of the family group being vested in its head, it was difficult to define the rights of the ordinary tribesman.

When a new tribesman was born into the tribe, both parents being of full tribal blood, he remained, according to Welsh custom or tradition, more or less rigidly adhered to, under the paternal lordship of his father, and was maintained by his father till he was fourteen. At fourteen, he claimed from the kindred, and not from his father, his full tribal rights. That is, he was apparently provided with cattle, independently of his father, and became liable to answer for his own misdeeds, and his father was no longer obliged to maintain him. When he married, if not before, he was allowed to establish himself in a separate homestead or *tyddyn*, and became, like his fellow-tribesmen, a small dairy farmer on his own account, putting his cattle into the common herd along with the rest. He also had a right to join in the common ploughing of portions of the waste. This tribal provision for his maintenance he got from the kindred to which he belonged, and not by inheritance from his father. But he also had a prospective right or chance of one day, if he lived long enough, becoming the successor of his father's rights or privileges, and of becoming, on the death of his ancestors, the head of a wele. The ordinary tribesman, therefore, was in a double position : he was a member of a kindred with tribal rights of maintenance, and not a joint tenant of any particular land. And at the same time, prospectively, and by possibility, he might succeed to the headship of a *wele*, and so become the person in whom the landed rights of a family group were vested.

This, according to traditional theory, and to some extent in practice, was the complicated condition of things in North Wales at the conquest as regards the free tribesmen. The English surveyors described it as best they could, and the Crown lawyers judged it right under the terms arranged on the conquest to let these Welsh family units of land occupation continue under Welsh custom.

The statute of Rhudlan left them alone, to follow the natural course of disintegration sure to result from the relaxation of customary ties and the division and sub-division by gavelkind generation after generation, till the statute of Henry VIII., when English law was extended to Wales, and the laws of primogeniture and English tenure were introduced.

Then, at last, after many generations of confusion, it became necessary for the Crown lawyers to bring whatever remained of the tribal rights of the descendants of the free tribesmen under some category of English law, and so define their rights for the future.

But there is also the case of the non-tribesmen or strangers in blood to be considered before we go further.

The distinguishing mark of this class was the absence of tribal blood, and this, in North Wales, was technically and under tribal tradition an impassable barrier between the stranger and the tribesmen for ever; whilst in South Wales it only could be bridged by continued residence under a chieftain for nine generations, or by repeated inter-marriage with tribeswomen for four generations.

The typical tenure of these non-tribesmen—who were settled upon the estates of the chieftain or head tribesmen, and called taeogs or aillts or alltuds—was that which in the extents is called by the common name of "trefgevery," the holding of *tir cyfrif*, or "register land," as opposed to the tribesmen's holdings in gwelys. Its peculiarity was that there were no rights of inheritance, no family groups with their heads, but that in the hamlet or group of these non-tribesmen there was absolute equality between all males above fourteen. Parents and children, side by side, all were treated alike, except that the youngest son kept house with his father, and had no separate recognition.

This was the normal tenure of non-tribesmen, but as regards some classes of strangers, after residence for four generations in the same place, kindred was recognised in the non-tribesman's family, but from that moment and for ever after its descendants became *adscripti glebæ.*

Hence the surveyors when they came to make the extents found two classes of non-tribesmen : those living in groups or hamlets with no rights of inheritance and in what was called trefgevery, and others occupying in families or gwelys, like the free tribesmen, though not acknowledged as belonging to the tribe. Both these classes of non-tribesmen were permanently attached to the land of the chieftain or of some landed tribesman, and hence, rightly or wrongly, were naturally classed by the surveyors as *nativi* or bond tenants, and so regarded until Tudor times.

Before tracing the after history of the tribesmen and non-tribesmen, there remains to be noticed the position of the chieftain and his family and the territorial arrangements which were connected with the chieftainship.

Now at the time of the extents and long before, in the time of the Welsh princes, the country was divided into *cymwds*, two of these generally making a *cantref.*

In each cymwd or sometimes in each cantref there was a tract of land set aside for the chieftain's residence. It formed an estate which the surveyors very naturally called a manor, and which in many respects resembled a manor. On this estate was what may be described as the home farm of the chieftain, called his *maerdref*, worked by groups of non-tribesmen or *nativi* under the management of a land maer and other officers. The chief also had pasture land allotted to him for his cattle, and all this he held in severalty.

There was one prince of North Wales with his chief palace at Aberffraw in Anglesey. But the prince was not an isolated chieftain chosen from the ranks of the tribesmen, but the head of a family of chieftains, a kind of royal family with aristocratic privilege. And though the palaces

of the other cymwds in his jurisdiction nominally belonged
to the chieftain, they appeared to have often become the
residence of sub-chieftains, members of his family, and in
later times came easily to be regarded as the property of
the subordinate chieftains under the prince.

Upon the home farm or maerdref were settled families
of non-tribesmen.   They were called the men of the
maerdref, and by their services the maerdref was cultivated.
Besides this, there were at Aberffraw groups or hamlets of
non-tribesmen holding in *trefgevery* and more closely
attached to the chieftain's estate than the other similar
groups scattered over the cymwds like the *gwelys* of the
free tribesmen.

The revenue or provision for the prince or chieftain
consisted mainly of—

(1) the produce of his maerdref or home farm worked
by non-tribesmen ;

(2) the rents in kind and various services due from the
clusters of non-tribesmen, including his right to quarter
his retinue and dogs upon them when on his hunting,
hawking, or other expeditions ;

(3) the food rents of the free tribesmen which had long
been commuted into money under the name of tunc.

This brief statement of the main features of the tribal
system [1] must be taken as applying chiefly to North Wales.
Though from the evidence of the Welsh codes the system
was prevalent at one time in South Wales also, the latter
had been subject to the disintegrating effects of Norman
conquest centuries earlier than the final conquest of North
Wales by Edward I.   And this remark applies also to the
border districts which had fallen under the power of the
Lords Marchers.

---

[1] For the authorities on the main points of the foregoing brief summary,
see "The Tribal System in Wales," by Mr. F. Seebohm, one of the Commissioners, who has for many years made a special study of the subject.

§ 2.—*Results of the Conquest of North Wales.*

Such being the positions of the chieftains, tribesmen, and non-tribesmen under the tribal system, the next question is how they were severally treated at the time of the conquest of North Wales by Edward I.

First as regards the chieftains. All their rights were transferred with but little alteration to the Prince of Wales or the Crown. The chieftains' demesnes seem to have been maintained in the same position as before. They were naturally regarded as manors to which were attached the old chieftains' rights within the cymwds of which they were the centres. Thus both tribesmen and non-tribesmen—now regarded as free tenants and *nativi*—became tenants of the Crown, with no mesne lord between them and the Crown, until from time to time grants were made of the manors or cymwds, and the rights appendant thereto, to subjects, who thereupon assumed the position of lords of manors or cymwds as the case might be.

As regards the tenants, at the time of the surveys made after the conquest, the value of the customary rents in kind for services both of tribesmen and non-tribesmen were severally ascertained and recorded, and probably thenceforth in the case of both tribesmen and non-tribesmen money was more often paid than the actual services.

During the period which followed it turned out to be a great protection and advantage to both classes of tenants —both the tribesmen and non-tribesmen—that their services and dues of all kinds had been commuted, for the most part, into fixed money payments. It not only saved them from any attempt to grind more out of them, but also closed the door against arbitrary exactions and oppressive use of the services. The extents made after the conquest became, as the Domesday survey did to the English tenant, the authority to which both classes of tenants could appeal, for it seems to have been tacitly assumed by the English surveyors that the money value of the food rents and services recorded in the surveys was to be religiously followed ever after without alteration.

In several special cases examined, the amount of the quitrents thus arrived at on the conquest of North Wales remained substantially unchanged through all vicissitudes (not excepting the Black Death and the rebellion of Owen Glyndwr), notwithstanding great reduction of population and forfeitures for joining in rebellion, and death in the wars.

The reason of this seems to be that the commuted food rents and services were regarded as chargeable upon a certain place or district rather than upon the persons or families occupying it.

Vast numbers of the ancient quitrents remain payable to the present day to the Crown or to grantees of the Crown. Others have from time to time been bought up and got rid of, and all are very trivial in their amount, very many of them under one shilling.

No doubt in part the extreme smallness of the quitrents is the natural result of the sub-division of holdings among heirs by gavelkind between the time of the conquest of Edward I. and the statute of Henry VIII., by which the law of primogeniture was extended to Wales.

There was, however, another economic cause at work, which in Wales, as in England, silently acted in favour of the peasantry whose services had been commuted in the fourteenth century into fixed money payments.

Granted that the descendants of the old tenants continued to pay the same quitrent in shillings in 1600 as their ancestors or predecessors in title did in 1300, they gained by the fact that the quitrent of 1600 was paid in shillings which contained only 93 grains of silver, whilst the shillings of 1300 contained 266 grains, *i.e.*, nearly three times as much.   Nor was this all, for in addition there had taken place during the interval, apart from the depreciated weight of the coin, a general rise in prices and in the value of the land.

The Welsh tenants were chiefly dairy or cattle farmers, and during the three centuries since the conquest the price of cattle had increased at a much higher rate than the price of corn.

Some measure of the enormous amount of relief which accrued to the tenants through the change in prices may be arrived at by a comparison of the burden of the payments of the tenants of the Prince's manor of Aberffraw at the time of the conquest and in the time of Queen Elizabeth.

The dues and services of the tenants of Aberffraw, as valued in the extent of 1294, amounted to 21*l.* 1*s.* 7*d.* per annum.

A few years after, in an assessment made for a 15th, the cattle of the tenants (including oxen, cows, bullocks, horses, and sheep) were valued at 137*l.*   The annual payment of the tenants to the chieftain amounted thus to about one-sixth of the value of their cattle.[1]

The descendants of these tenants in the time of Queen Elizabeth paying, as, in fact, they probably, roughly speaking, were doing, the same quitrent of 21*l.* 1*s.* 7*d.*,

[1]

A.D. 1300.	£	A.D. 1600.	£
137 oxen at 5*s.*.	34	at 60*s.* (Rogers, Vol. V., 382-348)	411
262 cows at 3*s.* 4*d.*	44 } at 50*s.*		750
38 three year olds at 2*s.* 6*d.*	5 }		
91 two year olds at 2*s.*	9	at 40*s.*	182
71 horses at 5*s.*	18 } at 100*s.*		535
36 mares at 5*s.*	9 }		
735 sheep at 6*d.*	18	at 8s.	294
	137		2,172

would be paying only about $\frac{1}{100}$th part of the value of precisely the same head of cattle at the increased prices of the day.

Thus the burden of the quitrents in the time of Queen Elizabeth throughout Wales may be taken as only a small fraction of what their payments had been under the Prince of Wales before the conquest. In other words, supposing that there had been no disturbance from pestilence, rebellions, or wars, and that the descendants of the old tenants had remained in occupation of their old holdings during the three centuries following the conquest, they would have practically grown, as English copyholders generally did under the same circumstances, into absolute owners, charged with a merely nominal and trivial quitrent of a few pence at most per acre.

But it must be remembered that the customary tribal tenures in gwelys or family groups with ultimate divisions among great-grandsons in gavelkind had been left to follow its natural course till the introduction of English law by the statute of Henry VIII. The case, therefore, was not so clear as the case of English copyholders of holdings in individual ownership. How far the old tribal custom of vesting the landed interest of the gwelys solely in the patriarchal head had survived or worn itself out under changed circumstances may be a matter of doubt, but so far as it may have survived it might well have resulted in confusion by raising the obvious question whether the head of the gwely was not the only person to be regarded as the tenant, and what were the rights, in that case, of his more or less numerous descendants.

The abolition of the custom of gavelkind, and substitution of the law of primogeniture, would, in such case, ultimately disinherit all but one son of the person regarded as the tenant, whether tribesman or non-tribesman.

Such a statute, however, was not likely to take general

effect all in a moment, and accordingly it fell upon the Crown lawyers of Queen Elizabeth for the most part to disentangle the knotty questions which, after 300 years of silent decay, the tribal system had left behind it.

The Application of English Law under Queen Elizabeth in North Wales.—This was the condition of things when the Crown lawyers of Queen Elizabeth had to undertake the task of bringing the various classes of Welsh tenants within some category of English law. Welsh tenures had been abolished, and it had to be settled what the future status of both classes of Welsh tenants was to be. The families of free tribesmen had, during the interval since the conquest, been regarded in a vague way as freeholders under the lordships which had grown out of the cymwds. And the non-tribesmen, classed by the surveyors as *nativi*, naturally had been treated very much as English copyholders ; but the status of both classes to the eye of the English law courts was vague and undefined, and had now to be settled.

The evidence of the quitrents and their general existence down to the present time, except when extinguished by purchase, may be taken as presumptive evidence that no radical change in the position of the successors of the free tribesmen was made on the substitution of English law for the old Welsh customs. But we have seen that even under the latter the free tribesman was not individually a freeholder, that, in fact, the land ownership and the rights of grazing, which formed so large a part of it, were vested in the head of the gwely or family. So that even as regards the successors of the tribesmen the Crown lawyers had no easy task to perform.

But this was not all. There were other difficulties to be dealt with besides the legal ones. The successors of the old free tribesmen were paying, presumably, the same quitrents as of old, and no other services. They held their homesteads or *tyddynau* in severalty. Some had been extinguished by escheats and forfeitures. But new ones had now and again been made out of the waste as families had increased. They had made encroachments and extended their inclosures out of the waste, and besides all this their most important right as mainly pasture or dairy farmers consisted in their ancient user of their undivided rights of pasture and co-aration over the districts in which they were located. Were they to be reckoned as freeholders under English law, or in what other class were they to be placed? Again, who was to be reckoned the owner, the head of the family, or the individual tribesman? It would be hardly possible to deal with each tribesman separately, as they were not under tribal custom joint tenants, and some of them had only rights of maintenance.

Side by side with these successors of free tribesmen were the successors of the non-tribesmen. They also had grown by long residence into the possession of family rights. But under Welsh custom, as understood by the lawyers, unless enfranchised, they had been for 300 years considered as *nativi*, and the land they occupied had for so long been regarded as bond land. They were the *nativi* of the old chieftains, and now of the Crown, but they had been *adscripti glebæ*, and had traditions of long-continued possession. Whether distinguished or not from the free tribesmen, they also had to be brought under some category of English law so that their future rights might be defined and known.

We have taken some pains to ascertain by careful examination of typical cases what really did happen to the two classes of tenants; and to the material facts of these cases attention will now be turned.

One typical case was brought under our notice by the agent of the Wynnstay estate, and is given in full in the

evidence.[1] It was that of two entire cymwds in Montgomeryshire (Arwystli and Cyfeiliog), which for 700 years,
with the exception of a short interval, had descended
together in one ownership, finally becoming a part of the
Wynnstay estate.

Now a cymwd under Welsh rule was, as we have seen,
a wide district embracing generally the chieftain's palace
and maerdref, now regarded as the demesne manor, and
the various groups of families of tribesmen and non-tribesmen scattered over it and loosely regarded as freeholders
and *nativi.*

The two cymwds thus easily came to be regarded as a
lordship, or as two distinct lordships, of which the Crown
farmers or grantees for the time being were the lords.

But what became of the two classes of tenants under this
lordship ?

In the year 1574, when the Earl of Leicester was in
possession under the Crown, a survey of the two cymwds
was made. The jurors were "the ancient and chiefest
freeholders," and six of them were chosen, with the consent
of the rest of the said jurors and of the freeholders of the
two cymwds, to petition the Earl for a composition.

The quitrents at the commencement of Queen Elizabeth's
reign amounted to 120*l.*, but some of them had ceased
through escheats, &c.

The composition agreed to seems to have been (1) the
reduction of the total of quitrents to $\frac{60}{100}$ in respect of
these escheats, &c. ; and (2) an addition in respect of the
encroachments made on the waste. Thus the old rents
were in principle left unaltered, though modified to meet
the changes that had taken place.

Next, effect was given to the composition by feoffments

---

[1] Qu. 76,408. Though not within the area to which the Stat. of Rhuḍlan
applied, the case of these two cymwds may be taken as typical of the application of English law to a thoroughly Welsh district.

by the Earl of Leicester under licence from the Queen, dated 1578, made to four gentlemen, who appear to have acted as trustees, for the whole body of tenants, of the whole messuages, lands, mills, tenements, &c., now in the occupation of the freeholders, reserving to the Earl a certain forest, and also all the waste and common lands not retained in severalty, and also reserving mines, &c.

This assumed that the freehold of the waste, &c., was under English law in the Earl, and put him in the position of the English Lord of the Manor or Lordship.

But then after this reservation of the freehold in the waste he granted to the four trustees " common of pasture in all the mountain lands, wastes, and in all common places in the commots (except those in demesne) for their sheep, animals, cattle, and herds (but not for agistment) as apertaining to the aforesaid messuages, &c., with right to take reasonable estovers, house bote, hay bote, plough bote, and car bote, in the common woods, &c., not then enclosed or appropriated, saving the Earl's right of having as many animals, &c., on the said waste, and of enclosing such portion of the waste as any previous lord might have done."

The four trustees were to hold the above in free and common socage as of the Earl's manor by fealty and suit of court, by the rents therein named amounting in all to 191*l.* 3*s.* 11*d.*, and by a relief after the death of every tenant in lieu of all other service.

The four feoffees were not expressly called trustees, but they became under these feoffments seised of all the tenements and common rights of all the freeholders to the intent, in the words of the Crown auditor, " to establish the same (freeholders' estates) to such as pretend to have them according to the composition made for the renewing of decayed rents."

In other words, this was the perhaps somewhat clumsy, but effectual, method by which English lawyers, acting under instructions from the Crown, to secure the descendants of the old tribesmen in their holdings, effected that object. According to the evidence of the present agent of the Wynnstay estate, it succeeded so far that there are still numerous survivors of these *quasi* freeholders paying the old quitrents as freeholders of the manors, and regarded to all intents and purposes as f ee-holders. At the same time, in the natural course of things, many of the old freehold tenants have from time to time sold their holdings to the lord of the manor or otherwise, so that by a gradual and natural process of purchase the extent of land in the lord's direct ownership has from time to time increased, and at the same time with it the area let to tenants from year to year.

So much for the descendants of the free tribesmen. Their rights were respected, and they or their successors in title still remain freeholders, paying the old and now trivial quitrents.

But the question remains, what became of the so-called *nativi?*

The agent assured the Commission that there was no evidence or tradition on the estate, to his knowledge, of the existence of any class of tenants, copyhold or other, representing the ancient non-tribesmen or *nativi.*[1] Whether in the case of these cymwds the class of *nativi* had become in the interval between the conquest of this district of Powys and the statute of Henry VIII., by long residence and the acquisition of family rights, merged in the class of the somewhat vaguely denominated freeholders, and so included in the class whose "pretence" to have freehold rights was admitted, or whether, on the other hand, they have become tenants from year to year on what, under English law, could be regarded probably as the lord's demesne lands, does not appear in this particular case.

[1] Qu. 76,471-480.

If this may be taken as a typical instance of the manner in which English Crown lawyers of Queen Elizabeth's reign dealt with the descendants of the old free tribesmen, it may fairly be said that their rights were carefully considered, both as regards the lands held by them in severalty, and also as regards their tribal rights over the wastes.

But when it is considered what the ultimate result of such a settlement would be, even in the case of those families whose practically freehold rights were thus carefully respected, it is obvious that the application of the law of primogeniture must have confined the settlement with freehold rights on the land at least to the heads of families, and thus there would arise at once the beginning of a class not sharing in the succession to land, and therefore if remaining on the land becoming hangers-on to the family holding and desirous of becoming tenants from year to year or with leases on the lord's demesne land or on the land of the larger freeholders. This result was obviously inevitable, and may have 'largely promoted the increased prevalence of the normal English year to year tenancy, accompanied, as historically it seems generally to have been, with the usage of succession from father to son, generation after generation.

But to pass on to another typical instance with special reference to the treatment of the non-tribesmen or *nativi.*

The result of a special search very ably made at the request of the Commission in the Public Record Office by Mr. Edward Owen, of the India Office, who has given much attention to the subject, brought before us interesting evidence of what happened to the so-called *nativi* or bond tenants of the manor of Dolwyđelen, in the cymwd of Nant Conway and county of Carnarvon.[1]

[1] Qu. 76,947, *et seq.*

The rights of these descendants of the old non-tribesmen came directly before the Court of Exchequer in 1590. They claimed to hold their land as freehold on the ground that their ancestors had been enfranchised under a charter of Henry VII., along with all other native and bond tenants of North Wales.

This charter still exists on the Patent Roll of 22 Henry VII. (part 3, and membrane 22), and the following is a translation of the passage above alluded to :—

"We have also granted on behalf of ourselves and our heirs that all our native tenants or inhabitants of our counties aforesaid (*i.e.*, Anglesey, Carnarvon, and Merioneth), their heirs and successors as well as the natives of the said Bishop of Bangor and of any abbots whatsoever (who are) bound by some obligation of law shall by the tenour of these presents obtain a general emancipation and liberty and henceforth have the full benefit and enjoyment of the same. And that they shall hold their lands in future by a free tenure paying annually both to us and to the forementioned Bishop of Bangor and the abbots the rents which were usually paid in former times, in lieu of every exaction, service, and custom which were previously due, rendered and paid, as our free tenants who reside in these our counties aforesaid do or have been in the habit of doing." [1]

It appears from the proceedings in the Court of Exchequer that the aforesaid charter was not held to be good in law "for some imperfections therein," but nevertheless the position of the *nativi* was fairly taken into account by the Court, and although their claim to a freehold estate was not allowed, their continued holding was secured by the grant of leases for twenty-one years and "renewal of grant after grant."

[1] The full text of this document is printed in Appendix to vol. v. of the "Minutes of Evidence" (p. 643, *et seq.*).

The Court, by a decree given in the Easter Term of the 33rd Eliz. (1590), held that "the freehold and inheritance" of the messuages and lands in question "are in her Majesty." But the decree goes on to state, "yet neverthelesse the saide Compl[ts] and theire ancesto[rs] and those under whome they do claime have of longe tyme bene suffered to hold and enjoye the said messuage and Landes, w[ch] possessions by sufferance this Court doth not like to be whollie frustrated for that the Compl[ts] and there ancesto[rs] have of longe tyme bene in possession thereof w[ch] possession this Court doth thinke good to p'serve, and that the Compl[ts] an other poore Tenants of the sayd Manno[r] w[ch] have likewise hold on there Lands by sufferance under the like Cullo[r] of Estate may not be (by) harde dealinge or exacc'on of her Ma[ts] ffarmors of the sayd Manno[r] be put from there sayd tenancies yt is therefore this day ordered by the Lord Treasurer and the Barrons of this Court that the sayd Compl[ts] and all such tenants as clayme the said customarye estate shall give over their clayme unto the ffreehold and fee simple of the sayd p'misses as ffreeholder by the Comon Lawe, yet newthelesse for the p'servacon of her Ma[ts] people or tenants of the sayd Man[rs] yt is ordered that the syyd Compl[ts] and all other her Ma[ts] tenants that hold theire lands under the p'tence of the sayd custome and there children wyvfes or assignes in succession for ever shall and may hereafter have the same to them and theire heires or assignes by renewinge of graunt after graunt to them to be made of the sewall tenants in succession. To hold for xxj[tie] yeres as at will to her Ma[tie] and to her Ma[ts] ffarmo[rs] of the sayd Manno[r] or Towneshipp of Dolewethelane, doinge and payinge th useuall rents for the same as heretofore hath bene usualye payed used and done and for the bett[r] assurance of the sayd Tenants so chellengeinge by custom, to every tenante and his heires or assignes successively yt is ordered that at thend of the sayd terme of xx^{tie} yeres so made to every tenante either by the expirac'on of the terme or by surrender theire shalbe newe graunts in succession made for the like number of yeres to there heires wivfes or assignes as at the tyme of the new taking⁰ shall be founde tenante or as uppon the surrender thereof shalbe agreed upon, to hold as aforsayd, payinge such fynes for the same as shalbe rated and assessed by theis Court or by any other authorised from this Court for that purpose." (Exchequer, Decrees and Orders, 33 Eliz., series 1, vol. xvii., fo. 175b) (76,953).

In order to be informed what lands were in question, a Commission had previously been issued which reported that they had " by the full assents and consentes of both the said p'ties ordered the matter in variaunce betweene them in mann'r and forme followinge viz. That the said Natyve Tennants shall accordinge to your honors said Decree enjoye their sew'all tenements for xxitie yeres yelding and payinge therfore to her highnes said ffarmors foure yeres rent of the old rent for a ffyne, and that terme of yeres expired to doe the like for the Residewe of yeres remayninge then unexpired and contayned in their leases ratably after that sort as they doe for the xxjtie yeres . . . We have c'tyfied herin the names of the tennants w'th ther sew'all rents de antiquo answered. (Signed) Robert Wyn ap Cadd'r, Jo. Heymys . . .

" M(emoran(d)um) . . . and the foresaid sew'all tennants auncestors have bene alwayes reputed and taken as Natyve tennants or bondemen of the said Prince's in his said Towneship of Dollw'thllan who now disclayme from any state of inheritance in their sew'all tenures but doe submytt and yeld up their tytles therin to her Ma'tie." (Exchequer, Special Commissions : Carnarvon, 32 Eliz., No. 3383.) Thus the tenants expressly renounced their pretensions to the estates of inheritance which they had originally set forth as being in all respects similar to freehold. A final decree to the intent already expressed was made in the Michaelmas Term, 33 Eliz., 1590–91, in these words :—

"It is this day ordered adjudged and decreed by this Court that the sayd Compl^{ts} and all other her Ma^{ts}.tenants that hold there lands under p'tence of the sayd custom and theire children wivfes or assignes in succession for ever shall and may from tyme to tyme and at all tymes hereafter have hold occupy and enjoye there sayd sewall lands and ten'ts to them and to theire heires wifes or assignes by renewinge of graunt after graunt to them to be made of there sewall lands and tennts in succession to holde for xxj^{tie} yeres. As tenants to her Matie and to her Ma^{ts} ffarmo^{rs} of the said Manno^r or Towneshipp of Dolewethelan, according to the first order doinge and payinge the usuall rents for the same as heretofore hath bene usually paid used and done. And such ffynes as by the sayd Commission are certified to be agreed upon, without any other exaction of ffynes or rents hereafter to be required by any ffarmo^r or ffarmo^{rs} of the said Manno^r or Towneshipp or any p'te thereof."

Mr. E. Owen[1] also brought before us the case of the so-called Manor of Dinorwick, which in the Record of Carnarvon is described as entirely composed of *nativi* (p. 21).

A suit in the Court of Exchequer (1594) established the right of the native tenants of this manor to renewable leases for twenty-one years or for three lives, and further set forth that a lease of any ancient lands could not be granted to a third party so long as the ancient tenant in possession, his heirs or assigns, desired to have it. But a later decree of 1600 held that the claim of the native tenants to rights of inheritance or estates in fee simple was invalid, seeing that the freehold was in the Queen, and the complainants and their ancestors tenants at the will. of the Queen, a decision perhaps not at variance with the practice of giving them leases before sanctioned by the court. They could not

[1] Qu. 76,959.

sustain their claim to the freehold and take renewable leases at the same time, and following English precedents, they seem to have been considered, like English copyholders in some instances, as tenants at the will of the lord, the leases being granted as a practical way of giving them a permanent tenure though at law tenants at will.

There is another remarkable instance to hand which runs nearly on all fours with the above, and which is given by Mr. A. N. Palmer in his "History of Ancient Tenures of Land in the Marches of North Wales."[1]

It is the case of Bromfield and Yale. In this case also there was a charter from Henry VII., granted in the twentieth year of his reign (1505) just two years earlier than the one last mentioned. It practically repealed the provision of the statute of 2 Henry IV., which prohibited Welshmen from acquiring lands in fee simple or fee tail, and at the same time altered the tenure of tenants under the King holding in gavelkind making the lands descendible to the eldest son according to English common law and freed from several customs or services which by their names are distinctly to be recognised as ancient tribal services mentioned in the early extents.

But it does not appear that this charter any more than the other charter of Henry VII. was held by the courts as having acknowledged or conferred a freehold estate to be recognised under English law. The decree makes no mention, moreover, of the class of *nativi*.

Thus, notwithstanding this charter, the whole question had to be gone into afresh in the reign of Queen Elizabeth and the position of the old tribal tenants of Bromfield and Yale was accordingly examined *de novo*, the inquiry going back to the time of the conquest, as though no point of law had arisen in the meantime.

In 4 Eliz. it was found that there was a "decay of the

[1] See his Appendix, pp. 127 *et seq.*

sum of 105*l.* 6*s.* yearly rent which in ancient times had been answered for the said lands."

By ancient times is evidently meant the time of the conquest to which throughout Wales the quitrents went back, for the document proceeds to state the explanation of the decay in these words—"which decay (as by ancient records appeareth) did grow by reason of the great mortality and plagues which in former times had been in the reign of Edward III., and also of the rebellion of Owen Glindor and troubles that thereupon ensued . . . by reason of which mortality and rebellion the country was wasted, the tenants and their houses destroyed in so much that the then Lords of the soyle were constrayned by their stewards and officers to graunt the said lands at a lesser rent than formerly was paid for the same to such as could be gotten to take it."

The reference to the great mortality is clearly to the ravages of the Black Death in 1349, of which and the many escheats caused by it, the Record of Carnarvon contains frequent mention.

The Crown, as lord of the manor, was not getting the whole of the rents mentioned in the extents made after the conquest.   And the jurors go on to say that in 4 Eliz. a commission under the great seal made a survey of the lordships of Bromfield and Yale "to revise the said decayed rent, and to compound and agree with the tenants of the said lordships for a lease of forty years of the lands in their several tenures at and under the covenants and conditions in the said Commission specified." As the result of the composition the tenants surrendered their copies and customary estates and agreed to accept leases of forty years instead of them.   They agreed to pay again the ancient rents of their holdings, as well as a fine of two years' rent upon the taking out of their leases.   The Queen then granted to the said tenants " several leases for the term of forty years of the lands then in their several tenures."

Then follow the words upon which would doubtless be determined the vital question, whether these leases were renewable *once only*, or for ever.

"And in every of the said leases (the Queen) did covenant and grant for her and her heirs and successors to and with the several lessees, their executors and assigns, that upon the determination of the said leases, or otherwise upon surrender of the same, the said tenants, their executors and assigns, might, and should have, another new demise or grant of the premises in their several tenures for the like term and rent and under the like covenants, as by the said first letters-patent were granted, reserved, and specified, they, the said lessees, and their executors and assigns, paying to the said Queen, her heirs and successors, two years' rents of the premises only, for a fine of the said new devise, so to be made over and above the rent by the said new devise to be reserved."

The intention of the Crown lawyers of Queen Elizabeth to do substantial justice to these Welsh tenants is obvious.

Now at least, after an interrupted tenure of 200 years under somewhat vague and decaying Welsh custom, practically abolished by the statute of Henry VIII., the tenants on these manors had leases granted to them giving them at least an eighty years' uninterrupted tenure, and very possibly in intention a perpetual right of renewal. During those 200 years, it would seem that the descendants of the old free tribesmen had retained their free tenure as customary freeholders, and it would appear that the *nativi* also had become recognised as permanent tenants holding by copy of court-roll, and considered by English lawyers as somewhat analogous to copyholders or customary tenants on English manors. This seems to be implied in their surrender of their *copies* and customary estates before the grant of the leases.

The evidence in this case seems to show that the

expedient resorted to by the lawyers of Queen Elizabeth sometimes in the cases both of the successors of the free tribesmen and of the *nativi* was the surrender of their former estates, whatever they were, and the substitution of leases, renewable on payment of a reasonable fine, as on many English manors.

The Commission had before it, in various parts of Wales, evidence of the prevalence of leases for three lives, which will be subsequently alluded to, and which very possibly, in the absence of other evidence, may be taken as survivals of the same system of granting renewable leases in lieu of the doubtful and vague claims to rights of permanent occupation put forward by the successors of the ancient tenants both free and *nativi*. In some cases the two classes had apparently been mixed up together, and the granting of renewable leases appears to have been the rough way out of the confusion.

Had these tenants remained tenants of the Crown, they would, no doubt, have fared better than in some cases they did. But during the Tudor period another cause of difficulty complicated the problem, and requires some notice, though applying only to individual and exceptional cases.

The result of the general view taken of the position of the Welsh tenants under the Crown placed the Crown very much in the position of a territorial lord with, no doubt, some land in demesne, increased from time to time by escheats, yet still very limited in area, and exercising little more than a seignorial jurisdiction over the greater part of the territory, consisting mainly in the right to receive the quitrents from the successors of the tribesmen and non-tribesmen in the ancient cymwd or lordship, which quitrents seem to have been continued unchanged under the system of leases above alluded to.

The quitrents, as already mentioned, had become divided into fractions by the prevalence of gavelkind, and further by a natural process great irregularity had arisen between the various tenants from the fact of one or more of the freeholders having steadily increased their holdings by buying up the lands of others, whilst others had succumbed in the battle of life and disappeared altogether.

At the same time the Crown seems to have commenced, in the time of Henry VIII., the practice of granting leases of the manorial rights or lordship over portions of the Crown possessions in Wales, sometimes to one or more of the chief freeholders, and sometimes to Court favourites, who thus became farmers of the rights of the Crown, the quitrents being reserved to the Crown, but the profits or improved value of the Crown demesne lands passing to the lessee.

There are many such Crown leases to farmers mentioned in the calendars of State papers, some with express mention and some without mention of bonds or covenants for the protection of the tenants. Some of these leases were intended apparently by the Crown to be made for the benefit of the tenants.[1]

The case of the royal manor of Aberffraw may be taken as a typical instance of the confusion arising from this practice, and also of the quarrels of rival families of freeholders competing with each other for these leases of the lordship over their district.[2]

This case illustrates the practice of the Crown giving a lease to a farmer of the lordship, he giving a bond that upon any controversy between him and the tenants he should abide by the order of the Lord Treasurer and Chancellor of his Majesty's Exchequer for the time being.

In one case the lease was transferred to a third party, who tried to get out of the obligation by denying that he had any notice of the bond. Again, where a second lease

---

[1] Qu. 76,957.
[2] Mr. E. Owen's evidence (76,962).

in reversion of the old one had been ordered to be made to another person, "to the use of the tenants," the lease itself contained no mention of the tenants, and the decree of the court held that this third party had no knowledge that the lease was to be to the use of the tenants. Hence arose disputes, confusion, and injustice.

At Aberffraw there were two great parties, one following one of the larger freeholders, and the other party following another, and by the habitual use of the ancient tribal practice of the fosterage of children with tenants exercised on both sides, the lesser tenants had become partisans and almost retainers and tenants of the two rival freeholders. No doubt such a case as this, and the litigation arising from it, should put us on our guard against the assumption that even after the decree of a Court of Exchequer, everything went on smoothly. However careful the courts might be to secure the rights of the tenants, it was not every injustice or oppression which came into court, and the case of Aberffraw shows that sometimes long periods elapsed before the protection of the court could be obtained, and that sometimes a claim was, in the end, as happened in the case of Aberffraw, abandoned by the tenants owing to the cost of litigation.

On the whole the general result of the evidence from North Wales seems to be that as regards the successors of the free tribesmen their rights were respected by the Exchequer Court of Queen Elizabeth, their ancient quit-rents being allowed to continue unaltered, so that, speaking generally, their successors either still remain freeholders paying the quitrents, or have sold their holdings with the common rights attached to them. The tendency towards large estates seems to have extended to Wales. The often repeated process of mortgages and subsequent sales seems to have often ended as in England, very generally in the ultimate addition of holding after holding to the larger

estates.   The lord of a manor or lordship, having acquired
by grant from the Crown, or having purchased an estate
honeycombed by the *quasi* or customary freeholders, was
mostly as ready in Wales as in England to buy up any
holding which might come into the market.

As regards the *nativi,* when not merged or confused with
the free tenants and sharing their treatment, it would seem
from the typical instances examined, that in most cases
they passed through the stages of renewable leaseholds
for lives or terms of years, which may or may not have
been renewed.

§ 3.—*Evidence from South Wales.*

The instances alreac'y examined have been confined to
North Wales.   As already mentioned, South Wales came
earlier under the influence of Norman law, and therefore
passed through somewhat different experiences from those
already described as regards the districts conquered by
Edward I., and the adjoining districts, once a part of
Powys.

In a valuable report,[1] supplementary to the evidence
given by Mr. Edward Owen, will be found a survey taken
in 1609 of the honour or lordship of Kydweli in Carmarthenshire, at that time one of the possessions of the Duchy
of Lancaster.   It shows that in South Wales the country
was divided into cymwds, and in many other respects
retained traces of tribal custom.   But South Wales had not
passed into the hands of the Crown in the same sense as
had those parts of North Wales which were conquered by
Edward I.   Earlier conquests had long before introduced
and firmly established the manorial system in South Wales
and thus the survey above-mentioned, instead of disclosing
a process by which the ancient tenants were being for the

---

[1] See Appendix to vol. v. of " Minutes of Evidence," pp. 643—677.

first time brought within English law by the Crown lawyers
of Elizabeth, describes them as already ancient tenants
on long established manors, with ancient and recognised
customs, representing a singular mixture of Welsh and
English traditions. The manors were sometimes divided
into two divisions, in one of which English tenants and
English customs were said to prevail, whilst in the other
Welsh tenants and Welsh customs were prevalent. The
differences between them were, however, very minute. For
instance, the English followed English manorial customs
and paid the "best beast" as their heriot, whilst the Welsh
still adhered to the Ebediw of the Welsh Codes of 10s.
Till the statute of Henry VIII. the tenants are said to have
held their lands in "gavelkynd," some being "bond" and
some "free men," transferring their holdings by the rod.
The survey goes on to say, "They are now for the most
part freeholders," some few copyholders remaining only in
one manor. These copyholders are described as "taking
for two lives only in possession and no reversion," and on
the death of the second life the copyhold became void
except that the next heir might "have the refusal at 12d.
less than any other will give." The fines were "uncertain,
such as the tenant could agree or compound for with the
lord or his steward." Hence we may assume from this
survey that, broadly speaking, a manorial system had long
been established in this part of Carmarthenshire with its
customary freeholders and copyholders and immemorial
customs, resting some on Welsh and some on English
traditions, varied only in Tudor times by the abolition
under Henry VIII. of the division among heirs.

Further light may be derived from what took place at
a similar period in Pembrokeshire.

It is well known that the boundary line between the
English and Welsh districts of Pembrokeshire goes back
to a very early date.

George Owen (who lived 1552—1613) wrote his "Description of Pembrokeshire " in 1603. His knowledge extended, therefore, over the critical period during which the rights of Welsh tenants of North Wales were considered by the law courts of Queen Elizabeth.

He describes the Welsh peasantry as still clinging to their old open field system of agriculture, with its holdings of scattered strips, and as still exercising the common right of pasture over them after removal of the crops.[1]

Now we know from the extent of the estates of St. David's made in 8 Edw. III. that the tribal system of occupation in *gwelys* was prevalent in the Welsh districts of Pembrokeshire and the estates of the see in Cardiganshire, Carmarthenshire, and Glamorganshire. And from the large number of quitrents of " customary freeholders " still collected by the Ecclesiastical Commissioners from these and other ecclesiastical estates,[2] it may be judged that in these districts, as in North Wales, the free tribesmen had come to be regarded by English law as " customary freeholders."

As regards the non-tribesmen or *nativi* it would seem from Owen's description that up to about the year 1500 they had been regarded at law as " *tenants at will according to the custom of the country*," but that owing to the absence of any pressure of population and the dearth of tenants the tenancy continued without alteration of rent and with only nominal fines for renewal as a practically permanent tenancy.

He says:[3] "And first I will begin with the tenants of the country whereof I speak in general, including therein the greatest number which in times past were tenants at will, and few sought leases, for most commonly the

[1] Owen's "Pembrokeshire," p. 61.
[2] Qu. 76,329—76.342.
[3] Owen's "Pembrokeshire," p. 190.

landlord rather made suit for a good tenant to take his land
than the tenant to the landlord, such was the scarcity of
good tenants in those days there to be found that glad was
the lord to hit upon a good thrifty and husbandly tenant."

He then contrasts this state of things with what had
happened in his own time, during which there had been
a rise in prices and a competition for farms, and during
which, in consequence, high fines had become general for
renewal of leases, whilst there was no security of tenure
without them.

"As for fines to be paid it was not a thing known among
them a hundred years past, saving only an earnest penny
at the bargain making, which the plain men called 'a gods
penny,' and which in these 60 years the poor tenants were
wont to say the paying of fines was an ill custom raised
among them of late."

And he gives an example of how insignificant were the
fines and how little they were thought of in the old days.

"The letting of lands was of so small commodity that
I know lands in coparceny between heirs, when the next
to the land hath had the setting and letting thereof these
60 years and more, the other contenting himself with his
part of the rent not esteeming what might be made by
fines thereof."

He continues to complain that during the last forty
years, *i.e.*, from 1560—1600, all this was changed.

"For now the poor tenant that lived well in that golden
world is taught to sing unto his lord a new song, and the
landlords have learnt the text of the damned disciple,
'*Quid vultis mihi dare, et ego illum vobis tradam*,' and now
the world is so altered with the poor tenant that he standeth
so in bodily fear of his greedy neighbour that two or three
years ere his lease end he must bow to his lord for a new
lease, and must pinch it out many years before to heap
money together, so that in this age it is as easy for a poor

tenant to marry two of his daughters to his neighbour's sons as to match himself to a good farm from his landlord."

This is precisely the same complaint as that made in England at the same period. Harrison, in his "Description of England" (A.D. 1577), says :—

"Although peradventure four pounds of old rent be improved to forty or fifty pounds, yet will the farmer think his gains very small toward the middest of his term if he have not six or seven years' rent lying by him therewith to purchase a new lease . . . for what stock of money soever he gathereth in all his years it is often seen that the landlord will take such order with him for the same when he reneweth his lease (which is commonly eight or ten years before it be expired, sithe it is now growen almost to a custom that, if he come not to his lord so long before, another shall step in for a reversion and so defeat him outright) that it shall never trouble him more than the hair of his beard when the barber hath washed and shaven it from his chin" (fol. 85).

Recurring to the position of the Pembrokeshire tenants, the successors of the non-tribesmen, though in some sense recognised as like English copyholders, were evidently not protected by custom from the payment of increasing fines on renewal, resulting from the keen competition for farms.

Their case had been dealt with by English lawyers centuries earlier than that of the *nativi* of North Wales.

They seem to have been regarded from early times as only *quasi* copyholders, as holding in law only from year to year, and yet they were subject to heriots at their death. The following passage is useful as showing how a kind of middle stage had grown up in these Welsh manors of South Wales between the ordinary customary tenant and the tenant from year to year.

"This use of tenants at will was so common that there were many other customs grounded upon the same, for they were not tenants at will at the common law to be put out at the lord's will at any time of the year, but they were tenants at will according to the custom of the country, and were not removable without two lawful warnings to be given at usual feasts, that is the one on our lady's eve in March, the other at May eve, and then was the old tenant at Mid-summer to remove out of the hall house and to lease it to the new tenant and the pastures to be common between them till Michaelmas, and then the old tenant to depart *cum panim* and to leave it wholly to the new comer, divers orders then are duly observed as yet amongst these tenants which for brevity's sake I here pass over.

"This kind of tenants by the custom of the country were to pay heriots at their death, viz., their best beast, and also were chargeable to the repair of their houses, hedges, &c., and therein is observed an order worth the noting . . . viz., that if the tenant suffer his houses, hedges, or buildings to grow ruinous the landlord used to swear a jury of six of his tenants of the like tenure and custom (whose turns may be next to taste of the same sauce) to view the decay who must and ought accordingly upon their oaths present the same indifferently between the lord and his tenant, which done the landlord by his bailiff or servant useth to arrest so much of the tenants goods upon the land as is found of decay and . . .

"This custom of repair held only for thatched houses, but for slate houses the landlords were to repair them except it were by special covenant . . ."

Thus, so far as it goes, the Pembrokeshire evidence so far as it can be regarded as typical of the early conquered districts of South Wales seems to show that, whilst the free tribesmen became "customary freeholders" under English law, the non-tribesmen had become regarded at law very early as "tenants at will under the customs of their respective manors" like English copyholders. But at the same time it would seem that the customs of the manors in their case, as in the case of many English manors, afforded no adequate protection as regards the amount of the fines. Owing to this lack of adequate custom controlling the amount of fines, and to the general rise in fines following the general rise in prices, they became subject to the competition of outsiders on the renewal of their tenures, and were obliged to pay what they considered exorbitant fines to obtain renewals. Thus, in their case, owing to the at one time harmless prevalence of the system of fines, they were prevented from reaping the advantage enjoyed by the customary freeholders whose quitrents remained the same through all vicissitudes notwithstanding the rise in prices.

§ 4.—*The Growth of Tenancy from Year to Year in Wales generally.*

Regarding the foregoing evidence drawn from the typical cases above mentioned as fairly representing the general experience of Welsh tenants under the application to their case of English law, it can hardly be represented as involving intentional injustice or hardship.

The compositions and settlements of the Crown lawyers of Queen Elizabeth were apparently in intention at least, on the whole, fair attempts to deal with the difficult circumstances of the ancient Welsh tribal tenures. The substitution of renewable leases for other and vague tenures was not confined to Wales, and the question when and how and why they ceased to be renewed is as much an English question as a Welsh one. Renewable leases disappeared in England as they did in Wales. Whether there was some legal flaw in the creation of leases with perpetual right of renewal, or whether the right of renewal once exercised was held to be exhausted, or whether the renewals ceased to be sought for by the tenants, or how much economic causes had to do with it, it is not easy to ascertain. To the more modern aspects of this question we shall have to recur hereafter. One thing, however, seems to be clear. The fines on renewal in the absence of express limit by the custom of the particular manor were it would seem held by the courts to be *uncertain*, and owing to the rise in prices and in the value of land the uncertainty might easily lead to prohibitive increase in their amount. Whatever hardship resulted from this, English and Welsh tenants shared it together.

John Norden, a land surveyor, whose surveys of parts of Wales show how great was his experience of Welsh as well as English tenures, in his " Surveyor's Dialogue," written in 1607, thus described the position of things at that date as regards fines on renewal of copyhold tenures.

Farmer : " You have not satisfied me . . . touching the fines of customary tenants of inheritance . . ."

Surveyor: " This kind of tenant hath seldom any competitor to emulate his offer, because the tenant leaveth commonly one either in right of inheritance, or by surrender to succeed him, and he by custom of the manor is to be accepted tenant *always provided* he must agree with the lord, if the custom of the manor hold not the fine certain, *as in few it doth.*" [1]

If in but few English manors fines were fixed and made certain by custom, it may well be that uncertainty was the rule at any rate in the newly-constituted manors of Wales, inasmuch as English law did not admit of the recognition of customs unless clearly going back beyond legal memory. It was not till after a series of later decisions that the amount of a "reasonable fine" was fixed by the courts to be two years improved value of the holding.[2]

Under the actual circumstances of the case, the year to

---

[1] Ashley's " Economic History," i. 297.

[2] See " Scriven on Copyhold," ch. vii., on " the lord's fine." And see also Ashley's " Economic History," book ii., c. 4.

year tenancy may have afforded a more comfortable prospect of permanence than the renewable lease. The year to year tenancy at a fair rent of the improved value of the land may have afforded a better prospect to the tenant than that of a smaller rent with the recurring uncertain fine. The recurring period of uncertainty and disturbance was hardly likely to be popular with tenants whose traditions were of permanent tenancy. And there can be little doubt that both in England and in Wales the year to year tenancy in most cases was in practice, as well as in intention, the more permanent tenure. At the same time, to fresh tenants the year to year tenancy would, for the same reasons, be the more popular one.

That the class of fresh tenants was in Wales a large and increasing one must almost necessarily have resulted from the two causes already mentioned. First, the substitution of primogeniture for gavelkind inheritance, by stopping division of holdings would add to the number of applicants for new ones ; and secondly, the large proportion of the land not as yet occupied in severalty, but subject only to common rights of pasture, in most districts would make easy the creation of new holdings out of the waste by gradual increase of inclosures, and without special legislation.

The homesteads and inclosures of the original tribesmen and non-tribesmen and their successors, originally occupied in severalty, as we have seen, but a very small part of the area of the district over which they had rights of pasture. No doubt the multiplication of homesteads during the two centuries after the conquest, before gavelkind was abolished, had involved encroachments on the waste, and set in motion the general practice of encroachment and inclosure, legally or illegally accomplished, which has a survival in the squatters of more modern times. This gradual increase of inclosures in Wales, resulting in the present prevalence of scattered farms, held in severalty, involved questions very different from those which the common form of the English Inclosure Act for an open field township was intended to solve.

The Welsh inclosures were, probably, very gradually and silently made as the pressure of population required new holdings to be provided out of the waste, and finally, when the aid of Inclosure Acts was sought, it would be mostly to divide up large tracts of mountain and other land which remained in common pasture.

The question of commons and inclosures is dealt with separately in the Report, but the mention of their position in the history of Welsh land tenure is not irrelevant in this connection as explaining, to some extent, the facility with which the system of separate farms, and year to year tenancy, was extended without legislative action.

§ 5.—*Summary of the Historical Result.*

To sum up the historical result, it will be seen, in conclusion, that many causes have combined in producing and afterwards perpetuating what is the marked and peculiar feature of rural economy in Wales, viz., the prevalence of a large number of small separate farms of what may be described as the peasant and family type. So that, on the one hand, the year to year tenancy in Wales has not become generally associated as in England with the system of large farms of the more commercial type, nor, on the other hand, has it been associated as in Ireland and the crofter districts of Scotland with that excessive subdivision and subletting which leads to the congestion of a rural population upon holdings too small to maintain the occupiers. Had the system of renewable leases continued, it might easily have led to the Irish system of throwing upon the tenant the obligation to make and maintain the buildings, and this in its turn might have introduced into Wales the complications of divided ownership.

The natural inherited instinct to live by the land, and the consequent competition for farms in Wales as in Ireland, furnished all the necessary factors for producing these results. But somehow or other the transition from tribal to modern forms of tenure in Wales has been accomplished without them.

No doubt the mountainous character of the country, the large areas of land under common grazing, and the pastoral character of the farming have had something to do with it, but much also must be attributed to the hereditary instincts and traditions of both landlords and tenants, and to the customary relations which grew out of them.

The relation of landlord and tenant in Wales gradually passing through the stage of leases for years or lives into a year to year tenancy has made possible the continuance of a useful control on the part of the landlord combined with a large measure of permanence in the tenure of the tenants; but it can hardly be doubted that the traditional element has had a great deal to do with the customary relations which have existed for generations on many estates.

The more modern aspects of some of the questions involved in the historical survey—the growth of large estates and the gradual dying-out of the system of renewable leases—receive more detailed attention in the Report and below, but it is important before leaving this part of the subject that the full extent of some of the before-mentioned peculiar results of Welsh economic history should be adequately realised as far as possible in actual figures.

The Census of 1861 enables us to trace some of these results with remarkable clearness.

First, the comparative smallness of the farms is shown very clearly by the statement of the number of labourers employed upon them. The annexed map No. 1 shows the number of labourers to each farmer and grazier in the various counties of England and Wales. It will be seen that if a line be drawn from the Wash to the Axe, there would be, roughly, about ten labourers to each farm in the Eastern Counties. If a line were drawn from the Humber to the Dee and from thence to the Severn, the average for middle England would be about five to each farm; whilst in 'Wales the number would not exceed one and a half to two labourers per farm.

The other counties of England nearly approaching Wales in this respect are Cornwall, Lancashire, Westmoreland, Cumberland, Durham, the West and North Riding of Yorkshire, and Derbyshire, all of which resemble Wales more or less in being hilly and chiefly pasture.

Again, the number of farmers and graziers according to the Census of 1861 was as follows:—

	North Wales.	South Wales.	England.
Males	14,660	18,102	194,193
Females . . .	2,202	4,862	15,714
Total . . .	16,862	22,964	209,907

It will be seen that the proportion of women for the time being returned as occupying farms is, roughly, as one to five in Wales, while it is only as one to twelve in England. This is more than a slight indication that the continuance of farms on the death of the occupier as family holdings was more general in Wales than in other parts of the kingdom. But the family or household character of the Welsh farms is still more clearly shown by a comparison which the same census enables us to make between

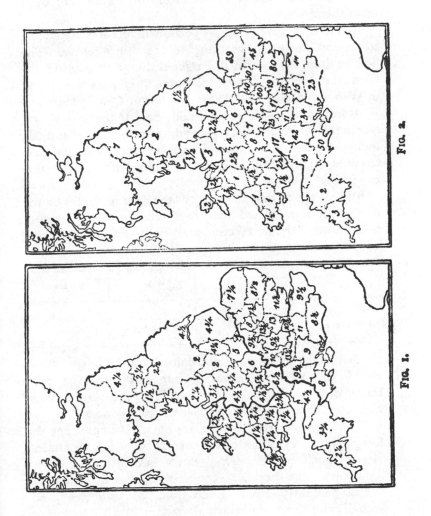

FIG. 2.

FIG. I.

the indoor and outdoor character of the labour employed upon them.

Map No. 2 gives the proportion of outdoor labourers to indoor labourers according to the same census. The figures show that whilst in England the great mass of the farm labourers are outdoor labourers, it is quite the reverse in Wales and the analogous counties of Cumberland and Westmoreland. Whilst about one-half of the agricultural labourers in Wales, Cumberland, and Westmoreland are indoor labourers, the proportion becomes less and less towards the east, till in Essex the proportion is only one to eighty.

Adding the number of indoor labourers in Wales to the number of farmers and their sons, &c., the total of household indoor labour as compared with the outdoor was as follows :—

	Wales.	England.
Household and indoor . . .	82,291	428,166
Outdoor	35,775	902,085

So that whilst in England not quite one-third of the labour was household and indoor labour, and more than two-thirds outdoor, in Wales less than one-third was outdoor, and more than two-thirds household and indoor.

These figures from the Census of 1861 supplement the foregoing survey of historical causes by giving a practical view of their results. They throw inferentially a strong light upon the peculiar economic process by which the Welsh peasantry have passed from the primitive patriarchal conditions of the tribal system into their modern conditions under year to year tenancy.

In conclusion, we have not attempted to minimise the extent to which the still lingering instincts and traditions of Welsh tenants may have their roots in the past, and yet be important factors in modern economic problems.

Their existence is one of the present facts which have to be acknowledged. But beyond this we have found no reasonable ground for importing into modern economic problems historical considerations which, however powerful at the time when the lawyers of Queen Elizabeth had to attempt to bring Welsh tribal custom within some category of English law, have been long superseded or rendered inoperative by the economic changes of the past three centuries.

The present year to year tenants of Wales cannot claim to be the direct successors of the ancient Welsh free tribesmen. The successors in title of these are still paying their ancient and now trifling quitrents. That more of them have not survived is owing to natural causes, and, perhaps more than all, to their having enjoyed for centuries, like English copyholders, the right of selling their holdings in the open market. On the other hand, if some of the present year to year tenants are the successors of the ancient non-tribesmen or *nativi*, then the most probable general conclusion seems to be that their ancestors have passed through various vicissitudes, out of which, through stages of leases for lives or years (which for some reason were not renewed), they have passed into the position of year to year tenants.[1]

§ 6.—*Formation and Continuity of Estates.*

It appears clearly enough from what we have said that the bulk of Welsh land is, for agricultural purposes, now divided into areas possessed by estate owners and cultivated by tenants from year to year, or by lessees for terms of years. From the legal point of view there is no

[1] Mr. Seebohm's contribution ends here; but as Commissioner he subscribed he remainder of the chapter.

difference between the tenant in fee simple of 100 acres and the tenant in fee simple of 20,000 acres. But from the economist's point of view there is an immense distinction. An " estate " is an economic unit, an industrial, organic entity, having a life of its own, and influencing in many ways the progress or retrogression of a county or district The owners of these estates collectively form an aristocratic class in the community, exercise a general superintendence over the management of their estates, and depend upon the rent and profits of their land for the maintenance of themselves and their families. To the actual cultivators of the soil, and, in many respects, to the people at large, they stand in a relation similar to that in which the lords or barons of mediæval times stood to the peasants of those days. If we go back some six hundred years to the time before the Edwardian conquest of North Wales, we find that the class in the community who occupied the position most analogous to that of the modern estate owner was the order formed by the lords marchers and the Welsh princes and lords. We find the land cultivated (so far as it was utilised at all) by the free and servile tenants of these lords, holding on customary terms. With the way in which these customary tenants have become tenants from year to year we have just dealt.

The further question how the feudal lord marcher and the Welsh *arglwyd* have been replaced by estate owners is one which may reasonably be asked, but which neither our research nor the evidence enables us to dispose of fully or confidently. The answer to it depends upon historical data which, though they are even now extensive, are not complete, and accordingly we cannot pretend to give a final solution to the problem. The question may be expressed more definit ly thus : How have these Welsh estates been formed ? Some few observations may be made with confidence. First of all, the process of formation has been very gradual, and there has never been any real break in its continuity. The points at which the continuity of the process became most nearly broken are the Edwardian conquest itself, the accession of Henry Tudor, the dissolution of the monasteries, and the civil wars of the seventeenth century.

The system of settlement and re-settlement from time to time with the view of keeping the estate together, and of vesting it continually in a tenant for life in possession, and tenants in tail in remainder, subject to charges in favour of younger children, was introduced into Wales as in England, not of course universally, for in most cases the estates were small, and in some cases the entail having been broken, no re-settlement was made.

In the next place, considerable distinction in the rate at which the change from the old order to the new went on must be made between the principality proper and the marches; for in the former the custom of dividing an inheritance was continued down to the reign of Henry VIII., while the laws and customs in vogue in the courts of the lords marchers were very rapidly assimilated in essential points to those of the English courts, both royal and manorial.

In the third place, the process was not fundamentally dissimilar from that which went on in the English counties; but even if it did not proceed (as is probably the case) more slowly than in those districts, yet it began later, and the modern type of estate, on a considerable scale, appears later in the Welsh counties than in most parts of England.

Now, in the century after the Edwardian conquest, the actual state of things in Wales and the marches was this: at the top of the social and economic structure there were the Norman or Norman-Welsh lords marchers and the heads of the Welsh noble families (*uchelwyr* of the royal or princely caste) who had survived the conquest without attainder. These by their bailiffs and officers, servants and tenants, cultivated their demesne lands, but the greater portion of the then cultivated area was probably in the actual occupation of free tenants (whether *uchelwyr*, *bonedigion*, or *alltudion*) and of tenants practically corresponding to the villein class in England—bond or native tenants.

The total effect, from an economic point of view, of the whole process we are trying to describe may be (making due allowance for the distinction between the principality and the marches) stated to be the survival of the free tenant or tribesman—the occupying *uchelwr*, *bonedig*, or *alltud* of free or gentlemanly degree (*i.e.*, entitled to bear arms in the host)—and the decay of the princely or baronial class, as such, on the one hand and of the servile or non-tribal occupier on the other.

§ 7.—*Causes of the Change.*

The leading causes or forces which have produced this great change, and which have resulted in the creation of the modern estate, may, in more abstract terms, be thus expressed :—

First, the seigniorial rights, owing to the change in the value of money, became less and less valuable (measured in current coin).[1]

Secondly, the price of land held on the least burdensome tenure (*i.e.*, freehold land held of the Crown or a mesne lord upon payment of chief or quit rents), and therefore most disposable by sale or mortgage, went up continuously and very greatly.   Before the development of manufactures and commerce on the modern system, land was not simply the most desirable and safe, but in the remoter and less-advanced districts the only readily available investment for any capital which a freeholder might possess, beyond what

---

[1] See the case of Maelor Saesneg in the Report, par. 190 ; and the Hon. Mrs. Bulkeley-Owen's evidence, Minutes, iv. p. 114, qu. 57, 149, *et seq.*

could be prudently used in actual farming. Accordingly, the saving and provident freeholder employed such money as he had to invest in the purchase of other parcels of freehold land. The mortgage of land, too, by the unsuccessful or improvident freeholder, offered another mode of investment, and in many cases the transaction ultimately led to foreclosure or sale, and·the consequent disappearance of the mortgagor and his family from the list of owners. As the feudal aristocracy of the marches decayed, and it became possible to purchase seigniorial rights and to enforce them in courts of law without recourse to arms, there was clearly every inducement to the freehold tenant who was accumulating land to acquire those rights, especially such as were exerciseable over his own or adjoining land. The astute and vigilant exaction and use of these rights by such a freeholder, living on his own estate, also tended to produce an enlargement of his property. So also the obtaining of leases or grants of Crown lands gave opportunities of which the progressing freeholder readily availed himself.

Thirdly, the Act of Union between England and Wales made the structure of Welsh society and political organisation similar to that of England, and the calling of members to Parliament from the Welsh counties and boroughs greatly added to the power and influence of the larger freeholders. Those freeholders who possessed areas of land so large that they had ceased to be merely farmers, but subsisted mainly on rents paid by the actual cultivators, had by this time, owing to the operation of many causes (*e.g.*, traditional sentiment), come to be a distinct class, sharing amongst themselves the Crown offices incident to the management of the principality, and the judicial and other posts connected with local government, and excluding all others (outside the boroughs, which were small and unimportant in Wales) from any share in county affairs. They already formed a *quasi*-aristocratic class, rapidly taking the same place in the social and political structure that had been previously occupied by the feudal baronial families, who had almost disappeared, but with whom this new class had many points of connection. Intermarriages among members of this comparatively limited class and succession by settlement and devise naturally became potent factors in the process of aggregation.

Fourthly, the assimilation of the Welsh and English law, completed by the legislation of Henry VIII., powerfully tended to enlarge the consequence and power of this class, and to produce an aggregation of land in a few hands. This involved the abolition of the Welsh system of dividing the inheritance, and the introduction of the law of primogeniture. The statute 12 Charles II. c. 24, abolished tenures by knight service and by socage *in capite* of the king, and converted all tenures into free and common socage. This Act in Wales, as in England, materially benefited the then existing estate owners, while the introduction of the modern method of settlement and re-settlement in tail into Wales was an additional means of preserving the estates intact in the possession of the same family.

§ 8.—*The Effect of the Chief Historical Events.*

Such, stated in general or abstract terms, appear to us to be the main causes of the displacement of the feudal aristocracy, the substitution of the Welsh country gentleman or squire, and of the rise of the modern system of estates. But a succession of concrete historical events, which cannot be logically classified, facilitated the process on most important points in the development. As we have seen, the Norman of South and Central Wales introduced into those parts of the country the Norman-English theories and systems. The Edwardian conquest of North Wales partially did the same for the principality proper. We

have examined above the method of settlement adopted by
Edward I. and his successors, and the later management of
affairs by the advisers of the Tudor monarchs. Generally
speaking, we may say the effect was to dissolve tribal
notions of real property law, and to replace them by the
more fully developed theories of the English lawyers.
That the change involved (whatever may have been the
intentions of the English Crown) grave injustice, there
can be no doubt. In theory the rights of the Welsh
freeholders, or free tribesmen, were admitted and preserved, but in practice the officers of the Crown and
the lords who surrounded or acquired a footing in the
principality were guilty of oppressing the Welshmen
of every degree. Speaking of the pre-Tudor times,
Sir John Wynne (a competent and trustworthy writer)
says : " The exactions were in those dayes soe manifold that not onely the bondmen ranne away from the
king's land, but alsoe freeholders from their owne land."[1]
From what Sir John says, it seems that the process or writ
called *cessavit per biennium* gave a ready weapon to the
unscrupulous Crown official. This writ appears to have
lain against a tenant in freehold under the king or another
lord who ceased for two years to do his service. Among
instances of oppression that he recounts he mentions that
Henry Lacy, Earl of Lincoln, to whom the king granted
the "Denbigh land," "minding to make a princely sea
of the castle of Denbigh, per force compassed the children
of the said David ap Gruffith to exchange their possessions
about Denbigh Castle (which were great) with him for other
lands of less value in the said lordship in the furthest part
from him."[2] The probable result of this state of things
was a diminution of the number of the freehold tenants
during the time between the Conquest and the time of

[1] " History of the Gwydir Family," p. 83 (edition of 1878).
[2] *Ibid.*, p. 25.

Elizabeth. But while this fact lessened the number of the freeholders, it should be noticed it increased the strength and opportunities of those of the class who were able to survive.

Another event which was of far-reaching economic effect in Wales, as in England, was the Black Death, which, at intervals, desolated the kingdom in the fourteenth century. The Record of Carnarvon and other documents contain entries which prove that this pestilence lowered the population, including, of course, the free as well as bond or native tenants.

The series of rebellions that took place after the Edwardian settlement and also the Wars of the Roses were also historical events which led to the decay of the wealth and power of, and the disappearance of, many of the individual families forming the feudal baronage, as well as of the survivors of the Welsh princely houses. The decline of the one class of proprietors naturally, in the long run, brought about the rise of the other class. It is often said that the ruin of the early feudal aristocracy was brought about by the conflicts between Lancastrians and Yorkists. This seems an error; the lessening of their power commenced before,[1] at any rate if one speaks of the whole kingdom; but everything points to their retaining their power and influence to a later time in Wales and the marches than elsewhere. For the two hundred and fifty years that passed after the conquest by Edward I. this western part of the Island was in a practically continuous state of disorder. The peace of the king and of his feudal tenants was ill kept. Life and property were everywhere insecure. Private wars were constantly breaking out between the lords marchers themselves and between the lords marchers and the descendants or reputed descendants of the Welsh princely or lordly families. The leaders of the

[1] Green's "History of the English People," vol. ii., p. 14.

Welsh, of course, too, quarrelled among themselves, and only occasionally took anything like real concerted action against the vexatious and oppressive conduct of the Norman-English settlers. The result of a period of confusion like this was naturally adverse to the persons who played the greatest part in the affairs of their times. The leaders habitually fought with their own hands, and therefore ran the risks of the battlefield in their own persons. Defeat oftentimes meant death or attainder, and sometimes both. All this is true of England as well, but this state of things lasted longer in the principality and the marches. It is easy, however, by wrongly interpreting the general phrases of chroniclers and historians, to form an exaggerated picture of the ills of this period. It should be noted that under the Welsh tribal system it was only the free tribesman (*uchelwr* or *bonedig*) who formed part of the host, and the bond tenant was left at home or attended the army in menial capacity. Nor was the matter for a long time very different after the Conquest. The right to bear arms belonged only to those of gentle blood or to those persons who were received as retainers of the lord marcher or Welsh prince or lord. A war did not mean that all the cultivators of the soil actually left it; when any of them did so they were away only a short time.[1] The operation of such agriculture as existed went on as usual. There was no such dislocation of rural life as modern war brings about in occupied districts. While, then, the consequence of the condition of things in Wales in the fourteenth and fifteenth centuries was disastrous to the aristocratic families, it was not fatal to the progress and permanence of the freeholders as a class, though no doubt their growth in prosperity was retarded and their comfort and happiness diminished.

Another historical event which had a marked influence

---

[1] This remark must be qualified by stating that on many occasions there was recruiting for the king's army in the marches and in Wales.

in improving the position of the descendants of the Welsh freehold tenants, who had by this time attained a considerable position and had acquired in many instances the position of the squire or country gentleman, was the fact that the Act of Union (besides its assimilation of the private law of Wales to that of England) gave Wales the right of representation in the House of Commons. Of course great lords or barons who owned lands or lordships in Wales or the marches had been summoned to the House of Lords, but one gentleman only of Welsh name and descent had, before the time of Henry VII., been advanced to the peerage in the modern sense—Sir William ap Thomas, created Earl of Pembroke by Edward IV., from whom the important family of the Herberts trace their descent, and who was in his time the " only and entire commander of Wales." [1] No Welshman in the true sense was summoned by Henry VII., upon his accession, to Parliament. Of the twenty-nine peers summoned by him to his first Parliament not a single one was Welsh by name and descent, or had his principal property and lordships in the principality or those parts of the marches that ultimately were apportioned to Welsh counties. No doubt some of these twenty-nine peers had property in the marches and possibly in Wales proper, but not one can be fairly described as a Welshman. Members had been returned to the House of Commons at an early date from Anglesey, Merionethshire, and Carnarvonshire,[2] but from the time of Edward II. to the stat. 27 Henry VIII. c. 26, there was an intermission. From the time of Henry VIII.,[3] however, Welsh members were sent up to Westminster regularly, and this fact had a

[1] Owen's " Pembrokeshire," ed. Henry Owen, 1892 (Lond., 8vo, Cymmodorion Record Series), p. 28.

[2] Williams's " Parliamentary History of Wales " (Lond., 1895, 4to, p. i. : Introduction).

[3] Certainly from 1541. As to the Parliaments of 1536 and 1539 *quære.* See Williams, p. i. : Introduction.

rapid and far-reaching effect upon the fortunes of the Welsh gentry. From the condition of the times and the nature of the franchise it was members of land-owning families who were elected for many generations. The effect upon these families of their joining in the general political life of the whole kingdom was to enlarge their views, to increase their importance, to bring them into contact, on a favourable basis, with the members of their order in the English counties, to lead to intermarriages between Welsh and English families, and to give, to the able and ambitious, opportunities of worldly advancement on a considerable scale in many directions, especially in civil affairs, which had theretofore been denied to the Welsh gentleman. The more wealthy and influential among these men were not slow to perceive and to use the advantages which this contact with the English Court, official life, and society afforded them, and many were able to add to the extent of the family estate and strengthen or consolidate their positions.

The dissolution of the monasteries, practically contemporaneous with the summoning of Welsh members to the House of Commons, had also a marked effect. Those members of the Norman-English baronial and Welsh princely families who still maintained a connection with Wales and the Welsh marches, as well as those freehold tenants who by steady accumulation had acquired a superior status, found in this event an opportunity for adding to the acreage of their estates or of retrieving the family fortunes. A large area of the most fertile and desirable parts of the principality fell into new hands, and this led to the enlarging of the estates and improving of the position of the larger Welsh freeholders, and brought things from the estate owners' point of view into a condition not very dissimilar to that which exists at the present time, and cleared the way for dealing with the tenants (the actual cultivators) in the time of Elizabeth in the manner which has been explained above.

The rebellion and civil wars of the seventeenth century had a great effect in regard to the formation of new estates, and the destruction or the partial breaking up of older ones. The Welsh gentry, as a rule, were Royalist in inclination and action ; though there were no doubt exceptions, as well as much uncertainty and tergiversation on the part of individuals and families. The triumph of the Parliament and the sequestrations and fines during the Commonwealth (especially in South Wales during the rule of the Cromwellian major generals) caused the ruin or impoverishment of several of the leading Welsh families, brought land "into the market," and gave opportunities to many of the lesser gentry, and in some cases to persons of "mean extraction." But on the whole there was no rush of new-comers into Wales ; there was no wholesale destruc- tion and splitting up of estates ; no general extinction of the families of gentle blood. The Restoration undid a good part of what had taken place, and the general effect was that the more prudent, unenterprising estate owner of moderate opinions, living quietly at his own place, found the trend of events tell in favour of his own aggrandisement.

Some of the Welsh gentry seemed to have suffered in the Revolution of 1688, but from that time no political troubles have interfered with the operation of the general and economic causes which told in favour of the increase of the wealth and power of "the landed interest" down to the middle of this century. The policy of enclosing land added to the acreage of many estates, while the great industrial development (especially in South Wales on account of the extension of coal-mining operations) com- bined with a large and steady increase of the population of Wales, involving necessarily, both in town and country, a greater demand for land for all sorts of purposes, added enormously to the capital value and yearly revenue of real property.

The preceding considerations lead us to infer that by the time of James I., Wales, like England, was divided into estates not dissimilar in character to those of our own day. They varied no doubt very greatly in size and in yearly value. Many freehold owners had only small parcels of land which they cultivated themselves. Others had freeholds of great extent.[1] The social line of demarcation between classes was drawn primarily between those owners who lived by farming and those who depended for their main income upon the rents and profits of their land ; but the distinction was emphasised by the respective length and purity of the family pedigree, by connection with the older and then existing great families, by serving in or the possession of offices (*e.g.*, the Lord-Lieutenancy, the Shrievalty, Justiceship of the Peace), and the scale and character of the domestic establishment. The gentry class was already separated from the yeoman class, formed an order apart, was possessed of prejudices and notions that tended more and more to exclusiveness, and was able to assume, justifiably enough, the social importance, as they had already obtained the political power of the older aristocracy.

Speaking broadly, the estates of the gentry in Wales in the seventeenth century appear to have been small— possibly many may have been extensive in area, but certainly from the point of view of annual value they were as a rule very small. Major-General Berry, writing to Cromwell, says : " You can sooner find fifty gentlemen of 100*l.* a year than five of 500*l.* "; and, going back to Tudor times, the conclusion to be formed from the observations of at least one contemporary observer of Wales—John Leland—is that the Welsh estates were then, as a rule

[1] See Report, par. 186.

small, both in extent and revenue. Rowlands, too, in his "Llyfrydiaeth y Cymry" (p. 195), has preserved some lines, which he describes as ancient, concerning Radnor-shire, which are to the same effect:—

> "Alas! alas! poor Radnorshire,
> Never a park, nor ever a deer,
> Nor ever a Squire of five hundred a year
> Save Richard Fowler of Abbey Cwm-hir."[1]

But perhaps the most striking piece of evidence upon this point is afforded by looking at the list of baronetcies con-ferred up to 1682. The order of baronet was revived by James I. with a view of raising money, but it probably partly owed its real origin to the desire of the noble families to prevent that increase of their numbers which was inevitable if something was not done to meet the reasonable demands of the wealthy English country gentle-men for hereditary titles. James offered the title of baronet to all persons of good repute, being knights or esquires possessed of lands worth 1,000*l.* a year, upon the terms of their paying 1,080*l.* in three annual instalments.[2] More than 200 baronets were created during his reign, and by 1682 there had been 866 creations. Only twelve out of the 200 were Welsh owners, and only thirty-seven out of the 866.[3] No precise conclusion can be drawn from this, but it seems a fair and probable inference that the number of estate owners having more than 1,000*l.* a year from land was proportionately less in Wales than in England.

[1] Richard Fowler was originally a London merchant, and held Abbey Cwm-hir for the king in 1644 ; he was afterwards High Sheriff of Radnorshire under Cromwell in 1655, and was probably the father of Catherine Philips, "Orinda."

[2] Gardiner, "History of England," vol. ii., p. 112.

[3] See the official list of 1682, published in Dugdale's "Ancient Usage in bearing Arms," etc. (Lond. 1682).

It is, however, clear from the list of baronets with their description that by the end of the seventeenth century some estates which have mostly become enlarged since then (though they may have changed hands), and which were even then considerable or large, had been formed. Mr. Lecky says : " At the beginning of the century (*i.e.*, eighteenth century) there still existed in England numerous landowners with estates of 200*l.* to 300*l.* a year. The descendants in many cases of the ancient yeomen, they ranked socially with the gentry. . . . From the early years of the eighteenth century this class began to disappear and by the end of the century it was almost extinct."[1] Similar remarks appear to be as true in regard to Wales, but the available sources of information appear to indicate, first, that the annual rental of the corresponding class in Wales was even less as a rule in the beginning of the eighteenth century, and secondly, that the existence of this smaller gentry as a class was more prolonged. The same general causes which, in the period from the Revolution of 1688, and even earlier, operated in England to extinguish the smaller gentry and the yeomen, were at work also in Wales. As to the inferior gentry class it is not possible to trace in detail their decline. Owing to various causes some sank to be mere ordinary farmers ; others sold their lands to substantial neighbours, or, having mortgaged their interests, foreclosure and ultimate sale took place. Many a house that was a small mansion-house and a centre of social life has become now a mere farm-house.

The whole tendency of legislation and administration, as well as of agricultural and even industrial progress, was in favour of the larger estate owners. Accumulation of land in the hands of the fortunate survivors of the mediæval and Reformation troubles was facilitated and encouraged. The estate owners of Wales had their share of the benefits

[1] " History of England," vol. i., p. 557.

conferred on the landed interest by the rule of the great families and the political system it involved, and their growing association with the same class in England led to their intermixture by marriage and the gradual assimilation of the former to the latter in speech, tastes, ideals of domestic comfort, and general habits.

CHAPTER X.

THE RELIGIOUS MOVEMENT.

IT is impossible to understand the evidence which the Commission received as to the condition of agricultural Wales, without taking into account the special ecclesiastical and religious circumstances of this part of the country. We desire in this chapter to avoid, so far as we can, entering upon the controversies which are continually carried on between the adherents of the Episcopal Church in Wales and those of the great Nonconformist bodies—controversies which have been accentuated by the introduction in the last Parliament of the Suspensory Bill and a bill for the Disestablishment and Disendowment of the Church in Wales. The existence of grave differences of opinion in reference to church organisation and doctrine, and the acute social and religious divisions created by the continual rivalry between different branches of the Christian Church, were forced upon the attention of the Commission at almost every sitting. There can be no doubt that this rivalry and these differences, with all the consequences that may be naturally expected to follow, are very important factors, even at the present time, in determining the relations of landlord and tenant. It is admitted on all hands that Nonconformity (including in that term all religious organisations other than the Established Church) is the predominating religious power in Wales in the sense that a large majority of those who habitually attend places of worship as communicants, members, and hearers, worship in Nonconformist chapels.

Much controversy has arisen recently as to the numbers of Nonconformists and of Churchmen. We have no means of obtaining exact statistics upon the subject, and none of the attempts which have been made to supply correct figures can be regarded as entirely satisfactory. Even supposing that the question of the relative strength of Non-conformity and Anglicanism is properly to be measured by counting heads, we would point out that in the attempts that are made to ascertain the facts the opposing parties do not seem to be agreed upon the terms of the issue. Most of the Church supporters appear to rely upon the presumption that every one who does not habitually attend a Nonconformist chapel is a Churchman. Now, of course, there can be no doubt that the legal *primâ facie* presumption is that every man who does not avail himself of the rights given by the Act of Toleration is a member of the Church of England, but we need hardly point out that in measuring the forces of religious organisations no such presumption can in fact be allowed any weight. The question is not what number of men in Wales are *de jure* members of the Church of England, but how many men are *de facto* conscientious believers in Church principles, communicants of the Church of England, and attendants at its services. In deter-mining to what extent in the average Welsh parish the inhabitants are Nonconformist or Church people, it is necessary to bear this point in mind. Our impression is that, however the question be put, the majority of the people inhabiting the area of the inquiry of the Com-mission are Nonconformist and not Anglican ; and if the question be more accurately put, *i.e.*, if we ask what propor-tion of those who habitually attend or connect themselves with any place of worship are Nonconformist or Church people, there can be no doubt that the former class is in a very large majority, especially in the agricultural districts in which the use of the Welsh language predominates.[1]

For our purpose it is quite unnecessary to go into statistical details. The evidence which the Commission received as to the condition of things upon most of the estates in Wales convinced them that the immense majority of the tenant farmers in the country districts of Wales were Nonconformists, and that a state of things in regard to religion was disclosed that found no parallel in any part of England of equal area. We, from our point of view, do not attach so much importance to mere numbers as to what may be called the organic structure of rural society, or of the ordinary estate considered as an economic unit. Looked at in this way what we find is : That on the most typical estates in Wales the landlord and his family belong to the Established Church, while the bulk of the tenants belong to one or other of the Nonconformist organisations. We are not aware that a similar state of things exists in any English county, and there can be little doubt that this remarkable fact has had a powerful influence in creating a marked divergence between the opinions of the landowning class and the mass of the people, and in emphasising the opposing interests of landlord and tenant. It is not necessary to summarise the evidence received upon this matter exhaustively. A few extracts illustrating what we have said and confirming the impression which even a superficial observation of the Welsh counties would produce will suffice.

---

[1] On this question of numbers see, among more recent contributions, "A Handbook on Welsh Church Defence," by Dr. Edwards, Bishop of St. Asaph (Lond., 3rd ed. 1895), "A History of the Church in Wales," by the Rev. H. W. Clarke, B.A. (Lond. 1896), "The Case for Disestablishment" (Lond. 1894). See also "Wales," by Sir Thomas Phillips (Lond. 1849), and "The Causes of Dissent in Wales," by A. J. Johnes (Lond. 1831, new ed. 1870).

Speaking in reference to this matter, Mr. John Morgan Davies, of Froodvale, Carmarthenshire, an agent for five considerable estates in the counties of Carmarthen, Pembroke, Cardigan, Glamorgan, and Brecon, stated that the families of the present tenants had been in the same places for many generations, and that they nearly all habitually spoke the Welsh language, and were Nonconformists " to a man pretty nearly." [1]

Mr. Lewis Bishop, agent for the Dynevor estate in Carmarthenshire, informed the Commission that the tenants of Lord Dynevor were all Welsh-speaking men, and mostly Nonconformists. He thought that there were about half a dozen Churchmen or so, but that there might be more.[2]

Mr. Charles Bishop, in reference to nine parishes in Upper Carmarthenshire, said that the Welsh language was "their Bible and hearth language," and that " by far the greater majority are Nonconformists." [3]

Mr. John Davies, of Landwr, Mydrim, St. Clears, speaking of the parishes of Mydrim, St. Clears, Landowror, and others immediately adjoining St. Clears, said they were Welsh-speaking parishes, and that for the most part the farmers and the labourers were all Nonconformists, though he added there were Churchmen in Mydrim.[4]

Mr. James Thomas, of Troedyrhiw Lanfynyd, churchwarden of the parish, said that nearly all the farmers in his district were Nonconformists, and that the adherents of the Church of England were a very small fraction.[5]

Mr. John Emlyn Jones, of Penlan Uchaf, honorary secretary of the Tregaron Farmers' Club and a teacher of agriculture, said that in the parish of Nantcwnlle ". . . there

---

[1] Qu. 37,524 and 37,621–3.
[2] Qu. 38,370 and 38,544–6.
[3] Qu. 39,493, 39,503, and 39,506.
[4] Qu. 41,943, 41,970, and 41,972.
[5] Qu. 42,056 and 42,059.

are 84 tenant farmers holding over 4 acres. . . . Of those 84, 24 are Churchmen, making 29 per cent., but out of 46 freehold occupiers of over 4 acres in the parish there is not one Churchman except the vicar. There is one man doubtful, and I count him a Churchman. That gives them 2 per cent. of the freehold occupiers."[1] The same witness further stated that in his parish 7 out of every 10 were Nonconformists, and that, taking the country round, three-fourths of the inhabitants were Nonconformists according to the best estimate he could give while as to the Nonconformists the proportion of Nonconformists to Churchmen was 60 or 70 per cent. But he admitted that this was a guess or estimate made from observation of the immediate neighbourhood.[2]

Mr. Owen Price, tenant farmer of Nantyrharn, in the parish of Cray, Breconshire, said that a very large majority of the tenants round Brecon, where the people habitually speak the Welsh language, were Nonconformist, though the Church was pretty strong in that neighbourhood.[3]

In the counties of Anglesey, Carnarvon, and Merioneth, there can be no doubt, both from the evidence and from our own observation, that on nearly all the estates, if not indeed on all, a large majority of the tenant farmers belong to Nonconformist bodies.

The Hon. R. H. Eden, the agent for the Crogan estate in Merionethshire, belonging to Lord Dudley, said that there were very few Churchmen on the estate. He really could hardly point to more than one or two, and we have every reason to believe that this is the case with regard to most of the estates in those three counties.[4]

Mr. Wynne, of Peniarth, said that the majority of his

---

[1] Qu. 46,622 and 46,649.
[2] Qu. 46,752–6 and 46,760.
[3] Qu. 50,505, 50,705, and 50,706.
[4] Qu. 9,116, 9,123, 9,207, and 9.208.

tenants were Nonconformists, and stated that of the tenant farmers on his Merionethshire estate about 46 were Nonconformists and 16 Churchmen.[1]

Mr. W. Cadwaladr Williams, junior, of Bendy Manor, Festiniog, told the Commission that most of the farmers spoke Welsh almost exclusively among themselves, and that, with very few exceptions, they were Nonconformists in that part of Merionethshire.[2]

Mr. Morris Owen, tenant of Mr. Wynne, of Garthewin, said that most of the tenant farmers on the estate were Nonconformists, and added he did not think his landlord cared what they might be.[3]

Turning now to Glamorganshire, the Rev. T. Howell, of Longland, Pyle, in the Vale of Glamorgan, said that in that district seven-eighths of the population were Nonconformists.[4] Similar evidence and the information which reached the Commission from many sources confirm the view that of the tenant farmers and labourers in that county a very large majority are Nonconformist.

No statistics, no dry statement of facts, can adequately explain the hold which Nonconformity has obtained on the Welsh people. It would be interesting to attempt to trace the historical causes which have led to the peculiar ecclesiastical condition of Wales, but it is quite beyond the scope of this work to try to perform any such task. We must content ourselves with only a few general observations upon the matter, which tend to show the special points in the religious development of the Welsh people.

The first thing to notice is the opposition between Celtic and Latin Christianity, which was ended by the triumph of the Roman organisation and the subjection of

---

[1] Qu. 9,448 and 9,459.
[2] Qu. 10,074 and 10,075.
[3] Qu. 14,419.
[4] Qu. 24,926.

the Welsh clergy to the Roman see,[1] and next the conflict between the Welsh bishops and the see of Canterbury, which resulted in the four Welsh dioceses becoming part of the southern English province.[2] So far as the materials permit us to form a judgment from the time that Latin Christianity prevailed over Celtic usages, there is little to differentiate the history of the Church in Wales from the course of development in England. The parochial system was gradually introduced into the Principality and the marches. The clergy obtained from time to time considerable grants of land from the Welsh princes and other lords. Tithe became, under the same influences as in England, a definite charge upon land, and the ecclesiastical law enforced in the spiritual courts of England was applied in Wales. A considerable number of religious houses were founded and endowed throughout the Welsh counties.

To attempt to estimate the extent to which the principles of the Christian religion obtained a real hold upon the Welsh-speaking population before the Reformation

[1] The literature connected with the early history of the Church in Great Britain and Ireland is very extensive. The student will find "Chapters on Early English Church History," by Dr. Bright (Oxford, 2nd edition, 1888), most serviceable and trustworthy. See also Green's "Making of England" (Lond. 1882), pp. 310 *et seq.*, and "The Celtic Church in Wales," by J. W. Willis-Bund, F.S.A. (Lond. 1897). As to the Church in Wales, see the following papers in "The Transactions of the Hon. Society of Cymmrodorion" for 1893-4 (Lond. 1895) :—"The Ancient Church in Wales," by Lord Justice Vaughan Williams; "Welsh Saints,' by J. W. Willis-Bund, F.S.A.; "Some Aspects of the Christian Church in Wales during the Fifth and Sixth Centuries," by the Rev. Professor Hugh Williams, M.A. See also, in the Transactions of the same Society for 1897-8 (Lond. 1899), a paper on "The Character of the Heresy of the Early British Church," by F. C. Conybeare, M.A. Consult, of course, Haddan and Stubbs's "Councils and Ecclesiastical Documents relating to Great Britain and Ireland" (3 vols., Oxford, 1867-73), and Pryce's "Ancient British Church."

[2] We cannot refer to all the sources bearing on this conflict. The matter is discussed in Clarke's "History" cited above; see pp. 34-66. The petition of the Welsh Princes to the Pope will be found in Gir. Camb., *Opera*, vol. iii., p. 244.

raises a question of grave difficulty, for the answer to which the data are few and uncertain. As late as the end of the seventeenth century, and perhaps even afterward, there is evidence of the survival of pagan ceremonies and notions.[1] Probably bardic traditions, which were maintained with considerable vitality, contributed to the continued existence of an ancient order of ideas, while the effect of the Norman-English gradual conquest and the loss of national independence clearly arrested the progress of the Welsh people. It is evident from the account given by Giraldus Cambrensis that even after large tracts of territory had been occupied by Norman invaders the Cymric people displayed powers intellectual and æsthetic of no mean order when measured by the general standard of Western Europe at the same time. The breaking up of their older social organisation, the troublous and almost continual warfare that took place down to the accession of Henry VII., appear to have reduced the great bulk of the Welsh-speaking people to a condition of intellectual torpor. The real Welsh aristocracy, who had been the leaders of the people and the fosterers of their literary development, gradually disappeared or became merged in the English upper classes. When, at the end of the Wars of the Roses, more peaceable times arrived, the condition of the Welsh-speaking people gradually improved, but it must be remembered it was chiefly the landowning class, as distinguished from the actual cultivators of the soil, that reaped the advantage of the comparatively friendly attitude of the Tudor monarchs to the Principality.

It is a curious fact that, so far as appears from the sources of information which we are able to command, the

---

[1] See Lecky, " History of England," ii., pp. 602-3 ; Paxton Hood, "Christmas Evans" (Lond. 1881), pp. 26 *et seq.* ; Edwin Sidney Hartland, ''The Legend of Perseus'' (3 vols., Lond. 1894-6),·i. 149, 176; ii. 167, 175-7, 197 n., 202, 229, 230, 290, 292-4, 299 n., 427.

Reformation produced, so far as the Welsh people were concerned, little or no popular excitement. The series of statutes which, from the lawyer's point of view, constituted the reformed Church, produced little movement of opinion in the Principality among the Welsh-speaking people. The aristocratic families for the most part appear to have remained at heart, if not in outward observance, Catholic ; but by the bulk of the population it seems that the events of the sixteenth century were practically unnoticed. There was no Welsh Pilgrimage of Grace, nor did the statutes for the dissolution of the lesser and greater monasteries and religious houses create any movement of an insurrectionary kind in the counties with which we are dealing. The property of these religious houses was bestowed upon laymen, many of whom were the descendants of the Norman invaders, for small sums of money which, even at that time, appear to have been hardly the market value of the lands in question. In all this, however, so far as we can ascertain, the Welsh-speaking people took little interest. They were plunged into a deep sleep from which even the civil wars and religious turmoil of the seventeenth century were only able very partially to arouse them.

A statute passed in the fifth year of Elizabeth (1562) had made provision for the translation into Welsh of the Bible and the Book of Common Prayer. Twenty-six years, however, elapsed before the work of translation and publication was completely accomplished. It was by the meritorious labours of Dr. William Morgan, afterwards Bishop of St. Asaph, assisted by other clergymen, that this great work was performed. The Church thus rendered an inestimable service to the cause of religion in Wales, and indirectly, as pointed out elsewhere, gave a new life to the language and literature of the country.[1]

[1] See below, p. 505. We ought to add it is Dr. Richard Parry's revised edition, published in 1620, that is the standard version. In 1546 a translation

The beginning of Nonconformity in Wales is usually associated with the names of William Wroth, William Erbury, and Walter Craddock, who, having been ejected from the Church, adopted an independent attitude, and became itinerant preachers throughout the country. The work of these men and others (such as Vavasour Powell, Morgan Llwyd, Hugh Owen, and James Owen) during the seventeenth century seems to have been very largely confined to the English side of Welsh life, that is to say, to the towns and more Anglicised portions of the Principality. We do not mean to ignore the fact that many of the Welsh Dissenting causes can trace their origin to the work of these active and earnest preachers, but simply to emphasise what appears to be the case, that the bulk of the Welsh-speaking population was untouched by their ministrations. So far as the outward legal organisation went, the position of the Church in its reformed condition was practically unaltered by the existence of a very considerable number of sporadic Nonconformist organisations, chiefly in South Wales, at the end of the seventeenth century.[1]

of the Lord's Prayer, the Ten Commandments, and the Creed, by Sir John Price, LL.D., was published. William Salesbury's translation of the New Testament appeared in 1567. Twenty-one years afterwards (1588) Morgan's translation of the Old Testament, with a revised edition of Salesbury's New Testament, was published. The first edition of Parry's revised translation was published in 1620, for the use of the churches, and in 1630 a new edition, more suitable or the use of families, was issued. For the lives of Price, Salesbury, Morgan, and Parry, see "Dict. Nat. Biog."; Rees' "History of Protestant Nonconformity in Wales" (Lond., 2nd ed. 1883), pp. 13 *et seq.*; "Bywyd ac Amserau yr Esgob Morgan," by C. Ashton (Treherbert, 1891).

[1] For accounts of the men here mentioned (except Wroth) see "Dict. Nat. Biog." and Rees' "History." As to the Act for the Propagation of the Gospel published in 1649, during the Commonwealth, and the controversy provoked by the proceedings of the Commissioners appointed under it, see Rees' "History," pp. 73 *et seq.* The Act is printed in the appendix to that work (p. 511). At least 106 ministers were ejected in Wales in consequence of the Act of Uniformity (1662). *Ibid.*, p. 153. The first organised Nonconformist church founded in Wales was the Independent cause at Lanvaches, which dates from 1639.

The fact appears to be that as a result of the historical circumstances rural Wales was at the commencement of the eighteenth century in a condition of extreme languor. What spiritual earnestness there was, apart from the instances of exceptional parishes and exceptional clergy-men of the Established Church, was due to the energy of Nonconformist (chiefly Baptist and Independent) itinerant preachers. The majority of the clergy of the Established Church contented themselves with a perfunctory dis-charge, in a somewhat listless and inadequate manner, of their spiritual duty. The services were held irregularly, preaching in Welsh was comparatively rare, and it is not too much to say that there was a general neglect on the part of the parochial clergy to inculcate the truth among their parishioners or to give practical instruction in regard to the conduct of life. The upper classes, speaking broadly, were virtually English, and in their manners and social habits reflected the prevailing condition of things in England. There can be no doubt that one of the principal difficulties was that created by the fact that in most of the rural parishes, except those of the border counties, the people habitually spoke the Welsh language. The stipends of the parochial clergy were so inadequate that the type of man who took orders and accepted the average Welsh living cannot, upon the most favourable construction, be deemed to have been cultured or efficient. We are not without some definite information as to the precise condition of things in the seventeenth century as well as in the eighteenth, and this information enables one to understand how it was that earnest and able men, throwing over the bonds of ecclesiastical discipline, were enabled to obtain a hold upon the affections and minds of their countrymen to the detriment of the more formal organisa-tion of the Established Church.

We will give two illustrations. First of all we will take

an extract from a report of an episcopal visitation made by Dr. Lewis Baily, Bishop of Bangor, in 1623 :—" Ɫlanfairpwɫlgwyngyɫl and Ɫlandyssilio.—There had been only two sermons in these places for the last twelve months, which were delivered by the rector, Sir (or Rev.) John Cadwalader. Penmon.—No sermon preached there five or six years last past. Ɫlandona.—No service here but every other Sunday. Ɫlangwyɫlog.—No sermons at all. Ɫlanddeussant and Ɫlanfairynghornwy.—The curate here is presented for not reading service in due time, for not reading of homilies, and for not registering christenings, weddings, and funerals. They had but three sermons since last Whitsuntide twelvemonth. He spent his time in taverns, was a public drunkard and brawler, quarrelling with his parishioners and others. Ɫlanfwrog and Ɫlanfaethlu.—But two sermons here these last twelve months." These remarks relate to parishes in Anglesey, but there are similar accounts in regard to Carnarvonshire, Merionethshire, Montgomeryshire. As to several places it is reported, "No sermons," or only two or three in the last twelve months. Of the clergyman at Aberdaron, in Carnarvonshire, it is complained that he neglected to bury a dead child, which lay uninterred from Saturday to Sunday, and that on one occasion when he came to the church he seemed drunk, and went straight from the service to the tavern.[1]

The next illustration is furnished by " A View of the State of Religion in the Diocese of St. David's, about the Beginning of the Eighteenth Century," by Dr. Erasmus Saunders, which was published in 1721, nearly a hundred years after the visitation of the diocese of Bangor, from the report of which we have quoted, had taken place. According to the account given by Dr. Saunders it appears that both

---

[1] See the " History of Protestant Nonconformity in Wales," by the Rev. Thomas Rees, D.D. (Lond. 1st edition 1861, 2nd edition 1883), p. 8.

the material and the spiritual condition of the Church in Wales was deplorable. He states that some churches were decayed and "do only serve for the solitary habitations of owls and jackdaws ; such are St. Daniel's, Castelhan, Kilvawyr, Mountain, Capel Colman, and others in Pembroke-shire ; Mount Llechryd, in Cardiganshire ; Aberllynog, in Breconshire ; Nelso, in Gower, Glamorganshire ; and others in Carmarthenshire. And it is not to be doubted, but as there are districts of land, so there were originally just endowments of tithes that did belong to all those several churches ; but, whatever they were, they are now alienated, the churches, most of them, demolished, the use for which they were intended almost forgotten, unless it be at Llanybrec, where, I am told, the impropriator or his tenant has let that church unto the neighbouring Dissenters, who are very free to rent it for the desirable opportunity and pleasure of turning a church into a conventicle. As the Christian service is thus totally disused in some places, there are other some that may be said to be but half served, there being several churches where we are but rarely, if at all, to meet with preaching, catechising, or administering of the Holy Communion. In others, the service of the prayers is but partly read, and that perhaps but once a month, or once in a quarter of a year. . . . The stipends are so small that a poor curate must some-times submit to serve three or four churches for 10*l.* or 12*l.* a year. . . . And now what Christian knowledge, what sense of piety, what value for religion, are we reasonably to hope for in a country thus abandoned, and either destitute of churches to go to or of ministers to supply them, or both ? Or how can it well consist with equity and conscience to complain of the ignorance and errors of an unhappy people in such circumstances ? They are squeezed to the utmost to pay their tithes and what is called the Church due (though, God knows, the Church is to expect little from it), and at the same time most miserably deprived of those benefits of religion which the payment of them was intended to support, and delivered up to ignorance and barbarity, which must be the certain consequence of driving away the ministers of religion, or of depressing or incapacitating them from their duty."[1]

We might easily multiply testimony to a similar effect as to the religious condition of the Principality.

Summing up the condition of things, we may say that there were an indifferent upper class, a clergy wretchedly paid, of low moral and spiritual type, and a people ignorant to the last degree cultivating the soil, for the most part unable to read and write, and habitually speaking a language unknown to their superiors ; the fabric of the churches in a large number of parishes had been suffered to go out of repair ; the discipline of the clergy was very lax ; the bishops were often non-resident pluralists ; there was a general neglect of Church services and administrations ; and, lastly, there was no zeal and enthusiasm for religion either among the clergy or their flocks. This condition of things, due to the historical causes operating for centuries in the Principality, was aggravated by the fact that the population was by race and language distinguished from those who ruled them, and still more by the fact that the bishops and other dignitaries of the Church who formed the more educated portion of the Welsh clergy exercised little control for good in their respective dioceses and spheres of influence.

We state these things not with a view to asserting that they have any necessary relevance in regard to modern controversy, but as statements of fact connected with the Church which tend to explain the rise of Noncon-

---

[1] See Saunders' "A View of the State of Religion in the Diocese of St. David's" (1721) ; Lecky, "History of England in the Eighteenth Century" (Lond. 1888), vol. ii., pp. 602-4.

formity in Wales upon a large and even extraordinary scale.

Now, such being the state of things in the Principality at the commencement of the eighteenth century, one might have expected that in days of comparative enlightenment the rulers of the Church would have attempted to cope with the ills and grievances that existed. Far from doing that, the policy of the ministers of the early Hanoverian sovereigns—a policy apparently acquiesced in without remonstrance in any effective degree by English archbishops and bishops—was one that ignored the special needs of the Principality, especially the necessity of supplying the Church in Wales with a clergy able to speak the Welsh language and to satisfy the spiritual requirements of the people. One would have thought that the dictates of self-interest, without considering higher motives, would have led the leaders of the Church party in England to encourage the education of the Welsh clergy, and to secure the appointment to office in the Principality of men who were able to preach and administer the sacraments in the Welsh language. It became, however, the apparently determined course of action of English ministers to appoint to the Welsh bishoprics and to the most lucrative offices connected with the Church, persons entirely ignorant of the Welsh language. Whether this was due to an intentional attempt to crush out Welsh, or whether it was due simply to ignorance of the condition of things in the Principality, and to a misunderstanding of the vitality of racial and linguistic conditions among a free people, we will not try to decide. Suffice it to say that from the time of George I. down to 1870 none of the bishops appointed to the four Welsh sees were able to preach effectively in Welsh, and, speaking broadly, the episcopate during that period was English and not Welsh, judged by whatever test one may be pleased to adopt. Most of the persons who accepted the Welsh bishoprics during the years to which we allude took their appointments simply with a view to further preferment. Of the six bishops appointed by George I. all were translated to English sees. George II. appointed twenty-one bishops, and fifteen were translated to England. During the reign of George III. twenty-three bishops were appointed to Welsh sees, and of these eleven were translated to England.

Another evil was clerical absenteeism. Some of the parochial clergy did not reside in their parishes, but the chief offenders were the bishops and dignitaries. The Bishops of Llandaff were absentees from 1706 to 1820, and similar, but not such gross, instances may be given in the case of other prelates.

But probably a still greater abuse was the system of pluralities. The most celebrated instance of the abuse of episcopal patronage in Wales is the case of Bishop Luxmoore, who was first of all Bishop of Hereford and was made Bishop of St. Asaph in 1815. He seems to have regarded his office as merely one of profit. The bishop himself had several clerical offices, but it was the exercise of his patronage and of his influence in favour of members of his own family that forms the principal indictment against him. The Rev. C. C. Luxmoore, his eldest son, was (1) Dean of St. Asaph (1,988*l.*) ; (2) Chancellor of St. David's (tithes 868*l.* with 400*l.* a year from fees) ; (3) Rector of Whitford (902*l.*) and Darowen (155*l.*) ; (4) in Hereford, Rector of Cradley (1,024*l.*) ; (5) Vicar of Bromyard (513*l.*) ; (6) of portion of Bromyard (1,400*l.*) ; (7) Prebendary of Hereford (50*l.*) ; (8) lessee of the manor of Landegle, belonging to the bishop and leased to him by his father ; (9) he had a lease of the tithes of Landegle (117*l.*) and of Landsa (651*l.*) for life from his father for 100*l.* a year. His total annual income, therefore, was 7,618*l.* commuted value, which was equal to 9,522*l.* non-commuted value ; also 450*l.* from other sources, total 9,972*l.*, or, deducting the 100*l.* for the lease, 9,872*l.*

The Rev. J. H. M. Luxmoore, another son, held (1) the sinecure rectory of Lan-yn-yâl (462*l.*) ; (2) the rectory of Marchwiail (636*l.*) ; (3) Morton Chapel (600*l.*) ; (4) Prebendary of Melford (65*l.*) ; (5) he had 200*l.* a year as joint registrar of Hereford Cathedral.

The Rev. C. Luxmoore, the bishop's nephew, received (1) the vicarage of Berriew (445*l.*) ; (2) the rectory of Lanymynech (385*l.*) ; and one Coryn Luxmoore received 300*l.* a year from Guilsfield. The total income from Church sources of the five Luxmoores, therefore, was about 25,225*l.*, and in contrast with this it may be mentioned that the working clergy of the diocese of St. Asaph received only 18,000*l.*[1]

It is unnecessary to multiply instances of abuses in connection with the Church system of the eighteenth and the earlier part of this century, as it actually worked, or to make further comments upon the matter. We have mentioned this case not with any hostility to the Church in its present more active condition, but in order that the causes which led to the predominance of Nonconformity in Wales may be understood.

The religious aspect presented by Wales at the commencement of the eighteenth century, so far, at any rate, as the rural districts where the Welsh-speaking population chiefly resided were concerned, may be compared to that of the Irish Church ; and the Church was utilised by the

---

[1] For these facts see Clarke's " History," cited above, p. 142 *et seq.* *Cf.* Spencer Walpole's " History of England," vol. i., p. 149. Luxmoore was an opponent of Romilly's attempts to amend the criminal law of the time. He is specially mentioned by S. Walpole as one of seven bishops "who thought it consistent with the principles of their religion to hang a man for shop-lifting." See his Hist., vol. ii., p. 133. It is said Majendie, Bishop of Bangor, held eleven parochial preferments (*ibid.*, vol. i., p. 153).

eighteenth century governments rather as a political machine than as a spiritual force. The inhabitants of the Welsh counties were divided into two classes very unequal in numbers : a landowning class, aristocratic in type, speaking for the most part the English language alone, in close touch with the same class in England, actuated by the same motives and imbued with the same prejudices ; and the other class chiefly cultivators of the soil, habitually speaking the Welsh language, retaining many views of life, ideas, and traditions belonging to an earlier stage of civilisation, lively in character, imaginative, quick in action, passionately devoted to music and country pursuits. Both classes appear to have been equally indifferent to religious duties, and unconcerned with those deeper problems of a philosophical and spiritual character which have occupied so large a part in the intellectual life of Wales since the revival to which we must now allude.

In 1735 there were only eight Nonconformist places of worship in North Wales ; in South Wales there were very numerous Nonconformist causes, some of them strong and flourishing, and most of them served by able and worthy ministers. But the Nonconformity characteristic of this earlier phase of the movement was of a type analogous to that of the Independency and Presbyterianism of the time of the Great Rebellion. Speaking broadly, it may be looked upon as the result of the spread of seventeenth century Puritanism in the Welsh counties, and, as we have stated above, it was mainly English rather than Welsh in its character, and affected rather the towns and the more English districts than those parts of the country which were distinctively Welsh. It is probable that the Welsh farmers and their families had hardly progressed intellectually as a class from the time of the Conquest. Every indication that we possess shows that hardly any one of

them could read or write, and it is clear that the provision
for education was of the scantiest possible description.
Wesley, writing some years after the description given by
Dr. Erasmus Saunders, to which we have referred, says that
the people were as ignorant as the Creek or Cherokee
Indians, and allowing for rhetorical exaggeration and
applying it to their culture rather than to their acquire-
ments as agriculturists, the phrase is probably true.

One is tempted to say that the intellect of the Cymry,
which had been active and progressive in the days of their
independence, became practically dormant and non-pro-
gressive with the loss of their cherished liberty. The effects
of the Conquest arrested their mental development, and
what progress there may have been was confined chiefly
to members of the landowning class, to whom, after the
accession of Henry VII., the colleges and universities of
England were thrown open, and in a less degree to the
inhabitants of the towns, who were enabled to take
advantage of the scanty and inefficient education afforded
by the grammar schools founded in some of the boroughs.
Of course some fortunate members of the tenant farming
or very small yeoman class under exceptional circumstances went to the English universities and carved out a
career for themselves in England. But from the people
as a whole hardly a voice comes during the centuries
from the Norman Conquest to the middle of the eighteenth
century. They tilled their land, attended to their flocks
and their herds, married and died in complete obscurity,
without being to any great degree touched by the intellectual
movements of the sixteenth and seventeenth centuries. It
is obvious that we have here all the elements nechssary for
a sudden intellectual and moral expansion. The renaissance
of Wales during the eighteenth century came, as might have
been expected, in the form of a religious revival which in
its intensity and its consequences can only be compared to

the analogous movement in Bohemia hundreds of years before, and the awakening of Scotland in the sixteenth century.

In 1730 the Welsh-speaking people were probably as a whole the least religious and most intellectually backward in England and Wales. By 1830 they had become the most earnest and religious people in the whole kingdom, and in the course of their development had created powerful Nonconformist bodies stronger than those to be found in any other part of the country, while the adherents of the Church had in the Welsh districts dwindled down to a comparatively small class. The Methodist revival which produced this striking result, and which in many respects resembled that which took place under Whitfield and Wesley in England, was commenced within the bounds of the Church. Its origin is usually associated with the name of Griffith Jones, of Llandowror, but it was Howell Harris and Rowlands, of Llangeitho, who carried the movement to a triumphant success. In the face of continual and violent persecution these men by their extraordinary preaching aroused the people from their lethargy. We need not give details of their methods, nor the steps by which the work was accomplished, but in order that the conditions under which it was carried on may be understood, and to illustrate the state of feeling at the time, we extract from an impartial and unimpeachable source the following facts as to Harris :—

"He seems to have given great provocation, and he certainly met with extreme hostility. He made it his special mission to inveigh against public amusements, and on one occasion during the races at Monmouth, when the ladies and gentry of the county were dining together in the Town Hall, under the presidence of a duke, H. Harris mounted a table which was placed against the window of a room where they were, and poured forth a fierce denunciation of the sinfulness of his auditors. The people and clergy were furious against him. I have already noticed how Seward, who was one of his companions, was killed by the mob. On one occasion a pistol was fired at H. Harris; on another he was beaten almost to death; again and again he was stoned with such fury that his escape appeared almost miraculous. He was repeatedly denounced from the pulpit. The clergymen were seen distributing intoxicating liquors among the mob to excite them. Another, who held no less a position than that of Chancellor of the diocese of Bangor, stirred up whole districts against him. Women in his congregation were stripped naked. Men were seized by the pressgangs, and some of his coadjutors had to fly for their lives."[1]

The movement was fortunate in its leaders. A series of great preachers continued the work of Harris and Rowlands. The example set by these men infused new energy into the earlier Nonconformist bodies, and in connection with them also a number of remarkable preachers, whose eloquence and skill in pulpit oratory have rarely, if ever, been equalled, arose to carry on the religious work of their denominations.[2] The result was that by the middle of this century a very large number of Nonconformist causes had been created in Wales, a powerful and efficient clergy had arisen, and the organisation of each denomination had been brought to a state of great efficiency. We are not for the moment concerned so much with the religious aspect of this movement as with its effect upon the character and capacity of the Welsh-speaking people, and its influence

[1] Lecky, "History of England," vol. ii., pp. 604-5.

[2] For the lives of the more important among the long list of Welsh preachers see Rees's "History." A good account of the characteristic methods of Welsh preaching will be found in Paxton Hood's "Christmas Evans" (Lond. 1881).

upon economic and social progress. By many persons unacquainted with the facts the whole revival is looked upon as one of those manifestations of dissent which have arisen from time to time to disturb the peace of an organised Christianity. It may be looked at in that light; it was no doubt a religious revival, but the moment its inner meaning is penetrated, the circumstances of its origin and its progress understood, it becomes apparent that it was a good deal more than that. It was, in fact, the new birth of a people. It would be going too far to say that it created a new national character—that, of course, was impossible; but it profoundly changed and strengthened the mental and moral qualities of the Welsh-speaking people. In the highly-strung and sensitive natures it produced a saintly type equal to any afforded by the literature or tradition of the Church. Among the people, who, as a whole, threw themselves into the movement, it developed intellectual powers which may have before existed, but which were only imperfectly utilised. It induced men who had never indulged in speculation to raise and to discuss fundamental religious and philosophic problems, and stimulated to an extraordinary degree the argumentative and imaginative faculties of a naturally quick-witted race.[1] It turned the attention of men to the art of oratory and to the capabilities of language.

[1] In support of this statement one of us can vouch for the following story. About thirty years ago an English professor of theology and a Welsh preacher were taking a morning walk in a very Welsh county, and sat down to rest awhile in a field. Near by two farm labourers, who were finishing their mid-day meal, were talking in Welsh. Their loud tones and excited gestures attracted the attention of the visitors. Said the Professor : "Are they quarrelling?" "Well," replied the Preacher, "they are not quarrelling more than is usual in a debate on a theological point. They are discussing the question whether Christ had two wills or one. The Monothelite controversy is revived." For the benefit of the professor the preacher translated the conversation as it proceeded, and the judgment of the former was that the arguments urged by each disputant were as subtle and absurd as any of those to be found in the old books.

Fortunately the Welsh translation of the Bible currently used is as good a specimen of Welsh pure and undefiled as the current English version is of the language of England. Practically every Welsh-speaking person became acquainted in a very high degree of familiarity with the text of the Scriptures ; and, lastly, it improved the general moral tone of the people, though perhaps it made them, when its results were quite fresh, take a somewhat one-sided view of life and of culture.

The principal result of the movement may be thus summed up : First, it was the chief agent in the preservation of the Welsh language. It is probable that but for the immense impetus given to the study and use of the Welsh language by reading the Welsh Bible and by listening to pulpit oratory it would have more and more tended to die out as the habitual language of the majority of the inhabitants of the whole of Wales. Secondly, it led to general and greater literary activity. This is shown by the increase, gradual but certain, of the number of books, in the early days chiefly of a religious character, published from time to time, and by the rise of Welsh periodical literature and Welsh journalism. Thirdly, it stimulated a demand for education. The necessity of a trained Nonconformist clergy became at a very early stage evident to the leaders of the movement, and theological seminaries and colleges were founded.[1] And this demand for an educated ministry in its turn gave rise to that general and spontaneous demand for education for all classes with which we deal in the next chapter. Fourthly, in a smaller degree, but still by no means ineffectively, it did what at an earlier date the Church generally had done for England and other parts of Western Europe. The Welsh Nonconformist clergy, placed under the very gravest disadvantages from the absence of all provision

[1] See as to the Welsh Theological Colleges p. 483, n. 1.

for any education in the Principality, and shut out from
the English colleges and universities by the tests there
imposed, triumphed over obstacles to a much larger extent
than is generally known.   It is true that even down to
the early years and middle of this century many of the
Welsh Nonconformist ministers were deficient in scholastic
attainments, and few, if any, could be described as
scholars in the strict sense of the term ; but in their
own special departments—in theology and philosophy,
and in regard to Welsh and even English literature—
many of them attained a high standard of knowledge.
In all cases their culture was so much higher than that
of the average farmer and labourer that their intercourse
with the latter on social occasions, quite apart from their
religious services, produced a most beneficial effect in
nearly every district.   Fifthly, it operated continually in
the direction of improved morality.   It is admitted
that there is no part of the country more law-abiding
and possessing a higher degree of immunity from crime
than the Welsh agricultural counties.   This must be very
largely attributed to the religious revival.   Lastly, it produced a great change in the Church itself.   No impartial
observer can fail to be struck with the immense improvement in the character of the clergy of the Established
Church in Wales.   In place of the negligent and generally
ignorant and incompetent clergy of the early part of the
eighteenth century there is to be found in Wales as active
and competent a body of parochial clergy as in any equal
area in England.   And it is to be observed that some of
the most distinguished among them are persons sprung
from Nonconformist families.   We will not discuss the
question whether the Church is developing its power and
influence at the expense of the Nonconformist bodies, or
whether the latter are declining in power.   We will content ourselves with saying that nothing we observe either

in the evidence or from sources of information opened
to us by our journeys in the Principality supports any
such inference.[1]

[1] Since about the middle of the century Welsh and English Nonconformists
have been brought into much closer touch. The high level of excellence
attained by Welsh pulpit orators has resulted in a considerable demand for the
services of Welshmen in English churches. Taking, for instance, the Independent denomination, and confining ourselves to men who have passed away,
we may mention the following instances of ministers who began their careers
in Welsh churches and afterwards became pastors of English causes :—Caleb
Morris, J. R. Kilsby Jones, and Thomas Jones of Swansea (see "Dict. Nat.
Biog."). Six bi-lingual preachers have been elected to the Chair of the
Congregational Union of England and Wales :—David Thomas, of Bristol
(1865) ; Thomas Jones, of Swansea (1871) ; Thomas Rees (1885) ; John
Thomas, of Liverpool (1885) ; Herber Evans, of Carnarvon (1892) ; and John
Morlais Jones, of Lewisham (1896).

CHAPTER XI.

THE EDUCATIONAL MOVEMENT.

IT would take an undue portion of the space at our command to attempt to trace fully the progress of education in the Principality, and we must content ourselves with only the very briefest statement of the way in which the present system has been established. It may be worth mentioning that in the century that elapsed between the conquest of North Wales and the rebellion of Owain Glyndwr, a considerable number of Welshmen seem to have gone to Oxford, but in the disastrous period that followed its suppression this influx seems practically to have ceased. Glyndwr himself, as is evident from a letter of his addressed from Pennal to the king of France in 1405,[1] projected the establishment of two universities in Wales, and Henry VII. (according to a Welsh bard of the period) promised to establish a Welsh university in Neath Valley ; but though the dreams of Glyndwr and the promises of Henry Richmond remained unfulfilled, the accession of the latter marked the commencement of an important period in the social and educational progress of the Welsh people. The attitude of the Tudor monarchs towards the

---

[1] See Wylie's "History of the Reign of Henry IV.," v. ii., pp. 313-4, where an account of the negotiations between O. Glyndwr and Charles VI. of France is given. In a letter dated March 31st, 1406, from Pennal, Glyndwr suggested that two universities should be established, one in North and the other in South Wales, the exact places to be determined afterwards.

Principality was distinctly encouraging and friendly, and with the advent of a period of peace after the battle of Bosworth Field, the Welsh people found themselves able to take advantage with comparative ease of the educational institutions of England. The Universities of Oxford and Cambridge, and the schools which had been in the Tudor or at an earlier period established, were in a large measure thrown open to the sons of the Welsh gentry and, in some instances, of the actual cultivators of the soil.

In the sixteenth and seventeenth centuries a considerable number of grammar schools were founded in the towns of Wales, and gradually attracted to them a large number of distinctly Welsh pupils. It must be borne in mind that one of the features of Welsh society from the time of Edward I., down to the Reformation, was the marked distinction between the people of the towns and the country districts. The towns were for the most part more English than Welsh, while it was in the country districts that the Welsh-speaking people were numerous. The distinction between the Englisherie and the Welsherie found in the borough charters and the oppressive legislation of the fifteenth century long continued, especially in the marches bordering upon the English counties. From the time of the accession of Henry VII. it gradually disappeared, and towns which had been practically Norman-English garrisons slowly became markedly Welsh; but for a long time traces of the older order of things remained, and it was not difficult, even at the commencement of the century, to find a market town almost entirely English, while the surrounding country was occupied by people who habitually spoke the Welsh language. The grammar schools established after the Reformation in accordance with the policy of the reformed church, no doubt, were attended not only by the sons of the town burgesses, but also by the sons of yeomen and

small landowners, though probably it was only exceptionally that the Welsh-speaking people availed themselves
of the opportunities thus afforded. The foundation of
grammar schools was in the main associated with the
Established Church, and they were carried on under its
auspices. The country districts were entirely neglected,
and down to the time of the religious revival of the
eighteenth century, it is hardly too strong to state that
no opportunity was afforded to the great majority of the
Welsh-speaking people for the education of their children.
All accounts show that the condition of the Welsh people
in regard to education was most lamentably backward
down to comparatively recent times, but especially so until
the time of the religious revival.

The foundation of a Welsh university was the subject of
a correspondence between Oliver Cromwell and Richard
Baxter,[1] whilst a remarkable attempt was made in the
latter part of the seventeenth century to provide instruction in Wales in the English tongue, and to circulate the
Bible, the Common Prayer, and other books in the Welsh
language. The Rev. Thomas Gouge, son of Dr. William
Gouge, with the assistance of Dr. Tillotson (first Dean
and afterwards Archbishop of Canterbury), Dr. Stilling-
fleet, and many others, formed a voluntary society for this
purpose, and considerable funds were collected in pursuance
of that object. The society, with the assistance of Gouge
and of James Owen, who ultimately became a Nonconformist minister, did a very large amount of good educational work in Wales, and, according to the funeral sermon
of Gouge, preached by Dr. Tillotson, by the exertions of
the society there were every year eight hundred, sometimes
a thousand, poor children educated, while a " new and very
fair impression " of the Scriptures and Liturgy of the Church
of England was distributed. The work of this society was

---

[1] See " Wales," vol. iii., pp. 121–4 (March, 1896).

to some extent carried on in Wales by the Society for Promoting Christian Knowledge. As early as 1701 the attention of this then new society was directed to Wales. It decided in 1707 to set up lending libraries in the Principality, and in 1711 a supply of books to furnish four such libraries was sent to Carmarthen, Cowbridge, Bangor, and St. Asaph.

The next considerable movement in this direction took place under the influence of the Rev. Griffith Jones, Vicar of Landowror, in Carmarthenshire, who was admitted a corresponding member of the society in 1713. It was in the year 1730 that this eminent divine opened at Landowror the first circulating school. By 1738 thirty-seven circulating schools had been established by his agency in South Wales, in which 2,400 persons received instruction, and by 1739 the number in North and South Wales had risen to seventy-one, wherein 3,989 persons were taught. In 1746 the number of the schools of Griffith Jones had risen to 116, and in 1760 to 215. The system according to which this movement was carried on was, as the name " circulating school " implies, itinerant ; the schools were only carried on for a short time each year at one place, and the manner of instruction was chiefly catechetical. The instruction in the schools was not confined to children, and it appears that in many of them quite two-thirds of the pupils were adult men and women, and most of the masters taught for three or four hours in the evening, after school time, very many who could not attend during the day. At the time of the death of Griffith Jones in 1761 these schools appear to have increased in number to 218, and as many as 10,000 persons are said to have been taught to read in a single year. The schools were continued until 1779-80, when, owing to a dispute respecting the funds which had been bequeathed by Griffith Jones for the carrying on of the schools, and consequent litigation, they were closed for many years. The charity came again into operation in 1809, under a scheme made under the direction of the Court of Chancery on the 11th July, 1807.[1]

In the meantime, however, Sunday schools, as a means not only of religious instruction, but of elementary secular education, had originated and spread to Wales, chiefly under the influence of Thomas Charles of Bala. These schools introduced into Wales by Charles quickly spread over the whole Principality, and are now carried on in connection with the Established Church as well as with the various Nonconformist bodies. It is unnecessary for our purpose to detail the efforts of a voluntary kind made by the National Society and the British Society for elementary education in Wales during the first half of this century, but, as the report of the Commissioners appointed in 1846 clearly shows, these efforts, creditable though they were, were wholly inadequate having regard to the increase of population and the exigencies of modern times. At the present moment the public educational system of Wales is equal to that established in any part of the Empire, and is the result partly of a general movement throughout the whole kingdom, but in a still larger degree its completeness and success are due to the spontaneous desire for education among the Welsh people themselves. The modern educational movement originated among the Welsh-speaking people largely as an indirect result of the religious revival which we have described in outline in the preceding chapter, aided (as it undoubtedly was) by the literary renaissance of the early part of the century, and, so far as education other than that of the public elementary schools is concerned, has been principally fostered by

---

[1] For a fuller account of the movements summarised in this paragraph, see "Wales," by Sir Thomas Phillips (Lond., 1849), ch. 7, pp. 247–314. See, too, Lecky, "Hist. of Engl. in the Eighteenth Century," ii., pp. 603–4.

the remarkable sacrifices made by all classes of persons in Wales. Even before 1846 the spread and success of Nonconformity had resulted in the formation of seminaries chiefly designed for the education of persons intending to become Nonconformist ministers, to whom the grammar schools of Wales and the universities of England were closed by reason of the imposition of religious tests.[1]

[1] For an account of the principal seminaries, see Rees's "Protestant Nonconformity in Wales" (Lond., 2nd ed., 1883), c. 8. The earliest Nonconformist Academy was that at Brynllwarch, near Bridgend, Glamorganshire, started soon after 1662. Its founder was Samuel Jones, M.A., for some time tutor at Jesus College, Oxford (see *sub nom.*, "Dict. Nat. Biog."). It was on his death moved to Abergavenny, but it was afterwards removed to the neighbourhood of Bridgend, and the Rev. Rees Price, the father of Dr. Richard Price, of London (as to whom see *sub nom.*, "Dict. Nat. Biog."), for some years presided over it. After some vicissitudes the institution was transplanted to Haverfordwest, and thence to Carmarthen. It was not a corporate body, and its constitution was entirely uncertain. Such as it was, it was dissolved in 1794 ; but a voluntary theological school, which traces its origin to the earlier academy, was re-established at Carmarthen in 1795, and still exists as the "Presbyterian College, Carmarthen." We give these particulars because this institution is directly connected with the work of Samuel Jones, and is open to all Protestant Nonconformists. The Theological Colleges recognised by the University of Wales under its statutes are : The Theological College, Bala ; the Baptist College, Bangor ; the Congregational College, Bangor ; the Memorial College, Brecon ; the Baptist College, Cardiff ; the Presbyterian College, Carmarthen ; the Baptist College, Aberystwyth ; St. David's College, Lampeter ; the Calvinistic Methodist College, Trevecca. (See Statute x., and Standing Order viii. ; Calendar of the University of Wales, 1898 (Newport), p. 47.) The Brecon Memorial College may justly claim to be an offshoot of Samuel Jones's Academy. Its existence as a separate institution dates from 1755, when it was established at Abergavenny. After several changes in the locality of its work, it settled at Brecon in 1836. (Rees's "History," pp. 495. 497 ; "Album Aberhondu," edited by the Rev. T. Stephens, B.A. (Merthyr Tydfil, 1898).) The Baptist College, Cardiff, was founded in 1807 at Abergavenny, transferred to Pontypool in 1836, and thence to Cardiff quite recently. There was an earlier Baptist seminary established at Trosnant, near Pontypool, about 1732, which carried on work for many years. (Rees's "History," p. 504; "Hanes Athrofeyd y Bedyddwyr yn Sir Fynwy," by the Rev. J. Rufus Williams (Aberdare, 1863).) The organised Calvinistic Methodist Colleges are of later date, as the denomination separated formally from the Church of England only as late as 1811. By its charter the Welsh University has the power of conferring degrees in the faculty of Theology or Divinity (Art. xiv., 7), and has exercised it. Grave fears were entertained that in the divided state of public opinion on matters

It is unnecessary for us to detail the history of these institutions, but we must advert for a moment to the Commission appointed on the 1st October, 1846, in pursuance of proceedings in the House of Commons on the motion of Mr. William Williams of the 10th March preceding, for an address praying her Majesty to direct an inquiry to be made into the state of education in the Principality of Wales, especially into the means afforded to the labouring classes of acquiring a knowledge of the English language.[1] The Committee of Council on Education appointed three Commissioners (Mr., now Lord Lingen, Mr. Henry Robert Vaughan Johnson, and the late Mr. Jelinger Cookson Symons). The Commissioners appointed as assistants a certain number of gentlemen possessing a knowledge of the Welsh language, and conducted their inquiry between the middle of October, 1846, and the end of the summer of 1847, and their reports were published separately before the close of that year. Incidentally they contain a considerable quantity of material which illustrates the conditions of the agricultural population at the time. It does not appear that the Commissoners went beyond the topics included within the scope of their inquiry by the remarks which they thought

of religious profession serious difficulty might arise in this faculty. In fact, this has not been the case. The Court (the legislative and executive authority of the University) established the faculty of Divinity by Statute xxiii., and created a Theological Board (Statute xxi.) on a representative basis. The duties of the Board are to recommend to the Court schemes of study in the faculty, the names of examiners, and to report on other matters. Such has been the admirable spirit displayed by all connected with the University from the first that nearly every form of Christian belief has been and is represented on the Board. Under its advice regulations for the B.D. and D.D. degrees have been made, upon which the only criticism has been that the standard of learning which they postulate is high.

[1] The motion for the inquiry was made in 1846 by William Williams (b. 1798 ; d. 1865), who was M.P. for Coventry, 1835–1847, and Lambeth, 1850–63. He was a generous supporter of the Welsh educational movement. See App. to Report, p. 43.

fit to make upon the moral and religious condition of the
people, but their observations aroused considerable controversy in Wales, and were widely challenged by representative
men of all shades of opinion.[1] It was, perhaps, unfortunate
that they did not confine themselves more strictly to the
educational questions with which they were primarily
directed to deal. The inquiry became known among
Welsh people as " The Treason of the Blue Books" (*Brâd
y Lyfrau Gleision*). For a time the cause of Welsh education may have been prejudiced by the introduction of
sectarian and social questions into their reports, but, on
the whole, the very fact that attention was drawn to the
state of education in Wales in a very forcible manner was
ultimately productive of good. It is hardly too much to
say that the chief event in the special history of Wales
during the last fifty years has been the modern educational
movement which has culminated in the system now existing,
and which may be traced directly to the agitation produced
by the observations of these Commissioners.

We must content ourselves with a very brief account
of what has taken place. Dealing first with elementary
education, we may mention that the report of the Commissioners of 1846 disclosed the very greatest inadequacy
in the provision for elementary schools. There were a
certain number of schools in receipt of a share in the
education grant, but in many parishes there was no school
at all, except a merely voluntary school started as a private
adventure. To some extent the opposition of the leaders
of the Nonconformist organisations to the receipt of money

---

[1] The Reports were criticised by Dr. Lewis Edwards in *Y Traethodydd*
for 1848 ; by the Rev. Evan Jones (Ieuan Gwynedd)—some of whose essays
were republished under the title of " The Dissent and Morality of Wales," by
the Rev. William Rees (Gwilym Hiraethog) in *Yr Amserau ;* and by Mr.
Henry Richard, afterwards M.P. for Merthyr, in a lecture. See Mr. Lleufer
Thomas' notes and analysis of the Reports in App. to the Report, pp. 43
et seq.

from the Government for educational purposes (*i.e.*, purposes looked on as quasi-religious) retarded the spread of "British" schools and the securing for Wales of the benefits of the Government grant. There was a gradual improvement down to 1870, when the Education Act was passed. In no part of the country has that Act been productive of more beneficial results than in Wales, and it may be observed that in proportion to the population there are a greater number of school boards than in any other part of England and Wales. The system at work is, so far as elementary education is concerned, assimilated to that of England in nearly every respect.

One of the great difficulties of education in Wales discovered by the educational reformers was the want of adequately equipped teachers speaking the Welsh language. Mr. Symons reported that "the meagre prospect of income which presents itself to a schoolmaster in Wales deters all but those whom poverty or want of activity compel to have recourse to so unenviable a status for their means of livelihood." At that time (1846) only one normal school existed in Wales, and that owed its establishment to the efforts of the Rev. Henry Griffiths, of Brecknock, aided by a few other friends of education. This school appears to have been established under the mastership of Evan Davies, M.A., LL.D. in 1846, and was afterwards transferred to Swansea, where, however, it lost its character as a normal school, and was continued for many yea s as a secondary school where many Welshmen who have subsequently distinguished themselves received their education. In 1862 there was established at Bangor a normal college for the training of male teachers for elementary schools in Wales, and the last few years have witnessed the development of training schools or colleges, both for male and female teachers, which are now worked under the auspices of the university colleges recently established. During the same period Church training colleges for school teachers were established at Carmarthen and Carnarvon, the latter being subsequently removed to Bangor. In 1849 Mr. (afterwards Sir) Hugh Owen addressed meetings of school teachers and educationists at Bangor on the importance of establishing a connecting link between the elementary schools and higher places of education. This led to the formation of the North Wales Scholarship Association, which was wound up on the passing of the Intermediate Education Act, after awarding upwards of 3,000*l.* in scholarships on the results of examinations at different centres.

Turning to intermediate education—that is to say, to the kind of education preliminary to higher or university education—there appears to have been a gradual improvement from the middle of the century down to the time of the passing of the Intermediate Education (Wales) Act, 1889, which has since resulted in a complete system of secondary education. Fresh energy was infused into the grammar schools, their constitutions were in many instances improved, and the character of the teaching changed very greatly for the better. In the meantime the movement for higher or university education had outstripped that for the improvement of intermediate education, and the establishment of three university state-aided colleges at once disclosed the necessity for a further improvement in the character of the education given at the middle-class and grammar schools. For it was found when the colleges began their work that the pupils who came to them at the age of sixteen, or even later, were in most instances hardly fit to enter upon university studies. Attention being thus directed in a pressing manner to the defects of the provision for secondary education, the Intermediate Education Act of 1889 was passed. This Act provided for the levying of a ½*d.* rate in the Welsh counties by the then recently constituted county councils, and for the appointment of joint education

committees in every county, who were to be charged with
the duty of preparing schemes utilising existing educational
endowments and buildings, and, where necessary, supplementing them by the establishment of new schools of a
public character to be carried on under county governing
bodies constituted under each scheme.   Schemes under this
Act have now been passed for every county, or nearly every
county, in the Principality.

It was found as the system was being gradually
developed that for many purposes it would be expedient
for the county governing bodies to combine to a greater
or less extent for the carrying on of their work, especially in
regard to using any general funds that might be available
for scholarships and exhibitions, and for the purpose of
inspection and examination of the intermediate schools ; and
accordingly it was proposed that a Central Board for intermediate education, controlling in some degree the action
of the different county governing bodies, should for those
purposes be established.   A contribution of 500*l.* a year was
promised by the Treasury.   Ultimately the scheme for
establishing a Central Board was laid before Parliament,
and was, in the course of the session of 1896, passed.[1]

We turn now to higher or university education.   At the
commencement of the century there was no college giving
real university education in Wales.   A certain number of
theological colleges or seminaries had, as we have seen,
been established in connection with the Nonconformist
bodies, but from want of means and an inadequate
conception of education they could hardly be considered
as institutions of university rank.   The Established Church,

[1] The Central Board was constituted in the course of 1897.   Mr. A. C.
Humphreys-Owen was elected chairman ; Principal Viriamu Jones, F.R.S.,
vice-chairman ; and Mr. Owen Owen, M.A., chief inspector.   For a fuller
account of the Welsh system of intermediate education and its history, see
vol. ii., p. 1, of "Special Reports on Educational Subjects," issued by the
Education Department, 1898 (c. 8943).

which, as we have pointed out above, had sunk in the early years of the eighteenth century to a low condition in point of spiritual energy and practical power, had under the influence of the evangelical revival in Wales and England considerably strengthened its position, largely, no doubt, stimulated by the formation of a Calvinistic Methodist organisation, and by the immense increase of Nonconformity. One of the principal needs of the Church at that time was the securing of an adequate supply of Welsh-speaking clergymen with a proper range of theological learning and general culture. Among all classes of Welshmen this need was felt, and, it appears, it was in regard to the necessity of training young men for the Christian ministry that the idea of equipping the Principality with institutions giving higher education originated. It was under the influence of this impulse that St. David's College, Lampeter, avowedly intended to be associated with the national Church, was founded in the year 1827 and incorporated in 1828. By charters granted in 1852 and 1865 it was empowered to confer the degrees of B.D. and B.A. upon its students.

Nothing further of an important character was done in the direction of higher education for many years in Wales, though the equipment of the theological colleges was gradually improved ; but the general controversy about education led to the suggestion in 1853 that a national university, open to all, without distinction of creed, should be founded. Mr. B. T. Williams (barrister-at-law, afterwards judge of county courts) wrote an essay in which the claims of Wales to a university were ably set forth. In the next year a meeting of London Welshmen, in conjunction with representatives of different interests in the Principality, took place in London, and among those who were present at this memorable gathering were Mr. Hugh Owen, the Rev. Henry Rees, Mr. (afterwards Sir) George Osborne Morgan, the Rev.

Richard Humphreys, Dr. David Charles, Dr. Lewis Edwards of Bala, Mr. Richard Davies (afterwards Lord-Lieutenant of Anglesey), and Mr. Enoch Gibbon Salisbury. To the interchange of opinion at this and similar meetings held about that time, and a little later, may be traced the origin of most of the modern developments of the Welsh educational system. The idea of a university did not take definite form till several years had elapsed, but the movement initiated by these gentlemen led, as we have seen, to the establishment of the Bangor Normal College in 1862, which, in its turn, led to a further development.

Mr. George Osborne Morgan and Mr. Morgan Lloyd, in 1863, convened a conference upon the general subject of Welsh education on the 1st December in that year at the Freemasons' Tavern, London. The meeting was held under the presidency of Mr. William Williams, M.P. for Lambeth, and subscriptions for considerable amounts were promised by those interested in the subject. Resolutions in favour of establishing a university were passed, and an executive committee appointed. Dr. Nicholas (who had read a paper on the subject at the Swansea National Eisteddfod a few months previously) was made secretary, under the control of Mr. Osborne Morgan and Mr. Hugh Owen as hon. secretaries. Mr. Williams, M.P., accepted the office of treasurer, and Mr. Morgan Lloyd that of sub-treasurer. Dr. Nicholas acted as secretary until 1867, when he was succeeded by Dr. Charles, who held the post until 1871.

Negotiations then took place with Dr. Perowne, Vice-Principal of St. David's College, for the establishment of an unsectarian university college in combination with his college. Differences, however, as might naturally have been expected, arose, and the executive committee were obliged to pass a resolution on June 16th, 1864, that further consideration of that " which appears to us an admirable arrangement " should be deferred. At the same time the executive committee prosecuted with the utmost energy during the following year the carrying out of the scheme for a Welsh university. No opportunity was lost by these energetic and patriotic men of enlightening public opinion upon the matter and enlisting every interest on behalf of the proposed institution. The original idea of the executive committee was the establishment of a degree-giving university, but as the movement more and more took practical shape, it was seen that the best way of attaining this was in the first instance to secure the foundation of a college giving university education of a high standard, whose students should be encouraged to graduate at the University of London.

The efforts of the executive committee being concentrated upon this definite object, from 1865 to 1872 it made frequent appeals to people of all classes in the Principality, or those connected with Wales, for funds. From 1871 until his death Sir Hugh Owen acted as secretary and organiser, and gave up all his time to the work. Buildings at Aberystwyth were secured for 10,000*l.*, and the college was opened under the principalship of Dr. Thomas Charles Edwards, assisted by two professors, in the following year (1872). The balance of the amount collected (about 12,000*l.* in all), after payment of the purchase-money, was applied to the completion of the buildings and the maintenance of the staff until 1874, when a new fund was created by congregational and house-to-house collections, local committees being organised for the purpose in North and South Wales. The middle and working classes, especially the tenant farmers, contributed most nobly in proportion to their means, while generous contributions were made in London. For ten years the institution received no grant or aid from the Treasury. The contributions of the Welsh people to a college which they learnt to look upon as national were cordially continued, and it is calculated that in all some 60,000*l.* were found by the Welsh people.

The foundation of the college had the result of exposing the inadequacy of the provision for intermediate education, and ultimately the leaders of the movement induced the Government in 1881 to appoint a committee to inquire into the condition of intermediate and higher education in Wales. The committee was presided over by Lord Aberdare, and with him were associated Viscount Emlyn, M.P., the Rev. Prebendary Robinson, the late Mr. Henry Richard, M.P., Professor Rhỳs, and Mr. (now Sir) Lewis Morris. After taking evidence very exhaustively, the committee reported on the 18th August, 1881. In their report they explained the then condition of intermediate and higher education in Wales, summarised the evidence as to its educational requirements and the suggestions offered as to the way in which they should be met, recommended the reorganisation of the Welsh endowed schools, and the formation of additional schools. It is unnecessary for us to go into the details of the report. In regard to higher education the committee said : " We have no hesitation in avowing our conviction that colleges of this kind (provincial colleges) which have been recently founded in many of the larger towns of England, are desirable in the circumstances of Wales, and would be found conducive to the advancement of higher education in the country. Amongst a people like the Welsh, who, though defective in regular scholastic training, have a natural turn for some forms of literary culture and self-improvement, such institutions would tend to stimulate the desire for more advanced education by providing opportunities for obtaining it under the conditions most suited to the position and requirements of the nation. The experience of the University College at Aberystwyth, where various adverse causes have operated, must not be taken as conclusive against the success of such colleges in Wales." They recommended that for the present only one college in addition to that already existing should be provided, the establishment of that college in Glamorganshire; and that either Aberystwyth College should be retained, or re-established in North Wales at Carnarvon or Bangor. In regard to the constitution of the colleges they expressed the opinion that they should be adapted to the circumstances of the country, that science and modern languages should occupy a prominent place, that they should be unsectarian, and that their benefits should be accessible to women. As to the question of a degree-conferring university they reported that, notwithstanding certain drawbacks and difficulties, the existence of a Welsh university would almost certainly exercise a beneficial influence on higher education in Wales, and they suggested the extension of the charters of St. David's College, Lampeter, to the other colleges.

The recommendations of this important report have been given effect to in almost every particular. In 1882 an annual grant of 4,000*l.* was given to Aberystwyth College,[1] but difficulties arose as to the adoption by North Wales of the college at Aberystwyth as the North Welsh College, and ultimately it was decided to establish a college at Bangor, in Carnarvonshire, while in South Wales immediate steps were taken for the foundation of the proposed college in Glamorganshire. A grant of 4,000*l.* to each college was promised by the Treasury, and generous contributions to both were made by all classes of the community throughout the Principality. The site of the South Wales College was a matter of dispute between Cardiff and Swansea, and ultimately was fixed at Cardiff,

[1] The relation of the Aberystwyth College to the Treasury was special. In 1882 a grant of 4,000*l.* was accorded ; but on the establishment of the college at Bangor in 1884, this was transferred to that body, but a separate grant of 2,500*l.* was given to Aberystwyth. In 1885 the grant was raised to 4,000*l.* ("Reports from University Colleges," etc., Education Department, 1897, c. 8530.)

by the award of Lord Carlingford, Lord Bramwell, and Mr. Mundella, to whom the dispute was 'referred. The college was started at Cardiff in the year 1883, and the North Wales College (by the award of the same arbitrators as between thirteen competing towns) at Bangor in 1884. A petition had been duly presented for a charter for the establishment of the college at Cardiff, and such a charter was granted by her Majesty on the 7th October, 1884. Somewhat similar charters were granted to Bangor College on the 4th June, 1885, and to Aberystwyth College on the 10th September, 1890.

The establishment of the three colleges has been amply justified, and the number of students has steadily increased at each institution.[1] It was, of course, natural that when the three colleges came into working order the demand for a degree-granting national university, which had never been lost sight of, should be revived. It was at a meeting of the Cymmrodorion section of the National Eisteddfod, which met in London in August, 1887, that the first definite step

---

[1] According to the " Blue Book " of the Education Department, published in 1901, containing reports from the University Colleges (1901, cd. 845), the number of students pursuing regular courses of study in the Welsh Colleges for the session 1899–1900 was as follows :—

Aberystwyth	437
Bangor	305
Cardiff	568

In October, 1901, the number at Aberystwyth was 474.

The figures only deal with university students. Cardiff College, however, works in connection with the County Councils of Cardiff, Glamorganshire, and Monmouthshire. The number of students in attendance at the technical school of the county borough of Cardiff was 2,716 in 1895–6. According to the " Report of the Principal of Cardiff College for 1897–8," the number of regular students had risen to 470, and we understand there was an increase for the same session in the other colleges. In addition to the faculties of Arts and Science, Cardiff has established departments in Medicine, Engineering, and Mining and Metallurgy, while Bangor and Aberystwyth have established Agricultural departments. (See " Report," pp. 801–810, and Principal Reichel's observations quoted on p. 816.) Day training departments have been founded at all three colleges.

was taken. The late Principal Viriamu Jones, of Cardiff, opened a discussion on Welsh education with a paper in which, among other things, he advocated the formation of a degree-granting university to crown the "educational edifice." He pointed out that without university organisation it was impossible to have a well-arranged educational system, and that the efficient development of all grades of education in Wales was bound up with the foundation of a properly constituted university, which, he urged, would order the scattered and disconnected results of previous action as a magnet arranges the iron filings within its field of force. The views advanced met with immediate acceptance. The Cymmrodorion section passed the following resolution, which was proposed by Professor John Rhŷs and seconded by Mr. (now Sir) Lewis Morris : " That it is the opinion of this meeting that definite action should be taken to impress on her Majesty's Government the desire of the Welsh people for the establishment of a Welsh university." And it was further resolved, " That in the opinion of this meeting a conference of the representatives of colleges, intermediate schools, and elementary schools should be summoned in a convenient place in the near future, and that the Society of Cymmrodorion be requested to take the initiative in convening it."

The conference was summoned by the Cymmrodorion Society to meet at Shrewsbury in January, 1888, and in due course the conference was held, under the presidency of Professor Rhŷs. It was resolved, " That in the opinion of this conference it is expedient that the provision for intermediate and collegiate education in Wales and Monmouthshire should be completed by a univers ty organisation, and that the inspection of State-aid d intermediate schools should be committed to the Welsh university, due provision being made for the representation of such schools on its executive body; that the

executive committee should be requested to make arrangements to enable the members of the conference to meet
the Welsh peers and the members of Parliament for
Wales and Monmouthshire at an early date." This
conference with members of Parliament took place on
the 16th March, 1888.

At a meeting of the Court of Governors of the Bangor
College on the 27th April, 1888, the following resolution (the
late Earl of Powis being in the chair) was passed, after much
discussion, on the motion of the Rev. Ellis Edwards,
seconded by Professor Rhys : "That the Courts of
Governors or the Councils of Aberystwyth and Cardiff
Colleges be invited to appoint four (subsequently increased
to seven) representatives each, to meet an equal number
appointed by this court, to formulate a draft charter for a
degree-conferring university." In the early part of July in
the same year, a conference so constituted assembled in
London and passed the following resolutions : "That this
meeting, representing the three Welsh university colleges,
is of opinion that the time has come when these colleges
should conjointly apply to the Government for a charter
for the establishment of the University of Wales ; " and
"That an application be made to the Government for a
charter to constitute a university for Wales on the same
general lines as the charter already granted to the Victoria
University, with such modifications as may be required by
the peculiar conditions and circumstances of Wales." In
the course of discussion some differences of opinion revealed
themselves, but the above resolutions having been passed it
was decided to present them to the Lord President of the
Council, and they were accordingly submitted on July 15th.
Nothing further, however, was done for some time, chiefly
owing to the divergent ideas as to the character of the
university, to which allusion has been made, and it was felt
by those concerned that it was best to allow opinion to

form itself by continual discussion, with a view, if possible, of arriving at practical unanimity.[1]

At a meeting of the Court of Governors of the Bangor College on April 1st, 1891 (Mr. Wm. Rathbone, M.P., in the chair), the following resolution was carried, on the motion of the Rev. Ellis Edwards, seconded by the Lord Bishop of St. Asaph:—" That a committee be appointed by this court to consider again the means of obtaining a degree-conferring University of Wales; and to deliberate upon this question, with, if possible, similar committees appointed by Aberystwyth and Cardiff Colleges, and with the joint education committees of North and South Wales; and to report the result of its deliberations at the next half-yearly meeting of the court." The conference so constituted met on November 8th of the same year at Shrewsbury, and it was found that the effect of deliberation during the preceding two years and a half had resulted in the general conclusion that the university ought to be a teaching university in the sense that no candidate should be admitted to a degree unless he should have pursued a course of study at one of the colleges of the university, and it was also resolved to appoint a committee to prepare the outlines of a draft charter. The committee met many times in the course of 1892, and as a result were able to present in a series of clauses the substance of the proposed charter to a conference which met on January 6th, 1893, and after full discussion, and with slight alteration, it was adopted by that body. In the framing of this, the original draft, a very large part of the work fell upon the three principals of the national colleges, the late Principal Viriamu Jones, Principal Reichel and Principal Roberts, and Dr. Isambard Owen, but they had the benefit of efficient

[1] The chief difference of opinion was on the question whether the university should be a teaching university or an examining Board, constituted on the lines of the then University of London.

assistance from many men whose names we cannot here record.[1]

In the meantime Mr. Acland, Vice-President of the Council in the Government newly formed in 1892, who had for some years specially associated himself with the Welsh educational movement, appointed Mr. O. M. Edwards, M.A., of Lincoln College, Oxford, to report on the condition of the colleges in relation to the proposition for the creation of a university.   Mr. O. M. Edwards duly made his report, and though it has not been made public, we may assume that it represented that the case for a degree-granting university for Wales had been made out, from the fact that when the petition was presented by the Draft Charter Committee to the Privy Council, it met with ready acquiescence.   The instructions for the charter having been approved of by the conference of January, 1893, the preparation of the formal document was left to Dr. Isambard Owen in conjunction with Mr. David Brynmor-Jones, Q.C., M.P., and Mr. Cadwaladr Davies, while Mr. Maynard Owen undertook to act as honorary solicitor to the petitioners.   In February and March, 1893, the charter was drafted in general accordance with the instructions laid before counsel.   It was then submitted to a representative conference, held in London in the latter month, and presided over by Lord Aberdare. After prolonged discussion it was adopted with slight alterations.   A petition for the granting of a university charter in the terms of the draft thus settled was presented in the names of the three University Colleges to the Privy Council ; the prayer of the petitioners, notwithstanding an adverse petition from St. David's College, was acceded to, and the charter as settled, with however an additional clause, was laid in due course on the table of each House of Parliament.

It met with opposition in both places.   In the Upper

[1] See note, p. 500. For the history of the University see "The University of Wales," by the late Principal Viriamu Jones, F.R.S. (Cardiff, 1896).

House the Bishop of Chester (Dr. Jayne), on the 29th August. 1893, acting in the interests (as he conceived them) of St. David's College, moved a resolution praying the withholding of the consent of the Crown, framed in terms which showed an imperfect acquaintance with the provisions of the charter.[1] After a short debate the House, against the advice of Lord Knutsford, one of the leaders of the then Opposition, and of Lord Kimberley, Lord Aberdare, and Lord Herschell, passed the motion. In the Commons it was Mr. Bryn Roberts, one of the Liberal members for Carnarvonshire, who led the attack, by moving the rejection of the charter on the ground that it only provided for the granting of degrees to students of the three University Colleges. In a clear speech he explained that his opposition was based on the contentions that the charter gave privileges to three State-aided colleges which might be used unfairly as against other Welsh institutions, and that no opportunity was afforded by the charter for the obtaining of degrees by non-collegiate students. He received no substantial support, and after a brief debate, during which the motion was opposed by Mr. Brynmor-Jones, Mr. S. T. Evans, Mr. Kenyon, and Mr. Acland, it was negatived without a division. Under these circumstances the Government ignored the ill-grounded resolution of the Lords, and on the 30th

[1] The Bishop of Chester asked the House to express the opinion " that the assent of her Majesty be withheld from the draft charter of the proposed University of Wales until such portions of the aforesaid draft charter shall have been omitted as prevent the inclusion of St. David's College, Lampeter, in the county of Cardigan, as a constituent college of the aforesaid university " ("Hans. Parl. Deb.," 4th series, col. 1321). In fact, there is nothing in the charter to prevent the inclusion of St. David's College, or any other Welsh college, in the university. The Crown, by the charter, expressly reserved to itself the right to make by supplemental charter any college in Wales a constituent college (see Lord Knutsford's speech in the debate). St. David's College never asked to be included as a constituent college, and the late Bishop of St. David's very candidly admitted that he had made no representations on the subject, though he was "visitor" of the college. The House was a small one. The numbers on the division were forty-one contents and thirty-two non-contents.

November, 1893, the charter was duly sealed. The petitioners (still actively represented by the committee whose labours had procured the charter) now found that there was literal truth in the saying that "Nothing succeeds like success." The Court of the University (the governing body) was easily constituted, as the greatest eagerness to join it was manifested by members of all classes in the thirteen counties. It met for the first time at the Privy Council Office in London, on the 6th April, 1894, and the proceedings began with a sympathetic address by the Lord President of the Council (Lord Rosebery). Upon his withdrawal from the meeting Lord Aberdare was voted to the chair, and the proper steps were taken for converting the then real but inchoate University into an active working body. It would lead us beyond the scope of this work to follow them in detail. The late Lord Aberdare was, with the unanimous approval of the Welsh people, elected the first Chancellor. After his death Albert Edward, Prince of Wales, was, with remarkable enthusiasm, chosen without a dissentient voice for the office, and he having accepted it, was duly installed as Chancellor on the 26th June, 1896, at a "congregation" of the University held at Aberystwyth.[1]

[1] For the names of the officers of and full information as to the University, see the "Calendar of the University of Wales" (Newport, Mon.), 1898. The first Calendar was published in 1897. In a short sketch of a movement like the one dealt with in this chapter, one carried on for many years and supported from different quarters, we have found it impossible to refer by name to all the men who have rendered assistance. Among those whose experience enabled them to give valuable expert service at different stages, but all of whom we have not had occasion to mention in the text, are certainly the following :— The Rt. Rev. John Owen, D.D., now Bishop of St. David's ; Mr. R. D. Roberts, D.Sc. ; Mr. Marchant Williams, J.P. ; Mr. Ivor James, now Registrar of the University ; Mr. Geo. T. Kenyon, lately Member for Denbigh Boroughs ; Mr. Lewis Williams, J.P., of Cardiff ; the Hon. W. N. Bruce ; Lady Verney ; and Miss E. P. Hughes. The strenuous support of the movement by the late Dr. David Thomas, of Stockwell, in the Press should not be forgotten. (See his life in "Dict. Nat. Biog.") The late Earl Powis, the late Marquis of Bute, Lord Tredegar, Lord Kendel, Mr. William Rathbone, LL.D. (formerly M.P.), the late Mr. T. E. Ellis, M.P., Mr. Alfred Thomas, M.P., and Mr. Stephen Evans, should be remembered as having been very helpful friends at all times.

CHAPTER XII.

LANGUAGE AND LITERATURE.

THE position of Welsh among the kindred languages
has already been sufficiently indicated : genealogically, so
to say, it is on a level with old Cornish and with Breton,
which was carried over to Armorica by Celts who left this
country in the fifth and the sixth centuries under the
pressure of West Saxon aggression. In all respects old
Cornish was the least important of the three sisters, and
of the other two Welsh is philologically the more important, partly because of the more conservative nature
of its vowel system, and partly because of its more extensive and varied literature, some of which exists in manuscripts dating from the twelfth century. Welsh is,
indeed, the lineal descendant of the Brythonic of the
Ordovices : it is true that it must have been modified by
the later people, who introduced the early form of the
Powys dialect, and also probably by the Silures and
Demetæ of the southern portions of Wales, and by the
Venedotian tribes of northern Wales, when on both hands
they gave up Goidelic and adopted Brythonic as their own
tongue. They must have introduced peculiarities characteristic of their previous vernacular—they could not help
it. Nevertheless the language must have remained, as
we have suggested in the first chapter, the same in most
essentials as it was when first brought to Mid-Wales by
the westward conquests of the Ordovices. From them it

spread itself doubtless towards the north and towards the
south, though the Silures in the south were probably subjected to the influence of the Brythonic of the tribes also
to the east of them.

This state of things had begun before the Roman occupation, when the question of the linguistic conditions
becomes complicated by the introduction of Latin. But
however much the language of imperial Rome may have
prevailed in the towns, and as the official speech of both
Romans and Brythons during the period of Roman rule, it
is probable that Brythonic continued uniformly dominant
as against Goidelic, until the latter was at length silenced
in southern Britain in the sixth and seventh centuries.
In the presence of the Latin of the Roman occupation
Goidelic may have appeared on a level with Brythonic ;
nay, the invention of Ogmic writing and the existence of
Goidelic inscriptions in that writing may perhaps be rightly
interpreted as the fruit of a transitory effort to rehabilitate
Goidelic speech and to assert Goidelic nationality. But, so
far from Latin and Goidelic having silenced Brythonic, the
latter may be dimly descried as the dominant figure in
the background even of Goidelic monuments themselves.
The grammarian who invented the Ogam alphabet lived
probably in South Wales, and he must have been familiar
with Latin letters ; but that is not all, for he, or some
improver of his system soon after him, had to borrow some
of their orthographic expedients from Brythonic phonetics
and spelling : we allude to the use of *cc* and *tt* for the
sounds now written in Welsh *ch* and *th*[1] respectively.
Further, when a Goidel in Wales indulged in a bilingual
epitaph and used Latin and Goidelic, the Latin forms of
the names prove, in some instances, to be not the Goidelic
names Latinised, but the Goidelic names transformed into
Brythonic, and then equipped with the Latin terminations

[1] See Chambers's Encyclopædia, *s.v.* "Ogam."

required. Thus a bilingual monument at St. Dogmael's, near Cardigan, reads in Goidelic written in Ogam, *Sagramni maqui Cunatami,* and in Latin, *Sagrani fili Cunotami.* Here the genitive *Cunatami* is translated into the Brythonic genitive *Cunotami,* and probably the same remark might be made as to *Sagramni* and *Sagrani.* A still more remarkable instance occurs on a recently discovered stone at Lanfaltteg, in Carmarthenshire. The name involved is that possibly of the king of the Demetæ who is called (in the vocative) *Vortipori* [1] in the Latin of Gildas, his contemporary. This we should, in that case, have to correct into *Votipori;* and the presence of the consonant *p* in the name of a Goidel, whose language had at one time little use for that consonant, is explained by the fact that the name in the Latin form is a Brythonic translation of the original, as will be seen from the legends on the stone respectively, in Latin: MEMORIA VOTEPORIGIS PROTICTORIS; and in Ogam the genitive *Votecorigas.* We are not convinced that these and similar upcroppings of Brythonic on Goidelic ground can be explained on the hypothesis, sometimes suggested, that Brythonic became extinct in Wales during the Roman occupation, and was reintroduced by the Sons of Cuneda and their people. From before the occupation began it must have existed in the country, and more than that, it must have gradually spread, since it finally became for a time the only vernacular of the west of the Island. That it should have done so in Wales is no more surprising than that it did the same in the Dumnonian peninsula, or than the fact that there is an actual Breton language in Armorica.

For the earlier stages of Brythonic we have no literature, but merely the proper names of men and places mentioned

---

[1] The latter element in this compound occurs as a separate name *Porius,* on the Lech Idris stone, in Merionethshire (Hübner's *Inscr. Brit. Christiana,* No. 131); and one finds it borne by an *essedarius* who was probably a Gaul: see the *Caligula* of Suetonius, 35.

in works written in Latin or Greek from the time of Pytheas down. The earliest Welsh glosses do not in all probability reach back to the eighth century, but they fairly cover the ninth and the tenth. To this, the Old Welsh period, may be ascribed several boundaries and other bits of Welsh in the Book of Lan Dâv, otherwise called *Liber Landavensis.* But no manuscript appears to be extant in Welsh dating before the Norman Conquest, which, among its other effects on Wales, brought about a great change in Welsh hand-writing and spelling. The old orthography was discontinued and another introduced more in harmony with English and French ideas; it had also the advantage of being more nearly phonetic than the old historical spelling, which was displaced by it, and which resembled to a great extent the spelling usual in Irish down to comparatively modern times.

The mediæval period of Welsh opens with two manuscripts dating from the latter part of the twelfth century, one of poetry known as the Black Book of Carmarthen, and the other of prose, namely, the Venedotian Version of the Laws of Wales. To a somewhat later date belong the manuscripts of the Book of Aneurin and the Book of Taliessin, as to which, especially the former, it may be said that the contents point to an earlier period than that of the manuscripts themselves. The same may also be said of portions of the Red Book of Hergest, one of the treasures of Jesus College. The contents of the Red Book are various, consisting partly of poetry and partly of prose, embracing the tales known as the Mabinogion, and referred to originals dating before the fourteenth century, to which the manuscript belongs. The same remark applies to some of the Arthurian stories which that collection contains. In this period translations into Welsh, or Welsh adaptations, were made of such stories as those in vogue on the Continent about Charlemagne and his companions, also of the lives of famous saints, and of treatises on Latin theology, such as that of the Elucidarium, put into Welsh by an anchorite of Landewi Brefi in the year 1346.[1] The greatest poet of this period was Dafyd ab Gwilym, who may be regarded as a Welsh troubadour, whose lyric muse was devoted to singing what the French called the *Amour Courtois.* The nature of that theme, and possibly other reasons which are not recorded, made Dafyd and the monks of his time sworn foes, a fact which cannot be construed wholly to the discredit of the monks and the clergy of the Middle Ages.

With the Reformation began another period, characterised by the publication in the Welsh language of the Anglican Book of Common Prayer, the New Testament, and then the whole of the Bible. These were followed by various works, both original and translated, on theological and religious subjects. But the men engaged in the translation of Holy Writ complained of the low ebb at which they found their countrymen's knowledge of their language and its literature. Among others may be mentioned Lichard Davies, Bishop of St. David's, who utters this complaint repeatedly in his " Letter to the Cymry," prefixed by William Salesbury, his friend and collaborator, to his New Testament printed in London in the year 1567. The publication of th: Scriptures in Welsh made little difference in this respect until, at any rate, an inexpensive edition had been a long time in print, namely, the five-shilling Bible issued in 1630, and recommended to the people with all the fervour of his eloquence by Vicar Prichard. The Vicar's own version of the teaching of the Bible and the Church, put into easy verse, and entitled *Canwyll y Cymry*—" The Candle of the Cymry "—was not completely published till

---

[1] The whole manuscript, the property of Jesus College, has been edited by Jones and Rhys, and published in 1894 by the Clarendon Press in its quarto series of " Anecdota Oxoniensia."

1672, nearly thirty years after the author's death; but it was destined to exercise great influence over his country-men. Nevertheless one finds the language reaching its lowest depth of neglect towards the close of the seventeenth century.[1]

The actual or current period of Welsh may conveniently be regarded as opening with the establishment of the Sunday School, which, originating in England, is regarded as introduced to Wales by the Rev. Thomas Charles, of Bala, about the year 1785.[2] Charles was educated at Jesus College, and ordained deacon in the Church of England in 1778. His career was somewhat like that of Wesley, and he became practically one of the principal founders of one of the most influential and powerful religious bodies in the Principality, the Calvinistic Metho-dists or Welsh Presbyterians. It was a time of religious revival in Wales, and the ground was prepared for Charles's labours by the earnestness and eloquence of the Rev. Daniel Rowlands, of Langeitho, and the genius of the Rev. William Williams, of Pant y Celyn, the chief of Welsh hymnologists; not to mention other men

[1] For valuable information on this and several other questions touched upon in this chapter, we gladly acknowledge our indebtedness to Mr. Ivor James's brochure, already mentioned : see more especially pp. 5-8, 18, 19, 22, 39.

[2] See a monograph by the Rev. D. Evans, M.A., of Barmouth, on "The Sunday Schools of Wales" (London, 1883), in which the date of Charles's Schools is clearly established. Some writers have endeavoured to prove the previous existence of Sunday Schools in Wales, *e.g.*, "Morien" in a series of articles published in the *Western Mail* of June, 1880, and the late Dr. Rees, of Swansea, in his "History of Protestant Nonconformity in Wales," 1883, p. 394. The latter, however, admits that the schools which he mentions "were properly catechetical meetings, such as every nonconforming church in that age held regularly every week," and not "Sunday Schools in the modern form." There is, however, scarcely any doubt that an occasional Sunday School had been established in Wales before 1785, the best authenticated instance, perhaps, being that conducted by Jenkin Morgan on Sunday evenings from 1770 onwards at Crawlom, near Lanidloes; but to Charles belongs the honour of having begun the type of schools which spread and lived in Wales.

of lesser fame, but of hardly less influence over their countrymen in a generation which was passing away as Charles was attaining to the full enjoyment of his powers. As one of the events of his life may be regarded the publication of his *Geiriadur Ysgrythyrol* or Scripture Dictionary, in 1811, and his Sunday Schools were intended to be devoted to the reading and exposition of Scripture. Charles's schools (like those of Griffith Jones, of Landowror) were in the first instance day-schools stationed for fixed periods at various centres, and their chief object was to teach people to read. These circulatory schools were conducted by men who regarded it as part of their duties to carry on evangelistic work in the districts where for their allotted time they remained as teachers. From their point of view, children and young people were taught to read, chiefly, that they might peruse the Scriptures themselves.

As there were many unable to read who could not attend school on week-days, these teachers, supported by the influence of Thomas Charles, took the bold course of combining their efforts on Sundays, for the sake of such as could not attend on week-days; and, to speak with more precision, this was the real origin of the Welsh Sunday School of Wales. The teachers would not have worked in this way without the religious motive which ·in their minds justified the new departure. Their labours in this new form met with strong resistance, and were extremely unpopular with the stricter portion of the congregations. But amid the fire of opposition the Sunday toil took more definite shape in the matter of Scripture reading and catechetical work, the more elementary task of teaching mere reading being confined to children. But there must have intervened a period when these efforts, mainly on the part of the teachers paid by the funds placed at the disposal of Charles, were sporadic. This was an interval of four or five years, between 1785 and

1789. By the latter date Sunday Schools had become common, conducted by teachers and superintendents from among the people themselves. Nevertheless, owing to the strong prejudice that had still to be encountered, the full tide of success did not come until about the year 1807–8, when Thomas Charles started the large gatherings called *Cymanfaoeð Ysgolion,* or School Associations. After this, opposition gradually died away and the institution found, on the whole, a fair course. Sunday Schools continue to be conducted on the same lines in Wales, and they retain the peculiarity that they are attended by men and women of all ages. Moreover, they form an institution recognised and encouraged by all Protestant denominations alike. Their importance from the point of view of Welsh and its literature consists in the fact that the Welsh are taught in these schools to read in their own tongue. The work done in them, it is true, extends further, namely, to the exposition of the words of Scripture, the only text read in them ; but it does not come within the scope of that work to do anything directly to teach the people to write their language or to compose in it. So it happened that, before the Elementary Education Act of 1870 had been some years in force, it was a common thing for numbers of Welsh people of both sexes to be able to read Welsh in print, but not in ordinary handwriting.

The work of the Sunday School covers the whole extent to which the bulk of Welsh people are taught Welsh at all outside their hearths and homes ; for the public elementary schools have till lately been almost wholly devoted, so far as language is concerned, to the teaching of English, and not a few of them continue so still, though the Code now recognises Welsh as an optional and special subject. Looking at the Sunday-school teaching of Welsh as a whole, one may say that the edifice is in a manner made complete by the *rôle* played by literary societies, and literary competitions in which prizes are given for singing, for writing Welsh, both prose and verse, and for translating from English into Welsh, and *vice versâ*. These competitions do not occur more than once a year even in the neighbourhoods where they are the rule ; and, speaking generally, they are sporadic and depend for their origination on individuals who feel interested in Welsh and Welsh music. They are altogether a very indefinite quantity, but literary societies have been of late becoming more general and somewhat more permanent. They all serve, however, as feeders to the Eisteddfod, and they have in recent years exercised great influence on the cultivation of Welsh and Welsh literature. It is needless to remark that, so far as regards Welsh prose, the style of the authorised version of the Welsh Bible is the ideal of those who try to write and speak good Welsh. The fact that the Bible forms the earliest prose reading of the youth of Wales, and that they commit a great deal to memory under the direction of the Sunday School, makes that result unavoidable ; and this is not to be deplored, as the style of the Welsh Bible is on the whole excellent. But this literary or standard Welsh is practically a dialect to itself, distinct from the colloquial language consisting of the dialects mentioned in the chapter on the ethnology—as distinct as standard English is from the dialects, let us say, of Somerset or Lancashire ; but it is familiar to the people from reading their Bible, and from listening to their best public speakers. In fact they would regard the colloquial placed in the position of the literary language as a violation of their sense of dignity, though they might condone a certain margin of deviation from the literary style in the direction of the speaker's own dialect. It is somewhat the same as regards a country gentleman, let us say a landed proprietor or the squire, who learns Welsh in order to be able to converse with the men in his employ. Thus if he addresses them in literary Welsh, he commands their respect without appearing too affable or provoking familiarity, but if he learns his Welsh from a stable-boy, his style of speaking provokes derision. For the Welsh have a keen sense of the dignity of speech, and what would strike them as most congruous under the circumstances would be a conversational style pitched perhaps between book Welsh and their own domestic colloquial. An educated man talking the latter would not be willingly listened to unless he happened to have a fascinating sense of humour : his language as such would not command a hearing.

Unfortunately this position of supremacy of literary Welsh is now more and more contested by the shoddy Welsh which prevails in many of the newspapers published in Welsh. Possibly the tendency of journalism generally, with the hurry and scramble attendant on its periodicity, is in the direction of inaccuracy of language and a loose application of its terms. Perhaps the French, who take much trouble thoroughly to master their own language, are the nation most successful in resisting the tendency to this kind of degeneration. It exists undoubtedly in English, and it does in Welsh ; but that is not the whole of the evil in the case of Welsh, for it is found to be the readiest way to fill the blanks of a Welsh newspaper to translate from English ones. Now translation is never satisfactory from the point of view of the language into which it is made, unless it is by men who are competent and not too hard pressed for time. Neither of these is always one of the conditions under which English ideas appear in Welsh journals. Sometimes the translator is wofully restricted in the matter of vocabulary, but his most grievous sins are to be found in the foreign idioms which he introduces. To such a pitch is this sometimes carried, that to be sure of the meaning which he intends to convey one has to translate the individual words back into English, whereupon one discovers perchance the sense intended. Unfortunately for the unskilled or hurried translator the syntax of Welsh is very unlike that of English, especially in the matter, already mentioned, of the position of the verb and its nominative, and in that of manipulating the verbal noun. It is to be feared that crude and loose Welsh of the kind here in question may, by dint of familiarity, become general; and the style of some of the younger speakers on Welsh platforms and in Welsh pulpits shows a tendency that way. The task of writing good and close Welsh is, it is true, of the same nature as that of writing Latin prose; but short of the elegancies of such an exercise and the closeness of texture of such a production, it is possible to write without violating the elementary rules of the syntax. On the other hand, it is perhaps inevitable that, when a language which has been much devoted to religion and theology, to poetry and romance, becomes the vehicle of journalistic tattle, it should put on a looser dress, so to say, and undergo divers changes tending to make it altogether more free and easy. It is to be hoped that in the process of adapting itself more and more to the purposes of journalism, the language will issue from the trial with its syntax essentially intact. At all events the dialects, which are the force behind literary Welsh, are up to the present time sound as a rule in the matter of idiom, and can be relied upon as the spring of a power to check the deteriorating tendencies of translation, especially when the language is handled by skilled teachers, such as the professors of Welsh at the colleges of academic standing in the Principality. But it is impossible to conceal the fact that good writers of Welsh are scarce at the present moment, and hard to find.

Such are the prospects of Welsh as they appear from the point of view of language and literature, and they are not wholly reassuring; but a great deal may be expected from the present awakening of interest in all things Welsh. This now demands a word of notice before we proceed further ; and first of all we may say that it would take up too much of our space to inquire minutely into its origin. But we may trace it back to the efforts of a few patriotic Welshmen, with the late Sir Hugh Owen foremost among the number, to establish a university college in Wales, the realisation of their more immediate object in the college at Aberystwyth, and the publication in the year 1881 of the report of Lord Aberdare's Departmental Committee on the state of Higher and Intermediate Education in Wales. Many other things have contributed to this result, and the tide has been steadily flowing. It has assumed the form of antagonism to the philistine wish to see all parts of the United Kingdom reduced to uniformity worked out on the level of the most characteristically Saxon parts of England. The more conservative idea has of late been gaining ground, that Wales and her people are more likely to contribute to the greatness of our Anglo-Celtic Empire by developing themselves on their own lines, so to say, and in their own way, rather than by slavishly aping the south of England. This view extends to the Welsh language and its literature ; and, among other proofs, we may mention that Welsh seems to be far more read and studied now than perhaps at any time in the past. But nothing is more remarkable than the change which has come over the old families of the Principality in their attitude towards the language. Not many years ago all care used to be taken that the children of the gentry should not be accustomed to Welsh, lest it should spoil their English accent for the rest of their lives, whereas now the fashion of having them taught Welsh is growing. This change, so far as it goes, makes for improved relations between their class and those dependent on it.

Taking a comprehensive view of the history of Welsh

and its literature from the close of the eleventh century down, one may say, perhaps, that the period when it flourished most vigorously consisted of the couple of centuries preceding the conquest by Edward I. Wales happened then to produce a number of very able princes, under whose rule and after whose example Welsh men of letters showed great activity, and Welsh bards especially distinguished themselves.[1] At a later time, chiefly under the Tudors, Welshmen seemed to have been looked at with favour at court, as one may gather from Shakespeare's plays and Ben Jonson's masque, "The Honour of Wales ;" nor can the Welsh language have been altogether despised. But in time the well-known Act passed by Henry VIII. in 1535, incorporating Wales with England, began to bear fruit in a way which threatened the Welsh language with certain extinction ; for before the close of the sixteenth century we find evidence of a desire on the part of many Welshmen to get rid of the language, which they regarded as a sign of subjection. This was the attitude, doubtless, of the bulk of the educated and well-to-do classes, and of some men who were thoughtfully anxious for the welfare of their nation. They held it to be the best thing for the Welsh to adopt English, and some of them did their utmost to help their countrymen in the acquisition of the latter language. Among others may be mentioned William Salesbury, who wrote and dedicated to Henry VIII. a Welsh and English dictionary, which he published with that object in view.[2] By the beginning of the seventeenth century few educated Welshmen could speak Welsh and few monoglot Welshmen could read it. The gentry with

[1] See Thomas Stephens's "Literature of the Kymry during the Twelfth and two succeeding Centuries," pp. 332—342.

[2] This was quite compatible with the zeal which impelled him afterwards to take a laborious part in the translation of the Scriptures into Welsh, as that might be made the indirect means of acquiring a knowledge of English in the way suggested by the following proviso, annexed to the original Act of

few exceptions no longer maintained family bards,[1] and the Eistedfod had been almost forgotten.[2]

Parliament passed in the fifth year of Elizabeth's reign, enjoining on the five Welsh Bishops—the Bishop of Hereford has the first place among them—the duty of seeing that the Act was carried out :—

"Provided always and bee yt enacted by thaucthoritee aforesaid, That one Booke conteyning the Bible, and one other Book of Cōmon Prayer in Thenglishe Tongue, shallbee bought and had in every Churche throughout Wales, in wch the Bible and Book of Cōmon Prayer in Welshe ys to bee hadd by force of this Acte (yf there bee none alreadye) before the first daye of Marche wch shallbee in the yere of our Lorde God XV c lxvj; and the same Bookes to remain in suche convenient Places wth in the said Churches ; that suche as understande them may resorte at all convenient times to reade and puse the same, and also such as doo not understande the sayd Language maye, by conferring bothe Tongues together, the sooner attayne to the knowledge of the Englyshe Tongue ; Any thyng in this Acte to the contrarye notwithestanding."

See also pp. 39 and 47 of Southall's "Wales and her Language," a work from which we have derived much useful information.

[1] Yet down to the close of the sixteenth century a knowledge of Welsh was in some cases considered almost indispensable for a country gentleman even in the border district around Montgomery, which is now among the most Anglicised parts of Wales. The first Lord Herbert of Cherbury (1583—1648) in his "Autobiography" (ed. Sidney L. Lee, 1886, pp. 37—38) makes the following statement :—" After I had attained the age of nine, during all which time I lived in my said lady grandmother's house at Eyton [Shropshire], my parents thought fit to send me to some place where I might learn the Welsh tongue, as believing it necessary to enable me to treat with those of my friends and tenants who understood no other language ; whereupon I was recommended to Mr. Edward Thelwall, of Plas-y-ward in Denbighshire. . ."

The practice of maintaining domestic harpers, which was once so prevalent among the Welsh gentry, survived in several instances till well on in the 19th century, and has in fact not wholly ceased even at the present-day, domestic harpers being still kept by the Dowager Duchess of Londonderry and the Marquis of Bute, while the late Lady Lanover (who died early in 1896) always maintained quite a group of harpers in connection with her house. In the last century the celebrated Blind Parry was domestic harper to the first and second Baronets of Wynnstay, and the post, subsequently filled by less distinguished harpers, was discontinued only about fifty years ago. In the 19th century Thomas Blayney is mentioned as harper to the second Earl of Powis, in "the thirties;" Wil Penmorfa held a similar post at Tregîb, Llandeilo, as late as 1823, if not later; Thomas Lewelyn, of Aberdare (1828—1879), was harpist to the Aberpergwm and Dyffryn (Lord Aberdare's) families; while Griffith Owen, who died only in 1879, discharged for many years the double functions of butler and domestic harper to the late Mr. Edward Corbett, of Ynys y Maengwyn, near Towyn, Merioneth.

[2] See Mr. Ivor James's brochure, pp. 5—8, 18, 19, 39—41.

The language, it need hardly be said, did not die out, but it was left uncultivated and uncared for, a condition of things which may be accurately characterised in the words of a humorous English traveller in the year 1682 : " Their native *gibberish* is usually pratled throughout the whole *Taphydome*, except in their Market-Towns, whose inhabitants being a little rais'd, and (as it were) pufft up into *bubbles* above the ordinary *scum*, do begin to despise it. Some of these being elevated above the common level, and perhaps refin'd into the quality of having *two suits*, are apt to fancy themselves above their Tongue, and when in their *t'other cloaths*, are quite asham'd on't. 'Tis usually cashier'd out of Gentlemen's Houses, there being scarcely to be heard even one single Welch tone in many families ; their children are instructed in the *Anglican* Ideom, and their schools are *Pædagogu'd* with professors of the same ; so that (if the stars prove lucky) there may be some *glimmering* hopes that the Brittish *lingua* may be quite extinct, and may be *English'd* out of Wales, as *Latin* was barbarously *Goth'd* out of *Italy*."[1] The Great Rebellion was the turning point ; it left the strong castles in ruins, and the property of very many of the Welsh gentry passed into new hands, while others found their estates crippled to the last degree by heavy mortgages. From that crisis forth the prospects of the Welsh language began to improve ; they still continue to improve, and that, we are happy to say, without boding ill to the landed gentry of

[1] See " Wallography," by W. R., p. 123. For calling our attention to that work we were indebted to the late Judge David Lewis, who contributed an interesting paper on " The Welshmen of English Literature " to the "Cymmrodor" for the year 1882 : see pp. 238—240. The title of the book runs as follows :—" Wallography ; or the Britton described : Being a pleasant relation of a Journey into Wales, wherein are set down several remarkable Passages that occur'd in the way thither. And also many choice Observables, and notable Commemorations, concerning the State and Condition, the Nature and Humor, Actions, Manners, Customs, &c., of that Countrey and People. By W. R., a mighty Lover of Welch Travels."

the Principality or even failing to enlist their sympathies
and good will. On the one hand we behold this going on
before our eyes, while on the other we see that a day must
come when English is the universal speech of the United
Kingdom : we strike a balance of our feelings and venture
to predict that the future has yet in store for the Welsh
language many long years of prosperity.

We have alluded in passing to the Eisteďfod, and we
cannot close these remarks wĩthout some further notice of
an institution so characteristic of the Welsh. It consists
now of a meeting for competition in Welsh poetry and
prose, and in music, both vocal and instrumental. One of
the oldest assemblages of the kind of which we have any
account is called a *gwleď* or banquet, given in the year 1176
by Lord Rhys at his castle of Cardigan : notices of it a year
in advance had been published, we are told, not only in
Wales, but also in England, Scotland, and Ireland.[1] We
observe a difference between it and the Eisteďfod of the
present day in that not only the best poet was then awarded
a chair, but also the best musician, whereas now the former
alone gets a chair. In other respects the Cardigan banquet
was like the modern Eisteďfod, namely, in that the men,
for example, of South Wales excelled in music, and those
of Gwyneď in poetry. The Eisteďfod, the name of which
means a sitting or session, appears to have been a regularly
constituted court, bearing all the marks of antiquity. Its
principal function was to license or aᴄmit duly qualified
candidates to the position of recognised bards or minstrels ;
and the legal position of the adjudicating bards or others
assisting in the decisions of the court was that of experts or
assessors to the sovereign, prince, or chief under whose
authority the court was held. The business of the court
must have been of a serious nature in proportion to the
value of the privileges which it granted, and those privileges

[1] See Rhys and Evans's "Bruts from the Red Book of Hergest," p. 334.

included among them the right of the qualified professionals to make the circuit of the country, billeting themselves on the nobility and gentry in their turn.   One of the Eisteɗfod proceedings which has most attraction for those who are interested in ancient ceremony is that of chairing the bard. It is referred to in one version of the Laws of Howel in the following clause : " From the person who shall conquer when there is a contention for a chair, he [the judge of the court] is to have a buglehorn and a gold ring, and the pillow placed under him in his chair." [1]   One of the chief places of meeting for Eisteɗfod purposes in North Wales appears to have been the ancient town of Caerwys, in Flintshire ; there Gruffyɗ ab Cynan has been supposed to have held a great Eisteɗfod about the year 1100.   And in Tudor times we read of an Eisteɗfod taking place there in the fifteenth year of the reign of Henry VIII., at which Richard ap Howel ap Ieuan Vychan, of Mostyn, and Sir William Gruffyɗ, and Sir Roger Salusbury presided. They were assisted by a gentleman of learning and distinction as a bard, named Gruffyɗ ap Ieuan ap Lewelyn Vychan,[2] and by Tudur Aled, who is well known to have been one of the ablest bards of the time.   The position of the "expert men" is still further defined by the wording

---

[1] See Aneurin Owen's edition, i. 369. We abstain from saying anything about the " Gorseɗ," as its antiquity is contested. See *Cymru* for 1896, where the reader will find several articles on the subject by Professor J. Morris Jones, whom we have to thank for calling our attention to the passage concerning the chair contest.

[2] We are indebted for this information to a note in Pennant's " Tours in Wales," vol. ii., p. 93, of the edition of 1810.   In the same volume also (pp. 89—93), is to be found at length Elizabeth's commission for holding the Eisteɗfod of 1568, which we ,have, by the kind permission of Lord Mostyn, inserted in the text from the original manuscript in his possession.   As to the reputation of Gruffyɗ ap Ieuan ap Lewelyn Vychan see Salesbury's marginal note (*b., i.*) to the Bishop of St. David's Letter to the Cymry, already mentioned, also Williams's " Dictionary of Eminent Welshmen," p. 185. Salesbury took Gruffyɗ to have been uncle to his friend the Bishop, and there is no reason to suppose that he was mistaken.

of Queen Elizabeth's commission for holding an Eisteḍfod at Caerwys in the year 1568. We print this important document at length, as it illustrates many other points in the history of the Eisteḍfod, and among them the position which the nobility and gentry of Gwyneḍ continued to occupy with regard to the language, literature, and music of Wales in the time of the Tudors :—

"ELIZABETH by the grace of god of England ffraûnce and Ireland Quene defendoʳ of the fayth &c. To our trustie and right welbeloued Sʳ Richard Bulkley knight, Sʳ Rees Gruffith knight, Ellice Price esquioʳ, doctoʳ in Cyvill Lawe, and one of our Counsaill in our marches of Wales William Mostyn, Jeuaⁿ Lloyd of Yale, John Salusbury of Ruge, Rees Thomas, Maurice Wynne, Willᵐ Lewis, Peres Mostyn, Owen John ap Hoᵘ Vaughan, John Willᵐ ap John, John Lewis Owen, Moris Gruffyth, Symound Theloall, John Gruffyth, Ellice ap Wᵐ Lloyd, Robᵗ Puleston, Harry aparry, William Glynne, and Rees Hughes esquioʳˢ, and to euery of them, Greating. Wheras it is come to the knowledge of the Lorde President and other oʳ said Cunsaill in oʳ mʳches of Wales that vagraunt and idle persons, naming theim selfes mynstrelles Rithmʳs, and Barthes, are lately growen into such an intollerable multitude within the principalitee of North Wales, that not only gentlemen and other by theire shameles disorders are oftentymes disquieted in theire habitacions. But also thexpert mynstrelles and musicions in tonge and Coñyng therby much discouraged to travail in thexercise and practize of theire knowledges and also not a litle hyndred in theire Lyvinges and prefermentes. The refourmacõn wherof and the putting of those people in ordʳ the said Lorde President and Counsaill have thought verey necessarye and knowing you to be men both of wysdome and vpright dealing and also of Experience and good Knowledg in the scyence, have apounted and aucthorized you to be Commission·s for that purpose. And forasmuch as oᶠ said Counsaill of late travayling in some parte of the said principalite had perfect vnderstanding by credible report that thaccustomed place for thexecucõn of the like Commissyon, hath bene heretofore at Cayroes in our Countie of fflynt, and that William Mostyn esquioᶠ and his auncestors have had the gyfte and bestowing of the sylver harpe[1] appertayning to the Cheff of that facultie, and that a yeares warning at the least hath bene acustomed to be geaven of thassembly, and execucõn of the like Commissyon. Our said Counsaill have therfore apoynted thexecucõn of this Commissyon to be at the said towne of Cayroes the monday next aftᶠ the feast of the blessed Trynitee wᶜʰ shallbe in the yeare of oᶠ Lorde god 1568.

"And therfore we require and command you by the aucthoritee of these presentes not only to cause open proclamacõns tᵒ̇ be made in all ffayoᶦˢ, mᶠketts, Townes, and other places of assembly within our Counties of Anglizey, Carn'von, Meryonneth, Denbigh and fflynt, that all and euery person and persons that entend to maynteigne theire lyvinges by name or Coloᶠ of mynstrelles, Rithm'ᵉˢ, or Barthes, within the Talaith of Aberfrowe comprehending the said fyve Shires, shalbe and appeare before you the said daye and place to shewe furth theire learninges accordingly. But also that you, xxᵗⁱᵉ, xixᵉⁿ, xviiiᵉⁿ, xviiᵉⁿ, xviᵉⁿ, xvᵉⁿ, xiiiiᵉⁿ, xiiiᵉⁿ, xiiᵉ, xiⁿ, xᵉⁿ, ix, viii, vii or ˙ of you, whereof youe Sᶠ Richard Bulkley, Sᶠ Rees Gruffith, Ellice Price, and Wᵐ Mostyn Esquioᶦˢ or iiiᵉᵉ or iiᵒ of you to be of the nomber to repayre to the said place the daye aforsaid, And calling to you such expert men in the said facultie of the Welshe musick as to you shall be thought convenient to proceade to thexecucõn of the premisses, and

---

[1] This silver harp is in the archives of Mostyn Hall, and was kindly exhibited to members of the Welsh Land Commission by Lord Mostyn on the occasion of their visit to Holywell and the vicinity.

to admytt such and so many as by your wisdomes and Knowledges you shall fynde worthy into, and vnd^r the degrees, heretofore in semblable sort to vse exercise or folowe the scyenc*es* and facultes of theire p*r*ofessyons in such decent ord^r as shall app*er*taigne to eche of theire degrees, and as yor discrèc͠ons and wisdomes shall prescribe vnto theim geaving straight monyc͠on and co*m*maundm*en*t in o^r name, and on o^r behalf to the rest not worthy that they returne to some honest Labo^r and due Exercise, such as they be most apte vnto for mayntenaunce of their lyving*es*, vpon paine to be taken as sturdy and idle vacaboûndes and to be vsed according to the Lawes and Statutes p*r*ovided in that behalf. Letting you wytt o^r said Counsaill looke for advertisem*en*t by due c*er*tificatt at your handes of yor doing*es* in thexecuc͠on of the said p*r*emiss*es*, forseeing in any wise that vpon the said assembly the peas and good order be observed and kept accordingly asscertayning you that the said Willm Mostyn hath p*r*omised to see furnyture and thing*es* necessary p*r*ovided for that assembly at the place aforsaid. Yeven vnder o^r Signet at o^r Citie of Chester the xxiiith of October the nynth yeare of o^r Raigne.

" S*i*gned her highnes Counsaill in the m'ches of WALES."

The state of things complained of in Queen Elizabeth's commission was remedied, no doubt, for a time by the Eisteďfod held at Caerwys in 1568 in obedience to it ; but the same unsatisfactory condition of the Welsh professional world, as far as concerned the bards and musicians, had again become prevalent by the year 1594. At any rate that is what one is led to believe from perusing a petition,[1]

---

[1] This is a document which Lord Mostyn only discovered in 1895, and his Lordship was good enough to sub.nit it at once to Professor Rhys, an act of courtesy for which we desire to record our hearty thanks. The petition may now be read at length in Mr. J. Gwenogvryn Evans's " Report [to the Historical Manuscripts Commission] on Manuscripts in the Welsh Language," vol. i., pp. 293-5.

signed then by a number of the gentry of North Wales, praying to have another Eisteðfod held.   We may mention in passing that according to this document the recognized prizes were by this time the silver chair for poetry, the silver harp for harping, the silver crowd for crowthing, and the silver tongue for singing.   It does not appear that the petition was granted, and the Eisteðfod is found to have now fallen on evil times, at any rate as far as regards North Wales.   Without attempting, however, to trace its history down to the present day, suffice it to say that it had probably become uncertain and sporadic in its occurrence in the different parts of the Principality long before the sovereign, the prince, or nobleman under whose auspices it was held, had disappeared from the position of central figure, and given way to a more democratic order of things, with a president appointed as a matter of form. At length, about the middle of the present century, it struck some of the leading Welshmen of the time that the Eisteðfod was to a considerable extent a neglected force which might be utilised for the benefit of Wales.   So Sir Hugh Owen and his friends undertook the attempt to regulate it and to add to its meetings opportunities for discussing social and economic questions connected with the future of Wales.   Their reforming work has proved lasting, and it is now carried on by the National Eisteðfod Association under the auspices of the Honourable Society of the Cymmrodorion, which has its headquarters in London.   One of the results is, that no more than one Eisteðfod claiming to be national is held in each year, and that no year now passes without one such an Eisteðfod being held, after an announcement a considerable time in advance.   Regarding the work of the National Eisteðfod in general, it may be said, that it continues to encourage Welsh literature, prose and verse, but that it has achieved its most striking successes in regard to music, while it has all but failed in the domain of art. Those, however, who expect the Eisteðfod every now and then to turn out a Shakespeare or a Milton are wholly mistaken as to its nature. It is not a union of learned or famous men like the French Academy, or even like the British Association, but a thoroughly popular assembly representing the rank and file of the Welsh people. Nevertheless it has now and then helped to bring to notice young men who succeeded afterwards in distinguishing themselves in the honour examinations of the older universities and in their subsequent careers. Besides the immediate work of the National Eisteðfod, it is valued as a rallying point by Welshmen who live apart from one another, whether in Wales or other parts of the United Kingdom. During the Eisteðfod week they make or renew their acquaintance with one another, and they form a sort of literary parliament for Wales, in which the steam of spent discussions may, so to say, be let off or new departures made.

After all, perhaps the chief importance of this the National Eisteðfod attaches to it, not as a structure complete in itself, but as a part of a larger and wider edifice. The National Eisteðfod is, in a sense, the coping-stone of the provincial and smaller Eisteðfods, and each of the latter depends for its success on how the ground has been previously worked by the smaller literary associations to which we have already alluded as in a sense following up the teaching of Welsh by the Sunday School. Considering the absence of any stimulus, economical or political, and the evident advantage of learning English, which the Welsh do not allow themselves to forget, the system we have sketched does them not a little credit. At all events, in the present state of hopeless division as regards religious views, it deserves to be encouraged by all who care for the welfare of the people. The Eisteðfod—and we here mean the Eisteðfod of all grades, from the national institution

down to the competitive meeting of a local literary society
—knows no politics or religious distinctions. Under the
auspices of the Eisteddfod men of the most divergent
opinions may meet without fear of prejudice to the politics
or dog nas of any. Its platform is the most neutral ground
one has in the Principality, and if the landed proprietors
had more generally been accustomed to take advantage,
especially of the humbler Eisteddfods and literary meetings,
to assist and encourage the people in the development of
their own ideas of culture, it would have gone a long way
to meet the complaint that they keep themselves aloof and
show little or no interest in the pursuits and ambitions of
those around them. Economically speaking, the men of
whom their dependants complain most loudly on the score
of their alleged aloofness are frequently and readily
admitted to be most generous as regards the material
welfare of their people. They may be ever ready to give
prizes for the best ploughing, and they may spend lavishly
on the improvement of the breeds of horses or cattle
on their estates, all excellent objects so far as they go.
The Welsh character has a point of greater sensitive-
ness than even the pocket ; but the landowner who
has never taken part in a small Eisteddfod or literary
meeting among his people has in all probability never
discovered it.

These remarks do not apply, it is needless to say, to the
larger and more ambitious Eisteddfods, to preside at which,
especially the National Eisteddfod, has come to be regarded
an honour not to be rashly rejected. It is, in fact, sometimes whispered, that the position is a matter of some real
competition and rivalry, though they mostly escape the
observation of the public. Suspicion of this has given
currency to a modern couplet, which, while wafting
the echoes of an old Welsh hymn, gives expression to
the sentiment that the voice of an English-speaking

president at an Eisteđfod is sometimes regarded as the bray of the silver trumpet :

Lais gwr o Sais mewn 'Steđfod,
Lais udgorn arian yw.

But when the people of a Welsh countryside are making an effort on a smaller scale to develop their ideas of culture in their own Welsh way, any encouragement they receive is accepted with a deep sense of gratitude ; and to see the gentry among them on such occasions brings home to the hearts of all a conviction that their superiors in rank and education are not ashamed of them and their humble aspirations. The feelings of friendliness and attachment thus engendered could not fail to tend in manifold ways to smooth the dealings between the farmers and those dependent on them with the members of the land-owning class.

Besides the Welsh language, English has long existed in the Principality partly as the official language of people who habitually talk Welsh, and partly as the only language used by certain of the inhabitants. As the official and business language English has prevailed to a large extent, especially wherever any kind of show had to be made ; for instance, when one enters a country churchyard one notices that epitaphs in Welsh only began to make their appearance in comparatively recent years. Indeed, when one considers how ubiquitous, so to say, English has been, and continues to be, in the Principality, it becomes a surprise that Welsh still exists, and exists in such comparative purity and vigour. The official language has depended on the intimate connection between England and Wales, but English as the vernacular of certain portions of the Principality has had its own history. Thus in the Anglo-Flemish districts of Pembrokeshire and Gower we have an English dialect which has been discussed in the first chapter, and we need not notice it any further. In the Vale of Glamorgan English and, to some extent, French must have been introduced over a considerable area, where Welsh was afterwards able to become the language of the hearth, not even excepting Cardiff and its immediate vicinity.[1] Similarly, with regard to Tegeingl or the Flintshire coast from the neighbourhood of Chester to the river Clwyd at Rhyl and Rhuðlan, such names as *Prestatyn*, *Mostyn*, *Acstyn*, *Bychtyn*, *Brychtyn* (Broughton), and the Point of *Ayre*, seem to show that English (and Scandinavian) once prevailed there, where Welsh became again dominant.

The spread of the language of the peasantry of one parish to those of another is not a change of a nature calculated quickly to attract the attention of the historian, and the propagation of English as the vernacular of the inhabitants of the Marches of Wales is accordingly involved in obscurity. Certain indications remain of successive stages in the westward advance of the tide of English; thus in English Maelor or the detached piece of Flintshire,

---

[1] A recently discovered "Directory and Guide to the Town and Castle of Cardiff," published in 1796, throws considerable light upon its linguistic condition (*inter alia*) about a hundred years ago. (See the *Western Mail* for 27th December, 1895.) At that time the town was chiefly an agricultural centre for the surrounding district, and "great quantities of oats, barley, salt butter, and poultry of all kinds " were sent from it to Bristol. In the Directory Welsh names largely prevail : *e.g.*, out of 127 traders 79 had Welsh names ; in the professions of law and physic four out of the five names were Welsh, though under gentry there were only three Welsh names out of nine. Mr. John Ballinger, who kindly made inquiries on behalf of the Welsh Land Commission among "the oldest inhabitants" of the town, informs us that he has come to the conclusion "that early in the 19th century Cardiff was a bilingual town, that English was freely used and understood by most of the inhabitants, but that a large amount of Welsh was spoken, particularly in the houses, and that, so far as Cardiff was a centre for markets and fairs, it was almost exclusively a Welsh centre." He also adds that there is an old Welsh proverb that the best English was spoken in Cardiff, Cowbridge, and Carmarthen, while a variant of the same saying substituted Crickhowell for Cowbridge.

most of the field names are still Welsh, and as to Monmouthshire, which was treated as an English county from the passing of the "Act of Wales" in 1535, the dialect of the English portion is considered to be a more recently introduced language than that of the greater portion of Herefordshire or Shropshire ; in fact, the English of Monmouthshire has been pronounced [1] to be decidedly Welsh in tone and to some extent in vocabulary likewise. Then, with regard to Shropshire, the vernacular of the corner of that county between Chirk and Lanymyneich has been described by the same authority to be English spoken as a foreign language ; and at Oswestry, the largest town in the district, a good deal of Welsh may still be heard. More to the south in the same county and nearer to Radnorshire, we come, in the parish of Clun, on a locality where the spoken English is said still to contain some Welsh vocables, such as the word for a *pig*, which is there called a *muchyn*, pronounced with the guttural spirant as in Welsh.[2] As for Herefordshire, Welsh appears not to be quite extinct there yet, and in the valley of the Wye it was spoken at Landogo, close on the border of Gloucestershire, as late as the year 1830.[3]

Within the actual boundaries of Wales this quiet and unobserved invasion of English has covered most of Radnorshire, a portion of Brecknockshire, and a considerable part of Montgomeryshire. It is the English spoken by the peasantry of the west of England and as learnt by the peasantry of the tract in question of Mid-Wales. It is not a particularly intellectual dialect, and, rightly or wrongly, the inhabitants of Welsh-speaking Wales do not regard the Welsh people who speak it as being among

[1] By Mr. Alexander J. Ellis. See the "Cymmrodor" for 1882, pp. 186–8.

[2] See Miss Jackson's " Shropshire Word-book " (London, 1879).

[3] See Southall's "Wales and her Language," especially the ninth chapter (pp. 336–56), where the author mentions various recent traces of Welsh in the Marches.

the most intellectual or the most enlightened of their nationality. In fact, some of the religious communities of Wales, such as the Calvinistic Methodists, have been in the habit of sending missionaries to the districts (chiefly in Radnorshire) near Offa's Dyke, or, as they call them in Welsh, *Gororau Clawd Offa.* The probability is that during the transition from the one language to the other the people suffered intellectually : they were cut off from the movements, religious and other, which took place among those of their countrymen who continued to speak Welsh, at the same time that their change of language failed to bring them into anything like the atmosphere of English culture. Here we might, perhaps, cite as relevant the words of one of the commissioners who reported, in 1846, on education in Wales, when he wrote (p. 519) as follows : —" As the influence of the Welsh Sunday-school decreases, the moral degradation of the inhabitants is more apparent. This is observable on approaching the English border." And it is believed in Wales to be their condition still to some extent,[1] but how far that may be really the case it would be hard to say. At all events, we may mention, by way of comparison with the Anglo-Flemish part of Pembrokeshire, that some of the tenant farmers of this area are among the most contented we have met in the course of our inquiry, especially those of Radnorshire. In other parts of Wales even the tenants who think most highly of their landlords usually join in the general chorus of their class that rents ought to be reduced, but, in one or two instances in Radnorshire, we met with the exceptional phenomenon of farmers who denied on their own behalf the cherishing of any such a wish.[2]

Whatever may have been the circumstances under which the Midland dialects of English invaded the borders of

---

[1] See also Qu. 54,167-72 ; 54,187 ; 54,754-73 ; 54,929.
[2] Qu. 53,007 ; 53,986 ; 54,137-44.

Denbighshire and Flintshire, and the Southern dialect of English spread into Mid-Wales, no English dialect seems any longer to possess the secret of spreading itself in Wales. The linguistic boundaries in Pembrokeshire and Gower appear to have been fixed long ago, and the same remark applies, on the whole, to Mid-Wales. Welsh has nothing to fear, so to say, at the frontier, but rather from innumerable points within its own boundaries : from the towns as the centres of commercial life, from her pleasant watering-places crowded with English visitors, and from the public elementary schools in every parish in the land. In some of the towns the number of English people who have taken up their permanent abode in them is not inconsiderable ; but, excepting the English-dialect districts already mentioned, the bulk of the English spoken in Wales is book English in various stages of assimilation to English as spoken by the middle classes in the towns of the west and south of England. English visitors who happen to have no partiality for dialect often express their surprise at the purity of the language as spoken in Wales ; but that is a subject of no surprise to any one who knows the circumstances, for it is the language daily taught at school.

Phonologically speaking, it is characterised in some parts of Wales by not allowing the voice to fall at the end of a proposition in the usual English way. With regard to individual sounds, it has some trouble in observing the distinction between the vowels of words like *hole* and *hall*, it vacillates between the two sounds of *s*, and it finds a difficulty with *sh* in such words as *shilling* and *fish*, which may still be heard pronounced *silling* and *fiss* in North Wales. Lastly, it trills the *r* in a way foreign to standard English ; but, on the other hand, it avoids the latest atrocity in English pronunciation, namely, the appending of *r* to words like *idea* and *potato*, and it never transgresses with regard to *h*, except in Monmouthshire and Glamorgan, where *h* is uncertain both in Welsh and English. In the case of Welshmen who have to learn English as a foreign tongue, there is a conscious effort to attain to the standard of English pronunciation. In other words, the Welsh accent is not a fixed quantity in the pronunciation of English under these conditions: it varies in point of intensity inversely with the length and success of the teaching. This applies especially to the country districts, whereas in the towns it tends to become fixed, the most decided instances of the prevalence of Welsh accent being the largest towns, Cardiff, Swansea, and Newport.

The code regulating public elementary schools now allows Welsh to be taught as a special subject, but it is still doubtful whether Welsh will be very eagerly taken up, such is the anxiety of Welsh parents to have their children taught English, and such is the reliance which they place on the Sunday School as the means of teaching the mother tongue. As a rule, however, the children in the country districts leave school before they have so far mastered English as to be able to make a free and comfortable use of it in conversation. Only a very small minority of them become really bilingual, as proved by their habitual use of Welsh for all purposes, domestic, social, and religious. At most they retain perhaps enough of the English learnt at school to be able to answer simple questions addressed to them in very plain terms. That they should shrink from giving evidence in English in courts of law is perfectly natural, as any Englishman possessed of a moderate acquaintance with French would at once comprehend, if he were called upon to undergo a cross-examination in that language in a court of law.

We have hitherto dealt with the quality, so to speak, rather than the quantity of Welsh literature, but, before we quit the consideration of this subject, we may, perhaps, attempt a brief statistical analysis of Welsh bibliography during the last four centuries.

The art of printing was probably not introduced into England before about 1477, though a few English books had been printed on the Continent prior to that date. It was not, however, before 1546 that the first book written in the Welsh language was printed, and it is a significant fact that this contained a translation of certain portions of the Bible. For the next hundred years the number of Welsh books was comparatively small. Thus the total number of books by Welshmen, or about Wales, published between 1546 and 1642, was 269, of which 44 were in Latin, 184 in English, and only 41 in Welsh. Of the Welsh books, four only were of an exclusively literary character, while the remaining 37 were purely religious, including three editions of the Bible, one of the New Testament, two selections from Scriptures, four Psalters, one Litany, five Liturgies, one book of Homilies, together with 13 religious works by Protestants, and five by Roman Catholics.[1]

In the next period, that of the Civil War, extending from 1643 to 1660, there is a most marked difference between the character of the productions of the Welsh and English presses respectively. Thomasson's famous collection of political tracts, which contains almost every known specimen of the ephemeral and controversial literature of the period, numbers over thirty thousand, all in English, but intended, however, for distribution in Wales as well as in England. As against this, we do not find that a single pamphlet or other publication of an exclusively political character was issued in the Welsh language, those that approach nearest to this definition being two works, which

[1] This estimate is taken from Mr. Ivor James's brochure (pp. 20, 21, 39), which has been already repeatedly mentioned. The figures for 1643–1800 are based upon the entries in Rowlands's "Cambrian Bibliography," edited by the Rev. D. Silvan Evans (Llanidloes, 1869).

are "strange mixtures of politics and religious mysticism," written by a North Wales Puritan, Morgan Lwyd, of Wrexham. The total number of books published in the Welsh language in this troublous period appear to be 36, as compared with 166 in English (mostly pamphlets, however), and four in Latin. It was after the conclusion of the Civil War that perhaps the first great opportunity of the Welsh language occurred, and we consequently find that in the next sixty years, from 1660 to 1720, the Welsh books numbered 247, as compared with four Latin books and 137 English works by Welshmen or about Wales.

It was not till the last year of the period, namely, 1719, that a book was first printed, or, in other words, that a printing-press was established, within the limits of the Principality itself. Almost all the earliest Welsh books had been printed in London, excepting a small number printed on the Continent, especially at Milan and Paris, though other works by Welsh authors had also been printed at Cologne, Amsterdam, and Heidelberg.

After London we find that Oxford and Shrewsbury, and still later Bristol and Chester, came to supply the Welsh book market during the seventeenth and eighteenth centuries. In the days of packhorses Shrewsbury enjoyed a geographical position of great advantage for all purposes of communication between Wales and England, and there is a long roll of Shrewsbury printers whose names are most closely associated with the Welsh literature of that period. It is now generally conceded that the first Welsh press was set up by one Isaac Carter, in 1719, at Adpar, a suburb of Newcastle Emlyn, on the Cardiganshire side of the river Teifi.[1]   Carter eventually removed to

---

[1] See the Rev. D. Silvan Evans's statement in Rowlands's "Cambrian Bibliography," p. 321, and two interesting articles (in Welsh) on "Old Welsh Printers" ("Hen Argraffwyr Lyfrau Cymraeg") by Charles Ashton in *Y Geninen* for October, 1891, and January, 1892, where a list is given of all the printers of Welsh books prior to the present century, and references are also

Carmarthen, which was then the chief town of South Wales, and soon became the main centre of the Welsh book trade,[1] at least for South Wales, a position which it has, on the whole, held to the present day.

During the latter half of the last century, the great revival which manifested itself, not only in the religious, but also in the literary, life of the Welsh people, resulted in a considerable increase in the number of Welsh books, an increase which has been steadily maintained from 1740 even to the present day.

The estimated numbers of Welsh books issued within each period of twenty years subsequent to the Civil War are exhibited in two tables, which we here append. The first comes down to (and includes) the year 1800, and is based on Rowlands's "Bibliography"; for the second, which covers the period from 1801 to 1895, both inclusive, we are indebted to Mr. Charles Ashton, of Dinas Mawddwy, who for the last ten years has been collecting materials for a Welsh bibliography of the nineteenth century, and who has kindly favoured us with the result of his researches up to the year 1896.[2]

given to the chief authorities on the subject of Welsh bibliography. A brief general summary of the question is also given in a paper by Mr. W. Eilir Evans on "Welsh Publishing and Bookselling," read before the Library Association at Cardiff (September, 1895) and published in the *Library* for December, 1895 (vii. 391 *et seq.*).

[1] John Ross (a Scotchman), who, after a London apprenticeship, settled at Carmarthen in 1743, and acquired a knowledge of the Welsh language, very largely contributed to this result. He used to describe himself as "the only printer in those parts brought up to the trade."

[2] Mr. Ashton has also sent us the following explanation of his list :— "Between Welsh books, etc., and those in some way or other relating to Wales, I have already recorded a total of 11,613. All these are different publications. Some of them are very small in size ; indeed, hundreds of them contain only about four pages each. Many of them are periodicals, tracts, and leaflets. But a book of any number of volumes, such as 'Y Gwyddoniadur,' or 'Welsh Cyclopædia,' or a monthly periodical (such as *Yr Eurgrawn Wesleyaid*, which has had a continuous existence since 1809), is only counted as ONE, and entered under the year it first appeared, but a second or any

WELSH BOOKS, 1546—1800.

	1546 to 1642.	1643 to 1660.	1661 to 1680.	1681 to 1700.	1701 to 1720.	1721 to 1740.	1741 to 1760.	1761 to 1780.	1781 to 1800.
Welsh . . .	41	36	35	74	138	115	177	423	440
English . .	184	166	48	35	54	55	80	91	155
Latin and other languages . .	44	4	1	2	2	4	4	—	1
Total . .	269	206	84	111	194	174	261	514	596

WELSH BOOKS, 1801—95.

	1801 to 1820.	1821 to 1840.	1841 to 1860.	1861 to 1880.	1881 to 1895.	Total 1801 to 1895.
Welsh . .	890	1,670	2,065	2,195	1,605	8,425
English, etc. .	415	500	550	995	728	3,188
Total . .	1,305	2,170	2,615	3,190	2,433	11,613

The earliest of the Welsh periodicals made its appearance in 1770, as a fortnightly publication, bearing the title of *Trysorfa Gwybodaeth neu Eurgrawn Cymraeg.* After

subsequent edition of the same work is separately counted. The column 'English, etc.,' includes a few historical books, written in Latin, and a small number of French and German books which relate to Wales, but the total is largely made up of Acts of Parliament relating to enclosures, canals, highways, railways, etc., in Wales, while there is also a good number of books recorded which treat of different districts in Wales—topographical works, guide-books, and some historical books of considerable size and much value. I have every reason to believe that there are still many books, in Welsh and relating to Wales, published in this country which I have so far been unable to record. I know practically nothing of the Welsh literature published in America, with the exception of an occasional book which has found its way over here."

the issue of fifteen numbers it was discontinued. It was succeeded by the *Cylchgrawn Cymraeg*, a quarterly, of which only five numbers appeared, between February, 1793, and February, 1794. Several other periodicals were started and had a short existence in the early years of the 19th century, but *Yr Eurgrawn Wesleyaid*, a denominational magazine, established in connection with the Wesleyan body in 1809, has continued to appear uninterruptedly to the present day.

In the year 1828, "the monthly press of Wales issued no fewer than fourteen hundred periodicals, and what is an anomaly in the history of literature, to the pages of these the peasantry were almost the only contributors,"[1] a statement which is very largely applicable to Welsh periodicals even of the present day.

Up to 1850 there had been started from time to time as many as—

(*a*) Fifteen Welsh quarterlies, of which only one, *Y Traethodyd*, which is an undenominational review, is still in existence, being now issued as a bi-monthly.

(*b*) Two bi-monthlies, both of which have died.

(*c*) About one hundred monthly magazines, of which ten are still in existence, all of them being published in connection with the various religious denominations.

(*d*) Eleven fortnightly and four weekly publications, of which only one has survived, that is *Yr Amserau*, started in 1843, and incorporated in 1859 with *Baner Cymru*, and now appearing under the title *Baner ac Amserau Cymru*.

In the year 1896 there were publishing in the Welsh language two quarterlies, two bi-monthlies, twenty-eight

---

[1] Speech by the Rev. John Blackwell at the Denbigh Eisteddfod in 1828 (quoted in Rowlands's "Bibliography," p. 8).

monthlies, and twenty-five weeklies, making a total of thirty-two magazines and twenty-five newspapers. Excepting one Welsh newspaper, published in Liverpool, all of them were published within the Principality, the chief publishing centres for North Wales being in the counties of Carnarvon, Merioneth, and Denbigh, and for South Wales in those of Glamorgan and Carmarthen. Of English newspapers published in Wales, eleven were dailies, which were issued from Cardiff, Swansea, and Newport, and seventy-nine were weeklies (about one-fourth of which have a Welsh column or two), not to mention half a dozen more that were published in the border counties, and circulated largely in Wales. Besides these there were at least twelve magazines periodically issued in the service of Wales or of Welsh literature, being for the most part the transactions of learned societies.[1]

We cannot pass on from this subject without stating that the Welsh Land Commission experienced very great difficulty in obtaining definite information with reference to Welsh publications generally. This was especially the case with their endeavour to have a bibliographical list compiled of all books relating to agriculture or land tenure in Wales, with the view of illustrating the history of the development of those subjects. On this subject the Commissioners speak as follows in their Report, p. 92 :—
"Out of a total of over four hundred books (exclusive of our supplemental lists) which are entered in our bibliograp hy, not more than about one half of that number are to be found in the British Museum. During the course of our general inquiry in Wales, we were repeatedly assured that no translation into Welsh of the Agricultural Holdings

[1] Further information as to the history of the periodical literature of Wales is printed in Appendix C to the Report of the Welsh Land Commission, which, in addition to other particulars, contains a list of all the periodicals (both Welsh and English) issued in Wales or in connection therewith in the year 1895.

Act, 1883, had ever been published. We subsequently discovered an edition brought out by a Welsh barrister ; but we very much question whether a copy of it is to be found in any public library, either in or out of Wales, and we fear that, owing to the circumstances which govern Welsh bookselling, it is unknown to the farming community outside the immediate district in which it was published. The explanation for all this seems to be that there is in Wales no central emporium where Welsh publications can be procured." According to a recent critic,[1] "every Welsh publisher plays for his own hand, and no more. No general Welsh catalogue is ever published, and scores, nay, we could say hundreds, of Welsh books never find their way to the British Museum." Private enterprise and a more enlightened policy on the part of Welsh publishers might do much to remedy this unsatisfactory state of things, but in the matter of collecting and preserving the varied and numerous productions of the Welsh press a national library and museum in Wales might effect what the British Museum in London is at present, through no fault of its own, wholly incapable of doing. The establishment of such an institution, and its endowment by the State, has been recommended from time to time,[2]

---

[1] Mr. Eilir Evans, in the article already mentioned. In the course of the discussion which followed the reading of his paper, it was suggested that the county councils of Wales might register the existing printers and obtain complete lists of the works issued by them.

[2] *E.g.*, by Rowlands, in the preface to his " Cambrian Bibliography" (p. xxii.) ; by various speakers at the National Eisteddfod (Langollen) of 1858 (see *Cambrian Journal*, 2nd ser., i., p. 297) ; by J. E. Southall, in "Wales and her Language" (1892), pp. 308–9 ; by Mr. D. Brynmor-Jones, in an address delivered before the Cymmrodorion section at the National Eisteddfod held at Pontypridd in 1893 (see " Thirteenth Annual Report of the National Eisteddfod Association ") ; and by Mr. Romilly Allen, in *Archæologia Cambrensis* for July, 1896. Several societies, having their headquarters at Cardiff, also promoted a scheme for celebrating Her Majesty's Jubilee in 1887 by establishing in that town a national institute for Wales, but the project was not realised.

and has recently been urged on more than one occasion in Parliament.[1]

Their experience led the Commission to the conclusion that such an institution is not only desirable, but most essential for the preservation of the scattered productions of the unorganised publishing trade of Wales. For the historian no tract or broadsheet, ballad or penny almanac, is without its value. They all contribute to make up the record of a nation's life, they are all expressions of local thought, and without them the mosaic of a country's past cannot be pieced together.

But there are many objects, other than printed works, that should find a receptacle in such an institution : drawings of implements and articles illustrating the industries of Wales and collections of the fauna and flora of the country. Nothing could throw such a light upon the development of agriculture in Wales as a series of drawings illustrative of the implements in use among Welsh farmers at the end of the last century. It is well-nigh impossible now to trace the local varieties in the form of the rake, the shovel, and the sickle, and it is difficult to ascertain with certainty what manner of implement the

---

[1] The National Institutions (Wales) Bill (No. 411), 1891, which was backed by Mr. Alfred Thomas and nine other Welsh members of Parliament, contained a clause [21(5)] which empowered the National Council "to establish a national museum for Wales, to apply for a charter of incorporation of the same, and to apply to Parliament for an Act to enable the trustees of the British Museum to give to such museum for Wales any books, manuscripts, works, objects, or specimens which, in the opinion of the said trustees, especially concern Wales or the Cymric race." The Established Church (Wales) Bill (No. 144), 1895, also provided that the objects (specified in the first schedule) to which the residue of the Church property were to be applied should include "technical and higher education, including the establishment and maintenance of a library, museum, or academy of art for Wales." The question has also been raised on other occasions, *e.g.*, on 20th August, 1894 (see Hansard, 4th ser., vol. 29, pp. 29 *et seq.*), on 28th August, 1895 (Hansard, 4th ser., vol. 36, pp. 1044 and 1048), and on 21st February and 10th July, 1896.

old Welsh plough was, or the fan, made of frame-wood and canvas and turned by hand, for winnowing purposes. The introduction of manufactured articles, in place of those formerly produced by domestic industry in every farm-house and cottage during the long winter evenings, will soon drive out all recollection of the Welsh peasant's skill in wood carving and other kindred handicraft, both of profit and recreation, while a few spinning wheels are almost all that survive to testify to the industry of his wife and daughters in converting the fleeces of his flock into all manner of woollen goods.

Apart, however, from what may be regarded as the duty of the State with reference to the collection and the preservation of such specimens and objects as have been indicated, whether literary, artistic, or industrial, the Commission was also greatly impressed with the inadequacy of the present means for bringing to the knowledge of the Welsh-speaking rural population the provisions of Acts of Parliament passed for their especial benefit, and the work done by the various Government departments with the direct object of improving their condition or of facilitating them in the pursuit of agriculture. Owing to this want of adequate information, the result has been that Welsh farmers have not been able to avail themselves, to the extent that Parliament has intended, of those ameliorative provisions which have of recent years altered in a considerable degree the relationship of landlord and tenant. The most prevalent instance under this head was the ignorance, well-nigh universal in some districts, as to the provisions of the Agricultural Holdings Act and the Ground Game Act. Almost all the tenant farmers in the Welsh-speaking districts believed that these Acts, especially the former, could be totally excluded by means of a contracting-out clause. Many appeared to be quite unaware that the Act of 1875 had been amended by the subsequent statute of

1883. Even where there was a knowledge of the existence of the latter Act, its provisions, especially as to procedure, were accurately known only to a few, and consequently in most districts the Act was for all practical purposes a dead letter.

To take another example, only very few of the witnesses examined by the Welsh Land Commission appeared to possess copies of the "Official Analysis of Railway Rates,"[1] published by the Board of Trade, though it is of great importance that farmers should be able to ascertain the legal charges for the conveyance of agricultural produce, feeding stuffs, artificial manures, and the like commodities.

In view of these facts, it was more than once suggested to the Commission that it would be of great advantage if in rural districts the service of the Post-office were utilised for the sale and distribution of Acts of Parliament and Government publications. If, for instance, a farmer could procure a copy, say, of the Agricultural Holdings Act by merely giving a verbal order for it to the local postmaster in his own district, or even to the rural postman, and prepaying for it its published price, with a fractional charge, if necessary, to cover its transmission,[2] we believe that such Acts would so penetrate to places which they never reach at present, and that there would result therefrom a more enlightened understanding of the civic rights and duties of those concerned in the occupation and cultivation of the soil.

---

[1] Parliamentary Paper C.—6,832 of 1893, price 1*s.*

[2] See, for example, Qu. 3142—3. We understand that in some foreign countries a system of this kind is in vogue for the sale and distribution of newspapers. According to the *Times* (5th December, 1894, p. 13), "it is possible in Egypt, for example, to order at any post-office any newspaper from any country in the world. The subscription to the newspaper, plus a small commission, is paid down in the local post-office, and the Egyptian Postmaster-General sees the rest of the business through."

Short, however, of establishing a system of this kind in connection with the Post-office, it would probably facilitate, to some extent, the sale of official publications, if a special depôt for that purpose were established in the Principality by means of commissioning some Welsh bookseller, or other person able to carry on correspondence in Welsh, to be the duly constituted representative of Her Majesty's Stationery Office in that respect. It may be pointed out that there are already such accredited agents in Edinburgh and Glasgow for Scotland, and in Dublin for Ireland, in addition to Messrs. Eyre & Spottiswoode in London; and that the names of these respective firms are imprinted on every Parliamentary paper issued.

But it is not the mere system, or want of system, in the distribution of these publications that is alone defective at present; the language in which they are couched is a much greater obstacle to their being read and understood by the Welsh-speaking population of Wales. The difficulty we refer to here is that which arises from the Welsh farmers' ignorance of English, rather than from the technical phraseology which, even in England, frequently renders Acts of Parliament far from being easily intelligible to the less educated classes. Technicality of language by itself is, however, so serious an obstacle to the general understanding and interpretation of official documents that it has been deemed expedient by the State to publish abstracts of such statutes as the Mines Regulations Acts and the Factory and Workshop Acts, with the view of more effectively bringing home to the persons carrying on, or employed in those industries, the conditions and regulations imposed on them by Parliament. In the particular instances mentioned, Welsh translations of such abstracts have been officially prepared and published by the Home Office, for exhibition in the precincts of mines and factories. The General Register Office, as early as 1837, had two of its official papers issued in Welsh, and since then a vaccination notice and the form of instructions for filling in the census schedules have also been translated by that department. Several other departments have also, from time to time, recognised the desirability of translating their notices, etc., into Welsh, notably the Local Government Board, which has so issued several Acts of Parliament and administrative orders, and these translations, now that they are becoming better known in the Principality, are, it is said, greatly appreciated by the Welsh-speaking population.[1]

Several witnesses[2] suggested to the Commission that Acts of Parliament directly affecting the rural districts should be translated into Welsh, while Sir Joseph R. Bailey, in objecting to such a course, recommended as an alternative that "there should be published in Welsh a short epitome of such parts of Acts of Parliament as concerned Welsh interests, cutting out what are called words of skill, and making the Acts of Parliament a *résumé* so simple that in fact persons not well educated could understand them."[3]

This was the view also taken by Mr. W. O. Brigstocke, formerly chairman of the Carmarthenshire County Council,[4] who observed that in the case of the Irish Land Act there are very concise and plain summaries published, and he thought that if a summary were published in Welsh it would be better than a complete translation, owing to the difficulty of turning English legal phrases into Welsh.

But not one Act that directly affects the agricultural

[1] A list of all the Parliamentary papers and State documents that have thus been officially translated into the Welsh language is given in Appendix A. to the Report.

[2] Such as Mr. O. Slaney Wynne, at Qu. 8,326 ; compare also Qu. 14,561, 23,224, 48,152.

[3] Qu. 49,786.   [4] Qu. 43,432.

community as such—from the Ground Game Act and the Agricultural Holdings Acts to the Allotments Acts and the Fertilizers and Feeding Stuffs Act—has been officially translated into Welsh, either in its entirety or in the form of a popular summary.   Nor does it appear that an official translation has at any time been issued of a single leaflet out of the very considerable literature published by the Board of Agriculture in the service of the agricultural interests of this country.   The practical suggestions, the timely advice or warning, and the valuable information about the agricultural methods of other countries which are contained in the publications of the Board, reach and influence but an infinitesimal fraction of Welsh agriculturists, owing to the fact that no translations of these leaflets and other publications are ever issued.   The evil is to some extent aggravated by the further fact that few, if any, of the inspectors of the Board who travel in Wales possess any knowledge of the Welsh language.[1]   This non-utilisation of Welsh as a medium for reaching the cultivators of the soil is all the more regrettable inasmuch as there is no exclusively agricultural newspaper or magazine issued in the Welsh language, and consequently the ordinary Welsh farmer, whose reading is confined to his own language, is not able to inform himself as to points concerning which his English brother receives gratuitous advice from the State.

To remedy this inequality, and to enable the farmers of Wales to reap the full benefit of the valuable literature issued by the Board of Agriculture, it seems to us highly desirable that in future Welsh translations should be issued of all the Board's leaflets, except such as contain matter wholly inapplicable to the conditions of agriculture in Wales.   A paper dealing with hops, for example, need

[1] On this point see Hansard's "Parliamentary Debates," 4th ser., vol. 36, pp. 739-742.

not, perhaps, be translated, as Wales is not a hop-growing country—unless, of course, it were decided to suggest the promotion of that industry in the Principality. In certain circumstances the peculiar conditions of Welsh agriculture might also render it necessary to prepare special leaflets for distribution in Wales alone, or even in the Welsh-speaking districts only. A Welsh edition of the "Journal of the Board of Agriculture" should also be published, but it would not, perhaps, be desirable that it should be entirely a translation of the English edition. Some of the English articles might, with advantage, be replaced by original articles in Welsh having special application to Welsh agriculture. An example in the nature of a precedent is to be found in Cape Colony, where the Colonial Government publishes an agricultural journal in English and in Dutch for the use of the respective races in that Colony. Owing to the more backward condition of agriculture in Wales as compared with England—taking the country generally, and also owing to the remoter situation of the country and the greater inaccessibility of portions of it, stronger efforts than are necessary in England should be made to enable the Welsh farmer to become thoroughly acquainted with the latest improvements and the most modern methods, unless his lot in the future is to continue, as in the past, much behind that of the ordinary English farmer.

The census returns for 1891 furnish for the first time a record of the number of persons speaking Welsh only, English only, or both English and Welsh within the confines of the Principality. The accuracy of these returns has been questioned by two different parties, one complaining that the number returned as speaking Welsh *only* is too large, the other that the number of those stated as speaking English *only* is too large. Thus, on the one hand the compilers of the census, in their general report,

state that abundant evidence was received showing that
the instructions appended to the householder's schedule
"was either misunderstood or set at naught by a large
number of those Welshmen who could speak both
languages, and that the word 'Welsh' was very often
returned, when the proper entry would have been 'Both';
on the ground, it may be presumed, that Welsh was the
language spoken habitually or preferentially." It appears,
however, that at the time of the taking of the census it
was generally understood that no mere smattering of either
language was to count, and that consequently most people
assumed that the real test as to the column under which
they should be returned was whether they could give
evidence in a court of law in the language specified at
the top of that column. This, it has been pointed out,
would cut both ways inasmuch as many who possessed only
a smattering of the Welsh language would naturally return
themselves as speaking English *only*, instead of returning
themselves in the bilingual column. The same would also
be the case with Welsh people possessing only a smattering
of English. There is thus the possibility that not only the
Welsh, but also the English column was, for some districts,
perhaps, unduly large at the expense of the bilingual one.
It was also suggested that in many cases census schedules
without the language column were through some error or
other not distributed in every district,[1] so that the result
would presumably be that those persons (whether Welsh or
English speaking), who were furnished with such schedules,

---

[1] "From various parts of the country there were complaints that papers
were sent round to householders which contained no columns for entering the
language spoken ; the Registrar-General does not inform us as to the way in
which such papers were dealt with, whether they were treated as English only,
or entered under 'No statement'": see Southall on "The Welsh Language
Census of 1891," p. 7. See also the report of discussions of this question in the
House of Commons (August, 1894), in Hansard's "Parliamentary Debates,"
4th ser., vol. 29, pp. 33 *et seq.*, 179 and 321 *et seq.*

were ultimately entered as English only. The opinion
expressed by the census authorities in their report, however, is that "the number of monoglot Welsh persons is
considerably overstated, and the number of persons who
can speak both languages correspondingly understated."
Most of those who have subsequently made a study of
these returns seem, however, to favour the opinion that
the returns are substantially correct, and that the doubts
raised by the Registrar-General as to the *bona fides* of some
of the returns were capable of only a very limited application. Having thus stated briefly the different views as to
the accuracy of these returns, we have no choice but to
deal with the figures as they stand. It is unnecessary that
we should here consider them in great detail.[1] Briefly
summarised, however, the population of Wales and
Monmouthshire, in regard to language, was composed as
follows :—

Speaking only English	759,416
Speaking only Welsh	508,036
Speaking English and Welsh . .	402,253
Speaking foreign languages . . .	3,076
No information (over two years) . .	12,833
Infants under two years . . .	90,791
Total . . .	1,776,405

It is thus seen that those who spoke English only,
759,416 in all, outnumbered those who spoke Welsh only,
who amounted to 508,036 ; while 402,253 were returned as
bilingual. Or the figures may be put in this other way :
Of the total population who spoke one or other or both of
the two languages, 1,161,669 could speak English, while
910,289 could speak Welsh. The total number of those

---

[1] This is done in the memorandum on the census statistics printed in the
Commissioners' Appendix, Tables 27 and 28.

who could speak Welsh, however, outnumbered those that could not, for while the latter numbered 759,416, the former amounted to 910,289.

The territorial divisions for which the returns as to language are given are registration districts and registration counties. It follows that the totals are, therefore, given not for Wales proper, according to its ancient and well-known boundaries, but for *registration* Wales and Monmouthshire, which, as the Commissioners show in the Appendix to their Report, is less by 14,116 acres than Wales and Monmouthshire; but the total population of this registration area exceeds that of Wales proper by nearly 5,000 persons. The registration districts are for all practical purposes the poor law unions of the country, but their boundaries are not generally known to any great extent outside their own limits though the name of their chief or capital town affords a general indication of their situation, inasmuch as such a town is usually found to be the natural centre of the district which has been formed into the poor law union as well as the registration district that bears its name. The boundaries of the registration counties differ in most cases so very widely from those of the ancient and administrative counties that it would be entirely misleading if we were to present here the result of the linguistic returns for such counties only. By grouping together several registration counties the vagaries of the boundaries of each individual county are pretty evenly balanced, and there is, in consequence, less difficulty in fixing in the mind the general characteristics, the contour, and the boundaries of a large area than of a small district with artificial or arbitrary boundaries little known except by officials whose business it is to be acquainted with them, and for whose convenience they have chiefly assumed their present form. We shall, therefore, give here the ratios of the Welsh and English-speaking population for such large areas only as can be easily apprehended or borne in mind even without the necessity of referring to a map.[1] We wish, however, to add that in order to render these linguistic returns of real value, if they are to be continued, in future censuses, both the civil parish and the ancient county should be adopted as additional units for which the numbers of those speaking Welsh only, English only, or both languages should be stated in the published returns.

The following table represents the result of such a grouping of registration counties as we have just suggested, so far as the returns as to language are concerned :—

	Proportion per Cent. to Total whose Spoken Language was stated, of Persons speaking.			Ratio of Total Number of Persons able to speak Welsh to Total *not* able to speak Welsh.	
	English only.	Welsh only.	Both English and Welsh.	Welsh.	Non-Welsh.
Six Northern Counties.	23·6	49·5	26·9	76·3	23·7
Five Western Counties (excluding Pembrokeshire) .	8·3	66·8	24·9	90·9	9·03
Six Western Counties (including Pembrokeshire) .	17·7	59·1	23·2	82·2	17·8
Six Eastern Counties .	49·1	22·8	28·0	50·7	49·2
Six Eastern Counties and Monmouthshire .	56·8	18·7	24·4	43·1	56·9
Six Southern Counties.	44·8	29·1	26·1	55·1	44·9
Six Southern Counties and Monmouthshire .	53·0	23·9	23·1	46·8	53·1
Wales	38·3	35·3	26·4	61·5	38·5
Wales and Monmouthshire .	45·5	30·4	24·1	54·4	45·6

The ultimate result of these statistics is, that of the total population whose spoken language is recorded, 54·4 per

[1] A Linguistic Map of Wales, showing approximately the exterior limits of native Welsh in 1890, is published in Southall's "Wales and Her

cent. were returned as able to speak Welsh, and 45·6 per cent. as unable to do so.

Though there are no definite statistics to show what were the respective numbers of the Welsh and English-speaking population of Wales previous to 1891, still various estimates have been made of their relative proportions at different periods during the present century.

Thus Mr. Thomas Darlington, who has given consider-able attention to the subject,[1] estimates that in 1801 the number of the English monoglot population of Wales was somewhere between 100,000 and 120,000. In other words, out of a total enumerated population of 587,245, about 20 per cent. were English-speaking, the remaining 80 per cent. being Welsh-speaking. Sir Thomas Phillips, the author of a most valuable work on the social condition of the Principality,[2] published in 1849, estimated that in 1841 the proportion of the Welsh to English-speaking popula-tion was as 67 to 33. But the population of Wales during the period that had elapsed since 1801 had increased by more than 60 per cent., and when it is realised that this increase included very large numbers of immigrants from England into industrial districts of the Principality, the Welsh language must be said to have held its own ground with remarkable tenacity. Thirty years later, after the census of 1871, Mr. Ravenstein made a careful and exhaustive inquiry as to the numbers of the Celtic-speaking populations of the United Kingdom, and the result, so far as Wales was concerned, showed that, according to his estimate,

---

Language " (2nd ed., 1893). A later map, based on the census returns of 1891, and showing the percentage of the Welsh-speaking population in the fifty-two registration districts of Wales, was published by the same author in his " Welsh Language Census of 1891 " (Newport, 1895).

[1] See " The English-speaking Population of Wales " in " Wales " for May, 1894, pp. 11–16.

[2] "Wales : The Language, Social Condition, Moral Character, and Religious Opinions of the People, considered in relation to Education," p. 7.

the proportions of the Welsh and English populations had not greatly changed since 1841. According to his conclusions on the subject,[1] the Welsh-speakers of Wales represented in 1871 66·2 per cent.

These various estimates can perhaps be best understood if cast in a tabular form, where they can also be placed in juxtaposition to the ascertained results of the census of 1891 :—

	1801.		1841.		1871.		1891.	
	Persons.	Per-centage.	Persons.	Per-centage.	Persons.	Per-centage.	Persons.	Per-centage.
Welsh . . . English (only) .	(About) 470,000 100,000 to 120,000	80 20	700,000 346,000	67 33	1,006,100 406,500	66·2 33·8	910,289 759,416	54·4 45·6
Total enumerated } Population. }	587,245	100	1,046,073	100	1,412,583	100	1,669,705[2]	100

Assuming the first estimates to be substantially correct, the result of this table may be stated thus :—The whole population of Wales has trebled during the 90 years from 1801 to 1891 ; the Welsh-speaking population has rather more than doubled in that time; but the purely English population has increased nearly sevenfold.

That the great increase in the English population of Wales has to some extent been brought about at the expense of the Welsh-speaking population is a conclusion which has already been forced upon us when we were

---

[1] Quoted in the "Report of the Committee on Intermediate Education in Wales, 1881," p. xlvii. The results of Mr. Ravenstein's inquiry were stated in a paper read by him before the Statistical Society, of which the portions relating to Wales were reproduced in "Bye-Gones" for May 7, 1879.

[2] This is the total for registration Wales and Monmouthshire, omitting infants (a) under two years of age, (b) adults who spoke neither Welsh nor English, and (c) those who made no statement as to their language.

considering the encroachment of English on the border districts of the counties of Radnor, Brecon, and Montgomery.[1] But this growth of the English-speaking population is probably due, even in a larger degree, to the immigration of English people into Wales, concurrently of course with the emigration of Welsh-speaking persons from Wales.

[1] See above, pp. 526-7.

CHAPTER XIII.

RURAL WALES AT THE PRESENT DAY.

IN estimating the moral and intellectual condition of the Welsh, it will be convenient to discuss facts of two distinct orders together, to wit, the natural disposition or racial characteristics of the people, and the circumstances under which they live. Under the latter heading we proceed to consider the questions of food and clothing, of farmhouses and cottages.

We begin with the diet of the farmers and labourers, premising that we have found no reason to draw any distinction in these matters between tenant farmers and small freeholders ; and in a general way we may say, that in the matter of food as in many others the difference between the small farmer's family and that of the labourer is very trifling. Nay, in some instances, the farmer in a small way lives quite as hard as his labourer, and harder than the artisans or miners of his district. This harmonises with the fact mentioned more than once in the evidence collected by the Welsh Land Commission, that a labourer frequently expects to become a farmer and succeeds in doing so, while, *vice versâ*, the sons of a small farmer find it sometimes more advantageous to work as labourers than to help at home. This is much the same all over the Principality, but when a farmer was asked the question as to his meals, he was not always willing to answer. Evidently a sort of pride came into play which made the witness put on the best appearance possible consistently with the wish not to depart too widely from the truth.   In other words, questions as to diet were apt to be regarded—unnecessarily we think—as inquisitorial ; and sometimes a witness could only be got to speak freely on the understanding that he was not describing his own household, but those of his neighbours or the people generally whose houses he visited in his district.   In some cases the witness seemed to be apprehensive lest his own neighbourhood should not appear to advantage as compared with other parts of the country.   This is a kind of local pride which we should be sorry to discourage ; it is self-respect writ large, and it cannot but tend to produce beneficial results.

We now proceed to cite some typical portions of the evidence[1] as to the diet of the farmers of Wales.   Mr. Hugh Williams spoke as to Lanfair Mathafarn Eithaf, and the adjoining parishes of the Anglesey Union, to the effect that some of the farmers there live " on bread-and-milk " for breakfast, on "potatoes with butter-milk, and potatoes with butter " for dinner, adding that some get salt meat, but very seldom any meat except salt meat, that is to say, bacon and beef.   He went on to say that they have bread-and-butter and tea in the afternoon, and porridge and butter-milk for supper.   Lastly, he said that " there are many farmers who cannot afford to get a piece of fresh meat once a year."

Mr. David Davies, a labourer living in the parish of Langybi, in Carnarvonshire, made the following statement[2] as to the diet of the farmers in his neighbourhood : " The farmer's food is not of the best.   It generally consists of salted meat, which is kept for a year or so until it is hard and difficult to eat.   It is not often that the farmer's family or the servants get fresh meat, but when they do

[1] Qu. 19,895, 19,932 –46.   [2] Qu. 11,766.

get it, it is only the head of a cow or pig when one is killed. Generally when a cow is killed for the farmer's use it is one which could not be sold to a butcher. If a cow is a good one it is always sold to pay the rent. The bread is better than it used to be, because they have failed to bake barley these last few years, and the farmers are compelled to buy wheaten bread. The butter is generally fresh and good, but the farmers can afford to give but very little to the servants, and little even to their own children."

Mr. Ivan Thos. Davies, giving evidence at Bala, stated it as his opinion that the hill farmers have much the same fare now as he had when a boy on a farm, and that fare he described as follows :—" First of all we had in the morning bruised oatmeal cake and butter-milk ;[1] then we had some bread-and-butter and tea. For dinner we had bacon and potatoes. For tea, at about three or four o'clock, we used to have a lot of *sucan*, followed by a cup of tea. *Sucan* is a kind of thin flummery, or something like that. Then we had porridge or bread-and-cheese and butter-milk for supper."[2]

Mr. Gomer Roberts, a native of Merionethshire, who now farms in the upper part of the Vale of Clwyd, gave us his view to the following effect :[3] Being asked as to the usual fare of a small farmer and his family, he said that they had as their breakfast bread-and-milk or *pôtes* (a kind of

---

[1] This kind of food is very common in Gwyned, and it goes by the English name of "shot"; but in Anglesey and parts of Carnarvonshire it is known also as *picws màli*. The oatmeal cake is bruised quite small, and butter-milk is mixed with it. It is then mostly eaten forthwith, but we have sometimes heard of its being left standing to give the bread time to swell. Even without that delay, however, it proves a very satisfying food, and the farmers know from experience that a servant who partakes of it freely will not require much else to complete his meal; and, above all, they regard it as conducive to economy in the matter of butter and cheese and meat.

[2] Qu. 6,961—4, 6,934.

[3] Qu. 61,156—78, 61,225—9, 62,264—5.

pottage or broth), and that this was followed by bread-and-butter and tea. For dinner they had " meat always, bacon or mutton or beef"; but he proceeded to explain that "bacon is the backbone of the meal"; and they had fresh meat occasionally, as, for instance, when a sheep was killed or when, within the last few years, a farmer found butchers' meat pressed on him at a very low price—a lower price, in fact, than that at which he could cure his own bacon. In the afternoon they would have bread-and-butter and tea, and for supper they had bread-and-milk or *pŏtès*, as in the morning. This witness stated that the bread in his present district had for the last few years been all wheat, and by way of comparison he stated that more oatmeal bread was made in Merionethshire, and that a good deal more porridge was eaten there. He considered that the food eaten in Merionethshire was better than the food prevalent in the Vale of Clwyd, and further that the less tea people take, and the more milk and meat, the better; this he considered " the strongest food and the best."

Mr. David Rogers, farming in the parish of Forden, in Montgomeryshire, spoke to the following effect[1] as to his own farm : They had breakfast at six o'clock, which in the case of the men consisted of broth ; between nine and ten they had a meal which he called a bait; then came dinner, with mutton or beef, or whatever meat there might be ; and between four and five in the afternoon came another meal, involving cold meat, cheese, and butter ; and, lastly, there was supper. He remarked that in harvest-time his men had meat at all their meals except breakfast, and that the meat was fresh; but he was of opinion that they had not always fared so well.

Nevertheless it is a tradition, probably of long standing in other parts of Wales, that the farmers of Montgomeryshire near the English borders fared, comparatively

[1] Qu. 65,797—808.

speaking, better than those of other parts of the Principality, say, for instance, Cardiganshire. In this latter county it used, in the days before the making of the railway connecting Aberystwyth with Shrewsbury and Oswestry, to be related of them that it was their custom to begin dinner with the pudding ever since one of them had chanced to die before reaching that course. The alleged change was supposed ɩv a people who rarely tasted pudding to embody the rule of securing the best thing first. As to the five meals, however, they will be found referred to in other parts of the evidence.[1]

In the adjoining county of Radnor the fare appears to be much the same as in Forden, except that less fresh meat is eaten there; and one witness, Mr. Lewelyn Pugh, from the parish of St. Harmon, an old man of eighty-four, gave it as his opinion[2] that when he was a boy people did not live in his neighbourhood "the tenth part as well" as they do now.

Mr. W. O. Brigstocke, speaking generally of the farmers in the unions of Cardigan and Newcastle Emlyn, used the following words:[3]—"The Welsh tenant farmer is most thrifty and frugal ; and his diet, though somewhat rough, is healthy and sufficient. It consists of tea, bread, butter, cheese, milk, bacon, and vegetables; fresh meat is rarely seen at table, and the diet of the ordinary farmer differs but little from that of the labourer." But Mr. J. C. Jones, trading at Lanarth, in the neighbourhood of Aberayron, Cardiganshire, spoke from a minute knowledge of a more circumscribed district, and described the usual diet as follows :[4]—"The fare of the tenants as a class is hard, and I am almost sure if I commenced describing the same it would carry on the face of it the air of exaggeration. The

---

[1] For instance, under Qu. 43,281 and 70,795—800.
[2] Qu. 52,996—53,005.
[3] Qu. 43,281.   [4] Qu. 48,103.

chief meal of the day is *cawl* or broth, with bacon or dried beef and potatoes. Fresh meat is out of the question."

Mr. John Davies, a tenant farmer living in the parish of Landeusant, Carmarthenshire, says [1] of the food there, that it, "especially the bread, is better than it used to be." "Farmers," he proceeds to say, "very seldom touch butchers' meat, but generally live on bread-and-cheese, potatoes, and some salted meat. They sell nearly all their cattle, butter, and eggs, and all the best things in order to pay the landlord." In his cross-examination he gave the details of the usual meals in harmony with the summary from which we have cited these words.

Miss Kate Jenkins, speaking as to the parish of Langadock, said,[2] "The living is exceedingly frugal and scanty, even in large farms ; fresh meat only on Sundays, often never at all ; no butter or meat for breakfast. They will not eat butter if dozen tubs in dairy ; it goes to pay rent. Broth for dinner daily, with a little salt meat ; I have been in a farm where they were only eating broth of oatmeal and potatoes, with no meat at all. Farmers will offer you tea and bread-and-butter for dinner as a luxury. Very hard-working, very little recreation, except to market. No holidays, except, perhaps, the sons go by an excursion train for two days, or the daughters for a few days to the seaside. No reading-rooms or entertainments, or where they have been tried unsuccessful. Singing schools and Eisteddfods almost the only recreations. A weekly newspaper looked upon as a luxury."

Mr. J. A. Doyle, of Pendarren, near Crickhowell, who reported to the Royal Commission on Agriculture, in 1881, on the state of farming in Wales, gave evidence to the Welsh Land Commission as to a district on the borders of

---

[1] Qu. 39,554, 39,575—82.   [2] Qu. 38,024.

Brecknockshire and Monmouthshire, saying,[1] "I should say from observation of some of the quite small farmers that I should think their standard of comfort was hardly, if at all, higher than that of the labourers. As to a former tenant of mine on a small farm, which I now occupy myself, of sixty acres, I do not think his standard of comfort, so far as I could observe, was materially better than that of my labourers."

Mr. Lewis Llewelyn, a tenant farmer living in the upper portion of the Neath Valley, gave the Commission the details of the farmer's meals as follows : [2]—" The breakfast consists of tea, bread-and-butter or cheese, and, in many places, bacon. At dinner, they have potatoes and meat, mostly bacon, but sometimes butchers' meat ; then comes in the afternoon some tea and bread-and-butter. For supper they have milk or broth and bread-and-cheese, but a cup of tea for those who are fond of having it again." He considered that the bread was good, and that they fared pretty well, but he suggested that those living higher among the hills lived harder.

Mr. James Jenkins, a tenant farmer and member of the Pembrokeshire County Council, gave his evidence[3] at Letterston, and stated that they have for breakfast tea or coffee and bread-and-cheese and butter, for dinner *cawl*, a broth or soup containing meal and meat, sometimes beef or mutton, but more usually bacon ; and it is very seldom that they have any fresh meat. Besides this the dinner has the usual complement of potatoes and bread. Lastly, the supper is sometimes tea and sometimes *cawl*, of the nature already described. Mr. Jenkins stated that the smaller farmers had been living harder than that, but in the Anglo-Flemish part of the county—his farm is near the boundary—people fare, according to him, considerably better. Asked as to the difference between the Welsh and

[1] Qu. 50,005.   [2] Qu. 2,507—20.
[3] Qu. 31,403—30, 28,929—37.

the English in the county, he answered, " We are hardier,
and we live harder."   *Q.*—" You think you live harder ? "—
" Oh, a deal ; there is no doubt about that."   *Q.*—" You live
harder in the Welsh part ? "—" Yes ; their landlords—Lord
Cawdor, for instance—he is very glad to get a Welshman
down Castle Martin way."   *Q.*—" Do you say they are
hardier or harder?"—" Hardier and harder, living harder—
we can do with commoner things."   It is to be noticed
that this evidence appears to coincide with the charge of
excessive eating sometimes brought against the Anglo-
Flemish, as, for example, by George Owen.[1]

We have dealt thus far with the food of the small farmer
and his household ; and it has been suggested to us more
than once, that the food provided by large farmers is
better ; but we can draw no distinction of importance
between the fare of the small farmer and his labourers who
eat at his table.   Those who have to find for themselves,
however, live probably harder.   Among other things, they
get less milk, especially in districts remote from towns ; it is
not worth the farmers' while to sell milk, and though they
may give the labourers milk when they send to ask for
some, the latter naturally feel reluctant to trouble them
too often, and the result is that they and their families fall
back on tea more and more.   The labourers probably fare
better in the neighbourhood of great centres of industries,
such as the ironworks of Glamorganshire or the slate
quarries of North Wales ; for a hard fare would act

[1] See his " Pembrokeshire," p. 43, where we read as follows :—" In one
thinge these our Ffleminges have altered their stomackes from the rest over the
sea, for in that excesse with which the Dutchmen are taxed for drinkinge are
these theire kinsmen for excessive eatinge, for of custome at certeine seasons
and labors they will have fyve meales a daie, and if you will bestowe the sixt
on them they will accept of it verye kindly, and if they be but a litle intreated,
they will bestowe laboure on the seaventhe meal."   To most men who have
travelled in Belgium and noticed the ample meals habitually consumed at the
hotels patronised by Flemings, George Owen would seem to have slightly
overrated the change in "stomackes."

powerfully to make them leave the land and seek other employment.[1]

The Commission did not systematically take evidence on the question of drink ; but we infer, from incidental remarks made by witnesses, that the small farmers seldom have beer at home ; and it is only on some of the larger farms that beer is given to the servants and labourers, which happens mostly in harvest-time, and on special occasions. Difficulties have arisen here and there in consequence of beer being supplied to the labourers, and the tendency is to discontinue the supply. In one instance the employer, Sir Joseph R. Bailey, of Glan Usk Park, Crickhowell, in speaking of the management of his home-farm, described the circumstances which led him to put an end to the custom of providing beer for his workmen in harvest-time ; but they receive each extra pay in that season of the year, and the rule appears to work satisfactorily. The ordinary drink of the small farmer and those dependent on him is milk, tea, or cold water ; but in some instances water with a sprinkling of oatmeal has been tried. We have it in evidence that this is pretty generally enjoyed in harvest-time in the neighbourhood of Bala ; and we understand that the custom is much the same in the neighbourhood of Lampeter, Lanybyther, Landyssul, and the adjoining districts on both sides of the Teify, together with the whole of the country between that river and the Towy.[2]

In looking over the evidence generally as to the diet of the small farmers of Wales and their households, one is greatly struck by the remarkable improvement which has taken place throughout the country. Among other things may be mentioned the fact that before the use of foreign

---

[1] For the evidence for the statements made in this paragraph see Qu. 10,774, 19,946, 24,866, 4,162—7, 10,225—6, 4,161—7.

[2] Qu. 3,727, 5,347—8, 7,304 – 7, 49,802, 49,841—5, 3,649—51.

flour became general the small farmers tried to grow corn for their own bread, and that in all the upland country they lived mostly on barley bread. If the harvest happened to prove disappointing or the weather continued wet, which it often did, they suffered in their fare accordingly, and anybody who remembers the forties or the fifties will not readily forget the sort of bread on their tables, how it looked more like lead than food for human beings. But they no longer rely on corn crops of their own, and very little barley bread is now made. One may say, that there has been an advance all along the line. In the course of the examination at Bala of Mr. Thomas Davies, a tenant farmer, who undertook to speak to the general condition of things on the Rhiwlas estate in the parishes of Lanycil and Lanfor, the following extract relating to the former fare of small farmers in Merionethshire was read from a " Prize Essay on the Agriculture of North Wales " : [1] " For dinner you will see a small farmer have half a salt herring, with potatoes and butter-milk (very poor food for a working man) ; his wife and family must content themselves with butter-milk and potatoes, or, perhaps, after the farmer has finished his part . herring there will be a scramble amongst the youngsters for the bones to suck as a treat. They sometimes have a little skim-milk cheese with oaten bread, some, better off than others, bacon."   The witness was then asked as to that extract : " Is that a fair average truthful picture of what you remember in your youth ? " He answered, " Yes, it is certainly so ; I remember it very well " ; [2] and, in answer to a further question, he said as to the

---

[1] Printed in the Journal of the Royal Agricultural Society of England for 1846 (vii. 572). See also Qu. 3,726, 5,346, 8,507—9, 8,072.

[2] If we go further back, to the seventeenth century for example, we find the extreme disparity between the food and drink of the rich and those of the poor attracting the attention of strangers : the reader may be referred for an instance to " The Account of the Official Progress of his Grace Henry the first Duke of Beaufort through Wales in 1684 " (London, 1888), p. 249.

diet that " it is very much better now." This statement as
to improvement is practically borne out by the evidence
of Mr. Price, the owner of the Rhiwlas estate, who said in
his evidence :[1] " Unmarried men prefer living in the farmhouses, because they get food and lodging free ; and the
master is bound to see to their comforts, and one of my
tenants told me that they now insist on meat and tarts and
pudding at dinner."

It is needless to produce more evidence on this point :
it is so generally admitted that we have as a rule taken it
for granted. Nevertheless there is no denying that some
of the small farmers have still a hard fare ; we need only
recall the words of Mr. J. C. Jones which we have already
cited. But there is also evidence in point from Mr. R.
Foulkes Jones, headmaster of the board school at Lwyn-
gwryl, between Towyn and Barmouth.[2] Asked concerning
the food of the children of the farmers in his district, he
answered as to those who came from a distance and ate
their midday food in the schoolroom, especially in winter,
as follows : " I have seen farmers' children in the school
eating barley bread and a red herring divided between two
or three of them, and drinking butter-milk with it." He
characterised them as " very badly fed indeed," and he did
not regard the fare as adequate to keep the children in
health. Even in the districts where the fare is still hard,
we have no doubt that it was harder half a century ago,
not to go back to the hard times before the repeal of the
Corn Laws ; and speaking of the country generally, the
advance in the people's ideas of comfort cannot readily
be exaggerated.

There remain, however, a few remarks which we wish
to make with respect to that progress itself in so far as
regards food. We would refer again to the little importance attached to milk as part of the food of the labourers'

[1] Qu. 16,318.   [2] Qu. 16,035—8.

families, since we do not think it altogether satisfactory
that tea should take its place. We have it in the evidence [1] given to the Commission at Bridgend, in Glamorganshire, by Dr. Wyndham Randall, medical officer of health
in the district, that the diet of the outdoor labourer and
his family " might be improved if more milk were made
use of, particularly by the children." Similarly, the Rev.
R. W. Griffith, whose ministry was carried on among the
people of the parish of Landeiniolen, in Carnarvonshire,
stated [2] that the workmen in the quarries " live to a great
extent on tea," while the agricultural labourers "get a
good deal of milk food." Asked to compare the results
so far as his observations went, he said, " Those who take
milk food as a rule are broader men and stronger men."

We cannot help deprecating the increasing consumption
of tea, and the change to the modern diet has not been,
perhaps, in other respects wholly beneficial. The old
regime is exemplified in Welsh parlance as represented by
the triad *F'ewyrth a modryb ac uwd*, " Uncle and Aunt
and stirabout;" as contrasted with the newer regime, with
its *Mistres a mistyr a thê*, " Mistress and Master and tea."
Porridge or stirabout, called in Welsh *uwd*, has probably,
in some form or other, been an important part of the daily
fare of the Welsh peasantry from time immemorial. For
we are carried back far into the past by the suggestive
fact that the Welsh word has its exact equivalent in the
old Cornish *iot* and in the Breton *iôd* for a dish cooked in
a somewhat similar fashion, from which the sturdy peasants
of Brittany are sometimes called *paôtred-iôd*, or " porridge-
boys.' In Wales *uwd* is altogether made either of oatmeal
or of groats, and it is mostly taken with milk. But it is
not the only food of the sort made from oatmeal, for
flummery, called in Welsh *llymry*,[3] is also made of oatmeal,

---

[1] Qu. 16,035—8.   [2] Qu. 12,256—9.
[3] Flummery is made by placing oatmeal to soak in water until it has become

and is eaten a good deal in parts of Wales instead of *uwd*, as it is also in Brittany, for instance, in the neighbourhood of Lanion, in the Côtes du Nord. But flummery is not such good food for a man who works, as porridge ; and the latter continues, on the whole, to be preferred in most parts of the Principality, as it does in Scotland.

At one time oatmeal cake used to be more commonly eaten in Wales than it is now ; but in such matters the Principality comes readily under English influence, and had England been so well known for its bannocks as Scotland they would have continued more in favour in Wales probably than they are. In the case of porridge the fact of its appearing on the breakfast-table of well-to-do English people will prevent the tendency to drop it. The fashion in such matters spreads from the houses of the rich in England to those of the bourgeoisie, and from these it reaches in many ways the houses of the small shopkeepers in the towns and watering-places of Wales. Thence it propagates itself in the farmhouses, and it may do good or the reverse, according to the nature of the change. In the matter of porridge its influence would be on the

---

sour, when the solid stuff, or bran, is squeezed out of it, and the rest passed through a strainer or sieve. It is then boiled to the consistency of a blanc-mange and taken with milk : with sweet milk it makes very palatable food. A thinner or fluid kind of flummery is made in Wales, chiefly for supper, and is called *sucan* in North Wales, and *bwdran* in South Wales ; with the latter vocable compare its mediæval Irish name *buaidrén*. The names vary : thus *sucan* is pronounced *sican* in North Wales, and *sycan* in parts of South Wales, where it is partly used instead of the word *llymry*, while in South Cardiganshire the longer term *uwd sucan* is heard for *llymry*. In Brittany the flummery is, we suspect, partly made of wheat flour, as is the case still more with the *iôd ;* and in 1888, whilst on a visit at M. Renan's house at Ros map Ammon, near Perros Guirec, Professor Rhys had an opportunity of making a comparison. Mme. Renan took Mrs. Rhys one day to visit some farms in the neighbourhood, and came across a family partaking of a dish of the flummery kind. This led her to mention how fond her husband was of it, whereupon the farmer's wife insisted on sending some at once to Ros map Ammon. M. Renan relished it thoroughly, but the Welshman, though fond of *llymry*, could not make much way with the Armoric variant.

right side ; but in the matter, for instance, of broth or
soup, the influence of the fashion is the reverse. For the
making of a cheap and nutritious soup is a problem which
it is not given the national genius of England to solve, and
when the Welsh farmer visits a shopkeeper or tradesman
in the town where he does his marketing, he finds no kind
of soup on the table. So he goes home convinced that
such a dish is not fashionable, and though some kind of
soup should continue to be made in his own house, he
would not consider it the right thing to place any of it
before a stranger who happens to be his guest. We mention this, as the art of making an excellent soup is not yet
extinct in certain parts of the Principality, such as Cardiganshire : it is made by boiling meat in water in which are
put a little oatmeal and a certain quantity of vegetables,
such as leeks, cabbages, turnips, or carrots. This and other
cheap dishes, in the making of which Welsh women have
some experience, should serve as the starting-point in the
cookery schools to be established in the Principality, at
any rate if they are to produce beneficial results in the
near future.

This leads us to touch on the question of cookery among
the farmers. The wife of a small farmer usually takes
part in the cooking, or at any rate tries to superintend it,
and a good deal beyond the immediate comfort of the
family depends on her skill and on that of the maid who
does the cooking. For at hiring time the state of the kitchen
at each farm is pretty well known in the neighbourhood,
and the qualifications of the maid who has charge of it
are freely canvassed. In case she has a bad name, as
unsuccessful in baking, for instance, or in boiling potatoes,
the farmer who engages her cannot readily get the best
servant-men to enter his service. Further, the depression in
agriculture tends to the same result, namely, by compelling
the farmers to engage young and incompetent servant-

maids, who lack the teaching and experience necessary to make them fit for their work in the kitchen. The Commission made no systematic inquiry into this matter, but it was occasionally brought under its notice, as, for instance, by Mr. Richard Rowlands, a farm labourer from Gwalchmai, in Anglesey. While admitting that there had been improvement in the food-stuffs which the farmers procured for their households, he found fault with the cooking, and said : [1] " The servant-girls, as a rule, are very young ; they are too young to know. They have no experience in cooking, and, of course, farmers employ them because they get them for little wages." He admitted that the farmers' wives understood cooking, but he characterised it as " cooking for themselves," not for the servants or labourers. Evidence to somewhat the same effect was given us by a man of a different standing, namely, Dr. Rowlands, physician and surgeon, practising at Lanaelhaiarn, in Carnarvonshire. Asked as to the diet of the labourers and peasantry on whom he attends, whether he thought it satisfactory for men engaged in manual labour, he answered,[2] " No, it is not. Their food is almost in a raw state. That is a reason why I should suggest a school of cookery for the farm servants to learn cookery, and to manage the house when they get married." We think that this witness looked for the remedy in the right direction, namely, that of improved education and better training, which the other witness did not regard as having yet reached the Isle of Anglesey.

On the question of clothing the Commission seldom held it necessary to ask for evidence. There is very little difference in this matter between Wales and England, and hardly any between the Welsh farmer and his labourer. In the case of farmers' children who work on their fathers' farms this last point is well illustrated by the correspondence

[1] Qu. 22,545—55, 22,588—95.   [2] Qu. 11,722

which Mr. Gee had had with thirty farmers in the Vale of Clwyd as to their condition, and of which he gave the Commission a summary in his evidence.[1] Concerning his children working on his own farm, one farmer wrote : "They get only food and clothing, and they are worse clothed than the servants." Another used the words, "They work like slaves, but are not clothed as they should be, and their shoes are worse than their clothes." And a third wrote : "They get food and clothing, but are worse clothed than labourers' children." Lastly, in answer to a question of Lord Kenyon's as to the farmers' daughters more especially, Mr. Gee said : "When you see farmers' daughters in Denbigh they are in their best, but if you saw them at home, as I have seen them, I am sure it would touch your feelings."

There are two or three remarks of a more general nature which it occurs to us to make at this point ; and among other things we may mention, that as regards the relative importance of respectable clothing and good food, the former stands higher in the estimation of the average Welsh man or woman of the farming or of the labouring class than it does in that of an English person of the same sex and position in life. Formerly, when the communication with England was more costly and precarious than it has been ever since railways have become available, a Welsh rustic who happened to have relatives settled in the west of England was not more struck by anything than what he considered their extravagance in the matter of food and their lack of proper pride in that of dress. His own tendency would be rather to stint himself in food in order to spend more on clothes in which to appear on Sunday, and, however desirous of attending the Sunday School or the other meetings at his chapel, he would stay at home rather than attend in his week-day clothes. This tendency is still more perceptible among the mining portion

[1] Qu. 64,004, 64,014.

of the population, and especially the quarrymen of North Wales. It is needless to say that it is sometimes carried to excess, leading to pecuniary difficulties; but, on the other hand, the way in which the women, for instance, in the quarry districts can dress, gives evidence to a natural taste, to a sense of colour and proportion which may be sometimes looked for in vain in ladies of a higher position in life in England. The ideal of the well-wisher of the Welsh people, in matters of this kind, should be to encourage economy without discouraging what artistic instincts they may have inherited as a part of their natural endowment.

From an antiquarian point of view there is probably little to be said of Welsh dress from the Tudor times to the present day, except what might be said of the fashions in England during the same time. Even the so-called Welsh hat which was still to be seen worn in the sixties by women in Cardiganshire, less frequently in Merioneth, Carnarvonshire, and Anglesey, has nothing distinctly Welsh : it was introduced from England, as may be seen from the examination of paintings dating from the Stuart times. How early Welsh dress had been assimilated to the fashions prevailing in England it is impossible to say in the absence of a systematic investigation of the subject. But if one pursues it back into antiquity, one will find peculiarities of dress becoming synonymous with marks of race. Thus we have a *Gallia Bracata*, which was characterised by the men wearing the *bracæ*, "breeches or trousers," and the poet Martial, in the first century of our era, speaks of the *bracæ* of a Briton, alluding, probably, to some of the Brythons who still lived on the Continent ; but the dress of those in this country was presumably the same. On the other hand, the Highland kilt probably represents the dress of the Goidels of this country in former times. This is found delineated on an old figured stone preserved at The Knoll, near Neath. Its surface is occupied mostly by a rudely-carved human figure interpreted, according to the late Professor Westwood, to be in the attitude of prayer, the only dress represented being a short apron or kilt, reaching from the waist to the middle of the legs; this garb is formed of a series of longitudinal strips radiating from a waistband, and giving the appearance of a short and very thickly quilted petticoat, just as in several of the Irish figures on the shrine of St. Manchan.[1] Another stone appears to show a figure clothed in a similar short kilt: it is at Landevailog, in Brecknockshire, and bears the minuscule inscription, *Briamail Flou*,[2] that is to say, the cross of *Brigomaglus Flavus*, and Professor Westwood ascribed it hesitatingly to the eleventh century, but it may well date considerably earlier.

An inscribed stone of the same class as that of *Briamail* occurs at Lanamlech, near Brecon, and shows two figures, regarded by Professor Westwood as clad in long shirt-like garments reaching down to the knees; he supposed one of them to represent St. John. The inscription states in faulty Latin that the stone was put up by a certain Moridic, whose name wears a somewhat Goidelic aspect; and the whole is supposed by the same authority to date before the neighbourhood of Brecon had felt the pervading influence of the Normans.[3]

Giraldus Cambrensis, in his "Itinerarium Kambriæ," written in the twelfth century, describes the personal appearance of Kynwric, son of Rhys, prince of South Wales, and remarks, as to his dress, that he was clad in a thin cloak only and a shirt, and that his shins and feet were left naked, regardless of thistles and thorns.[4] The rude

---

[1] We take this account of the stone from the late Professor Westwood's "Lapidarium Walliæ," p. 37; see also his plate xxv., fig. 3.

[2] *Ibid.*, p. 59, plate xxxiii.

[3] See the "Lapidarium Walliæ," pp. 68, 69, and plate xxxviii., figs. 3, 4, 5.

[4] Giraldus's words are to be found in book ii., chapter iv., and run thus :—

"*Adolescens ipse* [*Kenewricus filius Resi*] *flavus et crispus, pulcher et procersus,*

drawings of the officers of the Welsh court, given in a
Hengwrt manuscript of the early part of the thirteenth
century, present the same general appearance as regards
dress.[1] The same may also be said of the pen-and-ink
sketches of Welshmen to be found in the margin of the
Registrum Munimentorum (*Liber* A), a volume made up
of documents belonging to the reign of Edward I. now
preserved at the Record Office.[2] The Welshman of that
period appears to have been somewhat more scantily
clothed than the Irishman, if we may judge by their
respective figures in this manuscript, but while the latter is
quite unshod, the Welshman wears one shoe, namely, on
the left foot. Even as late as the commencement of the
present century, many of the poorer peasantry went about
barefooted. An English barrister resident in the neighbourhood of Newcastle Emlyn, in giving evidence in 1843
before the Commissioners of Inquiry for South Wales,
referred thus to the matter (Qu. 5,566): "Formerly, twenty
years ago, you saw the women walking about without shoes
and stockings, but now you never see such an occurrence in
this part of the country." At the present day the children
of small farmers, and of labourers or shepherds, are allowed
to go barefooted for a month or two in summer : otherwise
shoes and stockings are the rule in every countryside. To

---

*ut patriæ gentique morem gereret, pallio tenui solum et interula indutus, tibiis,
et pedibus nudis tribulos et spinas non formidantibus ; vir non arte quidem, sed
natura munitus ; plurimum quippe dignitatis ex se træferrens, ex adjuncto
parum.*" See p. 252 above.

[1] See Aneurin Owen's edition of the "Ancient Laws and Institutes of Wales"
(Public Record Office, MDCCCXLI.), vol. ii., pp. 749—814, and the Editor's
preface, vol. i., p. xxxii.

[2] See Thomas Wright's "History of Caricature and Grotesque," pp. 177—
180 ; and "Y Cymmrodor," x. 201. Two of these sketches of Welshmen are
reproduced in Wright's work ; the first "represents a Welshman armed with
bow and arrow, whose clothing consists apparently only of a plain tunic and a
light mantle," while a shoe is worn on his left foot. "The second [Welshman]
carries a spear, which he apparently rests on the single shoe of his left foot,
while he brandishes a sword in his left hand."

return, however, to the mediæval peculiarities of dress to which we have referred, it is impossible to say at present how far we should be justified in regarding them as survivals of the dress characteristic of the Goidels of Britain in early times. In any case, the analogous survival of their idioms and laws suggests it as a proper subject of an inquiry which we, unfortunately, cannot prosecute.

In this chapter we have abstained from discussing either diet or dress from the economical point of view : it is all the more necessary to observe the same distinction with regard to the large mass of evidence taken by the Commissioners on the next subject, namely, the housing of the farmers and those immediately depending on them. So we shall here deal with the questions of dwelling-houses chiefly in so far as they exercise obvious influence on the habits and mode of life of the people engaged in agriculture. A great many complaints were made to them from tenants as to their houses being out of repair; and in some cases they proved almost incredible neglect on the part of all concerned, while in some instances the houses were so old and so poor that the landowner did not think it worth the while to put them in repair. Here and there he appeared to be improving the houses on his estate as fast as the outlay of capital would admit, which meant that some of the tenants who had to wait for their turn experienced hardship for years. Now and then also the rebuilding of an old house involved the tenant in great discomfort for a shorter time. In some instances[1] we were told of the walls having to be propped up to prevent their falling and killing the inmates ; in others we were informed of a family having for a time to live in a barn, or in a stable. In one case we heard of frogs leaping about the bedroom, and in several mention was made of snow falling on the

[1] Qu. 45,560. 45,564, 41,846. 42,857, 44,443, 46,421, 64,407, 38,745, 42,367—72, 42,813.

beds. But however great the inconvenience and hardship which such cases as these involved, it is right to distinguish those which may be regarded as more or less temporary and transitional from those in which the bad or inadequate accommodation has been normal, and more or less permanent. We may here cite the words of Mr. J. C. Jones, of Lanarth, who expressed his opinion, with regard to the neighbourhood of Aberayron, as follows:[1] "Although great progress has been made of late years in regard to better buildings, I venture to say some landlords house their dogs and horses better than they do their tenants;" and Mr. Richard Rowlands, an Anglesey labourer, whom we have already cited, expressed himself to the same effect as regards the housing afforded the labourers by the farmers of Anglesey.[2]

Mr. Henry Jones, a tenant farmer, representing the farmers of Clynnog, in Carnarvonshire, stated in his evidence[3] that there are but few comfortable houses in his neighbourhood, and those but recently built. The rest are, according to him, old houses, with very inadequate sleeping accommodation, and very rarely provided with proper sanitary arrangements.

One of the most general complaints was that as to insufficient accommodation, especially for men and women to sleep. Mr. Richard Edwards, a tenant farmer from Pennal, in Merionethshire, gave the following description[4] of what had been his home: "The house was an old-fashioned one, a kitchen and two bedrooms downstairs, and two bedrooms over the kitchen and dairy. There was no flooring, and the fire was on the ground. The chimney was a big old-fashioned one, through which the sky could easily be seen, and through which the rain and snow came down freely. The sleeping accommodation upstairs was

---

[1] Qu. 65,031, 49,103.   [2] Qu. 22,557.
[3] Qu. 12,769 72.   [4] Qu. 70,536.

very deficient, inconvenient, and unhealthy. The female inmates of the house had to pass through the men's bed-room to their own. The house being a low one the beds were quite close to the slates of the roof, and we had to bend down so as not to touch the roof. The roof was also in a bad condition; there was no ceiling and no kind of plastering. The wind drove the rain and snow between the slates, and I remember on many occasions in winter being covered, when in bed at night, with about five inches of snow. We lived in the house in this condition for many years. I mention these facts because there are still farmers living in such houses."

The Rev. William Williams, a Baptist minister, living at Knighton, speaking of the houses in that district, used the following words : [1] "Of course, there are some excellent farmhouses and excellent cottages, and particularly in this neighbourhood. There are a good many excellent cottages, better than small farms up in the country ; there are others again, especially small farmhouses, that are not at all well arranged internally, and not with sufficient room. Had it not been for the presence of ladies in the court, I could give you dreadful instances, shocking instances, of the way sleeping accommodation is arranged, tending greatly to indecency and immorality." He explained in another answer that he alluded to houses where there would be, for instance, a father and mother, and children between fifteen and twenty years of age, all sleeping in the same room ; and he added that he had himself known cases of that kind.

Miss Kate Jenkins, while speaking [2] as to farms in the Vale of Towy, and admitting that the buildings are on the whole improving, instanced several bad cases known to her, adding, as a general remark, that " Welsh farmers will inhabit houses no English farmer would live in."

[1] Qu. 54,947—9, 54,966.—7.   [2] Qu. 38,024, 38,033 - 9, 39,745.

Mr. Thomas Davies, a tenant farmer, who gave his evidence at Lansawel, in Carmarthenshire, specified certain very poor buildings, and spoke[1] in particular of one farmhouse as " having one sleeping-room upstairs, where both the sexes sleep, with no divisions between them, no ceiling overhead between them and the slate roof, and the wind and the snow getting in through the crevices."

Mr. John Thomas, tenant farmer and butter merchant, specified in his evidence,[2] given to the Commission at Landeilo, a number of farms with bad buildings, and gave certain particulars, in which he spoke of " one farm where all the buildings are deplorably bad, the farmer and his wife sleeping downstairs, and the men and maid-servants, the carpenter, the tailor, and the sons on their holidays, all sleeping in the same room upstairs, for there are a vast number of farmhouses which have no partition at all upstairs ; another farm, rent 80*l.*, where a visitor would have to sleep either with the servant over the cows, or in the same room with the servant-girl." We make one more extract from his evidence to the following effect :—" In another farm, whose rent is 88*l.*, there is only one fireplace, and that is in the kitchen, the only room where the women can do their work. The son of this farmer has a high social position, but when he comes home for his holidays he has to sleep with the servant-man on the *dowlod* over the cows, or in the loft where the servant-girl sleeps, and which is not partitioned." He added the following remarks : " If the doctors of Wales told all they knew on the subject, they would put to shame many landlords who talk glibly of morality. It is sheer hypocrisy on their part to talk of it, when they know that the hearts of many of their tenants bleed because of this perilous inconvenience."

[1] Qu. 39,745   [2] Qu. 38,252.

Mr. Jenkin Thomas, son of a tenant farmer, living in the neighbourhood of Cardiff, gives the following description[1] of the house in which he was brought up : " We were a family of thirteen—eleven children and our parents—living in this house on the farm.   There were three bedrooms in the house and two front rooms, and a small back kitchen, a small pantry, and a small dairy.   In consequence, we, as a family, had to put three beds in the same room, and seven of us slept in the same room, and we had not room even to walk between these three beds.   We had to go over a bed to get into bed.   The servant-men, in consequence, had to sleep out in the buildings, and that was a great inconvenience to us."

These extracts lead us to mention the accommodation for farm servants, and, first of all, to say that in some districts servant-men sleep in the farmhouses, or adjuncts to the farmhouses ; but in the case of the counties of Flint and Denbigh, and in some instances in Anglesey also, it is not unusual for the access to their bedrooms to be by means of outside stairs.   The prevailing custom in the greater part of Wales, however, is for them to have their beds made in the lofts of the outhouses, such as the barns, cowhouses, or the stables.   This has been spoken of repeatedly as highly unsatisfactory for more reasons than one.   In Anglesey, Mr. John Hughes, a farm labourer appointed to give evidence by a committee of the farm labourers of that county, spoke to the lack of accommodation for the servant-men in the farmhouses, and added the following words : " The day-schools teach the children until they have passed Standard V., or until they are thirteen years of age, and then they go to the farmers, and they are put to sleep and live with the cattle, and they lose all that they have learnt in the school, and become

[1] Qu. 26,530—1.

of the same nature as the beasts. That is the truth of the matter."[1]

Mr. David Davies, a farm labourer from Langybi, in Carnarvonshire, spoke as follows:[2] "The places allotted by the farmers to their servants to sleep are altogether improper on account of size and situation, being only small rooms, with very limited head room, scarcely sufficient for an ordinary man to stand erect in. Other servants sleep in lofts above the cattle either in stables or cowhouses. There is seldom room in the farmhouses themselves; they generally are very small, and without rooms upstairs. They try and place one bed in such a position as to screen another. I have been sleeping one of six in a loft above cows : there was not sufficient room for a person to stand erect in. There were three beds placed in the room. The narrow space between the beds was all the room we had. I have been walking miles during the half-year in order to sleep elsewhere than in this room."

Another point at which the inadequacy of the farmhouse accommodation was pointed out to the Commission more than once is in connection with the question of the treatment of the servant-men or labourers resident on a farm. In some cases we have been told that they are welcome to pass their evenings in the kitchen; but in the majority of instances[3] that seems to be hardly the case, and for the valid reason that there is no room to spare for them. On this point, Mr. Samuel Hughes, chairman of the Anglesey County Council, stated[4] that "the farm labourers are not looked upon kindly if they stay in the house on a winter's night; they expect them to go," he said, "to their stable, and to their loft." This statement is corroborated by the evidence[5] of one of their own number, Mr. Richard

---

[1] For the evidence see Qu. 55,564—8, 56,428, 59,063—6, 63,106, 63,123—8, 19,611, and also 20,889, 20,903, 42,588—9.

[2] Qu. 11,766.

[3] Qu. 31,463, 47,235—9.

[4] Qu. 21,964.

[5] Qu. 22,561.

Rowlands; for, according to him, they may go to the kitchen for some time, but he adds that in most places they will be turned out, as the farmer may want to make some other use of that room; and another Anglesey labourer, Mr. John Hughes, who has already been cited, spoke concerning the Aberffraw district as follows : "There is no accommodation whatever provided for the labourers for the evening, only let them go where they will." Against this, however, must be placed the evidence[1] of Mr. Thomas Prichard, farmer, landowner, and agent of the Bodorgan estate and other properties in Anglesey, who stated that some farmers welcomed their servant-men to spend their evenings in the kitchen, and some did not.

Dr. Rowlands, speaking, as already suggested, of the district around Lanaelhaiarn, in Carnarvonshire, stated that the servant-men have no accommodation for the evenings except the lofts of the stables. And the same state of things was spoken to as prevalent in the western portion of Denbighshire by Mr. Hugh Owen, whose evidence was taken at Conway, and by Mr. William Jones, who spoke as to the district of Cerrig y Drudion, in that county.[2]

The same deficiency of accommodation for the evenings is proved by the evidence[3] of Mr. Thomas Davies, who came forward at Lansawel. The servant-men, according to him, besides having poor sleeping accommodation in the out-houses, "have no place to sit down or read, or anything."

On the other hand, Mr. J. M. Davies, of Froodvale, who spoke from his extensive acquaintance with estates especially in Carmarthenshire, said, in answer to the question whether servant-men have fire and light in the evenings, that "they live in the kitchen, with every comfort." The Commission had evidence[4] to the same effect from Mr. D. E.

---

[1] Qu. 20,889.

[2] Qu. 11,679, 15,132—52, 17,275—87.

[3] Qu. 40,002—25.

[4] Qu. 37,645, 43,131—3, 46,209, 44,235, 31,463—6.

Stephens, a landowner in the same county ; and Mr. J. C. Harford, a landowner in the neighbouring county of Cardigan, was of opinion that the complaint as to a lack of evening accommodation in the farmhouses would not apply to his estate. Similar evidence was given by Mr. W. Saunders Davies, a tenant farmer, living in the parish of St. Dogmaels, in Pembrokeshire, and by another Pembrokeshire farmer, Mr. Jenkins, of Brimaston Hall.

In most farmhouses of modern construction there is, besides a kitchen and a back kitchen, a room which is usually called the parlour, and that is commonly reserved for emergencies, such as when strangers call to whom the farmer or his wife wishes to show respect—for instance, ministers of religion. We have heard of the parlour being used for keeping corn or butter or other things for which the farmer has a lack of room. But it is more usual to find it furnished with a biggish table in the centre, with a show Bible on it and other books which are seldom disturbed, and with a number of chairs, each provided with its antimacassar. But as motives of economy prevent the room having a fire regularly lit in it, a visitor finds it the least comfortable in the house. It is in fact a kind of old-fashioned drawing-room, ill-ventilated as a rule, and very musty, not to mention that practically it is in many cases a clear waste of so much available space, to the inconvenience of those whose occupations have to be carried on in the kitchen.[1]

We have received a great mass of evidence as to the labourers' cottages, and we may briefly say that they vary in kind from the older cottage—not yet extinct—which consists of a square box with two or three holes for a door, a window, and a chimney, to the more modern specimens described by Mr. Davies,[2] of Froodvale, as having each three rooms upstairs, and a parlour and kitchen on the

[1] Qu. 11,818–20, 20,938, 21,960–8, 39,933.
[2] Qu. 19,594, 37,646.

ground floor. Of the old ones Mr. Davies spoke as follows :
" They are going out of fashion ; it is only the old-fashioned
who live in them ; the young people do not go into them
—there are not many of them." A much less encouraging
view is expressed by Mr. Thos. Prichard in his answers to
questions concerning certain cottages at Aberffraw, in
Anglesey. He admitted that they were built long ago
under old leases, and that they are very bad, but this he did
not consider the worst feature of the case, as the following
words[1] used by him go to show : " It is the people's habits :
that is the difficulty. They keep ducks there. They are
very fond of keeping ducks, and the floors are made of
mud, and they will make duck-ponds inside their houses ;
they feed the young ducks in those duck-ponds inside.
No matter how good a cottage may be, if people will keep
their poultry and their filth in the house in that way you
do not know what to do with them. It is hopeless. Yet
if I turned out a person because he had a duck-pond in his
floor, I should be called I do not know what,—a regular
brute." Then, on being asked whether a better class of
cottages with wooden floors would not bring about a
change for the better in the people's way of living,
Mr. Prichard answered, " Well, I think they would make a
hole in the floor : they would have a duck-pond." We
agree to a certain extent with the witness ; for there is
nothing more certain than that habits of cleanliness do not
spring up in a day. People who have been used to live in
dirt in bad cottages would hardly keep new and better
cottages in a state of exemplary cleanliness and order.
The disgraceful state of things described by Mr. Prichard
as actual at Aberffraw, the headquarters in ancient
times of the kings of Gwyneđ, will probably require
several generations to wipe away ; but in time, we
doubt not, better cottages will render their inmates

[1] Qu. 15,593–609.

disposed to lead better lives and cultivate habits of cleanliness.

This last remark may be applied also to the housing of the farmers themselves, and will serve to explain why we have written at so great a length on the subject, and why we attach so much importance to it. If we summarise the evidence from which we have made these extracts, it comes to this : improvement is going on steadily in the dwelling-house accommodation of the farming population of Wales, but much remains to be done to give the farmers proper houses and to supply the number of passable cottages required for the labourers in certain districts.

Now that we have passed under review the conditions under which the agricultural population exists as to diet and dress and dwellings, we propose to consider the kind of life which they ordinarily live. It has been stated more than once in the evidence collected by the Commission that the Welsh farmer leads a much harder life than the English farmer, and that it is not unusual for him to take a part himself in the work on the farm, as well as to superintend and direct the work of those whom he engages. The hours of his labourers have of late years been shortened, but hardly those of the servant-men who have the charge of the horses required for the tilling of the land ; and there has been no shortening of the service required of the female servants. As a rule they know little respite from early morning till late at night, and only one person has more than they to do and more care on her shoulders : that is their mistress, the farmer's wife. It is, however, needless to say that the pressure of work varies very greatly with the season of the year, and that the men of the household have their slack times and a good deal of leisure, not to mention one day regularly every week, namely, Sunday. Furthermore, the farmer or his wife, or both, devote most of one day to attending the nearest market for the disposal of the farm produce and the purchase of necessaries for the house.   This has become in some cases so completely a habit, that many a farmer may be found regularly in the town on market-days whether he has any business to transact there or not.

As a rule a farming neighbourhood is a model of peace and quietness, and when one of the inhabitants dies almost everybody hies to the funeral, as in all other Celtic lands. As an exception to the general peace one may perhaps mention[1] the bickering and squabbling which arise between farmers or shepherds in the upland districts owing to the lack of fences to keep the sheep within their boundaries. In the oase of some of the larger estates a better state of feeling has been established as one of the results of proper fences having been put up.   As a rule, however, the country districts are comparatively free[2] from all serious crimes, but men are now and then brought before the magistrates for trespassing in quest of game or fish.   Let us add that the Commission heard a complaint from Anglesey as to the roughness and recklessness of the farm labourers in that county.   We allude to Mr. Thomas Prichard's evidence[3] where he says that the men's accommodation is not so good as the women's, and explains that " it is not entirely owing to the farmer's fault."   For he proceeds to say : "The men are such ruffians, they will break or spoil anything in the shape of furniture which is put into their rooms. When Mr. Leufer Thomas went round we visited many sleeping-places,[4] and it so happened that we saw a man doing mischief in one."   When asked further to explain his meaning and to say whether he charged them with

[1] Qu. 70,158.

[2] For some criminal statistics in point, see the Report of the Welsh Land Commission, Appendix E., Tables XXXV., XXXVI.

[3] Qu. 19,462, 19,465.

[4] This was when Mr. L. Thomas was acting as Assistant Commissioner on the Labour Commission.

wilful damage, the answer was, "Certainly I do. They break things : if you put pots and pans and things of that kind into a room like that, you will find them all broken in the morning." We have no reason to doubt this evidence, and we cannot help noticing that it coincides with the bitterest complaint made to the Commission by labouring men as to the treatment which they, on the other hand, receive from the farmers. The evidence in point has already been mentioned, and we may add that one of the witnesses in question used words to the effect that the gulf between the farmers and their labourers is widening.[1]

One other question remains to be mentioned here, namely, that of immorality. This has long occupied the attention of every one who is interested in the improvement of the condition of the agricultural population, and of the morals of the country generally ; and, as far back as we can remember, the pulpits of all religious denominations in Wales have more or less persistently thundered forth against it. It has been repeatedly pointed out to us in the course of the evidence how inadequate accommodation in farmhouses and cottages must make against chastity and in favour of immorality. One of the witnesses, Dr. Rowlands, already cited concerning Lanaelhaiarn, in the Pwltheli union of Carnarvonshire, drew a comparison[2] between the agricultural labourers and the quarrymen of Trefor, in the same parish, to the disadvantage of the former. He did not consider the moral state of the country very bad, though he admitted that illegitimacy did occur ; but he stated that to the affiliation cases brought before the magistrates at the petty sessions the parties were always farm labourers, and he used the following words : "I have not seen a single case brought before the magistrates between people that are working in the quarry. They live quite differently. I never saw a young man and

[1] Qu. 20,957-44.   [2] Qu. 11,691-3.

young woman belonging to the quarry bring a case before the magistrates to Pwllheli since I have been in Lanaelhaiarn. There are several hundreds of people living in Trefor, but I have not seen a single case there. In the farmhouses it is different ; therefore I conclude that there must be some mischief in the sleeping accommodation, and in the connection between them and the farmhouses."

The Commission had evidence to somewhat the same effect,[1] but based on facts of a more reassuring nature, from the late Rev. Sir T. H. Gresley Puleston, rector of Worthenbury and landowner in the detached piece of Flintshire. Asked whether he found the morals of the people better in consequence of the great improvements which he had mentioned as having been effected in their cottages, he answered, " Very considerably. I can answer both as a clergyman and as a magistrate. I could give very strong proofs of it, but I think perhaps it is unnecessary; you will guess what I mean : there is a very considerable moral improvement in the district."

The same view was also expressed by Mr. Thos. Davies,[2] tenant farmer from the parish of Lansawel, in Carmarthenshire, who, though he ascribed the decrease of immorality in his neighbourhood chiefly to the teaching of religion, thought that proper accommodation for the men-servants would cause a material improvement in their morals. For, as he proceeded to say, " it would keep them at home " ; and he added the words, " I think that we ought to get an out-kitchen for them, so that they might have a fire and books, and they might read and write, and spend their leisure hours there."

The charges brought against Wales on the score of immorality are doubtless based to a certain extent on the survival in some of the agricultural districts of the old custom of night courtship, which is not peculiar to Wales,

[1] Qu. 57,064, 57,033, 57,135-45.   [2] Qu. 40,020-5.

but occurs likewise among various European peoples as a survival from the life of the Middle Ages. It is frequently referred to in the poems of the fourteenth-century Welsh poet D. ab Gwilym, and it may be briefly described thus : the lover sallies forth at night and approaches the house where his fair one lives ; then he attracts her attention by gently tapping at her window. In some Welsh districts this is called *cnocio* or *streicio*, and in parts of Germany it is termed *fenstern*, as when Hans Sachs sings,—

> "Erstlich da ich brewtgam worden,
> Da *fenstert* ich schier alle nacht."

A similar practice is implied in several of the songs of Robert Burns, such as that to Mary Morrison :—

> "O Mary, at thy window be,
> It is the wish'd, the trysted hour !
> Those smiles and glances let me see,
> That make the miser's treasure poor."

At the window, as in the case of Romeo and Juliet, a conversation ensues, which sometimes ends in the admission of the lover into the house ; and in that case he and the young woman sit up together the greater part of the night. The charge of assuming a different position, for which the vocabulary of the English language provides the term *bundling*, is usually denied and resented as a calumny.[1]

We have already cited evidence to the effect that Wales

---

[1] By way of further references to night courtship we may mention that in old Norse literature the work which makes the most frequent allusion to the practice is probably "Kormak's Saga" (edited by Möbius, Halle, 1886, also published with a Latin translation, Copenhagen, 1832). For the German terms for it and references to it in German literature see Grimm's Dictionary under the words *fenstern* and *kilt*, which latter belongs to Switzerland. The Dutch colonists seem to have carried the custom to South Africa, where one finds it, for instance, in Olive Schreiner's "Story of an African Farm" (see Part II., chapter v., concerning "Tant' Sannie's Upsitting" ; also "Thoughts on South Africa," by the same writer, in the "Fortnightly Review," August 1896, pp. 244–51). As to the custom in England see the volume entitled "Barthomley," by the Rev. Edward Hinchcliffe (London, 1856), p. 139, where he touches on the "sitting up" for which he regarded Cheshire and

is improving in the matter of the morality of its agricultural population, and more could be cited if necessary.   On the other hand, one witness, Mr. Thos. Prichard, whose evidence has already been referred to more than once, called our attention to statistics which show an increase of illegitimacy in certain parts of the Principality.[1]   His reference was chiefly to the following table given in Dr. Leffingwell's chapter entitled " A Study in Morals."[2] Of each thousand births, how many were illegitimate in the following registration districts of England and Wales during the periods mentioned below ?   That is the question put, and the table supplies the answers as follows :—

Name of Registration District.	County, &c.	Annual Average, 1884—8 (Five Years).	1842.	1893
Longtown . . .	Cumberland .	177	172	129
Alston . . .	,, .	132	125	99
Clun	Shropshire .	122	109	76
Rhayader . . .	South Wales .	121	145	85
Brampton . . .	Cumberland .	117	172	121
Pwltheli . . .	North Wales .	114	76	93
Lanfyllin . . .	,, ,, .	103	80	86
Church Stretton .	Shropshire . .	98	109	105
Downham . . .	Norfolk . .	96	86	91
Docking . . .	,, . .	96	104	90
Bromyard . . .	Hereford .	96	125	79
Machyntleth . .	North Wales .	93	80	92
Anglesey . . .	,, ,, . .	89	78	94
Newtown . . .	,, ,, . .	95	103	67
Walsingham . .	Norfolk . .	83	104	88
ALL ENGLAND .	. . . .	47	67	42

parts of the counties bordering on it as enjoying an unenviable notoriety.   In the valley of the Thames, in the neighbourhood, for instance, of Henley, it appears to be known as "courting on the bed."   An early instance of "bundling" is mentioned by Chrestien de Troyes in his poem the "Conte du Graal"; the lines in point are quoted in Nutt's "Studies in the Legend of the Holy Grail," p. 135. See also Rhys's "Arthurian Legend," p. 175, and Thomas Wright's "Womankind in Western Europe from the Earliest Times to the Seventeenth Century," for instance, pp. 166-8.

[1] Qu. 120,90–210.

[2] The title of the book is "Illegitimacy and the Influence of Seasons upon

From this it will be seen that, as in certain districts in Cumberland and Shropshire, there has been up to 1888 an increase in illegitimacy in certain districts in North Wales, namely, Anglesey, the Pwllheli district of Carnarvonshire, and the two districts of Lanfyllin and Machynlleth, in Montgomeryshire, at the same time that there has been a decrease in the average for the whole of England and Wales. We are sorry that for the purposes of comparison we have not been able to procure the figures for all the Welsh districts, but those we have given show that, though the worst Welsh spots are not so bad as the worst English ones, there is plenty of room for improvement still.

We think it right, however, to say that we do not believe that the increase of immorality in the Welsh districts in question has been as great as represented in this table between the years 1842 and 1888, for we suspect that the numbers for 1842 are too low, in consequence of the concealment of illegitimate births and neglect on the part of the registrars to do their duty conscientiously. So we are glad to be able to add the figures for the year 1893, from which it will be seen that Welsh illegitimacy is decreasing, except in Anglesey.

Taking a somewhat wider view of the question, living men of ordinary habits of observation who have lived in the Principality can testify that ideas of chastity have made great progress within their memory. Thus it was far more common in the forties and the fifties for farmers' daughters to be married at last in a hurry than it is now, and we are inclined to ascribe the improvement more to the spread of education than to the influence of the pulpit.[1] In such

Conduct : Two Studies in Demography," by Albert Leffingwell, M.D. (London, 1892). The above table is given at p. 33 ; and we have added to it the figures for the year 1893.

[1] We cannot help suspecting that the influence of the pulpit is in some measure neutralised by a wide-spread acquaintance with the biography of certain Old Testament worthies whose ideas of morality, if they had any, can

matters abstract notions of virtue and vice play a far lesser rôle than the ever-present question, "Is it respectable?" The farmers' daughters who were sent from home to school learned that the old fashion to which we have alluded was disgraceful, and that it was regarded so by educated people. So they set their faces against it when they returned home. In time the conduct of the better behaved of the farmers' daughters would tend steadily to establish a better fashion among the maid-servants. We may here remark that it would not only give the latter a much-needed interval for recreation, but also conduce to a higher state of morality, if they could be allotted, each in her turn, an afternoon a week for visiting their friends, as is usually done in the case of women in domestic service in the towns. At any rate, this might be done, probably without any serious inconvenience, during seasons of the year when there is no great pressure of work at the farmer's home. In any case we feel confident that the improvement proceeding in the housing of the agricultural population and the spread of education cannot fail to accelerate the improvement in morals to which we allude, and to extend it in the near future to the most remote country districts.

The same influences make in manifold ways for temperance: for instance, it is now regarded among the agricultural population of Wales a disgrace to be found drunk. The Commission did not ask many questions as to drunkenness in the rural districts. But they noticed that every farmer and every labourer who came to give evidence was sober at the time, a statement which they could not make of another class of witnesses who came before them. As to the farm labourers and men-servants in particular, we have very little more to say, except that it is

only be referred to a comparatively low level of civilisation—a level, however, above which, at any rate in the matter of the sexes, the East has never shown any great hurry to rise very much.

expected that, with more adequate accommodation for their passing their evenings at home, they will frequent the public-houses less. Where the accommodation is inadequate they have to go out somewhere, and those who cannot find room in the kitchen naturally gravitate to the public-houses, where they are certain to find a welcome, and to hear the gossip of the countryside. Some evidence touching on this point we have already given whilst dealing with the question of dwelling-houses, so we do not think it necessary to produce it here. Thanks to the pulpit and the advocates of total abstinence, it would be difficult, as regards temperance and sobriety, to exaggerate the change which has taken place for the better in Wales within the last fifty years. And were we to go back to remoter generations, we might illustrate the improvement by references to the jest-books of the early Tudor period, where one finds the bibulous propensities of Welshmen frequently satirised. Take, for example, Skelton's "Merye Tales," the burden of one of which is "How the Welshman dyd desyre Skelton to ayde hym in hys sute to the kynge for a patent to sell drynke."[1] We have possibly a survival of this notion of the Welsh character in the fiction, stereotyped in English literature of a certain order, that Welshmen never mention *cwrw*, "beer," without calling it *cwrw da*, "good beer," a combination of words resented by the Welsh-speaking Cymro of the present day, as he construes it, rightly or wrongly, to involve the insinuation that the whole people regard beer as the one thing good and needful.

No survey of the life of the Welsh farmer would be complete without some account of the great place which religion and religious observances occupy in it. His

[1] This tale is to be found in Hazlitt's "Old English Jest-books" (London, 1864), vol. ii., pp. 7–9, and it is reproduced in Thomas Wright's "History of Caricature and Grotesque" (London, 1875), p. 239.

Sunday is not a day of rest except in so far as a change of occupation answers the purpose of rest. In the morning he and as many of his household as can be spared from the farm go to a service, mostly a sermon, at the chapel which they attend. If the distance is not too great they return home for dinner, and most of them attend the Sunday School in the afternoon. They come home again, and go back in the evening for another service at their chapel. These three meetings partake of the nature of fixtures not only at the dissenting chapel, but also at the parish church. To these fixtures must be added various subsidiary meetings, such as those for musical practice or for catechising the young, so that even a farmer who is not an elder [1] or the bearer of any other office at his chapel has the hours of Sunday pretty strictly allotted. Besides Sunday there are meetings at the chapel in the evening on week-days. One of these, called the *Seiet*,[2] occupies at least one evening of every week ; it is confined to communicants and their children. Another evening there may be a prayer-meeting : occasionally there is a sermon, and sometimes a lecture or a musical practice, not to mention that in a Welsh-speaking district there usually exists a literary society, which meets regularly during the winter months. In fact, in a fairly populous neighbourhood there are chapel meetings of one kind or another held on most of the evenings of the week, but where the population is sparse and scattered the week-day meetings are not so numerous.

---

[1] The Welsh word is *blaenor*, which literally means a leader ; but the growth of ecclesiastical ideas is all in favour of *diaconus*, which is rapidly gaining ground in the form of *diacon*, with the un-Welsh pronunciation of *dëiacon*.

[2] It is needless to say that this word *sëiet*, pronounced in Gwyneď *sëiat*, is only an abbreviation of the English word *society*. In fact, the elders have till lately given the preference to longer forms of the word, namely *sysëieti*, *sysëiet*, and *sëieti*, which are now nearly obsolete. Lastly, the English origin of the name suggests that the institution which it represents may possibly be of English origin likewise, though it has acquired a thoroughly Welsh character.

With regard to the *Seiet*, one may say that it undertakes the religious initiation of the children. It reviews the sermons of the previous Sunday, elicits the religious experiences of the members, strengthens the weak-kneed, admonishes the erring, and in due time expels those whose conduct is held to be a scandal to the community.

The *Seiet*, comprising every church member, is, in a word, a miniature democracy, with the power residing in the elders and the other communicants, and not in the minister, whose presence, though usual, is not essential to the working of the system. Where there is a minister he is the mouthpiece of the *Seiet*, not its ruler. This is, roughly speaking, and in so far as concerns questions not requiring the attention of the denomination on a larger scale, the machinery of Calvinistic Methodism, an organisation which is to be traced back to the great religious awakening of the eighteenth century as inspired by the teaching of the Puritan fathers and guided by Whitfield rather than by Wesley, on the points where those reformers differed. It is a denomination of Welsh origin, and not a part of an organisation with its centre of gravity in England or Scotland. So its administrative work and the business of its chief assemblies are conducted in the vernacular; and it has the distinction of being the only organisation covering the whole of the Principality and embracing Welsh Churches in many of the towns of England, that has endured without breach of continuity or disruption for about a century and a half.

Its Calvinism is extensively shared by the two Nonconformist denominations of older standing in the Principality, namely, the Independents or Congregationalists and the Baptists, both of which have by degrees adopted to a large extent the organisation of Calvinistic Methodism by the establishment of county unions and national unions of their Churches in Wales.[1] In other words, the Church polity of the three great denominations[2] to which the overwhelming majority of Welsh Nonconformists belong, is virtually the same, and almost the precise antithesis of the polity of the Established Church, where the clergyman is practically responsible for everything. We do not feel called upon to estimate the respective merits of the two systems, but we notice with a certain amount of curiosity that most of the reforms mooted of late years by clergymen of the Established Church have as their object the securing of the more systematic and active co-operation of the lay element. It is needless also to mention what opportunities their chapels afford Welsh Dissenters of learning the art of self-government, and of successfully managing their finances; and as this lesson has been more and more thoroughly learnt it is but natural to find that divisions and internal feuds have been far less rife in Welsh religious communities of late years than they used to be formerly. On the whole we think that the tone of the following passage in the evidence of the late Mr. Thomas E. Ellis,[3] the parliamentary representative of the county of Merioneth, is not pitched too high : "The people in these Welsh villages have learnt during the last 150 years the most valuable lessons of self-government. Their chapels have been to them a splendid education in self-government ; they manage these chapels and manage their organisations with admirable skill and success."

Those who are pleased to generalise on the supposed characteristics of different races hold it as an axiom that

[1] On this and kindred questions see a suggestive letter by W. E. in the "British Weekly" for September 15th, 1892 (p. 330).

[2] We have said nothing of the Wesleyan Methodists, for they are not only numerically less important than the three denominations mentioned, but they are the same in Wales as in England.

[3] Qu. 17,065 ; see also footnote 3 at p. 646 of the Report.

the Celt is more impulsive and imaginative than the
Teuton ; and we should perhaps be safe in assuming that
the Welsh, for reasons which cannot be examined here,
participate in this greater impulsiveness and liveliness of
imagination. At any rate the assumption of such liveliness
of imagination would help one to account for the comparative rarity of suicide among them, and also for certain
phenomena observed in the sphere of religion in Wales.
We allude, in the first place, to the *Diwygiad*, or religious
revival, which every now and then comes over the Principality. The last (but one) of any magnitude spent its force
about the beginning of the sixties. Its most conspicuous
feature was great excitement at religious assemblages, men
and women, with their emotions intensified by the mag-
netic sympathy of numbers, being moved either to exceed-
ing ecstacy under a vivid realisation of the glory of "things
invisible," or to an uncontrollable terror by a discovery of
their "lost condition." They had, as it were, in full prospect
one or other of the spheres of Dante's "Divina Commedia."
Regarded from the point of view of the conduct of those
concerned, it may be mentioned that men who criticised
the *Diwygiad* from without sometimes alleged that it was
mere religious hysterics, that it led to certain wholesome
conventionalities being forgotten, and even to a laxity of
morals among people of an unstable disposition. But when
the spiritual storm had blown over it was found that it had
done more good on the whole than harm. This was proved
in most districts by the beginning of a new life by men who
had been till then given to habits of intemperance and to
the spending of their leisure hours in harvesting sorrow for
their families. It is but right to add that most of them
are believed to have withstood all temptation to fall back
into their old ways.[1] We cannot help perceiving that

[1] Since these words were written our attention has been called to some
eloquent passages dealing with the Welsh pulpit in Henry Richard's "Letters

what we have said of the *Diwygiad* may appear to recall the religious services of the Salvation Army ; and at first sight the comparison would seem a fair one to make. At any rate it might be so if one could conceive the spontaneity of the Welsh meetings being subjected to system, and the ebullitions of religious fervency which characterised them being made chronic. But it is a fact of some relevancy here that the Salvation Army, with its Saxon methods, has never met with any conspicuous success among the Celts either in Wales or elsewhere.

We have already hinted that the Welsh are well endowed in the matter of imagination and fancy. This faculty has sometimes played a great rôle when it was found combined with a certain kind of faith. The faith we mean is that which has sustained nations like the Jews in their expectation of a Messiah to come, or at one time inspired the Spaniards with the belief that the Cid Rodrigo was to return to restore the glories of Castile ; and other instances might be mentioned. From this combination there sprang up among the Brythons of yore a spirit of romance which held the Europe of the Middle Ages bound, as it were, under a spell. There is no great literature of the Continent which does not betray the influence of the Brythonic hero Arthur, whom his people as late as the time of Henry II. expected to see returning from the isle of Avallon hale and strong and longing to lead his men and countrymen to triumph over the foe and the oppressor. So real was this sanguine expectation that it is supposed to have counted with the English king as one of the forces which he had to quell in order to obtain quiet from the Welsh. So the monks of Glastonbury proceeded to

and Essays on Wales" (London, 1884), pp. 26–30. Alluding to the religious revivals which we have in view, Mr. Richard gives his opinion of them as follows :—" With some serious drawbacks, no one acquainted with the inner life of the country can doubt that they have been of incalculable value to Wales."

discover there the coffin of Arthur, his wife and his son. This was to convince the Welsh of the unreasonableness of their reckoning on the return of Arthur, who had been dead some six hundred years. The Welsh, however, went on believing here and there in the eventual return of Arthur ; and in modern times a shepherd is now and then related to have chanced on a cave where Arthur's Men are sleeping in the midst of untold treasure, awaiting the signal for their sallying forth to battle. This is located in various spots in Wales, as also in the Eildon hills, near Melrose, in South Scotland. Similar expectations have been connected in Ireland with the names of several of the heroes of local stories current in that country. Take, for instance, The O'Donoghue, who is supposed to be sleeping with eyes and ears open beneath the lakes of Killarney till called forth to right the wrongs of Erin, or the unnamed king who sleeps among his host of mighty spearmen in the stronghold of Greenan-Ely, in the highlands of Donegal, awaiting the peal of destiny to summon him and his men to fight for their country.

Nor was Arthur the only hero of the Brythons who was expected to return from the other world. One gathers from certain passages in the thirteenth-century manuscript of the poetry associated with the name of Taliessin that a similar expectation once attached to Cadwaladr, sometimes called the Blessed, the last king of the Brythons to contest the lordship over what is now the north of England with the Angles of Deira and Bernicia in the latter part of the seventh century. Indeed, there is reason to think that this sort of superstition did not wholly die out in certain parts of the Principality till, so to say, the other day. The Rev. Benjamin Williams, a clergyman and Welsh antiquary who has not been dead many years, contributed to the "Brython" for 1858 an article in which he alluded to a certain Owain Lawgoch, "Owain of the Red Hand."

Popular imagination, we learn, represented Owain Lawgoch as a hero expected to return eventually to reign over Britain. In the meanwhile he was by some supposed to be biding his time in foreign lands, and by others to be slumbering in a treasure cave, where certain intruders once on a time beheld him, a man of seven foot in stature, sitting in an ancient chair with his head resting on his left hand, while the other, the red hand, grasped a mighty sword of state which had come down to him as an official heirloom from the ancient kings of Britain. This Owain Lawgoch was the subject of ballads sung at Welsh fairs, and Mr. Williams quotes the following couplet :—

Yr Owen hwn yw Harri'r Nawfed,	" This Owain is Henry the Ninth,
Syd yn trigo 'ngwlad estronied.[1]	Who tarries in a foreign land."

Mr. Williams's statement is, that this "*is* sometimes heard sung"—"*clywir canu weithiau*"—which means that he or some of his friends had heard it sung not long before the time of his writing. Now it turns out that the original of Owain Lawgoch was a historical man ; he lived, as we have found (pp. 343—4), in the time of Edward III. and his son, the Black Prince. His deeds of valour in the French wars fill not a few of the pages of Froissart.

The faith and fancy which have combined to waft across five centuries and more the echo of Owain Lawgoch's name to our time will help one to understand a phenomenon touched upon in the evidence ; we mean the success which

[1] Since the above was written we have learned from a Welsh scholar, the Rev. John Fisher, of Ruthin, that this comes from a ballad in a twopenny book published at Carmarthen in 1847, entitled *Prophwydoliaeth Myrdin Wyllt*, " The Prophecy of Merlin the Wild." The booklet contains two poems or ballads, both of which speak of Owain Lawgoch : the couplet cited occurs in the first of the poems, while the second, which is similar, closes with the date of the year 1668 in rhyme. Mr. Fisher has never heard either ballad sung, but there are, he says, old people still living in his native Valley of the Lwchwr who could repeat scraps here and there of both ballads. We are indebted to Mr. Fisher also for calling our attention to Froissart's account of Owain, and for other valuable hints. See above, p. 343.

at one time used to attend the efforts of Mormon missionaries among the people of certain parts of Wales. It appears to have been most remarkable in the mining districts of South Wales, but it now and then involved the inhabitants of rural districts, such, for example, as the village of St. Bride's Major, in the south of Glamorganshire, mentioned by Mr. J. M. Randall, one of the agents engaged in the management of Lord Dunraven's Welsh estates. We refer to the following passage :[1] " You say about forty years ago there was a large exodus of the working classes from your district ? "—" Yes, particularly from the village of St. Bride's Major. There was a large exodus to Salt Lake City. I think they went to join the Mormons, on religious grounds."

Now there were two things in the preachings of the Mormon missioners which were calculated particularly to attract the ignorant in Wales, namely, the imminent approach of the end of the world and the coming of Christ in the flesh to reign with His saints in a temporal kingdom in the West. The latter doctrine belonged to an order of ideas which we have shown to have been far from unfamiliar among the Brythons and other nations. Probably, however, a certain class of people was still more influenced by an apprehension of the immediate approach of the end of the world ; for even now the crazes on this subject which are propagated from time to time by a certain type of English divines, whose favourite study seems to be the Apocalypse and the Prophet Daniel, are apt to command, perhaps, a more anxious hearing in Wales than they usually obtain in England. And in the earlier fifties apprehension and fear were helped by the uneasiness created by the Crimean war, and it was in some measure prolonged by the strange appearance somewhat later of Donati's Comet. Many timid people there

[1] Qu. 5,625—6 : see also p. 53 of the Report.

undoubtedly were who connected these things with the events set forth in the sixteenth chapter of the Book of Revelation, including among them the stealthy coming of Christ and the gathering together of mighty hosts to Armageddon. These and other reasons of the same nature seem to have made Wales a favourable arena for the activity of the Mormons for a time, and the success which attended that activity had the effect of giving the Welsh the reputation of being a very superstitious people. A great change, however, has come over the country within the last thirty years, as any one can testify who attempts nowadays to collect folklore in the Principality. His task has become an exceedingly difficult one so far as regards the Welsh men and women of the present day, for not only have they ceased to give any credence to the stories and legends of the past, but they go so far as only to own with reluctance to having ever heard them. In fact, such folklore is rapidly passing into oblivion as far as concerns the rustic of the type that formerly revelled in it ; and so would the creed of the Latter-day Saints too but for its apostles continuing to haunt the Principality. Some have been seen and heard preaching there the peculiar tenets of that creed within the last few years ; but the success of earlier days appears to have deserted their ministry, leaving it to interest solely the student of psychological pathology.

A word must now be said as to the opportunities for recreation and the means of improvement within the reach of the agricultural population. Few country places have any ground set apart for recreation and athletic exercise, and even where ground had been reserved for that purpose under the Acts of Parliament authorising the enclosure of common land, the Commission usually found that it was little used, or not at all.[1] The growth of interest in such

[1] Qu. 543 *et seq.*, 643—695.

games as that of cricket and of football belongs chiefly
to the younger part of the population of the towns and
mining centres, though football is by no means a new
game in the Principality. It used to be a very popular
pastime prior to the Nonconformist revival, but as the
principal day for it used to be Sunday it was put down
with stern severity by all the Nonconformists, who held
decided Sabbatarian views. In Catholic times there were
numerous saints' days and festivals on which the game
might be played, but as these holidays have nearly all
ceased to be observed and Sunday is out of the question,
football mostly ceased in the country districts. There is,
however, we think another and a deeper reason why
neither football nor any other athletic exercise is regularly
practised in country places, and that is the natural lack of
inclination to further physical effort on the part of men
who have to work through a long day in the open air.
Recreation to suit them must, we think, partake largely of
the nature of cessation from serious bodily exertion ; they
want some change of occupation which involves rest for
the limbs wearied by the day's toil. In other words, they
may be expected to prefer something of the nature of
reading, singing, chatting together, playing some easy
game of the nature of chess, or at most a game of quoits ;
not to mention that the hours of labour of the farmer and
his servants make it impossible that their recreation should
be found for them out of doors, at least for a considerable
portion of the year.

In winter the farmers and their families have long
evenings at their disposal, and it is interesting to notice
how they spend them. A few generations ago the household of an upland farmer on the Cardiganshire side of
Plinlimmon would sit round a good peat fire ; some of the
women would take up their knitting, some would peel
rushes for rushlights, a servant-man would carve a wooden

spoon or a ladle, and somebody would read to the company. When they grew tired of that, somebody would relate a story or propound riddles ; and so things went on till all retired to rest. Somewhat the same domesticity is suggested by the evidence of Mr. W. L. Williams, who, speaking of Carmarthenshire, said :[1] " I remember the time when servants had a kind of domestic competition on the hearth as to who could make the best wooden spoon or basket, or string onions. There is now nothing of the kind : the servants are gradually losing their character as members of the family, and do not remain as much in the farm kitchen. They have little or no domestic life." At Beddgelert and other places in the Snowdon district the neighbours used to spend their evenings in one another's houses on what they termed " knitting nights," when they used to knit and entertain one another with stories about fairies, bogies, or any other popular subject.[2] In the parish of Lanaelhaiarn, in Arfon, an evening of that description used to be called a *pilnos* or " rush-*peeling* night," though we read of the occupation of the company gathered together being rather the dressing of hemp and the carding of wool. But the entertainment consisted chiefly in telling stories, a fact which need surprise no one in a district which forms the classical ground of the old-world tales of the " Mabinogion " and has a topography that re-echoes the names of the goddess Dôn's descendants.[3] In Merionethshire, Bala and its neighbourhood were formerly celebrated for the trade done in them in woollen stockings, and Pennant, alluding to what he terms a " knitting assembly " or *Cymorth Gwau*, uses the following

---

[1] Qu. 37,829.

[2] See " Y Cymmrodor," vol. v., pp. 49, 50.

[3] *Ibid.*, vol. vi., p. 169. See also pp. 162—165, rom which it appears that it is in this part of Arfon alone that the name Dôn has survived in the language of the hearth : elsewhere it has been obtained from books, as proved by its being pronounced *Dòn* or *Donn* and treated as a masculine.

words:[1] "During winter the females, through love of
society, often assemble at one another's houses to knit ;
sit round a fire, and listen to some old tale, or to some
ancient song, or the sound of a harp."

The happy gathering of the family round the winter fire
continues in most countrysides much as in years gone by,
except on the one hand that the comforts now enjoyed are
frequently greater, and that on the other the charmed
circle is apt in our day to be somewhat encroached upon
by the frequency of evening meetings at the chapel, unless
that happens to be situated at too great a distance to be
often attended. In any case this raises the question of
the extent of the accommodation afforded by the farm-
house for those who would like to spend their evenings at
home, but we have already considered it at some length.
So we revert to Mr. W. L. Williams's words to the effect
that for some reason or other the servant-men tend, as
stated by him, to consider themselves or to be considered
by their employers less intimately members of the family
nowadays than they did formerly. This forms a third
exception to our general statement, and it is to be
regretted, we think, on the ground of morality and
temperance, and of honest service ; but it is a tendency
which is growing and likely to grow the more completely
labour becomes, like other commodities, ruled by the
highest bid without any predilection for person or place.
So the question of resorts and recreations in country
villages must become a more and more pressing one. The
labourers and servant-men who quit the farm kitchen
cannot all be accommodated in the smithy or the shoe-
maker's workshop ; and all are agreed that it is not
desirable that they should make a habit of frequenting
the village public.

The Commission took some evidence on this point,

[1] Pennant's " Tours in Wales," ii., pp. 210, 211, of the edition of 1810.

and beginning with the least ambitious order of suggestions made to them, we quote first the views of Mr. J. M. Prichard, farmer, magistrate, and barrister-at-law, who came before them at Langefni, and spoke as follows :[1] " Now Lady Reade has shown an example which I should very much like to see Class A landlords who are able to afford it, follow. She had three public-houses at Lanfaethlu, and, being a temperance reformer, she did away with two licences. She thought that one was quite enough, and that is, I think, the policy which is followed now. She did it without appealing to us as magistrates at all. She dropped these two licences ; she wanted to see less drink in the villages. The only result of dropping these two licences was to create more drinking. The three houses that were there before did not pay at all ; you might have bought both licences for 100*l.* each or 50*l.*, but when there was only one public-house, that house was immediately enlarged and made very comfortable and nicé ; three or four parlours were added, and the result is, there is more business done at that one than was ever done at the three. That, I suppose, did not suit Lady Reade ; she naturally did not like to see so much drinking in the neighbourhood, so near by, she built a coffee-house, which has been a very great success. I think if the landlords would build more of those—not make an attempt at once to do away with the few places that the workmen have to sit down in, but first of all build coffee-houses, or build them some places of entertainment, where they can enjoy themselves of an evening, and afterwards petition the magistrates to do away with the licences, that would be a good policy."

Mr. Prichard in dealing further with this subject instanced Lanfachreth, Bodedern, and Trefor as centres where places of entertainment might prove a great boon to that part

[1] Qu. 18,623, 18,624.

of Anglesey, and he thought it best to entrust the establishing of them to the County Council. A little later this view was advocated by Mr. S. Hughes,[1] the chairman of the County Council himself, who, however, in representing the desirability of having places for refreshments in every country village, gave some prominence to the intellectual requirements of the persons concerned : " I think there should be some sort of temperance house there," he said, " with periodicals and some books."

This brings us to the evidence about reading-rooms. As regards the majority of country districts, it was simply negative : there are none. But in one instance a witness went further, namely, Mr. William Edwards,[2] Lecturer on Agriculture under the Cheshire County Council, formerly Secretary to the Anglesey Farmers' Society, and otherwise intimately acquainted with that county. After dwelling in severe terms on the lack of a reading-room or any recreation-ground at the village, for instance, of Lanfair, in Anglesey, and the responsibility of the neighbouring landowners in the matter, he drew a contrast between that county and Cheshire in the following terms : " During the last fortnight I have been in Cheshire, I could not help noticing that there was a very vast amount of difference there in the small villages, as compared to ours." He went on to say : " In almost every small village you go to, there is a public room, all the papers come there, there are science classes and that sort of thing, and lectures are given on all conceivable subjects."

On the other side we feel bound to quote the evidence of Lord Stanley of Alderley, who owns land both in Anglesey and Cheshire : we refer to the following passage, Question 19,831.—" Have you done anything in the way of encouraging libraries in the villages, in order to prevent the prowling around the neighbourhood by the farm boys

---

[1] Qu. 21,971—2.   [2] Qu. 43,085—6.

at night ?"—"Yes, I have. I did one thing, and tried to do another. I have made a beginning with a library of Welsh books in my principal farm at Bodewryd; it is in the middle of the property I have there. Then at Bodedern I heard that Archdeacon Wynne Jones, when he was the owner, had attempted to establish a reading-room, and that the project had fallen through. I offered to build an additional room, either as a school class-room, or simply as a reading-room adjoining the school at Bodedern. The schoolmaster was perfectly willing to keep it open at night, and to receive people there for amusing themselves, for reading and so on ; but although I have offered to provide the building, I have not been able to get further than that. They have not yet said that anybody would be glad to have it, nor made any proposal to me as to which spot the building should stand on."

We have dwelt so long on the case of Anglesey partly because it is a typically agricultural county, and partly because the Anglesey evidence on this question happens to be explicit and concrete. But the same apparent lack of intellectual interest, which is suggested by Lord Stanley's words cited above, meets us elsewhere. In some instances where reading-rooms have been in existence they are not conspicuously successful, and in others they have failed altogether. As regards the Anglesey instances, his Lordship does not offer any explanation why his generosity was not more appreciated either at Bodedern or Bodewryd ; and we turn to another part of the Principality and cite a case which is explained by the witness dealing with it, namely, Miss Kate Jenkins. She spoke, as already stated, of the parish of Langadock, in the Vale of the Towy, and used the following words :[1] "I do not think the right people take it [the reading-room movement] up, or if they do they do not take it up in the right way. We had a

[1] Qu. 38,053.

reading-room at Langadock. I did not go to it at all ;
I happened to be away from home at the time, but when
I came back I found it was not a success. The farmers'
sons did not go there, only just the Church people went.
I asked them why they did not attend, and told them it
was very bigoted. They said instead of forming a committee and getting all the farmers together in that way,
which would be self-government by the people, the vicar
arranged everything, and when everything was finished he
called a committee together. It was very kind of him
and I have no doubt he wanted to do it, but it was all
finished at that time, and when the people came they
found inside the books, 'St. Cadog's Church Lending
Library,' and the Nonconformists (of course foolishly) took
umbrage and never came near, or very few of them. It is
now dead because nobody goes there."

The habit of turning into a reading-room to seek information or mental improvement has probably got to grow
among the rural population, and to do so under the
fostering influence of careful and protracted cultivation.
This is the first point to be considered in any attempt to
account for the failure of reading-rooms in country villages.
But reasons of the kind assigned by Miss Jenkins in the
case cited by her are not imaginary : they constitute a
vera causa. Any undertaking which labours under the
least suspicion of aiming at proselytising or of being an
act of patronising, whether on the part of the Church of
England or any dissenting body, of noblemen or wealthy
commoners, is in the present temper of the Welsh people
doomed to certain failure. In the long run the people
will not have it, even though that attitude should expose
them to the charge of indifference or ingratitude. We
cannot help referring here to the instances of reading-rooms
mentioned in the evidence[1] of Mr. Price of Rhiwlas, given

---

[1] Qu. 18,492.

in the course of one of the Commissioners' sittings at Bala. They do credit to the generosity of those who originated them and carried them on, in some cases with considerable success ; but we cannot admit that the references to them successfully rebut, as they were intended to do, the following passage in the evidence of Mr. Thomas E. Ellis :[1] " Now these figures speak for themselves. The occupiers pay the land tax, the poor, public health, education, highway, police, and county rates, yet in Merioneth, where 140,335*l.* was paid as rent in 1889—90, the county is ill-provided with public institutions. In a land and among a peasantry singularly devoted to social converse there is not a public village hall—keenly fond of reading, there is not a public library. In a changeable climate mainly damp and with homes small and confined there is not a single hospital or public dispensary. In a land whose people are singularly attached to the soil and its associations the dwellings of peasants and cottagers are allowed to fall to ruin. I venture to think this is too severe a strain and cannot last."

Mr. Ellis maintained his position and explained, as follows, the meaning which he attached to his words : "When I say a public village hall, I mean not a couple of rooms, which may be let with or without rent for a time and at the will of the landowner or of a resident, but a building with rooms and conveniences which is the property of a parish or of a village. Of such a building I believe there is not a single instance in the county of Merioneth." Reviewing Mr. Price of Rhiwlas' instances, he spoke of one of them as follows : " The Llanbedr room and hall is a very admirable one, and does a very great deal of good, but the hall is the property of Mr. Pope, and with great generosity he has allowed these rooms, I think, to be used freely by the public. But it is not the property of Llanbedr ; and if Mr. Pope went away from the district I

[1] Qu. 16,918, 18,508—10.

do not believe there is any guarantee except the guarantee
of his generosity that would leave it as a public institution.
It is in no sense the public library of Lanbedr." Further
on he speaks of the instances adduced from Corwen and
Dolgelley as little spasmodic attempts made by small groups
of individuals in those two towns. " There is no continuity
whatsoever," he added, " about these reading-rooms, and
they are in no sense public libraries." Of a reading-room
at Lanuwchllyn he said : " It was started by getting one
or two rooms in a house, and a certain number of books
was placed there, but they were the mere surplusage of
other libraries, and a good deal of the literature was about
such subjects as the Lost Ten Tribes." Lastly, with
regard to a portion of the old barrack utilised at Bala as
a reading-room, and supported by subscriptions, his words
were : " They have two or three comfortable rooms, so far
as they go. There is a little room which is called a library,
but I do not believe the Commission would give more than
about 5l., if they would give 5l., for the whole stock of
books that are there. They are antiquated, and the
majority of them perfectly useless and unserviceable. But,"
he added, "these subscriptions to what one may call a
casual reading-room, which is rented in an old barrack here
in the town, is a very different thing to a handsome building
which is owned by the people, and controlled by them."

These utterances of Mr. Ellis's as a farmer's son and
a man enjoying a position of eminence in the political
party to which he belonged, fix, probably, a minimum of
reform below which no future well-wisher of the agricultural population of Wales can well allow his demands to
fall. Even the seemingly otiose adjective referring to
architecture is, if we mistake not, fraught with future
significance.[1] But we have cited Mr. Ellis's evidence at

[1] After the visit of the Commission to Bala Mr. Ellis addressed more than
one meeting of Welshmen on the subject of architecture in the Principality.

so great a length, mainly because he lays his finger on two of the weak points in the present reading-room system : we have used the wrong word—there is no system, but there ought to be a system. And one essential part of such system must be the exclusion of all possible suspicion of proselytising and patronising, as we have already hinted ; or in other words, suggested by this evidence, the unequivocal ownership and control of the reading-room or library by the people for the people. The other weak point indicated by the evidence in the case of some of the well-meant efforts, already mentioned, to encourage reading is the lack displayed of discretion to select or of means to buy suitable books. The surplusage of other libraries, antiquated and unserviceable volumes, cannot be expected to form good intellectual pabulum for a farmer or even a farmer's man, and a reading-room that relies on the Lost Ten Tribes must speedily find itself more lost than they.

Having dealt at so great a length with the question of reading-rooms, we may remark that the evidence did not show that they were all unsuccessful, and that, even had such been the case, we should not feel compelled, seeing what the history of these undertakings has individually been, to consider that their want of success forms adequate proof that the rural population of Wales cares nothing about books. In fact the contrary statement has been more than once made to us—for example, by Mr. Ellis in the evidence already quoted ; not to mention the curious instance given at Lansawel by Mr. Thomas Davies. Being asked as to farm servants whether they take a delight in reading, Mr. Davies replied :[1] "Yes, I had a farm servant who left me last year : he had been with me nine years, and he was reading the Bible once a year every year right through, genealogies and all." On this we have to remark, on the one hand, that the man in question

[1] Qu. 40,026—8.

did his reading under difficulties as regards accommodation, and on the other hand that his case is probably not a pure instance of love of reading, but to a certain extent, at all events, of a sense of religious duty. We think it a mistaken sense of religious duty, but it is by no means uncommon in the Principality, and has in the estimation of strangers earned for the Welsh people the character of being devoted to Bibliolatry. It probably is a survival from a time when the Bible was almost the only extensive book which was as a matter of fact accessible to all in their own language ; and it is to some extent the result of the Bible being practically the only Sunday-school book still. On the principle, however, that a fact or two may prove of more value than a mass of opinion or theory, we have had the curiosity to inquire what has happened in one of the most rural parishes in the neighbourhood of Bala subsequently to the time when the Commission took the evidence there which we have in part cited, and above all since the machinery of the Parish Council has come into existence. We refer to Lanuwchllyn, and our inquiry was directed to one of the best known men in Wales, Mr. Owen Morgan Edwards, Fellow and Tutor of Lincoln College, Oxford, and a native of Lanuwchllyn, where he spends more than half of each year. He has been good enough to send us the following letter bearing the date of Lincoln College, Oxford, February 1, 1896 :—

"We adopted the Public Libraries Act at Lanuwchllyn almost as soon as our Parish Council got into working order. The parish is entirely agricultural, and its scattered village is a very small one. All took an interest in the movement for a library : 114 voted for it, and only 19 against.

"We started with a little over 400 books, and the number is continually increasing, the farmers and labourers themselves presenting many.

"Within the first two months after opening it, 354 books were taken out, the demands upon the library is increasing, and in spite of the Parish Council's willingness to spend money and of continual gifts, we find ourselves unable to cope with the demand. Books on agriculture, Daniel Owen's novels, books on history, and books on technical subjects are in greatest demand—all in Welsh, of course.

"The success of the movement we attribute to the fact that the people feel the library belongs to them, and is under their sole management."

For details concerning the growth and volume of the periodical literature published in the Principality we refer the reader to our chapter on the Language and Literature;[1] and we confine ourselves here to one or two remarks on those of our periodicals and newspapers which are in Welsh. There is no daily paper published in that language, but there are a good number of weekly ones, of which some are more or less closely identified with individual religious denominations.

Speaking generally of the Welsh newspapers, we may say that they agree in eschewing news about horse-racing and in devoting but little of their space to games of any kind. They are chary in their accounts of divorce cases and indecent assaults, but they are rather more accessible to accounts of murder and tales of horror. They are more literary than English papers of the like standing, and they are always open to poets and versifiers. The editors hail with delight anything of an antiquarian nature, and any history or biography, especially relating to Wales. They may be said to be on the whole Puritan in their tone. The majority of them are devoted to the interests of the Liberal Party, and only one has adopted a socialistic or collectivist attitude.

[1] See pp. 533—5, above ; also the Report, pp. 653—5, and the Appendices to it, especially C. III., pp. 195—200.

This brief survey of the journalistic literature current in Wales will serve also to indicate the general characteristics of the monthly and quarterly periodicals, as well indeed as of all the other books which are in request in Wales. The tone of all is expected to be more or less religious ; and even if they happen to be novels, they must devote ample space to the religious aspects of the characters which they delineate. Books of biography and travels are always acceptable ; and so are those that deal with Welsh history and antiquities. The world of fancy has its unfailing charm for the Cymro, and he is always accessible to the muse of poetry. Lastly, it is to his credit that the *Gwyddoniadur*, a high-class encyclopædia in the Welsh language, has found ready acceptance. It began to be issued in the year 1854, under the editorship of the Rev. Dr. Parry, of Bala ; and the late Mr. Gee, the originator and guiding spirit of the series, had in the year 1896 the gratification—as editor, this time, as well as publisher—to see completed a second edition of the work in ten massive volumes, comprising nearly 10,000 articles. Inquiries made by one of us have elicited the information that the whole undertaking has cost more than 20,000*l.*, and that the veteran publisher was satisfied with the way in which his enterprise had been backed by his Welsh-speaking countrymen. We leave these bare facts to speak for themselves as to the current literature which Welshmen read, and more especially the rural population.[1]

[1] Since this chapter was written, our attention has been drawn to an interesting essay in Welsh on "Rural Life in Wales" (" Bywyd Gwledig yn Nghymru "), by Mr. Charles Ashton. This is printed at pp. 36—92 of the "Transactions of the National Eisteddfod of Wales," Bangor, 1890.

APPENDIX A.

LIST OF THE CANTREFS AND CYMWDS OF WALES.

THERE are several lists of these ancient divisions extant; of these, the three oldest, each however representing a distinct text, are :—

1. The list in the *Red Book of Hergest*, which has been diplomatically reproduced as an appendix to *Brut y Tywysogion* in Rhys and Evans' Oxford series of Welsh texts, vol. ii. (pp. 407—12), and was previously printed, but very inaccurately, at the bottoms of pp. 606—12 of vol ii. of the *Myvyrian Archaiology of Wales* (1st edition, or at pp. 737 *et seq.* in the 2nd or Denbigh edition).

2. The text from the *Cwtta Cyfarwyd*, printed by Mr. Gwenogvryn Evans in *Y Cymmrodor* ix. 327—31.

3. A list copied in the 15th century from (ultimately) a lost MS. of the 12th or 13th, preserved in MS. Cott. Domitian, A. viii. (Brit. Mus.), and printed in Leland's Itinerary, edition 1769, vol. v., folios 16—18.

Among other lists which are of later date, being in fact composed subsequently to the division of Wales into counties, the more important and most frequently quoted are :—

4. The list given in Sir John Price's *Description of Wales* (of which the oldest known MS., dated 1559, is that marked Caligula A. vi., among the Cottonian MSS. in the British Museum). This list was edited by Humphry Lwyd, and is printed in Dr. David Powel's *Historie of Cambria*, 1584, pp. 1—22 (and presumably in all subsequent editions of that work; in the Merthyr edition of

1812 it occupies pp i.—xxiv.). It was also printed in a separate form by William Hall at Oxford in 1663, where it is said to have been merely "perused" by Humphry Lwyd (*Y Cymmrodor* xi. p. 54).

5. A list, virtually identical with No. 4, is the *first* of the two printed in the *Myvyrian Archaiology of Wales*, vol. ii., at the tops of pp. 606—13 (in the 1st edition ; or at pp. 735—7 in the 2nd edition), and erroneously thought to be and quoted as being from the *Red Book of Hergest*. There are also numerous other less important lists in existence.

We reprint here the list from Sir John Price's *Description of Wales*.

"About the year 870, Rodericus Magnus, king of Wales, divided the country into three territories, which they called kingdoms, and which remained until of late days.

These three were :—

GWYNEDD, or North Wales ;
POWYS LAND ; and
DEHEUBARTH, or South Wales.[1]

"GWYNEDD had upon the north side the sea, from the River Dee at Basingwerke to Aberdyfi, and upon the west and south-west the River Dyfi, which divided it from South Wales and in some places from Powys Land, and on the south and east it is divided from Powys, sometimes with mountains and sometimes with rivers, till it came to the River Dee again.

This land of old time divided into four parts :—

(1.) *Mon*, having three cantrefs or hundreds which were sub-divided into six commots, namely :—

(*a.*) Aberffraw, with two commots, Lleyn and Malltraeth.
(*b.*) Cemáis, with two commots, Talibolion and Twrcelyn.
(*c.*) Rossyr, with two commots, Tyndaethwy and Maenai.

---

[1] As to the alleged division by Rodericus (Rhodri) see above. p. 144 *et seq.*

(2.) *Arfon*, having four cantrefs and ten commots, namely : —

(*a.*) Aber, with three commots, Y Llechweddochaf, Y Llechwedd-isaf, and Nant-Conway.
(*b.*) Arfon, with two commots, Uwch-Gwyrfai and Isgwyrfai.
(*c.*) Dunodig, with two commots, Ardudwy and Efionyth.
(*d.*) Lleyn, with three commots, Cymytmayn, Tinllayn, and Canologion.

(3.) *Meirionydd*, containing three cantrefs, and each cantref three commots :—

(*a.*) Meireon, with three commots, Talybont, Pennal, and Ystumaner.
(*b.*) Arustly, with three commots, Uwchcoed, Isboed, and Gwarthrenium.
(*c.*) Penllyn, with three commots, Uwchmeloch, Ismeloch, and Michaint.

(4.) *Y Berfeddwlad*, containing five cantrefs and thirteen commots :—

(*a.*) Rhyfonioc, with two commots, Uwchalet and Isalet.
(*b.*) Ystrad, with two commots, Hiraethog and Cynmeirch.
(*c.*) Rhos, with three commots, Uwchdulas, Isdulas, and Creuddyn.
(*d.*) Dyffryn-Clwyd, with three commots, Coleigion, Llannerch, and Dogeulyn.
(*e.*) Tegengl, with three commots, Cynsyled, Prestatyn, and Ruthlan.

"The second kingdom was MATHRAFAEL. To this kingdom belonged the country of Powys and the land between Wye and Severn. Which part had upon the south and west, South Wales, with the Rivers Wye and Tywy, and other mears. Upon the north Gwynedd, and upon the east the Marches of England, from Chester to the Wye, a little above Hereford.

This part called Powys, was divided into Powys Fadoc and Powys Wenwynwyn :—

(1.) *Powys Fadoc*, contained five cantrefs and fifteen commots :—

(*a.*) Y Barwn, with three commots, Dynmael, Edeyrnion, and Glyndyfrdwy.

(*b.*) Y Rhiw, with three commots, Yal, Ystratalyn, and Hop.

(*c.*) Uwchnant, with three commots, Merffordd, Maelor Gymraeg, and Maelor Saesneg.

(*d.*) Trefred, with three commots, Croesfain, Tref y Waun, and Croesoswallt.

(*e.*) Rhaider, with three commots, Mochnant Israiader, Cynllaeth, and Nanheudwy.

(2.) *Powys Wenwynwyn* had likewise five cantrefs and twelve commots :—

(*a.*) Y Fyrnwy, with three commots, Mochnant uwch Raiader, Mechain Iscoed, and Llannerch Hudol.

(*b.*) Ystlic, with three commots, Deuddwr, Corddwr Isaf, and Ystrad Marchell.

(*c.*) Llyswynaf, with two commots, Caerneon and Mechain Uwchcoed.

(*d.*) Cedewain, with two commots, Conan and Hafren.

(*e.*) Conan, with two commots, Cyfeilioc and Mowddwy.

(Arustly was in old time in this part, but afterwards it came to the princes of Gwynedd.)

(3.) *The third part belonging to Mathrafael, was the land between the Wye and Severn*, containing four cantrefs and thirteen commots:—

(*a.*) Melienydd, with three commots, Ceri, Swyddygre Rhi-walallt, and Glyn Erthon.

(*b.*) Elfel, with three commots, Uwchmynydd, Ismynydd, and Llechddyfnog.

(*c.*) Y Clawdd, with three commots, Dyffryn Teyfediad, Swyd-dynogen, and Pennwellt.

(*d.*) Buellt, with three commots, Swydd y Farn, Dreulys, and Isyrwon.

"The last kingdom of Wales, called DYNEFAWR, was divided into six parts :—

(1.) *Caredigion*, containing four cantrefs and ten commots :—

(*a*.) Penwedic, with three commots, Geneurglyn, Perfedd, and Creuthyn.

(*b*.) Canawl, with three commots, Mefenyth, Anhunoc, and Pennarth.

(*c*.) Castell, with two commots, Mabwynion and Caerwedros.

(*d*.) Syrwen, with two commots, Gwenionydd and Iscoed.

(2.) *Dyfed*, containing eight cantrefs and twenty-three commots:—

(*a*.) Emlyn, with three commots, Uwchcuch, Iscuch, and Lefethyr.

(*b*.) Arberth, with three commots, Penrhyn ar Elays, Esterolef, and Talacharn.

(*c*.) Daugledden, with three commots, Amgoed, Pennant, and Efelfre.

(*d*.) Y Coed, with two commots, Llanhayaden and Castell Gwys.

(*e*.) Penfro, with three commots, Coed yr haf, Maenorbyrr, and Penfro.

(*f*.) Rhos, with three commots, Hwlffordd, Castell Gwalchmai, and Ygarn.

(*g*.) Pubidioc, with three commots, Mynyw, Pencaer, and Pebidioc.

(*h*.) Cemais, with three commots, Uwchnefer, Isnefer, and Trefdraeth.

(3.) *Carmarthenshire*, having four cantrefs and fifteen commots:—

(*a*.) Finioc, with three commots, Harfryn, Derfedd, and Isgeneny.

(*b*.) Eginoc, with three commots, Gwyr, Cydweli, and Carnwill eon.

(*c*.) Bychan, with three commots, Mallaen, Caio, and Maenor Deilo.

(*d*.) Mawr, with four commots, Cethinoc, Elfyw, Uchdryd, and Wydigada.

(4.) *Morganwg*, containing four cantrefs and fifteen commots :—

(*a.*) Croneth, with three commots, Rwngneth ac Afan, Tir yr Hwndrwd, and Maenor Glynogwr.

(*b.*) Pennythen, with four commots, Meyscyn, Glynrhodny Maenor Talafan, and Maenor Ruthyn.

(*c.*) Brenhinol, with four commots, Cibowr, Senghennyth, Uwchcaeth, and Iscaeth.

(*d.*) Gwentllw, with two commots, y Rhardd Ganol and Eithafdylgion.

(5.) *Gwent*, having three cantrefs and ten commots :—

(*a.*) Gwent, with three commots, Y mynydd, Iscoed Llefnydd, and Tref y grug.

(*b.*) Iscoed, with four commots, Brynbuga, Uwchcoed, y Teirtref, and Erging ac Ewyas.

(*c.*) Côch.

(6.) *Brecheiniog*, having three cantrefs and eight commots :—

(*a.*) Selef, with two commots, Selef and Trahayern.

(*b.*) Canol, with three commots, Talgorth, Ystradyw, and Brwynllys or Eglwys Yail.

(*c.*) Mawr, with three commots, Tir Raulff-Llywell and Cerrig-Howel."

APPENDIX B.

(See page 23.)

PRE-ARYAN SYNTAX IN INSULAR CELTIC.

" The notion of a ' mixed language ' must have much more weight assigned to it than has heretofore been allowed."—O. Schrader, *Prehistoric Antiquities.* Eng. trans. p. 113.

THE syntax of Welsh and Irish differs in some important respects from that of the languages belonging to the other branches of the Aryan family. Professor Rhys suggested many years ago that these peculiarities are due to the influence of a pre-Aryan language; this suggestion led me to make the comparisons summarised in this paper. The substance of that part of the paper which deals with Egyptian was communicated to Professor Rhys in April, 1891 ; the other omparisons were made later ; but hitherto they have all remained unpublished. I now gladly avail myself of the opportunity kindly offered to publish them in the pages of "The Welsh People."

When one language is supplanted by another, the speakers find it comparatively easy to adopt the new vocabulary, but not so easy to abandon the old modes of expression ; and thus, whilst the old language dies, its idiom survives in the new. The neo-Celtic languages, then, which are Aryan in vocabulary, and largely non-Aryan in idiom, appear to be the acquired Aryan speech of a population originally speaking a non-Aryan language. This view does not necessarily imply that the ancestors of the Welsh and Irish belonged almost exclusively to the conquered pre-Celtic race : we may suppose that the invading armies of Celts destroyed a large part of the aboriginal male population, and took possession of their wives, thus producing an amalgamated race, who, however, learnt their speech from their non-Celtic mothers.

These non-Celtic inhabitants of Britain are believed by anthropologists to be of the same race as the ancient Iberians, and to have migrated through France and Spain from North Africa,[1] where the race is represented by the Berbers and the ancient Egyptians. "The skulls of the pure Iberian race, such as those found in the long barrows of Britain, or the Caverne de l'Homme Mort, are of the same type as those of the Berbers and the Guanches, and bear a considerable resemblance to the skulls of the ancient Egyptians."[2] Again, on the linguistic side, M. de Rochemonteix has shown in his "Rapports grammaticaux entre l'égyptien et le berbère,"[3] that a relation exists between the Berber languages and ancient Egyptian, which are now usually included in one family, called the Hamitic. If the Iberians of Britain are related to the speakers of these languages, it is natural to expect that their language also belonged to the Hamitic family—in other words, that the pre-Aryan idioms which still live in Welsh and Irish were derived from a language allied to Egyptian and the Berber tongues. And if there is evidence that this is so—if we find, on comparison, that neo-Celtic syntax agrees with Hamitic on almost every point where it differs from Aryan, we have the linguistic complement of the anthropological evidence, and the strongest corroboration of the theory of the kinship of the early inhabitants of Britain to the North African white race.

Egyptian preserves a very ancient form of Hamitic speech ; and we can assume with confidence that it approaches much nearer to the primitive Hamitic type of language than the Berber tongues which we are acquainted with only in their modern form. Egyptian may therefore be expected to agree more closely in general structure with our hypothetic pre-Celtic dialect ; and it will be convenient to consider first those parallels which are offered by it.

---

[1] A. H. Keane, "Ethnology," 1896, pp. 135-6.

[2] Isaac Taylor, "Origin of the Aryans," p. 220. See also Sergi, "Origine e diffusione della stirpe mediterranea " (Rome, 1895), p. 79.

[3] In the "Mémoires du Congrès international des Orientalistes," 1re Session, t. ii., p. 66 et seq.

1. *The order of words in the sentence.*—As the relations of words in an Aryan sentence are sufficiently shown by inflexions, the order of the words may vary; but normally the verb comes *last.* In Welsh and Irish the verb usually comes *first:* thus in Welsh, *Darllennoð Ifan y llyfr,* "Evan read the book"; in med. Irish, *Aliss Patricc Dubthach,* "Patrick requested Dubthach." O'Donovan in his "Irish Grammar" (p. 357) says: "In the natural order of an Irish sentence the verb comes first, the nominative, with its dependents, next after it, and next the object of the verb." Compare with the above the following rules given by Renouf in his "Egyptian Grammar" (p. 57)[1]: "The order of the words in an Egyptian sentence is constant. When the verb is expressed it precedes the subject. If both the nearer and the remoter objects of a verb are nouns, the former is placed after the subject and the latter comes last." [2]

But there appears in Welsh another form of sentence in which the noun comes first. No distinction is made in any of our Welsh grammars between this and the simple form of sentence in which the verb comes first; and the Welsh translators of the Bible constantly misuse it for the simple form; as *Job a ateboð,* instead of *ateboð Job,* for "Job answered." This misuse of the construction is absolutely unknown in the spoken language; and such a phrase as *Job a ateboð* is never heard except when the fact of some one having answered is known and the doubt in the hearer's mind is as to *who it was* that answered. In short, the verb "to be" is understood with Job, and *a* is the relative pronoun; thus *Job a ateboð* means "(it was) Job who answered." [3] In Egyptian, says Renouf (p. 57), "a noun at the beginning of a sentence implies the ellipsis of the verb 'to be.'"

But a noun may also stand quite independently at the beginning of a sentence. In Irish, writes O'Donovan (p. 357), "when

---

[1] The references in this paper to Renouf's "Grammar" were made to the 2nd edition; but as the 3rd seems to be an exact reprint of the 2nd they hold good of the 3rd also.

[2] See also Brugsch, "Grammaire hiéroglyphique," p. 100.

[3] The full meaning is seen when the contrast is expressed: *Paul a lefaroð, nid Pedr,* "(it was) Paul who spoke, not Peter."

the noun is placed before the verb, it does not immediately connect
with the verb, but rather stands in an *absolute* state." [1] So Renouf,
speaking elsewhere of a noun coming first, says : "The noun is
not the grammatical subject of the verb, but what grammarians
call the 'nominative *absolute*'" (p. 47).

In Welsh and Irish an adjective or a noun in the genitive case
is placed after the noun which it qualifies ; as, Welsh, *gwr mawr*,
Irish, *fear mór*, "vir magnus"; Welsh, *Cân Selyf*, "the Song of
Solomon"; Irish, *inghean Shaidhbhe*, "the daughter of Sabia." So
in Egyptian *pa netàr āa* [2] (Welsh, *y duw mawr*), "the great
god"; *t'ruu tà* [3] (Welsh, *eithafoet daear*), "the ends of the earth."
Of course, the same order is preserved when the relation of the
genitive is expressed by means of a preposition. Now, M.
Bergaigne [4] has shown that in the primitive Aryan sentence the
qualifying word, whether adjective or genitive, came *before* the
word qualified. In Welsh and Irish, then, we have a divergence
from the primitive Aryan order, and an adoption of the same
order as that found in Egyptian.

2. *Personal Suffixes.*—In Egyptian "the suffixes representing
the different persons are :—

SINGULAR.			PLURAL.		
1st person		*à.*	1st person	*n.*	
2nd „	masc.	*k.*	2nd „	*ten.*	
2nd „	fem.	*t.*	3rd „	*sen.*	
3rd „	masc.	*f.*	3rd „	*set, u,* or *un.*" [5]	
3rd „	fem.	*s* or *set.*			

These suffixes (which, with one exception, do not exist independently) are added to verbs, prepositions, and nouns. In

[1] This construction, he says, is "unquestionably faulty." Similarly in some
Welsh grammars, such as that of Tegai, distinctively Welsh idioms, if found
at all, will be found under such a heading as "Common Errors."
[2] Renouf, "Eg. Gram.," p. 51.
[3] *Ibid.*, p. 21.
[4] "Mémoires de la Soc. de Linguistique de Paris," iii. 1, 2, 3, quoted by
Sayce, "Sc. of Lang.," i. p. 425.
[5] Renouf, "Eg. Gram.," p. 17.

Welsh and Irish they are represented (1) by inflexional personal endings already existing in Aryan; (2) by agglutinative personal pronouns. In what follows, I use a dot between an inflexion and a root in writing Welsh and Irish, thus *gwel·af*, "I see"; and a hyphen between a suffixed pronoun and the word to which it is attached, thus *gwêl-hi*, "she sees."

Welsh grammarians say that in Welsh, usually at any rate, the verb agrees with its subject in number and person; and most writers, notably the translators of the Bible, have attempted to some extent to observe the rule. But natural spoken Welsh knows nothing of such an agreement; the verb is always put in the third person singular (which is thus virtually an impersonal form[1]), except when the subject is the personal pronoun implied by the inflexion; thus, *daethant* is "they came," but "the men came" is *daeth y dynion*. This principle was stated as follows, in an article contributed by me to the Welsh quarterly *Y Geninen*, in October, 1890, before I was aware of the existence of anything analogous to it outside Celtic: "The 'inflected' forms *daethum*, *daethoch*, *daethant*, and the like, may be called *pronominal* forms, and they should not be used except when the pronoun is the subject of the verb. If the subject is a noun, the simple impersonal form *daeth* should be used: *daeth y dynion*, not *daethant y dynion*. The meaning of *daethant y dynion*, if it has any meaning, is 'the men they came.'" I now quote the rule of Egyptian grammar as given by Renouf (p. 47): "The suffixes stand for pronouns, and as such take the place of the subject when the latter is not expressed. When the subject is expressed, the suffix must be omitted. We say *ānχ-sen*, they live; but *ānχ netāru*, the gods live. *Netāru ānχ-sen* would signify 'the gods, they live.'"

The coincidence is absolute. The pronominal suffixes in Egyptian are not mere signs of relation; each has a substantial meaning of its own, and must not be used when that meaning is

---

[1] It will be understood that this is what I mean in this paper when I speak of the impersonal form. Etymologically it is the Aryan 3rd pers. sing., but actually it is impersonal—that is what Welsh and Irish have made it.

already expressed by another word. In Welsh the idea of pronominal suffixes has been completely transferred to the Aryan inflexions of the verb.

It is the same in Irish. "It must be confessed, however," says O'Donovan (p. 357), "that in the Irish language, ancient or modern, no agreement is observed between the nominative case and the verb, except in the relative and the third person plural, and that even this agreement would appear to have been originally adopted in imitation of the Latin language." Indeed, in Irish, the impersonal form of the verb, besides being used when the subject is a noun, may be employed with a suffixed pronoun to take the place of an inflected personal form. This, of course, represents the Egyptian method still more faithfully; and it has almost wholly supplanted verbal inflexion in Scotch Gaelic.[1]

In Irish an ending of an inflexional character may be used to denote the object of the verb. "These same pronominal elements," says Windisch, in his "Irish Grammar" (Eng. trans., p. 56), meaning the elements attached to prepositions, "also become suffixed to verbal forms in the sense of subjects *and objects;* thus, *ainsiunn,* protegat nos (*ainis,* protegat), *taithiunn,* est nobis (*taith,* est)." Renouf says of Egyptian (p. 48): "The suffixes appended to verbs, either directly or with the intervention of particles, may represent the *object* as well as the subject of a verb; thus, *mās-sen,* superat eos, *tes-nek,* nectit tibi." In Welsh, the object is expressed by the ordinary suffixed pronoun; thus, the Egyptian *nehem-ten-uâ,* "defendite vos me,"[2] may be rendered literally into Welsh *diffynn·wch-fi.*

The neo-Celtic passive voice is more properly an impersonal verb[3]; its inflexional ending, which is the same for all persons, stands for the indefinite subject, and the suffixed pronoun denotes the object; thus Welsh *cer·ir-fi,* "on m'aime." In Egyptian, the passive is formed by the suffix *tu,* which also means the same as

[1] Professor Rhys notes : "One tense at least has remains of inflections, the so-called past subjunctive."

[2] Renouf, op. cit., p. 58.

[3] Anwyl, "Welsh Gram., Accidence," p. 41; O'Donovan, "Irish Gram.," p. 183.

the French "on";[1] thus *ī-tu er tét,* "on vint pour dire," Welsh *deu·wyd i ddywedyd.* The Egyptian *tu* is feminine in form ; and in Welsh, when the indefinite subject is denoted by a suffixed pronoun, that pronoun is the third person singular feminine *hi ;* as *mae-hi yn glawio,* "it is raining."

In Welsh and Irish, when the object of a preposition is a personal pronoun, it takes the form of a pronominal suffix which is so fused with the preposition as to be indistinguishable from an inflexion ; thus, in Welsh, "for us" is not *er ni,* but *erom.* In Welsh, three "conjugations" of prepositions may be distinguished—those in which the first person singular ends in *-af, -of, -yf.* It is needless to point out how un-Aryan this conjugation of prepositions is ; but, as above stated, in Egyptian the endings which form personal verbs are also affixed to prepositions. Thus, Egyptian *em,* "in" (*àm* in combination), Welsh *yn,* Irish *in ;* Egyptian *àm-à, àm-ek, àm-ef,* "in me, in thee, in him," Welsh *ynn·of, ynn·ot, yn·do ;* Irish, *ind·ium, ind·iut, ind·id.*

The Egyptian suffixes are attached to nouns in the sense of possessive pronouns : thus, *tfe-à,* "my father" ; *tfe-f,* "his father." I believe we have in Welsh a few nouns taking pronominal suffixes, which, like those attached to prepositions, are of the same form as verbal inflexions. *Hyd* means "length," *hyd hyn,* "the length of this," *i.e.,* as far as this ; *ar hyd Gwy,* "on the length of the Wye," *i.e.,* along the Wye (Zeuss-Ebel, p. 685). Now, "along me" may be expressed by *ar fy hyd,* in which *hyd* is plainly a noun, or by *ar hydof,* or simply *hydof ;* and so for all persons. With *hyd,* "length," and *hydof* or *ar hydof,* "along me," compare the Egyptian χefi, "face," and χeftà or *em* χefta, "before me." The Welsh noun *eido,* "property," has not hitherto been satisfactorily explained. It may have prefixed to it a possessive pronoun, as *fy eido,* "my property" ; or it may take a personal ending, with or without the article *yr* prefixed ; thus, *eidof,* or *yr eidof,* "my property" ; *eidot* or *yr eidot,* "thy property." It is usually explained as a possessive pronoun. and equated with the

[1] Pierret, "Vocabulaire hiéroglyphique," p. 665 ; Renouf, op. cit., p. 18.
[2] Brugsch, "Grammaire hiéroglyphique," p. 57.

Irish *ái*, "his" or "her";[1] so that *eidof* means "my his." This explanation, though not impossible, leaves something to be desired, especially as the old first and second persons plural are *einym, einwch*, which again cannot be explained from the first plural possessive *ein*, since this was invented by Salesbury in the sixteenth century, the old form being *an*.[2] But even if *eidof* is a pronoun, it is like no Aryan pronoun; rather it resembles the Coptic series of pronouns: *pōi*, "il mio"; *pōk*, "il tuo"; *pōf*, "il suo";[3] or the Berber *oua-i*, "le mien"; *oua-k*, "le tien."[4]

But instances of nouns with personal inflexions are rare in Welsh; and (unless *eidof* be one) are confined to prepositional phrases.[5] This, indeed, is only what we should expect; for in the Aryan language acquired by our Iberians the noun had other endings for which personal inflexions could be substituted only in very exceptional cases. The possessive pronoun is usually prefixed to the noun in Welsh and Irish (which may also be done in Egyptian); but a suffixed pronoun is frequently added to the noun, as if it had been felt that the force of the old suffix ought not to be altogether lost. In written Welsh, as a rule, this suffixed pronoun is artificially suppressed; but it is always heard in spoken Welsh, except when it is reflexive:[6] thus, *Pan wel-o i dad*, "when he sees his (suum) father"; but *Pan wel af i dad-o*, "when I see his father"; and *Pan wel-o i dad-o*, "when he sees his (ejus) father."

3. *Periphrastic Conjugation.*—Speaking from the point of view of word-building, one may say that the base of the verb in Egyptian consists of a verbal noun or infinitive, as *ānχ*, "living"

---

[1] Zeuss-Ebel, "Gram. Celtica," p. 337; Brugmann, "Grundriss," Eng. trans. iii., p. 339.

[2] Professor Rhys writes: "They may all contain a noun etymon corresponding to A.-S. *āgen*, 'property,' related to the modern *own*."

[3] Rossi, "Gram. copto-geroglifica," p. 64. These are mostly adjectival in ancient Egyptian : see Brugsch, op. cit., p. 11.

[4] Hanoteau, "Grammaire tamachek'," p. 33.

[5] So also in Coptic, Rossi, op. cit., p. 66.

[6] In which case the need of it is not felt; just as in many languages the pronoun when reflexive is replaced by the article : thus in Italian, Mi doule *il* capo, not *mio* capo.

or "to live"; but it becomes a verb by the addition of a subject, as in the instance above quoted, *ānχ netàru*, "the gods live," or of a pronominal suffix, as *ānχ-à*, "I live," *ānχ-ek*, "thou livest." The element *n* or *àn* added to the root forms a tense-stem, whose meaning however seems to be somewhat vague : *meh-nà* or *meh-àn-à*, "je remplis" (pres. or pret., Brugsch), *reχ-nà*, "io ho saputo" (Rossi). There is no other simple form of verb, but a large variety of tenses can be expressed periphrastically.

(*a*) Perhaps the most common form of periphrastic conjugation is the following: (1) verb "to be," with personal suffix or other subject; (2) preposition; (3) crude form of verb as verbal noun. In Welsh and Irish, although these languages retain many of the Aryan tenses, this construction is extremely common; and, in Welsh at any rate, has long tended to supplant the synthetic form of conjugation, as being more precise, though weaker. The three prepositions commonly used for this purpose in Egyptian are *em*, "in," *er*, "to," "for," *her*, "above," "upon," indicating the present, future, and perfect respectively. These correspond in use with the Welsh prepositions *yn*, "in," *am*, "for," *wedi*, "after." Thus :

Egyptian : *àu-k   em meh.*[1]
Welsh : *wy't   yn ffanw.*
English : art thou in filling ; *i.e.*, thou art filling.

Egyptian : *àu-à er šem er ta ànt.*[2]
Welsh : *wy'f am fynd i 'r mynyḏ.*
English : am I for going to the mountain ; *i.e.*, I shall go, &c.

Egyptian : *àu-f her kem taif hemet.*[2]
Welsh : *mae-ef wedi cael ei wraig.*

English : is he $\begin{Bmatrix} \text{upon} \\ \text{after} \end{Bmatrix}$[3] finding his wife ; *i.e.*, he has found, &c.

A very large proportion of simple assertions heard in spoken Welsh, probably about a third of the total number, are cast in

---

[1] Brugsch, op. cit., p. 45.
[2] Renouf, op. cit., p. 50.
[3] Compare *thereupon* and *thereafter*. In Welsh, "after hearing from you" and "upon hearing from you" would both be *wedi clywed oḏiwrthych*.

this form. In the present sense we have in English a similar construction : he is *a-coming* (*i.e.*, *on coming.*) This is not Teutonic ; is it not borrowed from Celtic? In the perfect sense it has been transferred from Irish into Irish-English; as when an Irishman says " I am after having my dinner," meaning that he *has had* it. Of course the English comic papers always mistake him to mean that he is in quest of it, which shows how foreign the construction is to English.

(*b*) There are also in Egyptian periphrastic verbal forms without prepositions, of which the following are the most common types. " He knows" may be expressed : (i.) *àu reχ-ef*, literally " is knows he"; (ii.) *àu-f reχ-ef*, "is-he knows-he"; (iii.) *àu-f reχ*, "is-he knows." With (i.) may be compared the use in mediæval Welsh of the impersonal proclitic form *ys* of the verb "to be" before a finite verb; *e.g.*, *ys attebwys Owein*,[1] "is answered Owen," *i.e.*, Owen answered ; *ys ethyw gennyf deuparth vy oet*,[2] "is went with me two parts of my life," that is, two-thirds of my life are spent. With (ii.) and (iii.) the use of *sef* (*ys-ef*, est is) or *syd* (*ys-yd*, est id) at the beginning of a sentence ; *e.g.*, *sef yw hwnnw*,[3] " est-is est ille " ; *yssyd yssit cussul a rodaf itt*,[4] " est-id est-id consilium quod do tibi." The verb "to be," which serves only to mark an assertion, would be liable to drop, leaving behind its affixed pronoun ; and this is possibly the explanation of the fact that the verb in simple assertions in spoken Welsh has usually a pronominal element before it : *fe wnaeth ef hyn*, " he did this " ; *yr oed ef yno* (*yr* = mediæval *yd*), " he was there." At any rate, this is what actually took place in Egyptian itself, where the old auxiliary frequently disappears in Coptic, leaving its personal affix to stand at the beginning of the verb.[5] It may be objected to this explanation that the pronoun is always followed by the relative in mediæval

---

[1] Skene, "Four Anc. Books of Wales," ii. p. 189.
[2] Rhys and Evans, "Mabinogion," p. 104.
[3] *Ibid.*, p. 3, l. 1.
[4] *Ibid.*, p. 118.
[5] De Rochemonteix, *op. cit.*, p. 97. In Welsh, the conj. *ac* is *a* before a consonant, but we say *ac mi welais*, etc. (see Rev. xiii., xiv., xv., xx., xxi.), which shows that *mi* was preceded by a word now lost beginning with a vowel.

Welsh, *mi a welaf, ef a daw.* Mediæval prose writers certainly had a tendency to reduce everything to this form ; but in these cases the *a* is mostly artificial. In the oldest piece of written Welsh now in existence, the Juvencus fragment, we have *Ti dicones,*[1] not *ti a dicones ;* and in the Gododin, *Ef diodes gormes, ef dodes ffin ; ti disgynnut,*[2] and so throughout : so also in the Black Book, *mi disgoganafe.*[3] In some cases, however, the *a* may be legitimate, slightly modifying the sense : *ac yssef a dygyrch,*[4] "and is-he that snatches," *i.e.,* and he snatches. This seems to be similar in form to the Egyptian *au-f pu mer,*[5] "is-he that loves," *i.e.,* he loves, "egli ama."

Periphrastic forms with the verb "to do" are very simple in Egyptian : *àri-à mer,* Welsh *gwna·f garu,* "I do love" ; *àri-k mer,* Welsh *gwne·i garu,* "tu ami."[6] In Welsh, the verbal noun is very commonly placed first, followed by *a* and the auxiliary verb ; thus, *mynet a oruc Kei y 'r gegin,*[7] "go that did Kay to the kitchen," *i.e.,* Sir Kay went into the kitchen. Compare :

Egyptian : *seper pu àr-nef er paif pe.*[6]
Welsh : *dyfod a wnàeth-ef i 'w dy.*
English : come that did he to his house.

4. *The preposition yn.*—The syntactical similarity of the Welsh preposition *yn,* in all its uses, to the Egyptian preposition *em* is so remarkable that it deserves a section to itself.

(1) Like other prepositions, both take pronominal suffixes :

Egyptian : *àu-k àm-à, àu-à àm-ek.*[8]
Welsh : *wy·t ynn·of, wy·f ynn·ot.*
English : art thou in me, am I in thee.

That is, "thou art in me, I am in thee."

---

[1] Skene, op. cit., ii. p. 1.
[2] *Ibid.,* pp. 69, 74.
[3] *Ibid.,* p. 18.
[4] "Mabinogion," p. 127.
[5] Rossi, op. cit., p. 113.
[6] *Ibid.,* p. 114.
[7] "Mabinogion," p. 163.
[8] Renouf, op. cit., p. 21.

(2) In periphrastic conjugation both mark the present tense, as above noted ; *àu-f em meḥ, mae-ef yn ḥanw,* "he is filling."

(3) Renouf says (p. 56): "The usual sense, however, of the [crude form of the] verb preceded by *em* is participial or gerundive." Similarly few Welsh grammars omit to say that the present participle is formed by prefixing *yn* to the infinitive : as Dr. Davies, "ex Infinitis fiunt participia, præpositâ præpositione *yn*, vt *yn caru*, amans." [1]

(4) Both are used in the sense of "in" before the name of a place; *e.g.*, Egyptian *em Abu*, "in Elephantine," Welsh *yn Ḷundain*, "in London"; Egyptian *em ṭet-à*, Welsh *yn (fy) ḥaw-i*, "in my hand." Also before a noun of time : Egyptian *em ḳerht*,[2] Welsh *yn (y) nos*, "at night." In this sense both form a large number of prepositional expressions : Welsh *yn ol*, Egyptian *em sa*, "derrière, après, d'après, selon, par suite de." [3]

(5) The Egyptian *em* and the Welsh *yn* are used to introduce the complement after the verbs of being, becoming, &c. Thus, "I am a child," "thou art a god," "he is a servant of Osiris":

Egyptian :	*àu-à em šerà.*[4]		*àu-k*	*em neter.*[5]
Welsh :	*wy·f yn blentyn.*		*wy·t*	*yn ḍuw.*
English :	am I	child.	art thou	god.

Egyptian :	*unn-ef em šes*	*en Asàr.*[6]	
Welsh :	*mae-ef yn was*	*i Asar.*	
English :	is he	servant of Osiris.	

No English word can represent the preposition here; occasionally it may be rendered approximately by "as," thus *χā em neter cyfod yn ḍuw*, "rise as a god" ;[7] but it means more than "as" or "like": it implies absolute identity. It is true that *into*, εἰς, etc.,

---

[1] "Antiq. Ling. Brit. Rudimenta" (A.D. 1621), p. 95.
[2] Birch, "Egyptian Texts," p. 18.
[3] Brugsch, op. cit., p. 86.
[4] Renouf, op. cit., p. 32.
[5] Birch, op. cit., p. 38.
[6] Rossi, op. cit., p. 105.
[7] Birch, op. cit., p. 16.

may occur sporadically in Aryan languages in a similar manner after verbs of "making"; but the peculiarity of the Welsh construction is that the preposition introduces every kind of complement, and to omit it is the exception, not the rule. It comes, like the Egyptian *em*, before an *adjective* as well as a noun; *e.g.*, "thou art mighty" :

> Egyptian : *unn-ek   em   user*,[1]
> Welsh :   *wy't   yn gadarn.*
> English : art thou   mighty.

(6) Allied to the above construction, but sufficiently distinct from it, is the use of *yn* before any adjective to form an adverb. This is the only way in which adverbs can be formed from adjectives in Welsh, and the same method is always employed in Egyptian. Thus, Egyptian *em neχt*, Welsh *yn gryf*, "strongly" :

> Egyptian : *āq-es   er pet   em seχen.*[2]
> Welsh :   *aeth-hi   i   nef   yn ebrwyd.*
> English : went she to heaven   suddenly.

The use of the preposition *yn* before an adjective has long puzzled writers on Welsh grammar ; but the difficulty disappears if we suppose that the idiom was taken over from a language in which, as in Egyptian, no line could be drawn between an adjective and an abstract noun.

The preposition *yn* in Welsh is followed by different mutations of initial consonants ; but these differences imply no more than that the word in constructions (5) and (6) was originally similar in form to the archaic Latin *indu*, as Zeuss [3] saw it must have been in construction (1). It is not, however, upon the sameness of the preposition that I wish to lay stress : the preposition may, and does, vary ; thus, in Egyptian, *er* is used as commonly as *em* in construction (6). But the remarkable thing is that every one of these Welsh constructions, all of which, except the fourth, are

---

[1] *Ibid.*, p. 3S : " *User*, victorieux, puissant, riche."—Pierret, "Voc. Hiér.," p. 97.

[2] Renouf, op. cit., p. 32.

[3] Zeuss-Ebel, p. 44. The suggestion that predicative and adverbial *yn* might also have been of this form is due to Professor Rhys.

more or less peculiar, should have its exact counterpart in Egyptian.

These constructions are also found in Irish; but the preposition in (2) and (3) is *oc, ag,* and in (6) *co, go,* though *in, ind,* appears in the older periods;[1] while the "in" of (5) has been made into "in his," partly perhaps on account of the aspiration after it corresponding to the Welsh soft mutation, but chiefly from an attempt to make the construction logical. At any rate, it does not seem to be old in this form.

We should expect the parent Berber language to form a link between Egyptian and Iberian, and to have developed in common with the latter certain features not found in the former. This is, indeed, what the evidence seems to indicate; for, though the modern Berber dialects have been greatly modified by early contact with Semitic, they furnish parallels to most of the peculiarities of neo-Celtic syntax which we have not already found matched in Egyptian.

1. The Berber dialects agree with Egyptian and neo-Celtic in

---

[1] Zeuss considered (Z.-E., 609) that the Irish adverbial *ind,* with the allied Welsh adverbial and predicative *yn,* was the dative of the article. There is extremely little to say for this view; but the interchangeability of the Irish *ind* with the preposition *go* affords at least a strong presumption that *ind* is also a preposition, and this is confirmed by the fact that its evident meaning is utterly at variance with that of the article. Compare *in-biuc,* "a little," where we have adverbial *in,* with *in-diu,* "this day," where we have the article; or contrast the Welsh *yn fore* and *y bore,* which Zeuss seems to think mean the same thing (Z.-E., 617),—*yn-fore iawn,* λίαν πρωὶ (Mark xvi. 2), *y bore,* ἐπὶ τὸ πρωΐ (Mark xv. 1). The use of Welsh predicative *yn* is, if possible, even more decisive. (*a*) *Mae-ef yn frenin* means "he is a king," not "he is the king," which must be quite otherwise expressed. (*b*) The predicative *yn* precedes words before which the article is inadmissible, *e.g.,* pob, "every" (1 Cor. ix. 22). (*c*) The predicative *yn* may take the accent: *mae-ef* YN *barod,* yn AWR; but the article *yr* cannot be accented, nor can the article *yn* of *yn awr* (Irish, *ind-ór-sa*). (*d*) The predicative *yn* softens the initial consonant of a plural as well as a singular noun or adjective, *yn gochyon* (Mab., p. 2, l. 1), and the dative *plural* of the article certainly never ended in a vowel. (*e*) The predicative or adverbial *yn,* which softens the following consonant, is often replaced by the *yn* which nasalises the consonant, and which is admittedly a preposition; *ymhell* for *yn bell;* *ynghynt* for *yn gynt;* *yngham* for *yn gam,* contrasted with *yn ddi-gam,* J. D. Rhys, Gram. (1592), p. [xvi].

the arrangement of the different parts of the sentence. "Il semble que la construction la plus générale soit la suivante : le verbe, puis le sujet, enfin le régime : Chekkadh a tué un lion, *inr'a Chekkadh ahar*" ;[1] in Welsh, *Hadod Chekkadh lew.*

But, as in Welsh, a noun or its equivalent may come first (as complement of an implied verb "to be") followed by a relative pronoun (expressed or implied) with the verb and the rest of the sentence. The pure relatives so used are *a* (= Welsh *a*), *as* (= Welsh *yd*, *y*).

Tamashek' :	*midden*	*a*	*nemous ourger'*	*tidhidhin.*[2]
Welsh :	*gwyr*	*a*	*ym nid*	*gwraged.*
English :	(it is) men	that we are no	women.	

Tamashek' :	*s*	*tamachek'*	*as*	*isioul*	*ourger's tarabt.*[3]
Welsh :	*yn*	*Tamashek'*	*y*	*sieryd*	*nid yn Arabeg.*
English :	(it is) in Tamashek' that he speaks not	in Arabic.			

Tamashek' :	*s*	*takouba*	*as*	*t*	*inr'a.*[3]
Welsh :	*a*	*chledyf*	*y*	*'i*	*Hadod.*
English :	(it is) with (a) sword that him he killed.				

Tamashek' :	*nekkou a*	*t*	*inr'an.*[3]
Welsh :	*myfi a*	*'i*	*Hadod.*
English :	(it is) I	that him killed.	

Tamashek' :	*entenidh a*	*t*	*inr'an.*[3]
Welsh :	*hwyntwy a*	*'i*	*Hadod.*
English :	(it is) they	that him killed.	

The form *inr an* is called a participle in the grammars ; but there seems to be no reason for such a name. "En réalité, il n'y a la rien qui ressemble au participe français ou arabe" ;[4] it is an impersonal form of the verb used when the relative is the subject. Tamashek' has feminine and plural forms of it, not

---

[1] Masqueray, "Observations grammaticales sur la grammaire touareg" (Paris, 1896), p. 61.

[2] Hanoteau, "Grammaire tamachek'" (Paris, 1860), p. 84. *Cf.* above, "Paul a atebod nid Pedr."

[3] *Ibid.*, p. 100. The French translation of these sentences begins in each case with "c'est" or "ce sont."

[4] Belkassem Ben Sedira, "Cours de langue kabyle" (Alger, 1887), p. clv.

known in Kabyle ; but the last two instances show that even in Tamashek' the simple form is used after the pure relative, just as in the Welsh renderings given the third person singular, or rather the impersonal, *ɥaɗoɗ* is used after the *expressed* subject *a*, although its antecedent is in one case first person singular and in the other third plural. In spite of our grammars, no Welshman would venture in speaking to say *ɥaɗsant* for *ɥaɗoɗ* in such a sentence as the last quoted, for fear of being laughed at. So we have in the Gododin *Gwyr a aeth Gattraeth*[1] (not *aethant*), "the men who went to Cattraeth." So in Egyptian also :

> Egyptian : *na rotu à šem er t'est.*[2]
> Welsh : *y gwyr a aeth i('r) wlad.*
> English : the men who went into (the) country.

It is worthy of remark that the so-called participle of the Tamashek' verb "to be," *illan*, corresponds in use to the Welsh *syɗ*, "who is," "who am," etc. The third person singular, *illa*, corresponds to the Welsh *mae ;* as *illa r'our-i aiis*, Welsh *mae gennˑyf geffyl*, " is with me horse," that is, I have a horse ; and *imous* usually corresponds to *yw* (when the relative is the complement), thus, *anamahal a imous*, Welsh *gwas (a) yw*, " servant that he is," *i.e.*, he is a servant ; *ma imous aoua*, Welsh *pwy yw hwn*, " who is this ? "

I am tempted to think that the resemblance between *illan* and *syɗ* goes deeper than the surface, for the final *n* of *illan* seems to be, like the *yɗ* of *syɗ*, a pronominal suffix. When the verb is preceded by a particle, the suffix *n* (as is usual with Berber suffixes) becomes attached to the particle ; so they say in Tamashek', for

---

[1] Skene, op. cit., p. 64, etc. In the very few passages of the Gododin where *a* is followed by a plural verb, *a* is almost certainly the *object* of the verb. In Williams's hymn :

> " Fy meiau trymion, luoed maith,
> A waedod tua'r nen "
>
> (1811 ed., p. 742),

the ignorant editors of the new C. M. hymn-book have changed *a waedod* into *waedasant*, because *meiau* is plural, evidently thinking that this is the subject, and that the verb should *agree* with it.

[2] Brugsch, op. cit., p. 20.

"which is not," not *our illa-n*, but *our-n elli*,[1] just as we say in Welsh, not *na s-yd*, but *na-d oes*. Thus the Tamashek' *ma illan*, *ma our n-elli*? "what is, what is not?" *i.e.*, what news? would be in Welsh *beth s-yd, beth na-d oes*?

Sydd is the only distinctively relatival form in Welsh; but in Irish the regular verb has a relatival inflexion, with singular and plural forms, used like the Tamashek' " participe." These forms, as Professor Rhys has pointed out, are derived from the Aryan present participle with some (probably pronominal) suffix. Thus the Berber relatival verb with its pronominal suffix, which suggests a "participe" to the grammarians, corresponds to the Irish relatival verb formed from the Aryan participle apparently with some such suffix.

With regard to the position of the adjective and the genitive, it will suffice simply to mention that they *follow* the noun, as in Egyptian.[2]

If we adopt Prof. de Lacouperie's ideological notation,[3] the above observations on the order of words in the sentence may be summarised thus: the syntactical indices of primitive Aryan are 1, 3, 5, 8, III.; those of neo-Celtic, 2, 4, 6, 7, IV.; of Hamitic, 2, 4, 6, 7, IV. Thus neo-Celtic differs from primitive Aryan on every point, and agrees on every point with Hamitic.

2. The suffixed pronouns in Tamashek' are the following:—
Singular 1, *i, ou*; 2, mas. *k*,' fem. *m*; 3, *s, t*. Plural: 1, *ner'*; 2, mas. *koun*, fem. *kemet*; 3, mas. *sen, ten*, fem. *senet, tenet*.

The suffixes are added to prepositions and nouns in the same manner as in Egyptian, and the Celtic parallels need not be repeated. But it may be noted here that "to have" is expressed in Berber, as in Welsh and Irish, by means of the verb "to be" and a preposition with the necessary suffix; thus, Tamashek' *illa r'our-ek*, Welsh *mae genn'yt*, Irish *ta le·at*, "is with thee," *i.e.*, thou hast. So also in Coptic, *ou-nta-i*, "io he (è di mi)," *ou-nta-k*, "tu hai (è di tu)."[4] The verb "to be" is usually omitted in the present

---

[1] Hanoteau, op. cit., p. 89. The vowel change after *our* is not peculiar to the "participe"; see *ibid.*, p. 88.

[2] René Basset, "Manuel de langue kabyle," pp. 61, 67.

[3] "Trans. Phil. Soc.," 1885-7, p. 399.

[4] Rossi, op. cit., p. 108.

tense in Kabyle;[1] it may be omitted in Tamashek'; it may also be omitted in Irish.

In the Berber languages the suffixes are not used to form finite verbs, but a conjugation with purely inflexional prefixes and suffixes has been evolved, evidently under the influence of Arabic, for the prefixes agree too closely with those of the Arabic aorist to have been developed independently. It is perhaps due to the same influence that the habit has grown of making the verb agree wit its subject. This, however, is by no means always done; we have seen that there is no agreement when the relative is the subject; and even when the subject is a plural noun following its verb " l'accord peut n'être pas absolu en apparence entre le verbe et son sujet." [2]

The pronominal suffixes in Berber are added to the verb to denote the object direct or indirect: thus, Kabyle *izera-thent,*[3] Welsh, *gwelod-hwynt,* " he saw them "; Tamashek' *ekfet-i-tet,*[4] Welsh *rhowch-imi-hi,* " give (pl.) to me her," give her me.

When the verb is preceded by a particle or a relative or interrogative pronoun, the pronominal suffix which denotes the object is attached, not to the verb, but to the particle or pronoun. This is also the case in Welsh and Irish; and the suffixes so placed between the particle and the verb are called by Zeuss "infixed pronouns." Thus, Berber and neo-Celtic absolutely agree in the rendering of such phrases as the following:

Tamashek' :	*iouout*-I,	but *our*-K *eouiter'*.[5]	
Welsh :	*trawod*-FI,	but *ni*-'TH *drewais*.	
English :	he struck *me*,	not *thee* struck I.	
Kabyle :	*izera*-TH,	but *anou-a* ITH	*izeran*.[6]
Welsh :	*gwelod*-EF,	but *yrhwn-a* 'I	*gwelod*.
English :	he saw *him*,	he who *him*	saw.

Three examples of the suffix with a relative are given, with their

---

[1] Basset, op. cit., p. 15.
[2] Masqueray, op. cit., p. **62.**
[3] Basset, op. cit., p. 16.
[4] Hanoteau, op. cit., p. 96.
[5] *Ibid.*, pp. 95–6.
[6] Basset, op. cit., p. 16.

Welsh equivalents, in 1 above. Examples of the suffix so placed as indirect object are common in older Welsh and Irish ; *e.g.*, Welsh *ni'*M *oes*, "non mihi est." [1]

The objective suffix does not seem to be added to the particle in Egyptian, so that the construction was developed in Western Hamitic only. But the detachability of the suffix results in a very similar construction in Egyptian, where the *subjective* suffix is attracted by negative and some other particles, "de manière que les pronoms se trouvent parfois ajoutés à *la particule* au lieu d'occuper leur place *après le verbe.*" [2]

Of course a suffixed pronoun can only be used where there is something to support it ; and as a pronoun is often required to stand in an absolute state or as complement of an implied verb "to be," Welsh and Irish, like Egyptian and Berber, have series of independent pronouns to be used for this purpose ; as Welsh *mi, minnau, myfi, myfinnau,* Tamashek' *nek, nekkou, nekkounan, nekkouder',* ' I." Sometimes, in Berber, "nous avons affaire à un redoublement du pronom lui-même " : [3] in Welsh, we have a whole series of these pronouns formed by reduplication, *myfi, tydi, nyni,* etc. The grammatical resemblance between neo-Celtic and Hamitic is strikingly shown in the classification of personal pronouns. Zeuss in his great " Grammatica Celtica " distinguishes three classes in Celtic, which he calls *absoluta, infixa, suffixa,* but as the *infixa* are only a variety of the *suffixa* we have really two classes, *absoluta* and *suffixa.* So the Berber personal pronouns are classified into *isolés* and *affixes,* [4] and the Egyptian into *assoluti* and *suffissi.* [5]

3. Berber conjugation has only one form, which is commonly used in a past sense, but it may be made present by internal vowel change. The deficiency of tense-forms is supplemented partly by periphrastic conjugation, but chiefly by prefixing a particle to the simple verb.

The more common method of periphrastic conjugation is that

[1] " Ant. Ling. Brit. Rudim.," p. 177.
[2] Brugsch, op. cit., p. 66. Italics his own.
[3] Basset, " Etudes sur les dialectes berbères " (Paris, 1894), p. 78.
[4] Hanoteau, op. cit., p. 32 ; Basset, " Manuel," p. 10.
[5] Rossi, op. cit., p. 51.

in which the personal verb is preceded by a personal form of the verb "to be," as *ellir' zrir'*,[1] "was-I saw-I," *i.e.*, I had seen. This form is discussed under 3 (*b*) above. Traces of the form with the preposition are also found, in which, however, the verbal noun after the preposition is replaced by a personal verb, as *ellir' d'a zerrer'*, "I was seeing."[2] The alternative, and by far the most common, method of denoting time may originally have been the last-mentioned form without its verb "to be"; but in effect it is merely the prefixing of a particle to a personal verb; thus, *erser'*, "I descended," *ad' erser'*, "I shall descend."[3] The particles so used are, in Kabyle, *ad'* and *r'a* to mark the future, and *ai* to specially mark the past.[3]

Although Welsh and Irish with their Aryan tenses have little need of such helps, tense-particles are a familiar phenomenon in these languages also, especially in the older periods—such is the persistence of an old habit of speech. In Irish *no* is the sign of an incomplete action, and is used before the present and future tenses; *ro* and *do* denote completed action, and are generally found with a past tense : [4] "*ro* gives a *preterite* signification to the present indicative and to the present of habit."[5] In mediæval Welsh *dy* is occasionally met with, and *ry* very frequently. Thus Kabyle *ai zrir'* is Welsh *ry weleis*, "vidi."

These tense-particles in Berber, like other particles, attract the objective pronominal suffixes, which are thus placed between them and the verb. This is also the case in Welsh and Irish, where tense-particles may be followed by Zeuss's "pronomina infixa." Thus Tamashek' *ad-ı-inhi*, "he will see *me*," *ad-ᴀs-enner'*, "I shall tell *him*."[6] Compare Irish, *No-ᴛ-alim*, "I beseech *thee*," *ro-ᴍ-gab*, "he seized *me*";[7] Welsh *ry-ᴛʜ-welas*,[8] "saw *thee*."

---

[1] Basset, " Manuel," p. 32.

[2] *Ibid.*, p. 32.

[3] *Ibid.*, p. 27.

[4] Zeuss-Ebel, 411 *seqq.* The particle is *do* always in modern Irish; see O'Donovan, p. 157.

[5] Windisch, op. cit., p. 70.

[6] Hanoteau, op. cit., pp. 96–7.

[7] Windisch, op. cit., pp. 134–5.

[8] Skene, op. cit., p. 56. Zeuss says Welsh *ry* is an exception (p. 373), but surely instances like the above are far from rare. Cf. *ry'm gelwir*, Skene, p. 158.

4. As the Berber verbal system has been profoundly modified under Semitic influence, the equivalent of the Egyptian *em* is hardly to be found in it, though some of the verbal particles have often a distinct prepositional force. The equivalent of *em* before an adjective must also be rare, since statements such as " thou art mighty " (Egyptian *unn-ek em user*) are usually expressed by turning the complement into a verb, as can also be done in Egyptian (*user-ek*). But we have a distinct trace of the old preposition in *d'*, " in," placed before the adjective in such expressions as *aa'oud iou agui d' amellal*,[1] Welsh (*mae'r*) *ceffyl hwn yn wyn*, "this horse is white"; or in comparative statements such as *netta d' ar'ezfan fell-i*,[2] Welsh (*mae*) *efe yn fwy na-mi*, " he is bigger than I."

The whole structure of the neo-Celtic sentence and nearly all its distinctively non-Aryan features are embraced in the principles discussed above, and have been shown to have parallels in Hamitic. There are many minor points of resemblance which are important only as supplementing the above general principles. A few of these may be mentioned here.

5. The pleonastic use of a pronominal suffix after a preposition governing a relative, *e.g.*, Irish, *an fear* A *raibh tú ag caint* LEIS, "the man *whom* thou wert talking *to him*." This is considered incorrect by O'Donovan,[3] but it is common to Irish, Welsh, Berber,[4] and Egyptian. In Welsh, " the relative will stand alone at the commencement of the clause, and the preposition will follow the verb with a proper pronominal suffix ";[5] in Egyptian, "il relativo precede la frase, e la preposizione è rimandata alla fine, e spesso ricongiunta col soggetto per mezzo di un affisso pronominale."[6]

6. The omission of the copula, which is so characteristic of Hamitic, especially after a pronoun. Egyptian, *nuk Hor*, "I (am)

---

[1] Belkassem Ben Sedira, op. cit., p. cxxvi.

[2] Basset, " Manuel," p. 68. The prepositional meaning of *d'* given in the glossary of the " Manuel " (p. 50*) are "avec" and "dans." Compare the Irish adverbial *co* and *in*.

[3] P. 376.

[4] Basset, op. cit., p. 21.

[5] Hughes, " Welsh Syntax," in the " Transactions of the Aberffraw Royal Eisteddfod," 1849, p. 175.

[6] Rossi, op. cit., p. 72.

Horus";[1] Tamashek', *nekkou Mokhammed*, "I (am) Mohammed";[2] Welsh, *Mi Yscolan*, "I (am) Yscolan"[3] (the last two in answer to an inquiring stranger); Irish, *tu ar g-cruthuightheoir*, "thou (art) our creator";[4] Welsh, *pwy y marchawc*, "who (is) the knight?"[5]

7. The amplification of the negative by a noun placed after the verb, like the French *pas;* thus Kabyle OUR-*k zerir'* ARA, Welsh literally NI *'th welais* DIM, "je *ne* t'ai *pas* vu." This is common to Irish,[6] Welsh, Berber, and Coptic;[7] and may not the French construction have the same origin?

8. The numerals in Welsh are usually followed by a singular noun, *tri dyn*, "three man." This is probably an extension of the original construction as found in Irish, where all plural numerals take plural nouns, except twenty and higher multiples of ten, which take the singular.[8] Most of the Berber dialects have adopted the Arabic numerals; I have been able to examine only two in which the ancient system of numeration is preserved, and in these all plural numerals take the plural, except twenty and other multiples of ten, which take the singular in Zenaga[9] and the genitive singular (with a preposition) in Tamashek'.[10]

In the above comparisons I have confined myself strictly to syntax, and have not ventured to suggest any phonetic equation. But there is one point of contact which it is not easy to pass by. Perhaps the most remarkable fact of Celtic phonology is the total disappearance of Aryan *p* in Welsh and Irish. In Berber,

---

[1] Renouf, op. cit., p. 24.
[2] Hanoteau, op. cit., p. 244.
[3] Skene, op. cit., p. 42.
[4] O'Donovan, p. 365.
[5] "Mabinogion," p. 211.
[6] Zeuss-Ebel, p. 746.
[7] Rossi, op. cit., p. 148.
[8] O'Donovan strongly asserts that it is singular; it is always found to be so when the nom. sing. differs in form from the gen. plur. It is not often that they can be distinguished even in older Irish, and if, as Zeuss says, genitives plur. occur, they are probably artificial. The fact that the same numerals take singular nouns in Scotch Gaelic shows that this construction is primitive Goidelic.
[9] Faidherbe, "Le Zénaga," p. 28.
[10] Hanoteau, op. cit., p. 129.

" le *p* est excessivement rare, et ne se rencontre qu'en Zénaga." [1]
There are difficulties in the way of connecting the two things, but
the coincidence is certainly striking.

The occurrence in Semitic of many of the modes of expression
above quoted is due to the relation which undoubtedly exists
between the Semitic and the Hamitic languages. Of the precise
nature of this relation it is difficult to form a clear conception ; [2]
but it seems to involve an intimate connection of some kind
between the two families of speech in the prehistoric period,
though they are probably not actually cognate. It is with
Hamitic, however, rather than Semitic, that Celtic syntax is in
agreement ; for, as we have seen, it agrees with Egyptian where
both differ from Arabised Berber ; it also agrees with Berber where
the latter differs markedly from Arabic, as, for instance, in the shift-
ing of the pronominal suffix from the verb to a preceding particle. [3]

The case for the derivation as opposed to the independent
development of these idioms in neo-Celtic is strengthened rather
than weakened by their appearance in Semitic, since the connection between Semitic and Hamitic is generally admitted. Some
connection can probably be traced wherever any of them occur ;
thus, in Persian, the pronominal suffixes attached to nouns and
verbs, and the pleonastic pronoun after the relative (construction 5
above) may be due to Semitic influence. Is the influence of a
Hamitic substratum to be discovered in the simultaneous development on the same analytic lines of French, Spanish, and Italian,
in their use of infixed and postfixed pronouns ?

So far as I have been able to examine Basque, I have discovered little syntactical similarity between it and either Hamitic
or Celtic. Some attempts have recently been made to connect it
with Berber : there seems to be no reason why Basque should not
contain a number of Iberian words ; but Van Eys doubts that it
is related to Iberian, and Prince Lucien Bonaparte and others
have tried to show that it is allied to Ugric, in which family Sayce

---

[1] Basset, "Études," p. 4.

[2] See Budge, "The Mummy," 1893, pp. 3-5, where a *résumé* is given of
the opinions of leading Egyptologists.

[3] " Cette particularité, qui rend *mobiles* les pronoms régimes directs et
indirects, n'existe pas en arabe."—Belkassem Ben Sedira, op. cit., p. clix.

is inclined to class it.[1]　Taylor suggests that it is the language of the broad-headed French Basques, who belong chiefly to the Auvergnat race, and not of the long-headed Spanish Basques, who are chiefly Iberian.　These views as to the affinities and original speakers of Basque accord with the frequently-expressed opinion that the Auvergnats or Savoyards are of the same stock as the Lapps.[2]

That the pre-Celtic inhabitants of Britain were an offshoot of the North African race is shown by the cranial and physical similarity between the long-barrow men and the Berbers and Egyptians, and by the line of megalithic monuments which stretches from North Africa through Spain and the west of France to Britain, marking the route of the tribes in their migration.　It is not the object of this paper to dwell upon the anthropological evidence, but one further point may be mentioned. Schrader has proved beyond doubt that the primeval Aryan family was purely agnatic, counting every relationship through the father ; and Zimmer, in his remarkable paper " Das Mutterrecht der Pikten,"[3] has shown that the early inhabitants of Britain were cognatic: " Auf einen Piktenherrscher und seine Brüder folgt nicht etwa der Sohn des ältesten, sondern der Sohn der Schwester."[4]　This state of things has come down to our own times among the Berbers : " Quand le roi meurt ou est déposé, ce qui arrive assez souvent, ce n'est pas son fils qui est appelé à lui succéder, mais bien le fils de sa sœur."[5]

The idea of comparing neo-Celtic with Hamitic was suggested to me by the view just mentioned as to the origin of the Iberians. If they are the same people as those who speak Hamitic languages, then the explanation of neo-Celtic syntax which Basque had failed to supply was to be sought for, it seemed to me, in Hamitic.　The appositeness of this comparison of idioms may be illustrated by supposing a parallel case.　If Irish, like Iberian, had been irretrievably lost, and we were led by anthropological or other

[1] " Principles of Comp. Phil.," 2nd ed., pp. 21, 101.

[2] De Quatrefages, Topinard, and Dr. R. Cruel, quoted by Keane, "Ethnology," p. 405 ; A. C. Haddon, " Study of Man," p. 82.

[3] " Zeitschrift für Rechtsgeschichte," xv., pp. 209 *seqq.*

[4] *Ibid.*, p. 218.

[5] Hanoteau, op. cit., p. xv.

reasons to infer a relationship between this lost language and Welsh, a comparison of Irish-English with Welsh would suggest the derivation of the phrase, *he is after coming*, from the Irish equivalent of *mae ef wedi dyfod.* Now, as Irish is fortunately not lost, we know this to be actually the case. Further, the persistence of idiom as compared with vocabulary is shown by the fact that, although each word in this phrase agrees in meaning in Welsh and Irish, not even the word for " after " is etymologically related (Welsh, *wedi ;* Irish, *iar n-*) ; and this goes some way to show that they are both translations of a pre-Celtic word. These two languages have diverged considerably in the matter of phonetics ; is it likely that they would have independently evolved syntactical forms identical in the two languages, but differing from anything previously existing? The answer must be that these forms are not independently evolved, and do not differ from anything previously existing. The prevalence in Welsh and Irish of the very same analytical expressions shows that analysis, which is usually regarded as a modern development, goes back in these languages to the primitive period. It is the characteristic of the *language of the people*, and has been supposed to be modern only because it is not so apparent in the earlier literary language, which, besides being largely artificial, was based upon the dialect of a more or less Aryan aristocracy.

J. MORRIS JONES.

UNIVERSITY COLLEGE, BANGOR,
   March, 1899.

APPENDIX C.

LIST OF LORDSHIPS UNITED TO FORM NEW COUNTIES OR ADDED TO EXISTING COUNTIES BY THE ST. 27 HENRY VII. C. 26.

1. United to form Monmouthshire :—

"The lordships, townships, parishes, commotes and cantreds of Monmouth, Chepstow, Matherne, Llanvihangel, Magour Goldecliffe, Newport, Wenllonge, Llanwerne, Caerlion, Usk, Trelech, Tintern, Skynfreth, Grousmont, Witecastle, Reglan, Calicote, Biston, Abergevenny, Penrose, Greenfield, Maghen, and Hochuyslade, in the country of Wales."

2. United to form Brecknockshire :—

"The lordships, townships, parishes, commotes and cantreds of Brecknock, Creckhowel, Tretowre, Penkelly, English-Talgarth, Welsh-Talgarth, Dynas, the Haye, Glynebough, Broyulles, Cantercely, Lando, Blainllinby, Estrodew, Buelthe, and Lingros [1] in the said country or dominion of Wales."

3. United to form Radnorshire :—

"The lordships, townships, parishes, commotes and cantreds of New Radnor, Elistherman, Elue-les, Bongbred, Glasbury, Glawdistre, Mihelles Church, Meleneth, Blewagh, Knighton, Norton, Preston, Commothuder, Rayder, Gwethronyon, and Stanage, in the said country of Wales."

4. United to form Montgomeryshire :—

"The lordships, townships, parishes, commotes and cantreds of Montgomery, Kedewenkerry, Cawisland, Arustely, Keviliock,

[1] Lingors, according to Rastall.

Doythur, Powesland, Clunesland, Balesley, Tempcester, and Alcester, in the said country of Wales."

5. United to form Denbighshire :—

"The lordships, townships, parishes, commotes and cantreds of Denbighland, Ruthin, Saint Taffe, Kinllethowen, Bromfilde, Yale, Chirke and Chirkeland, Molesdale,[1] and Hopesdale, in the said country of Wales."

6. Added to Shropshire :—

"The lordships, towns, parishes, commotes, hundreds, and cantreds of Oswester, Whetington, Masbroke, Knoking, Ellesmer, Downe, and Churbury hundred in the Marches of Wales."

7. Added to Herefordshire :—

"The lordships, towns, parishes, commotes, hundreds, and cantreds of Ewyas Lacy, Ewyas Harold, Clifford Wynforton, Yerdesley, Huntingdon, Whytney, Wygmore. Logharneys, and Stepulton in the said Marches of Wales."

8. Added to Gloucestershire :—

"The lordships, towns, and parishes of Wollastone, Tidnam, and Bechley, in the said Marches of Wales, and all honours, lordships, castles, manors, lands, tenements, and hereditaments lying or being Chepstow bridge in the said Marches of Wales and Gloucestershire."

9. Added to Glamorganshire :—

"The lordships, towns, parishes, commotes, hundreds, and cantreds of Gowerkilvy, Bishops Town, Llandaff, Singnithe supra, Singhnithe subtus, Maskin, Ogmore, Glynerotheney, Tallagarney, Ruthien, Tallavan, Llanblethyan, Lantwid, Tyeryal, Avan, Nethe, Landewi, and the Clays in the said country of Wales."

10. Added to Carmarthenshire :

"The lordships, towns, parishes, commotes, hundreds, and cantreds of Lanemthevery, Abermerlese, Kedwely, Eskenning, Cornewolthou, Newcastle, Emel, Aborgoyly, in the said country of Wales."

---

[1] Altered as to Molesdale by st. 33 Henry VIII., c. 13, s. 3.

11. Added to Pembrokeshire :—

"The lordships, towns, parishes, commotes, hundreds, and cantreds of Harverfordwest, Kilgarran, Lansteffan, Langeharne, otherwise called Tallangharne, Walwynscastle, Dewysland, Llannehadein, Lanfey, Herberth, Slebeche, Rosmarket, Castellan, and Landofleure, in the said country of Wales."

12. Added to Cardiganshire :—

"The lordships, town, parishes, commotes, hundreds, and cantreds of Tregaron, Glenergine, Landway, and Ureny, in the said country of Wales."

13. Added to Merionethshire :—

"The lordship, town, and parish of Mouthway, in the said country of Wales."

N.B.—In the above extracts we have given the names spelt exactly as they appear in the Statute.

APPENDIX D.

NOTE ON THE WELSH LAWS.

SINCE Chapter VI. was printed the fifteenth report of the Royal Commission on Historical MSS. has been published.[1] We find in it the following paragraph, which no doubt expresses the opinions of Mr. Gwenogvryn Evans, the Assistant Commissioner who is charged with inspecting and reporting on Welsh MSS. :—

"Manuscripts of the Welsh Laws are numerous, and those (written on vellum) at Peniarth, the British Museum, Oxford, and Cardiff have been inspected. The oldest copy is a Latin version of the last quarter of the twelfth century, and the next oldest is the Welsh version known as the *Black Book of Chirk*, which can hardly be later than the year 1200. Both these manuscripts are at Peniarth, and their texts contain the substance of the other numerous recensions of later date. The prologue of the *Chirk Codex* states simply that Howel Ða, 'prince of all the Kymry,' finding no doubt much confusion in the administration of the law when his lordship extended over Gwyneð and Powys in addition to Dyved, summoned six men from every commote, four laics and two clerics, to examine the customs and laws of his dominion and to deliberate thereon. As a result some of the old laws were confirmed, some amended, some abrogated, and some new ones enacted. These were afterwards solemnly promulgated and confirmed in a general assembly attended according to the Latin text by 'all archbishops, bishops, abbots and priests.' But whether this took place before or after Howel's visit to Rome it is not stated. That Howel did go to Rome in 928 we know on the

[1] Parly. Paper (C—9295) 1899.

testimony of the *Annales Cambriæ* and the *Brut y Tywysogion;*
and if we may credit the prologues of the later manuscripts the
object of his visit was to submit the codified laws to the approval
of the Pope.　This statement derives some colour from the words
of an unedited thirteenth century manuscript at Peniarth, which
declares that the Laws were drawn up in Latin, in order that the
Church and the Pope might be able to judge of them, and that
the common people might hold them in greater respect from
their inability to understand them.　Linguistic tests, too, tend to
support this assertion of a Latin original, and probability enforces
it.　We should in this way get independent translations into
Welsh, which would naturally give rise to what came later to be
regarded as different 'Codes,' labelled respectively 'Venedotian,'
'Demetian,' and 'Gwentian,' though Howel was never King of
Gwent and Morgannwg.　The *Chirk Codex* represents Welsh
prose of any extent in its most primitive form, and the MS. must
be regarded as a transcript of an earlier one.　No one can doubt
this who will compare its style with that represented by the fragments of the *Mabinogion* in a MS. of about 1230.　In the latter
we find Welsh prose at its best.　How far the Laws of Howel are
purely Welsh in their origin can never, probably, be determined,
as no copy of the text in its original form is known to be now
extant.　The existing manuscripts refer to the 'Laws of Howel,'
which would not be possible in a pure text; and some of them
have admittedly been revised by later princes.　It is also instructive
to note that the older the manuscript the fewer the triads it
contains.　The two oldest do not contain a single triad between
them ! "

As to the assertion of a Latin original, we wish to call
attention to the reference in the Preface to the third book of the
Venedotian Code to "Hen lyfr y Ty Gwyn " (*i.e.*, the "Old Book
of the White House "), as one of the books from which Iorwerth
ab Madog compiled his Proof-book (see p. 182 above and notes 2
and 4 thereto).　The preface to this third Book is, if we understand
A. Owen aright, to be found in the Black Book of Chirk (the MS.
A on which he bases his text of the Venedotian Code, and which in
the above extract is referred to as the oldest MS.).　It looks like

the genuine work of a Welsh lawyer making a new edition of the Proof-book. He expressly mentions as among his authorities three books of Welsh judges or lawyers who were, according to the independent Preface of the Demetian Code, present at Howel's assembly. Of course, it may be that " Hen lyfr y Ty Gwyn " was in Latin, but we think it very improbable, not only because we can hardly suppose the Welsh judges and lawyers of the tenth or even the twelfth century to have been conversant with Latin, but because we think the main practical object of the Ty Gwyn convention was to promulgate an authoritative written set of laws which the king's officers could consult at all times for guidance— an object which would only be imperfectly attained by simply publishing a Latin book. We gather from A. Owen's Preface (" Anc. Laws," vol. i. p. xxxii.) that the first Latin version given in his collection is printed from the MS. referred to in the paragraph quoted above. There the Welsh technical terms are given first, and a Latin translation added in brackets. Thus :— "i. penteulu [prefectus familie]; ii. secundus offeyrat teulu [sacerdos familie]." (" Anc. Laws," vol. ii. p. 749.) The inference we draw from this—not a certain, but a probable one—is that the Latin text is a translation. The fact that the Venedotian Code is of greater length than the earliest Latin version may of course be accounted for by additions made from time to time ; but a comparison of the arrangement and treatment of the various topics or sets of rules suggests to us that the Venedotian Code conforms more nearly to what we infer was the form of the original Book of the Law, and that the Latin version, except as to the laws of the household or court, is an abridgement of some earlier work. The Venedotian Code as printed by Owen seems a new edition of an earlier work which was divided into three parts:—(i.) the laws of the court, (ii.) the laws of the country, and (iii.) the Proof-book or three columns of laws; and it looks as if Iorwerth ab Madog was editor and compiler; that in dealing with the first and second books of the original work he only added or modified, but when he came to the third book he found that the rules actually in force had so greatly changed from those contained in the old authorities that he made a fresh compilation, bringing the book up to date, as we should say. But while we think on the materials before us that the "Old Book of the White House" was in Welsh, it may well be that before the assembly was held a Latin version of the Welsh Laws had been prepared under Howel's auspices, and it may be that it was this book that was approved by the Pope when he visited Rome in 928. Notice, too, that the *Canones Wallici* contain texts identical with some in Owen's second Latin version. (See above, p. 177.)

On p. 184 we have given Owen's translation of the title of the triads in his Book xiii. ("Anc. Laws," ii., p. 474). It has been supposed that the word "mote" which he employs means moot' or meeting, and the word "*car*," cart or waggon. This is erroneous. The Welsh word *clud* has reference to motion ; and Owen probably used "mote" as equivalent to Latin *motus*, a moving. *Càr* does mean a carriage or van ; but *câr* signifies a friend or kinsman. So the most likely translation of this obscure title is—" Triads of movings and kin-movings," or "of flittings and kin-flittings." Motion seems the constant or essential conception in the mind of the composer of these triads, but no one word—neither "mote" nor any other—can be used throughout the series. The first triad, if our translation is right, refers to the travellings or circuits of professional persons or craftsmen. So perhaps we may render the first triad thus :—" the three roving professionalisms : bardism, metallurgy, and harp-playing"; and the second thus :—" the three things that constitute a travelling (or nomadic) home : race, status, and war." In triad xxiii. we find the king's *cylch* (circuit or progress) referred to. In triads x., xxviii., and xxxiii., we have, however, apparently a van (*càr*) introduced. This is probably due to the transcriber of the MS., or to the editor. From a lawyer's point of view, the whole book looks very forced and artificial.

INDEX OF NAMES AND OTHER WORDS.

INDEX OF PRINCIPAL TOPICS AND TERMS.